Martin Klein's eagerly awaited book is a history of slaves during the nineteenth and twentieth centuries in three former French colonies. It investigates the changing nature of local slavery over time, and the evolving French attitudes towards it, through the phases of trade, conquest and colonial rule. The heart of the study focuses on the period between 1876 and 1922, when a French army composed largely of slave soldiers took massive numbers of slaves in the interior, while in areas near the coast, hesitant actions were taken against slave-raiding, trading and use. After 1900, the French withdrew state support of slavery, and as many as a million slaves left their masters. A second exodus occurred after World War I, when soldiers of slave origin returned home. The renegotiation of relationships between those who remained and their masters carries the story into the contemporary world.

Slavery and colonial rule in French West Africa

African Studies Series 94

A list of books in this series will be found at the end of this volume

Slavery and colonial rule in French West Africa

Martin A. Klein

University of Toronto

CAMBRIDGE
UNIVERSITY PRESS

PUBLISHED BY THE PRESS SYNDICATE OF THE UNIVERSITY OF CAMBRIDGE
The Pitt Building, Trumpington Street, Cambridge CB2 1RP, United Kingdom

CAMBRIDGE UNIVERSITY PRESS
The Edinburgh Building, Cambridge, CB2 2RU, United Kingdom
40 West 20th Street, New York, NY 10011-4211, USA
10 Stamford Road, Oakleigh, Melbourne 3166, Australia

© Martin A. Klein 1998

First published 1998

Printed in the United Kingdom at the University Press, Cambridge

Typeset in 10/11.5 pt Times [VN]

A catalogue record for this book is available from the British Library

Library of Congress Cataloguing in Publication data

Klein, Martin A.
Slavery and colonial rule in French West Africa
/ Martin A. Klein.
        p.   cm. – (African studies series; 94)
Includes bibliographical references and index.
ISBN 0 521 59324 7 (hb). – ISBN 0 521 59678 5 (pb)
1. Slavery – Africa, French-speaking West – History. 2. Slavery –
Senegal – History. 3. Slavery – Guinea – History. 4. Slavery – Mali –
History. I. Title. II. Series.
HT1396.K54 1998
306.3′62′09660917541 – dc21   97-27996   CIP

ISBN 0 521 59324 7 hardback
ISBN 0 521 59678 5 paperback

In memory of
Etta Marcus Klein
1910–1993

Contents

Illustrations

Maps

Tables

Preface

Most histories have neither a beginning nor an end. They are part of a seamless web. We cannot say when slavery began in western Africa, though it was certainly long before the period I am studying. And we cannot say when it ended, though there is no place in the three countries being studied where persons are legally owned by other persons. There are still people who are referred to as slaves in various local languages, though very few of them are under the control of another person. Historians impose beginnings and ends in trying to order our understanding of the past. This is a study of slavery in three African countries. I chose to begin with the abolition of slavery by the French National Assembly in 1848, but I am not interested in writing a history of French policy. I am interested in slavery within Africa, which involves understanding how Africans related to each other and to the European intruders in their lands. This means that I had to step back and look at the world in which the French were intruding and which they helped to create. There is no concluding date. The heart of the study deals with the period between 1876, when a maverick prosecutor named Darrigrand tried to enforce the law, and ends about 1921, when the disruptions caused by the return of *tirailleurs* from World War I ended. But the struggle was not over, and in some ways is not over yet. In each generation, the terms of the struggle change, but the fact of struggle remains. It has often been repeated that the export slave trade integrated Africa into the world economy, but it is even more important that the horror of centuries of slaving and slave-trading have left their impact on the social structures, cultures and personalities of Africa.

I originally intended to study all of French West Africa because I was not sure how much data I would find. I had already been struck by the silences in the record. I ended up with more data than I could cope with, in part because I kept digging on and off for twenty-five years. The oral record was the most difficult because almost all people of slave descent are reluctant to acknowledge that descent, but the interviews I did provided me both with moments of truth and with a more profound understanding of the peoples I was studying. Most of my documentation came from archival sources. Though often disappointing in their gaps, those records provided extensive documentation every time there was a crisis. I was also helped by the missionaries who responded in a very humane way to the suffering of a system colonial administrators and military men accepted and provided an insight on both slavery and the colonial administration.

It has been a long and very rewarding voyage and it has been shared by some wonderful friends and colleagues. I cannot list all of the people who in one way or another have helped me or stimulated my analysis, but I must thank some of them. At the head of the list have been those who guided on my forays into the field. My trip with Mohammed Mbodj to Kaymor in Senegal in 1975 began twenty years of friendship. In Wasulu in 1988, Issaka Bagayogo taught me a great deal about research strategy. Jonkoro Doumbia traveled with us and enriched my understanding of Wasulunke history. Aly Kampo helped me in Bamako and did research for me in Masina. Almamy Malik Yattara also helped me in Bamako in 1981. The late Abdoulaye Barry translated many of my tapes. In Dakar, Boubacar Barry and his wife, Aida Sow, often provided me with a home, with introductions and with intellectual stimulation. Charles Becker gave generously of his knowledge of his adopted country. Abdoulaye Bathily often found time in his busy schedule to drag me off to lunch. Saliou Niang provided us with hospitality in Kabakoto in Saalum and the Ngom family in Kaolack and Dakar, especially Babacar, Boubacar, Doudou, Frankie, Habib and their father, the late Alboury Ngom.

I had some other partners. Richard Roberts and I have had a twenty-five-year-long conversation and Paul Lovejoy has provided me with more ideas than I could use. More than anyone else, Claude Meillassoux has shaped my thinking about slavery, though I have sometimes argued with him. Fred Cooper is probably the most perceptive critic I have ever had. I have leaned at times on the research and collaboration of Bernard Moitt and Ann McDougall. And I shared Senegal with Donal and Rita Cruise O'Brien, Wes and Marian Johnson, Jonathan Barker and Peter Mark. Richard Roberts, Fred Cooper, Paul Lovejoy, Charles Becker, Elka Klein and Suzanne Silk Klein all read this manuscript and helped me polish it. Parts of it were also read by Nehemia Levtzion, James Searing, David Robinson and Suzanne Miers.

I owe a debt to many archivists and librarians. I worked in more than a dozen archives, libraries and centers of documentation. I owe a special debt to Jean François Maurel in both Dakar and Aix, to his able successor, Saliou Mbaye in Dakar, the late Father Bernard Noël of the Holy Ghost Archives at Chevilly-Larue, to Father René Lamey of the White Fathers in Rome and Aly Onoigba in Bamako. Claude Ardouin was a guide to Mali and to Bambara cuisine. Of the many friends I made on archive staffs, special mention must go to Oumar Ba in Dakar and the gang in Bamako. Many fellow scholars sent me their theses or manuscripts, among them François Manchuelle, John Hanson, John O'Sullivan, Moustapha Kane, Andrew Clark, Kathryn Green, Maria Grosz-Ngaté, James Searing, Babacar Fall, Steve Harmon and James Webb. At different times, Judith Irvine, Commandant Louis Baron, Andrée Wynkoop, Salmana Cissé, Peter Mark and Robert Baum have discussed their researches. Each one of them helped me resolve one or more questions. Marie

Perinbaum enriched my work with her scholarship and her friendship. I mourn her recent death, as I do that of Moustapha Kane and François Manchuelle. All still had much to give. Commandant Baron kindly gave me a typescript copy of Charles Monteil's diary. Robert Harms provided a copy of Ismael Barry's thesis. I also thank Mamadou Diouf, Pathé Diagne, Papa and Francine Kane, Momar Diagne, Omar Kane, Samba Dieng, Amady Ali Dieng and Mbaye Guèye in Dakar. I am grateful to Alpha Konare, now President of Mali, and his historian wife, Adam Ba in Bamako. Denise Bouche probably started me off on this quest, but Roger Pasquier, Jean-Loup Amselle, Emmanuel Terray, Catherine Coquery-Vidrovitch, Marc Michel, Jean Bazin, Jean Boulègue, François Renault, Paule Brasseur, Jean Copans, Jean Schmitz, Gillian Feeley-Harnik, Sydney Kanya-Forstner, Myron Echenberg, Patrick Manning, Joseph Miller and Dennis Cordell have all helped. Countless grad students have done some research or translation for me, among them Maria de Sousa Lahey, Anshan Li, Chidi Nwaubani, Ugo Nwokeji and Chima Korieh. Igor Kopytoff has stimulated me by arguing with me. Philip Curtin has been a model of scholarship, though here too, I have sometimes honed my ideas in opposition to his.

This research has been generously funded over the years by the Social Sciences and Humanities Research Council of Canada. I also received grants from the Canada Council and the Social Science Research Council. A grant from the Woodrow Wilson Center in Washington made it possible for me to start writing in a wonderfully collegial atmosphere. I would also like to thank various editors from the Cambridge University Press for their patience. I originally promised this book to Robin Derricourt over fifteen years ago. In the final stages Jessica Kuper nurtured me through one final revision and Janet Hall was an eagle-eyed copy-editor.

Finally, I have three special debts. The first is to Suzanne, who got rid of both split infinitives and lapses into *franglais*. She has lived with this project since the beginning and has been one of its most perceptive critics. The second is to my mother. Her wit and her companionship have enriched my life and work. I wanted this book for her, but I think she understood that there were good reasons why it took so long. Finally, there are the elderly men with calloused hands and grey hair who received me into their lives, often lodged me and offered me their history. I particularly want to honor those who sought freedom and their offspring who have continued the rebuilding process. I thought at one time that I should keep the names of my informants secret, but as I got deeper into the research, I developed an admiration of those who overcame adversity and built new lives. The high points in my field research were small moments of self-affirmation. I remember Biraan Touré talking about how he worked by himself to create the settlement which is now a prosperous hamlet. I remember Dokoro Samake saying that those living in Ntentu were there because their parents returned from slavery and rebuilt the village. I remember most of all the old man in a village within sight of the trans-Gambian highway who kibitzed throughout the interview, and then at a certain point, told me to look at the trucks carrying the peanut crop up the highway. Many of them, he said, were owned by and driven by *jaam*. And then, he announced proudly that he had only one master, Leopold Sedar Senghor, then president of Senegal. I celebrate them and their achievement.

Abbreviations

AEH	*African Economic History*
ANG	Archives Nationales de la Guinée, Conakry
ANM	Archives Nationales du Mali
ANSOM	Archives Nationales, Section Outre-Mer, Aix-en-Provence
ARS	Archives de la République du Sénégal
AWF	Archives of the White Fathers, Rome
BCEHSAOF	*Bulletin du Comité d'Etudes Historiques et Scientifiques de l'Afrique Occidentale Française*
BIFAN	*Bulletin de l'Institut Fondamental de l'Afrique Noire*
CEA	*Cahier d'études africaines*
CHEAM	Centre de hautes études administratives sur l'Afrique et l'Asie
CJAS	*Canadian Journal of African Studies*
CSE	Archives de la Congrégation du Saint Esprit, Chevilly-Larue, France
HIA	*History in Africa*
HSN	Haut-Sénégal-Niger
IFAN	Institut Fondemental d'Afrique Noire (originally Institut Français d'Afrique Noire)
IJAHS	*International Journal of African Historical Studies*
JAH	*Journal of African History*
JHSN	*Journal of the Historical Society of Nigeria*
JO	*Journal Officiel*
JOAOF	*Journal Officiel de l'Afrique Occidentale Française*
JORF	*Journal Officiel de la République Française*
PRO	Public Record Office, London
PROB	Public Record Office, Banjul
RFHOM	*Revue française d'histoire d'outre-mer*
S&A	*Slavery and Abolition*
UNG	United Nations Archives, Geneva

Glossary

Abd. pl., Abid. Arabic for slave

Almamy. Common title for Muslim rulers in West Africa. Derived from Al-Imam, the leader of prayer

Ardo. Poular. Chiefs among nomadic Fulbe

Assaka. Wolof. Derived from Arabic zakkat (see below), but in Senegal a payment made by slaves or former slaves to former masters

Banniya. Songhay. First-generation slave

Baraka. Arabic. Blessing, God's grace. In some African languages has become synonymous with wealth

Bella. Songhay. Domestic slaves of Tuareg, usually born in slavery, who live in separate communities and farm

Beydan. Arabic. Members of the dominant tribes of Mauritania. Free, "white"

Bilad es Sudan. Arabic. The land of the Blacks. Used for savannah zone that stretches across Africa

Canton. Fr. Smallest administrative jurisdiction in French administrative system. Commanded by an African chief

Captif de case. Fr. Domestic slave. Used for the slaves born in captivity (woloso, woroso, horso, rimaibe)

Captif de traite. Fr. Trade captive. Used for persons enslaved in their own lifetime

Ceddo. Wolof and Poular. Slave warriors in service of king

Cercle. Fr. In administrative terminology, the smallest subdivision headed by a European officer

Cour de Cassation. Fr. Highest appeals court of French West Africa

Damel. Wolof. Title of rulers of Kajoor

Dara. Wolof. A community of disciples. Originally a group which gathered for religious instruction and labored for the teacher, but, under Mourides, a community that worked for a Shaykh. Important in colonization of eastern Senegal

Denianke. Poular. Ruling dynasty of the Futa Toro before the Torodbe revolution of the 1770s

Diwal. Poular. Province in Futa Djallon

Escale. Fr. A port-of-call. Used for river ports which were approved locations for trade. Later extended to railway towns and secondary commercial centers

Fama. Bambara. Traditional title of rulers

Farba. Title held by slave chiefs in many West African political systems. Term is of Mande origin

Feitoria. Portuguese. Agro-commercial centers. Along Guinea coast, they cultivated peanuts and were trading centers

Firdu. Workers in peanut basin who come for harvest. Originally from kingdom of that name on south bank of Gambia

Fulasso. Poular. Village communities of Fulbe in Futa Jallon

Futanke. The Umarian Fulbe in the Sudan

Geej. Wolof. A royal matrilineage in Kajoor

Ger. Wolof. The honorable classes. All who were neither slaves nor members of artisan castes

Grigri. Amulet

Griot. West African French. Caste of musicians, historians and praise-sayers

Guinée. Fr. A blue-dyed cloth much desired in western Sahara and Sudan used as currency in some areas

Habitants. Fr. Originally free African and Métis residents of Saint Louis and Gorée. Later, indigenous residents of Four Communes

Harratin. Arab. pl. hartani. Freed slaves

Hassani. Arab. Descendants of the Arabic-speaking nomads who invaded Mauritania from the fourteenth century. They are also often spoken of as warrior tribes since their victory in the Shurr Baba conflict in the first century disarmed their rivals

Hijra. Arab. Pilgrimage to Mecca

Homologation. Fr. An administrative and judicial review of lower court decisions to bring them into conformity with the legal code. Applied primarily to criminal cases

Horon. Bambara. Free person. Neither slave not caste

Horso. Songhai. Slaves "born in the house"

Indigénat. French colonial law code (1887). Gave arbitrary power to administrator

Jaam. Wolof. Slave

Jaka. Poular. See Assaka. Term used in Masina

Jamana. Bambara. In Wasulu and other southern Bambara areas, groups of villages that were linked socially and politically. Lacked any central authority

Jambuur. Wolof. Free man, noble, honorable

Jamgal. Poular. In Masina, obligation of the *rimaibe* to masters

Jassa (diassa). Malinke. Small temporary forts on a siege line

Jatigi. In various West African languages, refers to landlord or host

Jegom. Poular. A sixth of the harvest due to landowner in Masina after Tenenkou reform of 1908. Amount due has changed over the years

Jomfutung. Slave battalions in Umar's army

Jon. Bambara. Slave

Juula. Malinke. Mande-speaking trading communities; sometimes used for specific communities; sometimes used for all professional traders

Kafu. Malinke. Small Malinke states, which succeeded Mali empire in Malinke areas

Komo. Soninke. Slave

Komo xoore. Soninke. Freed slave remaining as client

Laptot. Fr. Sailors, interpreters, workers in Senegal River trade

Maccube. Poular. sing. mattyudo. First-generation slave

Mansa. Mande. Title of ruler

Mariage à la mode du pays. Fr. Temporary marriages by Europeans posted in colonies

Marigotiers. Fr. Small traders who worked the creeks of Senegal river

Métayage. Fr. Sharecropping

Métayeur. Fr. Sharecropper

Murgu. Arabic. Payments by slave to master for the right to cultivate for themselves; self-redemption. Used in Masina for a tax

Muude. Also moule. Measure used in West African grain trade. Meillassoux gives it as $2\frac{1}{4}$ kg. Standardized by Senegal in 1826 as 1.75 litres

Nansoka. Soninke. Contract for labor between masters and former slaves

Navetane. Seasonal migrants in Senegal and the Gambia

Nyamakala. Malinke. Artisan castes

Nyenyo. Wolof. Artisan castes of blacksmiths, leatherworkers and griots

Oussourou. Tax on trade. 10 percent under French military in the Sudan

Pileuses. Fr. Women who pounded millet and did other domestic services

Pulli. Poular. Fulbe herders in Futa Jallon

Razzia. Fr. Raid to gather booty or slaves

Rempeccen. Poular. Futa Toro. Sharecropping contracts

Rimaibe. pl. Poular. sing. dimo. Slaves born in captivity

Route de ravitaillement. French. The supply route from Kayes to Bamako

Runde. Poular. Slave village

Sahel. Arabic. Shore; refers to the areas just south of the Sahara

Sawal. Unit of capacity. Four muude

Shari'a. Arabic. Quranic law

Shaykh. Arabic. pl. Shayukh

Signares. Fr. Senegalese mulatto woman who were temporary wives of French men posted to Senegal. Became known for their elegance. Also were important property-owners and entrepreneurs in Senegal river trade

Sofa. Slave soldiers in various West African armies

Spahi. Fr. Colonial cavalry

Talibés. Arabic. sing. talib. Students, disciples

Tata. West African fortifications

Tefe. Brokers who specialized in slaves

Teug. Wolof. Members of smith's caste

Tirailleurs. Fr. Riflemen. French West African infantry were known as Senegalese Tirailleurs

Tonjon. Bambara. Bambara slave warriors. Literally, slaves of the "ton," the men's society

Torodbe. Clerical elite in Futa Toro who won power in late eighteenth century

Tubakayes. People from Tuba in Guinea. Important as merchants and planters

Ulema. Arabic. Clerical elite

Vuluoso. Khassonke. Slaves

Woloso. Bambara. Slaves "born in the house"

Woroso. Soninke. Same as woloso

Zakkat. Arabic. A charitable payment given to the poor. One of the five obligations of all Muslims. In theory, giver could chose those he wished, but many gave to a religious leader to distribute, and sometimes to a chief

Zawiya. Arabic. A religious establishment. Also refers to tribes disarmed after the Shurr Bubba conflict of the late seventeenth century. These are also referred to as marabout tribes

1   Slavery in the Western Sudan

> . . . in order to be exploited, the "alien" is rendered incapable of reproducing socially as a distinct social category.   Meillassoux 1986 (1991): 36

> Not only was the slave denied all claims on, and obligations to his parents and living blood relations, but by extension, all such claims and obligations on his more remote ancestors and on his descendants. He was truly a genealogical isolate.   Patterson 1982: 5

The Sudan is a broad belt of grassland that stretches across the West African continent. The word comes from the Arabic *Bilad es Sudan*, "the land of the Blacks." The Sudan's northern fringe, the Sahel, merges into the desert and has long been influenced by exchange with desert peoples. To the south, it merges with woodland and forest and with mountainous areas like the Futa Jallon of Guinea. Of all areas of Africa, it is the one that has seen the longest development of agriculture, of markets and long-distance trade, and of complex political systems. It was also the first area south of the Sahara where African Islam took root and flowered. This study is concerned with three former French colonies: Senegal, Guinea and the agricultural part of Mali.

For much of modern history, the western Sudan has been a source of slaves for other parts of the world.[1] Early in the first millennium, it began providing a steady stream of slaves for the Mediterranean world and, with the coming of the Portuguese in the fifteenth century, people were directed into the Atlantic slave trade.[2] The long period of involvement, over a thousand years for the Saharan trade and four centuries for the Atlantic trade, shaped its institutions, though areas further down the coast were able by the eighteenth century to provide more slaves. The upper coast trade was circumscribed both by low population densities and by the tendency of both slavers and slave traders to keep more and more slaves. In the past, historical interest has focused on those who left Africa. This book focuses on those who remained. It is probable that they were a majority of those traded.[3]

Slave traders, slave producers and slave users

When Portuguese navigators reached Senegambia in the middle of the fifteenth century, they found slavery well established. Slave labor was being used to feed the courts of coastal kings as it was used in the medieval empires of the interior.[4] In addition, slaves could be bought. This resulted from the fact that whether taken as a prisoner of war, enslaved as a criminal penalty or kidnapped, the slave had little value at the point of capture.[5] He or she could escape, knew the terrain and could often rely on kin. Only after being moved did the slave become valuable. Furthermore, between enslavement and incorporation into a new community, the slave had neither rights nor any social identity. Harsh treatment was most common at the moment of capture or on the trail. Identity came from membership in a corporate group, usually based on kinship. Thus, there was inevitably in any slave-using society a reservoir of slaves who could be bought and sold, could be moved, and who had no rights or privileges.

The traders who moved these slaves were the essential link between the slavers and those who used slave labor. Two acts were at the heart of any slave relationship, the act of capture and the act of sale. The second linked the slave-trader and the slave-user. For a relatively small number of societies, the appropriation of a surplus produced by slave labor became the major source of sustenance for both ruling elites and their merchant allies. Within these slave modes of production, slave labor tended to replace other forms of labor and created a hunger for more labor, both because slaves rarely reproduced themselves and because economic growth created a demand for labor that could not be filled in any other way.[6] This demand for slave labor called into existence partners who could provide large numbers of slaves, both those who could enslave others and those who could move them to where they were wanted.

Thus, the demands of American and Mediterranean markets and African production systems stimulated the growth of both military and commercial elites within Africa.[7] Warriors or aristocrats depended on traders to provide arms and luxury goods, to sell prisoners of war and to organize production and distribution. Traders depended on warriors for protection but feared the disorder and danger that war brought. In Meillassoux's terms, "Warfare and trade are complementary and opposed. The former feeds the second, uses it as an outlet, yet withdraws men from production. Hence two classes develop which are solidary and antagonistic."[8] They needed each other, but were also threatened by each other's values and way of life. Each developed its own ideology. For the traders, Islam provided a moral code and a set of legal principles that regulated interaction within the group. For the warriors, a code similar to those of warrior classes elsewhere stressed courage and generosity and sanctioned a rather hedonistic life style. Warriors, merchants and free cultivators were linked, however, by notions of honor, which separated them from slaves and from the artisan castes.[9] Both slaves and artisans were permitted to beg and encouraged to behave in a gross manner. The noble was expected to be courageous, generous, refined, with a sense of shame and control over his emotions. The Muslim variant of these codes also stressed piety and learning. Slaves were expected to behave in a manner considered ignoble, for example dancing nude or singing obscene songs.[10] Slave women were sexually available, to be commanded rather than courted. The exploitation of slave women degraded not only the women, but also men who could not protect their women. While slave systems were prosperous, these beliefs justified the hegemony of dominant social groups. They became even more important to those groups when the decline of slavery deprived them of wealth and power.

The growth of both aristocratic and merchant sectors was stimulated by the development of sugar cultivation in the West Indies. This was a watershed for African history. The price of slaves rose and slave supply networks reached deeper and deeper into Africa. The most visible development was the appearance of a series of military states, which used war and raiding to supply larger and larger numbers of slaves.[11] The process was facilitated by two other changes. First, Saharan horse breeders improved the stock of African horses by crossing small but hardy African horses with larger but disease-prone Barbary horses.[12] The improved horse gave slave raiders the mobility they needed. Second, from the late seventeenth century, muskets moved into West Africa in increasingly large numbers.[13] As guns became important for both predation and defence, Africans needed something to exchange.

Commercial towns grew during the same period. Both aristocratic and merchant sectors used slaves extensively but, as Meillassoux suggests, each did so in its own distinctive way.[14] Within the warrior or aristocratic sector, slaves were soldiers, servants, concubines and farmers. These farmers existed primarily to feed the court and army. The aristocratic state reproduced itself primarily through war and enslavement. By contrast, merchants approached slaves as an investment and developed slave modes of production. Long-distance trade encouraged an expansion of slave-based production. Slaves were used to produce food for caravans and trade goods, especially cloth. A merchant with large slave holdings was also free to devote his time to trade or religion. Merchants tended to live in separate communities, which were linked in various ways to aristocratic groups. The Maraka towns, for example, were subject to the Fama of Segu. Other Juula towns like Kong, Buna and Bonduku, were paired with a ruling dynasty, which lived either in a separate quarter or in a village outside the town.[15] Slaves often made up over two thirds of the population of closely cropped zones that surrounded these towns.[16] Most of the desert-side belt reported populations that were about 40 percent slave, largely because of the importance of slave production of grain and cotton for trade with Saharan nomads. Centralized kingdoms like Segu, Sikasso and the Futa Jallon also had large servile populations, often clustered near the political center or around the towns.

Meillassoux's analysis focuses on the two types of slavery, which developed in complex, politically centralized and market-oriented societies. Analytically, this is sound because these were the dominant sectors, but Boutillier talks of three: the merchant, the warrior and the traditional farming communities.[17] Some societies were even more complex. Thus, in Segu, we can differentiate the state sector based on warriors, Maraka merchant towns, Somono fishing villages, Fulbe pastoral camps and, at the base, the traditional Bambara farming communities.[18] Each exploited slave labor in a distinctive way. Finally, there were numerous societies that never received an overlay of warriors or merchants. Most of them were located in a belt of societies extending from the Guinea coast and Senegal's Casamance through eastern Senegal and along the southern tier of what is now Mali, where many peoples either did not keep or rarely kept slaves. The largest slave holders in the southern tier were intrusive groups of Fulbe or Malinke who came from further north and raided indigenous peoples.[19] People in these small-scale societies sometimes seized strangers or took captives in raids, who were usually ransomed. Women might be kept, but with the development of the slave trade, more and more were sold.[20] Analytically, it is useful to think about three types of slavery, the high-density systems of merchant and of aristocrat, and low-density systems which would include decentralized societies and traditional farming communities in larger states. High-density systems differed from low-density systems in patterns of residence, in demographic structure and in degree of economic rationality, the most visible distinction being the number of slaves. At the time of the French conquest, many cercles reported populations under 10 percent servile while others reported slave majorities.[21] In low-density systems slaves lived in households with their masters, participated in the master's culture, and engaged in face-to-face relations with the master and his family; in high-density systems, slaves lived in separate villages and made up a large part, often a majority, of the population.[22] In low-density systems masters worked alongside their slaves and often ate from the same bowl; in high-density systems, labor was considered the slave's lot, masters supervised, and face-to-face relations were limited. In low-density systems assimilation was rapid, often within one to three generations; in high-density systems manumission was rare and the status of a child differed little from that of the parent. Put in other terms, slavery in high-density systems reproduced itself within one of several slave modes of production, but not at a high enough rate to provide labor for growth. In low-density systems slavery did not reproduce itself because offspring were integrated into kinship systems.[23] Less centralized societies were more likely to be prey than predator.[24]

Most African slaves originated as prisoners of war. The desire for booty stimulated warfare, shaping the way war was fought and, as a result, the political systems of slaving states.[25] Major military campaigns generally took place during the dry season, but raiding and kidnapping could take place at any time of the year and generally involved small bands. They were more likely on the frontiers of kingdoms or desert-side, but kidnapping was a problem in many kingdoms and was often severely punished. The vast majority of male prisoners were sold into the Atlantic trade while women predominated in the Saharan trade. Most of those kept within Africa were women and children.[26] With the end of the Atlantic trade, it became common simply to kill male prisoners, who were more difficult to handle and assimilate.[27]

A second source of slaves was criminal penalties. Conviction for adultery or witchcraft often resulted in enslavement. The culprit was enslaved or the culprit's family had to provide a fixed number of slaves. A third source was debt. Famine and war were widespread. The failure of the rains, locusts, or the ravages of war often brought hardship and starvation. In these circumstances, poor families with inadequate grain reserves often had to buy food and to sell or pawn slaves or, if they had none, their children. A pawn differed from a slave in that the relationship was temporary and the pawn did not cease to be a member of his or her lineage. The pawn worked for the creditor until the debt was paid. His or her labor did not reduce the principal, but served the same function as interest. The female pawn was not supposed to be exploited sexually, but if she had a child, the child belonged to her lineage.[28] Pawning was widespread among the Malinke and Bambara, but was illegal under Muslim law and does not seem to have existed in more orthodox Muslim areas.[29] It is difficult to evaluate from archival sources the relative importance of pawning and sale because European observers often did not differentiate between them. Given economic inequality and the recurrence of drought, it is possible that the distinction was sometimes blurred and likely that sale or pawning of children by the poor was a significant source of slaves.[30] Voluntary enslavement also seems to have taken place, but it was illegal under Islamic law, and when asked, most French administrators denied its existence.[31] Where it took place, it probably involved the poor enslaving themselves in a quest for security and young men entering the service of kings or powerful chiefs.[32] Captives were generally preferred to volunteers because they were kinless and thus had no other loyalties.

Forms of slavery

The condition of slaves in the western Sudan varied greatly, but most French accounts make a distinction between *captifs de traite*, acquired by purchase or capture, and *captifs de case* born within the household.[33] This distinction is also made in many African languages. The Bambara *jon*, the Soninke *komo*, the Fulbe *maccube* and the Songhay *banniya* (*captifs de traite*) were people enslaved in their own lifetime.[34] Meillassoux makes a series of finer distinctions, which underline processes of incorporation. The newly acquired slaves were fed, housed and clothed by the master, were given the most onerous tasks, had no lands of their own, worked under direct supervision, and were watched more carefully than those born in the community. Meillassoux calls them *esclaves de peine* which Alide Desnois translates as "drudge slaves." Meillassoux believes that they were the great majority of slaves. I am not convinced of this. There was a seasoning process during which there was fear of escape and concern about the slave's acceptance of his or her condition. Newly acquired slaves and slaves who tried to escape were often required to sleep in irons, but if they accepted their status, their condition was ameliorated. The ultimate sanction for the slave who did not accept his condition was sale.[35]

The second category was born in slavery. The terms *woroso* (Soninke), *woloso* (Bambara-Malinke), or *horso* (Songhay) mean "born in the house."[36] The Fulbe called them *rimaibe*. These slaves were raised in the community, spoke the master's language, and lived in his compound or in his slave village. These terms are translated as *captifs de case* or domestic slaves. They went through the same or similar initiation ceremonies as the freeborn and were sometimes given a rudimentary religious education. Some writers call them serfs because they were supposedly not subject to sale or, in Meillassoux's usage, because they reproduced biologically and not through warfare.[37] I prefer the term slave for three reasons. First, it was their persons who were owned. They were not attached to the land, but directly to an owner. Second, they gave birth to other slaves, and it is not evident that the passage was always as clear as ideology would have us believe. Olivier de Sardan argues that the passage from *banniya* to *horso* sometimes took two or three generations and Meillassoux says that passage from one stage to another was subject to the master's arbitrary approval.[38] Third, slaves born in the house could be resold. Francis Moore explained the limits on sale:

An tho' in some parts of Africa they sell their slaves born in the Family, yet in the River Gambia they think it a very wicked thing; and I never heard of but one that ever sold a Family-Slave, except for such crimes as would have made them to be sold had they been free. If there are many Family Slaves and one of them commits a Crime, the master cannot sell him without the joint consent of the rest, for if he does, they will all run away, and be protected by the next kingdom to which they fly.[39]

Most informants, both slave and free, insisted that a slave was a chattel and could be sold.[40] Some administrators also took a sceptical position. Brevié, for example, wrote about the Soninke that custom forbade the sale of domestic slaves, "but no sanctions existing, the master violates it [custom] as soon as he has sufficient interest."[41] There is no contradiction between these remarks. Moore suggests that the slave's position depended in part on numbers, that his major "sanction" was flight, and that flight was most effective where others accepted its legitimacy. A slave born in the community was less likely to be sold than a newcomer, but the Sudan suffered from recurrent wars and famine, during which people sold or pawned their own children. No one was completely secure. Slaves were also exchanged within families. The insecurity of the late nineteenth century may have eroded previous safeguards. Brevié's remark that there were no sanctions to protect the slave recurs in other reports.[42]

Meillassoux divides domestic slaves into two groups. The first, *esclaves mansés* (translated as allotment slaves), worked five or six days a week on the master's lands, usually until afternoon prayer (about 2 pm), and could work the rest of the day on their own plots.[43] They were usually "married" and were generally fed one meal on the days they worked for the master.[44] In high-density systems, slaves worked longer hours, were supervised more closely, and in most cases worked only with other slaves. With the product of their plots, slaves could save, buy cattle and accumulate tools, but most of their product went toward subsistence. The second category was *esclaves casés* (settled slaves), who were liberated from labor on the collective fields, though they still had obligations to the master. Meillassoux stresses that this status was the master's gift and did not alter the slave's dependence.[45] The major obligation of the settled slave was no longer labor, but a fixed annual payment of grain, which has been reported as being anywhere from 35 to 337 kg a year.[46]

The chief problem in evaluating obligations is determining the value of a *muud*, the measure used for grain. If Meillassoux's figure of 2.25 kg is correct, the usual obligation was somewhere between 200 and 300 kg a year.[47] Monteil is thus correct in writing that a slave could free himself from other obligations by paying "a certain number of measures of millet, approximately enough to feed an adult for a year."[48] Meillassoux estimates the productivity of the average male at Gumbu at a little over a ton of millet.[49] Pollet and Winter suggest 300 muud, which would be a good bit lower.[50] If the latter is correct, the slave diet was sparse and there was little food for the unproductive young and old. The obligation of a woman or a child was about half that of an adult male. Settled slaves thus paid their masters between 25 percent and 40 percent of their harvest. Few sources say anything about famine years, but it is likely that most obligations were reduced or forgiven. Allotment slaves and settled slaves could accumulate property, even buy slaves, but the possibilities of accumulation were limited by their obligations, by the fortunes of weather, and by disease and accident. On death the slave's property reverted to his or her master. Meillassoux also discusses the manumitted slave as a fourth category; I will look at manumission later. There were differences of local culture and of personality that affected the rate of movement through stages and the slave's conditions within each stage. A person enslaved as a child could be fully assimilated and win his master's trust, and a female slave could become a valued concubine or wife.[51] Many African rulers were the sons of slave concubines, for example almost all of the Songhay Askias.[52]

Other slave work

Most slaves farmed. Slaves also wove. Cotton textile production was probably the most important industry in the Sudan, but unlike smithing and leather, it was not confined to a caste. In small-scale societies, both slave and free wove, but in more market-oriented communities, slaves worked systematically over the four months from the cotton harvest to just before the rains when it was time to start clearing fields again. Women spun and men wove.[53] Thus, where textile production was important, slaves were busy all year long. There was a brief slack time between the last weeding and the beginning of the harvest and another after crops came in, when there were weddings and other festivities. In a few areas, smiths and leather-workers were also slaves, most notably in the Futa Jallon, but this was rare.[54] Leatherworkers, smiths and griots often bought slaves or received them as a reward for services. These slaves were then taught the craft and worked in the master's shop. Caste members were rarely enslaved, but they were sometimes forced to enter the service of their captors.

There were also elite slaves. Wherever slavery existed, some slaves were powerful and privileged. In societies where slavery did not evolve into a mode of production, slavery was primarily a means to recruit people who served the elite: eunuchs, concubines, servants, soldiers.[55] The reason for this is fairly simple. Kinless and powerless, the slave's interest and well-being were tied to that of the family. He often exercised great power in the name of others

Fig. 1 Among the Soninke, the way a person sits displays his social rank: top left, chief; top right, noble; bottom, slave positions.

because he had neither power nor authority in his own name.[56] The most important privileged slaves in West Africa were the warriors. Slave warriors often farmed, though they preferred to live off booty or off the labor of their wives, who often were originally booty.[57] The number of slave warriors in western Africa grew during the seventeenth and eighteenth centuries. They served the state by fighting, but also by running messages, administering the court and holding important posts. In nineteenth-century Senegal, the *Farba*, the major slave chief, usually sat next to the king during meetings with the French and served as his closest advisor.[58]

Slave warriors were often a force for cohesion within a royal household. Normally, households split after becoming large, but when power was contested by several opposed lineages, members of each had an interest in sticking together. Thus, in Kajoor, the Geej matrilineage built up an inheritance of sixteen slave villages. These warriors, the *ceddo*, made the Geej dominant within Kajoor and they, in turn, could often control their own leaders.[59] Similarly, Bambara warriors, the *tonjon*, could make or break candidates for royal office.[60] Slave warriors escaped their powerlessness in two ways. First, that powerlessness made them preferred instruments of other men. They thus exercised real power in the names of others. Second, by becoming a corporate group, they could impose their will. At any given moment, relatively few slaves became warriors, and these were probably boys, old enough to be trained, young enough to be shaped culturally.

Slaves could also rise to positions of trust in merchant households. Any successful merchant family controlled a number of slave villages. Slaves were probably the best and certainly the most important investment an expanding merchant family could make. Those who farmed and wove cotton for merchant families were the most systematically exploited but here, too, slaves had different roles. Some became chiefs of slave villages, while others worked as porters and eventually were entrusted with trading missions. For example, boats working on the Senegal River and the Atlantic coast were staffed by and often commanded by slaves.[61] Here too, the structure of the domestic unit offered some slaves the opportunity to advance and enjoy some of the wealth they created.

Conflicting interpretations

The publication of Miers and Kopytoff, *Slavery in Africa*, in 1977, opened up a major debate on the nature of African slavery. Their most vigorous critic has been Meillassoux, though the two approaches have a lot in common.[62] Both see slavery within a range of coerced relationships, both stress a process of incorporation and both see the slave essentially as an outsider. Meillassoux, however, places more stress on violence, on the arbitrary nature of the master's authority and the chattel nature of slavery. Miers and Kopytoff have a more benign view, which sees slavery as one of a series of relationships, like marriage and parentage, which involve rights in persons. Most important, Miers and Kopytoff argue that the slave gradually ceased to be alien and that there was a transition from slavery to kinship. Meillassoux counters that slavery is the antithesis of kinship. Like Patterson, he sees slaves as persons socially dead and excluded from all prerogatives of birth. They had neither ancestors nor descendants and thus had no rights to either fields or marriage. They owed everything they had to their masters. Meillassoux also places more stress on economic exploitation of slave labor made possible by lack of kinship rights.

The differences in interpretation flow in part from the societies they studied. Meillassoux and most contributors to his 1975 book researched societies which are hierarchical, market oriented, and where the discourse of kinship is often a thin veneer over systematic economic exploitation, where, in Patterson's terms, "kinship, whether real of fictive, is at most a veil, never a cloak."[63] Kopytoff, Miers and most of their contributors studied less differentiated societies where kinship seemed more than a veil and slaves acted like kin. Meillassoux's analysis is more appropriate to the region discussed in this book. I did, however, have difficulty at first with his notion that slaves do not marry and have no paternity.[64] My data clearly suggest that slaves formed long-term unions and had emotional ties to each other and to their offspring. They often fled in family units or, as we shall see, tried to reconstruct family units created in slavery. To understand his argument, we must examine the household.

The head of the household was obligated to feed, clothe and find spouses for both free and slave dependants and all were obligated to work on household lands. When pushed on similarity in structural position, my Wolof informants denied the parallel and insisted that slaves could be worked as much as the master wished. Slaves were worked harder, but they had some privileges. They worked their own plots, the male slave could take a second wife and the slave menage could aspire to autonomy, but slaves could never hope to control their family life.[65] If the slave was an artificial kinsman, then the nature of his dependence lay in the artifice. The Wolof have a saying that a slave has no name. The first thing that happened after purchase was that the slave received a new name.[66] A slave could regain a previous name only by escaping and returning to an area where his or her family lived. Fear of escape was why adult men were not wanted as slaves and why the newly enslaved were treated harshly.[67]

With time, a new language and new ways, a slave became part of both household and community. Two key steps in the slave's advance through stages of integration were cohabitation and parenthood.[68] Sanankoua suggests that in Masina full integration came for male slaves only in the second generation, but for the female with the first pregnancy.[69] Patterson argues that masters in almost all slave-owning societies recognize some kind of marital union between slaves, but in none did "such recognition imply custodial powers over children."[70] The ratio of male to female in the Western Sudan was such that most male slaves had at least one wife, and most accounts say that the master was expected to find him that wife.[71] Cohabitation and parenthood tied both male and female slaves into the community, but did not create a network of kinship ties. In the absence of legal paternity, we see the essence of the male slave's subordination in the household. The word *rimaibe* means "those who have not given birth"; it refers to the absence of a social link rather than to a failure to reproduce biologically.[72] The slave child inherited his mother's status and belonged to his mother's owner. The owner of the hen, it is said, is the owner of the chicks.[73] His father could neither bequeath to him nor control his labor, and if the father could not bequeath, the child could not inherit. Some sources suggest that masters permitted children to inherit part of the father's wealth, but if so, it was not a right, but a gift.[74] Well into the colonial period, masters seized the property of deceased slaves. Similarly, the master could claim the services of a slave child, in some places after the loss of baby teeth, elsewhere after circumcision.[75] Thus, the father played a father's role only in the early education of the child.

In many areas slave children were given as part of brideprice. Thus, young slaves often moved to the master's compound or were permanently separated from their parents. In legal terms, the slave had no family except his or her master. Even in getting married, slaves depended on the master's decision and the master received the brideprice. A female slave escaped this isolation only by producing a male child for a member of her master's family. The slave couple had limited incentive to produce their own children, though they did so anyway. They bore the cost of raising infants, but could not count on the labor of an older child or the support of adult children in their old age.[76] Given the difficulty they faced in producing a surplus, they had good reason to control their reproduction. "Since slaves were not kin," Meillassoux wrote, "they had no right to the benefits of kinship or franchise."[77] This was as true of the privileged slave as of the poor drudge-slave, and was what made privileged slaves valuable.

West African slavery and the export trade

Would slavery have been as important without the export trade? Clearly, better weapons contributed to enslavement and increased commodity trade led to political centralization, which made possible the increased exploitation of slave labor, but conditions in western Africa made development of some form of servitude inevitable. A Dutch ethnographer, H.I. Nieboer, suggested that slavery was most likely to develop where land was plentiful, labor in short supply and work unskilled. Slaves were rarely used for productive labor where shortage of land was a more efficient way of forcing some persons to work for others.[78] This is why many great Asian empires did not develop slave modes of production.[79] Nieboer's analysis has been amended by more recent scholars. Goody argues that the development of slavery depended not only on a high land:labor ratio, but also on a centralized state and ruling classes interested in the extraction of surplus.[80]

This existed in Africa. Population densities were low and land was rarely not available. Thus Gray and Birmingham argue that "In Africa, the real key to production and prosperity was men and women; land was rarely in short supply and therefore, no special value was attached to its ownership."[81] Where struggle over scarce resources led some to become more powerful than others, forms of dependence evolved: clientship, new forms of marriage, pawning and slavery. Weapons made of iron, guns and horses made it possible for ruling elites to free themselves from the restraints of earlier, more egalitarian, social structures. Watson suggests that access to land also differentiated open models of slavery, found largely in Africa, from closed models predominant in densely populated Asian societies. Within open models, slaves were gradually incorporated into lineage groups, but they could never be incorporated in closed systems.[82] Watson argues that closed models were closed because land was scarce and dominant kinship groups had an interest in restricting rights to it. These were also societies where slaves played primarily service and not productive roles. American systems were also closed, not because of the high value of land, but because slave-owners could coerce and through coercion extract more labor from slaves. Cooper argues that slave-owning elites allowed the progress of the African slave through stages of incorporation because they were too weak to contain the conflict that would result if they tried to contain slaves within closed groups. Cooper also suggests that political struggle in Africa often involved opposed lineages increasing productivity, military potential and reproductive possibilities by incorporating slaves.[83]

The Western Sudan contained cities, centralized states, Islam, occupational specialization and long-distance trade, but its growth was not a product of natural wealth. Though traversed by a number of rivers, it was an area of poor soils and erratic rainfall. Its social development came from what people did with their scarce resources and, particularly, their human resources. Slavery was only one source of wealth, but probably the most important, at least during the late pre-colonial centuries. The use of slave labor was responsible for much economic development that took place during the period of the Atlantic trade, but reliance on slaving and slave use also put a cap on both economic development and population growth. There has been a long debate over whether the slave trade depopulated Africa. While a precise statement is impossible, it is certain that population experienced at best stagnant growth during a period when most of the world was increasing dramatically, and I believe that an argument can be made that, in many areas, population declined during the eighteenth and nineteenth centuries.[84]

Manumission

The final stage in the integration of a slave into a society came with manumission, which Meillassoux treats as a fourth stage of incorporation. We do not know how much manumission took place, but various forms were widely reported and were similar. First, the Quran's recommendation of manumission as a pious act meant that, in strongly Muslim areas, there were some death-bed manumissions, probably of elderly retainers. A slave who went to Mecca with his master or excelled in Quranic studies was also freed, but this opportunity rarely presented itself.[85] In general, slaves received little education. Second, the Quran provided for manumission in cases of mistreatment. The French used these verses to regulate slavery early in the colonial period, but it is not clear that they were actively used earlier. Third, the slave could purchase his freedom. The price was set by the master and often was the price of two replacement slaves. Freedom was granted in a public ceremony before the imam. In most societies, the freed slave no longer owed fixed payments, but he remained a client of his former master. He controlled and could bequeath to his offspring, but he gave gifts to his former master, took part in family ceremonies and spread the news when someone died. He distributed kola at a naming ceremony. In Meillassoux's terms, "the condition of the slave is transformed, but not their status."[86] Similarly, Monteil described the status of the freed Bambara slave:

The link is not severed, and the freed man is a kind of relative. He is interested in everything that happens in his master's community and is present on all important occasions, never coming with empty hands. Reciprocally, he is never treated like a stranger by the master. The master contributes to every event concerning him: helps him get his sons married and established . . .[87]

The major limit to manumission was that the individual alone was isolated. The slave capable of buying his freedom rarely had other ties elsewhere or was capable of forming a household of his own. Some of Roberts' Maraka inform-ants suggested that slaves preferred to buy slaves rather than freedom.[88] Certainly, for the slave with enough savings to pay for freedom, a slave or a second wife would provide more security in old age.

A fourth form of manumission, probably the most widespread, was for a slave woman to bear her master's child. In Muslim societies, she thenceforth was not likely to be sold, and after the death of her master was automatically freed. Her child was free on birth. When a slave woman bore a child fathered by someone other than her master, that child inherited the mother's status and belonged to the mother's master. A slave concubine was not married in any formal sense and could be sent away at her master's whim. Furthermore, she had no assurance that the master would admit to being her child's progeni-tor.[89] Like other slaves, the concubine was valued because she had no family and was totally dependant – and there was no brideprice. If she bore a son, her well-being was dependant on the son's success.

Restraints on slavery

Slavery was not an idyllic institution in Africa or anywhere else. Some slaves may have been economically better off in slavery, but even for this group there was a price. The slave was property. He or she was subject to the whim of others. Meillassoux reminds us that the slave was produced by an act of violence. Equally important, someone had to want the slave enough to pay for him or her. The purchaser may have been concerned with power or may have had enough wealth to afford non-productive slaves, concubines or servants for example, but the system had to pay for itself. There was thus built into a slave system an incentive to rationalization. Once the system reached a certain point, an economic logic pushed it further. Meillassoux suggests that a slave household at Gumbu could provide its master with the price of a slave in one to three years by weaving and producing grain for exchange with the Moors.[90] Similarly, an administrator at Podor calculated that a slave costing 250 francs could bring his master 40 to 50 francs a year and thus pay off his purchase price in four to five years.[91] Rationalization did not go as far as in American plantation systems because of lower produc-tivity. Southern cotton plantations involved labor from dawn to dusk. Slaves were fed well, but were worked hard. In the most market-oriented African systems, slaves worked for their masters about half as much as in the US South, largely because they had to provide their own subsistence, not an easy task with hoe agriculture.[92] African planters tried to get the largest possible profit from their slaves and to keep down costs of reproduction, especially food costs.

Low productivity was not the only restraint on slavery. The key restraint was the central contradiction in slavery, the slave's humanity. All slave systems try to reduce slaves to things which are owned and denied the social attributes of a person. Roman documents referred to slaves as "bodies."[93] My informants said their slaves were property, "like our cattle." Meillassoux describes slaves as desocialized, depersonalized, desexualized and decivilized, that is to say, totally deprived of any social, personal, sexual or civic identity.[94] There is, however, in all slave systems a tension between the legal definition of the slave's status and the reality of the slave's life. Patterson contrasts a stark picture of the slave's natal alienation and powerlessness to the existence in almost all slave systems of manumission and amelioration. For example, slaves have been given the right to accumulate property almost everywhere because it was the "best means of motivating a slave to perform efficiently on his master's behalf."[95] Patterson argues that the slave's struggle for recognition "made it necessary that the master, in order to make slavery workable, provide an opportunity for the negation of slavery. The conflict between master and slave became transformed from a personal into an institutional dialectic, in which slavery as an enduring social process, stood opposite to and required manumission as an essential precondition."[96] Also important was recognition of sexual unions. The household head was responsible for finding wives for male dependants. He probably took care of his sons first, but he had an interest in keeping his slaves satisfied. The masters sought to maintain control, but that control was never total. People can be reduced to things only when exploitation is not a concern, for example in prisons or death camps or when they are slated for sacrifice, but once there is a concern to profit from their labor, the system must recognize their humanity. Persons have will and intelligence. They can resist, can sabotage, can flee, or can just give up. Melancholy in a slave system can be as much of a threat as flight. As a result, slave systems combined coercion, rewards and hegemonic ideology.[97] Terray argues that in Gyaman intergenerational integration was rapid because the elite's control of the state was limited and they feared a class-concious slave mass.[98]

This is why I am sceptical of Meillassoux's claim that most slaves were drudge slaves. Meillassoux and I both disagree with the idea that African slavery was benign, but his argument goes too far. Stability and productivity depended on slaves accepting and working within the system. Besides, the power of masters was limited. Slaves were given their own plots because it was the most efficient way to feed them and were allowed autonomy because they were more productive when working on their own. The private plot was also important in East Africa and in the Americas. Slaves were encouraged to cohabit because that tied them to the community and made them easier to control. This does not mean that slaves passively accepted their lot. They did not, but the most common form of resistance was flight. Military conflict often led to flight, particularly in periods of instability or when rebels freed slaves of rivals.[99] Baba of Karo describes most of her grandfather's slaves leaving at the time of his funeral.[100] Flight was often irrational, a plunge into the unknown in an effort to get away or get home, but slaves did it. Where they were numerous, slaves could refuse to work. The more systematic the exploitation of slave labor, the more slaves formed separate communities with their own leaders and their own traditions. Collective action was probably most effective where slaves were not rebelling, but trying to shape participation in the system that exploited them.

In any struggle to define the status and condition of slaves, the very definition of slavery is a battleground. The debate is between those who define slavery in terms of kinlessness or natal alienation and those who define slaves as property. Most dictionaries define slaves as property, but most contemporary scholars lean towards natal alienation. I think that both are correct. The debate often misses the link between ownership and natal alienation. In the struggle between slave and master, the idea that the slave was chattel bolstered the master's efforts to keep slaves alienated, but natal alienation reinforced the chattel relationship and thus the master's ability to exploit the slave. Moses Finley said it more elegantly when he wrote: "The slave is an outsider: that alone permits not only his uprooting but also his reduction from a person to a thing that can be owned."[101]

The existence of sweeteners within the system was not enough. The establishment of a hegemonic ideology began at the moment of the slave's incorporation, when he or she received a new name and had to promise not to seek freedom.[102] While seasoning sought to break the slave's will, progressive amelioration encouraged the slave to accept his or her status and to hope for improvement. At the same time, social relationships were based on subordination. The slave addressed the freeborn as he or she would address a parent or older sibling. There were rules about how they behaved in the presence of the master, what they could wear, and often, what they could eat. The slave's continuing subordination was justified by what Roberts terms a moral economy, "a conscious ideological framework which contributed to the stability of servile relations of production by setting limits on exploitation . . . by establishing a set of mutual obligations for masters and slaves."[103]

For most of the societies discussed in this book, slavery was also justified in Islamic terms. This does not mean that either enslavement or the treatment of slaves met strict criteria of Muslim law or that there was anything that could be called Muslim slavery. Cooper suggests that we must ask how Islam was used in specific historical situations.[104] In the Western Sudan as on the east African coast, *shari'a* offered slaves a general protection against harsh treatment while providing divine authority for the masters. In this, it functioned much as Christianity did for Europeans. In fact, masters were often more flexible than the law. Under *shari'a*, slaves had no right to property, but masters allowed them to enjoy the proceeds of their economic activities.[105] Islam also provided an ideological basis for ideas of honor and respectability. I will return to these ideas of honor and respectability in the last chapter.

Emancipation

The story of emancipation is one of hesitant forward steps coupled to long periods of retreat, active complicity of the French state in slaving and the exploitation of slave labor.[106] Diverse interests and diverse ideological agendas competed with one another and changed over time. Throughout the period studied, there was pressure from metropolitan opinion, which considered slavery immoral, particularly after the Catholic Church developed its own abolition movement in the late 1880s. Colonial authorities could insulate themselves from these opinions by controlling what the metropole knew about what they were doing, They were successful only because many of those charged with colonial issues were ignorant of the issues or did not consider them important. Within the colonies, there were diverse interests. Senior administrators were more attuned to metropolitan concerns which shaped both budgets and possibilities of advancement, but they faced obstruction from bush administrators, who often ignored policy directives or carried them out lackadaisically.[107] Bush administrators were more concerned with order than with change and learned to live with the existing social order. The most compromised were the soldiers who conquered the empire.[108] They recognized that alliances were conditional on not threatening the control African authorities had over their slaves and often learned to enjoy the pleasures of slave society. French soldiers slept with slave women, enjoyed the services of slave servants and distributed slaves to their dependants.

Merchant groups were more ambivalent, sometimes willing to play the abolitionist card against governors and administrators they did not like, but always hostile to anything that threatened commercial interests or raised the cost of doing business. Like the soldiers, the merchants often bought and sold slaves and used their services even when it was illegal. Missionaries often found their first converts in slave markets, but they were divided into those who accepted the moral compromises of the state that protected them and those who were genuinely shocked by those compromises. Most members of all four groups, administrators, soldiers, merchants and missionaries, were committed to colonial expansion and recognized that expansion was possible only if the slavery of allies and subjects was tolerated.

Once they were firmly in control, the French banned slaving and slave trading which threatened order and peaceful development. They were more ambivalent about slavery itself, but when they acted, the results were more dramatic than was intended. Like the British in India in 1843 or in the Gold Coast in 1874, the French sought merely to distance the colonial state from complicity with slavery, but without the support of the state, slavery either collapsed or was radically transformed.[109] The slaves themselves were the key actors, either leaving their masters or forcing a renegotiation of relationships. Change was more decisive than in most British colonies. In French West Africa, in spite of the hostility of many administrators, slaves had only to leave. Their departures destroyed the most important form of wealth in many African societies. The state was, however, understaffed and underfunded and was generally unwilling to attack local compromises that resulted from renegotiation of social relations. Vestigial forms of slavery lingered on and, in some cases, still do.

Fig. 2 Slave women given by Mossi to French
explorer Louis-Gustave Binger.

Themes and arguments

This book will be concerned with the working out and intersection of tensions
within African slave systems and within the French colonial system. There are
a number of themes and arguments that will be woven through it. First, I will
try to depict how the logic of slave systems pushed different actors, both
European and African, toward greater exploitation of slave labor during the
nineteenth century and, after that, restrained pressures toward emancipation.

   Second, I will argue that slavery was throughout a difficult problem for
French colonialists caught between European public opinion and the conviction that their goals could only be achieved if they tolerated slave-trading and
slave use. This led to constant tension between Paris and Africa as Paris
constantly pushed the colonial administration to do things it did not want to
do. It also produced a tension between senior administrators fearful of scan-
dals and concerned about French opinion and commandants concerned
about order and stability.

   Third, I will argue that Islam played a complex role. Both slave holders and slave users found in Islam a justification for slavery. Islam recognized slavery, but also restricted the conditions under which persons could be enslaved and set restraints on exploitation. Both before and after the French conquest, some Muslims found in Islam a more egalitarian and revolutionary vision. Islam then played a crucial role in the emancipation process.

Fourth, I will examine the struggles between masters and slaves. As the masters lost the ability to call on the coercive capacity of the state, the balance of power between slaves and masters shifted. This did not end the struggle for control of slave labor, which continues in a few areas up to the present, but it shifted the terms of that struggle. I will examine this on a broad canvas within which differences of culture, geography and human response were great. The struggles always worked themselves out in the local arena.

2   Abolition and retreat. Senegal 1848–1876

Article 1. Slavery will be completely abolished in all French colonies and possessions two months after the promulgation of the present decree in each of them. From the date of the promulgation of this decree in the colonies, any corporal punishment or sale of non-free persons will be absolutely forbidden. Article 7. The principle that the soil of France frees the slave who touches it is applied in colonies and possessions of the Republic.

Article 8. In the future, even in foreign countries, it is forbidden for any French citizen to possess, to buy or to sell slaves, and participation, either directly or indirectly in any traffic or exploitation of this kind will result in the loss of French citizenship . . .   Law of 27 April 1848 abolishing slavery

The year 1848 was not the first time France had abolished slavery. It had done so in 1792, but slavery was re-established in 1802 after Napoleon came to power. With the end of the Napoleonic wars, France abolished the slave trade in 1818, but only with the greatest reluctance and at the insistence of a triumphant Britain.[1] There was little thought of abolishing slavery itself. Furthermore it was not just the monarchy that was hostile to abolition. The Catholic Church, unlike its British Protestant counterparts, had little interest in the movement. A generation of revolution left the Church hostile to the men and ideas of the Revolution, particularly to those like Abbé Grégoire who had supported the Civil Constitution of the Clergy.[2] There were influential people in Restoration France who favored abolition, but they organized no subscriptions and held no meetings. Lacking the popular following of their British counterparts, abolitionists preferred to work informally and behind the scenes.[3]

Slaving ships were still openly fitted out for the trade in France and it was actively conducted on the coast of Senegambia and Upper Guinea. The French maintained a naval squadron off the West African coast, but at least 482 French slaving ships sailed to West Africa between 1814 and 1831.[4] In 1830, the July Revolution brought to power a regime closer to that of the British and more willing to act against the trade. Abolitionists organized formally into the Société française pour l'abolition de l'esclavage in 1834. If there was a wide measure of agreement by then that slavery was immoral, there was little passion for its destruction and a concern that the rights of slave-owners to their property be respected. An 1831 law provided for effective criminal sanctions against slave traders, two to five years of imprisonment

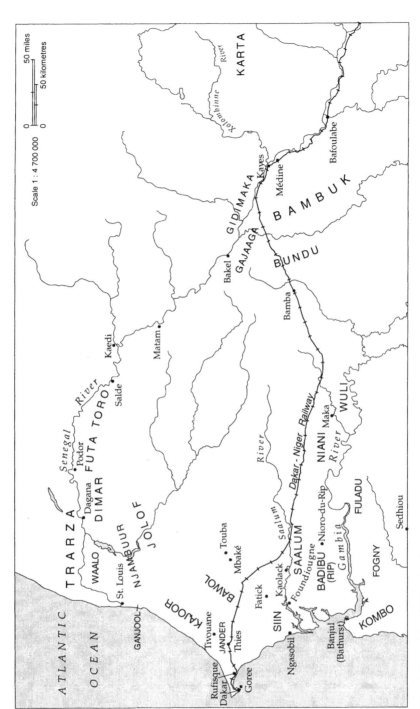

Map 1 Senegal and Mauritania

for the captain, ten to twenty for the entrepreneurs, as well as confiscation of ship and cargo. It forbade purchase, sale and resale.[5] Though the law was intended to apply only to the maritime trade, it remained for over seventy years the principal law under which slave traders were punished. Conventions were also signed with Britain in 1831 and 1833 giving each country the right to stop and search the other's ships.[6] Tighter enforcement reduced but did not eliminate slave exports. Curtin estimates that slave exports from Senegambia declined from about 680 a year in the 1820s to 400 a year in the 1830s and 1840s.[7] This trade was probably most extensive on the Upper Guinea coast, where deeply indented rivers made it easier to evade anti-slave-trade squadrons. Few of the slaves exported after 1831 came from the area between the Senegal and Gambia rivers.

A tale of two towns

Senegal was undoubtedly a minor consideration to French abolitionists in 1848. The vast majority of the slaves in the French Empire were in the West Indies.[8] The colony of Senegal consisted of two island bases, Saint Louis in the mouth of the Senegal river, Goree, off Cape Verde, and a number of forts along two axes, the Senegal river and the upper Guinea coast. At the forts French authority prevailed only within cannon range of the post. Saint Louis had a population of 12,000 to 13,000 in the 1840s and lived primarily off the gum trade in the Senegal river, which boomed during the first two thirds of the nineteenth century. In the lower river, which was high enough for trade all year long, the trading season corresponded to the gum harvest, January to June.[9] The gum was extracted by slaves, production and trade were organized by the marabout or *zawiya* tribes, and protection was provided by the warrior or *hassani* tribes.[10]

In the upper river, the trade began when the river rose in late July. A flotilla of small boats moved upriver to buy gum, hides, millet, gold, cattle and slaves.[11] By 1839, there were about 160 boats in the flotilla and about 3,000 people living off the gum trade.[12] Most boats were between 10 and 20 tons and had crews of ten to twelve. Boats were pulled upriver even after 1819 when steam began to replace sail.[13] The millet trade rivalled the gum trade in importance. The growing population of Saint Louis had to be fed and the gum-fuelled prosperity of southern Mauritania made the *zawiya* tribes a market for both slaves and millet. Higher rainfall and a fertile flood plain made the upper river a major source of grain since salinity on the lower Senegal limited productivity there. As a result, between 400 and 1,000 tons of millet moved down the river every year and were the major economic activity of the *marigotiers*, men who worked creeks linked to the Senegal. Soninke slave-owners produced a grain surplus in the upper Senegal and Xolombinne valleys. At the same time, French trading posts in the upper river, Fort Saint Joseph in the eighteenth century, Bakel and Medine in the nineteenth, were a source of guns, cloth and industrial products for the interior. By the mid-nineteenth century the river system was expanding. People on both sides of the river fitted into it and much profit was made moving goods between different points on the river. Kajoor and Waalo also provided food for Saint Louis.

Goree had about 4,500 inhabitants in 1848 and was less populous and less wealthy than Saint Louis. Goree traders regularly worked the Upper Guinea coast, and sometimes ranged as far as Liberia.[14] During the first part of the century, it was a mixed trade in hides, wax, slaves, local cloth, salt, ivory and gold, but from 1840 it grew rapidly as the market for peanut oil developed in France. Saint Louis was heavily Muslim and Goree was mostly Christian. Both had a small French population of officials, soldiers and merchants, several hundred in all, and a somewhat larger *métis* population issued from *mariages à la mode du pays* between French men and Senegalese women known as *signares*.[15] The *signares* were conspicuous not only by their stylish dress and life style, but also as crucial intermediaries between French and African societies. During the slave-trade years, many traded on behalf of their French spouses, who were forbidden to trade. When the French man died, his *signare* wife inherited and thus they accumulated wealth of their own. They owned much of the shipping and real estate in both ports. In the nineteenth century, they were increasingly folded into a community of French-speaking and Catholic *métis*. Many of their children were educated at mission schools and some benefited from scholarships to study in France. Some *métis* traders intermarried with Bordeaux trading families.

The major *métis* families played a key role in the two towns and generally dominated municipal politics, but it was largely Africans, mostly Muslim, who traded upriver and along the coast, working for themselves or for Bordeaux commercial houses that were developing the commodity trade. There was a hierarchy of traders, at the top a series of wholesale traders, European or *métis*, who provided European goods and credit, at the bottom a mass of petty traders, Muslim at Saint Louis and Christian at Goree, who moved back and forth on the river or along the coast, heavily dependent on goods received on credit from the wholesale merchants. The free people of the two towns were generally called *habitants*.[16] Those who worked the river and the coast developed political and economic ties there and learned to adapt to changes in supply, demand and price.[17]

In the first years of the river trade, free labor was recruited from areas near Saint Louis, but by the middle of the eighteenth century free laborers had been replaced by slaves.[18] Not only did slaves do heavy labor, but they were also the artisans and the sailors who went upriver and down the coast. During the 1820s, over 85 percent of the approximately 1,200 sailors (*laptots*) going upriver were slaves, as were over 90 percent of about 325 in the coastal trade.[19] As the river trade expanded toward mid-century, an increasing number of *laptots* were recruited from free men, mostly Soninke from the upper river.[20] Trusted slaves commanded trading expeditions, traded on their own account and accumulated wealth, including slaves. Many African merchant families descended from these slaves. Skilled workers were generally paid a wage, which they divided with their masters. Both French officials and *métis* families kept numerous servants. It was not unusual to see a *signare*

Table 2.1. *Census data, Saint Louis and Goree*

1758	Saint Louis	Goree
Free resident	292	
From mainland	301	
Slave	808	
TOTAL	1,401	
1767		
Free		326
Slave		718
TOTAL		1,044
1835		
Europeans	129	22
Habitants	750	607
Free Black	4,045	390
Indentures	634	95
Slaves	6,118	3,731
TOTAL	11,676	4,845
1845		
Europeans	166	68
Free African	5,346	1,099
Indentures	618	123
Slaves	6,008	3,735
TOTAL	12,138	5,025

Source: Charles Becker, Jean Schmitz and Monique Chastanet, *Les Premiers recensements au Sénégal.* Dakar: ORSTOM, 1983.

strolling with a slave holding an umbrella and several others following quietly behind. Slave ownership was widespread. A healthy slave with no skills cost about 300 francs in 1828 and could be rented out for 60 to 90 centimes a day. The slave received half of this for upkeep. A skilled slave cost as much as 1,500 francs and was hired for up to 3 francs 60 centimes a day. Many *signares* lived off the rental of slave labor.[21] Almost two thirds of the slave-owning households on Goree had fewer than ten slaves, but ten at Goree and seventeen at Saint Louis had over fifty. The largest slave-owners tended to be related to each other.[22]

Table 2.1 shows that censuses taken in Saint Louis and Goree reported a large slave majority. Only in the 1840s did the free black population increase, probably reflecting some manumission. In the decade before 1848, over 500 slaves had been freed.[23] Most skilled work was done by slaves and the vast majority of slaves had some skills. Table 2.2 shows the diversity of the Goree slave labor force. The same diversity is displayed in many individual holdings. For example, Marie Legrose owned thirty-nine slaves, among them nine laundresses, four masons, three *pileuses*, three carpenters, two cooks, a sailor and a dressmaker.[24] The largest group of female slaves was the *pileuses*,

Table 2.2. *Slave occupations,*
Goree, 1847

Male	
Sailor	312
Mason	118
Weaver	107
Laborer	92
Ship's carpenter	73
Cook	59
Servants	28
Blacksmiths	15
Other crafts	25
Traders	5
"Sans profession"	44
Others	105
TOTAL	983
Female	
Pileuse	965
Laundress	274
Seamstress	51
Cook	40
Servant	24
Trader	5
"Sans profession"	51
TOTAL	1,410

Source: ARS, 13 G 1/124, Pièce 2, 1847.

female grain-pounders who prepared millet. In general, there was one *pileuse*
for ten to twelve men.[25] Like other workers in the river trade, the *pileuses*
sometimes used their revenues to buy slaves for themselves and for others.[26]
Slaves were also given as gifts or as part of dowries. Marianne Pellegrin
received eight when she married Paul Holle, but Marie Valentin took forty-
seven into her marriage with Charles D'Erneville.[27] The predominance of
women in the slave population probably resulted from a clandestine trade in
small girls.[28] Indentured servants were mostly male. As we will see, this trade
in small girls persisted into the twentieth century. *Habitant* families had close
links on the mainland and often maintained residences and farms outside the
city. Slaves could and were moved, but never in any systematic way. As early
as 1823, French policy-makers were thinking and talking openly about emancipation, but officials and merchants seem to have accepted slavery as part of
the natural order of things and did not expect that change was coming.[29]

During the 1820s, an effort at agricultural colonization failed both because
of the hostility of local African states and because of the scepticism of local
commercial elites about agriculture.[30] To meet the demand for labor, the
naval ministry in 1822 approved a system of indenture under which slaves
would be purchased and then freed on condition of accepting an indenture

contract. Purchases of servants and workers were made in the same upriver markets where slaves were bought for military service. In 1823, introduction of new slaves into French possessions was prohibited. This was meaningless because indenture provided a convenient fiction for those seeking labor. The system was subject to numerous abuses. Most *engagés* were not freed when their contracts ended. Their children were often not registered and thus presumed to be slaves. Sometimes, an *engagé* was given the name of a deceased slave and the death was not recorded. The *engagés* were bought and sold in the market used for slaves, were sold on to the mainland, and were subject to the same corporal punishment.[31] In 1844, indenture was abolished except for military recruitment, where it persisted because the high mortality rate for whites meant upriver posts being largely staffed by black slave soldiers.[32]

The process of emancipation

Within the colony, the freeing of the slaves went as smoothly as could be expected. To be sure, there were vigorous protests from *signares* and some slave-owners tried either to sell slaves or to move them out of the colony.[33] During the two-month waiting period provided by the law there were discipline problems and some fights. Then, on 23 August, at 8 am, a proclamation was posted and an announcement made that the slaves were henceforth free citizens: "Vice and virtue, ignorance and merit, laziness and love of work will henceforth provide the only differences between inhabitants of this country . . . all are equal in the eyes of the law and enjoy an equal protection."[34] Many of the freed slaves went down to the sea for what seems to have been a spontaneous ritual cleansing. Then they gathered in front of the government offices to dance and sing the praises of the government.[35] In the weeks that followed, the transformation went relatively smoothly, in part because many were already working for a wage. Quite a few remained where they were.[36] About 200 freed persons, who found themselves without means of support, were housed temporarily in tents.[37]

Many freed slaves did quite well, especially skilled workers, but some slave owners suffered losses in the process of indemnification. At the time of abolition, indemnification procedures had not yet been worked out.[38] An indemnity of over 300 francs per slave was eventually given, but many *habitants* were in debt and could not wait out the bureaucratic procedures. As a result, they sold their indemnities. The biggest purchaser was Maurel Prom, the Bordeaux commercial house, which bought rights to 623 indemnities for less than a quarter of the final price. Some writers have suggested that this was crucial in establishing the control of the wholesale merchants over the river trade, but Mbodj has argued that while some masters lost out, the class of masters persisted and maintained their control over labor. They were able to do so because Saint Louis and Goree were islands with very limited amounts of land. Goree was separated from the mainland by what is now Dakar harbour. Land in Saint Louis was held as private property and marshes prevented the opening of new lands.[39] In 1851, the governor pointed out that land cost about 5 francs a square metre, a sum available only to privileged slaves who have worked as traders and ship's captains.[40] Where the slaveowner previously provided housing and took a part of the slave's salary, he now had no call on the salary, but charged rent. The same class of proprietors owned most of the boats, controlled most construction, and provided most of the jobs. They maintained control until the end of the century. The former slaves were freer, but for most, their economic conditions did not improve.

The reach of the law was also limited as the story of a twenty-five year old Bambara woman named Mariam Kamata illustrates. Taken prisoner fifteen years earlier in a Moor raid in Kaarta, she was sold in the Futa Toro and, when a famine struck, was freed to seek food for herself. In Kajoor, Mariam was re-enslaved and given to one of the women of the man who seized her. Mistreated, she fled to Saint Louis where her mistress found her and in 1846 sold her. When a census of slaves was taken Mariam was hidden and her name was not registered. She heard a griot announce the impending liberation, but her mistress forced her into the house and told her, "Yes, it is of liberty that they shout, but liberty for others and not for you." She was placed in irons, smuggled out of the city, and eventually sold to the Moors. She then escaped and returned to Saint Louis, where she finally claimed her freedom.[41]

Relations with neighboring states

The major problem was not within the colony, but with its neighbors. French authorities in Senegal feared a massive flight of slaves to Saint Louis and Goree, and perhaps war with the colony's neighbours.[42] These states had become dependent on the Atlantic slave trade which provided many goods on which the power of the increasingly centralized states depended. With the decline of the Atlantic trade, the rulers of these states found themselves deprived of revenue needed to buy weapons and consumer goods. The slave trade also saw the build-up of a Muslim minority, which was restless with continuing warrior hegemony, but was increasingly using slave labor to produce commodities. Three areas were important. North of the Senegal river were Mauritanian tribes organized in nomadic confederations. Slaves did much of the herding, all of the oasis agriculture, and extracted gum from trees found in the southern desert. While the clerical tribes, the zawiya, were valued trade partners, warrior tribes pillaged, raided for slaves and sought to establish their hegemony in the valley. Most of the Wolof and Tokolor of southern Mauritania had been driven south of the river and Trarza was trying to establish its control over the Wolof state of Waalo.[43] The second area of importance was the river route to the Sudan. Futa Toro controlled that route and provided some of Saint Louis' food supply.[44] Up river, the Soninke were important grain producers and intermediaries between nomads of the Sahara and agriculturalists of the Sudan. The upper Senegal was the gateway to the Niger valley, which provided most of the slaves used in or shipped out of both the Senegal and Gambia rivers.[45]

Third, the Wolof and Sereer states were the colony's closest neighbors.

Waalo was important because it was near Saint Louis and because it provided food for the town and salt for trade with the interior. Slaves regularly moved back and forth between Saint Louis and the adjacent areas of Waalo and Gandiole. Saalum was, like Gandiole, a source of salt for trade with the interior. Kajoor was the most powerful of the Wolof states. Along with western Bawol, it became the major area for peanut cultivation in the nineteenth century.[46] The Wolof and Sereer states were troubled by perennial internal conflict. Much of the agriculture was in the hands of slaves, and the caravans that brought trade goods to the two towns were largely made up of slaves.[47]

Thus both Muslim and warrior elites were threatened by Article 7, which provided that French soil freed. The authorities feared massive flight. Even before the emancipation law was passed, Governor Baudin was warned that it was coming and passed that on to rulers of various African states: "I am going to free all slaves introduced into Saint Louis . . . inform all of your subjects who possess slaves at Saint Louis . . . to withdraw them immediately from the island if they do not wish to see them freed."[48] François Arago, the Minister of Colonies, was not oblivious to Senegal's concerns. In informing Baudin of the law, Arago warned him not to encourage the idea that the colony was a refuge and reminded him that he "was invested with police powers necessary for surveillance of Blacks who come into our cities to seek their emancipation, and even to expel them from our territory if their presence becomes dangerous to good order."[49] Baudin was slow to see the implications of these instructions. Neighboring kingdoms, however, were quick to act, perhaps at the instigation of Saint Louis traders.[50] Trarza suspended the gum trade. Kajoor blocked a shipment of peanuts for which payment had already been made.[51] Waalo seized a herd of cattle destined for Saint Louis. The chiefs of Cape Verde villages refused to sell fish to Goree.[52] Baudin received a delegation of thirty-five Kajoor chiefs, who threatened war if their slaves were freed.[53] Baudin kept pleading for exemption from the law, pointing out that herds were pastured in Kajoor and that Saint Louis and Goree depended on food from the mainland. Besides, he argued, slavery in Africa was a mild institution.[54]

The Minister told Baudin that he could not present a change in the law to the Assembly, but reminded him again of his police powers.[55] Baudin told local police to expel from Saint Louis any slaves fleeing friendly states.[56] The merchants asked for more, submitting in February 1849 a petition with over 275 signatures requesting modification of the law.[57] It is not sure how much substance there was to the anxiety. Larcher, the prosecuting attorney, claimed in March 1849 that not one slave had taken refuge in Saint Louis.[58] Doors were closed effectively enough to discourage flight. Residents of Saint Louis were required to register any African visitors within twenty-four hours.[59] Baudin refused the right of residence and probably turned a blind eye to expulsion by local authority.[60]

Faidherbe

In 1854, Major Louis Faidherbe was appointed Governor of Senegal at the request of the Bordeaux commercial houses, which were unhappy about frequent changes of governors.[61] Senegal was ripe for change. Trade had multiplied seven times since the end of the Napoleonic wars. Gum was booming in the river trade and peanuts were becoming important along the coast from Kajoor south.[62] Faidherbe provided the conditions for the protection and expansion of that commerce. He was politically adept, a skilful liar, an effective soldier and a committed imperialist. At the time, France was committed to payments to major office-holders in every kingdom with which it traded. Faidherbe moved to suppress these fees, to eliminate Trarza control over Waalo and to reinforce French control over the river. In a three-year war, he forced Trarza to accept altered terms and he occupied Waalo. By time he left in 1861, he had also blocked Al Haj Umar's efforts to penetrate the Futa Toro, had established posts in Siin and Saalum, and had occupied the northern and southern extremities of Kajoor.[63] Faidherbe organized the Senegalese *tirailleurs* who, like earlier African soldiers, were almost exclusively recruited from slaves.[64]

In 1855, Faidherbe wanted to proclaim as French all villages on the river within cannon range of French posts, but he feared that the slavery could unite African rulers against him because slaves were numerous in riverine villages. At his request, Frédéric Carrère, head of the judicial service, prepared a report which provided the formula he needed. Carrère wrote that slaves were a recognized social class in African societies with rights and privileges. The law, he argued, forbade slavery in Saint Louis, and made it illegal for any French citizen to own slaves. France did not, however, need to recognize those coming under French authority after 1848 as citizens. As subjects, they could continue to live under their own law.[65] Faidherbe liked the distinction between citizen and subject, but felt he had to link his actions to abolitionist goals. The trade would be suppressed, he argued, only when it was abolished in areas that provided slaves. That would take many years. In other words, abolition was an important goal that could only be realized after conquest and, quite obviously, conquest necessitated discretion.[66] This argument, which was to be repeated regularly over the next half-century, persuaded not only Faidherbe's council, but also the Minister, Admiral Hamelin, who wrote back that toleration was necessary if African peoples were to be liberated from slavery, but that the governor had

the double duty to see to it that as in other areas increasingly subject to our action, no French citizen violates the prohibitions on slavery; on the other hand, to use . . . the full extent of his police powers to survey and if necessary to expel from our establishments all blacks who might seek manumission and whose presence might thus be a subject of trouble or danger.[67]

Faidherbe issued a decree in 1855 guaranteeing the right of subjects to keep their slaves. The prohibition against owning slaves applied only to French citizens. Citizens could, of course, hire slaves.[68] In 1857, he issued a circular repeating that subjects could retain their slaves and limiting the application of the 1848 law to areas under French authority at the time. He also stated that when France was at war with an African state, runaway slaves would be received and freed. However, slaves fleeing states at peace with the French would be expelled "as vagabonds dangerous for order and public peace" on the complaint of their masters. He accepted Hamelin's insistence that slaves not be turned over to their masters, but a master was free to seize the runaway once he or she was expelled, and the expulsion took place at the request of the master. Slaves accompanying chiefs making official visits to Saint Louis were also to be expelled if they sought freedom.[69]

In the same year, Faidherbe reformed a system of wardship set up by Baudin in 1849 to deal with minor children among the ex-slaves. Fearing the emergence of a rootless population, Baudin wanted to place these children in families or in apprenticeship programs. Committees set up to supervise the system never functioned effectively and responsibility for it was turned over to administrative personnel. Saint Louis families continued to buy children in the river area.[70] Faidherbe referred to this trade and charged that girls aged between seven and ten were bought to be used as household drudges and, two or three years later, their youth was "abused" or they were resold into marriage.[71] Under the new system, children could be purchased on condition that they be freed and registered within twenty-four hours after being brought to Saint Louis. If over eighteen years of age, they were free. If under eighteen, they were to be assigned as apprentices by a *conseil de tutelle*.[72] Though they were to be assigned to "respectable" families, the courts generally gave custody to whoever declared the children or, if bought for someone else, to that other party. There is no evidence of supervision. Few were put in apprenticeship programs.

From 1856, Carrère administered both the liberations and the assignment of children. In 1862, he submitted a report. A total of 433 had been liberated over the previous five years, 70 percent of them were female, half of them were children. Children who were not with families were assigned to Saint Louis families. The traffic in children continued until 1904 and provided families with a source of young servants, essentially replacing slave women in the domestic economy. Those taken in by French families were probably turned over to other French personnel or set loose when the French official died or returned to France. Most of those assigned to métis or Muslim families probably remained in some kind of dependent relationship, though certainly they were legally free to leave after reaching the age of eighteen. They were especially dependent when the family had wealth and power.[73] Moitt 1993 documents cases of sexual abuse and argues that some girls were forced into prostitution. Deherme also suggests that when girls became old enough, their owners "speculated in their charms, either selling them in marriage or cynically delivering them to prostitution."[74]

Table 2.3. *Slave liberations, December 1857 to October 1862*

	Total	Male	Female
Total freed	433	137	296
Under 18	216	65	151
To parents	63	30	33
To Saint Louis families	152	35	117
Free orphans	88	56	32
Apprenticeship	49	49	

Source: Report of F. Carrère, Chief of Judicial service on Counseils du Tutelle, October 1862, ANSOM, Sénégal, XIV 15 b.

After Faidherbe

Faidherbe served in Senegal until 1865 except for the period from 1861 to 1863 when J.B. Jauréguiberry was governor. Jauréguiberry's major contribution on the slavery issue was to extend Faidherbe's 1857 circular to Goree and its dependencies, essentially forts in Siin, Saalum, the Casamance and further down the coast.[75] A year later, a circular gave inhabitants of villages under French authority eight days to make a claim for a runaway slave. Only at the Casamance posts of Sedhiou and Carabane did runaway slaves pose a legal problem. Both posts had been created before 1848 and thus were technically covered by the 1848 emancipation law. Founded in 1836, Carabane was dominated by a *métis* planter who grew rice and produced lime with slave labor.[76] The slave trade was pursued there openly at first and then clandestinely until the early twentieth century. Sedhiou was founded in 1837. In 1843, the area around Sedhiou was disrupted by the first of the Marabout–Soninke wars that troubled Senegambia.[77] Marabout forces won a speedy victory near Sédhiou except for several villages near the French post. When the area opened up to peanut cultivation a decade later, the nuts were cultivated primarily by migrants from the strongly Muslim upper Senegal river area. The village of Dagorne, originally created near the French post for retired *tirailleurs* and a second village founded by a French commercial house became reception points for migrants, largely slaves brought there to cultivate peanuts. Jauréguiberry's 1862 circular was issued to provide a legal basis for expelling runaways from Sedhiou and Carabane. There were also cases involving flight both of slaves being traded and of slaves owned by local elders.[78]

By 1859, Faidherbe had asserted his ascendancy in the river area and had established a small mainland colony.[79] Once he had won in the river area, he turned to the Wolof areas. His major concern was to establish a telegraph line and a caravan route between Dakar and Saint Louis.[80] Lat Dior led the resistance. By 1863, Lat Dior had been driven out of Kajoor, though not before defeating the French twice, and had fled south to Nioro, where he joined Ma Ba, a Muslim reformer, who was waging war in the area between the Gambia and Saalum rivers. Though Lat Dior allied himself to militant Islam, the major goals of his twenty-five-year career were traditional political concerns: integrity of Kajoor, control of Bawol, his position within Kajoor, and control over his slaves.[81] By time Ma Ba was killed in 1867, storm clouds were gathering in Europe. Governor Pinet-Laprade was told that he could have no European reinforcements and should under no conditions provoke a war. In 1869, Pinet-Laprade died in a cholera epidemic that decimated French personnel. Lacking the military force to impose his will on Kajoor, Pinet-Laprade's successor, Valière, permitted Lat Dior to return to Kajoor and, in 1871, a war-weary France recognized him as Damel.[82]

The Franco-Prussian war ended the reign of Louis Napoleon. Though less revolutionary than earlier Republics, the Third Republic automatically recognized Senegal as part of France and gave it the right to send a deputy to the Chamber of Deputies. Within a few years, the colony received the right to elect a General Council with a degree of influence on policy and budget equalled by no other elected assembly in Africa. Finally, French municipal law was extended not only to Goree and Saint Louis, but to two new towns, Dakar and Rufisque.[83] Dakar was planned by Pinet-Laprade as the future capital of France's African empire. Construction of port facilities began in 1862. Its progress was briefly superseded by the unplanned growth of a competing port, Rufisque, which became the major port for peanut exports, largely because it was closer to areas where peanuts were grown. Recognition of the four commercial towns as communes extended political rights to their black and métis inhabitants. While the question of citizenship was not definitively resolved until the First World War, the *habitants* were treated as citizens and the arbitrariness that marked the colonial state was restrained by the rule of law. French law was applied and the legal structure of the French state was created in each of them.[84] In addition, elected officials could bring pressure on the colonial administration.

Nevertheless, for a generation French policy on slavery followed lines laid out by Faidherbe. Kidnapping could be severely punished, but in the interior the restraints of French law were minimal.[85] When in 1856 Lt. Pipy, the commandant at Bakel, took sixty-six Tokolor prisoners, he sold them and divided up the profits rather than letting African allies dispose of them discretely. Frédéric Carrère heard about the case because a Saint Louis trader and his two children were auctioned off. At least five children from the raid were brought to Saint Louis to be "freed." Faidherbe punished Pipy reluctantly, confining him to barracks for a month, and explained:

I have often recommended to M. Pipy that he be very circumspect in the division of prizes of war, when it cannot be avoided, not to get personally involved, to not let it take place on territory covered by the law of 1848 and to never permit soldiers, sailors or others in our pay to possess, buy or sell slaves.[86]

Pipy's error was that he had been imprudent, publicized the auction in and around Bakel, and attended it himself. Faidherbe allowed France's African auxiliaries to take and keep captives. The state was to receive one third of all booty, revenues that Faidherbe used to found an interracial social club.[87]

Lt. Pipy's problem was probably that slaves were openly traded and used in France's upper river posts even after 1848. There were active slave markets at Medine, Bakel and Senedubu. Merchants trading up river used slave labor and traded in slaves. It was here that children were bought as well as soldiers and indentured labor. The French often gave slaves to friendly chiefs.[88] Slaves were not only the most important item of trade. They were also the producers. When warfare and emigration decimated the population in the late 1850s, slaving and the slave market made possible a rapid rebirth of the economy.[89] Any slave fleeing friends of the French was returned. Only slaves of enemies were given refuge.

Even freeing slaves of enemies was often complicated, both because of the colony's interests and because of the arbitrary approach of some military men to social questions. Thus in 1865, and again in 1867, posts at Podor and Saldé in the river received many runaways from Jolof and Kajoor. Many were freed because they were fleeing enemies of the French, but two other problems arose. First, many Futa families complained that slaves were exploiting the situation to claim their freedom. Second, those from Jolof had little interest either in joining the Burba Jolof, an ally of the French, or in returning home. In February 1867, Governor Pinet-Laprade ordered commandants to tell those who had spent several months at the post that they would be expelled if their masters claimed them, and that if they wanted to avoid slavery, they should join the Burba or return to Jolof.[90] Several months later, the interim governor split some fine hairs in dealing with runaways from Kajoor in one of the same posts. They were French subjects. Masters who claimed them should be told this, but nothing should be done to "encourage the flight to our posts of people from Kajoor who have been captives in the Futa for many years, which would create difficulties with the populations of these countries."[91] Those who were slaves before Kajoor was occupied should be returned to their masters. Another commandant was told that he should "do nothing to displease people with whom we are friends."[92]

The Podor refugees

There are in the Dakar archives several lists of runaways who took refuge at Podor in 1866 and 1867.[93] The lists give a picture of disorder and enslavement in the mid-nineteenth century. Some were born in slavery. Two were Bambara from far away. Most were from nearby, the vast majority from Kajoor and enslaved within the previous four to five years. This was the period of a bad famine in 1865, several French invasions, civil war and religious conflict.[94] The runaways took advantage of the disorder to free themselves. More than half were female and almost 60 percent were children. They were enslaved in various ways, but none was taken in a siege or in a major military victory. Most, especially the children, were captured when they were outside their villages. Almost a fifth were seized in the woods where they were looking for firewood or fruit. Others were working in the fields, herding or going to

Table 2.4. *Some slave prices, Podor refugees*

Woman	Three matars of millet, two cows and one goat*
Woman	Ox and four pieces of guinea
Little boy	Two sheep and a piece of guinea
Little girl	One donkey
Boy, aged twelve	Two matars of millet
Boy, aged sixteen	Three matars of millet
Blacksmith	Ox
Wife of blacksmith	Four cows and one ox
Woman	Three matars of millet, 20 cubits of guinea and two large pieces of amber
Girl, aged ten	Three matars of millet
Girl	Gun, bull and cow

Source: Etat des captifs réfugiés à Podor, ARS, 13 G 124/11 to 14.
*Curtin 1975, II: 57–58 gives the matar as 40 *muud*. The *muud*, however, was variable. Curtin cites figures from 1 to 3 kg, and from 1.75 to 4 litres. The French treated it as 1.75 litres, but Meillassoux 1975b: 236 reports it as 2.25 kg.

market. One woman was traveling to a nearby village to claim some property of her deceased husband. Two were blacksmiths traveling with their tools and seeking work. Others were fleeing the invasion of Jolof and Kajoor by Ma Ba's warriors or were seeking food during a famine year. People were vulnerable because they could not remain inside their villages all the time.

Many were Muslims enslaved by and sold to other Muslims. One was a boy seeking alms, who was capable of reciting the Quran and should have been freed under Islamic law.[95] Slaving was a small-scale affair. Some were seized by people they knew or whose names they knew, others by bands of warriors or itinerant artisans. Some were enslaved by people with whom they took refuge. Those kidnapped were always sold, though most on these lists were not moved far from home and were therefore likely to be resold. Most were confided by the French to local chiefs, though some were assigned to a trader, an interpreter or a policeman. One list contains the governor's decisions. Eight from Kajoor were to be sent to Saint Louis to be repatriated because Kajoor was French territory. Two children were returned to their parents. Four from Jolof, not part of the French colony, were marked "When her master claims her, expel her." Three men joined the *tirailleurs* rather than be sent back to their masters, including a boy of twelve or thirteen recruited as *enfant de troupe*. French officers felt that it was immoral to enslave a free person, but were unsympathetic to other slaves. "Deserted for no reason," one entry says. Attitudes reflect both administration ties to elites and a belief that some persons were destined to be slaves.[96] Refugees given to local people were probably exchanging one master for another.

Extension of the law to Dakar and Rufisque

There was occasional pressure from above. In 1868, the Minister, Rigault de Genouilly, reminded Pinet-Laprade that the decision in 1857 to return runaways to their masters was exceptional and should be reviewed. "We should think about public opinion," he wrote, "and should not ignore that it would be embarrassing if it became aware of the actual state of things."[97] Pinet-Laprade had been warned by Faidherbe in 1865 that toleration of slavery might cause a scandal once Dakar was on international steamship routes.[98] French authorities also continued to worry about relations with their neighbors. In 1874, the commandant at Goree, Canard, asked how to handle slave complaints from Rufisque. He was told to go slow, talk to chiefs and elders and explain French intentions carefully so that they had time to "get rid of their slaves without too much loss."[99] Canard wrote back that he had been doing this for three years. He had also been telling slaves interested in buying their freedom to wait. Canard wanted to be able to free runaways not claimed in eight days and wanted the right of slaves to redeem themselves for 250 francs. The chief of the judicial service thought that few slaves had such funds.[100] The governor authorized the redemption fee but did not respond to the request for an eight-day rule and asked for a slave census.[101] Canard did not take the census for fear that too many questions would start a mass exodus.[102] Anti-slavery legislation was only extended to Dakar in 1877 and to Rufisque in 1879.

The early 1870s were frustrating for France's would-be empire builders. The army was defeated by Germany, the colonial administration was decimated by disease, their resources were limited and their instructions reminded them of this. Nevertheless, Faidherbe's move to the mainland had long-term consequences. France could no longer avoid conflict. There were continuing problems with Lat Dior, with Amadu Shaixu, a Muslim preacher and reformer in the Futa Toro, and with Sidia, the French-educated Brak Waalo, who allied himself with Amadu. A pragmatism based on weakness resulted in Lat Dior allying himself with the French first against Amadu and then against Sidia whom he turned over to the French in 1875.[103] The flight of his slaves was the subject of constant complaints from Lat Dior to the French. "If I whip a little runaway slave," Lat Dior wrote the Governor, "he flees to one of the villages that you have taken and I lose my rights to him."[104]

Slavery in the Gambia

In spite of Britain's anti-slavery policy, Bathurst was also closed to slave flight. Bathurst was founded after the abolition of the slave trade, its location was chosen to control access to the river and it was originally peopled largely by former slaves whom the British freed while occupying Goree. Information available to French abolitionists from their British counterparts suggested that Bathurst managed to survive without compromising with the odious traffic. If British abolitionists believed this, it was a tribute to the success of "perfidious Albion" in the arts of deception. The British tried to stop the export of slaves, but the Gambia could not have survived without tolerating slavery and slave-trading.[105] During the early nineteenth century, much labor at Bathurst was provided by slaves from Goree brought to the Gambia by their masters and generally returned to the more salubrious climate of that rocky isle during the rainy season. The British discouraged slaves who wanted to stay. Some were freed, but when they claimed refuge, it was often suggested that they buy their freedom. Governor Thomas Rendall lived with a woman who moved into Government House with her slaves. Rendall claimed that slaves working for him were using their wages to purchase their freedom. Even the Wesleyan Mission, the most resolute opponent of slavery in the colony, preferred redemption to abolition, perhaps because it minimized conflict with neighbors.

In 1829, an acting Lieutenant Governor signed a treaty with Combo, Bathurst's closest neighbor, providing for return of runaways. It was never ratified, but Bathurst periodically expelled vagabonds and undesirables. It also returned slaves charged with crimes, and masters could arrange for supporting testimony to prove that the runaway was wanted for criminal activity. The British set up an apprenticeship system much like the French, but as in Saint Louis, few children assigned to Bathurst families actually learned a craft. By 1840 most dry-season labor came from migrants, who were largely slaves. Like the French the British recruited most of their soldiers from slaves, and like the French they used protectorates to justify non-interference. In fact, till late in the nineteenth century, the British colony consisted of Bathurst and its small outlier on McCarthy Island. By the middle of the century, peanut cultivation was being extended rapidly up and down the Gambia. As Weil has described for Wuli, this involved a dramatic increase in the use of slave labor and in raiding to get that labor.[106] Limiting British control to Bathurst and McCarthy Island meant that the colonial administration did not have to sanction slavery. In 1868, the administrator wrote that he believed that "slaves are still debited and credited to accounts of the traders, and entered under the head of cattle."[107]

Conclusion

Abolition posed a threat to European colonial enterprises. We will examine in the next chapter the ways in which slavery shaped African political and economic development. For the moment, it is only crucial to recognize that these societies were so dependent on slave trading and slave labor that abolition threatened both political and mercantile elites. No colonial enterprise was possible without recognizing this. Furthermore, the communities from which colonial expansion began were themselves largely servile communities. Within them, slavery was accepted. Europeans in African colonies slept with slave women, used slave servants and slave labor, and depended on slave soldiers. The response of Saint Louis and Goree to abolition was to develop other methods of labor control, but these were strained in the 1880s when the demand for labor increased dramatically. Bathurst was similar to Senegal. By 1840, 40 percent of the population was made up of Liberated Africans, some of them were freed when the British withdrew to Bathurst in 1817, but most came from Sierra Leone.

The ability of Europeans in Africa to sustain an imperial agenda was based on their skill at deception. It was desirable that European public opinion not be informed about the real situation in the colonies and, in most cases, that metropolitan authorities be equally uninformed. For the French, this was easier than for the British. There was no colonial ministry until 1894. Generally, colonies were administered from the Navy Ministry. For most Navy Ministers, responsibility for the colonies was among the least of their charges. Most were profoundly ignorant of colonial affairs, and most colonial proconsuls had no desire to change that.[108] Control of information is crucial to the exercise of power in any bureaucracy. Paris wanted to avoid expensive commitments and politically embarrassing actions, but the adept or circumspect proconsul had a lot of freedom, particularly if careful about what he told Paris.

In 1876, a determined imperialist, Louis-Alexandre Brière de l'Isle, was appointed Governor of Senegal. The heir of Faidherbe, Brière launched France's conquest of the interior, but not without substantial difficulty. He ran afoul of judicial authorities dependent on a rival ministry, of mercantile groups opposed to expensive projects that promised little profit, and of missionaries who represented Europe's increasingly humane sensibilities. We will look at Brière's difficulties in Chapter 4, but first we must examine the way slavery and the slave trade shaped political and economic development in the interior.

3 Slavery, slave-trading and social revolution

> ... though the jihad was well nourished by a sincere religious passion, the desire to propagate the faith transformed itself into a more profane design: the effort to proselytize died out almost as soon as it was proclaimed, quickly, the distinction between Muslims and pagans came to justify the production of slaves for the domestic market and of captives for the international market.   Roger Botte[1]

> Endemic warfare had become so common in northern Dafina that people could no longer visit their ancestral shrines. Instead, each village developed its own religious custodians, who were usually from the grave-digger's caste, and each village looked to itself for protection.   Myron Echenberg[2]

The second half of the nineteenth century was a turbulent period throughout the area I have studied, a period of violent struggle, of transformations never completed, of dramatic changes annulled because the whole area eventually fell under the control of the French.[3] It was a period of increasing trade and production for market, of state-builders who tried to capitalize on the potential for change, and of increasing Islamization. Three themes intertwine themselves through the period: Islamic revolution, the increasing production of commodities, and new tools for making war. All were related to and often distorted by the region's tragic dependence on slave labor. All three of these themes were present earlier: to understand the history of slavery in the modern period, we must examine earlier transformations.

Slave raiders and slave traders

Philip Curtin has counselled us not to exaggerate the economic importance of the Atlantic slave trade to Africa.[4] Curtin argues that during the seventeenth and eighteenth centuries the slave trade was less than the total value of trade in salt and cattle with the desert or than the inter-regional trade within the Sudan.[5] The slave trade, both transatlantic and trans-Saharan, was important because it shaped the political and economic structure of the region. It did so not because slaves were more valuable than other items of trade, but because it strengthened the state. It provided weapons, trade goods to reward those who served the state, and the slave warriors who did most of the fighting. Curtin has argued that much of the resultant enslavement was political, that is, it was a result of wars that would have taken place anyway, and not

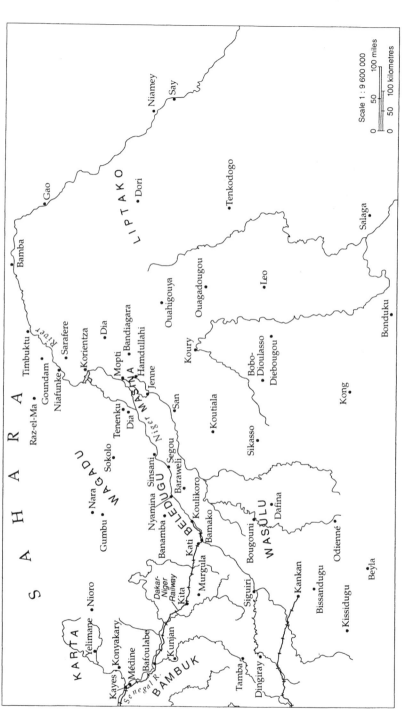

Map 2 The western African interior

economic, an activity pursued purely for economic gain.[6] Curtin's argument
has been rejected by many scholars, who believe that the slave trade shaped a
particularly predatory kind of state.[7] Thus Bazin and Terray write that "the
stock of slaves must be constantly renewed, either because the slaves are bit by
bit integrated and thus less exploitable, or because slaves must continually be
sold for the state to provision itself with firearms and horses."[8] Slavers neither
produced any value nor gave anything to the societies from whom the slaves
were taken. In essence, they exploited the societies they victimized by expro-
priating persons and converting them to commodities.[9]

The Atlantic slave trade thus contributed to a complex process of political
transformation. Along the Atlantic coast, foreign traders found their most
effective partners either in pre-existing states or in groups that moved down to
the coast to take advantage of trade opportunities. Kaabu, for example, began
as a Malian colony that provided sea salt and other coastal products to the
Mandinka heartland, but it moved early into supplying slaves to European
merchants.[10] On the upper Guinea coast, invaders like the Mane and, later,
the Fulbe of the Futa Jallon also provided slaves.[11] In the interior, there were
two processes, both of which involved the imposition of new kinds of states by
invaders. First, as medieval empires like Songhay, Mali and Jolof declined,
they were replaced by smaller, warlike states, often based on a relationship
between a group of armed invaders and indigenous agriculturalists.[12] Second,
a series of trading states appeared – Kong, Bobo, Buna, Wa, Gonja – each
based on a coalition between warrior and merchant, which were successful in
imposing themselves on local agriculturalists whose language and culture
were different from theirs. Warriors and merchants usually lived in separate
communities.[13] The more substantial merchant towns were surrounded by a
closely settled zone worked by slave labor, and in all, slaves either wove
during the dry season or worked as caravan porters.

Within a half century after the sugar revolution in the West Indies, we also
see the appearance of highly specialized slave-producing states – Oyo, Asante,
Dahomey, Segu, Futa Jallon. Like the merchant cities, they involved a symbiotic relationship between merchants and warriors. They also all developed
tributary and client networks. Asante obtained most its slaves as tribute from
states to the north of it.[14] In Masina the Ardos, chiefs of nomadic communities, increasingly became clients of the Segu Bambara.[15] Dahomey first provided European slavers with captives taken in its military campaigns, but as
the eighteenth century went along, also became an entrepot for slavers further
north.[16] In the nineteenth century these merchant-warrior formations expanded and new states, usually Fulbe or Mandinka intruders, often preyed on
decentralized societies like the Bwa or Minianka.

We cannot accurately assess the impact of the slave trade on other kinds of
economic activity. We assume that warfare and insecurity were deleterious to
economic growth, but we lack sound documentation.[17] We can only estimate
the level of economic activity in the early seventeenth century, but three things
seem clear. First, the increased number of merchant towns suggests an increase in commercial activity.[18] Second, a large number of slaves, probably a
majority, were kept within Africa even during the peak years of the Atlantic

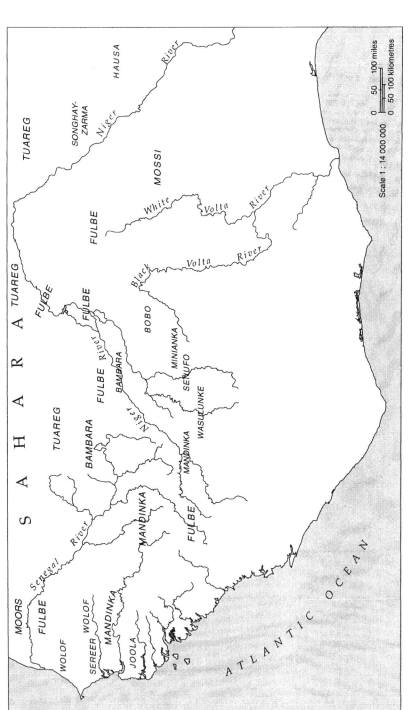

Map 3 Major ethnic groups

trade. This is obvious if we look at male:female and age distribution ratios. Most of those enslaved were women and children, but the majority of those shipped across the Atlantic were male. Slave traders did not want the very young or the old, and while they may have preferred men, they were also interested in healthy young women. The major reason for the predominance of men in the Atlantic trade was the preference for women and children within Africa.[19] Given the predominance of women among those enslaved and men among those exported, huge numbers of women and children must have been absorbed within the region. Men, or probably in most cases boys, were also absorbed as warriors, but in relatively small numbers.[20] The slave trade from Senegambia had a particularly high male:female ratio because most of the slaves came from the far interior.[21] The third is that economic activities which expanded seem to be those which depended on slave labor. The export of hides collapsed, and food security clearly suffered in many areas.[22] But production of gum, textiles and grain seems to have increased.[23] For traders (*juula*), slaves were even in the eighteenth century the best investment they could make. Those who stayed home were as important as those who went on trading expeditions because they produced the food reserves the *juula* needed. With their slave holdings, *juula* were in a position to exploit the development of a commodity trade.

Largely because the demand for slaves within Africa was high, British abolition of the slave trade in 1807 produced only a minor and transient drop in prices.[24] In fact, as slaves were directed to producing the palm oil and peanuts European merchants wanted, the demand for slaves increased.[25] The closing of markets elsewhere in the Americas and in the Maghreb had no significant impact on slaving or slave-trading, which actually increased during the latter part of the nineteenth century when new and more efficient weapons made slaving easier.[26]

There was also a slow but subtle transformation of many decentralized societies. Rodney has argued that most societies on the upper Guinea coast did not have slaves and that slavery was developed only as a result of the Atlantic trade.[27] While this cannot be fully supported, there were many societies that neither took slaves nor sold them, for example, the Jola of the Casamance. The earliest accounts of the Jola were of a people who refused to trade with others and who killed shipwrecked sailors.[28] By the seventeenth century, the Jola were interested enough in trade goods to ransom the sailors. There was also increasing conflict between Jola communities as population growth created competition for rice paddies, oil palms and fishing zones. Prisoners were usually ransomed and only sold when no ransom was forthcoming. Nevertheless, by the late eighteenth century, the Jola were not only selling slaves, but keeping some for themselves as slave ownership became a source of status.[29] We see a similar process in some interior societies, which tried a range of responses during the nineteenth century, regrouping into larger and better defended villages, or alternatively submitting, and sometimes raiding for slaves themselves. The Minianka, who did not have slaves, accepted the authority of war chiefs in resisting the attacks of powerful neighbors like Sikasso and Masina. Maintenance of a fragile authority and conciliation of powerful overlords involved them in taking, using and selling slaves.[30]

Islamic revolution

Trading communities were solidly Muslim and often centers of Islamic learning. Many clerics were from trading families and combined trade and religion.[31] They were not always the strongest supporters of the nineteenth-century jihads. Islam had taken root in West Africa toward the end of the first millennium, most deeply among merchants, who found in Islam not only a link to Arab trading partners, but a world-view and a legal system that regulated much of what they did. Merchants tended to be quietist.[32] As a minority dependant on the good will and protection of rulers, they rarely tried to force their religion on others. Islam was also the religion of a part of the political class, a group that tended to be more eclectic, balancing Islam and traditional religious systems. Many writers are convinced that with the decline of the great empires, the commitment of this group to Islam declined.[33] At the same time, Islam penetrated other parts of society. Merchant elites founded cities. Muslim leaders received gifts of land from rulers, often as a reward for services they provided. Muslim clerics increasingly competed in rural areas with traditional religious leaders. Rural Islam included both those who earned their living making amulets and providing magic and village schools based on real traditions of learning.[34] Crucial to this was the use of slave labor. Levtzion has argued that increased use of slave-farming by clerical elites made it possible for them to devote themselves full time to study and teaching.[35] Levtzion also argues that Islam was spread more by clerics than by merchants.

Throughout the seventeenth and eighteenth centuries, the argument for jihad was made with increasing intensity and often found fertile soil in communities who felt oppressed.[36] Their leaders were clerics who had done nothing but teach and study until undertaking jihad in mid-life. They often faced the opposition or passivity of merchant elites. Some jihad leaders were men like Usman dan Fodio or Umar Tal, known for their learning, but others were rural marabouts with limited education, scorned by the more compromised *ulema* of the major towns. They were important because they were an alternative elite, which responded to the challenge of a crisis. In Masina, Futa Toro and Futa Jallon, the learning revolution clearly took place after the jihad as a Muslim regime tried to create a class of people capable of running a Muslim state.[37] The struggle for power transformed these clerical elites. Many jihads started militarily weaker than their rivals, though a few used an early weapons supremacy. The victories were rarely complete, which meant that the new jihad states were forced to remain vigilant. Increasingly the Muslim cleric and the Muslim merchant were replaced by the Muslim statesman and soldier. While revolutions stimulated learning, leading families turned away from scholarship. In Futa Jallon, Robinson tells us, "most learned clerics were found once again outside the ruling group."[38]

The weapons revolution

These changes were magnified by a weapons revolution which took place in the second half of the nineteenth century. Between 1848 and 1872, most European armies retooled with breech-loading rifles.[39] Within a decade these breech-loaders were replaced by repeating rifles. The effect of military modernization in Europe was to make large numbers of recently obsolete weapons available for the African market. Arms salesmen also made available, albeit at a higher price, the latest weapons until enforcement of the Brussels Convention of 1890 cut the flow of arms.[40] The new rifles had greater range and accuracy. African armies often sought light field artillery, but both French and British refused to give these guns even to their friends. Umar's army used captured French field guns to good advantage, thanks to a French-trained soldier named Samba Ndiaye Bathily, but Samori lacked the capacity to breach African fortifications.[41]

Recent writers have downplayed the importance of the weapons revolution. They argue that it was not as decisive as had once been thought, that enemies either procured the same weapons or devised new tactics or that those who bought the new weapons did not learn the tactics necessary to utilize them adequately.[42] New weapons penetrated the interior slowly. The Sokoto and Masina jihads were fought largely with bows and lances.[43] Raiders in the Songhay area were still using bows and arrows in the late nineteenth century.[44] When Samori besieged Sikasso, the capital of Kenedugu, in 1887 and 1888, much of the Kenedugu infantry were still using bows and the cavalry were armed largely with flintlocks. Horses were probably more important than guns and harder to get.[45] Access to rifles and horses made possible the emergence of small mobile armies, but they remained largely infantry forces because they could not buy or maintain as many horses as they wished. With the new weapons, military units with no social bases could dominate large areas, and those with a social base could build empires.[46]

The problem was not simply that the weapons made possible the ascendancy of those who procured them. Unlike muskets which could be charged with any projectile, the new weapons used bullets and shells tooled to fit the weapons. Furthermore, the existence of field artillery doomed the kind of defensive strategy that was traditional in West Africa. Bah argues that without field artillery, African military leaders could not take a well-prepared walled town.[47] Those who competed for power had little choice but to seek superior weapons and learn how to use them. The greatest problem was how to pay for them. In areas close to the coast, cash crops facilitated rearmament. Muslim revolutionaries in Senegambia bought weapons with income from the sale of peanuts.[48] In the interior, however, that option was often not available. Gold and ivory were not easily expandable items of trade. The kola trade grew, but not as fast as the demand for weapons. State-builders like Umar and Samori could always sell slaves and use the revenue to pay for new weapons. As a result, the new state-builders all became proficient slavers, more proficient than any eighteenth-century slaving state.

Let us look at several case studies.

Futa Toro

The first jihad in the western Sudan took place north of the Senegal river, where for centuries Arab tribes had imposed themselves on and disarmed indigenous Berber tribes who came to be known as the *zawiya*.[49] In the 1670s the *zawiya* rallied under Nasr al-Din, a puritanical reformer, who called on rulers to practice Islam, to limit themselves to four wives, to dismiss their courtiers, and to stop pillaging and enslaving their subjects. The movement quickly spread south of the Senegal river where Nasr al-Din rallied Muslim minorities and overturned regimes in Waalo, Jolof, Kajoor and the Futa Toro.[50] The anti-slavery component of his ideology threatened the French, who feared the formation of a Muslim state able to dictate conditions of trade. They supported the warrior elites. In 1673, Nasr al-Din was killed and by 1677, the traditional rulers were all back in power.

The defeat of Nasr al-Din confirmed the distinction between *hassani* (warrior) tribes and *zawiya* (marabout) tribes. The *hassani* formed the emirates of Trarza and Brakna, which raided for slaves among and sought to dominate the Wolof and Tokolor. The disarmed *zawiya* paid tribute, but also developed their clerical vocation, devoted themselves to commerce and eventually became much wealthier.[51] Their schools became important to the spread of Islam, they controlled the trade in salt, gum and cattle, and in the nineteenth century took their camels south into Senegal to take over the transport of peanuts. A little over a decade after the death of Nasr al-Din, a former follower, Malik Sy, supported by refugees from the Futa Toro, created a Muslim regime in Bundu.[52]

The eighteenth century was a difficult period for the Futa Toro. The arable area is a narrow floodplain on both sides of the Senegal River, about 25 km across, open to external attack and difficult to keep united. The Futa suffered from both Moroccan invaders and Mauritanian raiders. Tokolor living north of the river increasingly found themselves forced to move south. Kane describes the impact of arms imports:

These weapons were used less to defend against increasing external aggression than to attack and enslave the innocent. It follows from this that the social disequilibrium increased because those charged with defending and protecting the people became their principal oppressors. Population decreased. In addition, manual labor was . . . increasingly debased in the popular mind because it tended to be reserved for slaves.[53]

The Muslim *torodbe* regrouped and increasingly defended themselves against both the Moors and the *denianke* rulers. In the 1760s, a Muslim coalition under Suleiman Bal put an end to annual tribute in millet. Then, after Bal's death, they regrouped in the late 1770s and formed a state under Abdul Kader Kan, a respected jurist. Abdul Kader consolidated his forces, confined the *denianke* to the Eastern Futa, and counterattacked against the Moors. Garrison villages were established at crucial fords on the river.[54]

Abdul Kader built mosques, encouraged Quranic education, and distributed land which had been confiscated or had fallen vacant. In 1785, he signed

a treaty with the French regulating tolls.[55] The French had just received Saint
Louis back from the British and were anxious to resume trading. The *torodbe*
insisted that Muslims not be enslaved, and since the inhabitants of the Futa
were all Muslim, they were not to be sold.[56] They did not limit the sale of
non-Muslims, but boats going down river were sometimes searched when
they stopped to pay tolls. The Futa had not, however, been a major source of
slaves. If anything, it was a net importer.[57] In 1796, when a new Damel of
Kajoor rejected Abdul Kader's attempt to impose his brand of Islam, he
invaded, but the Damel met his army with a scorched earth campaign, which
drew the Tokolor army into the heart of Kajoor and then crushed it. Many
Tokolor were sold into the Atlantic slave trade. Abdul Kader was taken
prisoner and kept in slavery for several months before being released.[58]
Finally in 1806, as his rigidity increasingly alienated supporters, he was
deposed and killed. With his death, a new political order emerged, dominated
by a series of powerful electors, whose power was based on control of land and
slaves. Robinson suggests that of all the Fulbe regimes, that in the Futa Toro
diverged most from the original ideals of the jihad.[59] Control of Saint Louis's
water route to the interior gave the Futa oligarchs access to slaves. The office
of *Almamy* changed hands regularly, leaving real power in the hands of
electors hostile to the emergence of a centralized regime. The more frequent
issue in the nineteenth century was not the enslavement of Fulbe, but the flight
or recruitment of their slaves.[60]

Futa Jallon

Rodney and Barry have argued that the jihad in the Futa Jallon was linked to
the Atlantic slave trade.[61] Fulbe pastoralists originally moved into upland
areas that Jallonke agriculturalists did not want and forged symbiotic relationships with the Jallonke. They traded with each other, and sold cattle,
hides, cloth and slaves on the coast. The Fulbe prospered so much that
Europeans in the late seventeenth century already knew the Futa as the land
of the Fulbe.[62] The original jihad coalition, however, was not built on ethnic
but on religious lines. About 1725, an alliance of Muslim Fulbe and Jallonke
tried to throw off the domination of non-Muslim rulers. During the fifty-year
struggle, the Fulbe pushed aside their Jallonke partners and established their
ascendancy. From the 1750s, they were pushing into non-Muslim areas, both
to extend their borders and to raid for slaves.

   Throughout the struggle, the sale of prisoners was a source of revenue. "The
growing supply of slaves," Levtzion argues, "was thus perhaps not only a
by-product of the jihad waged by the Fulani, but also an incitement to it."[63]
At the same time, most Jallonke were reduced to slavery. Slave villages called
runde became the basis of the Fulbe economy. The labor of slaves made it
possible for Fulbe elites to devote themselves to study, war and politics. There
was also a large population of pastoralists called *pulli*, who were late converts
to Islam. They were free, but received few of the benefits of the jihad. Finally,
the Futa also became a focal point for trade routes which drained slaves from

the interior and directed them down to the coast. Often they were traded for cattle, of which the Futa had a surplus. Relations were good with Juula traders and with Jaxanke clerics at Tuba.[64]

Futa Jallon had a distinct advantage over Futa Toro. Its mountain fast-nesses and interior location gave it a security Futa Toro lacked and enabled a homogeneous elite to seize power and construct the kind of society they wished. Islam remained the basis of political power. Schools were founded and a number of centers of learning developed. The office of Almamy alter-nated between families descended from the two first jihad leaders, the Alfaya and Soriya.[65] The power of Timbo, the political capital, was balanced by that of Fugumba, the religious center where the Council of Elders sat. Finally, the power of the Almamy was opposed to the Council of Elders and the nine *diwal* or province leaders, each descended from original jihad leaders.[66] In spite of internal conflict, the Fulbe state gradually extended its control over the coast and the area north and west to the Gambia.[67] This expansion was led by Labe, which became larger than all of the other *diwals* combined and came to control a large non-Fulbe population. The hierarchical nature of the Futa regime also led to the emergence of several religious movements, which rallied the disenfranchised in the name of a reformed Islam. The most important was the Hubbu founded by Mamadu Juhe, a cleric educated in the Futa Toro and Mauritania. For a while he taught the Quran at Timbo, but in 1841 he withdrew from the capital and gradually began to attract those fleeing the exactions of chiefs. Threatened by the regime, the Hubbu moved to the mountainous area of Fitaba and stepped up attacks on the regime. Though the Hubbu did not abolish slavery, many of those fleeing to Fitaba were slaves and were freed.[68] Barry also cites two other movements, that of the Wali of Gumba and that of Cerno Ndama, which contested the Futa regime.[69]

Masina

The most revolutionary of the jihads was that of Seku Amadu in Masina. Other jihads, like that of Usman dan Fodio, transformed existing state structures, but Seku Amadu created a totally new state. His regime, the Dina, changed the way of life in the delta for both the Fulbe and the dominated peoples, using the labor of slaves to underwrite new life styles. It also imposed Islamic law and a more uncompromising Islamic puritanism than any of the other major jihads. Masina is the inner delta of the Niger, a vast floodplain, where the river splits into numerous channels and floods every year. The size of the flood varies, sometimes causing disaster, but in most years it is ideal for both cattle grazing and rice cultivation. Much of the land was wild until recent centuries, a refuge for hunters and fishermen. Fulbe pastoralists began moving in as early as the thirteenth century, and from the sixteenth century systematic inroads were made by both Fulbe herders and Bambara agriculturalists.[70] The Bambara concentrated on dry-land areas, but the Fulbe found the alluvial plains ideal for transhumant cycles. In the rainy season, they would move north of the delta and then, as the flood receded, they moved their herds back to the well-watered grasslands. Gradually they established an ascendancy over pre-existing populations, reducing many to slavery or tributary relationships.[71]

Masina did not create a state before the nineteenth century. Brown speaks of the Fulbe of the delta as "loosely bound in anarchic little clans and matrilineages."[72] The leaders of fractions were called Ardos. Two processes began to transform them. First, each of the Ardos began to develop a group of warriors, often the sons of wives taken from neighboring agriculturalists. These warriors fought on horseback in contrast to the herdsmen, who fought as they followed their herds, on foot.[73] As elsewhere, a warrior subculture emerged. According to Brown:

They developed an ideal model of the intrepid cavalryman, innovative and courageous in battle, unyielding toward foes, stoic in defeat, and magnanimous toward lower classes . . . Military prowess, political power and material wealth did create something of a gap between the Dikko and the other Fulbe clans, and made the Dikko objects of envy and resentment.[74]

Second, as slave-raiding and slave use increased, the Ardos were pulled into the slave-raiding economy as clients of Segu. The Dikko, Brown writes, "policed and taxed the Pulo regions in the interest of the Diarra; they campaigned widely with the armies of Segu. They inter-married with the Diarra, and adopted some of the trappings and social practices of the Bambara royal clan."[75] The Ardos also became dependant on the labor of slaves, both earlier inhabitants reduced collectively and those taken in slave raids. The Dikko thus became slave raiders, slave traders and slave users. At the same time, Masina was increasingly the brunt of both Bambara and Tuareg raids. Vulnerable to attack because of their transhumant cycles, the mass of Fulbe found themselves more prey than predator. Once again, we refer to Brown: "They raided and exacted tribute indiscriminately among the Fulbe as well as other people – thereby stimulating other clans, including many of the scholars, to arm themselves and become partially militarized."[76]

The only alternative elite was the clerics. A diffuse group of varying ethnic origins, they did not compare in learning to their counterparts among the Hausa or along the Senegal river. Most were either makers of amulets or modest teachers of the Quran.[77] As outsiders, they did not participate in the patronage of established states and increasingly attacked not only the Ardos but also the syncretism and compromises that marked cities like Jenne and Dia.[78] During the period before the jihad, a number of clerics built up communities of disciples, possibly influenced by Sokoto and the two Futas. By 1818, Amadu felt strong enough to challenge Dikko power. As the story goes, one of his followers, acting on orders, killed an Ardo who had seized a disciple's blanket. The Jenne *ulema* then drove Amadu out of Jenne and forced him to take refuge at Nukuma, where he gathered elements hostile to the existing order.[79] In 1818, Amadu's army defeated an attacking coalition of the Dikko and the Bambara of Segu. With victory, the Muslims suddenly found themselves heading a national coalition as neutral groups joined the revolution.[80] During the following decade, they built a new state, destroyed the power of the ardos, provided increasing protection from Bambara and Tuareg attacks, and tried to guarantee efficient justice.

Seku Amadu created a standing army capable of protecting transhumant migrations and extending the control of state. He based the new order on the rule of the *ulema*, represented by a council of forty. He always transacted business with two other marabouts at his side.[81] The state moved actively to regulate economic life, asserting control over land and regulating transhumant rights. Every market was placed under the control of an official in charge of weights, measures and prices.[82] Islam was encouraged and its prohibitions strictly enforced. Every village was to have at least one person capable of teaching the Quran. Women were secluded. Alcohol and tobacco were prohibited and only the uncircumcised were allowed to dance. The most important change was sedentarization. One of Brown's informants explains:

... all heads of families were commanded to choose a place where they could be found in the ... season. The heads of villages were to watch over them. Each person had to be with the head of his village at some season ... They changed from straw huts to towns; they followed his [Seku Amadu's] example: only one or two sons would go with the animals because of Sekou and his example.[83]

Thus, only a small part of the community traveled with the herds. The rest remained in their villages, where they could study the Quran and supervise the labor of their slaves. Sedentarization made taxation easier and it altered relationships between the Fulbe and the *rimaibe*.[84] Before the jihad, *rimaibe* villages served as bases for nomadic migrations. From the time of Amadu, Fulbe and *rimaibe* either lived in the same villages or in adjacent ones.[85] Before the jihad, slave use was probably focused in the hands of the Dikko. After, it became generalized.

There is a certain irony about the question of slavery. Seku Amadu's jihad was a response to the inroads of slave raiding on the Fulbe pastoral life. Furthermore, *rimaibe* were probably a high percentage of his original supporters. Many free or noble Fulbe waited on the sidelines during the first stages. Oral traditions say that Amadu appealed for support to slaves and artisan castes. All slaves who fought at Nukuma were freed, but slavery itself was not abolished.[86] In later years, slaves who were conscripted received booty, but were freed only for valor. The regime used slaves from the early days. Those taken from the Dikko were often reassigned to men who served faithfully. As Fulbe infantry became cavalry, the army moved further afield, first to establish the regime's control within the delta, and then to raid for slaves outside the delta. Thus, as in the Futa Toro, Islam started as a liberating force and ended up rationalizing slaving military activity. The *rimaibe* of the delta became as much like serfs as any group in West Africa. The Dina lasted less than a half-century, falling to Umar's armies in 1862, but by that time the Fulbe of Masina had become sedentary, dependent on slave labor, and deeply committed to Islam.

The holy war of Umar Tal

Most West African jihads took place when a self-conscious Muslim community felt threatened by ruling elites. The jihad of Al Hajj Umar Tal began with conquest of societies hitherto resistant to Islam by a largely Fulbe invading force and ended up fighting some of the most orthodox Muslims in West Africa. David Robinson calls it an "imperial jihad" by contrast to the "revolutionary jihads" led by Seku Amadu, Usman dan Fodio and Suleiman Bal.[87] Umar is an example of what Cruise O'Brien calls a "charismatic career," that is to say, a career in which a leader consciously prepares himself for his mission.[88] Umar was born in about 1796 in a modest *torodbe* family. He grew up while memories of revolution were vivid, but the elan was gone and, for many, the revolution had failed. Umar left the Futa to make the pilgrimage to Mecca in about 1820. On his return, he settled in the Futa Jallon, wrote his most important book, *Rimah*, and began to gather arms and a small community of disciples.[89] After a Senegambian recruiting expedition in 1846 and 1847, he moved to Dingiray just outside the Futa, and in 1852 he began a jihad against the Mandinka kingdom of Tamba. In 1855, he defeated the Bambara kingdom of Karta after a brilliant campaign that mobilized support in the Futa Toro and Senegal river kingdoms hostile to Kartan domination. At this point, only Faidherbe barred his access to Futa Toro. The failure to take the French fort at Medine in 1857 and Faidherbe's subsequent success in controlling the upper river forced Umar to turn to the east. His 1860 treaty with the French confirmed his access to weapons, but was an admission of defeat. By this time Umar had begun the conquest of Segu, completed in 1862.

Throughout these campaigns, Umar fought as if he was doing God's work and seems to have assumed that if he got into difficulty, God would save him. He attacked entrenched states with larger and more powerful armies. To get the men he needed, he recruited in his native Futa Toro, appealing to flight (*hijra*) from the corruption of a Senegal increasingly dominated by the French.[90] Umar needed continued success to keep his armies going and booty to reward them. Umar also constantly pushed to the limits of his logistical support. During his campaign against Segu, he sent home women and children because he could not feed them. Mage described "a column of veritable walking skeletons who for a month or even more had not eaten anything other than leaves or grass."[91] Once victorious, Umar's hungry armies imposed themselves on conquered peoples. This led to revolts that sprang up within a year or two of almost each of his victories. In Karta, the Massassi aristocracy were deprived of wives and palaces and were reduced to the status of neophytes in Islam. They revolted in 1855 as did Umar's Jawara allies, who were offended by discrimination in the distribution of booty.[92]

This made it difficult for Umar to win the support of those he needed. Some Muslims like the Jaxanke of Tuba cited their quietist traditions in refusing to participate and others were among those who revolted. When his armies moved into the Niger river towns of Sinsani and Nyamina, local people anticipated the introduction of Muslim law, a more orderly system of justice and lower taxes. Instead, there was arbitrary confiscation of goods, higher taxes and, in some cases, humiliation. Muslims had to work the fields of the Umarian commander, a task they thought appropriate for slaves, and found themselves worse off than they ever were under the Bambara.[93] In 1863, both Nyamina and Sinsani revolted. Umarian Segu never regained control of Sinsani or of the vital river route to Timbuktu.

Up to 1862, Umar's enemies were not Muslim. In that year, he attacked the most orthodox Muslim state in the Sudan, Masina. Amadu III of Masina supported Segu against Umar, and when it lost, refused to turn over Bina Ali, the Fama of Segu. Nevertheless, Umar's attack was a clear violation of Muslim law.[94] The Kunta Moors, hitherto hostile to Masina, joined Amadu III, but Umar's forces prevailed in a bloody battle. Within a year of the fall of Hamdullahi, Masina rose, hostile to alien rule, offended by forced labor, confiscation of property and the execution of members of the royal family. With Amadu, Umar's son and chosen successor, tied down by revolts in Segu, Umar and a band of supporters escaped from Hamdullahi only to be tracked down to caves in the cliffs at Degembere, where he died.

Amadu in Segu and Umar's nephew, Tijani in Masina, rallied Futanke forces. For the next thirty years, Amadu struggled to maintain his ascendancy, fighting both his brothers and the remnants of the Bambara state. Amadu's major military concern was keeping open the trade route to the west, which provided arms and, in the 1880s, more recruits. The defeated Bambara withdrew, but rebuilt their army and harassed the Futanke until they returned to Segu in an alliance with the French. By the mid-1880s, the Bambara were operating from a fort only 14 miles from Segu.[95] The Futanke had weapons supremacy, but their tax resources were limited as was their ability to make war. Even more than their Bambara predecessors, the Futanke lived by the razzia which provided them with slaves who could be traded for weapons and, during periods of hardship, for needed food.

Hanson argues that there was never a "Tokolor empire," but rather a series of Umarian states.[96] Certainly Amadu never exercised authority over Tijani in Bandiagara and did so with only the greatest difficulty in Karta, where he twice deposed independent-minded brothers. Karta was the wealthiest and for Amadu the most strategic of the Umarian states. Umar's choice as governor of Karta was Mustafa Keita, a Hausa slave who distinguished himself in the conquest and successfully mediated between different ethnic communities in Karta.[97] Most Futanke emigrants in Karta rejected Amadu's pleas that they join his embattled forces in Segu. A split also developed within the Karta Futanke. Many first-generation migrants put their slave booty to work growing grain in the Xolombinne valley, which produces two crops a year, one rain-fed and one on the flood plain. The grain could be sold both to the Moors and to the French. By the 1880s, about 500 tons a year were being marketed at Medine and almost as much at Bakel. The grain growers opposed military adventures that would cut off access to the French market. By contrast, later migrants were often young men, who came to Karta to make their fortunes. They wanted slaves, and an aggressive military policy was the only way to get them.[98] The grain market also spawned an active slave market at Koniakary, where prices were often twice those in the river area.

Umar's nephew Tijani was probably the ablest of Umar's heirs.[99] When Umar was besieged at Hamdullahi, Tijani escaped and rallied support from Fulbe, who originally opposed Umar, and from the non-Muslim Dogon. His forces arrived too late to save Umar, but he exploited tensions between his rivals to establish an Umarian regime dependent on those groups most hostile to Umar's goals. The most important effect of this success was a thirty-year civil war between the Futanke, the Masina Fulbe and the Kunta. Tijani tried to move large populations from the Left Bank to areas he controlled, but he was never completely successful. The rival forces not only raided each other, but regularly raided into Bobo, Minianka and Dogon areas to get slaves necessary for the purchase of horses and weapons.

One reason that the jihads of the eighteenth and nineteenth centuries failed to achieve their goals was that they got entangled in the logic of slave-raiding, slave-trading and slave use. Umar's jihad was the most striking example of this. From the first, Umar's actions limited the revolutionary effect of his efforts. To be sure, careers were open to talent, and in the early years those who served him well advanced quickly. This was particularly true of slaves he received as booty or as gifts during his six-year stay in Nigeria.[100] He was, however, cautious and socially conservative, more so than Seku Amadu. While living in Futa Jallon, he was careful not to encourage slave flight.[101] When Umar seized Bambuk, he appropriated slaves or returned them to their owners.[102] He was at the time trying to rally those in the upper Senegal river area hostile to Karta's hegemony.

Slave booty was also important to his soldiers. Umar's forces often killed male prisoners.[103] The Atlantic slave trade had come to an end, and men were of little value. The Saharan trade did not want men. They were more likely to resist or escape. At Sirmanna in the upper Senegal, 600 men were killed, but 1,545 women and children were taken prisoner.[104] Nonetheless, many men were taken prisoner. One of Mage's informants said that Umar's *talibés* each took between ten and twenty prisoners in the suppression of the Karta revolt of 1855.[105] Robinson estimates that 9,000 captives were taken in the conquest of Segu and 13,600 in the suppression of the Segu revolts.[106] The most important exception to the killing of male prisoners was the slave soldiers, who were allowed to change sides. After the defeat of Karta, about 2,000 of Karta's *tonjon* were incorporated as *sofa* in Umar's army. They formed the nucleus of the *jomfutung*, "meeting of slaves" battalion, one of five in Umar's army.[107] In the 1870s, Amadu depended increasingly on the *sofa* and on a handful of Hausa, many also probably slaves. Slaves were important for two other reasons. First, superior weapons often compensated for the numerical inferiority of his forces. Against Masina, Umar was outnumbered by about 50,000 to 30,000, but Amadu III's army was equipped largely with spears, swords, bows and arrows. Umar also was able to use captured cannon to breach walls and attack fortifications that were hitherto impregnable.[108] Umar tried to control gold-producing areas in upper Guinea, but gold was not available in large amounts. Weapons and ammunition were bought either with slaves, or with goods like salt and kola which had been purchased with slaves. Umar's forces also needed horses, for which slaves were also important.

Slaves were also important to the individual warrior. The decimation of faithful disciples in battle created a constant need for more men, many of whom expected material rewards. Robinson describes Umar's dilemma during a difficult period: "Umar's problem between 1857 and 1860 was that he had no rewards for the masses for whom he had evoked such a glorious future. He had not mobilized these people to raise millet and cattle in Karta, *and they did not yet have the slaves to do the work for them*"[109] (emphasis added). Umar's soldiers treated physical labor as the lot of slaves. After failing to take Medine, Umar built a fortress at Kunjan. At one point, he carried rocks himself to set an example for his talibés.[110] In the twenty-five years that followed, Amadu's forces conducted themselves as their Segu predecessors had, living off the razzia, though with less success because it was linked to a political and economic base more fragile than that of the Segu Bambara.

Samori

Samori was a more effective state-builder than Umar. More realistic, less dependent on divine assistance, he was an effective organizer and an innovator, without a doubt the most difficult opponent the French faced in Africa. In spite of this, he got caught in the same slaving scissors crisis that destroyed the Umarian enterprise. Samori was from a Malinke area on the fringes of the forest.[111] This area's traditions refer back to the glorious days of Mali, but in the nineteenth century it was divided into small units called *kafu*. After mid-century, a series of new military leaders began building larger political units. Mostly Muslim, these new men had experience in trade and an appreciation of military hardware, but they were not clerics. Yves Person has described this phenomenon as a "juula revolution" because it involved new forms of political and military organization.[112] Samori started out as an itinerant trader and as a soldier in one of these armies. Tradition has it that he enslaved himself to redeem his mother, but was so successful as a soldier that he persuaded his superior to impose him as ruler of his native *kafu*. Starting about 1861, he gradually extended his control through the southern savanna. He was more successful than Umar in integrating conquered peoples because he started in a homogeneously Malinke area and, at first, demanded less of them. In his early years, he had neither weapons supremacy nor an ideological mission. In 1873, he founded his capital at Bissandugu. By 1875, he controlled about 20,000 square kilometres and about 75,000 people. By 1881, he controlled Juula Kankan and most of the Malinke area.[113]

When the French first collided with Samori in 1883, he had a large army recruited through a *levée en masse*. He learned quickly from the French and shifted in the late 1880s to a highly mobile cavalry force armed with late-model repeating rifles.[114] He also began using Islam as an official religion and tried to impose it on conquered peoples. Samori's elite troops were his *sofa*, well-trained cavalry, disciplined, intensely loyal and largely slave. Bissandugu was surrounded by a belt of slave plantations about 15 km thick. The slaves lived in hamlets of about a hundred and worked under the direction of retired *sofa*.[115] Samori had resources, but they were inadequate to the demands war placed on him. The most important came from outside: kola from the forest and salt from the Sahara. Ivory and gold were available in limited amounts. The rubber boom did not provide a real stimulus to the economy of the southern Sudan until Samori was on the run.[116] Faced frequently with larger armies and, in the case of the French, with a better equipped army, Samori had no choice but to slave. He did so more systematically and more efficiently than anyone before him. In spite of this Person calculates that Samori was never able to equip more than 5,000 to 6,000 men with modern rifles. With an army that numbered at its peak about 35,000 men, that meant that most of the army was equipped with dated weapons.[117] Horses were probably more important than guns, but Person calculates that Samori never had over 2,000 and often had fewer.[118] He tried unsuccessfully to acquire field artillery. The demands of warfare constantly created strains as raiding ravaged the population base on which he depended. Subject populations and those threatened by conquest often sought French protection, and when the French began chipping away at the empire in the 1890s, Samori found himself ruling a wasteland.

Sikasso

Samori's major rival was Tyeba Traore of Sikasso. The Traore were warriors from Kong who settled among the stateless Senufo of Kenedugu toward the end of the eighteenth century, bringing military skills and ties to juula trade networks. By the late nineteenth century, the Traores had been absorbed by the Senufo and the Senufo language was spoken at court. Traditional religion remained dominant, though some sources say Tyeba was a Muslim.[119] Tradition credits the Traore with the introduction of clothes, cowries and maize.[120] The establishment of a state involved two parallel processes. Villages submitted to new rulers and slaves taken in raids were resettled in areas under Traore control. After a battle, military commanders got first choice of the younger males to replenish or increase their numbers. The rest were either exchanged for horses, guns or trade goods or were resettled. As the state developed, it also became a major commercial center. Rondeau suggests that in a gerontocratic society warfare may have been attractive to young men frustrated by the hegemony of their elders.[121] Tyeba came to power toward 1870. In about 1875, he took the title of Fama, established his capital at Sikasso, and began construction of a *tata* (fortress) which became within a decade the most powerful defensive structure in the Sudan.[122]

Slave trade

The demand for slaves within Africa was high and grew higher during the century. Commercial reports from the early colonial period make clear that slaves were by far the most important item of trade in the markets of the Sudan, often a majority of the value of taxable trade. Slaves had to be moved away from the area in which they were captured for fear of escape. They were

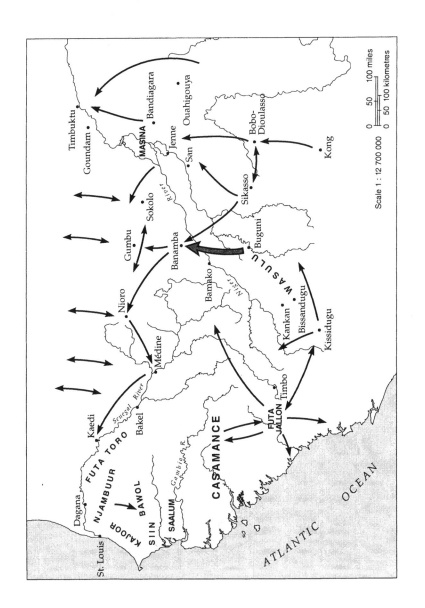

Map 4 Major slave trade routes of Western Sudan

Fig. 3 Slave caravan in Malinke area of Sudan.

moved in every direction and often sold several times and in many small transactions. The most important slave trade routes centered on Banamba, a town founded only in the 1840s, which had become the most important slave market in the Sudan.[123] Banamba had two advantages. It lay on Segu's western corridor, the economic lifeline to Senegal and was in an area suited to raising horses.[124] From the early 1870s, Samori's caravans and, later, Tyeba's, moved north to exchange slaves for horses. The demand for horses is indicated by the prices Binger reported: two or three slaves per horse among the Moors, six to ten in Karta and Beledugu, fifteen to twenty at Samori's capital at Bissandugu.[125] By the 1890s, Banamba was also the major distribution center for salt from Mauritania and, thus, the major source of slaves for Mauritania. There were about 1,500 Moors in the area.[126] The Futanke and then the French both tried to cut off the horse trade, but with only partial success. The trade went both ways. Maraka merchants brought horses to Samori and Samori's caravans brought slaves to the Maraka towns.

Slaves moved from Banamba in several directions. Some went into Mauritania, some to desert-side towns like Sokolo and Nioro. Many remained near Banamba which was surrounded by a closely cultivated, 50 km belt of slave-worked plantations.[127] They grew grain for trade to the north and wove cotton cloth for trade both north and south. Slave-based production also flourished around other Maraka towns, for example Baraweli, a major slave market on the route to Sikasso. Banamba was also a central location on a Sahel trade route that went from Medine and Nioro through Gumbu and Sokolo and from there to either Sinsani or across to Timbuktu.[128] Baillaud claimed that this was cheaper for goods coming from the upper Senegal than the river route through Bamako.[129] The most important slave trade, however, was from Banamba to Senegal and the Gambia. There was also an important route from what is now northern Ghana up through the Mossi states to the bend of the Niger.

Desert-side slave sector

The desert-side was second only to Senegambia as a market for slaves. Every year, Saharan tribes moved down into the sahel where they exchanged salt and stock for slaves, grain and cloth. The high return on slave labor shaped a very systematic and rigorous kind of slavery. Slaves worked in the fields during the rainy season and wove during the dry season. Slavery in this area very much resembled that which Lovejoy has described for the Sokoto Caliphate in that work was carefully regulated, discipline tight, and manumission rare.[130] At the beginning of the colonial period, desert-side cercles were all among the highest in percentage of slaves.[131] The only market north of the desert to remain important till the end of the century was Morocco. An annual caravan crossed the Sahara every year from Timbuktu to Tindouf and smaller caravans took the western route through Mauritania. Lenz traveled from Nioro to Medine with a caravan of about a hundred women and children destined for the western route.[132] Shroetter has recently estimated that this trade fluctuated between 4,000 and 7,000 between the 1870s and the French capture of Timbuktu in 1894.[133] This represents a substantial increase from previous estimates, but it uses tax records that were not used by others and it equates well with information about the earlier part of the century.[134] After 1894, the trade from Timbuktu dropped sharply. In 1897, Father Mahiet, a White Father in Timbuktu, estimated the northward movement from that city at 1,000 to 1,500 a year.[135] A French report suggested, however, that little of this movement went to North Africa: "Slaves at present are not the object of an important trade with the Arab countries . . . they are purchased primarily by tribes which exploit the salt mines, by the Ulliminden Tuareg, who form agricultural colonies in the East, in the Adar, and in the Immarauy."[136] Cordell and McDougall have also argued that the trade into the desert may have been more important than the trade across the desert. Certainly all across the Sahara slaves did most of the herding, most of the domestic labor and all of the oasis agriculture, in fact almost all the physical labor. High mortality among slaves, especially during drought years, meant that replacement was a constant problem.[137]

Organization of the trade

Some slavers moved long distances. A group of Senegalese traders arrested in Sokolo in 1902 were more than a thousand kilometers from home.[138] Binger describes Soninke from the upper Senegal engaging in complicated triangular voyages in which they started out with imported cloth, used it to buy salt, and then traded the salt for slaves.[139] More common was probably a dry-season expedition, in which the merchant's strategy was determined by his desire to return home before planting time. Binger also attributes such a strategy to the Koroko.[140] This means that a slave might be sold two, three or even more times before finally being settled somewhere, and given the nature of the market might well be marched back and forth over long distances. Binger talks of a young man taken prisoner by Umar's troops in Gajaga on the upper Senegal, moved first to Jenne, a trip of 700 to 800 km, then to Bandiagara, where he was sold to a chief from Kong, another trip of 600 km.[141] Cheikna Keita tells the story of a woman who grew old in his family's house. She had been enslaved three times, the first as a young girl. She claimed to have traveled in the course of a lifetime from the northern Ivory Coast to Gao, to Segu, to Kano, back to Gao and then to Nara.[142]

During peak periods caravans could be quite large. In March 1889, 40 percent of the slaves arriving at Medine came in caravans of over fifty slaves.[143] Most slaves, however, moved in relatively small caravans. Few of those stopped by the French seem to have included more than forty or fifty.[144] A lot of slave trading involved small traders moving two or three slaves. Binger describes much of the Mossi trade in such terms.[145] The size of caravans was probably influenced by concerns for security. In secure areas, smaller caravans were possible, but this meant that, in such areas, the trade took place everywhere. There were few formal markets though Mage described one at Nyamina. There were about a hundred slaves of both sexes and all ages, some of them in irons, sitting in a large hut surrounded by barriers. There were a dozen merchants in the hall. When a buyer approached, the merchant would show off the slave, often focusing on the teeth or the musculature. Mage commented, however, that it was the only place he saw slaves displayed for sale.[146] In general, slaves were sold privately within compounds and were not openly displayed. Binger reports: "Sometimes, but very rarely, the slave traders make a tour of the market with two or three unhappy individuals, not clothed, but well covered with shea butter. After several greetings, the price is discussed and the merchandise is selected in a hut."[147] In most trade centers there were brokers who specialized in slaves and often stocked small numbers. At Medine, for example, there were three brokers (téfé), who specialized in slaves, two of whom controlled most of the trade.[148] At Salaga, there was a formal slave market into the 1870s, but it gave way to the sale of slaves within broker compounds.[149]

Conclusion

The state-building efforts described in this chapter were only a few of the many that took place in the region during the nineteenth century. Some were short-lived. The jihad of Al-Kari of Bussé lasted only two years.[150] Few have been studied. Many state-builders started out as clients of the more powerful. Tyeba linked himself to the Futanke at Segu. Alfa Molo was a tributary of the Futa Jallon. The use of clients probably produced slaves without disrupting the core area of the state. Others sought external legitimation. Liptako in northern Burkina Faso was a distant outlier of the Sokoto Caliphate and Seku Amadu seems to have early sought legitimation from Sokoto.[151] The same forces in varying combinations shaped these lesser efforts. With a few exceptions, Islam provided the ideological basis. The expansion of commodity production and the extension of market relationships provided the opportunity. New weapons provided the means. Many started with bows, lances and flintlocks, but by the last quarter of the nineteenth century modern rifles were being used in most regions and made possible the domination of alien groups like the Futanke and the Zaberma.

In the end, however, the slave trade and the weapons revolution were the two prongs of a scissors crisis. Slaving limited the possibility of expansion of any of these states. Each of the great state-builders is reviled to this day in areas that suffered from his efforts. It also created large deserted areas virtually empty of people. New weapons facilitated conquest, but in few areas did they create more than small and temporary islands of stability. Power was illusory. The price paid for these weapons was the sowing of death and destruction across the Sudan. And in the end, as we shall see in subsequent chapters, the armies of the Sudan had neither the weapons nor the training needed to stand up to the Europeans.

4   Senegal after Brière

The concession of land whether for the route, for the stations, for stopping places can in no way involve rights over surrounding areas in favor of the French, nor serve as a refuge for subjects of the Damel who wish to withdraw themselves from his authority.

As a consequence, no subject of Cayor can enter the interior of the concession without the express authorization of the Damel.

Treaty of 1879 with Lat Dior[1]

When Brière de l'Isle arrived in Senegal as governor in 1876, Senegal was still largely a collection of commercial posts, but France ruled about 200,000 people. The population of the communes was almost twice what it had been in 1848, trade had increased, and peasant production was expanding on the mainland. French trade with Kajoor hit 3 million francs a year in 1874.[2] Millet, cotton and peanuts were being traded in the upper Senegal river area. Brière picked up where Faidherbe left off. In a series of military and diplomatic efforts, he tightened control over the Senegal river, the peanut basin and the Guinea coast.[3] He also initiated a railroad project that began the occupation of the Sudan.

Early in 1880, Naval Minister Admiral Jauréguiberry asked the Chamber of Deputies to approve construction of three linked railroads: one from Dakar to Saint Louis, a second connecting the Senegal and Niger rivers, and a third linking the other two railroads.[4] Work was to start almost immediately on the first two. Going through areas not under French sovereignty, these projects required military control. In August 1879, even before the project was presented, Brière sent Capt. Joseph Gallieni to the Sudan to survey possible routes, to negotiate treaties, and to make arrangements for a post at Bafulabe. The post was set up in December 1879, but Gallieni was detained for ten months at Segu by Amadu. By the time he was released, a separate military command had been established and France's forward position was at Kita. The conquest of the Sudan had begun. In the short run, the Dakar–Saint Louis railroad was more important. It led to the conquest of mainland Senegal, and stimulated a process of economic growth.

The Darrigrand Affair

From the beginning, Brière ran into problems. The first was waiting for him when he arrived in Senegal. Before the late 1870s few French leaders seriously considered a massive land empire in Africa. The empire consisted of substantial colonies in Algeria and the West Indies and a smattering of posts and beachheads elsewhere. The universalist heritage of the French revolution meant that not only did the colonies get representation in the Chamber of Deputies and many of the rights of metropolitan French, but administrative structures often paralleled those in the metropole. Thus both courts and prosecuting attorneys took orders from the Ministry of Justice and not from the naval ministry, which ran the colonies. This mirrored a similar conflict in France between the Prefects, depending on Interior, and the prosecutors, depending on Justice.[5] Irregular procedures in slavery matters were bound, in the words of naval minister Rigault de Genouilly, "to raise the scruples of men long accustomed to the rigorous formulas of the law."[6] In 1848, Larcher, the prosecutor, objected to efforts to deal with the slave question administratively, that is, without recourse to the courts. Carrère, his successor, was more pliant. In 1868, a prosecutor named Bazot refused to be involved in either expelling runaways or administering guardianship for freed children.[7] Then in 1874, Prosper Darrigrand, a lawyer with West Indian experience, arrived in Senegal.[8]

In 1875, Darrigrand brought slave-trading charges against two *habitants* in a case involving a thirteen-year-old girl enslaved in Karta and taken to Saint Louis by Mauritanian slave dealers.[9] The girl had been taken in a raid, in which the men were killed and the women and children sold for food. The case became known because the purchaser tried to avoid payment. Charges were brought under the 1831 law against slave trading. Governor Valière opposed prosecution on the grounds that the 1831 law applied only to sale for export, but he lacked the authority to stop the case from going forward. The accused were acquitted, but several months later Darrigrand tried again in a case that involved Jama Thiam, a slave from Coki, a Muslim town not far from Saint Louis which was involved in fighting between marabout Amadu Shaixu and Damel Lat Dior of Kajoor. Taken prisoner by Lat Dior's warriors, the slave was sold in Saint Louis, where she found out about the law and asked for her freedom. The Political Affairs department was willing to free her without asking how she got to Saint Louis, but Darrigrand decided again to prosecute. The purchaser, Samba Toute, insisted he wanted her as a wife, but he had not sought a certificate of liberty for her during the two months she was with him. She also fought with his first wife, who did not support her husband's testimony.[10]

Under pressure Darrigrand agreed at first to prosecute cases only within Saint Louis though he was disturbed by slave-trading in villages under French sovereignty.[11] In 1878, he charged four Senegalese with slave-trading. All four had slave-cultivated farms with fifteen or more slaves just outside of Saint Louis. Charges were dropped against three of the men, but Darrigrand refused to yield on the case of Ndiack Ndiaye. Ndiaye was the son of former slaves, hard-working and frugal, with eight children, fifteen slaves, and residences inside and out of Saint Louis. He had several times served in French military campaigns, on one occasion organizing a volunteer unit. He was also a rival of the village chief, who reported him as a slave-dealer. Ironically, the same chief had several times sold him slaves.[12]

The acting governor asked Darrigrand to drop the charges. When Brière de l'Isle returned from France, he was livid. Brière argued that political considerations should take precedence in slave matters. There were two political questions. First, Brière was afraid of hostility in occupied Waalo and in a Kajoor that he was eying covetously. Second, the sale took place at the home of Bou-el-Mogdad, a Muslim cleric and collaborator. Faidherbe and his heirs believed France needed Muslim collaborators if it wanted a Sudanic empire. To inspire confidence, he set up a Muslim court, encouraged Muslim cooperation and was careful about Muslim sensibilities. Bou-el-Mogdad was a key figure, cadi of the Muslim court, sometime interpreter and emissary, and the first Senegalese to have his way paid to Mecca. His ties with Mauritanian tribes were also a source of slaves for the Saint Louis area.[13] Brière tried to get Darrigrand removed, but was told that this would not be understood in France.[14] The minister wanted Darrigrand to show more deference in political questions, but he reminded Brière that local people had to be warned neither to trade slaves nor to mistreat them on French territory.[15] But Darrigrand kept at it. In January 1879, he brought slave-trading charges against two subjects from a village in the interior in a case that involved a deliberate challenge to the administration, first because the accused were clearly subjects and, second, because the Political Affairs Bureau was accused of turning slaves over to their masters.[16] By 1879, however, former Governor Jauréguiberry had become Minister. He insisted that the case not be pursued further.[17]

There are data on seventeen slaves involved in prosecutions. At least ten of them came from the upper river area, taken by either Bambara or Tokolor raiders. Two came from the Moors, one the offspring of a Moor and a slave woman, who claimed that he was given to Ndiack Ndiaye in payment of a debt. Only one was enslaved near Saint Louis. One spoke a dialect unknown on the coast, and presumably could not be interrogated. There were two major trade routes. Slaves were either brought down river by Soninke or Wolof traders, or were moved overland by the Moors. Most of them were relatively recent imports. In only one case, a fifty-year-old male, was there no indication of origin. He had two wives, however, who had been brought down river about four and eight years earlier. The demand was great enough that slaves were being moved to Saint Louis from as far as Wasulu.[18]

Victor Schoelcher

The slavery issue was one of three that isolated Brière de l'Isle within both Senegal and France at the very time when he was laying the basis for French expansion into the Sudan. Bordeaux commercial houses wanted free trade in the river area and elimination of a system under which licensed traders were protected in the *escales*. At the same time, the coming to power of the Republicans in France led to re-establishment of the General Council in 1879. Rivals in river markets, Bordeaux and Saint Louis traders were both hostile to Brière's expansionism because it involved increased taxes.[19] Though they favored continued toleration of slavery, they turned for support in France to men hostile to slavery.[20]

The French press focused on the issue of slavery. In 1878, a Protestant missionary in Senegal wrote an article about slavery and the slave trade in Senegal for a Protestant publication, *Eglise Libre*. This story was picked up by a number of other publications and was sent to Senator Victor Schoelcher.[21] Then, in January, *Le Petit Parisien* reprinted Jauréguiberry's confidential circular of 1862. Schoelcher was the leader of the abolitionist movement in 1848. He had devoted his life to a series of causes, of which the most important were the abolition of slavery and the well-being of freed slaves.[22] Schoelcher did some further research, and then, on 1 March 1880, he rose in the Senate to speak. He conceded that France had an obligation to respect the *statut personnel* of colonized peoples, but the law on slavery was clear and colonial policy violated it. The phrase in Jauréguiberry's 1862 decree that slaves would be expelled "where their masters would be free to retake them" disturbed Schoelcher. "Is this not to make ourselves gratuitously the master's gendarmes and to push the love of property further than respect for humanity permits . . .? What kind of a role is this for a France which prides itself in having abolished slavery?" Schoelcher cited the printed form used for the expulsions and regretted that runaways had to register to get their freedom. "Slaves are not freed where there is no slavery," he stated. He cited the case of a commandant who stopped a slave caravan and then was forced to return the slaves to their owners. He discussed Darrigrand. He talked about a slave who jumped off the bridge from Saint Louis rather than be returned to her master.[23]

The Minister, Jauréguiberry, resurrected in his own defense arguments made earlier in official correspondence. He called African slavery "a type of hereditary serfdom" and insisted on the need to respect local customs. He was afraid that caravans would be scared away from French posts and that the communes would become refuges for criminals, vagabonds and the discontented. The Senate accepted Jauréguiberry's explanations, but the story was out. In 1880, letters passed back and forth between Jauréguiberry and Brière. The Governor defended himself, but Jauréguiberry insisted on stricter enforcement of the law.[24] Brière could accept a ban on slave-trading, but not the freeing of runaways.[25] He had banned slavery in Dakar and Rufisque, and regularly insisted he was doing all he could do on slavery without compromising French interests. For example, he asked the Commandant of Dagana to investigate boats stopping at Dagana. Slaves were being transported there and then either sold or moved overland into Kajoor. In the next few years, many slaves were freed at Dagana.[26] In one case, it was a caravan of twelve children aged six to eighteen purchased in Nioro, Gumbu and Medine and being moved overland down to lower Senegal.[27] The Commandant at Dagana insisted that slaves were being moved by citizens: "the Bakel and

Medine traders help the trade by hiding masters and slaves in their houses till the boats are ready to depart. The boat owners, well paid by their passengers, are careful not enter them on their papers. Questioned at the post on whether they are importing slaves, the response is always negative."[28] The Commandant also told the local chief not to return runaways to the Moors without his approval.[29]

Jauréguiberry and Brière fought a vigorous rearguard action, but neither stayed in office long enough. The crucial years from 1880 to 1884 were unstable ones in both Paris and Saint Louis. In Saint Louis six governors served over three years, two of them dying on the job. In Paris Freycinet fell in September 1880, and Jauréguiberry was replaced as Minister by Admiral Cloué, with whom Brière did not get along. Cloué insisted that the notion that French soil freed should be applied as much as was "compatible with public security and with the maintenance of good relations between us and our neighbors," and that no one could own slaves within French posts or in villages under the protection of those posts. African traders were to be warned that slaves brought on to French soil were free and that masters could neither use force to make them leave nor call on French assistance.[30] Lacking ministerial support, opposed by a General Council hostile to his Sudan project, Brière resigned in February 1881.[31] That May, Cloué attended the annual banquet celebrating the abolition of slavery in 1848, as did several other politicians, including Gambetta.[32] De Lanneau, Brière's successor, reduced the waiting period for liberty papers to eight days.

Schoelcher greeted Cloué's letter as a victory for abolition, but soon, colonial authorities were waffling again.[33] Canard, an old colonial hand, who served briefly as governor, was hesitant about enforcement. He distributed a circular announcing that a runaway could be freed only after submitting written proof of three months' residence in a fixed location. If someone claimed to be free, the administrator was to ask for written confirmation from a village chief.[34] Canard also peppered the Minister with reports about problems. In November 1881, it was loyal allies from Bakel:

They complain bitterly about our way of acting on the subject of slaves. "They are property," they say, "and our wealth, and you have encouraged their desertion to increase the number of your soldiers. How can we cultivate our lands?" I succeeded in reassuring them, promising that Commandants would no longer sign up their slaves if they were claimed within a reasonable period.

In the margins, someone has written "Oh!!" In January and February 1882, the political reports speak of Lat Dior's demands about his slaves. In March: "The king of the Moors complains constantly of the liberty that we give his slaves."[35] Cloué's successor Rouvier was just as insistent that there be no toleration of slavery, but suggested that the administration go only as far as was "compatible with public security and maintenance of good relations with our neighbors."[36]

Within a few months, Jauréguiberry was back as Minister, and this time treading a tightrope. In June 1882, he told the new governor, Vallon, that he was to pay careful attention to French humanitarian sentiments. There was to be no sale, open or disguised, no transfer and no ownership of slaves on French soil. At the same time, he insisted: "It would be contradictory, in effect, to make so many sacrifices, on the one hand, to develop our relations on the river and on the African continent, while on the other hand, we drive natives away from our posts under the pretext of imposing on them a civilization for which they are unfortunately not ready."[37] He agreed with promises Canard made to Lat Dior not to interfere outside French territory and to the Emir of Trarza not to allow his subjects into Saint Louis without written authorization. Vallon was also reminded of his police powers and told that runaways who refused to join the army or accept work could be expelled.

Schoelcher, in turn, received letters from Senegal that little had changed. He wrote of the chief of a quarter in Saint Louis, who arbitrarily seized some runaway slaves and returned them to their masters. In another case, a French officer presented two freed slaves, who wanted to enlist. He was told that they could not be enrolled until they had spent three months in Saint Louis.[38] The new Chief of the Judicial Service wrote that

it is only too certain that slavery still reigns in Senegal, not only on French territory, in the posts, but in the city of Saint Louis and in the outskirts. On this point, no amelioration, absolutely none, for several years. Without doubt in Saint Louis, the shameful habits of slavery are practised secretly – authority is there, and people are afraid. But there is no pretence in the outskirts of Saint Louis, at the gates of the city at Leybar and Gandiole – it is there that the Moors come to sell their merchandise.[39]

Vallon was more disturbed about the character of the runaways, whom he saw as lazy and dishonest. He feared that they would involve him in unnecessary wars.

In 1883, Senegal's first civilian governor, René Servatius, arrived. Henceforth, runaway slaves had only to report to the judicial authorities to receive their papers without any formalities. On French territory, Servatius wrote, "there can be and there should be only free men, and no one has the right to claim or to take a captive. Such is the law."[40] Once again, the administration took what seems like a clear-cut action, but Servatius died suddenly after only six months in office. Under his successors, there was an increase in emancipations, but the administration limited the effects of its anti-slavery policies, most notably in Kajoor and the River.

The opening of Kajoor

In 1879, Brière signed a treaty with Lat Dior authorizing construction of a railroad across Kajoor. To win Lat Dior's approval, Brière accepted limits on French rights to railroad lands and promised that they would not serve as a refuge for subjects of the Damel.[41] This was really a promise not to receive Kajoor's slaves. Most of Lat Dior's correspondence with the French at this time was concerned with the flight of his slaves into French-administered areas that had once been part of Kajoor and were occupied twenty years earlier. Both slaves and free peasants were moving to Jander and Ganjool because the French provided security from incessant warfare and raiding. In addition, French commerce provided advances of seed for those interested in growing peanuts there.[42] The French also promised Lat Dior that there would be no military presence. In spite of this, the Damel expelled surveyors two years later and renounced the treaty. The French built the railroad anyway while fighting a war with Lat Dior, and completed it in 1885. A year later, both Lat Dior and his major rival, Samba Laobé Fall, were defeated and killed in separate battles several weeks apart. When Lat Dior fell, he had only eighty men left. The slave warriors under Demba Warr Sall, the major slave chief, had already accepted a role as intermediaries in the new peanut-based economy. Demba Warr became President of the Confederation of Chiefs of Kajoor.[43] Between 1887 and 1890, the French completed the conquest of most of the rest of what is now Senegal.[44]

Before completion of the railroad, peanut exports were inhibited by the bulky nature of peanuts, which were exported in the shell. It took place only where water transport or Mauritanian camel-herders were available, but only the northern part of Senegal was suitable to camels.[45] At the time the railroad was completed, production was growing slowly because prices were low, but the railroad changed that. Peanut exports for Senegal went from 24,000 tons in 1879 to 43,000 in 1883 to 140,000 in 1900, the increase coming largely in the railroad area, which produced about 70 percent of Senegal's peanut exports during this period.[46] The major constraint on growth was the low productivity of traditional agriculture. A strong man with a hoe could not hope, no matter how hard he worked, to cultivate much more than a hectare of land (2.5 acres). Those with land could significantly increase production only by purchasing slaves.

Thus at the very moment when political change in France imposed the principle that French soil freed, economic change increased demand for slave labor. Warfare in the Sudan also made massive numbers of slaves available during this period. The major market was Senegambia. Neither the Futa Toro or Waalo could absorb large numbers of slaves. Money to buy massive numbers of slaves was available only in the peanut basin. Slaves were brought downriver in boats or overland, and at Dagana were taken south through Muslim Njambuur into Kajoor. Thus, a later administrator wrote that "the river crossed, the wretched, having been sold, are immediately taken into the interior by *juula*, who will sell them principally in Kajoor, Bawol and the outskirts of Saint Louis."[47]

To make the import of slaves possible, the administration had to insulate Kajoor and Bawol from decrees and regulations that they had proclaimed in Saint Louis. In January 1884, a circular sent to all local administrators and post commanders defined the limits of French policy. It distinguished between French areas, the communes and the posts, and annexed territories where France was committed to respect the laws and customs of the conquered people:

French soil frees the slave who touches it, but only French soil, that is to say, the interior of posts and *communes de plein exercice*, Saint Louis, Goree-Dakar and

Rufisque. On the territories in question, there are only free men and no one has the right to claim or seize a captive. . . As for annexed and protected territories. . . the first step on the path of civilization is scrupulous respect for treaties passed and conventions signed.[48]

Emigration of the Fulbe

French intervention also produced problems in the river area, which had seen massive emigration. Umar recruited in the river area in 1846–47, and then in 1858 and 1859 recruited another 40,000.[49] When Amadu sent missions to the Futa during the 1880s, he again found fertile soil for his appeals. In October 1882, Governor Vallon placed Waalo and Dimar under direct administration. This meant that slaves were legally free there. Most contemporary accounts saw this as the sole reason for renewed emigration, though Hanson believes that efforts to control slave-raiding may have been more important. Most of the emigrants were young men who wanted to accumulate slaves and saw warfare as the only way to do it.[50] The movement was facilitated by the commercial house of Justin Devès, which provided boats and bought surplus cattle. In the 1860s, there had been 50,000 Fulbe in the cercles of Saint Louis and Dagana. In 1882, the number was down to 30,000. In 1888, a census reported 9,598. There were also Wolof who left for the Sudan.[51]

Many reports of emigration came from slaves who fled for fear of being taken to the Sudan.[52] The argument of slave masters was pushed home in letters from African rulers and from administrators. Thus an administrator in 1886 wrote that the chiefs "have assured me of their profound devotion to France, but they also said that if we continue to free their slaves, they will not be able to live and that it would then be necessary for them to leave the country, painful though that might be."[53] Abdul Bokar Kan, the most powerful of the Futa chiefs and an opponent of emigration, wrote in 1889: "it is impossible for us to live without slaves because they work for us. Slaves for us are as money and merchandise are among you; those who would have good relations with us should leave them in our hands or we cannot stay since we know only slaves."[54]

The problem was compounded by the resourcefulness of some slaves. Thus, in 1885, a Dagana slave named Samba Boubou fled to Saint Louis and then returned to his village with six sets of manumission papers. When hauled before the courts, Samba Boubou claimed that false papers were the only way to free his family because his master demanded four slaves to free one. His master also treated them as if they were newly purchased.[55] This is evidence that though society distinguished between the newly enslaved and those born in slavery, there were no sanctions to protect the slave. There were many cases of slaves returning to the site of captivity to claim kin or entice others to flee.[56] There were also many cases of conflict over children. Thus, in Dagana, the commandant upheld a slave master's complaint that an eighteen-month-old child had been illegally freed with its mother.[57]

The French prohibited sale of slaves to people outside the colony, which meant mostly export to Sudan and Mauritania.[58] Thus, slaves of people emigrating to Sudan were confiscated.[59] This then led to protests as masters reclaimed freed slaves.[60] There were movements in opposed directions at Dagana as slaves fled to the south shore to escape the Moors and slave-owners moved slaves to the north shore to escape French authority.[61] Increasingly, people asked the local commandant to seek relatives taken in raids.[62] Relations with the Moors were difficult. Policy was to keep the Moors north of the river and, particularly, to keep them from raiding or seeking runaways.[63] At the same time, the French wanted trade. Thus, the Commandant at Podor was told:

if the slave is not himself the subject of a Black state protected by us, who was victim of a raid by the Moors or their suppliers, if he had not been so mistreated that he would be freed under Muslim law, if he was seized immediately at the moment of his escape, that is to say, within three days, he should be given to the Moor chief . . . or should be asked to furnish a bond.[64]

Many commandants felt not that slavery was immoral but that it was wrong to enslave someone who was free. Some were also convinced that there were rules to the game. In one case, the female slave of a Moor was sent to Saint Louis to testify in a theft case. When she claimed her freedom, the commandant objected, arguing that she had not gone to Saint Louis to seek protection.[65]

The administration's first response to the problem was the 1884 circular cited above, but commandants wanted something more substantial. "It is necessary," Commandant Noirot wrote, "if not to stop, at least to make liberation of slaves more difficult."[66] In 1889, Governor Clément-Thomas proposed a protectorate. Talks with remaining Fulbe chiefs had stopped the emigration, but if nothing was done, the governor expected it to resume.[67] A protectorate was a device to enshrine commitments to indigenous rulers and to prevent implementation of French law. Ironically, most of Senegal was already conquered. The last major emigration was in 1890. As General Dodds closed in on his capital, Burba Jolof Alburi Ndiaye fled, first to Abdul Bokar Kan in the Futa, and then both moved east to join Amadu. But Segu had also fallen and Amadu had fallen back on Nioro. A year later, there was no place else to go.[68] The regime proceeded anyway. In 1890, many territories ruled from Saint Louis were disannexed and made into protectorates. Two years later, the same was done for those administered from Goree. Ironically, effective control being established over conquered areas made disannexation unnecessary except as a way to avoid having to free slaves.[69] All French posts were areas of direct administration, and thus a slave could claim his or her freedom there. The problem for the administration was how to dissuade them from doing so. The major restraint was the isolation of the post. A slave freed at a French post could never be sure of being able to move freely outside it.

War, peanuts and slavery in the Gambia

Cultivation of peanuts developed first in the 1830s in the Gambia and was important all along the coast from Goree to Freetown. For areas incorporated into the world market economy largely as producers and traders of slaves, it created a new form of integration and radically altered many social and economic relationships. Most important, it created a hunger for labor. Writing on the Gambia, Jeng suggests that labor was provided in four ways: intensification of family labor systems; increased use of young male age sets; purchase of slaves; and migrants called strange farmers in the Gambia and *navetanes* in Senegal.[70] Given the limits to the amounts of labor that could be extracted from family members or young men's age sets, the most important sources of new labor were slaves and *navetanes*.

Peanut production was easy to expand. Most cultivators already grew peanuts and there was a lot of free land available. Family labor was most important during the 1830s and 1840s. Slave ownership was not widespread. Most slaves were owned by chiefs, traditional leaders and merchants. Thus, one of Jeng's informants told him: "Before the coming of the Islamic wars, some people did have some slaves at home, but most of the slaves that there were belonged to the chiefs and the small sub-chiefs."[71] This was changed by the Marabout–Soninke wars.[72] The first of these began in 1861 when Ma Ba Jaxoo led a revolt against the Mansa Badibu, a North Bank ruler. Within a year, Badibu had been defeated and Ma Ba was at war with Saalum. Though at first looked upon with favor by both British and French, he rallied both Muslim factions and opponents of the French. Lat Dior was thus with him from 1864 to 1867. Ma Ba briefly controlled a large part of Senegambia before dying in 1867 while trying to conquer the resolutely pagan Siin.

Ma Ba left behind a strongly Muslim state under first his brother, Mamour Ndari Ba, and then his son, Saer Maty. Mamour Ndari exercised only a loose hegemony over the different Muslim leaders, each of whom commanded his own military force.[73] Thus, Biram Cissé, a former student and lieutenant of Ma Ba's, built a *tata* in 1877 and increasingly began raiding for slaves further up river in Niani.[74] In the same year, Fodé Kaba, a Jaxanke from Combo near Bathurst, returned to the South Bank where he fought Moussa Molo of Fuladu for a generation. The strength of the Muslim forces lay in their frugality and investment in weapons of income from peanuts. An 1866 report explains:

the Government of Maba has become of late a great slave mart; the demand comes from our own Liberated Africans, or Colony-born Traders, and the supply is furnished by Maba in this wise. He breaks a town in one of the neighbouring countries . . . returning to Baddiboo with a coffle of slaves! These he sells to our Traders cheap, who pass them over to the left bank of the river, where the people . . . eagerly purchase them to work their Groundnut farms.[75]

The British had no territorial ambitions, but they were increasingly alienated by ravaging and slave-raiding. Thus, another account suggests that "as soon as each has been able to purchase a horse and a gun, he considers himself a warrior, lives by plunder and works his fields by the slaves he captures in his expeditions, and thinks it beneath his dignity to perform any work whatsoever, which is left to women and slaves."[76] Ma Ba sought submission to Islam. Prisoners were given the choice of death or conversion.[77] After his death, many of his lieutenants were primarily slave-raiders.[78] Ma Ba used slaves to cultivate peanuts, but Fodé Kaba disdained agriculture. "I have nothing to do with groundnuts," he told a British Governor. "Ever since I knew myself to be a man my occupation has been a warrior, and I make it my duty to fight the Soninkis who profess no religion whatever."[79]

Fodé Kaba was one of several military leaders who saw in the densely populated Jola areas of Casamance a potential source of slaves. From 1883, Kaba raided largely into the Jola Fogny from Medina in the middle Gambia.[80] In Combo, another Jaxanke marabout-warrior, Fodé Sylla, also raided for Jola slaves.[81] From about 1883, a French citizen from Saint Louis, Ibrahima Ndiaye, also tried to stake out a military base, but he was defeated by Sylla in 1888 and by the British in 1894.[82] These wars dramatically increased the slave population of the Gambia. Jeng argues that they also displaced many peasants and rendered the size of the crop smaller than it would otherwise have been.[83] There was insecurity. Peanut cultivators would often go in caravan to Bathurst or to the river trading posts to sell their crop. Nevertheless, peanut exports increased to over 15,000 tons in 1867 and 25,000 tons in 1882, and in spite of war, epidemics and the vagaries of climate.[84]

Before 1889, the Gambia consisted of Bathurst at the mouth of the river and a post upriver at McCarthy Island. Then, a treaty dividing the North Bank gave the British control over land. When Administrator R.B. Llewelyn proclaimed British sovereignty in the area, he was told that his action

raises serious difficulty with regard to the existence within them of slavery. In the eyes of the law all the people who are held as slaves have, by the conversion of the country into British territory, been made free and I cannot doubt that the courts of the Colony would so decide if any case should come before them, or if any of the slaves should claim their liberty.[85]

The result was the Gambia Protectorate Ordnance of 1894.

Labor migrations: the navetanes

The migrants came early and largely from the upper Senegal river. Curtin has suggested that as least as far back as the 1780s, farmers from the interior came down to the lower Gambia, cultivated, and used their profits to buy trade goods. Many slave dealers also rented land near trading posts and put slaves to work while waiting for a ship to call.[86] Soninke and Jaxanke from the Upper Senegal dominated trade with the interior and by the 1830s were coming to the Gambia for dry-season labor. The 1848 Annual Report said that most of the peanuts were grown by "Tillibunkas and SeraWoollies coming from 500 to 600 miles in the interior."[87] Most of the migrants spent two or three seasons growing peanuts before heading home. Some also traded or sold their services as mercenaries. They worked under several kinds of contract, but generally the *navetane* received land and seed, and was fed in exchange for work on the landlord's lands.

Sedhiou saw a similar evolution. Peanut production grew to 390 tons in 1852 and 6,600 in 1867. Cotton was also grown there during the American Civil War.[88] The work was done by Soninke from the upper Senegal, who were lodged in several villages close to Sedhiou, one of which was set up by a French commercial house.[89] Most of the *navetanes* were probably not free men. Swindell explains the system:

> Merchants or chiefs from the interior assembled groups of free workers or domestic slaves and brought them into groundnut areas. Slaves could no longer be regarded as one form of merchandise transporting another, and their owners had come to realize that their labor represented a considerable asset. Although groundnuts could be grown in the interior, the loads porters could carry in no way recompensed the merchants or chiefs for the cost of feeding them en route; therefore the workers had to be brought to the most economic point of production.[90]

There were similar migrations elsewhere. In Guinea Jaxanke entrepreneurs from Tuba brought slaves to the coast to cultivate peanuts. The major difference was that on the Guinea coast, the Tubakayes became planters, while their Senegambian counterparts simply served as labor contractors for local landlords.[91] In Saalum, there were *navetanes* near Foundiougne in the mid-1870s, though it was a center of bitter warfare until 1887. In 1892, there was a group around Foundiougne, 600 to 700 in the area south of Kaolack, and a small group near Fatick.[92] Finally, entrepreneurs developed agrocommercial complexes called *feitorias* in the Rio Grande and on Bolama island, using both slave and contract labor.[93]

Slaves, migrants and Soninke society

The vast majority of nineteenth century *navetanes* were Soninke from the upper Senegal river. They were primarily slaves until early in the twentieth century.[94] Both the migrants and *juula* contractors who brought them to Sédhiou, Foundiougne and the lower Gambia were also involved in trade. The situation in the Senegal river was different. Increasingly, Soninke nobles worked there as *laptots*, servants, traders, gardeners and soldiers.[95] Some went from the French navy's river service to the Atlantic fleet, especially to vessels serving in tropical waters. During the eighteenth century, free Wolof workers in the river trade were largely replaced by slaves, but in the nineteenth century this trend was reversed and, by 1870, the *laptots* were mostly Soninke. Manchuelle asks why increasing numbers of Soninke were going into river work. Agriculture was prosperous, gum was selling well, the grain trade was increasing and peanut exports were rising. His answer is based on analysis of salaries. *Laptots* were earning 30 francs a month in the French navy's river service, more if they served on ocean-going vessels, up to 50 or 60 francs a month on commercial vessels. A Soninke *laptot* could earn more than an agricultural worker in France and as much as four times the income of a peasant cultivating peanuts. They were not, however, leaving the rural world behind, but migrating in order to compete within it. Some *laptots* served long years and, on return, became traders, but in general, there was a very high turnover, the *laptot* often introducing his "brother" who replaced him when he went home.

The key to *laptot* recruitment lay in the patriarchal nature of Soninke society. The *laptots* did not turn their earnings over to their fathers but, instead, used them to become patriarchs themselves. In a good year, a *laptot* could earn enough to buy two slaves. Frey wrote that "as soon as [a Soninke] has built up a small savings, he buys goods which he sends back to his home country. He entrusts a relative or a friend with acquiring one or more slaves whenever an occasion arises during his period of absence."[96] A French navy report corroborates this: "Among [the Soninke], almost all men go abroad for a shorter or longer period, they come to St. Louis in order to obtain *pièces de guinée* which on their return will allow them to settle after buying wives and slaves."[97] Frey was waited on by a servant who had purchased seven slaves in this way. Manchuelle distinguishes between Wolof workers, mostly former slaves, who did not own land and thus became full-time proletarians, and Soninke, who accumulated wealth in order to strengthen their position at home.[98] Wealth thus accumulated could be used both to strength the noble's political position and to underwrite trade with the nomads.

The freeing of slaves

In spite of the reluctance of the administration, many slaves were freed. Fewer than a hundred a year were freed between 1857 and 1862, but from 1875 to 1881, the number freed rose to 350 and then to 674. From 1881 to 1889, it varied from 1,058 to 2,198 a year.[99] These data are slightly different from those in Table 4.1 which is based on my tabulations from lists of freed slaves published in the *Moniteur du Sénégal* between 1868 and 1888. These lists are incomplete and there are problems of interpretation. Whole months are missing and the type of data presented changes. They do, however, indicate a similar pattern of increasing emancipation and they give data on who and how.

The lists contain two kinds of persons: first, slaves who fled their masters and sought freedom, and second, slaves bought upriver and redeemed in Saint Louis. They include the name of the slave, the person or persons declaring him or her and, if a minor, the person to whom the slave was "confided." Most were declared by an institution, the prosecuting attorney, the Political Affairs Bureau or a court. I have calculated the redemptions from two groups, those declared by an individual and assigned to the declarer, and those declared by an individual and assigned to another person. The latter clearly involved one person purchasing a slave for another. The lists for certain periods indicate the origin of the slave and the occupation of the person to whom confided. The number of liberations is lowest for the years after 1870, when the French were particularly anxious not to alienate African neighbours.[100]

About 60 percent of those freed were female, a majority in all years but one

Table 4.1. *Data on freed slaves, 1868 to 1888*

Year	Total	Male	Female	%	Minors	%	Children freed and adopted
1868	102				21	21	
1869	139	32	80	58	27	19	
1870	148	67	81	55	27	18	
1871	129	55	74	57	30	23	
1872	91	38	53	58	30	33	12
1873	55	15	40	73	32	58	24
1874	85	22	63	74	64	75	54
1875	328	64	259	79	255	78	189
1876	278	91	186	67	163	59	103
1877	349	164	176	50	152	44	99
1878	347	209	123	35	127	37	88
1879	440	219	220	50	116	26	60
1880	609	274	335	55	216	35	81
1881	643	220	422	66	271	42	129
1882	919	347	573	62	237	26	27
1883	1,266	542	719	57	428	34	17
1884	841	323	516	61	393	47	130
1885	1,060	470	585	55	403	38	6
1886	676	273	403	60	301	45	0
1887	not available						
1888	254	113	141	56	102	40	

Source: *Moniteur du Sénégal*.
The 1868 reports begin with a 9 June report covering the period from November 1867. The following are missing: July 1872, January and February 1873, October 1874, June 1883, May 1885, October to December 1886, and all of 1887. 1888 is available through 12 April.

and a majority even among runaways. Female slaves fled, often with their children. Almost 40 percent of those freed were minors. Of these, about 70 percent were girls. The percentage of girls was especially high among those redeemed, close to four fifths. Most of those who bought a child for redemption wanted young girls. This traffic was probably underreported. Deherme suggested in 1906 that the actual number of children purchased for redemption was three times the number declared.[101] Redemptions were less than 15 percent of liberations and fluctuations are so great that I believe that they were not recorded during certain periods. Many children, perhaps as many as half, came in with parents, usually their mothers. Other children may have been freed as a result of efforts to find lost children, particularly cases where one or more children were redeemed by a relative, who probably tracked down where the child was and either paid a ransom or arranged an escape. There also are a number of cases in the 1880s where children were confided to parents, but the parent was not on the list.

The children can be divided into those with family, the redemptions, and those with no known relatives. The latter two groups were assigned as wards.

Table 4.2. *Origins of slaves freed at Saint Louis*

Kajoor	21.4%
Other Wolof and Serer	26.2
Total Wolof and Serer	47.6
Western Mali	19.2
Upper river	12.7
Futa Toro	8.8
Guinea	2.3
Miscellaneous	0.9

Source: *Moniteur du Sénégal.*

The recipients of wards were very diverse. The largest group went to traders and merchants. The second largest was housewives. Almost all of the girls were assigned to women. In many cases, there is no indication whose wife the woman was. Well over half went to people linked to the river economy – traders, sailors, *pileuses*, ships' captains. All social groups took in children. A number of administrators, including several governors, adopted children. Mme. Brière de l'Isle adopted a nine-year-old girl four months before her husband resigned his post. Mme. Seignac-Lesseps adopted two girls, aged nine and twelve. About 10 percent went to *métis* households. Twice as many went to Europeans and almost two thirds went to African Muslims, some of them people of quite modest standing: a guard, washerwomen, ordinary sailors. Under 10 percent were assigned to craftsmen. Some of these, generally boys of ten to fourteen years old, were clearly destined to be apprentices, but some craftsmen also took small girls more likely to be servants. Quite possibly, others found their way into apprenticeship programs, but it is likely that most were used as servants and as laborers. Robinson has suggested that slaves in the river area were often enticed to run away, and that when losses were too large, Futanke pressed the French to reduce recruitment and return fugitives.[102]

Until the mid-1880s, most liberations took place in Saint Louis. There was a small number at Goree, rarely more than two or three a month, but almost none from the posts until 1882, after which they had a small but steady stream of liberations. Slaves freed at the posts were usually assigned to local notables, often poorly identified in the lists. Most of these persons probably became dependants and virtual slaves of the men to whom they were assigned. Almost half of those freed were Wolof or Sereer, over a fifth from Kajoor. They were not necessarily born Wolof, but came from Wolof areas or had Wolof names. Many had only personal names. Almost 30 percent came from the river economy, Futa Toro, the upper river states or the Moors. Many slaves certainly learned of the possibility of liberation from men in the river economy, who were often not disinterested. Sometimes a young woman was declared by a man, who probably intended her as a wife or companion. In other cases, women fled with promises of help from male friends or suitors. There were also freed slave children assigned to institutions, but relatively few.

A little over a dozen went to Protestant ministers, who seem to have run a refuge. Less than two dozen went to Catholic institutions, but these institutions also made purchases that did not find their way on to the lists.[103]

Recruitment of tirailleurs

Another group of freed slaves was the soldiers. In October and November 1877, thirty-nine young males were declared by a French captain, clearly intended to be *tirailleurs*. Over a three-year period, 181 were declared. They were the only such recruits who were processed through the formal emancipation structure and had their names published, though male slaves had long been purchased for military service.[104] African soldiers handled most military duty at upriver posts that were unhealthy for European soldiers. From the 1820s, some also served outside Africa. The Emancipation Act of 1848 expressly prohibited the recruitment of slaves and the military tried to rely on volunteer forces, but in the three years after emancipation, only three volunteers came forward. Military service was seen as the work of slaves and ex-slaves and the wages were much lower than those of *laptots*. There was talk of conscription, but by 1851 the army was buying slaves again and freeing them in exchange for an indenture contract of twelve to fourteen years.

Faidherbe's response was to organize *tirailleurs* into separate units, give them their own uniforms, better working and living conditions and better training. Though wages remained low, they had access to re-enlistment bonuses, pensions and booty. The number of recruits increased after 1857, but most were still either slaves purchased for military service or recently freed slaves who chose military life over the insecurities of freedom. Enlistment ensured that the freed man would not be re-enslaved and would be able to find wives from among slaves taken in war. Administrators often recommended enlistment to slaves who complained about their masters.[105] In 1866, when recruitment was slow, Governor Pinet-Laprade raised the enlistment bonus from 50 to 200 francs, the price demanded for most able-bodied male slaves. Commandants at river posts were told that the bonus was to be paid only when the would-be soldier was about to board the boat. This was to prevent recruits from taking the bonus and fleeing. There were intermittent efforts to break away from reliance on slaves, but they were of little avail. In 1880, Governor Canard raised the bonus to 300 francs for six years, 120 for four and 60 for two.[106] There was a fiction that the enlistment bonus was paid to the slave and that he paid off his master. In most cases, the master seems to have been paid directly.

Slaves were purchased in many areas, but there was a preference for the "bon Bambara," seen as loyal, brave and strong, the ideal soldier. Many were not Bambara, but Bambara became the language of the *tirailleurs*. Commandants in the river area had funds to buy slaves. One administrator in Bakel used his journal as an account book.[107] Often the purchases were large and the vast majority were direct: "Paid to masters of 40 slaves an enlistment bonus of 300 francs for the price of their purchase." Slaves were sometimes enticed away from their masters, but when that happened, it was often difficult to move them. The river is shallow in places and horsemen on sandbars could stop a boat from passing. One incident involved a descent of the river with twenty-five *laptots* who had signed up for Gabon. They were stopped, but when the commander insisted that he had no slaves, they were allowed to continue only to be shot at further down river. When they got stuck in the sand, the boat was boarded by a large body of men and then by the Almamy, who insisted that slaves be turned over. Six were taken. An effort was made to ransom them with payments from advances on their salaries.[108]

French authorities constantly discussed what to do with freed slaves. The most common answer for men was to put them into the army.[109] Canard was particularly worried that children confided to *habitants* would be raised hostile to French "civilization." He wanted "to make them good workers and good Frenchmen by confiding them to the Director of the Artillery or the Director of Public works."[110] He actually confided twelve to each of these pillars of civilization and twelve to the missions. The demand for labor was high at this time. The economy was expanding. The telegraph line to Bakel and Medine was completed in 1880, and the task of supplying the annual campaign in the Sudan provided a lot of work.

Conclusion

The victory of the Republicans in France in 1879 put the country back on the course of empire. If the Republicans tended to be colonialists, they were also often abolitionists. It is tempting in the absence of solid research to assume that abolitionist sentiments were nothing but window dressing, but republicanism and colonialism were part of the same ideological package, a package that also included a commitment to human rights, an opposition to restraints on the free movement of labor and a commitment to economic growth.[111] We see a difference in values and in objectives between those in the metropole who supported colonial expansion and those in Africa who actually created the empire. We also see a contradiction between the two goals of imperial ideology in Senegal in the 1880s. Public opinion and the increasing openness of the cities of Senegal forced Senegal to make manumission available to slaves. The number taking advantage of this increased from year to year. At the same time, the expanding peanut economy led to the greatest import of slave labor in Senegal's history. The Fulbe emigration provided an excuse to impose a legal fiction. Disannexation put slavery at arm's length. It was banned in areas of direct administration, but tolerated and protected in most of rural Senegal.

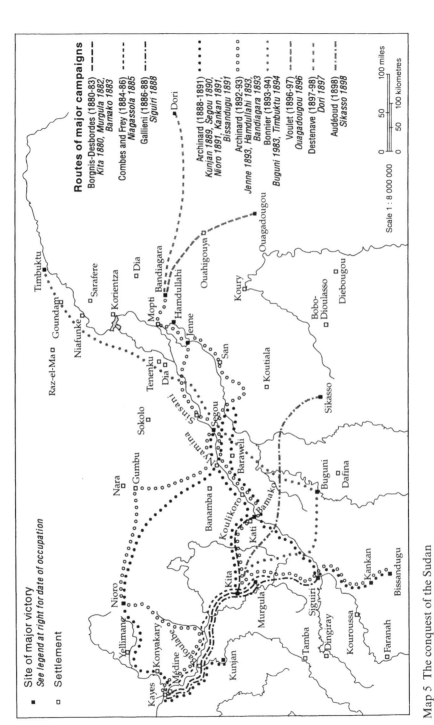

Routes of major campaigns

Borgnis-Desbordes (1880–83) — — —
Kita 1880, Murgula 1882,
Bamako 1883

Combes and Frey (1884–86) – – –
Niagassola 1885

Gallieni (1886–88) — - —
Siguiri 1888

Archinard (1888–1891) • • • •
Kunjan 1889, Segou 1890,
Nioro 1891, Kankan 1891,
Bissandugu 1891

Archinard (1892–93) o o o o
Jenne 1893, Hamdullahi 1893,
Bandiagara 1893

Bonnier (1893–94) ✶ ✶ ✶ ✶
Buguni 1983, Timbuktu 1894

Voulet (1896–97) ∞ ∞ ∞
Ouagadougou 1896

Destenave (1897–98) – ·· – ··
Dori 1897

Audéoud (1898) ⨯ ⨯ ⨯
Sikasso 1898

■ Site of major victory
   See legend at right for date of occupation

□ Settlement

Scale 1 : 8 000 000

100 miles

50

100 kilometres

50

Map 5 The conquest of the Sudan

5   Conquest of the Sudan: Desbordes to Archinard

> . . . the slave trade constitutes a majority of the transactions in these unfortunate countries.
>
> Gallieni on Sudan (1885)[1]

> On the day when everyone is free the first act will be the cessation of work, famine will follow, then pillage and a return to the state of perpetual revolution from which we have pulled this country. Only the slave safeguards our situation; armed with primitive tools, he works little but in a continuous manner.
>
> Commandant, Bafulabe (1894)[2]

From the first, the Sudan was different from Senegal. It was a military fief and remained so for a generation.[3] There were no concrete economic interests, only vague and illusory hopes. There was no French community. Information about the military and its operations there came only from the military. The Sudan was insulated from French politics and its would-be conquerors were determined to keep it that way. The only non-military group of any substance was the missions, but they supported colonialism and rarely went public when they disapproved of policies pursued by the military.[4] The exercise of power was thus unrestrained by either political opposition or civilian morality. Commandants often made their own policy and ignored instructions from political superiors.

The conquest of the Sudan also responded to no clear imperative of the French economy. At least one military commander, Frey, saw this. The only lucrative commerce, he wrote, was that of slaves. The Sudan was "a country without resources," underpopulated and without any future prospects.[5] To the degree that the military tried to rationalize what they were doing, they did so in terms of poor market research. The Sudan was underpopulated because the rains are irregular and the land is poor, often lacking significant topsoil. From an economic point of view, areas closer to the coast like Guinea or the Ivory Coast offered a better potential for commercial development. Reports of the Sudan's economic potential were based on delusion or deception.[6] Combes, for example, assured the Governor of Senegal in 1884 that the land between the rivers was incontestably of great fertility. "It is enough to scratch the soil and drop some seeds on it in order to have a magnificent crop, and that, two times a year." To the contrary, two crops were grown only on the floodplains of rivers, where a second crop could be grown as the waters receded.

There had long been a French fascination with the great cities and ancient empires of the Sudan.[7] These states existed not because of great wealth, but because small groups could gain control over the wealth and use it to build both cities and states.[8] If there was a logic to the conquest, it lay in the desire of peacetime soldiers to practice their craft and win promotions.[9] The men who conquered the Sudan were largely from the marines, the least prestigious French military force. For many of these men, the Sudan offered not only adventure and promotions, but a challenge, an arena within which they could demonstrate their military and political talents. They had larger forces than those who conquered the coastal colonies, but never had over 4,000 men. They prevailed because of better training, superior weaponry and a network of alliances.

First steps

In 1879, Brière de l'Isle sent Captain Joseph Gallieni to the Sudan.[10] His mission was to make preliminary surveys for the railroad, establish relations with the Malinke in the area between the rivers, and arrange for construction of a fort at Bafulabe. After completing his first mission, he was sent out again, this time to arrange for two further forts, to survey the route to the Niger, and to sign a treaty with Bamako, a market town already chosen as the French base on the Niger. He was then to proceed to Segu to negotiate a treaty of friendship with Amadu. The mission was a qualified success. An ambush cost the expedition its supplies and gifts destined for Amadu, and they spent ten months in detention, but Gallieni returned with a pocket full of treaties, including one with Amadu which was never ratified. More important, he knew that Amadu's writ was limited and that most of his subjects were hostile to Futanke rule. When he arrived at Kita, Borgnis-Desbordes, the new Commandant Supérieur, had constructed a fort there. The Sudan existed. In theory, the Commandant Supérieur was to report to the Governor of Senegal, but with the departure of Brière de l'Isle and a shift to civilian rule in Senegal, Sudanese officers increasingly dealt directly with Paris and Senegalese governors often had difficulty getting information about events there. The colony was based first at Bakel, and then at Kayes, a new river port and railway terminus constructed on the site of a Medine slave village.[11]

There was a profound difference in goals between the military men and their civilian supporters. The decision to build a railroad between the two rivers was crucial to the launch of the conquest, but Charles Freycinet, who pushed the railroad project, and many of his allies, thought in terms of peaceful penetration and loose commercial empire.[12] Borgnis-Desbordes, Brière de l'Isle and Jauréguiberry had no idea how far they were going, but they were committed to establishing effective control over the middle Niger.[13] In doing this, they were circumscribed both by politics and by climate. Politics meant that they had neither the green light they wished for nor the resources they thought necessary. Borgnis-Desbordes had 420 troops in 1880 and 349 in 1881.[14] Climate restricted them to an annual campaign. Supplies were accumulated in Saint Louis and moved up river to Kayes after the river rose in July. The annual campaign usually began in December and lasted until just before the rains came in June, when the troops pulled back to their posts and many French officers withdrew to healthier climes.

The first three campaigns were directed by Borgnis-Desbordes and operated within the triangle between the upper Senegal and Niger rivers, an area bordered by Segu, Karta and the rising power of Samori. The Futanke had focused their military strength into maintaining control of the western corridor to Senegal which brought them needed weapons. Their preferred route was a northern one through Banamba, Nioro and Koniakary to Medine. The Futanke writ was loose over much of the rest of their empire.[15] The French chose a more southerly route through Bafulabe and Kita to Bamako inhabited by Malinke and Beledugu Bambara. Not everyone in these areas welcomed them, but allies were not hard to find.[16] The area had been much raided for slaves by Karta. Bamako was a market town of under 2,000 people, more than half of them slaves, which was strategically located near the only rapids on the middle Niger. Desbordes exploited local conflicts to find allies within the town.[17] The French had taken a Futanke fort at Sabousire in the upper Senegal in 1878, and Desbordes had begun the 1882-83 campaign by forcing the evacuation of the Futanke fort at Murgula, but Amadu was anxious to avoid a confrontation. While a fort was being constructed at Bamako, the French had their first major collision with Samori.[18]

Slavery and first stage

The first years of the conquest involved little combat because the conquest took place in an area hostile to Amadu. The French acted to stop slave-raiding in the upper river, but in their campaigns they took prisoners, mostly women, who were generally given to friendly chiefs and to the *tirailleurs*. Thus, after taking Gubanko in 1888, a friendly chief was asked to found a village with the prisoners.[19] Some administrators were surprised that these slaves either disappeared, presumably sold, or were taken as "wives." In one case in Bafulabe, the commandant tried to do a count and found fifteen missing. The chief claimed they had died, but the administrator was sure they had been sold. One had also been taken as a "wife" by the chief.[20] Most of those who received "libérés" clearly saw them as slaves.[21] The problem was not simply booty. Administrators complained that they had to spend much of their time on slave matters: flight, enticement, and theft of slaves. There was scarcely a day, one administrator claimed, without either a runaway or the theft of a slave.[22]

By 1883, another problem had emerged. In establishing a base at Bamako, Desbordes sorely stretched his supply lines.[23] The original plan involved construction of a railroad, but the railroad made it to Bafulabe only in 1887 and then stopped. The decision to proceed militarily without waiting for the rail line was costly.[24] Local people were hostile to Futanke rule, but not eager to undertake even heavier obligations to the French. From the railhead to the Niger, goods and supplies had to be head-loaded. The French introduced wagons, but they were never adequate to the chore. The problem of moving goods was compounded by low population in the French area. From early on, thus, a constant concern was the *ligne de ravitaillement* and the supply of troops in the interior.[25]

When Desbordes laid the first stone for the fort at Bamako, he gave a flowery speech which set France's objectives in an anti-slavery context. "Even if our labors do little more than cause this great humanitarian idea to triumph, we will be rewarded for our efforts, and very few railroads will have so beautiful a dividend as that which will link the Senegal and Niger."[26] Whatever the "great humanitarian idea", Desbordes was concerned with slaves primarily as booty. Paris had different versions of this humanitarian idea. Desbordes' successor, Combes, received very explicit instructions that slaves fleeing into French territory were not to be returned and theft of slaves was to be repressed.[27] Slave use declined in some parts of the triangle. Thus, Khasso was a warrior state within which Medine, the commercial center, and Kayes, the political center of the new colony, were located.[28] Long allied to France, Khasso passed under more direct control as a result of seizure of the Futanke fort at Sabusire and construction of posts at Kayes and Bafulabe. From 1886, the slaves on whom the Khassonke elite depended began to leave, many of them moving into the upper river urban economy. It was largely the newly enslaved, not *vulusuo* (*woloso*), who left, but chiefs found their position much eroded. The movement increased after 1890.[29] The French originally hoped that Khasso would provide labor for railroad construction, but efforts to commandeer labor only led to increased slave flight and French prohibitions on raiding limited Khasso's ability to acquire more. Cissoko argues that the result was a decline in population and impoverishment of the elite.

The French army

The French army was also a Sudanic army. Gallieni remarked that many *tirailleurs* with him in 1879 met relatives, who sometimes tried to persuade the *tirailleur* to return home with them.[30] The *tirailleurs* were created by Faidherbe, but Gallieni in 1886 was the first to rely on an all-African fighting force. The only French soldiers were officers and some specialists.[31] In order to create the larger army needed for conquest of the Sudan, French commanders were given wide latitude to recruit the troops they needed, and few questions were asked about their methods. The normal method was the one used in Senegal:

> The enlistment bonus is 250 francs. If he is a free man, we give him the 250 francs and he serves you loyally. If he is a slave, we act as follows so as to not annoy the master: the master is told when the slave will receive his bonus and often he takes it and the slave has nothing.[32]

In one case, a French officer commandeered a body of porters, put them in uniform, drilled them and trained them.[33] More common was the recruitment of slave warriors. Attracted by the success of French arms, their superior weapons and the possibility of booty, defeated soldiers sometimes asked to be incorporated into the French army. Only thus could they preserve their life style and their privileges, most notably the slaves they had accumulated in earlier service.[34]

The French were usually outnumbered, but they found allies without difficulty among those threatened by more powerful states and among those earlier defeated by Muslim conquerors. Thus, the commandant at Niagassola on the southern frontier promised villagers the opportunity get back kin taken by Samori's *sofa*: "You can thus under protection avenge yourselves for all of the evil that has been done to you and win back that which is yours."[35] More important were the former rulers. Dama, the heir to the Massassi throne of Karta, had been given land in the upper Senegal valley. Near Segu, Amadu faced throughout his reign the opposition of several Bambara chiefs. The auxiliaries were useful as scouts, in harassing operations and in mopping up after a victory. Once a wall was breached or an enemy attack repulsed, the auxiliaries were set loose to round up prisoners.[36]

Booty was essential to the morale of the French army and slaves were the most important kind. One young officer was told when he asked for his troops to be paid before leaving on a campaign "that *captifs* should not be paid since they were going to war and would surely take captives which would be their reward."[37] The attitude of French officers is vividly depicted in Louis Carpeaux's racist *Mon Roman au Niger* about campaigning on the desert's edge.

According to customs of the country, my right, I would say more, my duty, would be to take all prisoners for myself and sell them just like the calves, cattle and sheep, unless I preferred to keep them for my service, in which case their children would also be my property.[38]

Many slaves taken by *tirailleurs* were sold. Others became part of the military community. The French army, like its African rivals, traveled with what one missionary called its "battalion of women." Every *tirailleur* had at least one woman who carried his personal effects, cooked and prepared camp at the end of the day. Each *spahi* also had a *gorgi*, a boy who took care of his horse. The *tirailleurs* generally carried only weapons and ammunition on the march in order to be mobile.[39] Sometimes, of course, feeding captives was a problem. Thus, after one military action, a commander wrote: "I am going to distribute the captives in order to not have useless mouths to feed. It is understood that I will keep a certain number of them for your men which they can have after the campaign; you can tell them this on my behalf in order to stimulate them a bit."[40]

Colonial memoirs were either carefully purged or tried to put such acts in a favorable light. Frey was not a strong defender of the imperial cause, but he tried to justify the distribution of women taken from Mamadu Lamine:

Liberty was given to them without exception. The women of Bundu were sent back to their families. Others were formed into groups and assigned to different detachments of *tirailleurs* and *spahis* to be used to pound millet . . .
They were full of joy to be free again and to discover among the *tirailleurs* sons of the

Fig. 4 Distribution of slave women after defeat of Mamadu Lamine.

same country, even of the same village, from whom they had been separated by the horrors of war. You can only guess the lot of these captives . . . Courted by *tirailleurs*, who when drunk with victory had acquired a perky and jaunty air, which in all countries renders the soldier irresistible, they became enamored of their conquerors and became their wives. It is the best possible fate for them, because without families, the fact of having been slaves would expose them to being enslaved again by the first native to come along once they left behind the protection of the column and of our posts.[41]

The fate of other prisoners varied according to the political and military situation. Those given to local chiefs and elders were to be given land, but often they simply disappeared.[42] Others were given to intermediaries. Mademba Sy, a Senegalese official, who built the telegraph line from Kayes to Bamako, was given 100 slaves when Archinard set him up as ruler of Sinsani.[43] The only limitation seems to have been that "white" Tuareg women were rarely given to African soldiers. On one occasion, Tuareg women were simply allowed to escape.[44] Even when a slave was "freed," she was a resource. A White Father in Segu took up the case of a thirty-year-old woman who was freed and confided to a political agent, who treated her like a slave. When the missionary complained, the commandant was reluctant but, under pressure, freed the woman.[45] The threat of enslavement was also used to force obedience. Thus, in 1888, the administrator at Bafulabe wrote a chief who did not respond when called to headquarters: "If he does not wish to see his village burned and its inhabitants sent into slavery, he should present himself immediately to the Commandant at Bafulabe."[46]

The military state

The Sudan was run by and for the army. Administration was in the hands of young lieutenants, captains and, in some cases, sergeants. They had no training for administrative work, but were often better administrators than the civilians in the coastal colonies because they were literate and accepted orders. Nevertheless, they did not want to sit at desks. Administrative service was the prerequisite to the military action they sought. They liked the freedom of colonial service and accepted the risks. Many came from Catholic families, but whatever they were like at home, in the Sudan they were not often restrained by religion or by due process. Many had difficulty with the heat and suffered a variety of tropical maladies, often compounded by excessive drink. The mortality rate was high. While foolhardy young officers sometime got themselves massacred, the worst killers were syphilis, dysentery and malaria.[47] In Boilève's campaign of 1883-84, there was no combat, but 18 percent of the European troops were lost. Others were posted home sick or transferred because of aberrant behavior. They were often brutal. Prisoners were frequently shot without a trial and on charges that seem trivial. The arbitrariness that marked their public acts also often marked their private lives.[48]

French officers often kept slaves for their own use both as servants and concubines, or distributed slaves to their servants. Many officers maintained a household. Thus, when children were divided up among officers after a successful campaign, it was largely as servants.[49] Even servants were sometimes rewarded. One missionary reported a conversation with a gardener who assessed commandants according to their generosity in giving out slaves. One gave him five, another only two.[50] Some servants used these gifts to trade and to accumulate a little financial reserve and some just maintained large households.[51] One of the rewards of putting up with the climate and sickness was a regular and active sex life. The French soldiers were mostly young, male and very interested in sexual partners. Some had mistresses, but many were quite promiscuous. Thus, the mission at Segu received complaints about a fifty-two-year-old sergeant, who had an African family but sent his interpreter and his political agent out every day to get him two attractive young women. When the missionaries complained, the local commandant was sympathetic, but suggested that he was not likely to get much help from a regional commandant who kept six women, five of them from ten to fifteen years old.[52] Another sergeant expelled his entourage of women when he feared that death from dysentery was near and he wanted to reconcile himself with his God.[53] Mission-educated males were often hired as servants because they spoke French. The missionaries were generally disturbed to see their converts exposed to behavior they saw as immoral.[54] After a battle, the officers often got the first choice of slave women. After the fall of Nioro, Archinard kept five of

Amadu's wives for himself.[55] In other cases, slaves were kept around for public works. Thus, after stopping a column of slaves being moved by one of Samori's generals in 1889, Archinard kept 200 for construction work and put the rest in a liberty village.[56] Similarly, after the fall of Segu, Archinard had 100 households of former slaves sent to Kita to finish some work being done there.[57]

Among the most important intermediaries of the colonial state were the political agents, who took great risks in spying or handled delicate missions and were usually well rewarded. There was also a network of clerks, interpreters and guards. Since most commandants spoke few if any African languages, these intermediaries possessed a great deal of power and could often manipulate colonial authority. Even after liberty villages were established, many commanders felt that gifts of slaves were the only way they could adequately reward these faithful servants.

The liberty villages

Between 1884 and 1887, the army made little progress. Inhibited by an unsympathetic government in Paris, French commanders had explicit orders to avoid combat and only to relieve and supply existing garrisons.[58] Boilève (1883–84) avoided combat. In 1885 Combes attacked Samori, but only succeeded in tying troops down in forts he could not supply. Samori's *sofa* continued to control most of the southern frontier. In 1886, Frey relieved Niagassola and defeated Samori, but then had to return to the upper Senegal, where the revolt of the Soninke Mamadu Lamine in the upper Senegal river kept French troops busy for over a year.[59] Only in 1887, after defeating Mamadu Lamine, did Gallieni resume the forward movement.[60] Before he could do much, he had to resolve logistic problems posed by the lack of population along the *route de ravitaillement*.

In 1886, Frey created new settlements for prisoners outside of Kayes and Bafulabe, much to the discontent of allied chiefs, who would rather have kept the prisoners.[61] Toward the end of the year, Gallieni began generalizing the experience:

It would be desirable . . . that we create little by little near each of our posts a village where we will receive slaves fleeing the Right Bank, who will be given their liberty while being used as laborers or as *tirailleurs*, persuading them in a word to group themselves around our establishments.

They will be fed the first two or three months and put to work. It will be good, I believe, to leave them one or two days a week to work their fields, whose location will be chosen by the commandant

. . . this measure will apply only to people fleeing the Right Bank and the possessions of chiefs seeking to limit our action and our influence in the Sudan.[62]

By 1888, there were settlements near most posts, though some commandants still assigned freed slaves to local notables. In December 1888 Archinard issued rules for the liberty villages which commandants were to place at the head of their order books. A runaway slave seeking refuge was to be inscribed

in a register and freed only if not claimed over a three-month period. Furthermore, liberty papers could only be issued by the Commandant Supérieur or,
on delegation, by a senior official.[63] The Commandant Supérieur reserved the
right to order the issue of such papers earlier, probably in cases where slaves
were fleeing enemies of the French, in particular Amadu or Samori.[64]

In 1891, Archinard amended the regulations to provide emancipation in a
month for those enlisting as *tirailleurs*.[65] He also set up a procedure by which
the French hired slaves and set aside part of the slave's pay as the price of
liberation. The master was allowed to ask up to 1 franc a day, but very few
workers were paid more than that.[66] Archinard guaranteed the right of a slave
to purchase his freedom for 300 francs, a price that was well above the cost of
replacement.[67] Later in the decade, that was reduced to 200 francs. The first
liberty village in Senegal was set up near Sedhiou in 1888 for slaves of two
defeated chiefs. By late 1895, there were forty-four liberty villages.[68] More
were set up during the early years of the twentieth century. Even where the
villages existed, some slaves were still distributed as before and the Catholic
missions received many orphans.[69]

Bouche differentiates between villages serving as simple refuges and those
where the administration sought to create a permanent settled community.[70]
The French wanted to tie down both freed slaves and those fleeing war zones
because of the need for labor. Freed persons were known popularly as the
"commandant's slaves," and were usually so regarded by the commandants.
They were generally placed near a post, sometimes on the site of a deserted
village. At Bafulabe, the liberty village was only 300 m from another village.[71]
In some cases, they were placed near a ferry or in a depopulated area, where
surveillance or porterage were desired. When a liberty village grew in size, it
was normal to split it and move part of the population to an area where labor
was needed. Thus, in Nioro in 1894, there were over 800 persons in the liberty
village. In 1895, 540 were sent to form new settlements strung out on the trade
route to Senegal.[72] There was less control and, therefore, fewer demands for
labor in villages far from the post. Often, the commandant had no idea how
many persons were in distant villages.[73] By contrast, in villages near the post,
comings, goings and demands for labor made it difficult to sustain agricultural production.

In the early years, most freed slaves were runaways. In 1887 alone, more
than 6,000 people fled Samori's *sofa*, many of them slaves. From 1893, there
were orders to free any slaves fleeing Moors or Tuareg.[74] Increasingly, slaves
entered villages from other sources. Caravans going to and from Samori were
stopped and their slaves confiscated. Slaves of refractory chiefs were often
confiscated. In 1893, Archinard ordered collection of the *oussourou*, a 10
percent tax on trade. This means that one of every ten slaves being traded was
placed in a liberty village.[75] Slaves were often also confiscated from persons
accused of crimes. Otherwise, slaves were only freed when there was evidence
of mistreatment.[76] Many commandants disliked the villages. When numbers
increased suddenly, they often lacked resources to feed newcomers. Humbert

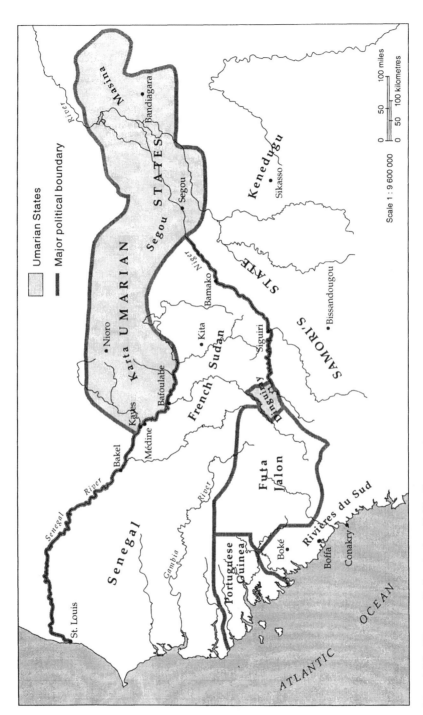

Map 6 The Western Sudan during Gallieni's campaigns

suggested that commandants try to feed all refugees, but if food was in short supply, the priority was feeding the troops.[77] The surplus of women and children was also a problem. In 1897, the commandant at Bandiagara explained that he could not set up a liberty village because he had no men.[78] Some villages had twice as many women as men (see Appendix 3). In addition to these real problems, many administrators lacked sympathy for the freed persons. A frequent complaint was that "most of the non-free who take refuge in our liberty villages are not pushed by a natural sentiment of independence, but by the much less noble goal of avoiding all work, and when they are declared free, quit the village . . . preferring to become vagabonds rather than pay the tax."[79]

Runaways had three possible tactics. The first was to flee to a distant cercle where they were unlikely to be reclaimed. The second was to hide their identity by changing names. One commandant complained that most runaways knew neither their own names nor those of their parents or their place of birth.[80] Many slaves were, however, reclaimed. Data on those returned to their master are rare, too rare for us to venture an estimate, but for some periods, it was a majority of those seeking refuge. In the four villages of upper Senegal, about half were reclaimed.[81] In Nioro, during the third quarter of 1900, fifty-one slaves were reclaimed and twenty-three were not. The third option was to spend several days or weeks recuperating and then move on, to use the liberty villages as way-stations. The number of slaves freed in liberty villages was not huge. In 1895, there were almost 8,000 in the villages.[82] There were large villages outside Kayes and Medine and from four to nine villages attached to each of the older posts – Bafulabe, Nioro, Kita and Bamako. Occasionally, people were authorized to leave when home areas were liberated, but the local commandant usually tried to keep them where they were. In spite of this, most freed persons did not remain indefinitely. This kept the population of the villages low. Appendix 4 gives some data on this. The local administrator rarely knew how many he had in the village because people came, returned and left without his approval. Administrators did not like it. They often referred to departures as "escapes" and punished those caught fleeing.

The "commandant's slaves" did most of the work around the post and could also be used as strike-breakers. Archinard explained: "they assure us in the chief place of our possessions a reserve of labor on which we can count completely and which constitutes a precious resource for our public works and transport when there is a strike among the local people, as happened recently when the Department ordered a salary reduction."[83] Gallieni asked that they be paid 50 centimes a day, but often money was lacking. Commandants used both the newly freed, who were still on rations, and older residents. Soldiers also often went to the liberty village to get women. The heaviest burden was porterage. From the first, the conquest was dependent on the ability of the French army to move goods over long areas. Eventually, the road to Bamako was improved to the point where wagons could be used, but

Fig. 5 Street in a liberty village.

porters were still necessary on ancillary routes and during the rainy season. The worst problem was that officers traveling during the rainy season would commandeer labor in the middle of planting or weeding. The Commandant of Bamako complained in 1887 that so many porters and laborers were being requisitioned during the growing season that people could not feed themselves.[84] Porters were often away for weeks on end. The work was hard and not always remunerated. Sometimes, orders were given limiting use of porters during the rainy season and restricting who could order them to work and under what conditions.[85] The best strategy for freed persons was simply to move on, but until at least 1898, they fled to a very insecure world.[86]

The defeat of Amadu

By 1886, attitudes toward the Sudan had softened in Paris. Within the Sudan, Amadu had moved from Segu to Nioro.[87] Though his position menaced the French flank, he was weakened by a French arms embargo and was interested in resuming trade. During a two-year stint as Commandant Supérieur (1886-88), Gallieni tried to stabilize the French base in the Sudan. He defeated Mamadu Lamine, extended the railroad to Bafulabe, and signed a series of treaties. Gallieni was probably the ablest French military commander in the Sudan, more patient than the others and more given to diplomatic methods.[88] In 1887 Samori agreed to a protectorate, guaranteed security for French commerce, and conceded the left bank of the Niger.[89] This freed Samori to attack his major rival in the southern savanna, Tyeba of Sikasso (Kenedugu).[90] Amadu also agreed to a protectorate, offered the French navigation rights on the Niger and guaranteed safety for French trade. In exchange, the French promised never to invade the Futanke empire or construct forts on its territory and to pay an annual rent.[91] It is unlikely that any of these parties expected the treaties to last. Gallieni certainly did not. He thought the Futanke empire would fall apart on Amadu's death. Gallieni also signed treaties with Tyeba of Sikasso and with Aguibou, Amadu's brother and ruler of Dingiray. Gallieni was convinced that Guinea was a better trade outlet for the Sudan than Senegal and sent a mission to the coast via the Futa Jallon. His only important forward move was the construction of a fort at Sigiri, which gave the French access to valuable gold fields and opened up possibilities of a Guinean trade route. Gallieni also organized administration within areas that the French controlled, and appointed canton chiefs.

In 1888, Louis Archinard was appointed Commandant Supérieur. Archinard was more than any other the conqueror of the French Sudan. A protege of Borgnis-Desbordes and a veteran of his campaigns, he was hungry for promotion and saw military action as the only way to get it.[92] For the first three of his four campaigns, he fought a three-front war: against Amadu and Samori within the Sudan and against a Paris opposed to war with either. To get the military action he craved, he either disobeyed orders or persuaded higher authority to approve his far-reaching plans. He started by attacking the Futanke fort at Kunjan in violation of his instructions. He then convinced both Senegal's Governor Henri Lamothe and a reluctant Eugene Etienne that conquest of the Umarian states would reduce the charge to French taxpayers. Finally, he got the troops he needed to do battle with Amadu's sizable force by using alliances with local chiefs. France's fragile links with the Bambara were based on a shared hostility to the Futanke, but many Bambara communities were hostile to each other, were wary about French objectives, and were dissatisfied with French reluctance to attack their common enemy. The French had difficulty getting the Beledugu Bambara to provide them with cattle, millet or labor. They were also unhappy about conflict between Nto, a Bambara slave chief, and Mari Jara, the Fama, who maintained two *tatas* across the river from Segu.[93] In April 1890 Archinard took Segu in a battle in which the French did not lose a single man. Barely had Amadu fled when Archinard expelled the Futanke from Segu. They were to leave for Senegal under armed guard and the Bambara were authorized to attack any Futanke remaining. This was essentially a license to kill or enslave.[94]

Indirect rule à la française

In order to free the French military from close supervision of a Paris reluctant to underwrite wars of conquest, Archinard relied as much as possible on local resources. This left him little choice but to seek some form of indirect rule. Archinard, however, was no Lugard. He was too authoritarian to concede African rulers much authority, too contemptuous to understand his African underlings and too insecure to trust them. The French restored Mari Jara in

Segu, but sharply reduced the Segu state. A part was given to Mademba Sy, a Senegalese official, who became Fama of Sansanding (Sinsani) and another part was assigned to Bojan from the Massassi Bambara of Karta, traditionally hostile to the Ngolossi Jara of Segu. Within his reduced domain, Mari Jara was to receive traditional taxes, but the French were to take half of the market tolls and the taxes on river and caravan trade. Archinard expected the French Resident to be "the real king."[95] Within two months, Mari Jara was accused of plotting to assassinate the French Resident and was executed along with twenty of his chiefs.[96] Bojan was made Fama and the rest of the Segu war machine withdrew to the south and east where a series of revolts was staged, which cost the French more heavily than the capture of Segu itself. Bojan was a harsh and unpopular ruler who was himself removed two years later. The inability of the French to work out any relationship other than total subservience complicated Archinard's task. Even in suppressing the Segu revolts, the French depended on their allies. Bojan provided about 3,000 men. Nto remained aloof at first, but Tyeba and Mademba provided forces.

At Segu, the issue of slavery was linked to the question of political authority. The area around Segu was populated almost completely by slaves.[97] At the moment of conquest, many Futanke, both slave and free, fled to avoid enslavement.[98] Amadu's slave warriors were expropriated by the colonial state and settled near Segu as a labor reserve.[99] Some Futanke slaves were freed to keep them from leaving and about 5,000 to 6,000 Futanke were redistributed.[100] Of these, about 1,000 were given to the Somono, whose loyalty the French wanted. A hundred were given to Mademba Sy, who needed supporters if he were to impose himself on his "kingdom." Archinard wrote Etienne that the *tirailleurs* "have taken enough booty to be happy," and auxiliaries did even better because the French could not control the process: "the Bambara, the Malinke and the Moors have done well. No one has made them return slaves so they may be given Liberty Papers. They do as they wish, keeping them, selling them or ransoming them. We do not even know what they do."[101] In addition, suppression of the Segu revolts allowed the allies to take many prisoners. When Bojan was removed as Fama, he had about 1,300 slaves, who were freed when he died in 1899, presumably in order to reduce Massassi power. Many refused to follow him and others tried to flee along the way. Then, when they reached Karta, some former slaves of the Futanke were claimed by previous owners.[102] Mademba Sy used these military campaigns to build up his army, his household and his harem.[103]

After fleeing Segu, Amadu returned to Nioro, where he could threaten the upper Senegal. Archinard seized Koniakary before the end of the campaign to protect French positions and then returned to the attack when the rains stopped. On New Year's Day 1891, Nioro fell and Amadu fled again, this time to Masina. Archinard exploited the fact that Karta was ethnically diverse and restored the Massassi Fama, but with only a fraction of the area his ancestors ruled.[104] Archinard restricted the Futanke to two areas, forbade them to travel without a pass or communicate with Senegal.[105] He had earlier expelled the Futanke from Segu. Now, he kept them in Karta for fear of seeing the area depopulated, but their life was hard. Many were enslaved in the wake of the conquest and were distributed as booty or used as laborers.[106] In the spring of 1893, Archinard finally expelled many Futanke.[107]

Archinard's departure and return

Between the two expulsions, Archinard ran into political storms. He attacked Karta without prior approval of Etienne and then compounded his difficulties in Paris by moving south and taking Kankan and Bissandugu. He returned to Paris a hero to many, but an anathema to others. He had ignored his civilian superiors, in particular the powerful Etienne, and had imposed his conception of the Sudan on them. As a result, he was replaced by Humbert, but he left Humbert in a difficult position. Archinard's 1891 victories extended French supply lines deep into Samori's territory. Samori's *sofa* were now armed with up-to-date repeating rifles and had perfected their tactics. They avoided set battles and harassed. This was not what Etienne expected when he approved Archinard's attack on Segu.[108] By the spring of 1892, Etienne was gone and Archinard's patrons secured his reappointment. Sudan was also reorganized. Bakel and Bundu were re-attached to Senegal and Sudan was removed from Senegal's control. The office of Commandant-Supérieur was to be purely administrative and was to report directly to Paris. Archinard sent Combes south to pursue the war with Samori, and then, in March, left Segu for Masina. In a lightning campaign, he took Jenne, Mopti and Bandiagara. Amadu fled east once again and his brother Aguibu was installed as Sultan at Bandiagara, where he proved a successful agent of French power. After Nioro fell, Gumbu submitted without a fight. Archinard put Mamadou Racine, a Senegalese officer, in charge and promised to make him a king like Mademba Sy, but he left before he could make good on his promise and never returned. He had, however, in five years quadrupled the size of the Sudanese empire.

   In conquering Masina, Archinard brought an end to thirty years of warfare between Umar's nephew, Tijani, the Kunta and the Amirou Masina, heir to the Dina. The French moved in at an opportune time. Tijani had died in 1887 and was succeeded by his brother, Muniru.[109] Though war left significant areas empty of population, Masina was marked by large slave-holdings. Many Bambara villages and Fulbe fragments seem to have accepted the authority of either the Futanke or the Kunta, presumably in order to protect slave holdings and their way of life.[110] In 1895, Commandant Destenave estimated that there were two *rimaibe* for each Fulbe, equal numbers of slave and free among the Bambara, and one slave for each two persons among the Futanke elite.[111]

   Slave-raiding was important in the area as was a slave trade north toward Timbuktu from Sikasso and the Volta river. There were also traders from Saint Louis and Kajoor in the area who bought slaves for export to Senegal. The period after conquest saw both flight by slaves, who took advantage of disruption to return home, and efforts by Aguibu to raid the same areas to restore his slave holdings. The relatively equal numbers of men and women suggest that much of the slave population was born within the community. D'Arboussier describes *rimaibe* as having interbred with Fulbe and absorbed their language, religion and customs.[112] Many accounts of Fulbe slavery speak of the rarity of manumission or marriage, but there was a distinction between red Fulbe and black Fulbe.[113] Red Fulbe were cattle people, some of whom were forced to farm because of loss of their herds. Black Fulbe were clerics, warriors and the political authorities. The tendency of ruling elites in Fulbe communities to blacken was rooted in Islamic law, which recognized equal rights of inheritance to all of a man's offspring. The rich and powerful had numerous wives and concubines. The son of a black concubine had the same status as that of a Fulbe senior wife. Black Fulbe were the most systematic users of slave labor. Commandants received explicit instructions to respect local customs. The Resident at Bandiagara was told to ignore slave raiding or trading done by Aguibu.[114] The new Commandant at Jenne was told: "do not get involved in the slave trade by opposing it. The time is not ripe and it would be maladroit. It would hurt our political situation and consequently, the progress of ideas of civilization we hope to triumph some day."[115]

Conquest necessitated not only a policy toward chiefs, but some kind of development policy. Archinard encouraged the penetration of the Sudan by the Senegalese traders who provisioned his columns, but he remained suspicious of the profit motive and imposed numerous regulations on them.[116] Most of the Senegalese were based in Medine and linked to Saint Louis trading houses. They supplied French garrisons, traded with African rulers, and bought a range of commodities. Until the late 1890s, the most important was probably the exchange of goods for slaves.[117] Throughout this period, the vast majority of caravans from any town in the western part of the colony was heading toward Medine or Kayes, and most of the taxable value of these caravans was in slaves.[118] In Wasulu, the representative of a Saint Louis métis trader was arrested only two months after French occupation.[119] The same year, traders from Saint Louis and Kajoor were reported in Masina.[120]

Much of the opposition to Archinard in Paris resulted from his overspending. When he sought permission to attack Segu, Archinard promised to reduce the cost of administration. Instead, his campaigns doubled costs. This aroused enemies of the Sudan operation and alienated many one-time supporters. It led to first his removal and finally in November 1893 to his replacement by a civilian governor, Albert Grodet. We will look at the Grodet interlude in Chapter 7. Archinard also refined a discourse on slavery that had its roots with Faidherbe. The essence of the discourse was that the end of the slave trade and of slavery was the goal of conquest, but that France had made promises to slave owners. Thus in the preamble to a law regulating the use of slaves by the state, he asserted:

That political necessity and even the interest of the native populations obliges us to respect the customs of the country. That as a result, we must assure the masters whose slaves we employ a benefit equal to the work that their slaves would furnish at home.[121]

A White Father claimed that Archinard prohibited the trade in the cercles of Bakel and Medine.[122] I have seen no such order. Father Cros, a Holy Ghost Father, wrote about areas near the old posts: "All that one can ask and does ask today is that merchants do not mistreat their slaves, do not display them in public markets, and are equipped with passes which should be counter-signed at every post."[123] There seems to have been a restriction on open slave markets, but many slaves moved through Medine and Kayes during the 1890s. One order rationalized the export trade because those sold to Senegal were from outside the colony, that is to say, from Samori.[124] Humbert banned any purchase of slaves by a Senegalese subject not followed by an act of liberation.[125] Liberty papers may have been provided for some slaves being moved into Senegal, but with the exception of the Grodet years, there seems to have been no limit on Senegalese traders buying slaves in the Sudan.

Conclusion

Given the reluctance of France to give them the resources they needed to achieve their goals, the soldiers tried to create resources. They had to be able to reward both their own men and their allies. This produced brutal methods of making war. They became an African army, recruited by African methods and organized in an African manner, but with modern weapons. The effect, however, was a bloodier and more horrible period than the Sudan had ever known. If the French were brutal, so too were their rivals. Amadu, Samori, Tyeba and the French were all caught in a resource squeeze, in which they financed increasingly costly ways of making war with the bodies of a servile mass of women and children. Archinard's departure in 1893 was the end of the period of unrestrained military rule. Archinard's disdain for civilian authority and his deception of both his superiors and his allies exacerbated hostility to the military. Paris was not the only problem the military faced. The success of their conquests forced them to create a state. It was not enough to run up the tricolor; they had to administer the lands they conquered. This meant, among other things, bringing in missionaries, who disapproved of much of what they did. They also had to pay for it. This meant incorporation in both the colonial empire and the international market economy. In this Senegal was sometimes a model, sometimes a link to the larger empire and world market. We must, therefore, look in the next chapter at what was happening in Senegal during this period.

6   Senegal in the 1890s

Fear God in the matter of your slaves. Feed them with what you eat and clothe them with what you wear and do not give them work beyond their capacity. Those whom you like, retain, and those whom you dislike, sell. Do not cause pain to God's creation. He caused you to own them and had He so wished, He would have caused them to own you.

Teaching attributed to the Prophet Mohammed[1]

There is no use crusading in a country you cannot keep after you have conquered it.

Sir John Kirk[2]

Faidherbe's success was in part due to his ability to control what his superiors knew. Brière's problems show that it became increasingly difficult to do that. Steamships stopped at Dakar. Travelers, missionaries and politicians regularly passed through. Furthermore, Senegal participated in French parliamentary democracy. The General Council discussed and controlled a large part of the colonial budget. Governors regularly clashed with councillors.[3] Municipal councils controlled local affairs and a deputy represented them in Paris. The deputy was usually linked to one or more of the political blocs on the General Council and could bring pressure to bear on the administration. Senegal was also being converted from a colonial backwater to the center of a colonial empire. This meant a demand for literate functionaries in both administration and commerce. Literacy in turn meant that people could write letters, frame grievances and make them known. Senegal was thus a modern legal state.[4] Arbitrariness was restricted by the existence of a corps of citizens with rights, by an independent court system, by a free press, by institutions before which the administration was responsible.[5]

The legal state

The way in which legality limited the operation of the colonial state is illustrated by two incidents that occurred in 1887. Both involved the distribution of captured women. The first took place after the capture of Rip. The French commander, Colonel Coronnat, explained:

The King of Saloum made war in his manner and took prisoners of both sexes. I had nothing to do with it . . . At Kaolack, after my departure, a certain number of women were put in the presence of a certain number of *tirailleurs*, drivers, and spahis, and after coming to terms, there resulted a certain number of unions in conformity with the customs of the country . . . The measures taken at Kaolack constituted real progress from a humanitarian point of view, by comparison with what happened in previous years in the campaigns of the upper river and elsewhere.[6]

The incident became known when a *spahi* tried to sell his "wife" for 75 francs. The woman had the good fortune to find her way to a lawyer. Court officials, aware of political implications, suspended the case and contacted the Governor. Neither the Governor nor Etienne felt the case could be suppressed, but Etienne insisted that neither Coronnat nor any other officer be mentioned. The case was simply a criminal action against the *spahi* who tried to sell the woman.[7]

The second case involved Senator Alexandre Isaac of Guadeloupe, who received information about the distribution of women after the defeat of Mamadou Lamine.[8] A sub-lieutenant, Samba Maram, was given three young women, who asked to return home and, when refused, ran away. They were seized by force and returned to him. Isaac wrote Etienne and Etienne wrote the Governor.[9] The commanding officer explained that "according to the custom of the region, the defeated becomes the slave of the victor. What concerns our regular native troops is that some female slaves were given to the *tirailleurs* as wives, marriage rendering them free."[10] He then explained that the women were not confided to Samba Maram, but to his wife and only pending their marriage to three younger men. He acknowledged that they tried to run away, but treated it as a whim of the most strong-minded of the group. The other two were interviewed, claimed to be happy, and wore jewelry, which testified to the high regard of their "husbands." Of the three women, one was in a caravan that was passing through the war zone. The others were picked up in villages that supported Mamadu Lamine. All were prizes of war. A laundered version of this account was passed on to Isaac.[11] Both tales end with the notion that the women involved were "freed" by being married. Neither in Senegal nor in the Sudan did a slave gain rights when she became a wife. Thus two Commandants at Bafulabe were told that a slave woman was freed by marriage to her master, but could not leave him.[12]

As one of the few parliamentarians to know Senegal, Isaac was for many years a thorn in the side of the administration. In 1894, he visited Senegal when François Devès was accused of libel. He also visited Sudan with Hyacinthe Devès and wrote the Governor about things that disturbed him: arbitrariness, the protectorate system, the judicial system.[13] Governor de Lamothe was convinced that Isaac was connected to attacks on the administration in two French newspapers. Links Devès developed with both African rulers and French parliamentarians troubled the administration.[14] For both Lamothe and his opponents the slavery issue gave leverage to the opposition in a struggle for control of colonial budgets and policy in the interior.[15] In 1897 the General Council debated a resolution moved by Hyacinthe Devès that criticized toleration of slavery in Kajoor, Bawol and the outskirts of Saint Louis and called for complete suppression in the disannexed territories. When a senior administrator denied that slavery existed in Senegal, Councillor

François Carpot suggested that he was the only one in Senegal who did not know about it. Carpot went on to discuss cases. Devès talked about active markets several kilometers from the site of the meeting and claimed that the protectorate was an excuse to avoid applying the 1848 law and the Act of Brussels.[16]

While democratic politics was changing within Africa, it was also transforming the situation in Europe. A key change was that the Catholic Church made its peace with the Enlightenment. A central figure was Cardinal Lavigerie.

Lavigerie and the Brussels Conference

Archbishop of Algiers and founder of the White Fathers, Lavigerie was originally concerned with relations between Islam and Christianity. Muslim peoples, however, resisted his efforts and the White Fathers increasingly found a more attentive audience in hitherto traditionalist populations south of the Sahara. This forced Lavigerie and his missionaries to confront the horrors of African slavery. With Brazil, the last Western state to tolerate slavery, on the verge of abolition, he appealed to Pope Leo XIII to lead a new anti-slavery movement. After winning the Pope's approval, he undertook a tour of Europe in 1888, calling for "a great crusade of faith and humanity." He left behind organizing committees in every Catholic country he visited and formed crucial links with older British organizations. The movement he created was completely new; he was wary of the anti-clericals of the earlier French movement and made no effort to join with them.[17]

An international conference met at Brussels in 1889 in response both to Lavigerie's campaign and to the desire of several powers to justify imperial expansion.[18] Many colonial powers tried to limit discussion. The French did not want serious discussion of slavery itself and objected to presentation of any evidence of slave trading in French colonies.[19] The conference produced a toothless treaty prohibiting the slave trade both on land and at sea and calling for "progressive organization of administrative, judicial, religious and military services in African territories placed under the sovereignty or protectorate of civilized nations." It also tried to restrict trade in arms and in alcohol.

Though the powers were all slow in implementing the convention, Miers claims that it contributed to the idea of international trusteeship.[20] Anti-slavery became crucial in legitimating the new imperialism. King Leopold, for example, cut his links with Arab slavers. All but one of the colonial regimes got their budgets from democratically elected parliaments, which were generally not eager to fund the grand projects of colonial proconsuls. Up to this time, most anti-slavery movements had focused on the maritime trade and on American slavery.[21] Many assumed that with the end of the export trade, the growth of "legitimate" commerce, and the progress of Christianity, African slavery would fade away. After Brussels, there was a continuing, though often discreet, pressure from anti-slavery and mission groups, as much in France as elsewhere.

Lavigerie's movement was closely linked to increased mission efforts. An anti-slavery fund set up by the Pope was used to create liberty villages and to purchase slave children, who were then educated as Christians.[22] In addition to the purchases, the Holy Ghost Fathers took in refugees and children given to them, deserted children, children taken prisoner after battles and, sometimes, servants of officers due to be posted back to France.[23] Lavigerie's success meant that, after 1888, slavery issues were most often raised within France not by radical anti-clericals but by otherwise conservative Catholics. In 1896, the Holy Ghost Fathers chose as their leader Alexandre Le Roy, who had been an anti-slavery militant while a missionary in East Africa and later served briefly as a bishop in Gabon. He was Superior-General for thirty-three years and was also active in the French Anti-Slavery society. He helped redirect anti-slavery from formal slavery to marriage, focusing on the "slavery" of women to their fathers and husbands.[24] The Holy Ghost Fathers wrote less about slave raiding than the White Fathers, but with the same sense of horror.[25]

Liberation by treaty

The Brussels Treaty was signed just about the time Senegal embarked on disannexation. When a copy of the Treaty was sent to Lamothe, he set up a commission to study how it should be applied.[26] The commission was headed by Martial Merlin, Director of Native Affairs, who was a key figure during the next thirty years. It proposed a new approach to the slave trade, treaties with "protected" states. Shortly afterwards, Governor Clément-Thomas met with several chiefs from the cercle of Saint Louis and agreed to the following:

1. Slaves were no longer to be sold within their lands.
2. All slaves were to be considered domestic slaves and were to be given the protections cited in the Quran.[27]
3. French subjects kept the right to buy slaves elsewhere.
4. Any slave had the right to purchase his or her freedom for a price not to exceed 500 francs. This ceiling was twice the price of the most sought-after young people.

The convention was signed in 1892 and in subsequent years was imposed on chiefs of other cercles.[28] In 1893, it was signed by the chiefs of Bawol, Dimar, Siin and Saalum. In 1894, some chiefs from Futa Toro agreed to transform slaves into indentured tenants. After ten to twelve years, they would be free and would only have to pay rent for lands they cultivated.[29] The administration was startled when three notables with about fifty slaves each actually freed their slaves.[30] In 1895, the Governor-General described these conventions as the administration's way of complying with Brussels: "Domestic slavery," he wrote, "involves only a form of clientship or domestic service, in which the obligations of the master are sometimes as onerous, if not more so that those of the servants."[31] The claim that slavery had been converted into a benign form of domestic servitude or the use of terms like *captif* or *serviteur* was an effort to alter Europe's image of a detested institution. As long as slaves could call on no sanctions, a change in terminology had no influence on the way they were treated.[32]

Many chiefs did stop caravans though it is unlikely that the regime expected them to do so. Thus, in the first six months of 1893, Tanor Jeng, the Ten Bawol, stopped slave traders and liberated at least 149 slaves. One trader had only a single slave. Others had as many as forty-one. Most were women or children being moved by Wolof traders, largely from Bakel, Segu or somewhere in the Sudan. Some traders protested that they had passes from the French authorities in the Sudan and no reason to think they were acting illegally. One hired a lawyer.[33] The probable reason for Tanor's zeal is that the freed slaves became his dependants. He was warned, however, that they were not to be sold and should be produced on demand.[34] One group of juula offered to keep the slaves on the same terms as Tanor, that is to say as "freed slaves."[35]

The situation was similar in other jurisdictions. In Niani-Ouli, the administrator wrote that "every time a slave escapes, he becomes the property of the chief of the province in which he is stopped."[36] The Bur Siin complained that since few trade routes crossed his kingdom, he did not receive as many slaves as his neighbors.[37] Chiefs were particularly eager to free slaves being sent to or fleeing from traditional enemies. This sometimes produced heated exchanges between administrators, as for example when Noirot in Sine-Saloum freed slaves being sent from Rip to Kajoor with the approval of the Commandant in Rip. Noirot discovered that the slaves had been taken in a recent raid, and had therefore been enslaved illegally. The Bur Saalum was, of course, quite happy to seize slaves being shipped by his enemy in Nioro.[38] He had to be reminded, however, that they did not become his slaves.[39] Slaves confided to chiefs were to receive subsistence, tools, land and a hut, and in return, the chief received part of the first crop, but "it is impossible to make them understand that they are only temporary protectors."[40] Administrators distinguished between slaves bought for trade and those bought for personal use, which was still legal.[41]

While chiefs proved surprisingly eager, administrators were often told not to intervene. In 1893, when the administrator of Matam asked what to do about caravans coming from Sudan with passes indicating the number of slaves they were moving, he was told: "Let them go by as if you were ignorant of their passage and do not countersign their passes."[42] Policy was to free only slaves of their enemies and slaves with clear evidence of mistreatment: marks of severe whippings, emaciation, or evidence of being tied up or held in irons for a long period.[43] Until 1904, the Commandant at Tivouane was obeying the following instructions: "this question is one of the most delicate in regions where agriculture and herding are done on a large scale and demand numerous hands . . . Subjects of protected countries keep the right to redeem slaves and raise them to the status of servants who should not be freed except when serious brutality is noted."[44] Other instructions justified such an approach on the grounds that freed slaves would only become vagabonds. The problem was keeping runaways from areas of direct administration: "If this slave finds himself on French territory, he will be free under law. You should under no pretext assist the agents of the Bur Saluum in their efforts to recapture him."[45] In some cases, administrators ignored the law or looked the other way when coercion was used. In one case, a runaway from Bakel wanted to purchase the freedom of his wife and child, but was told that he had to purchase his own first. He had only 250 francs.[46] Another administrator was told that slaves claiming liberation were to be kept under surveillance until it was ascertained that they were not being sought for criminal acts.[47]

The Gambia border

The Gambia border created opportunities for slaves. In 1895, the Gambia Protectorate Emancipation and Slave Trade Abolition Ordinance prohibited slave-dealing and provided for gradual emancipation.[48] As in Senegal, the ordinance was a hesitant and nervous response to Brussels that resulted from metropolitan pressure. In a minute on an earlier report, A.W.L. Hemming in the Colonial Office wrote: "If the Aborigines Protection Society were to hear that the existence of slavery was actually tolerated in what must now, I presume be held to be British territory, we might have a *mauvais quart d'heure*."[49] The ordinance provided that all slaves were to be freed on the death of their master and slaves born after a certain date or brought into the colony from outside were to be freed. Some slaves claimed their freedom, but in general the ordinance impacted more on the slave trade than on slavery itself.[50] Slaves were given the right to buy their freedom and some actually did.[51] In 1898, a registration system was set up to prevent the sale of slaves.[52] Some administrators used non-registration to free slaves. As in Senegal, the Gambia often claimed greater progress than it actually made.[53]

The slave trade was undoubtedly much reduced. By the end of the decade, there is a report that savings were being spent on cattle rather than slaves.[54] If there was a change in slavery, it resulted from the possibility of flight. In 1898, the Travelling Commissioner of the North Bank observed: "After the British occupation in 1893 all the Male Slaves, principally Jolahs, ran away leaving behind only the hereditary and old slaves and female Jolahs."[55] The 1895 law made it possible for any slave who crossed the border to complain about mistreatment and get his freedom. Elsewhere, the slave often had to present evidence of mistreatment. One French commandant wrote that British policy was "to free the slaves from our territory who flee to the Gambia, and not to free those of their chiefs, but to claim them if they come to our territory."[56] British administrators made the same charge about French policy.[57] Movement went both ways. Niani-Ouli in the upper Gambia was only organized as a cercle in 1897, but almost immediately found itself the center of slave problems. In 1903, the Commandant complained that every spring large numbers fled. In one case, twenty-six from the same village slipped away at night, probably because they feared that masters would try to keep them by force. The same report refers to slaves coming in almost every day from the Gambia.[58] Runaways from the Gambia were the major reason for setting up a liberty village.[59]

Persistence of the slave trade

While action was taken against the slave trade, slaves were still being shipped into Senegal and slaving was still going on in the Casamance. Fodé Kaba was defeated only in 1901 and Musa Molo broke with the French in 1903.[60] British policy made moving slaves across the Gambia difficult. The Saint Louis convention enabled the administration to deal with the slave trade on a cercle by cercle basis. By the early twentieth century, it had been reduced. Some chiefs had to be pressured. Thus, in Nioro-du-Rip, the trade was very active up to the signature of the anti-slavery convention, but five years later, the commandant claimed that it had been suppressed.

And yet, slaves still moved. Slave traders from Kajoor were in Niani-Ouli in 1897.[61] Increasingly, it was only children, who were moved in small numbers and often at night; but in 1904, slaves from the Sudan could still be purchased in Sine-Saloum.[62] One slave market remained wide open several years after the others. This was Kaedi, on the north bank of the Senegal river but administered from Senegal. Every year during the dry season, Moors moved to Kaedi to pasture and water their herds, to sell gum to the French and to exchange salt and cattle for grain and cloth. A post built at Kaedi during the campaign against Abdul Bokar Kan became a major market during the 1890s, probably because it permitted trade with the Moors.

The slaves were destined largely for the peanut basin: "the trade has begun at Kaedi, Moors coming from the desert, selling slaves in quantity to juula from different parts of the colony."[63] The trade was taxed and every purchaser told that the "slaves could not be resold and would become free on reaching the age of majority." Gov. Lamothe authorized purchase from the Moors and only from the Moors.[64] Ironically, this letter was in response to the Director of Native Affairs, who was surprised that a slave market still existed at Kaedi. Even the commandant learned about the system only from his interpreter. An earlier commandant, however, was told unambiguously: "while the administrator should not involve himself directly in these questions of slavery, he has an interest in using his authority to support orders given by the chiefs."[65] The existence of markets encouraged the persistence of slave-raiding along the river, where it remained serious well into the colonial period. While the French tried to bar the south bank of the Senegal river to the Moors, raiding persisted there long after it ended elsewhere.[66] One Moor protested that kidnappers made it difficult for masters to send slaves to harvest gum.[67] Once slaves were moved into Senegal, there was a chance that runaways would be freed. In 1898, Aubrey-Lecomte in Kaedi complained bitterly that Victor Allys in Podor was freeing Kaedi slaves:

It seems enormous that an administrator has the right to free slaves from a neighboring cercle without even asking the advice of the Commandant of that cercle . . . It is enough for a slave to complain of his master and show a few marks for him to get his freedom. This is contrary to all justice and the population is profoundly disturbed by such actions.[68]

Law, policy and the commandant

Thus, policy varied from cercle to cercle according to the political situation, the social structure and the views of the administrator, but the general rule was to discourage flight and reclamations. Caution was intensified by the desire of commandants to avoid disruption, by their dependence on slave-owning collaborators, and by their own conservative views. Many thought it more immoral to deprive a master of his property than to deprive a human being of his or her freedom. They often saw nothing but sloth in the efforts of slaves to free themselves.[69] Thus, after a period of slave resistance, Allys in Bakel suggested that fat and healthy slaves were complaining of not being fed. The problem, Allys wrote, was that the work season was approaching. "They want to be well fed and clothed without doing any work."[70] Given the views held by most commandants, the reception of runaways was probably even colder than the archives suggest. Administrators often avoided putting on paper actions that could cause them difficulty. Coercion of various kinds clearly operated to keep slaves in place. One administrator explained in 1893 how he discouraged slave claims:

... every time an individual presents himself at Foundiougne to ask for his/her liberty, I have always responded that on French territory no one can claim to be a slave, that by the sole fact of living in Foundiougne, he is as free as me, but that I cannot say what would happen to him if he returned to nearby territories where slavery still exists.[71]

Two incidents in Kajoor show how the administration often deliberately shut its eyes to the dilemma of slaves. The first took place in 1886, when a slave belonging to Demba Warr Sall, France's most powerful ally in Kajoor, obtained liberty papers in Saint Louis for his family. Demba Warr tried to retake them as they left and they sought refuge at the railway station in Tivouane. Fifty of Demba Warr's horsemen surrounded the station. This was only months after the defeat of Lat Dior. The chief of the station turned over the freed slaves.[72] A second incident took place a year later. Two female slaves from Saalum took refuge in the home of a French trader at Ndande, a station town in Kajoor. When the trader wrote the judicial service to ask for liberty papers, he was told that the women had to come to Saint Louis. In Kajoor, the courts only had authority within 300 m of the station. When the head of the judicial service asked the Governor what he should do, he was told

slave questions which arise in the interior between natives should always be examined with a lot of tact and prudence, and especially in Cayor, we must at all cost avoid intervening in such affairs under risk of seeing people of this country detach and distance themselves from us. If a slave had only to present himself at one of our stations for us to give him protection, before long, Cayor would be depopulated, all the captives would invade our establishments along the railroad and there would be a pretext for incessant recriminations and interminable conflicts and difficulties.[73]

With Demba Warr's men watching the house, the trader could not smuggle the women out. Eventually they were seized and no further questions were asked.[74]

There was often a conflict between French law and Muslim or customary law. A dossier from Bakel provides a series of illustrative cases. In one a freedman died without children. His wife inherited his granary and his clothes, but not his livestock or real property, which went to the post. In another case, two men were fined the value of a slave for adultery with the cadi's wife. In a third, a slave given as part of brideprice asked to be sold, but the administrator decided that he lacked the authority to force a sale. In traditional law, slaves were treated very much like livestock and were frequently given as fines or in settlement of debts. The Commandant objected only when a child of seven or eight was separated from his mother and given in payment of a debt and when a husband protested the sale of his wife. There was a case involving slaves given to chiefs by French officers and another involving slaves awarded in a civil action. There were also criminal cases. A slave dealer was given a 100-franc fine, fifteen days imprisonment and loss of his slave in a sale case. Paradoxically, three men were given fifteen days for inciting "captives to present themselves at the post and demand their liberty." [75]

Slave revolts

During this period at least two revolts took place. In both cases anticipation of change led slaves to withdraw their labor. The first was at Saba in the Gambia, an area with a slave majority and a large number of slaves born in the community. Slaves lived in separate hamlets of twenty to thirty huts, each with its own headman. In June 1894, thinking they were now under British rule, many slaves refused to work for their masters. One group submitted after a showdown with armed masters, but another refused. This led to a battle in which two slaves were killed. The British administration fined and jailed several village chiefs, but it is not clear what the final resolution was. Descendants of the two communities were still living there in 1963.[76]

In 1895, slaves of the Soninke near Bakel also rebelled. This area had been part of Sudan. From 1886 to 1890, the military freed runaways from Guidimaxa in order to press villages near the river to submit to France.[77] Many slaves also fled when Mamadu Lamine was defeated in 1888.[78] In 1895, Bakel was returned to Senegal, stirring hopes of freedom among the slaves. Slaves near Matam started to flee to Bakel and slaves from Bakel fled to Saint Louis.[79] Then, newly appointed Governor General Jean-Baptiste Chaudié visited Bakel and gave a speech to chiefs and elders explaining that slaves had a right to their freedom, that this right existed no matter how they conducted themselves, and that anyone making a claim would be freed.[80]

As *tirailleurs* from the area spread word about the speech, chiefs from Gwey reported that slaves from Bakel were getting ready to leave. The commandant promised that he would free no one, and "that those who come to me without a complaint against their masters would be severely punished." It is not clear how much flight there was between November and March, but some slaves took refuge in nearby cercles like Kayes.[81] In March 1896, a new administrator explained that the decision whether to return a slave or grant liberty papers depended on the slave's conduct and hard work.[82] Then, suddenly slaves started pouring in to both Bakel and the nearby post of Selibaby. It is hard to estimate the totals because many fled the region. On a single day in April, 130 slaves showed up at Selibaby, and three times that number in the weeks that followed, many with iron shackles on their feet. By mid-May, the commandant reported that there was neither room in the liberty village nor available land. Fearing starvation, he stopped issuing liberty papers and ordered the post of Selibaby to stop as well.[83] Both posts gave freed slaves one meal a day and hired some to build needed facilities. Many newly freed slaves tried to earn money selling firewood or pounding millet. The administrator asked Saint Louis to send grain and seed.[84]

Chiefs and elders pleaded for the return of their slaves. "We consider them like our children; we treat them well," the Tunka of Gwey said. The commandant responded that they lost their slaves because of mistreatment.[85] By late July, flights had stopped as they often stopped during the rainy season. A few returned to their masters, but there were at least 500 to 600 at Bakel and only work for about 40 a day.[86] Half of all salaries were being held to indemnify the masters.[87] The commandant suggested that if the state did not want freed slaves to disperse, it could deny them the right to emigrate or assign them to village chiefs, who were all former masters.[88] In July, a new commandant, De Roll Montpellier, arrived with instructions from Merlin.[89] To stop the migration, he made life more difficult for the slaves. They had to make their claims at Bakel, but official caravans were not to add refugees while on the trail. He brought together each master with his slaves, hoping to persuade slaves to return.[90] Slaves were urged to return to their masters as "free workers" and about a dozen leaders were expelled and returned to their masters as punishment for "having misled others and continued here to lead them and to give them bad advice, appointing themselves chiefs without any right to that." At its peak, there were about 1,000 refugees. Seven hundred to eight hundred returned to their masters. About sixty to one hundred were given liberty papers. But the number who disappeared to head to the cities, to the Gambia, or to earlier homes was probably greater.[91] Many were probably re-enslaved.

The Bakel rising of 1895–96 took place at a time of economic difficulty. Peanut prices had been low for over a decade. A cattle epidemic struck in 1892, and in 1894, the gum price dropped suddenly. The demands of the French army for millet and the increasing flow of slaves, who had to be fed, could only partially compensate for the losses. The area was a major peanut producer only from the 1860s to the 1880s. It is possible that slaves bore the brunt of economies forced by economic decline, but reports in the archives do not say this. Administrators attributed the revolt to Chaudié's speech, agitation by *tirailleurs*, trouble-making slaves and the desire of slaves not to work at all. Manchuelle argues that most of the slaves simply wanted to be transformed into *woroso*. This argument is based in part on an incident in 1897, when a master lodged a complaint against slaves who refused to work. When the administrator tried to mediate, the slaves said they wanted not liberation, but land and an ameliorated status.[92] Manchuelle is right in that slaves wanted to establish control over their own productive activities, but in 1895 and 1896, many of those north of Bakel saw leaving as the only way to accomplish this. After 1905, flights from this area were not as massive as from other Soninke areas, perhaps because of the 1895 rising, more likely because of steady erosion of slave holdings during the previous decade and the adaptation of masters to the possibility of flight.[93] By 1898, the local administrator was worried not about keeping slaves with masters, but about keeping them in the region.[94]

The quest for freedom

There were other ways in which slaves became free. Many freedmen enlisted in the *tirailleurs*. They began another life, were often given slave women and became clients of the colonial state. Former *tirailleurs* often received jobs as messengers, guards or interpreters after completing their service. Some former slaves also contracted to work as laborers or serve as soldiers elsewhere in Africa. Legally, it was important that when their military service was completed, they were free. At that point, they often returned to the site of captivity to look for children, parents, siblings or former spouses. They were not always welcome. Thus, in one case, four veterans returned to Kaedi to ransom wives and children. All had remarried. One, who had born three children for her subsequent husband, refused to leave, but the ex-*tirailleur* got his child.[95] The returned *tirailleurs* often faced the opposition of masters, but they could usually count on the sympathy of the commandant.

People sometimes tracked down lost members of their families, often in distant areas, and sought to purchase their independence or, later, when the law was favorable, simply to bring them home. Often letters were sent through the administration. Other times people went to find lost kin. Members of chiefly families were especially well received. Others used the services of a lawyer or public letter-writer in one of the communes. Thus, Fatou Camara found Louis Huchard, a métis lawyer and politician.[96] She and her seven-year-old daughter had been enslaved by Saer Maty Ba in Niani-Ouli. More than a decade later, in 1898, she escaped to Dakar. She knew where her daughter was and asked for her daughter to be freed. When the administration dragged its feet, Huchard had the question raised in the General Council, informed Senator Isaac about it, and used it to attack government policy. With Isaac on the case, the Governor General pressed the local administration to settle it and an assistant administrator was sent to find the woman. The daughter was now grown, had married another slave, had three children, and was about to give birth to a fourth. She told the administrator that she did not wish to leave her husband and children. The difference between mother and daughter probably lay in the daughter's fear of losing her children, who belonged to her master. The administration was willing to facilitate a redemption payment, but was not willing to call into question either the owner's right either to a slave or to her children.[97] This was only one of several cases of children who grew up in captivity and were no longer interested in their parents.[98]

Box 6.1

Fatou Camara and her daughter, Aram, were *teug*, members of the smith's caste, from Niani-Ouli. In the mid-1880s, they were captured by Saer Maty. The daughter was only seven at the time, but they were separated. The daughter and four other captives were exchanged for a horse. Both mother and daughter were sold in Kajoor, where they had intermittent contact. The mother claimed that the daughter pleaded for help in getting her liberty and saved the price of the horse for which she was originally sold. In 1898, the mother escaped and took refuge with a jeweler, a member of the smith's caste, in Dakar. Some time after Aram was bought, her master let it be known he had a female *teug* available for marriage, but no smith came forward. He therefore gave her to a slave. A free man would have refused to marry a *teug*. When her master died, she was inherited by his daughter, who was willing to free her for an appropriate sum. She claimed that she had last seen her mother seven years earlier. According to the administrator, she attested as follows:

I affirm that I have been voluntarily married to Matar Binta, a slave of Matar Fatimata. I declare that I do not wish to live with my mother. I do not wish to be freed and I desire to live at N'Daur with my husband and my children.*

*Procès-verbal of interrogation, 21 March 1900; Asst. Admin. to Dir. Native Affairs, 17 March 1900; and Fatou Camara to dir. Native Affairs, 25 July 1899, all in ARS 2 D 315.

The Futa Toro

In the Futa Toro, slave flight was frequent, but the area did not have the pattern of crisis and revolt that marked Soninke and Maraka areas further east, though all three societies were rigidly hierarchical and had a high concentration of slaves. The probable explanation lies in geography and economic history. The Soninke early developed from their position as the northernmost bastion of agricultural settlement a role as intermediaries between the desert and agricultural societies further south. Their commercial vocation dispersed Soninke traders across West Africa. They also developed production for exchange in their desert-side towns. Both sectors depended heavily on slave labor, but the Soninke inhabited areas with a fertile hinterland.[99] The Tokolor inhabited a narrow stretch of floodplain, to the south of which lay the dry Ferlo, inhabited only by their Fulbe cousins. When they spread out of the Futa in the nineteenth century, it was as preachers, teachers and soldiers. Soninke slave accumulations came from parsimonious reinvestment of commercial profits or wages. The Tokolor accumulated slaves as booty and were more likely to exploit them as patriarchal lords. Slavery was an issue during the *torodbe* revolt, when the Tokolor cut off the river trade, and it was an issue during the late nineteenth century, when Futa nobles constantly complained about the escape of their slaves to become *tirailleurs* or to seek freedom in Saint Louis. The nineteenth century saw the accumulation of slaves both in Futanke domains of the east and in the river area itself. In fact, emigration meant that lands were available that could be worked by slaves. The position of the Futa straddling a major river trade route facilitated accumulation of slaves. So too did continuous warfare. In spite of the strictures of Islam, Futanke even enslaved other Futanke.[100]

Then the exiles returned. After the capture of Segu in 1890, Archinard sent the Futanke back to the Futa. In 1893, over 10,000 Futanke from Nioro were also sent back.[101] Thus, twice, a large column of exiles wended its way home, broken, defeated, but encumbered with slaves and cattle accumulated in earlier successes. They were plundered by Mauritanian raiders and by French *spahis*, tormented by hunger and thirst. A French account describes their arrival at Matam: "All are in the most profound misery, and give out from a distance, a fetid odour. Many died of hunger on the way; many fall breathless while coming down or climbing the river's edge. One also notices many wounds..."[102] Furthermore, when they arrived, many of their cattle, horses, weapons and slaves were confiscated, they learned that their lands had been expropriated and that they risked execution. When village chiefs asked Administrator Molleur at Podor what they should do with people coming in from Nioro, he ordered that the slaves be freed and their horses and guns sent to Saint Louis for auction.[103] There were, however, numerous slaves who were not seized or who remained with their masters. It was probably, in the long run, the best way for them to have access to land. The return from Nioro contributed significantly to the high percentage of slaves in the Futa Toro.[104]

Conclusion

The partition of Africa began the conquest of Africa, and the conquest stimulated the demand for labor. Soldiers were needed for colonial armies. Sailors were needed to staff boats on river and ocean. Workers were needed to build railroads and port facilities. Those colonies that were wholly new, that did not build on old Eurafrican communities, had to seek much of that labor in the older colonies. Thus, there was heavy recruitment for the two Congos in West Africa and sometimes recruitment for Guinea or the Ivory Coast. The older colonies did not, however, have a surplus of labor. Most labor was tied up in slavery. We have seen that labor recruitment took diverse forms. While free labor staffed the boats on the Senegal and Gambia rivers, slave caravans brought the newly enslaved to the peanut fields of Kajoor. The colonial state remained hostile to freed slaves, seeing in them a problem of order, vagabonds and potential criminals who sought freedom not to work but to avoid work. And yet, in the 1880s and 1890s, these freed slaves were an increasingly important source of labor. They were not adequate to the colony's needs. The high wages paid to *laptots* testify to this. So too did the import of Kru to work on the port of Dakar in the 1860s, of Piedmontese for the Dakar–Saint Louis railroad, and of Chinese and Moroccan labor for the Kayes–Niger.[105] Not surprisingly, in 1894, the Senegalese government banned recruitment for the Congo Free State.[106] Keeping the labor at home did not necessarily solve Senegal's labor problems. Increasingly, the demand for labor in the upper Senegal led the military to rely on forced labor. Few in Senegal seem to have conceived of the potential of freed slave labor, in part because most observers believed that coercion was necessary to get people to work.[107]

The administration continued to balance between its opposed concerns up to 1903. It eliminated slaving, though slave-raiding persisted on its northern border, fed by a continuing hunger for slaves. It also gradually closed down the slave trade. Slaves were still, however, being bought and sold, though in reduced numbers, into the twentieth century. And slavery itself was protected, though the law promised freedom to those who could find their way to the right place. The problem of doing research on this period is that the administration was often concerned to hide what it was doing.[108] It had to do so. To extend colonial rule, it needed both the support of metropolitan legislators and a structure of allies and auxiliaries. To get the former, it had to present itself as abolitionist. To get the latter, it had to confirm the control of propertied classes over their slaves. The major restraints on colonial administration were the shortage of funds, the pressures of metropolitan humanitarianism, and the existence of representative government within Senegal. Lamothe introduced a head tax largely to create a source of funds that the General Council did not control.[109]

7   The end of the conquest

... many commandants de cercle are so used bush to life that they make no
effort to hide details of administrative life that would appear horrible in
France, for example tax rolls in which the merchandise consists only of slaves
or lists for rations in which we see under Changes, "shot."   Charles Monteil[1]

... what reward can we give in exchange for services rendered [to African
soldiers and auxiliaries] ... if not booty, that is to say, slaves ... It was
necessary for a period of time (that of the conquest, now it would appear
completed) to abandon the most precious ideas of civilization and of the
pacification of customs, and pushed by the hard law of necessity, submit to
the spirit and the customs of Blacks in distributing slaves as a reward for war
service.   Administrative report[2]

Archinard was dismissed for disobeying orders and for his continuing deficits.
The colonial lobby was as critical as anti-colonial elements in the Chamber
because Archinard's wars were not favorable to economic growth.[3] The price,
however, of his removal was bitter conflict both in Paris and within the Sudan
between the civilians and the military. The new Governor, Albert Grodet,
who had been a Governor in the West Indies and a colonial department
official, seems to have been chosen because he was believed to be strong
enough to stand up to the military. He certainly was not intimidated by them.
He was also tactless, though it is doubtful whether tact would have made a
difference. Grodet was told that "the period of conquest and territorial
expansion must be considered ... at an end."[4] He was to develop administration, extend the communications network and encourage trade.

Lt. Colonel Etienne Bonnier was the new Commandant Supérieur. Bonnier
was a friend of Archinard and protege of Borgnis-Desbordes. He left Bordeaux within days of his appointment and arrived in Kayes three months
before Grodet.[5] Though he had official instructions to undertake no military
action, he had secret instructions from Archinard and Borgnis-Desbordes to
continue the fight against Samori. His own goal was Timbuktu, but events on
the southern front forced him to change his plans. Ntentu, the major market
town of Wasulu, was under siege by Samori and had requested help. As soon
as his French officers arrived and the rains ended, Bonnier's *tirailleurs* were on
the march.

Samori, Sikasso and Wasulu

During the second half of the nineteenth century, Wasulu was the most important source of slaves in the Sudan. As early as the 1870s, Wasulu was mentioned and Wasulunke names were found on the freed slave lists in Saint Louis.[6] Wasulu proper is an area of mixed agriculture that straddles the borders of Mali, Guinea and the Ivory Coast. Its people claim Fulbe origins, but have long since lost any knowledge of the Pular language. They were grouped into *jamana* that could contain from eight to fifty villages, but all activities were organized and conflicts were resolved within kinship structures.[7] The Wasulunke spoke Bambara and resembled other Bambara speakers in the southwest corner of what is now Mali. Segu had long raided this area for slaves and collected tribute and recruits in it.

In the second half of the nineteenth century, Wasulunke methods of alternatively resisting and parrying foreign intrusions broke down, when they found themselves surrounded by increasingly powerful states dependent on the slave trade – Futanke Segu, Kenedugu (Sikasso), Futa Jallon and Samori's rising state. Some Wasulunke took military service with these states, but most communities simply built walls.[8] The Futanke raided in Wasulu, but did not collect tribute.[9] Samori's empire was often identified as Wasulu, but its base was further south. Samori's forces moved into Wasulu only in 1882. At the time, each of the *jamana* made a ritual sacrifice and swore loyalty to Samori.[10] Most Wasulunke accepted the new political order, but some fled. By 1887, Wasulunke communities near Bamako, Kati, Kita and other French posts supplemented liberty villages as a source of labor.

There were several revolts before 1887, but the real crisis came with the siege of Sikasso. By then, Samori controlled most of the Malinke of the southern savanna. His major rival was Tyeba, the Senufo ruler of Sikasso. Tyeba was weaker than Samori because he started later and had less access to arms. The major outlet for his slaves was north through Segu, which controlled his access to the Banamba horse market. Thus, he maintained close ties with Amadu and later with the French. His cavalry were recruited from free men and thus his ability to get horses was crucial to his ability to recruit volunteers.[11] Every cavalryman received a sabre and a gun, but most were armed with flintlocks. The bulk of his army was the slave infantry, many armed with bows and arrows. Confronted with better-armed enemies, Tyeba built the most formidable fortress in West Africa at Sikasso.[12] Lacking artillery, Samori could only break Sikasso's will by imposing a siege. To maintain the siege, his forces constructed small forts called *diassas* at strategic points around the perimeter, but Tyeba was Samori's match as a military strategist. Throughout the fifteenth-month siege, Tyeba was able to move men and supplies into the city. His *sofa* regularly attacked the *diassas* and forced Samori to spread his forces out along the siege line.

Samori had to feed and supply a large army tied down in a raid and counter-raid cycle in which Tyeba controlled the time and place of combat. To feed his troops, Samori imposed heavy obligations on his subjects. Wasulu was a fertile area adjacent to Sikasso. The Wasulunke had not only to grow

Fig. 6 *Tata* of Sikasso and Diassa, fort built by Samori's forces on siege line.

the grain, but to carry it to the troops month after month. Some fled without fighting. Others refused to continue serving. This became what Person called the Great Revolt.[13] Binger, who passed through this area in 1887, saw numerous ruins, villages completely empty or inhabited by a smattering of people, one with bodies still rotting.[14] But it got worse. Repulsed at Sikasso, Samori's *sofa* ravaged Wasulu, burning, destroying and enslaving. Tens of thousands of captives were moved north each year from the walled market town of Ntentu (Tenetou) to Banamba.[15] By 1893, there were not many people left, and they were clustered in a small number of communities in northern Wasulu in and around Ntentu. Pressed by the French, Samori decided to move his whole kingdom and ordered those communities still under his authority to join him.[16] Ntentu refused and got ready for a siege. People from the few remaining communities flocked into Ntentu and a plea for help was sent to the French. When Bonnier's column reached Bamako on the way south, they heard that Ntentu had fallen.[17] More than 3,000 men were massacred and long files of women and children were moved north to be exchanged for horses.[18] Almost three weeks later, Bonnier's troops arrived and defeated the *sofa* at Faragaran. The French then built a fort at Buguni. The stench of the rotting bodies at Ntentu was so offensive that the French regrouped survivors for several months at their new post.[19]

Bonnier did not remain at Buguni for long. Within days of the victory at Faragaran, his army was on the march again, hoping to be on the way to Timbuktu before Grodet arrived. He left behind a garrison to build a fort at

Buguni and defend northern Wasulu. The *sofa* withdrew to the south, but in 1894 there was almost nothing in the vast area from Ojenné to Bamako except an occasional wandering refugee or some unharvested grain.[20] The remaining inhabitants, a little over 6,000 people, gathered in several secure villages.[21] Bonnier recommended that no taxes be levied and that food be provided for returning Wasulunke.[22] Within a year, however, the French were trying to collect taxes, and at no time did they give assistance to Wasulunke who wanted to return home. The remnants of the once thriving Wasulunke community were still not safe. *Sofa* continued to raid in the area for several years and, with the retreat of Samori, forces from Sikasso also raided there. Tyeba and his successor, Ba Bemba, forged close relations with the French; there were even joint military efforts.[23] Sikasso was thus able to increase its slave holdings, even raiding areas nominally subject to the French. Where French control was weak, former *tirailleurs* or auxiliaries often imposed themselves, claiming to represent the French and demanding slaves and livestock.[24] Slaves stolen or taken in combat were often sold by *tirailleurs*.[25]

Grodet's war with the military

Bonnier knew that Grodet would muzzle him. On 26 December, the day Grodet was due to arrive at Kayes, Bonnier started down river by barge while a second force under Commandant Joffre moved overland. Bonnier took Timbuktu, then split his force, leaving a garrison in Timbuktu while the rest of his troops moved back to meet Joffre. At Gundam, Bonnier and eighty-one of his troops were massacred by the Tuareg.[26] The massacre at Gundam damaged the reputation of the colonial army, but it also created deep resentments against Grodet. Grodet had few options. Thus, he removed and punished officers, but he could only replace them with other officers. His task was compounded by the question of security. The Colonial Department (which became a Ministry in 1894) was unwilling to give up any conquests. Thus posts had to be staffed, allies protected and defences maintained. Neither tactful nor subtle, Grodet experienced constant conflict.[27]

Most of Grodet's fights with the military concerned his efforts to prevent combat, but he also tried to limit their privileges. Lt. Mangin was punished for distributing slaves to his servants.[28] When Grodet discovered that Comm. Quiquandon had accumulated 140 slaves and 37 head of cattle in military operations, he freed the slaves and confiscated the cattle.[29] More important than his attack on military privilege, Grodet tried to end the slave trade. He started by asking for an inquiry on slavery.[30] It was not, however, these reports that pushed him to act but the listing of slaves on regular commercial reports: "I cannot accept that on the territory of the Republic in the headquarters town of a Commandant de Cercle, representatives of the human species are among the articles for purchase or sale." Besides the trade was contrary to the Act of Brussels.

If in spite of this act we are forced for the moment for political reasons to ignore domestic slavery, we have the right and the duty to stop the sale of slaves. As a

---

Box 7.1

This is a story told by Edouard Guillaumet. At Gundam, he saw a group of *tirailleurs* leading some Tuareg prisoners back to the post. Two adult men were shot and the others were to be divided up among the *tirailleurs*. He rescued four children. He could not communicate with them or take care of them. He therefore let it be known that he wanted a female slave. The woman brought to him was an attractive Bambara of twenty to twenty-five years. He explained to her that he would be going back to France, that he would take her to Kayes, and free her there. When she agreed, he proceeded to negotiate with her master. After much haggling, they set a price of 75 francs.

Djidi, the young woman, had grown up in a village, married and had children. She was taken prisoner in a raid by Samori's *sofa*. Her husband died defending the *tata*. Her daughter also died, probably on the march. She changed hands several times before she was sold in Jenne. There, she was assigned the care of her master's children. Jenne soon fell to the French and Djidi found herself among the booty to be divided up by the *tirailleurs*. She was then sold to someone in Saraféré, when Guillaumet bought her. Guillaumet does not tell us what happened to her. He also does not tell what happened to the Tuareg children.*

*Guillaumet, 1894: 215–24.

---

consequence you will formally forbid in my name the sale of trade slaves . . . All slaves in this category will be immediately freed and placed along the supply route. Those who brought them should be immediately expelled from the colony and told that if they are found again with human merchandise, they will be severely punished.[31]

This order was quickly extended to other cercles.[32] Where there were no liberty villages, Grodet asked that they be set up. When explorer Edouard Guillaumet arrived back in Kayes with four Tuareg children, Grodet lashed out at the distribution of slaves.[33] Many Commandants were bothered by Grodet's actions. The Commandant at Segu wrote that local people were disturbed, but he reassured them that there was no intention to free existing slaves. Runaways would still be returned unless there was evidence of severe mistreatment.[34] The Commandant of the Northeast Region refused to apply the law until he had explicit instructions on what to do about the trade tax (*oussourou*), which was paid partly in slaves. He explained that *juula* had been told that they could keep and sell their slaves and wanted a warning to *juula* before such a policy was enforced. Finally, he pointed out that many *tirailleurs* possessed slaves, which they wanted to sell.[35] Nevertheless, the number of manumissions increased. In 1893, before Grodet's arrival, 641 certificates were issued, about 70 percent of them in the cercle of Kayes. In 1894, that increased to 1,258. There was also wider distribution, though in four cercles, Segu, Timbuktu, Bandiagara and Niagassola, no slaves were freed.[36]

Slave markets were closed.[37] At Medine, someone had placed a plaque reading "Place de la Liberté" on a tree under which slaves were often sold.[38] The export of slaves was prohibited.[39] Grodet was also bothered that at Segu, Jenne and Sinsani, former crown slaves were being used as the Commandant's slaves. A Commandant at Jenne wanted to reconstitute the state of Masina and proposed giving these slaves to the Amirou in the same way that Archinard set up Mademba Sy in Sinsani. Grodet insisted that the slaves were freed by the conquest and that this freedom should be made public in some striking ceremony.[40] He also insisted that no unremunerated labor be imposed on the crown slaves of Segu and that they should henceforth be on the tax roles.[41] Paul Marty wrote years later that all of this was *faite pour la galerie*. Slaves, however, were freed, though the small numbers suggest both that *juula* circumvented the new rules and that local commandants were not eager to enforce them. The missionaries did not like the anti-clerical Grodet, but one of them wrote:

He had a thankless task which he performed in a malicious and maladroit manner, but men of good will always be grateful to him for his courageous initiative against slavery, the great plague of the Sudan. This praiseworthy act earned him the hostility of men who are in general upright, but warped by absolutely false ideas on this important question.[42]

Return of the military

Grodet's term of office was a brief eighteen months. He was defeated not so much by military insubordination as by the effectiveness of military propaganda in France. Grodet was blamed both for the absence of economic growth and for the defeat by Samori of Monteil's Kong column in the Ivory Coast. Grodet was removed in July 1895, but there was no return to military autonomy. In June 1895, four West African colonies, Senegal, Sudan, Guinea and the Ivory Coast, were grouped in the federation of French West Africa. The Commandant Supérieur, Colonel L.E. Trentinian, was also to be Governor of the French Sudan, but under the administrative control of the new Governor General. Military insubordination remained a problem, particularly during the interim of Colonel Audéoud, but the heyday of military rule was over.[43] Trentinian cautiously resumed military expansion. The major concerns were the *boucle du Niger* and a jockeying for position with British and German rivals. Comm. Destenave occupied Ouagadugu and Ouahiguya in 1896. In 1897, the French took over Dori and Gurunsi while other French forces moved into the interior in Guinea, the Ivory Coast and Dahomey. In 1898, differences with Great Britain were settled in a treaty that divided many disputed areas, but left France's Sudanic empire intact. Operations were constant along the sahel as the French began the long difficult task of breaking Tuareg control over desert-side communities. The most important military successes, however, were the capture of Samori and the defeat of Sikasso in 1898, both during Colonel Audéoud's interim.

The first Governor-General, Chaudié, was told to obey the Brussels act, but also to respect local customs:

You should apply Monsieur Grodet's decrees and not revoke them because they are within the spirit of the Brussels act, but in interpreting them, you should consider the principles of Islam where slavery is of the first importance, that is to say, slowly bring those who profit from it to understand the benefits of liberty. We cannot take Black Society brusquely across a distance that it took European society 20 centuries to cover.[44]

Trentinian, however, had already taken action. In a circular, which is a masterpiece of coded messages, he suggested that Grodet's decrees were being enforced too strictly and that this could be prejudicial to the interests of the colony. He avoided revoking them, but suggested that all administrators keep in mind the statement of the Minister of Colonies: "We pursue an anti-slavery policy without respite in Senegal and the Sudan, which is to the honor of the administration, but we apply it with circumspection and caution dictated by the intellectual state of these peoples."[45] In 1897, Trentinian asked that the term *captif* be replaced by *non-libre*.[46] Within a few years, the *non-libres* became *serviteurs*.

Trentinian cut his cloth to fit the changed temper of the times. He devoted more attention to economic growth in the hope of increasing revenue and he acknowledged Chaudié's authority. He was also very discreet, which means that there was less documentation on slave activities. Only the diaries of the White Fathers make clear what was being done. Clearly, runaways were being regularly returned to masters and in most cercles the trade continued.[47] When the Segu mission questioned Trentinian, he explained:

As to the question of slaves, he spoke with difficulty . . . he assured us that resale is forbidden. He confessed to us that if there are written orders, there are verbal orders, which are less severe or less fair. It appears that it is necessary to deal gently with masters, the Muslims. But soon, the Commandant assures us, we will see our desires fulfilled. It will only be necessary to take Kenedugu, from which most of the slaves come, to end the sale.[48]

Trentinian's remarks help us understand one characteristic of the sources. The historian investigating slavery often finds periods of crisis during the early colonial period when slavery matters dominated correspondence; yet reports for the preceding period give no indication of what led to the crisis. It is thus difficult to see the issue evolve, but slavery matters were often dealt with by verbal communication. Most commandants saw the Governor twice a year. Tours were becoming common and commandants came and went.

Others were also discreet. Thus, instructions to a new Commandant at Gumbu told him to consult two orders on the slave trade already in the files and to talk to Capt. Mamadou Racine, whom he was replacing. The orders were specific only on runaways:

The Sarakollé of Gumbu are very hard on their slaves who are very numerous; you will constantly have unfortunates complain to you. Make careful inquiries on the facts, seek the truth in any way possible and when there is no proof, return the slave to the master. If the slaves have clear marks of beatings, place them in the Gumbu liberty village until you get my decision.[49]

Trentinian also gave instructions on the liberty villages. Chiefs were to be chosen from former *tirailleurs* and other employees of the administration or, if necessary, from among those with some personal authority. Slaves were only to be freed in cases of severe and repeated mistreatment or inadequate feeding. The lone slave was to be confided to a family head within the village who could give him or her land. He received his own land only when he married or was wealthy enough to be head of a family.[50]

Catholic missions

By time Trentinian took over, missions were important to the colonial enterprise. The Holy Ghost Fathers entered the Sudan from Senegambia. At Archinard's suggestion they started at Kita, then still resistant to Islam, in 1888.[51] The mission at Kayes, which opened in 1893, was staffed by a chaplain and nurses for the hospital; a year later an orphanage and school were opened at nearby Dinguira. The White Fathers started in North Africa and tried unsuccessfully to run their Sudan missions from Biskra in the Sahara. Missions were founded at Segu and Timbuktu in 1895 and at Bamako in 1897. In 1901, The White Fathers exchanged their missions in Guinea for those of the Holy Ghost Fathers in the Sudan.

Some French authorities were ambivalent about the Catholic missions. Gallieni feared that their presence would arouse Muslim fanaticism and Grodet was anti-clerical.[52] As the colony grew, however, it needed schools to train clerks, teachers, and petty functionaries for the administration, as well as orphanages, and chaplains and nurses for the hospitals. The missionaries were well received by the soldiers. They were invited to the officers' mess and shared some parts of the soldiers' lives. Many of the soldiers came from strict Catholic backgrounds and most saw no contradiction between their Christianity and what they were doing in the Sudan. The mother of Lt. Henri Gouraud gave him a lamp which burned in the Kayes chapel until he left the Sudan. Archinard, though Protestant, saw the Catholic church as the ideological arm of a struggle against Islam.[53]

Conflict was inevitable. The White Fathers were there not to bolster the colonial state but to search for souls. Many commandants did not like the way the Fathers distanced themselves from the state and their reluctance to accept its priorities, for example, teaching in African languages rather than in French. The missionaries, by contrast, were horrified by slaving, the slave trade and the sexual immorality of the military. In addition, there was a frustration that commitments locked them into areas where the strength of

Islam limited their prospects. Progress was slow in Muslim Bamako and Kayes, somewhat better in Segu and Kita, but even there Islam was growing rapidly. Astute officers like Gallieni knew that it would continue to grow. By the late 1890s, the White Fathers realized that their best prospects lay with people who had a limited exposure to Islam.[54] This meant the peoples of the southern tier, the Mossi, the Bobo and the Minianka, but the White Fathers lacked the funds and the colonial state refused to let them close their northern missions.[55]

If opposed objectives lay at the heart of their differences, the chasm between soldier and priest was widened by their attitudes toward slavery. As Lavigerie's disciples, the White Fathers came to Africa committed to the eradication of slavery.[56] They tended to see the officers as fine fellows, but somewhat misguided. Both religious orders bought slaves. The first caravan of the White Fathers was given two orphans by the Holy Ghost mission at Kita to get them started.[57] They often bought children who were near death and tried to nurse them back to health. They also bought relatives, often the mother or sister of someone already in their village, or spouses or would-be spouses. At the same time, they began receiving refugees of various kinds.[58]

At Segu, just after the White Fathers arrived, a large caravan was stopped. Augustin Hacquard, the head of the mission, offered to take charge of the freed slaves, providing huts, clothes, tools, seed and grain until the first harvest.[59] The mission ran a liberty village near Segu for a number of years, though the Fathers constantly had to cajole local commanders, many of whom still preferred to distribute slaves to their interpreters, political agents and servants. Hacquard was disturbed that female slaves were assigned to family heads within the villages who used them as concubines. The chief, Cros wrote, was often a former slave,

who dreamed only of increasing the numbers of unfortunates called freed persons, who have to work his fields and provide him with food. Sometimes, chiefs assist in police work and stop caravans, but it is always on condition that these slaves become theirs or that at least that with the price of their labor, they can buy slaves.[60]

Mission policy, therefore, became an effort to marry off the women as soon as possible.[61] The French Anti-Slavery Society was at that time looking for a way to use its energies in the struggle and had taken an interest in the liberty villages. In 1897, Hacquard persuaded the Society to make the villages a major subject of fund-raising. Eventually, thirty were created, ten of them in the Sudan, this in addition to the state's villages.[62] Bouche is not convinced that more than twelve mission-run liberty villages existed as distinct villages and suggests that many missions used the anti-slavery movement to get funds for other purposes. I am not sure of that, but the missions certainly used them and freed slaves provided most of their early converts.

Increasingly, other slaves looked to the missions for help. In 1896, when a slave woman from Nyamina walked for three days to seek refuge, a priest asked how she knew about the mission.[63] In other cases, a freed slave sought the help of the mission in freeing a spouse, a child or a sibling.[64] In some cases, the slave was being held illegally, or the mission put pressure on the master to set a modest ransom.[65] In one case, a woman asked for help because her husband wanted to pawn their daughter.[66] In May 1900, a missionary from Banankuru persuaded the Commandant to free two children, whose mother had been sold and whose father had been turned out because he could no longer do much work for the master.[67] Many people turned to the missions during famine years as they traditionally turned to the wealthy and powerful. Hacquard describes the response:

Masters turn loose their slaves so they will not have to feed them (reserving the right to resume possession at the end of the crisis); many families pawn their children – this consists of delivering children capable of work in exchange for a sum between 15 and 50 francs; the parent can withdraw them by paying back the sum. The interest of the lender is to advance enough money that the family will never be able to return it. The growing children will always bring a profit. They are essentially slaves purchased at a relatively low price.[68]

The missions took in many pawns, though sometimes it is unclear whether they were taking pawns or making purchases, and during most famines their resources were inadequate. During the 1899 famine, grain cost ten times the normal price. In the Niger valley (Segu and Banankuru), they bought over a hundred persons and would have taken more if they had had the resources.[69] In 1901 and 1902, famine struck again in the Niger valley. During famines, the mission was always offered more children than it could feed.[70] The liberty village in Segu posed particular problems.

The mission was often unhappy at the way the local commandant moved freed slaves around or imposed work on them, though the mission also moved its converts.[71] For example, it moved many Christians to the more isolated Banankuru, where they were freer from both the demands and the temptations of Segu. Moving did not solve one problem. Most of the former slaves were Senufo, Turka, or from one of the decentralized societies of the southern tier. They were eager to return to homes in much-slaved areas further south as soon as conditions improved. The mission had three concerns: first, that their converts offered no entry to Bambara society; second, that these converts wanted to leave the mission as soon as it was safe to do so; and third, that they were not free to follow their converts.[72]

The missions also began to care for mulatto children. When officers were posted back to France, they often turned children they had fathered over to the mission. The position of the mulatto child in the Sudan was very different from that of the Senegalese métis. There were some stable menages and some French men who acknowledged mulatto offspring, but most French officers spread their seed widely and cared little about where it sprouted. Some mulattos were killed at birth.[73] Both administration and mission saw mulattos as potential agents of colonization. The mission at Dinguira received a subsidy of 4,000 francs for the education of mulatto children on condition that they be taught in French.[74]

Most of the early students at mission schools were orphans, but an effort

Box 7.2

The best published account of a enslavement in the western Sudan is the biography of his father by historian Joseph Ki Zerbo. Alfred Diban was born in a Samo village near Tugan in northern Burkina Faso. During a famine that Diban attributed to destruction by invading French troops, the boy was sent to a maternal aunt. There, while working in a field, he was seized by raiders from a nearby village and walked first to a market in northern Burkina Faso and from there six days to Kabara, Timbuktu's river port. He was fed well on the march so he would be in good shape for market. At Kabara, he was sold to a Tuareg, who brought him to his camp north of Timbuktu. For four months he was harshly treated, chained every night with his left hand to his right foot. Then for three months, he herded with his master and was sent to gather wood, but the master chained him when he went to market. He was then given his own hut and allowed to participate in evening diversions. His master's wife said that after a year, he would be given a wife and allowed to trade. Three times he tried to escape. Twice he was caught because he did not know how to find his way in the desert. He was badly beaten and closely watched, but the third time he made it to Kabara, hiding in the water from those tracking him. He luckily made contact with a White Father. At the mission, there was a young girl who spoke his language. He was soon moved to Segu for his safety. He eventually converted, was given the name Alfred, and made it back to his home area, where he became a leader of the Christian community.*

*Ki Zerbo, 1983.

was made to recruit others. Every mission ran catechism classes, which produced a few converts. Africans who worked for the colonial state often put their children in mission schools. Mademba Sy had several children at Segu.[75] So too did some political agents. An effort was made to keep orphans in school until the age of fifteen. The mission tried to recruit the abler males as catechists and to steer others into manual training.[76] Most, however, became servants or took jobs with the administration. Trentinian was friendly to the missions, but he expanded secular education, often using military and civilian personnel.[77]

The missions played an important role in the Sudan by providing a refuge for those fleeing slavery. They also played a moderating effect on the soldiers. Nevertheless, their resources were never adequate for the demands made on them. They had to turn away the hungry during famines when they clearly had difficulty feeding their own people. Finally, the missionaries themselves were very much men of their times, courageous in risking themselves in a difficult climate, marked by Christian sympathy and compassion, but sometimes racist, authoritarian and paternalistic.

Sikasso and after

In February 1898, the French alliance with Sikasso came to an end and France attacked the fortress that withstood Samori. Sikasso emerged in 1888 from its lengthy siege strengthened and allied to the French. During the decade that followed, the French nurtured this alliance and new walls were constructed. Tyeba's ambassadors were invited to watch the attack on Segu in 1890 and a year later, Capt. Quiquandon and 3,000 Bambara joined Tyeba in an attack on one of his enemies. In 1892 Tyeba refused Humbert's request that he attack Samori and in 1894 his successor, Ba Bemba, refused a French garrison. Meanwhile, Kenedugu profited from the gradual withdrawal of Samori and its greater access to arms and horses. Ba Bemba's *sofa* ranged further and further from home, and slaves from Kenedugu became more and more important in Banamba and along the Masina–Timbuktu trade route.[78]

In January 1898, a French delegation was run out of Sikasso. The French decided that they had been insulted and, with the approval of Paris, sent an army south. They faced a fortress surrounded by 8 or 9 km of wall, in many places almost 2 m thick. After twelve days of siege and an intensive bombardment, French field guns breached the walls.[79] There is an account of the sack of Sikasso by Capt. Imbert de la Tour, which suggests what most such victories must have been like.[80] Sikasso was a large city, with a population estimated as high as 40,000 at the time of its fall.

After its walls were breached, people tried to flee. Imbert describes the killing of many adult males. "A cloud of human vultures, bands of two-legged jackals emerged from one knows not where, pillaged, burned and killed throughout the night."[81] Then, everyone joined in the pillaging – *spahis*, *tirailleurs*, porters, servants. *Spahis* pursued children, putting the smaller ones across their saddles and herding the larger ones to the camp, where they would be sold to slavers that evening. Before nightfall, "a convoy of several hundred women, they say 800, entirely nude, arrived at the camp . . . the seraglio of Ba Bemba . . . examples of the most beautiful races of the Senegal and Niger."[82] In all, about 2,000 people were gathered from the fortress. About noon, the call came to return to camp. There, prisoners of both sexes were turned over to relatives, and the slaves of Ba Bemba and the major chiefs were turned over to the troops. "Europeans were free to take whoever most pleased them, at least among those who remained. Those with copper or almost white skin were quickly taken."[83] At the end, there were a half a dozen no one wanted, but they disappeared during the night. Much of the horde of captives disappeared quickly. Imbert continues: "a non-com hid 11 under sacs, behind boxes of biscuits with the intention of selling them, a form of traffic many of the non-coms, and even some of the officers engaged in, without understanding the shame of such a trade, forbidden by rules, by French law, and by the most elementary human decency."[84]

Fig. 7 Samori prepares for prayer one hour after capture.

The missionaries pick up the tale: "A large caravan of slaves from Sikasso passed between the nuns' house and ours. For some time, one passed through every day. They say that the Governor had 3,000 slaves distributed to the soldiers. The Segu market is now well furnished. That is how we destroy slavery in the Sudan."[85] Some political agents received as many as twenty slaves for their services. Not everyone participated in the process. Imbert himself turned four little girls over to the mission. In the days that followed, other children were brought in: a boy of five from a *spahi* lieutenant, a child from an African carpenter, two from a captain, three from a sergeant.[86]

Later that year, a French unit stumbled on Samori's camp and took him prisoner. It was anti-climactic. The colossus that barred the path of the French was powerless, surrounded by a small band when he was taken. The conquest was not yet over. The soldiers still had to finish conquering the southern savanna and the Sahara, but the large states and great state-builders were gone.

Reoccupation and reconstruction in Wasulu

Bonnier understand that a tax holiday and food subsidies would help Wasulu to reconstruct itself, but his major concern was Timbuktu and Grodet's was reduction of the budget deficit. Wasulu was a low priority for both as it was later for Trentinian. Wasulu was not the only area ravaged by war and raiding, but no other area had been so completely depopulated. Wasulu's only assets were good land, reliable rainfall, and the desire of Wasulunke to return home. In spite of insecurity, Wasulunke refugees within the colony asked for the right to return home almost from the moment the French arrived. In most cases, these requests were refused because their labor was needed, especially along major supply routes. Commandants came and went at Buguni. There were five during the first fourteen months. Most pleaded for people, some for help in feeding people and one even suggested the import of slaves.[87] Gradually, however, people drifted back. Some came from the Left Bank of the Niger without French approval. Others were in caravans stopped by the French and many were fleeing Samori's retreating forces.

For those who did return, there were years of suffering and hunger. In most cases the land had returned to bush. The returning Wasulunke had no tools. They lived by hunting and gathering, but lacked the weapons to defend themselves against wild animals.[88] To make things worse, there were locusts in 1895 and for several years thereafter. Without any help from the French, the misery continued and new returnees were more mouths to feed. A clerk who did the 1899 census reported that a quarter of the population had returned since the previous year: ·

The natives are all in a state of misery almost impossible to describe; the great majority have no clothes. Only the old men wear a torn and dirty old boubou with no pants; all wear one simple piece of cloth that only covers their buttocks . . . the huts are empty with scarcely any kitchen tools. There is complete misery and the people who return bring nothing with them. Cattle and sheep have disappeared. There are whole cantons without a sheep . . .[89]

A liberty village was founded in 1894. The large number of comings and goings would suggest that some people used it as a staging post. Thus, at the end of the first year, there were 32 persons in the village, but during the year there were 181 entries and 191 departures.[90] In spite of this misery, the regime tried to collect a head tax from 1896.[91]

Last years of the slave trade

Though the largest slavers were gone, the trade was not over. At the turn of the century, the major sources of slaves were the southern savanna and the desert-side. There was still slave-raiding around Koury and Sikasso in 1900 and 1901. One chief in Koury had forty-three women and children stocked for sale when his operation was shut down.[92] The largest source was the Gurunsi of the northern Gold Coast. Another source was the first chiefs appointed by the French. In acephalous areas, the French often appointed agents or former tirailleurs. Like Mademba and Aguibou, these men supported their entourages by raiding and selling slaves.[93] The trade persisted throughout Mossi, Bobo and Minianka areas.[94] Caravans were small and consisted largely of children. Samori sent caravans north with hundreds of slaves. After 1898, caravans generally had under twenty, often only one or two, taken from raiding, kidnapping, sale by parents during famine years and criminal penalties.[95] Slaves were moved north to Masina and Bandiagara, where Aguibou seems to have protected the trade for a while.[96]

In areas where there was no state, the struggle for control was difficult, but the French were less beholden to masters and were better able to control the trade. Along the desert's edge, it was more difficult because of the mobility of the Moors and Tuareg. Even more than further south, the trade involved children, usually kidnapped or taken in hit-and-run raids. Timbuktu was a lonely base where the ability of French units to move outside of the city was limited. The city itself had about 4,000 people with about a thousand settled in camps outside the city.[97] In the city a veritable Babel of languages could be heard, but control was firmly in the hands of a Muslim elite, which up to 1894 paid tribute to the Tuareg. Timbuktu lived from trade. Unlike other Sudanic cities, there was little productive activity except for a local market with 250 to 300 traders and the caravan trade which brought salt, cloth and products of British industry from Morocco and major Saharan settlements. Though the trade was reduced, slaves were still the most important item of trade. According to Father Mahiet, 1,000 to 1,500 were shipped north every year.[98] On the slave trade, Mahiet wrote: "There are laws that forbid it and secret orders which tolerate it."[99] Many slaves were also sold into the desert.[100]

Most of the population of Timbuktu was probably servile. They herded, engaged in floodplain agriculture, incidental labor, petty commerce and prostitution.[101] The response to the mission was cold. They set up school within weeks of their arrival, but in spite of pressure from the commandant, they had only five students, three of them street children, who became servants as soon as they learned a little French.[102] They received children picked up in

Fig. 8 Mossi horsemen return from raid with captives.

raids, though sometimes they had to plead for them, and they picked up neglected children in the market. In April 1898, they moved the children back to Segu, where they could provide a more Catholic ambience.[103] Within a few years, Hacquard and Bazin wanted to withdraw from Timbuktu.[104]

As French armies moved into Niger and the Sahara, a movement began to repopulate deserted areas. Many Wasulunke groups asked permission to return home in 1898.[105] Some were allowed to do so, but construction had resumed on the railroad into Bamako in 1899 and labor was again in short supply. The call for forced labor fell largely on slaves: "Many villages furnished slaves who have disappeared from the work site and have not returned to the homes of their masters."[106] In cercles further south, some refugees were allowed to go home. In Bamako, many were allowed to return to Sikasso after the 1899 harvest.[107] The liberty village at Segu was virtually emptied as Senufo went home.[108]

In 1899, Trentinian was still not willing to act against the slave trade:

Some Commandants de Cercle report the sale in Sudanese markets of a certain number of slaves and propose measures to completely suppress the trade. I understand the humanitarian sentiments that inspire them and while I have decided to end the slave trade, I think that for the moment, commandants not at the periphery of the colony should not intervene. If surveillance is exercised over caravans or markets, it will certainly lead to vexatious and rigorous measures, of which the result will be to hamper trade and again plunge Sudanese peoples into the misery and apathy from which we wish to raise them.[109]

While the number of slaves marketed was high in 1898, Trentinian went on to suggest that the end of warfare would reduce it:

... submission of all of Sudanese chiefs and suppression of internal struggles have closed off this source of the commerce in slaves and have dealt the trade a mortal blow. Captives actually for sale who remain within the colony are protected by the very humanitarian measures which we have taken since the beginning of our occupation of the Sudan and which should set in progress a rapid evolution toward liberty.[110]

Trentinian's only suggestion was the suppression of slave exports. Slaves were being exported to Mauritania, to Sierra Leone and Liberia, but mostly to Senegal and the Gambia. Labor was needed within the Sudan. In distributing Trentinian's circular, the Commandant of the Western Region underlined its meaning:

I ask that you formally prohibit the trade in slaves from one colony to another and public sale of slaves within the colony; but you should close your eyes to the related clandestine trade which takes place between inhabitants of the colony . . .
   . . . you will levy no tax on the slave trade; you will not establish a license based on their value. When you must take account of the slaves accompanying a juula, consider them as porters and list them as you would list the donkeys, camels and oxen of the juulas.[111]

The juula were prohibited only from setting themselves up as full-time slave traders.

Conclusion

In October 1899, a new Minister of Colonies, Albert Decrais, reorganized the Sudan. The southern cercles were attached to coastal colonies. Two territories were left under military rule, one centered on Ouagadougou and the second at Timbuktu. In 1900, a new military territory was set up in what is now Niger. The largest part of Sudan was renamed Haut Sénégal et Moyen Niger and placed under the control of the Governor-General with a representative in Kayes called the Délégué Général. The first and only Délégué Général was William Merlaud-Ponty, one of the few civilian administrators in the Sudan. In 1904, Haut-Sénégal-Niger became a full colony once again and Ponty became a Lt. Governor. Ponty was more politically astute than Grodet had been. He also understood the Sudan and the soldiers, having served as Archinard's secretary. His appointment marked the end of military rule in the Sudan. Soldiers were gradually replaced and a more orderly administration took over. More than any other person, Ponty dominated French policy on slavery questions, first in the Sudan, and then as Governor-General.

   At the time when Ponty took over, most local administrators had no interest in moving on slavery, though slavery, the slave trade and the accompanying violence were clearly a major barrier to the kind of economic development colonial interests wanted. The picture of the world that the White Fathers paint in the period before the capture of Samori is an anarchic one in which anyone without protection could easily find himself, and more likely herself, in irons.[112] Even those in relative comfort, the women in the harems of the great and powerful, could speedily find themselves the instruments of the lust and greed of others. The French army was as much part of this savagery as any other, and their African agents often exploited French power to accumulate wealth and slaves.[113] Such a social order could not be justified and could not provide the basis for the rational exploitation of the Sudan's resources that Archinard's civilian backers wanted. Ponty's goal was to transform a military hunting reserve into a real colony. When he took over, slaves were already trying to regain control over their lives, and by doing so, were to shape the way in which Ponty's mission was realized.

8 The imposition of metropolitan priorities on slavery

> ... the status of captivity should be recognized neither by administrative authority nor by judicial, neither in civil matters nor in penal matters; any attempt on the liberty of the individual should be vigorously prosecuted.
>
> Instructions of Governor-General Roume[1]

Under Ponty, Haut-Sénégal-Niger moved more quickly on slavery than any other colony. Ponty had spent most of his short career in the Sudan, serving at one time as Archinard's secretary. He took from his Sudanese experience a concern to liberate ordinary Africans from the oppressiveness of traditional rulers and "barbaric" custom. His commitment to liberty was, however, strongly tempered by caution and a pragmatic streak.[2] Ponty could be absolutely ruthless when he had to be, as, for example, while trying to extend the railroad into Bamako during a period of famine. He clearly saw, however, that economic growth required both an end to the slave trade and the creation of a more mobile labor force. Equally important, he took office at a time when pressure was being placed on the colonial administration from Paris. He knew when to appeal to Republican principle and when to appeal to colonial paternalism. He could be cautious and he could be daring, but he had a clear view of metropolitan priorities and African necessities.

Albert Decrais and Ponty's first steps

On 11 December 1899, Abbé Lemire, a Catholic deputy, rose in the Chamber to speak on family questions in the colony. A large part of Lemire's speech dealt with the persistence of the slave trade, and in particular the trade in women. Albert Decrais, the Minister of Colonies, claimed ignorance of the problem, but promised to do all he could to see to it that such acts were suppressed.[3] Within weeks, Decrais wrote all governors a strong letter, which noted that reports received by the ministry made no mention of such problems. He asked that the governors make an inquiry, reminded them of the principles of the French Republic, and insisted:

It is important then to the progress of civilization and the honor of our country that natives are led to completely renounce the practice of slavery in all territories over which our control is established. It is especially important that the slave trade, their export from one country to another, confront a surveillance and a repression of such severity that where it still exists, it disappears as soon as possible.

I do not need to add that I rely on your prudence and experience, to consider in the measures you will have to take, the temperament, the customs and the traditions of the natives placed under your administration.[4]

One of Ponty's first acts was to distribute Decrais' letter to all administrators.[5] Later the same year, he distributed a circular which commented that many orders and decrees on the slave trade were not being enforced. He insisted that commandants stop caravans of slaves, put slaves in liberty villages and punish slave dealers with fifteen days in prison and a 100-franc fine for every slave. He was very careful, however, not to threaten slavery itself:

As for persons called domestic slaves, it is an improper designation for persons far from servitude who should rather be considered domestic servants. You will only free them in cases where the family head has mistreated them. To push them to abandon the families they serve would be a clumsy and imprudent act, which could provoke economic and political disturbances.[6]

Several months later Ponty's approach changed. A new circular pointed out that most administrators drew up separate tax rolls for slaves and free men. Though political necessity forced France to tolerate the continued existence of slavery, it could not officially recognize the difference between slave and free. He reminded them of the abolition of the trade and went on:

Today, we ask you, Messieurs, to be unrelenting in sending from your offices any person coming to claim an escaped slave and ask you henceforth in such affairs to treat all natives as "men." In the same order of ideas, we should attribute to those improperly called domestic slaves the rights which servants attached to the service of a family have among us. Let us not forget that it is in the name of Liberty and to combat such barbaric customs that European powers have come to the territories of Africa.[7]

Ponty was dealing with slavery by denying it recognition. This not only made it possible for the regime to keep its hands clean, but in the long run it undercut the basis of slavery, which could not function without the coercive power of the state. Not all local administrators received the message. Thus, in 1902, the commandant at Bamako assured elders at Tuba in the Banamba complex that runaways would be returned "when their flight was not well motivated."[8] Non-recognition became the major theme of French policy toward slavery. In October 1903, Ponty sent out another circular reiterating points made three years earlier and using much of the same language.[9] Ponty was ahead of his contemporaries, but he still moved cautiously because he feared both political disturbances and economic disruptions.

Decline of the trade

Slave trading was taking place all over the Sudan during Ponty's first years, but two routes were particularly active. The first involved Wolof and Soninke traders taking slaves across the Sahel into Senegal. Between 1902 and 1904,

Senegalese traders were arrested in places as far away as Sokolo and Jenne. Between May and August 1902, three caravans going to Senegal were stopped near Banamba.[10] The second was the trade route from Gurunsi via Ouagadougou and Bandiagara to Saraféré and Timbuktu.[11] Ouagadougou with over a million people was the most populous cercle in French West Africa. In the absence of personnel the administrator depended on the Mogho Naba, but when the Naba's horsemen stopped a caravan from Gurunsi areas, slaves went into the Naba's slave villages.[12]

The trade did not die immediately though it rapidly became risky. Local administrators increasingly cracked down on slaving bands, on chiefs who seized people, on former *tirailleurs* who claimed to represent French authority, and on slave traders.[13] The reduction in the size of caravans suggests that many traders were shifting the focus of their business. In 1902, some fairly large caravans were still being stopped, though nothing like the caravans of 400 and 500 that Samori sent to Banamba. Thus, in November 1902, caravans of thirty-nine and seventy slaves destined for Senegal were stopped in Sokolo. A month later, it was a caravan of forty-three from Saraféré heading toward Senegal.[14] One military commander described Saraféré as a major center of the clandestine trade, but claimed that "large slave caravans no longer circulate in the territory, but we notice . . . merchants coming from the south with several men, women and children, return six months later almost alone or with a woman and one or two slaves."[15] Slave-raiding remained a constant along the desert's edge and kidnappers operated not only in the densely populated and poorly controlled societies of the southern savanna, but also in and around major posts. During the famines of 1900–2, many people sold children.[16]

Enforcement of the new rules was uneven. Thus, in cases brought before the new native courts during the third quarter of 1903, there were no cases involving slavery in thirteen of the twenty-seven cercles reporting. Many of these were districts where the courts were little used, for example, Dori with two cases, Raz-el-Ma with four. This, in turn, usually reflected the limited authority of the new colonial regime. Overall, however, there were forty-four convictions on slave-related offences. Over half involved either theft of a slave or seizure of a free person. The courts were most severe with attempts on the liberty of a free person. There were fourteen slave-trade cases. One involved an effort physically to stop a woman from seeking her liberty papers. Another involved helping a woman escape. Sentences were anywhere from fifteen days to two years but, most important, the person lost the slave involved.[17] Administrators generally handled larger caravans, but from 1904 on, there were few of these. Slave trading persisted, but moved underground. The effort to control slave-raiding and slave-trading was part of a larger effort to impose order and, in particular, to make the chiefs agents of the colonial state.

Working on the railroad

Ponty's major task during his first years was to extend the railroad from Bafulabe into Bamako.[18] This time, there were no Moroccan or Chinese

Fig. 9 Forced labour levy gets ready to work on railroad construction.

workers. The result was a heavy reliance on forced labor. The work crews were mostly unskilled workers, camps had to be prepared, and porters were needed to carry food to the camps. The Commandant at Kita, where much of the construction was taking place, protested plaintively in September 1900 that all of his workers were used in building and supplying the camps. He could provide porters for neither merchant houses nor railroad construction. Poor rains and locusts meant that people were so short of food that they lacked the energy to weed their fields, and by September many were dying of starvation.[19] In addition, men were sought for a trading post in Conakry and for military service in Madagascar and there was a strike of Wolof workers.[20] Under pressure to complete the rail line, Ponty insisted on grain from drought-stricken areas and assigned Bojan's former slaves to work as porters.[21] In spite of a bad harvest in 1900, Nioro had to provide 25 tons of millet. In July, the administrator reported "an absolute dearth of grain . . . inhabitants have only the grass of the fields to eat, some of them are walking skeletons."[22] Ponty also recognized that people needed to work their fields and insisted that they had the right to return home to plant, that labor should not be requested during the rainy season, and that they should be paid.[23]

Almost all of those sent to work on the railroad were slaves. This led to flight: "Many villages provided slaves who have disappeared from the work camps and have not returned to the residence of their masters. Where are they? Without doubt in other cercles where they have increased the population of the liberty villages."[24] Often half of them were gone within a week. Even women brought to prepare the meals fled.[25] The first approach to the problem was to insist that slaves be allowed to keep part of their wages, which they could use to pay for their freedom.[26] In fact, workers fled without waiting for their wages. In 1900, 5,000 to 7,000 francs a month were not collected because workers did not wait till payday.[27] The regime dealt with the discontent of the masters by letting them watch the work camps and pursue runaways.[28]

The demand for labor merely exacerbated what was already taking place. The refugees from the Samorian wars were the first to try to go home, but by 1901 many cercles were also reporting slave departures. In Bafulabe, there were many reports of flight to Buguni and Segu from 1901. Some runaways went to the commandant knowing their masters could no longer claim them. Others simply headed south without stopping at the liberty villages.[29] Bafulabe showed a decline in population in 1902 and 1903. At Medine, so many flocked to the liberty village that the commandant could neither feed them nor find them work and many had to go looking for famine foods to feed themselves. As a result, more and more were fleeing the liberty village.[30] By 1902 there were fears of depopulation at Kita, though better counting showed a rise in population. Chiefs complained because they were often stuck with tax obligations for slaves who had gone.[31] By 1904, slaves were leaving Kita at a rate of ten to fifteen a month.[32] Many reports indicate that many administrators and chiefs were convinced that slavery was finished.[33] Ponty increasingly insisted that the movement should be allowed: "Today, peace reigns everywhere, the era of the great Black Conquerors is definitively ended, and I see no inconvenience in authorising the movement of natives who have the legitimate desire to live where they were born, while at the same time regulating it."[34]

Administrators were often frustrated by slave matters, which took up much of their time, but there were problems all over. Thus, a group of twenty-seven slaves fled Nyamina in April 1901, taking guns and lances. They were pursued by over 200 Maraka men. Fourteen of the fugitives and seven pursuers were killed. Only six slaves were returned to Nyamina. Ponty considered that this was "the first time that I record an act of energy on the part of blacks wanting to regain their liberty. Could this be a new era in the *morale indigène*?"[35] In 1904, two or three slaves a month were being freed at Gumbu, six or eight a month at Kayes.[36] At Léo, among the Mossi, a large exodus resulted from the rumour that the French were going to free the slaves.[37] In Karta, the Massassi chief was unhappy that the French would not force his crown slaves to work for him.[38] In Sinsani, many of the slaves given to Mademba Sy by Archinard asked the right to work for themselves. Though Ponty was sympathetic, the local administrator worked out a compromise under which they continued to work three days a week for Mademba. At the same time, he warned the Fama "that in the near future all of the sofas would enjoy complete liberty."[39]

In Aguibou's case, it was not his *sofa* who fled, but his "wives," twelve of whom fled his *tata* in May 1903 claiming that they were not well fed or cared for. Aguibou's men tried to take the women back by force, but three more came the next day and, finally, a group of thirty-eight. In May, the administrator asked for a census of the women in Aguibou's four *tatas*. Aguibou did not know how many women he had, and apparently at one point had asked every village under his authority to provide him with one.[40] There were numerous arguments with Aguibou during this period about jewelry he had given to these women and about his right to beat them.

In 1904, Segu reported that "several individuals in the service of others have asked the right to cultivate only for themselves," in effect rejecting their masters without flight to earlier homes.[41] This is coupled with reports that attitudes to porterage were changing. In Buguni, it was noted in 1903 that "porters who were recruited with such difficulty in the first quarter and had to be escorted by armed agents to stop them from fleeing, now accept this work without a murmur, and are being paid conscientiously and regularly, flight is rare though they are no longer accompanied by armed men."[42] The 1905 Annual Report from Bamako speaks of the increasing number of men seeking work.[43] Thus, what is striking about the first years of civilian rule is that famine and labor shortage made it difficult to loosen controls over labor but, in spite of this, there was increasing movement of both slave and free to return to earlier homes and to respond to opportunities for wage labor.

Situation in Senegal

In Senegal, during the first years of the new century the situation was much more ambiguous and policy varied from cercle to cercle. Decrais' dispatch seems to have had a more limited impact. A slave making it into an area of direct administration could claim his or her freedom, but the administration and the traditional elites did their best to see that few did so. In areas under protectorate, the conventions with chiefs were the only law that applied. There was still a large clandestine slave trade, mostly into the rail line area but also into Sine-Saloum, which was just beginning its rapid growth as a peanut producer. In many cercles, slaves were returned to their masters or were forced to purchase their freedom if they did not present evidence of mistreatment. In one case, the master was simply told to stop beating the slave and the slave was returned.[44] The best way for a slave to seek freedom was still to cross the Gambia–Senegal border.[45]

In 1903, Musa Molo broke with the French. After sacking some villages, he crossed the border into the Gambia with about 5,000 people, including slaves he was given when Fodé Kaba was defeated in 1901, among them wives and daughters of Fodé Kaba. The French charged that these slaves were forced to follow him and sought his extradition under the Brussels treaty. They claimed that he fled because they intended to force him to release the slaves they let him take only two years earlier.[46] The British insisted that Musa Molo renounce all dealings in slaves and, at the request of the French, that his "wives" be asked if they had wished to come with him. About 300 persons in Musa Molo's harem were interviewed. Over 100 women and children were freed, some to Bathurst, others to homes in Senegalese territory.[47]

Action on slavery

In January 1903, Victor Prom, an employee of a French commercial house was sent to Podor on business. A Senegalese friend, Amadu Fall, gave him 250 francs to buy a little girl for his wife. Prom did so and had another friend bring her to Saint Louis, where Fall got liberty papers for her. When the young girl's mother found her, Prom and Fall refused to turn her over. Under interrogation, Prom admitted that he often made such purchases. He was charged under the same 1831 law against slave-trading that Darrigrand had used. When the court acquitted him, the Governor-General ordered an appeal, but the Cour de Cassation, the French appeals court, held that it was not a "punishable infraction." Though he had purchased a slave, it was "to deliver her from slavery and assure her a better destiny."[48] Thus began a sequence of events that knocked the legal props out from under slavery in French West Africa.

The Governor-General was not an old colonial hand. Ernest Roume was a graduate of France's elite Ecole Polytechnique and an official of the Colonial Ministry. He had never served in the colonies, but was sensitive to metropolitan attitudes.[49] His mission was to create a modern bureaucracy, to lay the financial and legal basis for economic growth and to create infrastructure. Much of his term of office was spent in Paris trying to raise money for infrastructure projects. He created the office of Secretary-General and chose for it Martial Merlin, an able career civil servant who later became a conservative Governor-General. Camille Guy, the new Governor of Senegal, was a liberal who, like Roume, had never served in the colonies. All three were to play key roles.

Guy was shocked at the purchase and adoption of children though Prom operated within an established system that provided French and African families with servants. Discussion of the Prom affair centered on whether *rachat*, redemption, was also *achat*, purchase. Joucla, the prosecuting attorney, felt that it was, and Guy was persuaded.[50] In October 1903, Colonial Minister Gaston Doumergue asked for modification of the decrees of 1857 and 1858, which had set up this system. "The terms of these texts would suggest that the barbarous practice of slavery has not entirely disappeared in our colonies."[51] Guy agreed that this was a disguised slave trade that encouraged Mauritanian slave raiders.[52] Procedures laid out in earlier decrees were not being followed. Registers were poorly maintained, there was often no indication of a guardian's death, and guardians sometimes left for France without providing for the child. Apprentices had to turn 50 to 75 percent of their wages over to their masters and some girls were forced into prostitution.[53] In November, Guy presented Roume with a decree, which was immediately approved and which provided that all children freed were to be returned their parents. If the parents could not be found, the child was to be assigned to a public institution or a training school.[54]

The pressure was on. Governments which came to power during the Dreyfus affair were progressive. A 1904 inspection mission was told to examine the slavery issue and evaluate the administration's efforts.[55] In 1905, the Colonial Ministry inquired about the trade in eunuchs with the Ottoman empire.[56] The operation was reported only for Mossi regions, but what was important was not the issue itself, but the fact that Paris was paying attention.[57] It is not clear that Roume needed the heat. In late November 1903, right after signing the decree suppressing adoption, he toured the Senegal river area. He was surprised at lack of consistency and shocked by open conduct of the trade in Kaedi. There was little evidence of the trade at Matam or Bakel, but at Podor and Dagana it was clearly active. He immediately asked that all laws dealing with slavery be rigidly enforced and requested more personnel for the river area.[58]

The same month, Roume proclaimed a system of native courts applying customary law.[59] Drawn up primarily by Merlin, it applied a law code known as the *indigénat*, which gave extensive powers to commandants. The crucial clause for the slavery question was Article 75 which provided that "Native justice will apply to any matter of local custom except when it is contrary to the principles of French civilisation."[60] Customary law recognized the master's right to reclaim a runaway slave. Jurisdiction in cases of enslavement or slave-trading was removed from the chief's court and assigned to the administrator and the principles to be followed were spelled out by Merlin in a circular. Administrators were to pursue "actively and effectively the suppression of any social condition of the individual which is directly or indirectly reminiscent of the former state of things." Administrators were told to be prudent, but the approach to slave claims was clear:

Do not hesitate then in rejecting definitively any claim by would-be masters who call on rights over the person of other natives based on slavery, whoever they may be. You will warn any who try to seize those they claim as slaves that such an act will expose them to legal action. To those who come to complain against their masters or simply to claim their liberty, you will explain if they are adults or at least in a condition to understand their situation, that they are free under the law and that French authority will insist on respect for their freedom.

Merlin went on to insist that children should be given to their parents and to make provision for situations where that was not possible. Finally, he suppressed liberty papers. "Possession of this document would seem to indicate, in effect, that only those who have obtained it are recognized as free and that others who do not fulfil the same conditions could be considered as being held in a state of slavery with the agreement of French authority."[61] Merlin also distributed a questionnaire that asked a series of questions about slavery and solicited the commandant's opinion on what policy should be followed.[62]

Merlin's circular established principles which were eventually followed, but many administrators did not immediately accept changes in policy. This was clear in the answers to the questionnaire and the Diaries of the White Fathers. Some ignored Merlin's instructions and continued to free slaves only when they had evidence of cruel treatment. Guy's reform of treatment of minor children was effective in Saint Louis and Dakar, but not in all the cercles. Thus, Allys, who did not have a liberty village in Tivouane, distributed five young girls to his wife, the wife of the interpreter, the chief cadi, a chef de canton and a local merchant.

Roume had a good idea where he wanted to go, but was uncertain about his ability to get there without disorder. The circular explicitly warned administrators that, in making their inquiries, they were not to create "propaganda that might provoke among natives still living in captivity a movement of a collective or general character."[63] In other words, administrators were not to spread the word and were to see to it that slaves sought their freedom one by one. There were too many slaves for that to happen.

Slavery and the colonial administrator

The responses to the questionnaire were very uneven in quality.[64] Only one administrator, J.C. Brevié in Bamako, later to become Governor-General, seems actually to have interrogated slaves. Nevertheless, the responses are one of the most valuable collections of data available on African slavery and have been important for this study. The longest answers were to questions on policy. These underlined the chasm between senior administrators and jurists on one side, and field administrators on the other. There was a profound hostility to radical change aired by the vast majority, a hostility rooted in the insecurity of French men isolated in strange places among people they did not trust or respect.[65] The only suggestion aired in the questionnaire that drew any favorable response was the proposal that children be freed at birth. Obviously this would cause little disruption because the supposedly free children would be raised in slavery and little if anything would change but the label. Several, however, saw the difficulty of administering such a program without a registry of births (état-civil). Commandants tended to be conservative. They generally were more concerned about property rights than human rights. Several commented on the injustice of depriving masters of their property. Many believed that an indemnity would be necessary, but they often recognized that necessary funds would not be forthcoming.

The reports also underline their low opinion of the people they ruled. Many believed that slaves were so lazy that they would starve if not actually forced to work. "Suppress the slaves," Victor Allys in Tivouane wrote, "and the fields will remain uncultivated and the colony will be ruined."[66] If slaves were too lazy, masters were too proud to work. Freeing the slaves would cause a decline in population, and famine. To the degree that they identified with anyone, it was with the masters, though not all respected local elites. Some suggested that slaves could gradually free themselves while working as sharecroppers, but others thought that this would be too difficult to administer.[67] Most commandants minimized the harshness of servitude and quite a few compared the slaves to Roman clients. Many suggested that, with a ban on the purchase of slaves, slavery would fade into a kind of benign domesticity. Freeing slaves on the death of the master was seen as a violation of the legitimate rights of heirs.

The 1905 Comprehensive Slavery Decree

Decisive action came more quickly than anyone expected, and it did so largely because of another court case. Roume took a number of small measures, many

Box 8.1

A case from Tivouane illustrates the chasm between senior and junior administration. Vidal, the President of the Dakar Tribunal, had issued liberty papers for three children, whose mother and stepfather had been freed. He sent the woman to Victor Allys, the administrator in Tivouane, who refused to do anything about the children.* A year later, Allys explained his reluctance to carry out a court order. Anta N'Doye was a slave belonging to a woman from a village near Tivouane. Her husband had died and her mistress married her to Mallali Ba. She was allowed to live with her husband, but could not take her children with her. When Anta asked to have a daughter with her, the mistress turned her down. At this point, Anta and Mallali fell in with a former policeman, who persuaded them to seek liberty papers for themselves and for the three children. Allys found the request a violation of previous practice. The children themselves did not ask for their freedom and had never left the protectorate. Furthermore, the children said they had nothing against their mistress and did not wish to leave her.** Allys responded that it was politically unwise to interfere with slavery. It was also a violation of long-standing policy. To prove this he included a copy of Admiral Hamelin's letter of 1855 authorizing Faidherbe to ignore orders where political interests dictated. His letter is filled with prejudice. Anta N'Doye, he comments, was covered with jewels, which proved that Mallali Ba was well off. His failure to pay the brideprice was only an act of ill will. The mistress, by contrast, is depicted as someone who acted as a mother to the children. Anta charged that when she came to complain, she was tied up for two days. The mistress denied it and others in the village supported her.

*Vidal to Admin. Tivouane, 12 Aug. 1902, ARS, K 27, 24.
**Admin. Tivouane to Sec. Gen., 16 Aug. 1903, ARS, K 27, # 25. On a previous incident involving Allys, see Klein, 1968: 205–6.

of which involved deliberately ignoring slave status. For example, the forms used for juula licenses were suppressed because they asked how many slaves and free persons accompanied the trader.[68] When Roume and senior officials began looking for legislation available to deal with the slave trade, they found a vacuum. Memos passed back and forth between the Governor-General and the Chief Prosecutor.[69] The 1848 law only provided one sanction against slave ownership, loss of French citizenship, a sanction that was no threat to African subjects. This was why prosecutions were made under the 1831 law used by Darrigrand. Over seventy-three years, there were only ten prosecutions, three in the 1830s for maritime slave traders, and three under Darrigrand.[70] The problem with this law was that it was written with the maritime slave trade in mind. The Chief Prosecutor knew that it was a limited instrument, which was why Roume was investigating the possibility of a new law.[71] The regime, however, continued to use it until, in 1904, a local court held that there was no ground for prosecution in a slave-trade case. As in the Prom case, the Chief Prosecutor appealed and in April 1905 the *Cour de Cassation* held that the 1831 law could not be used against slave transactions within Africa.[72]

This left Roume in a difficult position. He had a hodgepodge of legislation, much of it not well crafted. He was being pressed by political superiors who saw no reason for further compromise and his major juridical weapon had been taken from his hands. He had just legislated an important role for customary law, but customary law quite happily accepted slavery and the slave trade. The results of the slavery study were in, but offered him few options. His response, therefore, was to ask the Chief Prosecutor to draw up a new law and to specify what should be in it.[73] He wanted it done quickly so he could present it when the Government Council met in December. Roume also asked one of his abler administrators, Georges Poulet, to prepare a report on the slavery questionnaires. In June 1905, he forwarded to Paris a copy of Poulet's report and one of his own, summarizing the situation and his thinking about what should be done.[74] His program involved tighter enforcement of some legislation, expansion of liberty villages, and the creation both of "places of refuge and temporary assistance and places for prolonged stay where the natives could work, both watched and protected by the administration, paying in kind for a grant in land."

But the most important question was his new legislation. Roume made clear that he had no funds either for indemnification of masters or for settlement and maintenance of a mass of liberated slaves. He was afraid of a collective mass movement, but he recognized that, politically, it was impossible either to accept categories of slavery or to set up some kind of officially regulated slavery. He rejected the freeing of children from birth because that would recognize the slavery of the parents. He therefore saw no choice. He wanted the law to ban any alienation of the liberty of another and any transaction in persons. He also insisted that it explicitly exclude the authority of husbands over wives and of fathers and guardians over minor children and that there be no legal prohibition against "certain individuals remaining voluntarily in the service of other natives." At the same time, like many of his predecessors, he was convinced that in most areas slavery was benign and that the slaves would often be worse off if they left their masters. He recommended that administrators try to arbitrate master–slave conflicts and was ready to use coercion if disorder threatened.

The decree, which was proclaimed by the President of the Republic on 12 December 1905, did exactly what Roume wanted. It did not abolish slavery, though within a few years people were discussing it as if it had. It only abolished enslavement and the sale, gift or exchange of persons. The reason the impact of the decree was exaggerated was the interpretation Roume gave it in opening the Government Council in December. He incorporated what Merlin had written two years earlier, using much of the same language. He insisted that the colonial state could no longer return slaves to masters, that it must assure those who claimed their liberty that they already had it and could do as they wished, and that the state could no longer recognize slavery in any way. "There is no longer," he insisted "an institution of slavery in any form whatever." Instead, the colonial state should and would in the following years substitute for coercive relationships new ones based on contracts between buyer and seller, lender and borrower, but, most of all, between boss and worker.[75]

Many Lieutenant Governors were not ready. Roume insisted that the new law and a copy of his speech be sent to commandants. In Senegal, Guy did so in a straightforward manner, quoting Roume directly.[76] He did, of course, recommend "prudence and tact." The Governor of the Ivory Coast explained both to Roume and to local administrators why the law could not be put into effect everywhere. He was legally bound to publish it, but French authority was precarious in some cercles and nonexistent in others. He insisted that local administrators not officially recognize slavery, but suggested that they distinguish between the slave-dealer and the small slave-holder. And he repeatedly urged prudence.[77] In Guinea, Lt. Gov. Richard was more careful in choice of language, but he also recommended caution in applying the decree. As we shall see, most administrators in Guinea did not apply it.[78] The Mauritanian circular stressed the need to end slave-raiding in the Senegal river valley, but then launched a discussion of the nature of Mauritanian society and the reasons for prudence.

Military territories

While civilian administrators like Roume and Ponty wrestled with the creation of a new colonial order, lands to the north and east were still playgrounds for the military. The soldiers who invaded the desert and finished the conquest of the sahel were more restrained by the hegemony of Dakar and Paris than Archinard had been, but they still had a measure of autonomy, especially in the Sahara. Lands beyond the Niger became the Third Military Territory in 1900 and remained under military rule until 1920.[79] Most of the Sahara remained a military area until the 1930s and some regions to the end of colonial rule.[80] This study does not deal with the Sahara, but it is hard to exclude it. Transhumant patterns brought Saharan nomads to the sahel and their *bella* and *harratin* settlements were found over much of the area.

In taking Timbuktu in 1894, the soldiers found themselves in conflict with the Tuareg, who controlled the city and the region around it. Their major goal was not control of the desert, but a share of the fertile Hausa lands of the central Sudan.[81] French forces occupied Say in 1897 and then pushed on toward Lake Chad. Other forces tried to establish a loose suzerainty in the desert. Many Tuareg tribes submitted in 1899, but raiding did not stop, many Tuareg continued to resist, and some of those who submitted revolted during World War I.[82] In Mauritania, there was a longer period of penetration. The commercial houses of Saint Louis had close links with Brakna and Trarza and had no desire to place them under colonial rule. Xavier Coppolani, administrator and student of Islam, was able to sell a program of peaceful penetration, but only over objections of authorities in Senegal. Coppolani's program involved a protectorate with very limited interference in local customs. In 1903, Coppolani signed such treaties with Trarza and Brakna and Mauritania, was recognized as a Civil Territory. Coppolani was assassinated in 1905 while on a mission to the Adrar. From that point, the military took over and completed the conquest by arms.[83]

In resisting the French, the greatest weakness of the Tuareg was the vulnerability of the *bella* to the French. The *bella* were traditionally left alone most of the year, and thus, unlike most slaves, were used to a certain measure of independence. They regulated their own affairs and paid their masters an amount of grain which was little over a third of that paid by *woloso* and *rimaibe*. They were also loaned cattle and sheep, which provided them with milk and manure.[84] The French were concerned to maintain population in desert-side areas, but they also wanted to weaken the Tuareg. Thus, they encouraged the autonomy of the desert-side dependants, both *bella* and tributary villages.[85] They were not, however, always happy with the results. Thus, in 1902, the Commandant at Dori spoke of the "turbulent and independent mood" of *bella* who were reluctant to give up one set of obligations for another and did not want to work as porters.[86]

Difficult as the *bella* often were, the French encouraged their autonomy in areas where the Tuareg resisted. In 1909, the Commandant at Dori was told:

We must make nobles understand that the Imrad and Bella are men like themselves . . . we must recognize them immediately as owners of herds they guard . . . we must make Imrad and Bella understand that they should raise their heads, that they should submit their claims directly to us without fear of the nobles, and finally should expect to become the owners of herds confided to their care.[87]

An interesting court case several years later at Timbuktu demonstrated French concerns. Two slaves of Abdullah Ould Mohammed fled. A nephew was sent after them with a camel. He caught them and was taking them to Arawan. During a halt, they took the camel and fled. The nephew died of thirst. The two slaves were sentenced to one year apiece. This was a light sentence, but was over-ruled. Higher authority suggested that it was Abdullah who should have been before the court, "guilty of having concluded with his nephew an agreement whose goal was the alienation of the liberty of a third person."[88]

There were a number of key questions: protection, land, possession of herds. As in agricultural communities, a central concern was control of children. The Tuareg claimed the right to take slave children to work in the camps, girls at domestic chores and boys as herders or to be given as servants to newlyweds. Many Bella broke away from Tuareg masters. In the Voltaic regions, they often submitted to the French before the Tuareg did, in essence using the French to free themselves from traditional obligations. Nevertheless, the attitude of both French and *bella* frequently changed. When discretion dictated, *bella* continued, renegotiated or resumed tribute relations.[89]

In the Gao region and in the southwest corner of what is now Niger, the

Tuareg were not the only large slave-holders. There were also Fulbe and Arma, descendants of sixteenth-century Moroccan conquerors. Olivier de Sardan estimates that slaves made up from two-thirds to three-quarters of the population.[90] Administrators who wanted to undercut the Tuareg by freeing *bella* were often reluctant to do so to Fulbe and Songhay. The French were reluctant to weaken the authority of local elites over their slaves. By 1899, there were reports of Songhay slaves fleeing or coming to the Commandant to seek their independence. Some fled Songhay masters, but most were trying to free themselves from Tuareg or Arma control.[91] They were often turned down. French policy remained relatively hostile to slave claims until 1906.[92] Events in the east were, in fact, a condensed version of what happened earlier in Bambara and Mandinka regions. The French wanted to occupy contested areas before the British or Germans could get into them, but they knew that their resources were limited and were not willing to commit necessary funds. The result was a very thin administration dependent on local intermediaries.

This weakness was demonstrated by the Voulet–Chanoine affair. In 1899, two years after the occupation of Say, a column of 1,700 men was sent toward Chad to join up with columns crossing the Sahara and coming north from the Congo. Captains Paul Voulet and Charles Chanoine were expected to live off the land, though the area was poor and its people had not submitted to French authority. To get the porters and the food they needed, Voulet and Chanoine burned villages, enslaved populations and massacred those they did not need. By time they were stopped by another French column, their ranks had swollen to about 3,000, mostly slave women. Historians have often treated Voulet and Chanoine as men who went mad in the tropical sun, but Fuglestad argues that the atrocities were simply an extravagant version of what the French military did elsewhere.[93]

Massacres were not an effective way of achieving what the French wanted. Other officers recognized the need for intermediaries. A number of "chiefs came forth not to submit to French authority, but to seek an alliance against neighbours."[94] They were able within a short time to use relations with the French to build small client-states similar to those Mademba and Aguibou created a few years earlier. Such a figure was Aouta, a Zarma political agent from Dosso in southwest Niger, who managed to persuade the French that he spoke for the Zarma, and the Zarma that he represented the French. For about four to five years, Aouta provided most of the intelligence on which the French acted and provided the bulk of French forces that conquered local villages. Every victory swelled the number of slaves he controlled. Some were sold in the Sokoto Caliphate or Dahomey. Others worked his fields.[95] During this brief transitional period, the tendency was either to refuse slave reclamations or to arbitrate them. In 1904, in one area in Niger, the French tried to produce an agreement between the Tuareg and *bella*, which would fix the *bella* commitment as one-twentieth of the harvest, one day of labor a year and the service of two children from each family.[96] Almost immediately, there were conflicts as both parties tried to test the new balance of forces.

If Tuareg resistance led the French to undermine their control over desert-side dependants, Songhay resistance led them to reinforce their control over slaves and clients. There was a series of revolts in the early twentieth century in Niger, which Arnaud saw as a struggle of established classes, chiefs, nobles and merchants, to protect the slave system.[97] The French were hesitant to undermine the chiefs. The French commandant, Lt. Col. Péroz, told commandants in May 1901 not to interfere with internal politics. Several months later, his second-in-command, Major Gouraud, was more specific: "slaves should be confiscated, turned over to French authorities and returned to their villages. All the same, we can close our eyes if Bayero or Aouta keep some slaves for themselves because it is necessary to give them an interest in restraining the movement."[98] Aouta raided to 1905. The 1905 decree was enforced in the eastern areas, but clandestine trading continued.

Conclusion

Roume knew, of course, that he had not abolished slavery. The contrast between the wording of the legislation and the wording of his public statements was important. To France and the world, he announced that he had erased the moral stigma of slavery. To the local administrator, he insisted that there be no act that would make evident to critics of colonial rule the limitations of what had been done. There is, however, no reason to doubt his vision of where he wanted to go. Roume and his colleagues were not egalitarians. They were profoundly sceptical of the potential of those they governed. Even those who developed a progressive reputation believed in hierarchy.[99] Had they not done so, they would have found service in a command system like the colonial state quite onerous.

At the same time, refusal of the colonial state to be the enforcers for conquered elites undermined their control. Slavery cannot exist without a structure of law and coercive machinery to back up the masters. Did Roume fully understand this? We cannot say for sure. What is clear is that most local commandants, whatever their attitude toward slavery, were nervous about social disruption. If they did not realize how lightly sat the hand of the masters on their slaves, they were well aware how fragile their own ascendancy was. Few fully understood what was happening at the very moment that Roume and Merlin were debating what to do, and none understood how the slaves themselves would take the issue into their own hands or, perhaps better, their own feet. The slaves would end up solving Roume's dilemma for him, and in the end make a handful of senior colonial administrators look good.

9   With smoke and mirrors: slavery and the conquest of Guinea

> ... poorly nourished, poorly treated and poorly paid for their work, slaves husband their resources as long as they can and work only as long as their masters are there to watch. Thus the latter are forced to stay nearby, seated under a tree reading several pages from their Qurans or chatting with several followers ... The Fula is poorly endowed by nature for physical labor, puny and sickly ... with no resource other than cultivation by his slaves ...
>
> Among Malinke there is no visible difference between master and slave, no disdain of the one for the other, no rancour, they eat the same food and work side by side ... flight and misery will soon deprive the Fulas of slaves they can no longer renew by war, while the Malinke preserve theirs, linked to them by community of interest, I would even say by appreciation and affection.   Paul Guebhard on Guinean slavery[1]

Even more than in the Sudan, the French in Guinea were on the side of the slave owners. There were a number of reasons for this. Most important, France put few resources into the conquest and control of Guinea in spite of the importance of rubber exports.[2] Only the Sudanese part of Guinea was actually conquered. Because of this, Guinea had few soldiers and administrators. Furthermore, problems of health and poor administration meant that there was a very high turnover. At one point, Faranah had ten commandants in four years. Ditinn had twelve in nine years.[3] The corps of administrators also included some of the dregs of the colonial service, men with few real qualifications for government, who enjoyed the freedom of life away from the restraints of civil society, but used that freedom only to realize some of their fantasies.[4] This was demonstrated by a scandal which we will examine below.

The heart of the issue however was the nature of Guinea. Slavery was as deeply entrenched as in the Sudan and slaves were more numerous.[5] Only in the mountainous eastern corner were there small-scale societies that did not depend heavily on slave labor, but even here the slave trade was important. Commercial reports for Beyla and Kissi for 1894 suggest that, for any given month, slaves represented anywhere from 54 percent to 94 percent of the value of trade.[6] The importance of slavery was historical. Political centralization on the coast and in the interior was often dependent on the use of slaves. It was also geographical in that Guinea lacked significant water transport routes and the use of animal power was limited in much of the country by the tsetse fly. There was no alternative to porterage. Even before the rubber boom, trade

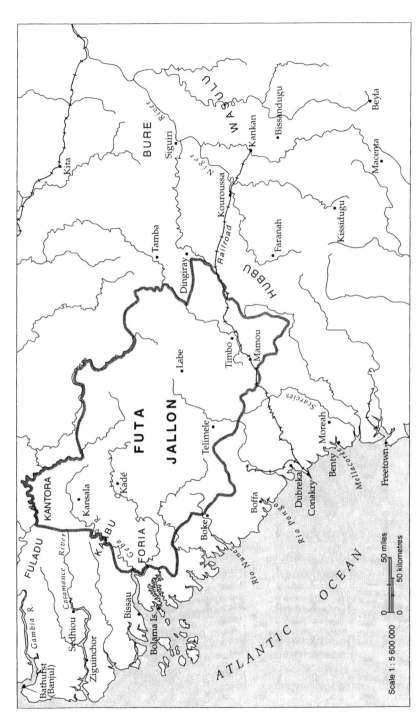

Map 7 Guinea

in Guinea depended on head-loading, but rubber was so remunerative during the boom that it paid the heavy labor costs involved in moving it.

As elsewhere, there were tensions within slave systems. Guinean rulers were concerned with protecting slave holdings. Fulbe elites in particular wanted the French to return runaways and to eliminate rivals like the Hubbu and the Wali of Gumba, who welcomed their slaves.[7] Futa Jallon resembled the Sokoto caliphate more than the reformist states of the western Sudan. The revolution had created a conservative slave-using regime which, in spite of its divisions, functioned well. The land-holding elite profited both from slave labor and from the trade in slaves. Militarily, Futa kept incorporating new areas and accumulating slaves. In the interior, they sold cattle and bought slaves and salt. Toward the coast, they sold slaves and cattle and bought manufactured goods.

Coastal society had an even higher percentage of slaves. At her death in 1880, Mammy Lightburn, a Eurafrican matriarch in the Rio Pongo, controlled 6,000 slaves. French and Senegalese traders depended on slave labor, dealt openly in slaves, took slaves in payment of debts or as pawns. When a French trader was accused of slave-dealing, he insisted that the slaves belonged to his wife. She swore in English: "I am right according to the country law of Rio Nunez to bye [sic] and sell slave because is the money of the country and I don't possess any things more except slave because that is my business."[8] Most administrative accounts of slavery talk of how well slaves were treated, but missionaries presented a harsher picture. Rations were minimal, the growing season went almost the full year, and many suffered from disease. When they could no longer work, they were sometimes released to fend for themselves.[9] The only protection slaves had were in their numbers. Thus, in 1881, over a thousand slaves surrounded the post at Benty to protest the whipping of one of them.[10]

The most critical indictment of slavery policy in Guinea came not from missionaries, but from the colonial ministry's inspectors. In 1908, Guinea was the subject of a series of reports of which the most important was a study of slavery in Guinea by an inspector named Saurin, who skilfully documented what the administration did, what it did not do, and how empty many of its claims were.[11] Saurin suggests that up to 1905 the administration in Guinea clearly sanctioned ownership of slaves and openly recognized the property rights of slave owners. Slaves were freed only when their masters were being punished for opposing the French. Redemption generally involved women being purchased by a third party. It was policy to return slaves to their masters. To back these statements, Saurin cited official reports, legal records and interviews, some of which are no longer available.[12]

French presence along the coast

The upper Guinea coast was to Senegalese traders the Southern Rivers. To their rivals from Freetown, it was the Northern Rivers. If French imperialism had been economically rational, Guinea would have been the major focus of French expansion out of Senegal. It is well watered with deep estuaries that made fine ports and it was dominated by a kingdom with a literate and effective ruling class. Furthermore, the French knew it well, having contested its trade for centuries. By the late nineteenth century, French and British explorers had been through Futa. The coast contained three French posts and trading operations based on Goree, and from 1880 almost to World War I the rubber boom made it economically the second most important French colony in Africa. If Sudan was the preferred goal of French imperialism, it was in part the ascendancy of Saint Louis over Goree, but even more the greater isolation of the Sudan, which allowed the military to do as they wished. And it was the marginality of Guinea to French imperial planning that most shaped policy toward slavery there, particularly the lack of military force and the shortage of capable personnel.[13]

As in Senegal, societies on the Guinea coast had long participated in and been shaped by the Atlantic slave trade, but geography kept both political and commercial authority highly fragmented. Each of the estuaries was politically separate, and contained different polities.[14] In the eighteenth century, a number of European slavers established bases along the coast, intermarried with local ruling families and created local dynasties that established a fragile political hegemony based on wealth and large slave holdings.[15] A clandestine slave trade continued into the second half of the nineteenth century as fast slaving ships took advantage of numerous estuaries to outrun British cruisers.[16] The commodity trade also began early. Coffee was grown on the Rio Pongo from 1826, peanuts from about 1840, and there was also a lively trade in rice, hides, gold, wax and ivory, mostly from the interior. This enabled traditional dynasties to reassert themselves, though major Eurafrican families continued to control thousands of slaves.[17] It also attracted increasing British and French intervention from the late 1830s.

The commodity trade brought in new entrepreneurs – French, Wolof and métis from Senegal, Creoles from Freetown, and Jaxanke from Tuba – to compete with existing entrepreneurs. Many moved quickly from trade to production and the creation of plantation complexes, which absorbed slaves and in some rivers attracted free labor migrants.[18] By 1840, peanuts were being exported along the coast from the Gambia to Sierra Leone. A large reservoir of slave labor, heavy rainfall and easy transport made the Guinea coast attractive, though the heavy soil made cultivation difficult and the extended rainy season often endangered the harvest. Peanuts dominated the coastal trade until the rubber boom began in about 1880 and made for a relatively smooth transition from slave trade to commodity trade. The peanut trade also facilitated establishment of French hegemony as French industry preferred peanut oil to the palm oil used by the British.[19]

In 1868, the commandant of the new post in the Rio Nunez referred to "numerous migrations of Tubakayes [people of Tuba] who have come to establish themselves."[20] Involved in agriculture, trade, and possibly religious proselytism, the Tubakayes rented land from Nalu and Landuma chiefs and used slaves to work it. The development of learning at Tuba was underwritten by large slave holdings and widespread commercial activity.[21] The most productive river was the Rio Nunez, which exported over 5,000 tons of peanuts a year in the 1870s and was the major outlet for Futa's trade. By contrast, the Rio Pongo exported only about 2,000 tons a year. The peanut boom collapsed in the 1880s as peanut prices dropped, while rubber exports took off.[22] The rubber boom started on the coast, but over-cutting speedily decimated the vines there and the rubber frontier moved into the interior. In spite of this, exports grew rapidly, to 770 tons in 1892 and over 1,500 tons in 1906.[23] By 1906, more than 50,000 porters a year were being used to head-load rubber to coastal ports.[24] Diversion of labor was so great that food was in short supply and had to be imported.[25]

While officers of the naval infantry dreamed of Sudanic empire, some navy officers thought about coastal expansion.[26] British governors in Freetown looked to both Futa Jallon and the rivers as a hinterland for commercial penetration.[27] From the late 1830s, both French and British actively intervened to eliminate the slave trade and to protect commercial interests. Among those protected by the French were the Tubakayes. An 1884 treaty with the Nalu chief in the Rio Nunez confirmed this: "The Tubakayes, who are a cause of prosperity in the Rio Nunez, depend only on the French government and can neither be troubled, requisitioned nor punished by the Nalou chiefs."[28] Both French and British wanted to control trade by putting forts at the mouth of each of the estuaries, but it was the French who actually did it. Protectorate treaties were signed in the Rio Nunez in 1865 and the following year in the Mellacorée and the Rio Pongo. By 1867 there were forts at all three. Though the British saw the Mellacorée as part of their sphere of interest, the Colonial Office was not interested in further annexations at this time. French authority was nominal for over a decade. The Almamy of Futa Jallon continued to collect tribute and local chiefs ignored the French outside cannon range of the posts. Commandants were told not to risk their forces outside the post, and could often do little but try to mediate disputes. Increasingly, the French used local conflicts to force treaties on various African rulers and extend their control.[29] In 1877, Brière de l'Isle proclaimed French sovereignty over much of the coast and in 1882 a Lieutenant Governor resident in Senegal was appointed for the Rivières du Sud. Only in 1885 was there a Lieutenant Governor resident on the coast, and only in 1890 did Guinea become autonomous from Senegal with its capital at Conakry.[30]

Social revolutions on the periphery of Futa

Throughout the century, Futa Jallon was expanding. The Rio Nunez and Rio Pongo fell under its control, but the French presence limited that control and was exploited by both traditional and Eurafrican chiefs. Futa, however, dominated the coast into the 1880s and expanded in other directions. Most of this expansion centered on Labé, which exploited social tensions on the fluid and fertile northwestern frontier to establish control over an area greater than the rest of Futa.[31] Labé's move into Kaabu, Foria and the upper Gambia was in alliance with Fulbe groups in each of these areas and profited from a social and political crisis similar to that in areas north of the Gambia. Originally a colony of medieval Mali, Kaabu became a major slave producer, but with the decline of the Atlantic trade its revenues declined, and the population of slaves and Muslims increased. Some of this increase came from overpopulation and social tension pushing Fulbe herders out from Futa in quest of better pasture and greater freedom. Initially welcomed because they brought revenue to financially strapped rulers, the herders resented their financial obligations. As the Kaabu state weakened, peripheral provinces sought more autonomy. Labé exploited the situation, alternatively raiding Kaabu for slaves and supporting Fulbe rebels. In 1867, after a generation of intermittent warfare, a Fulbe army took Kaabu's capital at Kansala.[32] In the Biafada state of Foria, a similar alliance of immigrant Fulbe herders and slaves overturned the state, again with help from Labé, in a war that lasted from 1868 to 1878. The difference in Foria was that slaves refused to lay down their arms and fought the Fulbe until Foria became part of Portuguese Guinea toward the end of the century.[33] The situation in Foria was compounded by revenues from peanut exports, which made possible the purchase of guns.

Fulbe slaves were also important in the upper Gambia, where Egge Molo, the son of a Mande slave and a Fulbe mother, was the catalyst. Molo studied the Quran in Futa and participated in the war against Kaabu. He then returned to Firdu, where he organized a revolt of Fulbe slaves against the Malinke of Tumana and Kantora. By time he died in 1881, his kingdom of Fuladu controlled much of the south bank of the Gambia. His son, Musa Molo continued the expansion, using an alliance with the French in 1883 to establish his independence from Labé, to extend his control of the free Fulbe, who were reluctant to accept a ruler of servile origin, and to build up his own slave holdings. He also fought a long and bitter war against Fodé Kaba in the lower river.[34]

The conventional interpretation of these events, based on oral tradition, stresses Fulbe–Malinke conflict.[35] Barry argues persuasively that Kaabu was destroyed by the intersection of two crises, both linked to the decline of the Atlantic slave trade.[36] Within Futa, the triumph of the revolution and the constant accumulation of slaves led to overpopulation which, when coupled with an exploitative social order, created an outward movement. In peripheral regions, the decline of the slave trade left centuries-old states incapable of coping with increased social conflict. The result was slave revolts, which involved both slaves of the Fulbe and Fulbe slaves owned by Malinke and Biafada elites. In each case, success was followed by conflict between the free, the Fulbe-rimbe, and the servile, the Fulbe-jiyabe, when the free expected former slaves to return to some kind of subject relationship.

There is a different dynamic in areas actually incorporated into Labé.[37] Most of the area around Labé was not very fertile. The areas to the north and west were fertile and well watered. Labé's conquests enslaved large numbers and drove others out. The major noble clans were given lands in the new areas, which they settled with both captives and purchased slaves. The new areas, most of them non-Fulbe, served as both a buffer against attack and the granary of Futa. The basis of power in them shifted from warfare and trade to the exploitation of slave labor. There was also a gradual assimilation to the Poular language and culture. Labé had a very high percentage of slaves and was the most centralized *diwal*. Both Ibrahima and his son and successor, Alfa Yaya, exercised more power than the Almamies to whom they were nominally subject.

Conquest of Futa Jallon

Much of what is now Guinea was conquered not from the coast, but from the Sudan. Gallieni saw the future of the Sudan in a link with Futa Jallon and the Guinea coast. To further this goal, he built a fort at Sigiri in 1888 and sent two missions to the Futa.[38] When Archinard replaced him, policy shifted back to an east–west axis focused on the Senegal and Niger rivers, but large parts of upper Guinea were brought under control in an effort to cut communication between Samori and Futa.[39] These areas were attached to Guinea only in 1899, when the Sudan was partially dismembered. Futa Jallon was solicited by three French colonies and by the British and Portuguese. Britain and France sent missions to Futa Jallon in 1881. A British emissary, Gouldsbury, signed a treaty of trade and friendship, but described the area as a poor one with few economic prospects.[40] The French were less troubled by economic reality. Their emissary, Jean Bayol, brought back two agreements, one of which was interpreted to recognize French control of the coast. The French text of the second provided for a protectorate, but the Arabic text spoke only of an alliance. For the next fifteen years, France tried to implement this protectorate while Futa rulers parried their efforts and claimed that no such concession had ever been made. Futa received subsidies from the British until 1895 and Freetown continued to see Futa as part of its hinterland.[41] In spite of this, in 1882 London accepted a border between the Mellacorée and Scarcies basins and, in 1889, a treaty that conceded Futa to the French.

Only the Fulbe resisted the idea.[42] They would not permit a residence, they objected to French troops passing through, and they asked Archinard to communicate with them through African messengers. They also continued to collect tribute and exercise suzerainty along the coast. Without an adequate military force, the French were reluctant to attack the mountainous Futa and tried merely to encircle it. The Fulbe were consistently hostile to the French. Almamy Bokar Biro aided Samori's resistance, and both Almamies sought to play off French and British. French emissaries were regularly told that the Futa was for the Fulbe and France for the French. Though Futa was completely surrounded by colonial possessions by 1893, a French embassy came back that year with a treaty inferior to the one they believed to be in force.[43]

The political weakness of the Futa lay in cross-cutting lines of social conflict and in frequent alternation of the royal office between two ruling houses. The French threat was the kind of crisis that usually pulled the two houses together. Until 1890, the system of alternation worked reasonably well because of regular consultation between the two houses and the moderating role of the Council of Elders. In that year, Ibrahima Sory Dongolfella died and a Soriya candidate, Bokar Biro, imposed himself by force over a brother preferred by the Council of Elders. He had opponents assassinated and he made clear his disdain for alternation. In a short period of time, Bokar Biro's autocratic style managed to threaten rivals within his own house, the leaders of the rival Alfaya, the major provincial chiefs and the Council of Elders.[44]

Bokar Biro surrounded himself with men of low status and tried to remove hostile chiefs. He regularly assured the French of his devotion, but also corresponded with Freetown and played on Fulbe anxieties about the French reception of runaway slaves from Futa.[45] In 1895, he was defeated when he tried to remove Alfa Yaya of Labé. With a full-scale civil war threatening, the French decided that the time was ripe. De Beeckman, the French resident at Dubreka, headed up to the Futa with 100 soldiers, but he failed to impose a resident. The French thought they had Bokar Biro's signature on a treaty, but when the document reached Saint Louis it was discovered that Bokar Biro had not signed it, but had merely written "Bismillah," which means "in the name of the Gracious and Merciful God." Then Amadu, the Alfaya Almamy, died, and Bokar Biro tried to eliminate the alternation. When the Council of Elders opposed him, he tried to eliminate the council and de Beeckman returned, this time in alliance with Umaru Bademba, the Alfaya candidate, Ibrahima Fugumba, the leading religious leader, and Alfa Yaya of Labé. Ten days after French occupation of Timbo, Bokar Biro was defeated and killed at Poredaka. De Beeckman became the Resident, Umaru Bademba the Almamy, and Alfa Yaya was recognized as sole chief of Labé.[46]

Noirot's private kingdom

Within months after Poredaka, a new protectorate treaty was signed.[47] In June 1897, Ernest Noirot became administrator of Futa Jallon. A former Folies Bergère set designer, Noirot first came to Africa as an artist with the Bayol mission of 1881. He liked Africa and soon afterwards moved into colonial administration. A verbose and passionate man, he was a dominant figure in Guinea for eight years, first in Futa and then as Director of Native Affairs. He cultivated a reputation as an abolitionist. In Senegal, he had to be warned in 1893 that the administration did not want a large vagabond population or the alienation of elites.[48] In Guinea he described slaves as superstition-ridden beings not ready for freedom and opposed any action against slavery.[49] Noirot liked to act through indigenous agency. Soon after arriving in Futa Jallon, he called an assembly of chiefs. Ismael Barry refers to this meeting as a "summit," but the chiefs seem to have done little talking before they accepted a new policy on slavery.[50] The assembly rejected immediate liberation of slaves as a threat to public order, but "agreed" to the following:

(1) Abolition of the slave trade with a sentence of five to ten years for buyer and seller, twenty years for the trader.
(2) No separation of husband and wife or mother and child.
(3) Guarantee of humane treatment under threat of a one-year prison sentence and immediate manumission of the slave.

(4) Absolute right of the slave to buy his or her freedom.
(5) In debt cases, the administrator could free slaves on condition that their redemption payments go to the creditor of the former master rather than the slave being given in payment for the debt.[51]

It is not clear what Noirot promised the chiefs to get their approval or whether he expected them to keep their agreement. Acting Governor Cousturier and Lt. Governor Ballay refused to approve the document, but Noirot later treated it as a precedent. The chiefs protested only against prohibition of the slave trade. One asked "Does not the Quran say that the Believer who has captives taken in war should keep them in his service and treat them well?"[52] Ballay vetoed posting of the agreement in mosques for fear, Noirot charged later, that humanitarians would see it as administrative complicity in slavery.[53]

Whatever Noirot expected, the chiefs did not intend to apply the agreement. Though Noirot remained a key figure in Guinea, there is no evidence of any cases being brought under the agreement.[54] The chiefs used delaying tactics in putting it off, as they were to use them in other conflicts.[55] They would agree to something and then just not do it. Whatever interest Noirot had in slavery – his memos are profuse – he saw the chiefs as the only possible agency of change but, to do what he wanted, he had to bend them to his will. He clearly had a conception of indirect rule, but was more interventionist than even Archinard and achieved less. The traditional state was simply the vessel through which he chose to act. At the 1897 assembly, he was opposed by Almamy Umaru Bademba and religious leader Ibrahima Fugumba. By 1898, he was thinking of authority devolving to the *diwal* chiefs, but the Almamy was still the focal point of the state, so he deposed Umaru Bademba and imposed Baba Alimu, a minor figure in the Soriya family, who would not normally have been a candidate.[56]

The dismissal of Umaru Bademba was the first step in a sequence of bizarre events. Noirot's key partner in reshaping the Futa was a former slave named Boubou Penda, who started as his servant and ended up exploiting his intimacy with Noirot to acquire wealth and power. Umaru Bademba later suggested he was deposed because his gifts to Boubou Penda were inadequate. He gave Boubou Penda a slave-born wife, but refused him a member of his own family.[57] Baba Alimu gave him a sister.[58] Baba Alimu turned out to be a brutal Almamy, using his militia to extract "gifts" from his subjects. The third key person in the scandal was Hubert, a clerk, whose only qualification for rapid promotion was that he was Binger's nephew and Noirot's protege. In 1899, Hubert became administrator of Timbi, and in 1901, when Noirot became Director of Native Affairs, Hubert replaced him as Futa commandant. Hubert had a slave "wife" during his previous tour, but he gave her up when he left. Now, he set himself up in truly regal style. He traveled on a white horse with a full entourage of slaves, five concubines carried in hammocks, and griots chanting his praises. His compound was large, as befitted a grand chief, and contained numerous huts for his concubines.[59] This life style demanded revenue. The militia had been deprived of their salaries in 1900, but they no longer needed salaries. They worked for both Baba Alimu and Hubert, collecting gifts from both peasants and traders: a chicken or a goat from one, six chickens from another, horses, cattle and gold from the wealthier and more powerful. When chiefs could not pay taxes, they were imprisoned and their slaves and cattle sold.[60]

From the very first, the system involved the use of violence. When Ibrahima Fugumba was deposed, he and his son were killed, one after a hasty trial, and the second arbitrarily. Three thousand slaves were confiscated, many of them distributed or kept by Boubou Penda or Baba Alimu, most kept in their slave villages and used by the administration.[61] There were other arbitrary executions and, on one occasion, Hubert had a village sacked and its inhabitants enslaved. Hubert's clerk, Meillet, distributed female slaves.[62] Boubou Penda wanted aristocratic women. When refused the wife of a well-placed noble, he seized and kept her for four days. He then seized the woman's sister, raped her and kept her for three months.[63] Noirot protected both Boubou Penda and Hubert. When interpreter Alioune Salifou was asked why he had not reported Boubou Penda's exactions, he said that Noirot had presented Boubou to everyone as his son. He asked that Boubou be treated as himself and said that he approved in advance of everything he did. It is amazing that a series of governors were either ignorant of what was happening or chose to ignore it. Frézouls, a reform Governor, became aware of the affair only when a settler on the Administrative Council charged that it was depopulating the area around Timbo. Frézouls arrested Boubou Penda, suspended Noirot and Hubert, and ordered the inquiry from which most of the data cited come.[64]

The Hubert–Noirot scandal led to a press campaign in France, which focused on slave trading, and to further investigation.[65] With charges and counter-charges being made, Frézouls was removed in early 1906. Both Lt. Governor Poulet and Governor-General Ponty denied most of the charges. The heart of their defence of Guinea's compromises was that Guinea was not conquered by force of arms, but "as a result of treaties passed with native chiefs and freely agreed to by them."[66] Noirot died in 1907. After years of investigation and a libel suit against Frézouls, the case was dropped in 1909 without Hubert so much as receiving a reprimand.

Reluctant action

To be sure, things did happen. Perhaps the most important is that, as in the Sudan, slaves freed themselves, seeking either refuge with Muslim reformers or security in French-run areas. Slave flight was a constant. Thus 1902 and 1903 reports from Satadougou in the Sudan speak of emigration from the Futa "motivated by the violence and the exactions of the alfas."[67] Slaves exploited differences in policy. In 1905, the Commandant in Labé was bothered that six slaves from Labé got liberty papers in the Casamance, that masters were not heard and that no redemption payment was made. They then returned to slave villages with new clothes to talk of liberty.[68] Some slaves joined the *tirailleurs*. Others fled to Portuguese Guinea or the Rio Nunez, where they could be protected by local agents of French commercial houses.[69] The largest group of runaways was probably people enslaved by Samori's *sofa* who were simply trying to get home.[70] Slaves from Futa and Dingiray fled all over upper Guinea. "Within the cercle," one commandant complained, "slaves flee without any plausible reason and go free themselves in other cercles, while slaves from other cercles come here for the same reason."[71]

The administration was primarily concerned in slave matters to win the confidence of Fulbe chiefs. Lt. Governor Cousturier wired a local administrator: "We have an interest right now in proving to the Foulahs that the Government is concerned about conservation of their wealth and guarantee of their property."[72] He wrote the Commandant in Kadé: "Involve yourself as little as possible with slave questions, which are an economic problem we do not wish to deal with right now. Apply the laws of the country which prohibit the sale of domestic slaves. In such a case, manumission of the slave is the best sanction."[73] Commandants were also concerned to build up or to protect their tax base. When the administrator at Faranah was told to return all runaway slaves to the Futa except free men enslaved by Samori, he freed those from Faranah claimed by relatives and returned others.[74] In most of the Futa, all of the land was cultivated. Nevertheless, Guebhard was concerned that the exodus could hurt Futa's economic interests.[75] On the coast, slave flight affected particularly the plantations of the Tubakayes.[76]

In Upper Guinea, some areas like Dingiray and Kankan profited from the slave trade of previous generations and others, like Sankaran and Faranah, were seriously depopulated.[77] There were different kinds of runaways. There were slaves who fled caravans, still important up to 1905, those who fled slavery itself, and old people who were turned out because they could no longer work. The most plaintive were emaciated Toma and Guerzé trying to get back from Futa to their homes in the forest zone.[78] Some people found their way to liberty villages, but their desire to return home and their fear of being reclaimed meant that the villages had a rapid through-flow. Dingiray was ruled by Umar's son, Aguibou, until Archinard brought Aguibou to Bandiagara. Authority at Dingiray then devolved to Maki, the son of Aguibou. Like his father, Maki used the first years of French rule to expand his slave holdings. When deposed and exiled in 1899, he was limited to an entourage of thirty-five, with only ten wives and fifteen selected slaves.[79]

Though the slave trade had not yet been ended, people were coming from Kayes and other old cercles of the Sudan to look for relatives, many of whom had long been in slavery. The administrator thought that they were enticing slaves who had quite happily taken root in Dingiray.[80] Over a seventeen-month period from May 1899 to October 1900, forty slaves were freed, eighteen because of beatings, burns, lack of feeding or excessive use of irons. Twelve were simply not claimed at the liberty village.[81] In spite of or perhaps because of this, Cousturier told the Commandant to leave slave matters to the chiefs.[82] There were also special concerns. One administrator reported that he had an excellent interpreter who had been taken hostage when Segu fell and spoke five languages. "We must leave him convinced that he is still our hostage," the administrator wrote, "because he will immediately leave to rejoin his relatives at Segu if he believes himself free."[83] In 1903, when Noirot visited Dingiray, the most important issue raised by the chiefs was maintenance of their authority over their slaves. Noirot responded, first, by asking confirmation of the rights of slaves, for example, to rest, to two days for themselves, and to the right of redemption, and, second, by asking that slaves refusing to work be hauled before the administrator.[84]

Construction of the railroad also stepped up slave flight. Construction began in 1899 and continued till 1913. At any given moment, there were between 2,000 and 6,000 men working on the railroad. Almost all were slaves sent to fill forced labor quotas.[85] As in the Sudan, many did not return to their masters. In 1906, for example, there were only 80 left out of 600 from Labé within a few days of arrival.[86] The problem was not simply slave flight. In 1901, Maclaud, the Commandant of the Futa, relayed a series of complaints from the chiefs. Wages were often not paid. Workers were fed only once a day, and then it was often rice without any meat. If a man fell sick and could not work, he received no rations and had to scavenge in the bush. Some ran away. Others tried to return home, but few made it. Many sick and hungry workers died. Others fled. Maclaud could find only four deserters to interrogate. The governor was told that if treatment of labor was not improved, it would be difficult to recruit more.[87] Similar complaints came from Faranah. Men worked up to three months without pay. Medical care was poor and, most important, there were no rations for the sick and injured.[88] In early 1903, the commandant in Faranah reported that many chiefs refused to send levies, saying that they had few slaves and were reluctant to part with their sons. He also indicated that the archives were full of complaints about treatment of railroad labor.[89]

The demand for porters was also great, and this too fell largely on slaves. Construction of the railroad did not reduce the demand for porters. As the railroad moved into the interior, the terminus was the point of convergence of trade routes. It was not unusual for a cercle to be using 500 to 1,000 porters at a time. As with railroad labor, demand for a constant supply of labor probably led to improved treatment. Porters in most cercles were paid 50 centimes a day with a ration of 650 grams of rice.[90] After 1905, there was an effort to create permanent teams of porters in the major centers. This reduced the time needed to recruit a team, but it was more costly. Porters had to be paid while they sat around waiting for work. Crews of 50 men each, sometimes 200 or 300 men in all, were kept ready to go. Often, the demand for porters strained a cercle's resources. Thus, in 1907, the commandant at Kurusa complained that he could not meet the demands for both porters and railroad construction workers. Kurusa could no longer feed itself. Villages along trade routes often moved so as to be less available for labor. In some cases, porters fled before being pressed into another trip.[91]

When asked to report to higher authority on slave matters, Governors regularly lied. "As for the trade in slaves," Lt. Governor Cousturier wrote Governor-General Chaudié, "properly speaking, it no longer exists in French Guinea where the natives know only domestic slavery . . . Besides, the government favours with all of its powers the emancipation of blacks by redeeming slaves who ask for their liberation and who reimburse the advances made for them with their labor."[92] As we have seen, the message that went out to local administrators was different. There was also no commitment to liberty villages, except in upper Guinea, where they were created before the area was transferred. Some administrators created them, for example, in Faranah with numerous refugees from Futa. There were only thirty-one liberty villages in Guinea compared to eighty-eight in the Sudan, but five of them were in Faranah.[93] As in the Sudan, they were placed along trade routes and used for porterage and to maintain facilities for traveling administrators. Elsewhere, they were not encouraged. The administrator in Benty was told that there was not enough money and that he should assign freed slaves to families in villages near the residence.[94]

Guinea seems to have insulated itself from the pressures that pushed change in Senegal and the Sudan. Up to 1902, there were no legal texts or instructions proscribing the slave trade.[95] Decrais' 1900 letter was published and ignored, but in 1902 the charge of a local trader that Guinea was protecting slavery led to questions being asked. Acting Governor Tautain defended Guinean policy:

We are obligated to respect the uses and customs of the inhabitants. We cannot from one day to the next proclaim the liberation of all the slaves our proteges possess. Beyond the injustice this would cause unless reasonable indemnities were given to the masters, there would be a great danger in acting thus because liberation would deprive the servile populations of all resources and reduce them to famine, which would lead to troubles and numerous acts of brigandage.[96]

But he had to act. At Noirot's suggestion, the Saint Louis convention and his Futa assembly were taken as a model. Tautain asked all administrators to hold meetings with chiefs and persuade them to prohibit the slave trade: five years in prison for a person already in slavery, eight for a free person, ten in cases of kidnapping or enticement of a minor, all to be handled by traditional courts.[97] Assemblies were held and agreements signed in all cercles. At Timbo, the new laws were quietly accepted by 1,500 Fulbe.[98] At Boffa, where elites were concerned to acquire more slaves, there was unhappiness and fear that once slaves were informed they would run away or refuse to work. The commandant promised that if they treated slaves well, the administration would continue to return runaways.[99] Tautain clarified his intentions in a dispatch to Boké: "Slaves should from this time forth be considered domestic slaves. Nothing is changed beyond that. Those who wish to buy slaves in foreign areas should in no way be bothered. Please reassure the chiefs in this regard in my name."[100]

Almost immediately, there was an effort to clarify the right to purchase slaves outside the colony. When Famechon, the director of customs, claimed that slaves were being sold to cannibals in Liberia to be eaten, which was almost certainly untrue, the import of slaves from Liberia was authorized, using wording taken directly from the 1892 Saint Louis convention.[101] Roume immediately vetoed this and questioned the validity of the convention as a precedent. Besides, the convention was no longer being used in Senegal.

Roume insisted that no trade in slaves be allowed and suggested the Decrais dispatch of 1899 as a basis for action until further notice.[102] In December 1903, Cousturier finally banned the trade, but the only penalty in simple trade cases was liberation of the slave.[103] The trade certainly continued but was less open.

The unreformed slave economy

The new policy resulted in an increase in the number of slavery cases, but mostly cases of theft rather than trade. Slave-trading charges were almost always accessory to either kidnapping or enticement.[104] In Ditinn, there were seventy-four slave-trade cases during 1903 and 1904, all of them involving theft of slaves. In Labé there were ten cases in 1905, all involving theft. Theft cases were also more severely punished than ordinary slave-trade cases. In trade cases, sentences ranged from fifteen days to six months, but theft or kidnapping a slave often drew a five-year term.[105] "Judgments," Saurin wrote, "in the mind of the tribunals that pronounced them, are more concerned to consecrate and safeguard the rights of property of the masters than the principle of individual liberty."[106] When the administrator of a commercial house wanted to free two slaves, he was told he had to indemnify their masters.[107]

Though administrators arbitrated some slave grievances, runaways were usually returned. Adequate proof of violence was hard to produce in cases of mistreatment. An administrator in Sigiri wrote that if mediation failed when a slave refused to work, he asked the court to punish the slave.[108] Flight was more common than redemption because slaves had difficulty getting the 150 to 200 francs demanded. Slaves were more likely to be freed for political reasons. In at least nine cases between 1896 and 1914, a large body of slaves was freed because the French wanted to destroy someone's power.[109] Over 3,000 of Bokar Biro's slaves were freed, but were kept in their villages under slave chiefs and were used as labor by the local commandant.[110] Many of Bokar Biro's slaves fled the Futa, but in 1907, eleven years after Poredaka, the population of his slave villages was still three fourths of what it had been. Ibrahima Fugumba's slaves were also freed, but nineteen were sent to Conakry to serve his widow.[111] The new law code was proclaimed in 1903. The only effect of Merlin's instructions was the suppression of the liberty papers, but in Guinea few liberty papers had been issued and suppression facilitated the perpetuation of servitude. Though the Guinean administration used the Sierra Leonean border as a justification for inaction, the British raised the issue of kidnapped children being sold in Guinea.[112]

When Frézouls was assigned to Guinea in 1904, he was the first outsider in many years. Closely linked to the Radicals in the Chamber of Deputies, he came out as a reformer, but he had little African experience and seems at first to have depended too much on "old hands" like Noirot. He was reluctant to disrupt local social structures even after the Noirot–Hubert scandal broke. But pressure was on from Dakar. In September 1905, Merlin responded to a

Tuba case in which the judge spoke of the "servile condition" of some witnesses and treated as legitimate the obligation of slaves to work five days a week for their masters. The judge addressed the slaves: "if you wish your rights to be respected, should you not respect rights of your masters, if those rights are not suppressed by mistreatment, by refusal of food or clothing or some other cause . . . there is one way to obtain liberty, it is to pay for it."[113] Merlin pointed out that this clearly violated his 1903 instructions and insisted that the government could not let slavery perpetuate itself.[114] Two months later, Roume wrote that Tautain's 1902 circular was not in the Dakar archives. The decree that followed the meetings and supposedly gave their decisions force of law did not specify penalties. He then pointed out that many actions being prosecuted were violations of Muslim law. More important, Roume insisted, "the condition of slave does not legally exist. It cannot then be juridically recognized." Furthermore, the distinction between direct administration and protectorate, which once made possible toleration of slavery, no longer existed. Since all persons were free, Quranic law could be used in prosecuting slave traders. Finally, he reminded Frézouls that the administration was under fire in the French press for defending slavery.[115]

Before responding to Roume, Frézouls asked for a review of slave policy. The review underlined the commitment France made to chiefs "to protect them in their persons and in their property." It cited the repeated sanction of slavery in such pronouncements as Tautain's 1902 circular and the administration's fear of disorder.[116] Frézouls added that it was difficult to find Africans willing to enforce the new laws and that administrators often pursued policies contrary to principles of French legislation. "Native chiefs, feeling themselves supported by functionaries whose power they have experienced, are not afraid to violate our orders." Some, he suggested, openly tore up liberty papers and re-enslaved those freed.[117] While writing this, Frézouls started to take a stronger line in instructions to administrators. In July 1905, he extracted the colonial state from a situation in which Noirot made it the owner of slaves taken from Bokar Biro. "It is inadmissible, in effect, that France considers as belonging to it in their status as slaves human beings found in the succession of a native chief."[118] A new administrator in the Futa asked for instructions, claiming that slaves were becoming more reluctant to work and quicker to flee.[119] Frézouls responded that there could be no slaves on French territory. A slave claiming his liberty was free. A slave choosing to change masters could do so. If a master wanted to marry a slave girl, he had to address himself to her mother and to respect her right to refuse. At the same time, he urged the administrator to explain that a man could no longer own another person, but he could engage the services of others. In other words, he urged a move toward contract relations.[120] A day later, fearing he had opened Pandora's box, he wrote again, suggesting prudence and the possibility of transforming domestic slavery into sharecropping.[121]

In the meantime, the 1905 law was proclaimed. Richard, the new governor, distributed copies of the decree, the Governor-General's circular, and one of his own. Richard underlined that slavery could no longer be recognized either juridically or administratively, but went on to cite Roume:

It is important, in effect, that natives understand that for the state of subjection consisting of the traditional rules of domestic slavery, a contractual state is substituted, based on individual liberty, within which masters and servants have rights and reciprocal duties, which we must guarantee, to the former as to the latter.

We will return to the idea of contract. Richard went on: "I ask you to take the greatest care in applying the measures contained in this extract . . . to apply the Act of 12 December without creating in the mind of the natives unjustified disquiet of such a nature as to compromise the public tranquillity."[122] Not surprisingly, little was done. Saurin and Guyho confirmed this in 1908. To be sure, Richard insisted that slavery could no longer be recognized officially. The number of trade cases increased, but most still involved theft – nine of thirteen submitted for review in 1906, and twenty-two of thirty-nine in 1907. Saurin charged that without precise instructions, administrators had too much freedom of action, but even after 1906, they rarely acted. "Slavery is no longer recognized," Guyho wrote, "but it still exists and ways should be examined to make effective the emancipation of voluntary slaves."[123]

The case for prudence was based on three arguments: first, that slaves were not mistreated; second, that emancipation of slaves would impoverish the country; and third, that emancipation would create political instability. Saurin took all three arguments apart. First, he was skeptical that slaves were neither mistreated nor interested in freedom. Second, he argued against the notion that production would fall if the slaves were freed. He suggested that the major cause of recurrent famine was that once slaves had paid their dues, they had little incentive to produce more. Once freed, they would be more productive. Third, he suggested that there was no evidence of a political danger. The slave owners were only about one eighth of the population. The recently enslaved would probably head home and the others would probably stay where they were. He then went on to argue that the administration had an obligation to aid the process, to give land to those who wanted it and to guarantee the right to acquire and transmit property. He saw no reason to think that freed slaves would become vagabonds.

Responses to Saurin were often simple lies, sometimes ignoring the evidence he clearly presented from their letters and judicial decisions. Administrators insisted that they rejected all claims based on slavery and that they pursued slave trade cases *impitoyablement*. They also retreated into the same ideological arguments that Saurin castigated. Freeing slaves would sow hatred and cause economic difficulties. Saurin saw these responses as delaying tactics. Thus, when Lt. Governor Poulet suggested that a registry office was necessary for emancipation to be effective, Saurin conceded that it was desirable, but argued that it would take too long for it to precede an emancipation already begun. Ponty, by this time Governor-General, conceded that Guinea had "evolved" less rapidly than other colonies, but suggested that progress had been made. Ponty's deceptions were more subtle than those of others, but then Ponty's record in the Sudan was praised by Saurin and Guyho, and put forth as a model for Guinea.

I have done less research in mission archives for Guinea, but missions seem to have been less important than in the Sudan. The Holy Ghost Fathers and the Church Missionary Society were established on the coast. In 1901, the Spiritans took over the White Fathers mission near Kissidugu. They bought children, received runaways, and were entrusted with freed slaves by the government. In 1901, they had 106 redeemed slaves at Kissidugu, but within a few years the mission was hard-pressed to maintain itself.[124] In December 1906, they were feeding 317, mostly children, but their resources were so strained that some slaves returned to their masters.[125] As in the Sudan, the missions seem to have been immobilized by the Church–State conflict.

Conclusion

How do we explain Guinea? The "Soudanais" were certainly more disciplined. Military men took orders, at least from other military men, and reluctant as they were to take desk jobs, they did so and filled out endless reports. Reports from the Sudan tended to be more detailed than those from Senegal, and certainly better than those from Guinea. More important, the colonies in general, and Guinea in particular, attracted a certain type of free spirit, restless at the restraints of ordered society, interested in a world where they could implement their fantasies, where they could be little kings of the bush. Hubert differed from sexually active counterparts in the Sudan in that he was not simply interested in night-time companions, but in living out a role day and night. A new breed was moving into the system during the first years of the century, many of them products of the Ecole Coloniale. Even here, the system failed. Colonial administration was built on a military model. A colonial administrator, like a soldier, was trained to take orders. The new group included a number of bright young men who later did well, but during the Hubert years they did not rock the boat. In a way, it was a dry run for Vichy.

In some ways, however, the rulers of Guinea read their situation accurately. All of the conquered states in the Sudan were relatively weak. Neither Samorian or Umarian states survived the conquest. France's allies in the Sudan were men like Aguibou, Nto, Mademba Sy, who wielded power because the French gave it to them. In Guinea, the Futa Jallon was an entrenched state with a century and half of history. Its existence was unquestioned, and its legitimacy was attacked only by several Muslim radicals. Many smaller states were also secure. Furthermore, few had been conquered. In Futa Jallon, De Beeckman won in alliance with Umaru Bademba. Archinard, like Lugard, understood the importance of military victory. Having defeated the Sokoto caliphate, Lugard could be generous to it. Having defeated the Futanke, Archinard could distribute their domains. Few Guineans had been defeated.

Slaves were the most important kind of wealth. For chiefs and elites, protection of servile property was the most important single issue once the conquest was over and they regularly told the French so. Administrators felt that order and stability depended on the chiefs. They also accepted the ideology of the chiefs. They seem convinced that most slaves were lazy and improvident, that most owners were generous and concerned about the well-being of their slaves – though there are references to slaves being poorly fed and to older slaves being left to their own resources when they could no longer work. Fulbe chiefs often made agreements that they had no intention of carrying out. They got away with it because they made themselves indispensable to the French.

10   The Banamba exodus

Since Logeais has come,
Since Papa Logeais has come,
Since the brother of the little slaves has come,
All men are free.
We no longer cultivate for our masters.
We no longer pound millet for our mistresses.
We can work for ourselves.
We can have children.
Thank you Logeais.
Thank you Papa Logeais.
The children of the slaves will be eternally grateful.
Thanks to you they are men.

Song of Praise to Resident of Banamba[1]

In the spring of 1905, when they were supposed to be preparing for the rains, the slaves of Banamba began to leave their masters. Most were persuaded to remain where they were for one more year, but in the spring of 1906 the exodus began again. For the next four or five years, all across the Sudan, groups of slaves trekked slowly and patiently across the dry savanna lands, braving hunger and deprivation to look for earlier homes. Often villages they sought no longer existed. Sometimes, those enslaved when young had forgotten their clans and even their villages. Many ended up in other places, but hundreds of thousands went home and began the difficult task of reconstructing destroyed communities. The effect of the exodus was the destruction of slavery as a labor system in much of the area covered by this study.

There were already tensions within slave systems, especially within those that most systematically exploited slave labor. Slave flight increased as the period of conquest drew to a close. Population growth in Wasulu and other areas that had been depopulated took place from the moment of French conquest and in spite of risks involved in the return. The Bamako Commandant reported in 1901 that so many Wasulunke wanted to return home that he had to reject all requests.[2] When a new Resident was assigned to Banamba in 1902, he was told to crack down on the slave trade.[3] The French did not, however, want significant flight or even separation of slaves from masters. Just the reverse, both senior and junior administrators were afraid of popular disturbances and assumed they would lead to economic decline. Convinced both of slave passivity and of the necessity of coercion to produce work, they did not want massive liberation. Roume, who felt he had to distance the colonial state from support for slavery, feared disruption and urged administrators to control the process of change. After the exodus began, Ponty extolled the virtues of a pool of free labor, but he did so only afterwards.

Showdown at Banamba

The exodus began at Banamba because it was new and was marked by intensive exploitation of slave labor.[4] Banamba was founded only in the 1840s, but by 1880 it was the most important market in the western Sudan. Many slaves who poured into the town were kept and redirected to grain plantations. By 1899 slave-worked plantations surrounded Banamba for 50 km in all directions.[5] Rapid growth of the slave economy meant that most slaves remembered another home or, if enslaved young, knew where they came from. It also meant rigorous exploitation of their labor, and thus a harsh regime. Finally, they were relatively homogeneous since most of them emerged from Samori's conquests. This facilitated cooperation.

Slave flight was common from 1896 and there was substantial slave dissidence from 1903. "This movement," the resident wrote in 1903, "will only increase."[6] In late 1904, a rich Maraka from Tuba died leaving an estate with 2,000 to 3,000 slaves. Many of them fled rather than be passed on to the heirs.[7] Then, in February 1905, others began leaving. When questioned as they passed through Bamako, they said they had no animosity to their masters, but wanted to go home.[8] By April, armed vigilantes were patrolling paths to the south, stopping all movement. Many slaves were also armed and traveled in compact groups. Administrators feared violence, and indeed, on May 15 a slave was killed by a noble on the road to Kulikoro.[9] This all happened as Roume was working on the new anti-slavery law. In late May, Roume sent a company of *tirailleurs* under Comm. Vidal to Banamba. He also ordered acting Lt. Governor Fawtier to mediate the dispute and if necessary to "arrest all leaders on one side or the other who are fomenting troubles, because even admitting the legitimacy of certain collective grievances, we cannot tolerate that public order be compromised."[10]

Nearby chiefs were ordered to halt the movement and the slaves were proclaimed vagabonds.[11] When Maraka chiefs claimed that they could not live without slaves and asked for their return, Vidal refused, but after the chiefs threatened to stop paying taxes, he authorized them to stop movements. A group of 200 slaves was returned to Kiba by force, but others slipped through. To halt the exodus, masters seized slave property, especially firearms, destroyed non-Muslim places of worship and sequestered wives and children in the walled city, which only incensed the slaves further.[12] When Fawtier insisted that the Maraka turn in their arms, over a thousand weapons were turned in, probably a fraction of their arsenal.[13] Fawtier put pressure on both sides:

Could we authorize an exodus of 4,000 to 5,000 persons at a time when Blacks must prepare planting for the year? . . . The exodus would be the ruin and maybe the death by starvation of Marakas incapable of cultivating their fields, as well as servants, who at this time of the year, could not prepare other fields, find necessary seeds and construct houses in the middle of the rainy season. This would be the return to bush of this beautiful part of Beledugu . . . It would also be the death of an important center of horse rearing.[14]

Vidal's efforts produced a temporary agreement. Masters promised that slaves would be well treated and their women and children would not be taken from them. Slaves would have two full days of the week for their own work and masters would supply seed. They would be fed on the days they worked for the masters.[15] Fawtier's report made clear that masters showed little concern for their slaves. Only a year earlier, Brevié documented Maraka treatment of their slaves:

. . . slaves are poorly fed, mistreated and poorly clothed. Masters rarely give them two days free [which is theirs] by custom. They prefer to feed them poorly and be assured of their labor all the time. . . a slave of Tuba belongs to a master who "generously" gives three moules [sic] of millet [about six kg] for rations of 25 slaves. The administrative services estimate that a daily ration is one kilo [of cereal] per person per day. Another slave . . . told us that twenty slaves of his master were given four kilos per day.[16]

Some administrators learned slowly. Thus, Vidal got twelve older slaves together to find out why they wanted to leave an area "where most of them enjoyed an almost comfortable situation." The slaves responded that the Marakas treated them worse than their animals.[17]

In the spring of 1906, the agreement came undone. At the first sign that the exodus was resuming, masters seized slave children and confiscated personal goods.[18] This was compatible with customary law under which masters owned both children and possessions of slaves, but the slaves were angry. This time, Ponty was in the Sudan and strongly supported slave rights. He insisted only that they pay their taxes and seek passes indicating where they intended to go. "Keep me informed on the incidents in Banamba," he wrote. "Protect the domestics who want to leave their masters."[19] A force of *tirailleurs* was sent to Banamba and, a month later, Ponty reported:

The exodus of servants proceeded with remarkable calm and order. With rare exceptions, they were all directed to Bamako where passes were issued to them for their home lands. Most of them were originally from Buguni cercle. Even before arrival of reinforcements, my instructions were strictly applied and the servants were able to leave for Bamako without being disturbed by former masters.[20]

Between April and late May 1906, about 3,000 slaves left Banamba and other Maraka cities.[21] Their plight was often desperate. Dispossessed, they often went for days with little or nothing to eat: "the emaciation and misery of most of these unfortunates deprived for many days of sufficient nourishment, despoiled of their modest savings by shameless masters can only arouse the most profound pity."[22] Many ended up in Bamako, where demand for labor was easily met that year, but most made it back to earlier homes.[23] By early June 1906, the exodus was temporarily over.

Table 10.1. *Month of departure, Gumbu, Kita, Kayes*

January	10.2
February	14.5
March	29.8
April	20.6
May	11.6
June	6.4
July	0.9
August	0.6
September	1.2
October	1.0
November	1.3
December	1.9

Sources: For Kayes, ANM, 1 E 44; for Gumbu, ANM, 1 E 38 & 39; for Kita, ANM 1 E 48.

The movement spreads

In May, a missionary in the isolated station of Patiana wrote: "They speak here of nothing else but the proclamation at Bamako: Slavery is abolished. For several days there has been a constant parade of ex-slaves . . . returning to their country. More than 500 have passed . . ."[24] The same month, Ponty approved the return of almost 2,000 Wasulunke who had repeatedly been denied the right to leave Kati. At Bafulabe, three slave villages disappeared in June 1906 without a trace.[25] In March 1907, slaves were coming "by the hundreds" to the post at Segu and by the end of June, 5,331 passes had been issued.[26] In May 1907, 400 sought passes at Bafulabe and others left without permission.[27] By spring of 1907, slaves were leaving Sokolo, Sikasso, Kita, Kury and Gao.[28] In January 1908, many Soninke slaves at Gumbu indicated they would leave as soon as their crop was in. By March, *rimaibe* were also leaving.[29]

The cercle of Kury (now Dafina in Burkina Faso), and much of what is now northern Burkina Faso and southern Mali, was populated largely by peoples with no state or diffuse state structures. They were preyed upon by stronger states that surrounded them.[30] Starting around 1905, many of those retained in the region simply picked up and headed back to Bwa, Samo and Marka villages. Most did not have far to go. They were joined by slaves returning from Sikasso, Segu and Masina.[31] Slave departures were also reported in Matam, Podor, Dori, Sokolo, Nioro, Jenne and Kayes.[32] By 1910, there were slave departures even in isolated desert posts like Bamba and Bilma.[33] Most movements took place over two to three years, though not the same two or three years everywhere. They continued into 1911 and 1912 and seem to have drawn to a close only with the famines of 1912–14.

In the Ivory Coast, Lt. Governor F. J. Clozel responded cautiously to the 1905 decree, but in June 1907, on a tour of northern cercles, he announced that slaves no longer had to redeem themselves. In two years, an estimated 40,000 slaves went home, many only recently enslaved in Samori's last wars. The movement continued until 1912.[34] It also spread into upper Guinea, where slaves left Kurusa and Dingiray from 1907. By 1908, Dingiray reported that most war captives had left and only those born to slavery or enslaved young remained.[35] From 1907 to 1911, there were constant reports of master–slave conflicts and of departures from Kurusa, particularly from the Muslim province of Oulada. One commandant tried to keep freed slaves within the province to meet demands for labor, but with little success. Tensions in Oulada were attributed to a harsh labor regime.[36] Many also left coastal cercles, Rio Pongo and Rio Nunez in 1907 and Mellacorée in 1908.[37]

All Futa Jallon cercles reported departures, particularly along the line of the railway.[38] At Timbo in 1907, it was said that "their servants are beginning to no longer obey them and from some places a very strong movement of emigration has developed to return to the country of origin, toward the cercles of Kankan, Wasulu, the upper Ivory Coast . . . I fear that we can do little to stop this disintegration because we consider these people free."[39] From Timbo, there were a few statistics: 199 identity papers in March 1908 and 279 departures in May 1908, then, in 1910, groups of over 500.[40] At Tuba, departures were estimated at between 4,800 and 8,000.[41] By contrast, Faranah was a cercle to which slaves fled. By 1910, three quarters of the population there were returnees.[42]

Departures even took place in recently conquered areas east of the Niger. Though many commandants were unhappy, slaves were authorized to leave in 1906 and 1907 and many did so.[43] Those who remembered earlier homes headed south, mostly to Mossi and Gurunsi areas. Others sought jobs with the French or as they learned of opportunities elsewhere. Archival sources are less rich than for the old colonies, but it seems the same pattern. Rothiot cites no statistics, but his informants suggest that those who remembered an earlier home returned to it. Those born or raised in slavery tended to stay. Slaves of the wealthy and powerful were more likely to stay than those owned by small households.[44] One of Olivier de Sardan's slave informants explains: "Some knew the village they came from; only force kept them. One day, those people got ready, some indicated they were going, others who were still afraid of slavery slipped away during the night. But no one pursued them. It was thus until all had left their masters."[45] Force was used, but slaves learned that they could complain to the authorities. As further west, emancipation was also a way of undercutting chiefs who resisted or might resist the French.

The archives contain less information about departures from Senegal. In 1911, the Commandant at Kaedi reported emigration of Bambara slaves because of "uneasiness experienced within the Tokolor and Soninke environment."[46] There were also departures from cercles in the middle and upper river, but probably not as many as in the Sudan.[47] Migration from the peanut basin was strung out over a longer period of time and was moderated by economic growth, which created an incentive for slaves to remain within the growing peanut economy. In Chapter 12, we will look at oral sources on processes of change in the Peanut Basin.

Strategies of slaves and masters

Most slaves seeking passes in Guinea and Haut-Sénégal-Niger did so in groups. The smallest were family groups, the largest a group of about 1,800 slaves who showed up on the same day in Kankan in 1911. In 1910, the chief of a *rundé* led a group of 585 from Timbo.[48] They moved throughout the year, but mostly between the end of the harvest and the planting of a new crop. Slaves took with them only what they could carry. Migrations were heaviest from the sahel, but they took place all over. Masters often tried to block departures and, if they could not prevent slaves from leaving, tried to keep their children. In a village near Kita, there was an armed conflict before 165 slaves were allowed to leave.[49] At Issa-Ber in the northern delta, there were three murders and a sequestration in 1911, all involving conflict over children. Sometimes, guards were sent with slave women looking for their children.[50] At heated meetings, slave-owners were often told they would be punished if they used violence.[51] At Gumbu, masters were prepared to use arms, but slaves showed up in village units and often with their own arms.[52] We can only guess how much coercion took place without the commandant knowing, or where he did not wish to know. Catholic missionaries, writing from isolated stations, often refer to violence.[53] The colonial state could not protect slaves in distant villages even when it wanted to do so. Saurin's reports on Sokolo and Issa-Ber suggest that some administrators in lonely posts kept their eyes closed.[54] Many masters had help from clerks and interpreters, themselves often slave-owners, in covering up their actions.[55]

Slaves who had been distributed to soldiers, chiefs and agents also picked up and left. Thus, at Bafulabe there was a village, where retired *tirailleurs* settled, each with a number of wives. From 1906, women began leaving "their husband-master" to return home. Some of the men then took their families to areas where it would be easier to control their women.[56] The French had to decide at what point a master's authority over a woman who bore his children became a husband's authority. A 1903 study suggested that "liberty papers given to a female slave can have no effect on the matrimonial union and can have no implication for recognition or the disavowal of the rights of the husband." This was probably the basis of Ponty's Circular of 25 June 1906, which held that paternal and marital authority were not slavery.[57] Key personnel could count on administration support. Thus, in July 1907, slaves of the interpreter at Kita asked for their freedom and were turned down. Samba, the interpreter, then locked up their children. The mission got involved when many of the slaves sought refuge with them. In September, the men were freed, but their wives and children remained at Samba's. Finally, in February 1908, the wives and children were freed after two men went to Kayes to plead for them. The commandant would probably have supported Samba if not for the presence of the mission.[58]

Tirailleurs often also spent time looking for lost family members and many returned to earlier homes. Thus, in 1911, an artilleryman named Bakary Traore wrote the Governor-General enquiring about his father, mother and sister still in slavery. Traore was a good soldier, so the administration tracked down his former master, who said he never had a slave named Bakary Traore. He had two runaways, one twenty-five years earlier, a second, named Ousman Dembelé, about eight years earlier. He assumed that Dembelé and Traore were one and the same and suggested that Dembelé's family was free to go where they wished.[59] They were, however, only one of many groups trying to find relatives. In Sikasso, for example, there were reports of people coming with passes to look for "relatives separated from them by slavery."[60] What is most remarkable is that information networks stretched hundreds of miles across cultural zones. Returning slaves brought news of other family members, often old, sometimes less courageous, who remained in slavery. In Senegal, relatives were tracked down in different parts of Senegal or in Mauritania.[61] Oral sources also speak of people walking back to the Sahel or to Senegal to find long-lost kin. People also went with passes to places where they were in slavery to look for children and spouses from whom they were separated.[62] Sometimes there was a kind of exchange. One Senegalese informant said that his father went to Mauritania to find a sister in slavery there, while his uncle had a female slave from Jolof, whose relatives came to get her.[63]

The French gave the go-ahead, but almost no help except liberty villages, which were used by returning slaves. The Resident at Yelimané wrote that many inhabitants intended to leave, but wanted to accumulate some resources first.[64] Near Bakel, several former *villages de culture* served as refuges for fleeing Tokolor and Soninke slaves. They had a high turnover because freed slaves often stayed only until they saved enough for the trip home or found something more interesting.[65] In other cases, men parked their women and children in a liberty village and went home. During the exodus, entries and departures were much in excess of the number actually in the village. Furthermore, they were mostly women and children, many of whom left during the third quarter, the growing season. Thus in the third quarter of 1907, two thirds of the population of the liberty village at Buguni left.[66] See Table 10.2. The "parking" is clearest in Buguni, but many liberty villages show a significant increase in population between 1905 and 1908 with a lot of entries and departures. Patterns, however, varied. Kayes increased from 937 in 1906 to 1,403 in 1909, but only in 1908 were there more than 300 departures.[67] Sikasso's village never had as much activity as Buguni's, but population gradually grew to 365, then, in 1907, 308 left.[68] Bandiagara, Issa-Ber, Kita, and Nioro also had a high flow-through.[69]

Many freed slaves heading home got diverted. Pressed by hunger and uncertainty, some sought work or other arrangements on the way. There was work in the cities, on the railroad and in the peanut fields of Senegal. Equally important, administrators tried to maintain their tax rolls and in desert-side cercles to keep a physical presence. In Gumbu, many *rimaibe* were persuaded to remain in the cercle. In Nioro too, many freed slaves broke with their masters, but remained within the cercle.[70] In Segu, almost 40 percent of those

Box 10.1

The village chief of our little village is overflowing with joy. Think of this: Not long ago, he had a nice little girl by the name of Dana. Dana was taken prisoner and led rather far from here, to a village on the Niger, not far from Bamako. Today, she returned to him big and strong. She escaped and fled back to her father. The abolition of slavery has been proclaimed in the Sudan. Everyone is free. Any person held chained in servitude can now break those chains, do what he wishes, go where he wishes and his master can do nothing. Dana has profited from this beneficent law and like many others, has returned to the ancestral hearth.*

*Diaire, Segu, 13 April 1907, AWF.

Table 10.2. *Entries and departures, liberty village, Buguni and Issa-Ber*

	Men	Women	Children	Entries	Departures
Buguni					
1902	14	9	2	27	81
1903	34	15	6	122	78
1904	22	13	5	60	140
1905	54	20	12	85	39
1906	30	27	16	101	120
1907	14	26	31	306	308
1908	0	10	4	251	298
1909	4	18	5	85	72

1902: Data is for two quarters. In June, village was down to 12.
1904: Data is for two quarters. 77 left in village in the third quarter.
1906: 98 leave third quarter.
1907: 104 arrivals second quarter; 215 departures third quarter.
1908: Activity mostly first two quarters, 195 entries, 256 departures. Report notes that many come only to be fed and find family.
1909: Briefly empty at end of March. No entries after 1909.

	Men	Women	Children	Entries	Departures
Issa-Ber					
1906	127	111	73	74	9
1907	154	155	74	331	64
1908	120	150	62	332	368
1909	188	221	66	305	277
1910	166	197	58	61	132

Source: ANM, 1 E133

who sought passes during 1907 remained within the cercle.[71] In Kita, many slaves simply moved permanently to their rainy-season sites.[72] In Sokolo, Niafunke and Gumbu, former slaves moved out of desert-edge cantons to settle in better-watered and commercially active riverine areas. In Sokolo, population in riverine cantons increased by 73 percent between 1900 and 1910, while the desert-edge cantons declined by 44 percent.[73]

Ponty's role

Throughout this period, Ponty regularly insisted that slaves were free and that freedom involved the right to go wherever they wished. In 1907, when the commandant at Segu wrote of his fears of economic decline, Ponty responded that the Banamba experience did not justify such fears. Not only did things go well there, but a free labor market held a bright promise:

... the happiest result of this exodus of servants will certainly be to definitively establish the principal of individual liberty in the region as a necessary principle . . . The population will quickly perceive by the results obtained that free labor is much more productive, and that this increase in production will largely compensate for the increase in expenses caused by the payment of salaries. Supply and demand will come as a result to naturally regulate the condition of work. These freely discussed conditions will be regulated by contracts . . . and the economic evolution of the colony will have taken a large step forward.[74]

In letter after letter to local commandants, Ponty hammered home both their legal obligations and the colony's economic interest. When the commandant in Gumbu worried about depopulation desert-side, Ponty insisted that his first obligation was personal liberty and warned him not to impose Fulbe chiefs on *rimaibe*.[75] Ponty clearly realized that commandants had to be reminded of their obligations. Thus, in late 1906, he sent out a circular criticizing the hesitant pursuit of the slave trade and the failure to use the full range of sanctions.[76]

If letters to administrators urged action, letters from Ponty and Roume to their superiors stressed the orderliness and calm of the migration, the resignation of masters and the eagerness of former slaves to work for themselves. Political reports went from cercle to colony, where they were merged into an edited synthesis, then to Dakar, where the same process took place. Ponty edited carefully, sometimes using the language of the local administrator, some times recasting information in his own words.[77] When the migration seemed over, Ponty treated the issue as one that had been resolved, often claiming more than he had actually accomplished. Thus in 1913, he wrote the Minister:

Slavery is neither abolished under law nor tolerated in fact. There are no longer either servants or slaves. Every man is recognized as free in practice and in theory. The prudent, but continuous application of this principle has given the best results. In many milieux, it was believed and repeated that the abolition of slavery would inevitably provoke a dangerous social and economic crisis. We have proceeded quietly, without making a stir, without proclamations. The slave has left his master quietly. He left simply, without fleeing, but he has not taken a step backward. Often, he has remained, but under the conditions of a contract. Liberty suddenly given or refound has in no way embarrassed him. He returned quietly to his homeland or has gone to offer his labor in our cities or our workshops.[78]

If slavery no longer existed, liberty villages were redundant. If everyone was free, "there is no longer any reason to maintain the vestiges of an organisation which might suggest the survival of a social status henceforth abolished."[79] When the railroad was completed in 1904, the French no longer needed the "captifs du commandant." In Sudan, more than a dozen liberty villages were created between 1905 and 1908, but only so they could be used as refuges for former captives who might become vagabonds. Other villages, primarily in older cercles, were to become ordinary tax-paying villages.[80] Then, one by one, just after their most active period, the villages lost their separate status. The last entries at Buguni were in 1909. By 1911, there seem to have been no more functioning liberty villages. Some disappeared. Many lost population. Others continued to exist as ordinary villages or as quarters in growing administrative centers like Bakel. Many kept names that indicated their origins: Françaiscouta near Bafulabe, Nioro-Refuge and Sokolo-Refuge, among others.

Bouche treats liberty villages as failures.[81] She argues that their greatest contribution was that labor of the commandant's slaves built roads and railroads, and church villages launched small Christian communities. It is true that they were rarely humanitarian institutions and did not last, but they provided labor that the conquerors wanted and options for slaves, who used the villages throughout their history, but never more than in the last brief, but active period of their lives. The flight from the liberty villages was not a sign of their failure but, from the slave's point of view, of their success.

In 1908, Colonial Minister Millies-Lacroix wrote asking if it were time to eliminate domestic slavery.[82] This dispatch pushed Ponty to decree that all labor was free and remunerated, that non-free labor was prohibited and that acts likely to prevent free exercise of the worker's freedom were prohibited. Ponty also encouraged labor contracts and in an accompanying letter raised the question of a registry office, which would give each individual a civic identity.[83] Later in the year, he used the opening of the Government Council to claim that "the exodus of former slaves toward their native land has taken place with calm and without the slightest incident. The principle of individual liberty having been put above discussion, former masters were at first discon-certed, but have accepted the new state of things. Thus a new class of free and salaried workers has been created."[84] Ponty's ideas were echoed by many senior officials. Clozel, his successor in Haut-Sénégal-Niger, reported in 1909 that the movement of emancipation "is almost finished without ever resulting in political and economic disruption that was feared; to the contrary they contributed to the equilibrium of productive forces in the colony."[85]

In spite of this, many commandants were reluctant to enforce the new policies. Contempt for slaves persisted. According to the commandant in Bafulabe, many slaves only left because of the "spirit of imitation"; the movement was caused by agitators "hoping to procure servants on the cheap."[86] Brocard in Haute Gambie thought it wrong "to destroy in a single blow fortunes sometimes painfully accumulated at a time when the slave was

Table 10.3. *Tax rolls, residence of Banamba*

1907 – 44,844
1908 – 44,844
1908 – 32,329
1909 – 38,638
1910 – 39,366

Table 10.4. *Tax rolls, canton of Ganadugu, cercle of Sikasso*

1899 – 4,842
1902 – 5,551
1905 – 23,256
1907 – 29,836

the only form of capital possible." He wanted to go back to slaves buying their freedom.[87] Rocaché, in defending his record at Issa-Ber against Saurin's criticism, explained that he wanted to return freed slaves to former villages.[88] Perhaps the best measure of zeal was the number of prosecutions on slave matters. Thus, during the second quarter of 1906, only six of ninety-five cases heard at Bandiagara involved sale or purchase of slaves. In Nioro only one of thirty-three involved slavery, and in Bobo-Diulasso, Kutiala and Kury, there was none.[89] Inspectors often checked court registers to test an administrator's commitment.

Reports from Banamba supported Ponty's position. Tax rolls dropped by over 12,000, but then immediately started to rise again.[90] Though Maraka saw much of their capital wiped out and their living standards reduced, results were not as disastrous as many administrators predicted. Many Maraka and their families were forced to do agricultural labor, but they also turned to free labor, sometimes former slaves, sometimes Koranic students, sometimes Bambara work groups, which provided services to Maraka in exchange for money or goods. The existence of work groups suggests that within Bambara villages slave labor never fully replaced traditional modes of labor organization.[91] Production dropped, but not drastically, and taxes were paid.[92] Many Maraka moved from towns to agricultural villages, and by 1909, there are reports of houses in ruins.[93]

There was also a drop in trade licenses from 14,611 in 1903 to 3,541 in 1909, but this began before the exodus and had other causes. Banamba's importance declined with the end of the slave trade and completion of the railroad, though it remained the center of the salt trade and a productive agricultural area. Many traders moved elsewhere and the town took on a more limited role.[94] A 1914 report suggested that this retreat to the countryside involved a decline in the intensity of Islam as children were sent into the fields instead of to school. From 1909 to 1914, the number of schools dropped from 58 to 47 and the number of Koranic students from 608 to 337.[95] This was a temporary phenomenon. The Maraka have remained strongly Muslim and may have used Islam to maintain their economic position. They probably played a key role in the proselytism in the Sudan at this time. In the long run, they did well, because of both their commercial skills and their learning. Most reports treat Banamba as a success. The 1910 annual report claimed with a bit of exaggeration that "every trace of personal constraint or of servile labor has completely disappeared."[96] Results elsewhere reinforced Ponty's position. Saurin also cited Segu as a success. In 1907 and 1908, over 10,000 passes were issued and many left without passes. In spite of this, taxes were paid without difficulty from 1907 to 1909 and reported population actually increased, perhaps because Segu also received returnees, perhaps because counting became more rigorous.[97]

How many?

We can only estimate the number of slaves who left. Most commandants made only qualitative statements such as the report "of increasingly large numbers of former servants returning to their country of origin."[98] In the old cercles of Kita and Bafulabe, the exodus involved as much as half of the population of many villages.[99] At Bakel, it was simply: "Numerous servants are leaving their masters and present themselves at the Residence."[100] Only for Gumbu is there a detailed report on passes issued and where the slaves said they were going. For a few others, there are data on a limited period. From Segu, over 10,000 had left by April 1908 from a slave population estimated at 25,100 four years earlier. Even these numbers are suspect. Many slaves left without seeking passes, an estimated 2,000 from Segu, probably more from Banamba. About 2,300 requested passes at Kita during 1908 and 1909, but the commandant estimated that 4,000 left without passes.[101] But on this, the commandant could only guess. With commandants coming and going, many did not know their districts well enough to make an educated guess. In 1910, the Governor of Sierra Leone, faced with claims from chiefs whose slaves were fleeing into French territories, asked for information. In his response, Ponty claimed that more than 500,000 slaves had left their masters in Haut-Sénégal-Niger and returned home. He claimed similar results without giving statistics for Senegal, Guinea and Dahomey.[102]

Another source of information is the head counts done for taxation purposes. There are two problems here. First, there was a tendency for counts to go up. Early censuses were often based on "eyeballing." Over 12,000 slaves left Banamba, but the head count dropped from 1905 to 1913 by only 3,800. Second, epidemics and other population movements shaped these figures. People were moving to Bamako, Kayes, and line-of-rail towns. Finally, slaves were significantly undercounted. The best measure of this was in Brevié's response to the 1904 slave questionnaire in Bamako. Brevié was the only administrator who clearly talked to slaves, and the results were startling. At Banamba, masters said they had 300 slaves, slaves said 1,500. At Tuba,

Table 10.5. *Registered slave departures*

Segu	1907 & 1908	Over 10,000
Gumbu	1908	2,956
	1909	2,598
	1910	703
	1911	240
TOTAL		6,497
Kita	1908	849
	1909	1,438 (plus an estimated 4,000 unregistered departures)
	1910	575 (first 5 months)
Kayes	1908	398
	1909	39 (Jan. and March only)
	1910	262 (April, May and June)

Sources: For Gumbu, ANM 1 E 38 & 39

Table 10.6. *Selected census data, 1905 and 1913*

Cercles	1905	1913
Sahel		
Kayes	71,421	74,691
Bafulabe	65,273	60,811
Kita	56,624	46,633
Nioro	114,228	122,166
Gumbu	66,947	63,117
Sokolo	34,770	44,717
Gao	46,011	34,703
Southern Sudan		
Buguni	95,592	162,343
Ouahigouya	92,566	310,000
Sikasso	164,410	223,719
Bobo-Dioulasso	236,000	270,000
Kury	224,266	322,083
Others		
Segu	140,610	206,869
Jenne	69,635	100,953
Bandiagara	197,870	268,060

masters said 500 and slaves 6,000 to 7,000. At Kiba, masters said 500 and slaves 6,000.[103] Table 10.6 shows a general decline in population in the sahel cercles. Bafulabe dropped almost 9,000 in a single year. Karta-Binné lost more than 40 percent of its population in a single year.[104] In 1908, Kayes lost 3,000, Nioro 1,000, but Gumbu only 500. During the same year, some southern cercles added much larger numbers – 19,000 in Sikasso, 14,000 in Buguni, 12,000 in Kutiala.[105] Some southern cercles lost and some gained. In Kutiala

Table 10.7. *Destinations of returning slaves*

From Gumbu, 1908–11*		
TO: Buguni	2,887	44.4%
Sikasso	856	13.2
Bamako	459	7.1
Jenne	267	4.1
Segu	271	4.2
TOTAL:	6,497	
From Kita:		
TO: Buguni	87	34.5
Guinea, Ivory Coast	102	40.5
From Bamako, April 1908		
TO: Buguni	95	89.6
TOTAL:	106	
From Kayes:		
Buguni	39	33.3
Sikasso	32	27.4
TOTAL:	117	
From Agades:**		
Buguni	58	65.2
TOTAL	89	
From Médine-Residence†		
Buguni	69	24.7
Korko	52	19.6
Sikasso	45	16.1
Bobo-Diulasso	20	7.2
Kutiala	12	4.3

*ANM 1 E 38 & 39.
**From two quarterly reports, 1909 and 1911, ANM 119.
†ANM, 1 E 134. These are departures from the liberty village. The list shows a greater diversity of destinations than the others.

and Kury, where there were islands of slave-holding Fulbe in a sea of stateless peoples, several thousand *rimaibe* had left by the end of 1908, but even larger numbers of Bobo returned.[106] In Sikasso, cantons with large slave holdings lost, while others gained.

Buguni was the largest gainer. Over 40 percent of those leaving Gumbu gave Buguni as their destination. A census taken of eight cantons in 1906 showed a 61 percent increase in population. Almost 80 percent of those leaving Gumbu were heading to the area ravaged by Samori and Tyeba – Buguni, Sikasso, the northern Ivory Coast and eastern Guinea.[107] If the net increase over the whole period was not as great as departures from the sahel would suggest, it was for several reasons. Returning slaves said that they wanted to go to Wasulu and most did, but many went elsewhere, to Guinean Wasulu or into Bamako and the railroad towns.

Ponty's estimate seems high, especially since the exodus was not over, but if I am right that there were over a million slaves in Haut-Sénégal-Niger, it is within the realm of possibility. The percentage leaving was certainly higher in the Sudan than in Guinea. In Senegal, emancipation was stretched out over a longer period of time and is harder to estimate. My own guess is that about a third of the slaves in Senegal and Guinea left their masters.[108] If that is true, we can probably talk about 800,000 to 900,000 slaves from the three colonies leaving their masters in the period between 1905 and 1913. If Ponty's figure was inflated, the real numbers would probably be somewhere between 650,000 and 800,000. The number for French West Africa was probably over a million.

Role of the missions

One of the great ironies of the process is that the one community in French West Africa concerned about slaves was totally immobilized while slaves were being freed. Between 1899 and 1905, a series of laws removed all links between state and Church in France. Overnight, the administration moved from aid and support to hostility and persecution. Local commandants charged the missions with treating their converts as slaves, especially when children were moved from one mission to another. Missions could no longer purchase children or take in orphans.[109] Subsidies given to Catholic missions were suppressed, nuns were dismissed from hospitals, and orphans paid for by the state were removed from Church-run orphanages.[110] The hard-pressed colonial state set up secular orphanages and schools and recruited civilian staff, who were usually more expensive and less qualified than Church personnel. Soldiers were pressed into service as nurses. The mission was denied the right to move into areas further south at the very moment when many of its converts were heading back to those areas.

The mission and its converts also suffered harassment which was often petty, and in one case perverted. The mission at Kupela in what is now Burkina Faso was founded in January 1900 and had instant success, especially among younger people anxious to free themselves from control of the elders. The Naba resented this and in December 1904, after a visit to Lt. Goguely, the Commandant at Tenkodogo, pulled his sisters out of the mission and began to harass converts. Goguely insisted that parents had the right to control their children. Father Menet responded that most were adults. Converts were beaten, placed in irons, forced to take part in rituals they had rejected. The Naba's men came to get former slaves, claiming them as children. Converts continued to come to the mission, some of them after being held for a while in chains. Finally, in June, Lt. Goguely came to interview children who came to catechism class. With his pants undone and his penis exposed, he asked the girls about their sexual activities and particularly whether they had relations with the priests. He ran his hands over their breasts and other parts of their bodies. One of the girls was called to Tenkodogo, where her persistent refusal of the lieutenant's suit apparently quelled his ardour and she was sent home without being raped. Eventually, Father Menet was told to yield to the Naba and after some negotiations, catechism classes resumed in November 1905. There was still some harassment. Thus, in 1907, another commandant, Carrier came through, asked for some girls "to refresh his august person," and was provided by the Naba with several of his Christian sisters.[111]

Runaway slaves were often caught in the middle of the Church–State conflict. Thus, in the spring of 1904 a young slave named Bedari and his wife ran away because Bedari's master planned to sell him. They took refuge at the mission's Banankuru liberty village, where Bedari's father lived. Though liberty papers had been suppressed and Ponty insisted that slaves were free, the missionaries sent Bedari with a note to Segu because they were nervous about constant visits from Bedari's master. The commandant insisted that he and his wife come to the official liberty village in Segu, this though they had already planted fields at Banankuru. When Bedari and his wife did not show up, the Commandant came to Banankuru to insist that they do so. They went to the Segu liberty village, but fled several weeks later.[112]

Thus, at the very moment when slavery was becoming undone, missions lacked the resources to feed extra people. They could only help small numbers of slaves, mostly those who were already part of their community. Thus in June 1905, the mission at Kita arranged for redemption of the sister of a woman in the liberty village, and later the same year, for redemption of a female slave by a man who wanted to marry her.[113] Redemption should not have been necessary in 1905, but local administrators often ignored policy directives and masters made constant efforts to retake runaways. Slaves did turn to the missions for help, but the numbers seem small. The Diaries of various missions report a slave here and a slave there, sometimes relatives of earlier converts, but there is no evidence of large numbers showing up at the mission door, nothing remotely equivalent to the numbers who passed through the state's liberty villages. During the period when thousands were leaving Segu, only about a dozen turned for help to the mission at Banankuru.[114] Furthermore, there is little evidence that large numbers were turned away. Thus in early 1909: "A large number of slaves have freed themselves during the last year. Many of them would have willingly come to settle near us if they had not seen that our people were the object of so much petty harassment."[115] In Timbuktu, the reaction was even stronger:

The Timbuktu Fathers have tried to intervene in the liberation of several slaves who asked for their protection. It seems, however, that in high places involvement of Missionaries in civil affairs is seen with mistrust. It has been impossible to bring about any liberation . . . As a consequence, it is in the interest of these persons that we have nothing to do with any claim they make at the Cercle.[116]

These dilemmas were exacerbated by intermittent famines. A particularly severe famine took place in 1908 in what is now Burkina Faso. Children were sold or pawned and thousands of people died of starvation. The administration was very insensitive, demanding payment of taxes while people had

> *Box 10.2*
> In 1906, two slave converts from Bendugu near Kita were married
> by their catechist in the chapel. Some time after, the man was to be
> returned to a previous master. Threatened with separation, the
> man went to the authorities, had himself declared free and settled
> at the mission, waiting for his wife to join him. The master,
> however, turned her over to another male slave. She eventually
> succeeded in running away and joining her husband. The master
> came to the mission several times to plead for her return, but the
> missionaries refused, saying that slavery was no longer recognized
> by law. They even offered to pay her brideprice, usually quite small
> in the case of slaves, but he refused and took the case to the native
> tribunal. She was declared free, but her husband was condemned
> to several months in prison for reasons the missionaries did not
> understand.*
>
> *Chroniques*, Kita, 146, Feb. 1908, AWF.

nothing to eat, but the missions could do little by themselves.[117] In the past,
missions took pawns, but in the changed climate after 1905 they were reluctant to do so. At Ouagadougou in 1908, people were trying to live off roots. In
many villages, fifty to sixty people died.[118] Famine struck a broader area with
even more disastrous consequences during the years just before World War I.
Missionary views on slavery also created problems with host communities,
many of whom were openly hostile to the missions. Every time a convert or a
badly beaten slave took refuge at the mission, the missionaries had to deal
with angry elders. In 1907 the mission at Patyana was warned by the Vicar
Apostolic that they possessed no land of their own and they were dependent
on the villagers. By receiving slaves, they were exposing themselves to
danger.[119] These tensions were exacerbated by missionary opposition to
circumcision and forced marriage.[120]
  Clozel was less hostile to the missions than Ponty was, and by 1912, the
mission was expanding again and able to shift resources into areas where
there was some promise of conversion. By this time, the slavery issue was no
longer important to them. With the end of warfare, there was no longer any
need for refuges or for orphanages for slave children. Many of the slave
converts had returned to homes further south. The missions increasingly
turned inward, concerned to nurture and expand small Christian communities. They looked to the expansion of those communities rather than growth
through redeemed slaves. Slavery remained important in much of the Sudan,
but mission concern increasingly moved to the family and the status of
women, which was articulated in anti-slavery terms.[121]

Box 10.3

A slave named Alla-ma-son was working for the mission for a month and decided he would like to stay with them. Knowing that Alla-ma-son wanted to escape, his master's son came for him, apparently with the intention of selling him. When the Superior of the mission said that Alla-ma-son had the right to stay if he wished, the son announced that he would never consent to discuss with a slave what he wished to do. The master had a reputation for being harsh to his slaves. According to Alla-ma-son, the master always carried a stick, which he often used to beat slaves. The next day, two elders came, and once again, when told that it was the slave's choice, they insisted that slaves had no choice. The master's son then proposed a redemption, which the mission refused. After about a week of this, the missionaries were awakened by a loud noise one morning and saw a group of young men dragging Alla-ma-son as if he were a piece of wood. The affair isolated the mission within the village, but eventually discretion won out, and the mission did not appeal to the commandant in Segu.*

*Diaire, Patyana, March 1907, AWF.

Conclusion

Jean Suret-Canale has argued that African slavery was not abolished for humanitarian reasons:

Patriarchal or domestic slavery, as practised in Africa, presented a serious obstacle to colonial exploitation. Under this system the master, in principle, did not work at all or very little, and the surplus labor of the slave did not so much provide him with additional luxury as relieve him of the need to work ... it was not a question of abolishing it to ease the fate of the slave, but rather of making them do more "work under the stimulus of self interest," which, in fact, was confused with necessity – to the advantage of the colonisers. As for the former slave masters, they were to be turned away from the "easy and lazy life," in other words, put to work under the same terms as their former slaves, and for the profit of the same colonisers.[122]

There is a certain truth to it. Slavery was a barrier to development and many saw it as such. Many were also pleased that former master and former slave had little choice but to work.

There are, however, several problems with Suret-Canale's argument. First, the administration was so nervous about order that it was hostile to anything that undermined authority. Roume wanted to extract the colonial state from its role as guarantor of slavery, but he did so for primarily political reasons and wanted as little change as possible within Africa. Second, though senior administration was sensitive to the demands of the French state and, by inference, of French capitalism, local administration was often hostile to industrial capitalism. Though they believed in the value of work, often as an end in itself, they also believed in hierarchy and property. That is to say, they believed that some should command and some should obey and they believed that people had a right to keep what they had accumulated, even property rights in other human beings. Finally, those who explained the success of the exodus in terms of the creation of a free labor market did so only after the fact, only when they had to rationalize a movement that was already taking place.

The exodus took place because slaves were willing to risk intimidation, hunger and hardship to return home or seek freedom elsewhere. Some writers have questioned whether slaves understood the concept of freedom. For the vast majority, freedom in whatever language they used meant in very concrete terms the right to work for themselves and to control their family life.

11   French fears and the limits to
an emancipation policy

> When the white man entered this land, they called a meeting of the Fulbe and the slaves and said that from that day slavery was over. They asked the Fulbe if they were satisfied with this. The Fulbe answered yes without any opposition to the colonial rulers who had the power. A scholar in the crowd walked to the middle of the circle and said: "You, Fulbe gathered here, listen to me. Keep this in mind. From today, you are like orphans. You have no slaves any more. Your only slaves are your cows. Take care of them like members of your family." Those who had land were saved from the humiliation of [farming] and working the land. The ones who did not own cattle became farmers. This is how some families became farmers.
>
> Amadu, a shepherd from Konna (Masina)[1]

The commitment of Ponty and other senior administrators to personal freedom had its limits and these became evident in the first years of the new regime. The return to earlier homes was very orderly, as Ponty repeatedly assured all who would listen, and the effect of emancipation was to free the energies of slaves for other kinds of productive activity. In spite of this, most administrators were cautious about freedom and believed in the necessity of both coercion and hierarchy. We see this in the way they responded to a crisis in fertile Masina and in hesitant efforts to force Guinea to catch up with Senegal and Sudan. The history of events in Guinea teaches us to beware of colonial documents for French officials there constantly assured superiors that something had been done until the next crisis came along and made clear that it had not been done.

The idea of contract

Frederick Cooper has suggested that a major debate took place in East Africa over the transition from slave labor to free labor:

To some abolishing the legal status of slavery was enough: deprived of court enforceable powers to engage in transactions in human property and of the shield ownership rights provided to arbitrary punishment, slaveowners would lose their power over a captive labor force and free labor would emerge as a consequence . . . Others, less optimistic about the transforming power of ex-slaves merely having the right to sell their own services, worried that the freed men might find it necessary to do so.[2]

In French West Africa, the debate was over whether to try to maintain some kind of servitude. Opposition to Ponty, prevalent in lower ranks of the administration, would have maintained servile ties under another name. Ponty and those around him articulated a belief that freedom would provide its own answer, but they were unsure about consequences of the exodus and sought in contracts a way of guaranteeing the labor of the former slaves. In this, their experience mirrored that of diverse British colonies that sought by Master and Servant laws to control the labor of recently freed slaves and invariably passed such laws soon after emancipation. These laws made it illegal for the ex-slave to contract for life or to commit members of his family, but within a short-term contract, they provided the master a great deal of control over the laborer.[3] Both French and British conservatives feared vagrancy, crime and disorder even more than they feared ex-slaves withdrawing from the market. These fears were not justified, though there was undoubtedly some vagrancy and theft. Implicit in the debate was a belief that order depended on authority, that human beings were inherently lazy and improvident and that without a well-defined hierarchy, the social order would crumble.

For the French, the key word was contract. Talk of contract began early. It was discussed in the 1894 slavery inquiry in the Sudan and was a popular theme in the 1904 inquiry. In 1906, as slaves were beginning to wend their way home, Governor-General Roume brought in legislation providing for employers and workers to register formal contracts with the administration. The Banamba exodus seemed to convince Ponty that labor was flowing to areas where it was needed and that former slaves would be productive, but he must have had some doubts. Certainly from the moment he became Governor-General in 1908, he faced pressures from below toward a more conservative posture: fear of a decline in production in fertile Masina, fear of depopulation in the desert-side cercles, and fears of resistance and disorder in Guinea. When he addressed the Government Council in 1908, he treated the exodus as a boon to the economy, but he proposed negotiation of written contracts as a way to control labor and tie a "new class of free workers" to their masters.[4]

Between 1908 and World War I, there was much talk of contract, which invariably meant one kind of contract – *métayage* or sharecropping. The contract the *métayer* had with his employer was not seen as a new bondage, but as an affirmation of his freedom because he contracted his labor of his own free will. *Métayage* was legitimated by the fact that it existed in France, and therefore, could not be seen as servitude.[5] No question was asked about the options the former slave had, but while the French pursued formal contracts, former slaves and masters developed their own forms of contract, which emerged from a struggle over the labor of the ex-slaves.

Crisis in Masina

Before the Great Exodus was over, a crisis in Masina illustrated anxieties about slaves and the limits to William Ponty's commitment.[6] Masina was the "granary of the Sudan." Its importance lay in its rich surplus of both cattle and rice. During the wars of the late nineteenth century, many Fulbe retreated to safe areas further south. Others submitted to Tijani or Abidin, the Kunta chief.[7] Though many Fulbe lost slaves during the wars and some were enslaved, many preserved their holdings. With establishment of the French regime, authority in the inner delta was redistributed. The northern part was within the cercle of Issa Ber, Aguibou ruled part of the delta from Bandiagara, but the largest part was under the authority of the Amirou, heir to the title of Seku Amadu. The social order at this time was still based on Seku Amadu's settlement and involved large slave holdings and a sharp distinction between Fulbe, who were scholars, administrators or pastoralists, and *rimaibe*, who farmed. Some *rimaibe* seem to have fled Futanke masters to return to former Fulbe masters, perhaps to get access to the land.[8]

At the time of the Banamba exodus, slaves produced an agricultural surplus, some of which was sold, some of which fed herders, scholars and chiefs.[9] As long as the river rose during the flood season, Masina produced greater yields than rain-fed areas of the Sudan. Many *rimaibe* were long-time residents of the Delta. The *jamgal*, the major obligation of the *rimaibe* to their owners, was about 200 *sawal* (about 550 kg) per man and 100 *sawal* per woman.[10] In 1909, the administrator estimated this at about one third of the crop.[11] That was about twice the usual slave obligation in the Sudan, but Masina was fertile enough for *rimaibe* families to pay their dues, feed themselves and produce a surplus during good years.[12] In bad years, slave obligations were forgiven. In addition, *rimaibe* children worked for their masters – boys as herders and girls doing domestic labor for Fulbe women. During the dry season *rimaibe* repaired houses.

The French feared that a massive exodus would jeopardize the colony's grain and meat supplies. Some *rimaibe* fled, especially between 1906 and 1908, but most did not want to leave.[13] "Liberty for these people," Saurin wrote, "consists not in leaving a country which has become theirs, but in being freed from all personal servitudes which alienate them from their labor and their children."[14] For them, as for Maraka and Soninke *woloso*, living in separate communities was an advantage. Thus, Cissé writes that "spatial distance separating them from their masters allowed the development of a system which gave them a rather large margin of economic manoeuvre."[15] It also meant distinct decision-making and leadership structures. *Rimaibe* hostility to their obligations was indicated as early as 1903 when the Amirou complained that an agitator was encouraging slaves to leave their masters and reject his authority. *Rimaibe*, in turn, complained that they were being over-taxed.[16] By 1905 *rimaibe* were growing restless about the authority of traditional chiefs and some refused to pay the *jamgal*.[17] Tension was exacerbated by extension of land under cultivation and by increase in herd size.[18] Increased agricultural production reflects either *rimaibe* response to the market or a Fulbe effort to squeeze more surplus from them, or, more likely, both.[19] Resistance to Fulbe authority may have been stimulated by the return of about 200 former slaves from Gumbu and Sokolo.[20]

The Tenenkou compromise

By 1907, many *rimaibe* were refusing to pay the *jamgal* and wanted to throw off other obligations.[21] Throughout 1908, there were a number of meetings as the French sought to avert an exodus. The Fulbe tried to parry, even offering to renounce the *jamgal* if they could keep *rimaibe* children.[22] Shortly after this, at Tenenkou, the Amirou's capital, representatives of Fulbe and *rimaibe* agreed to suppress slavery, serfdom and all personal dues. *Rimaibe* were confirmed in rights to lands they occupied and to further lands as they needed them, but the Fulbe were accepted as landowners. The *jamgal*, a personal obligation, was replaced by a rent of one sixth of the harvest, about half of what they were paying. Proprietors were to be present at the harvest and the division of the crop. The sixth came to be called the *jégom*. Each woman was also to provide one child to serve the proprietor in exchange for his renunciation of her jegom and a 5,000 cowry payment for every child then in service. *Rimaibe* leaders insisted that a reduction by half of their obligations was a condition of their acceptance.[23]

The solution was thus the transformation of slavery to sharecropping.[24] Clozel approved the agreement, but suppressed two parts which implied continuation of servitude: the rights of masters to the labor of minor children and to the brideprice of *rimaibe* girls. He thus confirmed both that *rimaibe* were free in theory and that Fulbe owned the land. The French thought that they were introducing modern concepts of property because they thought the Fulbe had a nomadic attitude toward land. In fact, Fulbe elites were not nomads and had a clear conception of property. Land rights were based on conquest and, in particular, on distribution of land by Seku Amadu to those who served him. There was a land registry and those who received land had the right to dispose of it under Muslim law.[25] French law confirmed these rights. Faidherbe had set up procedures by which land could be granted in full property. Then, a 1906 decree made possible registration of land where there were no opposed rights.[26] Use rights of the *rimaibe* were not seen as opposable rights. The decree was clearly advantageous to those in authority within lineage, village and state. Fulbe landowners used registration to override use rights held by the *rimaibe*.[27]

The compromise breaks down

The *rimaibe* were at first enthusiastic about the accord. The Fulbe, however, were more interested in their slaves and unhappy that Clozel had suppressed two concessions made to them.[28] Furthermore, the agreement solved nothing. From the first, there were reports of Fulbe hostility and fear of a *rimaibe* effort "to free themselves entirely of the very harsh yoke of their former masters."[29] Some administrators had reservations about the agreement, which Saurin registered:

The administration concedes exclusive right of property over all land to the Fulbe, that is to say, to a minority that represents about $\frac{1}{4}$ of the population. We are consecrating a right based on conquest and it is questionable whether we want to dismiss claims of those who have occupied and worked the lands. In my opinion, the essential drawback is economic. When *rimaibe* and former masters no longer accommodate themselves to the proposed compromise, we will be faced with 8,000 proprietors incapable of cultivating their lands and 30,000 cultivators without land. The crisis will be more difficult to resolve because we have created unfavourable conditions by establishing a bad land regime. The goal of agrarian laws has always been to make land available to those who cultivate it . . . there must be an agrarian law which divides the lands; we must not render this impossible in advance by sacrificing to the lazy and unproductive Fulbe the mass off whom they have long lived.[30]

At the end of the year, a senior administrator was sent on a two-month tour. He reported that *rimaibe* frequently found themselves faced with demands for two sixths, one from the former master and one from the proprietor of the land, not always the same. The administrator wanted written contracts, but the Fulbe were opposed and the *rimaibe* were not interested. He asked chiefs to divide land between families, but *rimaibe* simply wanted an end to Fulbe hegemony.[31] This situation led to a shift in French attitudes. Before 1908, they identified with the Fulbe. From 1910, faced with Fulbe duplicity and increasing intransigence of the *rimaibe*, many commandants were convinced that it would be best to give land to the cultivator. The Resident at Mopti suggested that the administration deny Fulbe land rights: "The *jamgal* has disappeared. It is essential that some day the real obligation which succeeded it ceases to be the rule. What is a *dimajo* [singular of *rimaibe*] today? Not a captive as in the past, but a serf on the glebe, with a softened lot, to be sure."[32]

The unstable compromise meant that the administration had to deal with constant conflict. *Rimaibe* kept trying to reduce their obligations. When they owed the *jamgal*, the size of the harvest was irrelevant unless it was a disastrous year. It was a fixed amount. Now that it was a portion, masters watched the harvest and took part in the division, constantly claiming that they were not getting their full share. By 1912, many *rimaibe* simply refused to pay.[33] *Rimaibe* also became less submissive. In one case, a Pullo herder lost nineteen head of cattle which drowned after being chased off *rimaibe* lands.[34] The Fulbe were sullen and sought to sabotage the accord. When asked to provide labor for public works at Mopti, Fulbe responded that they were free men and did not work.[35] When recruitment for the French army began, only *rimaibe* were sent.[36] And when drought in the Sahel brought Tuareg herds down to Masina, one chief assigned a herd to *rimaibe* rice fields.[37] Administrators considered increasingly radical measures, most notably suppression of all dues or a flat-sum payment, but Bamako was no longer responsive.[38] During World War I the issue disappeared from reports and did not reappear. We must look to more recent studies to understand what happened. According to Salmana Cissé, *rimaibe* have tried up to the present to render null the pretensions of the former masters of the country. Former slave hamlets manage their space without taking into consideration traditional rights or actual preoccupations of Fulbe pastoralists. Part of this space is divided among families long settled on it, who use it as if they were true proprietors . . . Everything happens as if *rimaibe* were trying in practice to eliminate from the collective consciousness any idea of traditional control of their lands by a group other than themselves.[39]

Some *rimaibe* acquired land, but most remained sharecroppers. Population growth strengthened the power of the Fulbe. Both individually and collectively *rimaibe* had room to maneuver that they did not have earlier, but not much. They ran their own villages and negotiated their own marriages, but did not take part in larger political structures and were in a dependent position because they had no land. The Fulbe kept the land and though they still saw the *rimaibe* as property, they no longer had to feed them when they were in need. Continued dependence created an incentive for *rimaibe* to perpetuate traditional forms of behavior if they wanted to be able to call on Fulbe when in need.[40] They worked under sharecropping contracts that provided the landowner between a quarter and a half of the crop.[41] They gave gifts on festive occasions and paid a variety of dues of which the most important were *murgu*, a kind of head tax, and *jaka*.[42] The subservience of *rimaibe* was forced in other ways. Their young might be required to work the former master's fields. They addressed the former master as "abba" or father, sat in the back of the mosque, and were charged with tasks seen as unclean, for example, cutting up a slaughtered sheep.[43]

Kampo's interviews in Masina confirm Cissé's picture of an incomplete liberation, but the masters still have a sense of what they have lost. One informant suggested that "very few slaves maintain good relations with their former masters. Those who do so assist in social rites like weddings and naming ceremonies that take part at the master's house. But even with these new relations, the master cannot exploit the slave, use him for other ends, or inherit his property."[44] In general, interviews suggest a lot of regional and individual variation with the crucial question that of wealth. Some Fulbe without dependants have been reduced to farming for themselves. *Rimaibe* with land and income show no deference. Where *rimaibe* are poor and landowners rich, the *rimaibe* show great deference. The crucial question is land. The rent the *rimaibe* pay is still called *jamgal*, which underlines that Fulbe still see the *rimaibe* as slaves.

Cissé argues that there was a continuous process in Masina that began when slaves became too numerous to remain part of the family.[45] It continued with transformation from control of persons to control of land, which involved the "depaternalization" of the relationship. *Rimaibe* gained a "margin of maneuver" and some control over work and family life, but they remained dependent.[46] There were contracts, but as in the East African case studied by Cooper, they were not contracts dependent on colonial authority, except to the degree that the government confirmed Fulbe control of the land. In 1935, the commandant reported that slavery was gone, but all of the land belonged to the Fulbe. Instead of personal dues, the *rimaibe* were paying rent.[47]

Sharecropping in the Sahel

French policy-makers quickly convinced themselves that sharecropping was particularly appropriate to Fulbe–*rimaibe* conflict. Colonial regimes often thought in ethnic terms. What worked for one group of Fulbe would presumably work for another. The Fulbe did have a few things in common. The quest for pasture led them to spread out from Senegal to the Cameroons and their slaves were usually physically distinct agriculturalists. But within these broad parameters, there were radical differences. They could establish sharecropping in Masina because there was a high population density, Fulbe control of the land, and a high yield for flood-plain rice. Most *rimaibe* did not want to leave.

The idea did not work elsewhere. An administrator in Koury proposed a tour "to demonstrate to Fulbe the advantages they could take from paid individual labor guaranteed by contract . . . in which conditions of work are freely discussed and determined in the presence of the administrator."[48] The idea failed. Unlike Masina, most Koury *rimaibe* were recently enslaved and came from nearby Samo or Bobo districts. Their places of origin were not so distant that they could not find their way back. Contracts might have appealed to Fulbe, but not to slaves. The administration was also concerned to establish sharecropping in the Sahel, where emigration was massive. Slave-based production in the Sahel was linked more to exchange with Saharan nomads than with the French. The French were therefore not as concerned with trade or food supplies as with maintaining population in the desert-side areas. With conquest of the Sahara incomplete and control over desert tribes tenuous the French wanted people there to provide a base for policing the desert fringes. In the spring of 1908, after a tour of Masina, Clozel urged other administrators to apply "the solution I have indicated to the Administrator of Djenné to all cercles inhabited by Fulbe and *rimaibe* . . . that is to say, that custom grant the Fulbe control over agricultural lands and that *rimaibe* sanction this right by payment of annual rent."[49] Clozel wanted to reduce *rimaibe* obligations, but he also wanted to establish the Fulbe as landlords. He asked commandants to determine a fair rent, taking into account the yield of the land, and to arbitrate between masters and former slaves.

The reason why the French wanted to keep *rimaibe* in the Sahel was the very reason why it was impossible. The balance of power was different. With other slaves moving, it was impossible to keep *rimaibe* in the Sahel without coercion. Dry years simply added to the pressure to move. Commandant Henri D'Arboussier in Gumbu pointed out that the Masina Fulbe were sedentary. They were proprietors of the land. The Fulbe Samburu of Gumbu ranged over large areas with few fixed points. If anyone conceived of landed property, it was Bambara and Soninke villagers among whom they wandered.

Rimaibe were often willing and even preferred to stay on lands they knew, but were not willing to re-establish a tie broken earlier that year.[50] Many *rimaibe* were persuaded to remain, but only by affirming their autonomy. Others left. By the end of 1909, there was no longer any talk of sharecropping. The same thing happened elsewhere in the Sahel. The Commandant in Hombori wrote that *rimaibe* awaited with impatience the day they would be free. He doubted whether anything would persuade them to remain with their Fulbe masters.[51] *Rimaibe* were also leaving masters in Bandiagara and Douentza.[52] Clozel retreated. He wrote Gumbu that the desired changes would work only if rooted in traditional law.[53] We shall see in Chapter 12 that control of land was important elsewhere.

Guinea

Controlling emancipation on the Guinea coast

An effort to impose registered contracts also failed on the Guinea Coast, but for very different reasons. There, slave labor was used primarily to produce goods for market. Population densities were not high and political authority was fragmented. Thus a maroon community like the Mikifores was able to establish itself. Flight was not very extensive, but it was increasing in 1904 and 1905.[54] Then, in 1906, in the Rio Nunez, requests for emancipation increased sharply even though it was still necessary to pay for one's freedom.[55] In 1908, Lt. Governor Poulet visited the area shortly after receiving Ponty's letter that the Minister wanted further action on domestic slavery and gave orders suppressing all payments for manumission.[56] The commandant was soon deluged by slaves "coming in mass to the Post to claim their liberty, to say that they were tired of working for their masters and wanted only to work for themselves."[57]

At first they came in groups of fifty or sixty, almost all of them slaves of the Tubakayes.[58] And then, towards the end of August, they stopped work. Happening in the middle of the growing season, this threatened not only the Tubakayes, but also French commercial houses which had advanced rice and peanut seed to the masters. Lands had been seeded. If they were not worked, weeds would destroy the crop and the investment would be lost. With the season threatened and pressure from the traders, the administrator worked out a compromise with slaves and masters. The slaves would remain through the harvest, but on three conditions. First, they would be free after the harvest. Second, the masters would return children who had been dispersed to their parents. Third, the masters promised good treatment and adequate food. One group, working for a particularly harsh master, insisted that the master and his family work alongside them, which they agreed to do. The slaves also insisted that the administrator give them an explicit statement that they were free and had a right to live and work where they wished. He also conceded them the right to use the land they worked.

The agricultural season on the Guinea coast is long. The rains last six months, the harvest is not finished until March, and in May the fields are already being prepared for a new season. This gave Commandant Treillard time to study three previous cases of collective emancipation. In the first, the slaves of a Eurafrican woman were allowed to remain in their villages when she died.[59] In a second, case, masters seized part of the harvest of 115 slaves who claimed their liberty. As a result, they sought land and protection from a Baga chief. In a third case, eighty of a master's eighty-four slaves dispersed.[60] Treillard was convinced that availability of land, political fragmentation and desire of chiefs to increase the number of their subjects made it unlikely that anyone could keep control over the slaves. He argued that slaves were most likely to remain in their villages if their emancipation was not seriously contested and suggested helping them find land.

By spring of 1909, there was a new administrator at Boké. Like his peers elsewhere, he was convinced that, if freed, slaves would stop working and both slaves and masters would starve. The Tubakayes exploited these fears and threatened to return to Tuba. When slaves from three villages came to claim their freedom, he insisted that they remain in their villages until instructed otherwise and that they work to meet their needs.[61] As more and more slaves left, the Tubakayes used force to keep control. In April, there was a fight when some Tubakayes tried to force slaves to work. Finally, the administrator called a meeting of 20 Tubakayes and about 300 slaves. The 300 were adult males, which implies that between 1,000 and 1,500 slaves were involved. The administrator suggested sharecropping contracts as a solution. The slaves were not interested. An old slave stood up. He thanked the administrator on behalf of his fellows and expressed their appreciation of previous decisions. They had, he announced, decided to work for themselves: "They were determined to work not only to guarantee their own subsistence and the well-being of their families, but also to increase their wealth, because thenceforth they would be sure of benefiting from the fruits of their own labor. None of them would agree to remain one day longer in the service of their masters."[62] They agreed to stay in their villages, to work hard and to pay taxes. They had collected on Treillard's promise and had been given the land they worked.

The Tubakayes recognized defeat and left the meeting in silence. The freedmen gathered their wives and children and went to the marketplace where they held a boisterous celebration. Several weeks later, the administrator reported that both former slaves and masters were at work in the fields. Almost none of the slaves stayed with their masters and no sharecropping contracts were registered. He was relieved that he would get no more visits from women seeking children held in servitude.[63] There was no other such confrontation on the coast, but there were constant departures. In 1907 and 1908, slaves were leaving their masters in the Mellacorée. One administrator there stopped giving identity papers because he did not approve of the way freed persons used their liberty.[64] Several months later, it was reported from the same cercle: "Natives often complain of the flight of their servants, but this sort of desertion would incontestably be more rare if masters treated their people with more kindness, if they secured for them more well-being and if they did not consider them beasts of burden."[65] In the Rio Pongo, the administrator reluctantly began freeing slaves in 1909 without demanding any payment.[66]

Many manumissions took place on estates of old Eurafrican families. Sometimes the first freed returned to slave villages to encourage others to go. The administrator tried to suppress such agitation, but he lacked the personnel to do so. There were efforts to impose sharecropping contracts, most notably in the Mellacorée, where an administrator simply wrote into the contract the traditional obligations of slaves. The Governor vetoed that.[67] By 1912, there were over 500 contracts in the Mellacorée, but it is not likely that these contracts lasted long or had any significant effect on social relationships.[68] In the Mellacorée, proximity to the Sierra Leone frontier made control more difficult, but nowhere did masters have much leverage. One commandant promised an amelioration of working conditions to some Turpin slaves, but this did not prevent their leaving.[69] In April 1910, several hundred in the Rio Pongo freed themselves. Several thousand still lived under control of their masters, but many were moving from villages to homes on lands they farmed, which undermined an already weak local authority.[70]

The odd man out: Guinea

The events of 1907 and 1908 dramatically reduced the importance of slavery along the coast, but we know little about the subsequent period. Elsewhere in Guinea, slavery showed greater resilience. Lt. Governor Richard did nothing to implement the 1905 anti-slavery decree except to urge that the terms *non-libre* and *captif* no longer be used, that slave cases come before European tribunals and that administrators respond favorably to slave demands.[71] In 1908, the choice of Ponty as Governor-General, a letter from the colonial minister and the Saurin report all increased pressure on Guinea. Acting Lt. Governor Poulet replaced liberty papers by identity papers, which were available to all, and asked for a "discreet inquiry."[72] Poulet and his successor, Liotard, insisted that slavery not be recognized. Poulet wrote Pita that he was surprised to find the categories slave and free on tax lists, "categories which seem to indicate that slavery still exists in your circumscription."[73] In 1909, Liotard told two administrators that they could not "free" a slave because France did not recognize slavery, but they could also not consider the claims of masters: "You should avoid any intervention in palavers based on the supposed state of subjection of a person, no matter which side the claim comes from, except to declare that no person can either confer or withdraw liberty."[74] Much of this was cosmetic. There was some reluctant action, for example, Poulet in the Rio Nunez in 1908. The same year, he told several commandants that they could not deny the right to emigrate nor return slaves to masters. They could only insist on prior payment of tax and administrative authorization.[75]

The situation in Guinea may have pushed Ponty to articulate his *politique des races* in 1909.[76] This policy had two thrusts, destruction of all *grands commandements* and removal of subject peoples from the control of alien conquerors. It was similar to Lugard's conception of indirect rule in its emphasis on "natural rulers" and "local customs," but the British had greater sympathy with the traditional rulers and felt more secure with them.[77] Ponty and the French made the chef de canton the key intermediary between the colonizer and the colonized, and used emancipation policy to reduce the power of those capable of frustrating the will of the colonizer. Cooptation took place, but at a lower level.

The Futa Jallon was an area of particularly intense resistance to French hegemony, a resistance that expressed itself not in revolt, but in a reluctance to bend to the French will and in a reserve that often exacerbated French insecurity.[78] The French looked warily at the commitment of Futa elites to Islam. In 1909, Ponty addressed the Lt. Governor a detailed memo proposing application of the *politique des races* to the Futa Jallon. He suggested hiving off areas, mostly subject to Labé, which were not Poular speaking, suppressing the Almamyat, breaking down centralization and freeing the slaves. Ponty recognized that the Futa was different from Banamba in that a good part of the slave population descended from the original Jallonke or was enslaved early in Futa history. He erred, however, on two points. First, he insisted, largely on a misreading of Banamba's experience, that loss of their slaves would lead to a decline in Fulbe commitment to Islam and a reversion of many to a nomadic life. Second, like Clozel, he assumed that what worked with one group of Fulbe would work for others and proposed the Masina agreement of the previous year as a model for the Futa.[79]

Camille Guy

A year later, Ponty sent Camille Guy to Guinea. Seen as a liberal for his role in Senegal, Guy was probably the only governor of Guinea that Ponty picked. Other choices were made by the ministry.[80] Ponty toured Guinea with Guy and gave him detailed instructions, which again focused on break-up of the Futa and destruction of slavery.[81] Ponty underlined that control of land by masters was the most important limit on emancipation. He suggested "in the first place . . . agrarian cantonment of the Fulbe aristocracy, inactive holders of all lands, on the other hand, a program of colonization by creating agricultural villages on lands effectively vacant, notably along the railroad line." Ponty saw the problem, but he was wary of radical solutions. Though he wanted to give former slaves control of land, he still spoke of sharecropping contracts, which meant he was reluctant to give the former slaves ownership.

Guy's mission was compounded by two events. The first, the ambush and murder of a French administrator named Bastié, took place in March 1909.[82] This was more than eighteen months before Guy took up his appointment, but it aroused French fears of an Islamic plot and began a debate that was resolved only after Guy's arrival. The French charged a follower of Cerno Aliou, the Wali of Gumba with the murder. Many French people in Guinea were convinced that the murder was not an isolated act, but part of a conspiracy masterminded by Cerno Aliou. The Wali was a saintly figure who advocated a reformist and egalitarian Islam. By this time, he was over eighty years old, feeble and almost blind. He had never given the French trouble and was much more an enemy of the Futa elite, whose runaway slaves he had welcomed for years.[83] Cerno Aliou had turned the accused in the Bastié case over to the French. After investigation by a local administrator, Lt. Governor Liotard was convinced that the murderer had acted on his own. Guy did not agree. He was told by Ponty to "put an end to Islamic clericalism" and his administrators convinced him that the Wali was an example of that clericalism.

At the same time and over objections of conservatives in Guinea, Ponty also authorized the return to Guinea of Alfa Yaya of Labé, who had been interned in 1905. Labé had been much reduced in size and many slaves fled his farms, but Alfa Yaya still had a lot of support.[84] On his return, former slaves, probably warriors, came to pay their respects and, perhaps, to swear loyalty. Within weeks, there were reports of stockpiling of arms and of what Suret-Canale calls an "imaginary plot."[85] The evidence for a plot is certainly not clear. What is clear is that key administrators hostile to his release showed Guy evidence which suggested an impending revolt.[86] In February 1911, Alfa Yaya was again arrested and interned. A month later, French troops seized Gumba and massacred over 300 of the Wali's disciples. The Wali fled, but was arrested in Sierra Leone, extradited and sentenced to death. He died in prison before being executed. The military force that seized Gumba also attacked Tuba and arrested two leading clerics also believed to be involved in the anti-French conspiracy.[87] Thus, before Guy acted on slavery, he had to deal with incidents which convinced him that French authority in Guinea was fragile and resistance could jeopardize the colonial enterprise.

When Guy did act, it was thus with caution. His circular of 4 March 1911 stated that

captivity suppressed under law and on paper exists in fact and captives themselves accept with good grace, and sometimes eagerly the ties of vassalage that link them to a powerful and feared chief. Our action has been impotent up to now, and in spite of perseverance, has failed to destroy prejudices and traditions several centuries old. We cannot accept that in one of our colonies, captivity, even in the familial form that characterizes it today, can last for long . . . It is not a question of a frontal attack on the social ideas of our proteges, nor of using force or constraint to suppress in a single day a traditional organization, which is for the people of Guinea an economic system with which they are happy.[88]

Thus, Guy accepted the notion of his administrators that slavery was deeply rooted in the Guinean psyche. The circular continued. Administrators were to inform slaves that it was "immoral for a man to possess another." They were to reject all claims of masters and to protect refugees. They were to pursue crimes against persons, to remove chiefs involved in such crimes and to protect any slave making a claim from reprisal.

In August, Guy insisted that the administration no longer ask how many slaves a chief had.[89] In September, he sent out more circulars. The first suggested that greater use of horses in the mountainous Futa would reduce reliance on porters.[90] A week later, he asked for a slave census. After enumerating slave settlements, Guy wanted to reorganize payment of taxes. Slaves had been counted and taxed as part of the master's household, even though they lived in different communities. Guy wanted to end this and, if possible, remove the rundés from Fulbe control. They were thenceforth to pay taxes directly through their own chiefs and, if necessary, to be placed under separate canton chiefs.[91] I have seen no evidence that this census was ever taken or that any rundé were removed from the authority of Fulbe chiefs at this time.[92] Guy's hesitation is explained by a memo sent to Ponty earlier that year. He described the Futa elite in negative terms, but he pictured slaves as an inert mass accustomed to their yoke and slavery as the major barrier to better relations with chiefs.[93]

During all of this and in spite of lack of sympathy from the French, slaves kept fleeing, encouraged by continued French attack on Muslim elites. The arrests of Alfa Yaya and Cerno Aliou and the occupation of Tuba were followed by confiscation of slaves and property. At Gumba, 1,500 slaves were freed and settled in two large villages. Cattle owned by the Wali and his followers were distributed among them.[94] Whole villages of slaves came to the post at Tuba to ask for emancipation.[95] For those who remained, it was a summer of threats and intimidation from the Jaxanke, which ended when about 2,000 slaves held a prayer meeting and then marched to the French post to sing the praises of their liberators.[96] Many freed slaves remained in the area and many rimaibe moved out of rundes to live in isolated households, where possible secluded from any road.[97] Slave flight and claims were frequent throughout the Futa and Upper Guinea between 1908 to 1911.[98] A 1909 report from Mamou spoke of abandoned villages and uncultivated fields as a result of twelve years of flight.[99] Faranah grew from 20,363 in 1898 to 51,141 in 1906. By 1910, three fourths of the cercle was former slaves.[100] Meanwhile, local officials feared that emancipating slaves alienated nobles. "The Foulahs," Maurice Roberty wrote from Timbo, "accepted our domination only on condition that we respect their customs."[101] In Kurusa, some slaves left and some created separate communities within the cercle. There were physical clashes as masters tried to force slaves to work.[102]

Then, seven months after his slavery circular, Guy issued one on sharecropping contracts.[103] He suggested that a slave exodus invariably impoverished the area they left. Contracts would keep slaves where they were while transforming relationships with their masters. He suggested that contracts be simple and that the worker pay either money or part of his crop. Contracts had been tried already, but this was the most systematic effort to develop them. They were not very popular. Five hundred were signed in the Mellacorée. In 1912, there were 27 involving 161 persons at Timbo. There were twenty-eight at Telimele, seventeen at Tugué. Only at Mamou were there over a thousand.[104] Ismael Barry suggests that some chiefs agreed to the contracts only to keep the administration happy.[105] The contracts varied. Most gave the landowner a share of the crop, usually a half, some a third. Others gave two or three days of work.[106] Guy thought that a fixed obligation might reduce conflict. Resistance came largely from masters, who distrusted the French and feared loss of their slaves.[107] Guy saw sharecropping as a temporary expedient and assumed it would lead to leasing and land ownership, but some chiefs saw contracts as a way to re-establish their authority over former slaves. Guy told some administrators to make sure contracts were not too onerous.[108] There were cases where contracts had to be edited because they used terms like "master" or implied servile status.[109]

Futa Jallon resembled Masina in that both areas were intensively cultivated by a slave majority long resident in the area. In both, *rimaibe* lived in a separate yet close relationship with the Fulbe, but Futa Jallon was much less fertile than Masina. In fact, given the dense population and limited resources of Futa, there was no economic reason to keep people there, but local officials feared the effects of the exodus.[110] Most political reports from the Futa during 1908 and 1909 speak of the profound hostility of slaves to Fulbe hegemony, and yet slavery remained resilient in Futa and for reasons Ponty understood. He knew that the slaves wanted land, that without land former slaves were not completely free, and that emancipation was most successful where masters and slaves were separated. But he also believed that it would be unjust to deprive the Fulbe of their landed property. Without property rights in the land they farmed, *rimaibe* who remained were dependent on masters who still considered them slaves.[111] As in Masina, Fulbe resisted conversion of slaves into sharecroppers, but in the long run it was control over land that enabled them to maintain control over their slaves.[112]

In many parts of both upper Guinea and the coast, slaves leaving their masters remained within the cercle and, in some cases, within the same village. Thus, in Kankan in 1911, there were many new villages, sixty-one of them former slave communities. In Kadé, too, new communities were founded by former slaves. In both areas, Guy was worried that fragmentation of authority would favor anarchic tendencies.[113] In 1913, when a new Governor, Peuvergne, was sent out, Ponty's instructions again stressed the *politique des races*, claimed success for suppression of large states and warned that division should not lead to fragmentation. Slavery remained a vital issue: "Some noble families of Fulbe origin defend step by step tyrannic ideas that they consider their privileges and linked to the maraboutic caste, keep their vassals and a mass of serfs under their control and far from our action."[114] He stressed the connection between emancipation and land, warned of the problem of a massive exodus, and suggested that one problem was the apathy of the slaves. But "it is on this laborious mass that we must depend in the fight against the conservative spirit of the higher castes. We should attach them to us . . . render them morally and materially independent of their former masters." But he was still convinced that the French had no right to deprive the masters of their property in land, and once again recommended sharecropping contracts.

In 1914, Inspector Rheinhart charged that many contracts approved were simple contracts for serfdom because they involved indefinite terms and committed the former slave's whole family.[115] Rheinhart saw one of Guinea's problems as "absence of continuity, absence of method, the inadequacy of general direction joined to frequent transfers of functionaries who are designated and moved without taking account of any competence or specialisation they have been able to acquire." In Timbo, there were twenty-five administrators in less than fifteen years.[116] Rheinhart was also troubled that there was a short and massive exodus at Kankan, and then, as suddenly as it began, it ended. The administrator claimed that the issue had been solved, but there were no claims and no complaints in the archives of the cercle.

There were simply not enough personnel to administer and supervise a massive system of contracts.[117] That does not mean that there were no contracts. Many social relationships, including that of *rimaibe* or *woloso*, were based on contracts. These contracts were oral or were based on unstated understandings, what is often called the moral economy. Where most effective, they reflected the balance of power between groups and operated in the interest of both contracting parties. The problem with many parts of Guinea and the Sudan, especially Futa Jallon and Masina, was that slaves had few resources and, where unable to get control over land, found themselves forced to acknowledge their own dependence.

Persistence of slavery in Futa Jallon

In spite of flight, hostility, claims, even the impact of World War I, which we will look at later, slavery persisted in the Futa Jallon. Only in the desert was slavery more deeply entrenched. In part, this was a result of the changing relationship between the colonial state and the chiefs. The French originally saw Futa chiefs as hostile and uncooperative, but they increasingly appreciated the ability of the chiefs to deliver and the chiefs learned that the French could protect them from the threat posed by the breakdown of authority within their own community.[118] Change took place within a social system that allowed traditional elites to maintain control over most former slaves.

There is no more vivid picture of the Futa between the wars than Oswald Durand's novel, *Terres Noires*. Like most colonial novels, it is both racist and ethnocentric, but gives a feeling for the Futa that we get from few other sources. It is about an effort to modernize. The leading character, Tene Kamara, is the son of a "good" noble and a slave woman, who is sent to Perigord in France to learn French farming methods. On his return, he tries to organize the "freedmen," introduce ploughing and reform society.[119] Durand's picture of nobles is harsh. The chief is miserly and arrogant with his inferiors, craven and submissive in the presence of Whites, and abusive to his "servants." Sons of masters "profited from their status to order, pillage and dishonor, sure in advance that they will not be punished."[120] When recruits or laborers were demanded, *rimaibe* were sent. Young free males cheated the slaves and took their women by force.

In the novel, the Fulbe oppose the use of oxen for plowing because they fear that with higher incomes *rimaibe* will become truly free. An old Pullo mutters in one scene, "A naked captive never speaks! If you dress him, he insults you and soon after, strikes you."[121] Durand had little confidence in the truly wretched. He described *rimaibe* as "tattered, frightened, bent for centuries underneath blows . . . they lack will."[122] Tene's supporters were the *libérés*, many of them former *tirailleurs*, others men who had been exposed to "French values" by school or work as servants. Durand believed that any contact with the French was enlightening, but French authority was distant. An ordinary person needed an intermediary to get access to the commandant and often had to pay a bribe. The climax is a plowing contest, which Tene wins before the governor. The novel is quite conservative. Durand does not question sharecropping. His argument is that plowing will liberate the "servant" from the "feudal" control of the chiefs while providing higher incomes for both tenant and landowner.

Other writers confirm this harsh picture of Fulbe control. Even the 1931 report to the League of Nations on slavery in Guinea conceded that in the Futa, "former slaves possess no property." Slaves still worked three days a week on the master's land and three on their own. The report's picture of the Futa contrasts to its discussion of other areas, where slavery was seen as finished.[123] Other sources are harsher. A slave was still a slave according to Gilbert Vieillard.[124] The French had meetings to announce that there was no more slavery. The slaves understood, but those who remained were still slaves. Before, they had Thursday and Friday for themselves, now they also had Wednesday. Slaves paid tax and did all of the forced labor that built roads and administrative housing. "The slave possesses nothing. His fields and his compound belong to his Peul," Vieillard wrote. The slave's master and his landowner were not always the same person, in which case the slave worked four days for the master, and three on a plot, for which he paid 10 percent of his crop.[125] The only change in work was from labor rent to sharecropping. Masters could generally count on support of the colonial state until after World War II.[126] As late as 1954, *rimaibe* spent more time on the masters' fields than on their own.[127]

The freedom the French gave came at a high price. Derman writes that "the suffering and exploitation of the serfs increased under colonial rule because the burden of forced labor fell mostly on them; on the other hand, the colonial period presented new opportunities for escape from their status and poverty."[128] The harshness of colonial rule and the introduction of money led to a reduction of obligations. Masters lacked the money to pay taxes for their slaves and were unwilling to do forced labor themselves. Both *rimaibe* and noble migrated, but *rimaibe* also sought out new occupations or used old ones to earn money. Thus, many started weaving for money. Blacksmiths, who were slaves in the Futa, began selling their services. Others became butchers, tailors, basket-makers, leather-workers or traders, all jobs not considered honorable. The major source of wage labor in the Futa, *rimaibe* could earn enough money to free themselves from obligations and even buy land.[129]

Rimaibe also achieved increasing control of family life. The master no longer received the brideprice for a slave woman, but *rimaibe* could still be inherited or given to Fulbe children at marriage.[130] *Rimaibe* negotiated their own marriages and bequeathed their holdings to their children. In the past, slaves belonged to their masters' lineages. Now, they developed lineage structures "fundamentally the same as that of their former masters."[131] Masters did, however, continue to select *rimaibe* concubines and young Fulbe men often imposed themselves on *rimaibe* women. They were also able to command the labor of *rimaibe* children in their households.[132] In spite of Islamic law, a concubine was not freed when she bore a child for her master unless he took her as a wife. Derman says that the child was sent back to the *rundé* and the mother might follow if she ceased to please.[133] Formerly, slaves had distinctive names. Increasingly, they took Muslim personal names like those of the nobles.[134] The only real manumission was under traditional law. A slave could be freed as an act of charity or could purchase his freedom, and a slave child could be adopted when a woman was sterile.

The poverty of the Futa made Guinea an increasingly crucial source of migrants, replacing the Sudan as the major source after 1950. Most came from the Futa. Wynkoop and Baldé argue that most were *rimaibe* and that coercion was often necessary to get them to go in the early years.[135] In contrast, Derman argues that more Fulbe migrated because they had fewer options at home.[136] *Rimaibe* were particularly important in Senegal as charcoal-makers.[137] Others went to cities, gold fields and banana plantations, and often stayed. Sometimes, traditional social relationships followed *them*. Baldé tells of a former slave in a Senegalese village who cared for his aged and weak former master.[138]

As a result of heavy migrations of the period from 1906 to 1921, the number of slaves in the Futa was much reduced, from over half of the population to about a quarter. Furthermore, some of those who remained improved their circumstances with revenue from work or from military service. Nevertheless, at the end of colonial rule about 200,000 people still accepted a form of slavery.[139] It is easier to explain persistence in Masina, where the land was rich. In the Futa, most slaves lived in poverty. Population densities were high for historical rather than geographic reasons. Furthermore, amelioration cannot explain much. Some did well, but many slaves were probably worse off than before conquest. *Rimaibe* had little power as long as the law recognized Fulbe ownership of the land. Baldé argues that changes took place only because of the departure of some and the refusal of others to accept the traditional rights of their masters.[140] I suggest two other variables. First, *rimaibe* lived in separate villages with their own chiefs and autonomous social structures. Second, their reaction to a limited emancipation was not to affirm a separate identity, but to become Fulbe, though their masters did not accept them as such.[141] Most important, they studied the Quran and became practising Muslims. Not at home in the Fulbe mosque, they built their own more modest places of worship.

Conclusion

Rheinhart's report criticized the lack of stability not only in the cercle, but at the center. There was clearly a problem of continuity. Between 1904 and 1914, not a single governor served a full term. In defending himself, Ponty said that most Governors sent to Guinea were not his choices. He then made biting comments on almost all. He criticized the early and healthy governors as "Governors-Mayor of Conakry." Cousturier made it into the interior once in his term, and then only because Roume wanted to tour Guinea. Frézouls met resistance from local administrators, Richard was inactive, and Liotard, who hewed to the Ponty line, had a tendency to leave things alone. Guy did not serve out his term for health reasons. Ponty suggested that most of Guy's circulars were not put into effect. Peuvergne's term was even shorter than Guy's.[142]

Guy's failure was rooted in deeper flaws. The house that Ballay built proved more durable than it seemed in 1905. It was administered by men who understood its fragility and were often more concerned to maintain their autonomy than to act on the governed. Local administrators tried to shape a new Governor just as subaltern staff sought to influence newly arrived local administrators. Both Frézouls and Guy were shaped by what they were told. The passion of administrators for inaction reflected their insecurity. They often reminded superiors that Guinea was not conquered and they recognized that in the Futa, Dingiray and Kankan there was deep hostility to French rule, a hostility reinforced by Islam and stimulated by French action against slavery. French action was also limited by a belief in property and hierarchy. In spite of his talk of drawing servile masses closer to colonial rulers, Ponty and those under him were incapable of mobilizing those masses against ruling elites. It was one thing to reduce the power of Bokar Biro or Alfa Yaya by freeing slaves, another to attack a whole class. Bothered as they were by determined opposition of Fulbe elites, they respected the control they exercised over their own society.

The Sudan was regularly cited by observers like Saurin as a model for Guinea. The early colonial years in the Sudan were dominated by two strong governors, but even the Sudan showed the limits to French action. Guy may have believed in liberal principles, but he was afraid to impose them on those below him. Ponty shied away from depriving Fulbe of landed property and was unwilling to gamble on Bamako's food supply. But there were other problems. In the vast colonial domains, chiefs and masters could coerce and intimidate, impose new arrangements, safeguard old ones and prevent complaints. In addition, comments of different Inspectors make clear that some commandants were petty tyrants and others bored and complacent. Many were hostile to policies they were supposed to enforce, both because it made life difficult for them and because they thought it wrong. In spite of claims that freed slaves increased the amount of land they cultivated, many were critical of the anti-slavery policy. An interim governor in Guinea wrote "The emancipation of domestic slaves has caused an agricultural crisis. The masters were not used to working the soil and freed persons have considered their new status a right to do nothing."[143] A decade later, Paul Marty wrote that

Many [slaves] have suffered from the new regime. When abandoned to themselves and not directed, they have not worked and have been immersed in misery. When hunted down and mistreated by former masters, who still hold political and judicial authority under our orders, they no longer work and are punished and imprisoned for imaginary crimes, chased from the country, pillaged under the pretext of fines, of damages . . .[144]

12   Looking for the tracks. How they did it

> ... knowledge of all human activities in the past as well as the great part of those in the present is ... a knowledge of their tracks.
>
> Marc Bloch[1]
>
> ... The slaves of Kayor were not happy men, but they knew when and how to seize a chance.
>
> Donal Cruise O'Brien[2]

Most slaves did not leave. I have several times tried to estimate the number of those in slavery and the number of those who left. Igor Kopytoff has used estimates made by me to minimize the importance of the exodus and to underline that most slaves chose not to leave.[3] We differ in how important we consider a movement of probably over a million people and what that movement meant to slave systems, but in one way, he is right. Most slaves did not leave; probably somewhat over a third did. Leaving was not easy. Nobody was offering to help slaves, and where the masters were able to do so, they were willing to coerce. Most important, the exodus involved a long walk home. Slaves often owned nothing but what they could carry with them and in most cases that was very little. For those going from the Sahel to the southern savanna, it was usually a walk of twenty to thirty days. It was about 230 km from Banamba to Buguni, more than double that from Nioro, and even further for Gurunsi slaves returning from desert-side areas. Furthermore, they had no idea what they would find when they got home. If they could get land and seed, it was three months from planting to harvest.

The vast majority of those who were born free left, some to return to earlier homes, some to go elsewhere. Those who left, often did so with great joy. At Gumbu, they marched out singing and shouting insults, telling their former masters to put their sons and daughters to work in the fields.[4] The majority of those born to servitude stayed, sometimes moving to new locations. In the 1890s, the French suggested converting all slaves into domestic slaves, that is to say, into *woloso*.[5] That is what happened, not through conversion, but through most of the others leaving. Those who stayed were *woloso* born to the language and culture. They had a more secure status, knew the land and how to make it produce. Many of the more privileged slaves also stayed. Women who married their masters often though not always stayed. Those who feared the uncertainty of the trip home stayed. Others stayed because they were too old or sick to undertake the long trip. For those who stayed, there was often a long process of struggle and negotiation.

The previous two chapters have said relatively little about Senegal. Around the turn of the century, use of slave labor seems to have declined in Senegal even while slaves were still being imported. Masters resisted change, but there was no major social disruption because there were new ways to recruit labor. Crucial changes took place without leaving significant documentation behind. And yet, the tracks are there, albeit often faint. Understanding what happened in Senegal is important to our understanding of what happened elsewhere. In this chapter, I would like to look briefly at Senegal, then examine how slaves all across the Sudanic zone established their autonomy, and finally, consider those who stayed behind.

Senegal: Where did the slaves go?

The data on movement of slaves into Senegal is overwhelming and has been presented in earlier chapters. The data on slave departures is most extensive for areas outside the peanut basin. The largest departures were from the Senegal and Gambia river areas, but there is little archival evidence of massive departures from the peanut basin. Thus, the register of slaves freed at Tivouane, then the most prosperous peanut-producing cercle, indicated only 139 liberations from 1903 through 1907.[6] Inspector Saurin saw this as evidence that slavery was finished there, but we know that slaves were still coming in to the peanut basin. Where archives are sparse, oral data is clear. Informants in diverse parts of Senegal refer to many slaves leaving between 1905 and 1914.[7] Some say that most left, others say that most remained, but all agree on large-scale departures. One informant commented wryly that his father had seven slaves and six left on the same night. The seventh was lame.[8] "Some left," one informant remarked. "Some stayed, a minority. We had many Sereer, who were found by their kin. The rest freed themselves and founded new households."[9] Many people tracked down kin. "A person could recover a relative by paying the purchase price."[10] One of Moitt's informants said that slaves who disliked their masters left. Others suggested simply that slaves left when they could.[11]

Slave matters occupied much time of local commandants. They had to deal with grievances of slaves and masters, efforts to find lost kin, and constant movement into and out of the Gambia. Nevertheless, with the exception of Bakel in 1895, Senegal did not have the kind of massive exodus that marked Guinea and the Sudan. This can be attributed to the adaptation of slave systems to a market economy between 1890 and 1905 and to the rapid economic growth taking place in Senegal during the period when slaves were freeing themselves. It is quite possible that as many slaves left as in the Sudan, but their departure has not been well described in the literature. The Wasulunke tell of relatives coming home from Senegal, but they undoubtedly blended into the migration of *navetanes* and they probably had resources their kin from the sahel lacked. Many also moved within Senegal, seeking to profit from the growing peanut economy. Any place within the peanut basin, one can ask today where the slave villages are. Some of them are former *villages de culture* that became autonomous, but many are communities that picked up and moved somewhere else.[12] These movements will be discussed more fully in Chapter 13.

The early years of the twentieth century were years of rapid economic growth. Senegal was the most important colony in French Africa. Peanut exports multiplied six times from 1897 to 1914, reaching 300,000 tons in the last pre-war harvest. From 1908, construction crews pushed the railroad south and east of Thiès, opening large areas to export agriculture.[13] This was also the rubber boom, less important in Senegal than Guinea, but a factor in growth. Dakar was the capital of French West Africa and its most important port. Thiès and Kaolack also grew as did most towns along the line of rail. The administration recruited most of its workers from among freed slaves.[14] There was work on the docks, along the line of rail and with merchants. Local textile production faced increasing competition from imported cottons, but it persisted.[15] Slaves were probably a majority of those moving into city and town, and of the new city-dwellers they had the least incentive to return to rural homes. Many took salaried employment, but an even larger number moved into the informal sector. In Senegal, for example, former slaves got involved in charcoal-making. Thus by 1910 a largely Bambara group of charcoal makers was producing about 3,000 tons of charcoal a year in the area between Pout and Sebikotane.[16]

The agricultural sector absorbed the greatest number of ex-slaves, providing opportunity for those from Senegal and from the other two territories. Many moved away from masters to form new communities. Moitt describes migrations from within Senegal, especially freed slaves from Ganjool and Njambuur moving further south to look for land or work.[17] Others formed their own households and sought increasing control of their productive activity where they already lived. Accumulation, however, often required migration. The form that migration took was determined both by existing patterns of settlement and by the availability of water. We can define three different modes of labor organization in the peanut basin. First, the old peanut basin, Kajoor, Siin and western Bawol, lacked surplus land and received relatively few *navetanes*. The tendency for entrepreneurs there was to intensify existing forms of exploitation, using family or dependent labor.[18] In the early years, this region was still attracting labor. Thus, when the liberty village in Podor closed in 1903, the commandant reported that "all the freed slaves left for Cayor and Baol attracted there by relatives who are already living in this area where millet is abundant and the possibility of acquiring money by cultivating peanuts exists."[19] Opportunities in this area were limited, however, and it soon became a source of labor for other areas.

Second, in part of the new peanut basin, western and southern Saalum, the major source of labor was *navetanes*. We have seen earlier how the *navetanat* probably evolved from the slave trade. In the early years, migrants often came for several years and had to cope with insecurity.[20] Then, from 1896 migration increased dramatically into both Senegalese and Gambian peanut growing areas. They came primarily from Soninke areas of the upper Senegal river, but increasingly from other areas. There were several possible ways to organize the *navetanat*.[21] In the most common, the *navetane* received land, seed, food and lodging in exchange for working on the master's field five days up to early afternoon prayer. This was clearly based on obligations of slaves, which in turn, were based on the obligations of male dependants. The difference was the context. The slave had no leverage. He or she had little recourse if asked to work extra time or if pushed to work harder. The *navetane* was sought. In most years, more than 70 percent of them went to Sine-Saloum. Furthermore, most of these went to the area west and south of Kaolack.[22] The *navetanat* was adapted to a situation where capital was short, land was available, and a reception structure existed. The successful *jatigi* (landlord) had to be able to provide a *navetane* with land and to feed him. In western and southern Saalum there were numerous villages, each surrounded by large uncultivated areas suitable for expansion. This is where expansion was most rapid before the First World War.

The third mode of labor organization was on the frontier of settlement. Eastern Bawol and eastern Saalum were areas where a low water table had long inhibited agricultural development.[23] In the absence of agricultural settlements, there were no landlords and therefore no one who could feed a *navetane*. New groups had to cope with water problems and provide for their own subsistence. The French never confronted these problems because the Mourides did it for them. As construction crews pushed the line of rail east, the Mourides usually arrived at least a year before the station opened, and two or three before the commercial houses arrived. And then, finally, the well-digging crews came in.[24] These became known as the Terres Neuves.

The Mourides

The Qadiriya of Bou Kunta and the Mourides of Amadu Bamba were as important as the existence of a free labor market in destroying slave labor systems. Bou Kunta was the son of a Mauritanian horse trader, born in Kajoor about 1840.[25] Though of limited education, he established a reputation for piety and learned to exploit both the development of commercial agriculture and the emergence of a pool of unattached persons. In 1886, after Lat Dior's defeat, many Kajoor *ceddo* joined his community. They were soon followed by others. His disciples neither studied the Quran, nor prayed or fasted. They worked for him, lived in villages he controlled, and when in need, benefited from his generosity. "The virtue of his *baraka* and the efficacity of their work are the only conditions necessary and sufficient to obtain paradise."[26] Bou Kunta acted like a Wolof chief, supporting griots and travelling in style, but he also invested in real estate and businesses. By his death in 1913, his community numbered about 50,000, most of them probably of slave origin.

At Bou Kunta's funeral, many of his disciples prostrated themselves before Amadu Bamba's son Mamadu Mustapha and speedily switched to the Mourides.[27] Marty recognized that Amadu Bamba was very different from Bou

Kunta. He and those around him were both learned and pious. Though his family was linked to Lat Dior and Mouride traditions make much of a meeting between the two just before Lat Dior's final confrontation with the French, Amadu Bamba kept his distance from both the old Wolof state and the new French one. His base was on the frontiers of agricultural settlement in eastern Bawol, where his family controlled the village of Mbacké. There is no evidence that Amadu Bamba ever amassed weapons or planned resistance. French fears, however, led to his exile in Gabon from 1895 to 1902, and then periods of controlled residence in Mauritania from 1903 to 1907 and in Jolof to 1912. Exile only contributed to his prestige and his community was well managed by his brothers and leading disciples in his absence. Like many charismatic leaders, Amadu Bamba does not seem to have sought fame or power. Much of the success of his movement can be traced to the more practical men who surrounded him.[28]

From an early date the Mourides attracted those "closely associated with the courts of the old states, the *ceddo* or warrior class, and those who had been the chief victims of the raids and violence of those states, the slaves and especially the recently enslaved."[29] Amadu Bamba and his closest disciples lived pious and ascetic lives themselves, but his teaching recommended submission to a spiritual guide (shaykh) and the religious value of work. Disciples not interested in study began gathering around Amadu Bamba soon after he established himself at Mbacké in 1886. The most important was Shaykh Ibra Fall, a minor marabout of aristocratic origin, who is supposed to have stripped naked and prostrated himself before Amadu Bamba, declaring "I submit myself to you, in this life and in the next. I will do everything that you order me. I will abstain from anything you forbid me."[30] Ibra Fall neither prayed nor fasted and was reputed to be a heavy drinker. He was crucial in attracting former *ceddo* to submit. He also organized the first working *dara*, a community organized not around study, but around work.

The *dara* became the crucial institution in Mouride expansion. A band of young men would submit to a Mouride *shaykh*. Under the *shaykh*'s direction, it would settle in a frontier area, eating and living as a community. Once the new village was established, on average, about eight years after submission, the young men would be given land and be freed to marry. From that time on these *talibés* were like any other Senegalese peasant. They had their own lands, paid taxes and presumably gave regular gifts to the *shaykh*. The *dara* was especially attractive to former slaves. Mouride organization and the commitment of the disciples made it possible for new communities to colonize the arid regions of the east. They often had to fight it out with Fulbe herders, whose lands they were taking by force.[31] They had to face wild animals, to walk long distances for water and to clear the land. Amadu Bamba is reputed to have told a would-be *talib* not to go against his father's will. Most men who lacked land and did not have to worry about a father's will were slaves. Most free-born Senegalese at the time had some claim to land. The vast majority of those joining the *daras*, at least during the early decades, and probably a majority of those submitting to Amadu Bamba, were slaves. Cruise O'Brien explains: "Freedom from their masters did not however provide increased economic security, often indeed the contrary . . . slaves and castes shared a common predicament in the marginality or non-existence of their rights to land in the traditional zones of Wolof agricultural settlement . . . Land in these areas was already overcrowded by the late nineteenth century."[32] The result was the creation of what Copans calls a *marché de talibés* in which the young and landless sought a *shaykh*.[33]

To confirm the widespread belief that many Mourides are of slave origin, I looked through files of the Ecole Nationale d'Economie Appliquée for studies of predominantly servile villages. I found three. In one, a solidly Mouride village where I later interviewed, everyone was *jaam* except for the village chief, who came from the founder's family.[34] In the other two, those of slave descent were heavily Mouride.[35] "Serigne Bamba is our liberator," one old *jaam* told the ENEA students.[36] A team led by Jean Copans studied three villages in Bawol, one of which was largely free (4 percent *jaam*). The other two were respectively 40 percent and 56.7 percent *jaam*.[37] The ORSTOM research team, of which Copans was part, stressed the degree to which Mouridism transcended old social barriers, largely because it stressed the equality of all in their relation to the *shaykh* and to God.[38] Within the Mourides, restrictions on marriage between *ger*, *jaam* and *nyenyo* still prevail, and some ritual obligations persist, including symbolic payments to the master. A *shaykh* will often use a *jaam* or griot intermediary.[39] Nevertheless, *ger*, *jaam* and *nyenyo* have equal access to land and there is no difference in who takes part in or benefits from collective work groups.[40]

Recruitment to the Mourides took place largely in the old peanut zone. In the three Bawol villages studied by the ORSTOM team, 50 percent of the families came from Kajoor, 40 percent from elsewhere in Bawol.[41] In 1900, the old peanut zone had a population density of between fifteen and thirty per square kilometre, and parts had over thirty.[42] Elsewhere, it was often possible for former slaves to find land for hamlets in the space between villages, but in densely populated areas all of the land was claimed and most of it was farmed. Recruitment also took place where Islam was weak. Most Tijani strongholds held fast to the Tijaniya, but their poorly educated slaves often found Amadu Bamba's version of Islam more attractive. In 1912, there were almost 70,000 Mourides and about 50,000 followers of Bou Kunta.[43] As the railroad started pushing east in 1907, Mourides poured into new areas.[44] Colonies increased during the inter-war years and provided an outlet for former slaves seeking land and community.[45] It is not clear whether marabouts of other orders also received former slaves, but it is quite possible that some did.

My argument therefore is as follows. The 1870s and 1880s saw a massive movement of slaves into the peanut basin, a movement that continued in reduced numbers into the first years of the twentieth century. As the system broke down, many slaves returned to earlier homes, but others looked for institutions that could provide land and security. Bou Kunta and Amadu Bamba responded to this. An important body of thought going back to Paul Marty sees Mouridism as a new slavery, but it clearly also provided land and social order for the former slaves.[46] It was most attractive to men born in Senegal or brought there young and, if so, also played a role in Wolofization.

The long march

For Guinea and the Sudan, the crucial question is how they did it. It was a long walk. They probably tried to take remaining food stocks, and cloth or jewelry if they owned any. Masters seized property, which they regarded as theirs, and returning slaves faced the danger of robbery. They ended up with little, probably scavenged, ate famine foods like "monkey bread," the fruit of the baobab tree, and went hungry. One informant talked of eating carrion and wild fruit on the way back to Wasulu.[47] Some checked into liberty villages, where they could get land and a ration. A few villages served as rehabilitation centers, and there, as at Buguni, the strategy of freed slaves was to place women and children in the camps and have the men head home. The men sent for women and children after they had planted or were sure that family was capable of taking care of them.

Many did not arrive at the destinations they gave. Most slaves had no idea what cercle their villages were in. Clerks probably wrote down Buguni for people going to Wasulu and, perhaps, for some who were just heading in that direction. Many stopped elsewhere. Others took two or three years.[48] Many went to Bamako, where some became what the French feared, vagabonds living by begging, casual work and theft.[49] Others plugged into communities of their own people, especially the Wasulunke, whose diaspora created communities in towns all along the French supply line. The one informant who made the trip back told of being welcomed by her father's brothers who provided seed.[50] Then, as today, people with similar backgrounds, meeting for the first time, would peel back family trees to discover where they intersected and who they knew. During the exodus, there are few reports of people starving to death. Such reports were common during famine years. I believe that they did not starve because they lived off the land and made contact with kin. From kin, they got food, land and work.

Reconstruction

If the return home was difficult, there were still more problems after they got back. They had to restore social networks, rebuild villages and reclaim land that had reverted to bush. They had to integrate former *sofa* as well as former slaves. If the returnees found relatives, they found help: "When they arrived, they depended on relatives. If they lacked food, it was the relative or the clan that fed them the year of their arrival. If there were unmarried men among them, the clan found them wives."[51] But for those who arrived first, there was little help. They lacked seed and there was no network of credit to provide them with start-up capital. The first groups lived largely from gathering and hunting small game. Most of the Wasulu interviews list the wild roots and fruit they lived from. All accounts speak of hardship. The greatest threat was wild animals. "The whites gave us no help, but we carried their baggage to Bamako and they paid us. This informed many Wasulunke living in Bamako about the reoccupation and enabled them to return to their villages."[52]

Those who left to seek work probably did so as much to be able to buy guns as to be able to feed themselves. The Wasulunke have become known as hunters, probably a response to the war with nature that marked their first years back home. That was probably also true in other depopulated areas like Sangalan and Faranah.[53] As population built up and lands were cleared, it became easier to feed returnees and provide them with land, but building up agricultural stocks or herds still took time. Crucial to reconstruction was not only hunting and gathering, but also the possibility of earning money elsewhere. Work was also important because the French imposed taxes from the beginning. I often asked informants whether work such as rubber-tapping or gold-mining aided reconstruction. I was told that porterage for the colonial state was useful in letting people know about opportunities to earn money, but these opportunities were most important not for reconstruction, but for payment of taxes.[54] Clearly, however, the eagerness of the recently freed to seek work reflected difficulties they faced in reconstructing their lives.

They sought different kinds of work. The most important option was Senegal. In 1911, the Annual Report for French West Africa claimed: "In 1910–11, we saw former slaves from the Sahel descend in bands to Senegal where they covered the area alongside the Thiès–Kayes Railroad with cultivated fields; at the end of the season, they returned to their villages, making clear their intention to return in greater numbers every year." For the Gambia, the number of *navetanes* went from 4,657 in 1904 to 21,979 in 1914.[55] From 1906 on, there are increasing reports of migrants from the Sudan in many parts of Senegal. Many of these reports underline the importance of freed slaves.[56] From 1902, there were also harvest migrants called *firdu* because many came from Musa Molo's domains on the upper Gambia. In the early years, upper Senegal and western Mali were the major source of *navetanes*, though other areas soon got involved. Buguni was particularly important.

Over the years, the number of days *navetanes* and other male dependants owed the *jatigi* was reduced from five to four and the work day increasingly ended at noon instead of at 2 p.m.[57] Most informants attribute the reduction in labor obligations to the *navetanes*. Parallel to the reduction in the number of hours worked by all dependants, there was a reduction in the size of the average household and in the authority of the *jatigi*. Brothers farmed for themselves. Sons paid their own brideprice and formed autonomous households soon after marriage or the birth of children. The French seem to have taken no interest in the arrangements Africans made between themselves until the 1920s.[58]

For a short period after 1903, rubber was probably more important to those seeking revenue than Senegalese peanuts. As the rubber frontier moved inland, the terminus of the railroad was at any moment the junction of a network of trade routes feeding wild rubber to French commercial houses. By 1903, those routes extended into the wooded savannah lands of Wasulu. The boom continued until plantation rubber came on stream in 1908 and 1909, but rubber remained an important option even after that, providing work for both tappers and porters.[59] Gold was also important. There are many gold workings in upper Guinea and adjacent areas of Mali. The important gold fields at Buré in Guinea experienced an early exodus of slaves, encouraged by a liberal administrator, but they were quickly replaced.[60] By 1908, there were eighty Europeans and a thousand Africans working around Sigiri. Yields were too low to give European enterprises an adequate return on investment, but provided dry season incomes for many Africans.[61] It is hard to measure the importance of gold because it was often sold to African jewellers without paying a colonial tax.

Freed slaves also became part of a reservoir of unskilled labor. There are isolated reports of men looking for work as early as 1902, but labor was in short supply until about 1908 and coercion was used to recruit it.[62] About that time, "Bambara" were hired for construction of the Thiès–Kayes and Conakry–Niger railroads.[63] As the railroad moved forward, some thought that it would reduce the demand for porters, but it increased it.[64] In Guinea, the colonial state had long been involved in providing labor for private commerce. The use of permanent teams of porters was rejected by 1909 because it was too costly, and besides, the problem was solving itself.[65]

From 1908, we read of "these Bambaras who come every year from Bamako and even further to work as porters between the last harvest and the beginning of sowing."[66] Faranah reported recruiting problems in January 1908 and, a month later, indicated volunteers offering to work on the railroad.[67] Another report suggested that "although it used to be difficult to find porters and laborers, they now present themselves and when they do not find work, they go elsewhere to look for it, sometimes very far."[68] In Niger, Zarma-Songhay migrations to the Gold Coast began about 1902 and involved mostly former slaves.[69] During the same years, we read in some cercles of free labor suddenly becoming available, and, in others, of labor shortages. Most migrants were freed slaves, but not all. During the same period, Dogon, Samo, Mossi and Bobo began going to the Gold Coast to work the cocoa fields or to Bamako, Segu and Bandiagara to work as porters during the dry season.[70] Some early migrants in these societies were undoubtedly returned slaves, but their migrations soon included others.

The emergence of a labor market created difficulties for the colonial army. The early twentieth century saw an increase in the number of soldiers recruited. Parts of upper Guinea, Niger and the Sahara were not yet conquered. Troops were needed to garrison the new empire and to conquer Morocco. The French still preferred their *bon Bambara*, but could no longer buy recruits in the slave market. They recruited primarily in ethnic groups with a good reputation as soldiers, but with the economy expanding, there were other options for those seeking work. The army was unable to meet quotas, though there was a steady if not always adequate flow of former slaves seeking military service, especially from Bambara-speaking areas.[71]

Those who stayed

Dramatic though the exodus was, most slaves stayed where they were. The exodus was largest in areas involved in commodity production and with a harsh form of slavery. Many other freed slaves asserted their autonomy, but remained in the same area. Some converted *villages de culture* into regular villages. Others moved to isolated homesteads. The French disliked the break-up of consolidated villages because it made control more difficult, but they could not control the process. Ex-slaves also moved within Sahel cercles from the desert-side to better-watered riverine areas. Some former slaves remained in contact with their masters. They were not only far from the protection of French posts, but most commandants were not eager to protect them. Furthermore, some relationship with former masters was often in their interest.

Archival reports of new relationships were almost always phrased within the discourse of emancipation and exaggerated the degree of freedom. Thus, a report from Bandiagara in 1911 reported that "we find ourselves really in the presence of free servants having the right to acquire and sell on their own account and only giving their patrons two days of work for each two days for themselves."[72] Masters provided land, paid taxes and, on some days, fed their "servants." The question of who paid whose taxes was central. Thus, from Labé: "Former servants, in effect, although they have acquired their freedom, continue to pay their tax to the chief of their original village – father, mother, and children often figuring on so many distinct tax rolls when they belong to different masters."[73] At Dingiray, many left, but those born in slavery either remained where they were or settled nearby.[74] In Kurusa, most slaves were willing to stay, but conflict with masters over how taxes would be paid persuaded many to leave.[75] Nevertheless, slaves could no longer be recruited and their numbers were reduced, especially in those societies that most systematically used their labor. There was significant amelioration, though it is difficult to date the process. Dues were reduced, sometimes to the point where they were symbolic, but former slaves continued to perform roles that slaves traditionally played, for example, cooking at weddings and naming ceremonies. Many continued to acknowledge the authority of the family head.

We can get some idea of the process by looking at the often terse comments of informants. Kaymor was a province of Saalum, which was experiencing rapid economic growth at the time of emancipation. It was in an area that received many *navetanes*, but there is a tinge of bitterness in informants of both slave and free status. Most informants stressed that slavery no longer existed and that the break was sharp. "No slave remained with his master," one *jaam* informant insisted.[76] But another informant, born in slavery, remembered the process somewhat differently: "The *jaam* remained a *jaam* though inalienable. Few knew their origins and almost everybody remained where they were. Those who remained in the household of a *jaambur* continued to have the same life until maturity. Then, he founded his own household."[77] Breaking away was not difficult in Wolof society. The newly enslaved and the very young tended to live within the compound or under the direct control of their masters, but even before colonization, *jaam* born in the house were allowed to work their own plots as allotment slaves and usually, soon after marriage, were given their autonomy. As settled slaves they were obligated only for certain fixed payments and services. Many informants stressed the assertion of greater autonomy.[78] The head of a freeborn lineage described the changes: "We had many of them [slaves]. Some remained at Thyssé, others at Sonkorong and others at Sokone. With the coming of the White Man, the slave no longer respected his master . . . Even calling someone a slave became a crime. But this does not mean that slaves hurried to leave with colonization. Some agreed to remain *jaam*, but no one dares to call them *jaam*."[79]

Why did so many stay? Many administrators assumed that it was inertia. That is an argument that minimizes barriers to emigration. A more important reason is that they were at home. Those who stayed were born there and often married in the community. They knew no other home. Undoubtedly, too, many accepted the status into which they had been born or raised. They also faced coercion. We have seen struggles over children, seizure of property, fights, murders and endless palavers that marked the emancipation process. Masters did not like the idea of contracts, but were willing to use them to maintain their ascendancy. "Contracts between patron and servants," an administrator in Fuladu wrote, "are for the moment only a continuation of customs that existed before."[80] They exercised both a moral and a physical ascendancy and were willing to use their power. They harassed, threatened and intimidated. Thus, when former slaves at Tuba planted their fields, they were told the masters intended to repossess them.[81]

A 1907 case from Guinea suggests the determination of some local slave-owners. The administrator received a letter from Bacary, a slave from Moreah in the Mellacorée. He was bought by the Almamy as a young boy, was married and had four children. In 1907, he heard that there were no more slaves. He wanted to leave because the Almamy had sold his nine-year-old daughter. He twice tried to escape, but was beaten and locked up. The Almamy seized his wife and other three children. When he tried to see the administrator, the interpreter would not let him in because he was a slave.[82] When the administrator inquired, the Almamy insisted that he had not sold the girl, but confided her to his sister. The girl then died of a fever.[83] Bacary's wife was permitted to join him, and they settled where they wished, but he would not have had a chance without finding someone to write a letter for him. Bacary was alone, the French commandant was far away, and the interpreter controlled access to him.

In spite of this, there was a complex process of renegotiation, which involved a struggle between former masters and former slaves for the control of the labor of the slaves. Success or failure in this struggle depended on many variables. Swindell and Weil suggest that in Gambia, potential profits from peanut farming persuaded masters to reduce the labor dues owed by their slaves.[84] Masters knew that if pushed too far, slaves would leave, but many found ways to intimidate, to control and to assert an ideological hegemony. The position of the masters was also weakened by a decline in the authority of household heads. The major battlegrounds were control of family life and work. The first major change was that slaves established greater control over family life. We have seen that slaves had no rights in their spouses, children or parents, but they formed all the emotional ties other people form with close kin. There are repeated references to families, and where available, statistics suggest family groups.

In most areas, former slaves established a control over marriage and offspring, the right to raise their own children and the right to bequeath and to inherit, but it was often a struggle. The fights over children were especially bitter. This was the point at which slave families were often split and was difficult because some local commandants did not wish to impose the new order. Thus, at Tenenku in 1908, the Masina Fulbe insisted on control over *rimaibe* children. The labor of children was also often an issue. One *jaam* informant explained that the slave became autonomous. "From that time he owed only the *assaka*. He cleared his new field himself. The master kept with him the sons of slaves, who worked for him."[85] In Gumbu, one of the factors inhibiting emigration was that children of many slaves of the Moors were working in the camps, and many feared never to see them again.[86] At Timbo, sharecropping contracts gave parents control over the labor of their children, but the Fulbe often refused to sign, or if they signed, still insisted on traditional rights over the children. This was a factor in continued emigration.[87] The struggle over the right to bequeath and inherit went on even longer.

The second major change was increasing control over the conditions of work. One consistent theme in slave grievances was the desire to work for themselves. They "kept the name of *jaam*, but they no longer worked for anyone else," a Kaymor informant suggested.[88] "They remained where they were, but worked for themselves," another explained.[89] Others stressed mobility. "Everybody is free to settle where they wish. Now, it is everyone for himself," explained a *jaam* in Kaymor. Those who were locked into sharecropping relationships had very heavy obligations, but as Cissé makes clear, they fought to maintain their autonomy and their control over their productive work. In most cases, obligations of slaves were reduced substantially. In southern Saalum, when I asked in 1975 about the obligations of former slaves, I was told that they still paid the *assaka* (*zakkat*), which was a tenth of the harvest. The only budget of a slave family I saw indicated a much lower payment, a purely symbolic amount. If this is correct, the *assaka* persisted as a symbol of submission and a way for former slaves to maintain linkages with those more powerful than themselves.[90]

Land and emancipation

For those who remained with or near former masters, the key to the struggle was land. In Masina and the Futa Jallon, though masters resisted the change, control of land helped them maintain control over persons.[91] Freeing slaves was often a way of reducing the power of the chiefs, but once deprived of their autonomy, chiefs became faithful partners of the French, and were often able to use their position to define traditional law and land rights. Customary law was used to construct the interface between colonial state and traditional authority systems. The move from military to civilian bureaucracy system required law, but there was no reason for the French to impose French law or to create a completely new legal code. If order was to be maintained, it was best to administer people under their own legal traditions, as it were, to create law rooted in tradition. The law code of 1903 provided for use of both Muslim and customary law. In order to have information on traditional law available, Roume asked commandants to study it. In 1903, Ponty asked commandants to write monographs on their cercles. In 1909, Clozel asked them to add sections on customary law to these monographs.[92]

Crucial in this effort to mobilize tradition was a group of scholar-administrators. The most distinguished was Maurice Delafosse, whose *Haut-Sénégal-Niger* contained a synthesis of African law based on the studies Clozel commissioned.[93] While some, like Delafosse and Marty devoted all or most of their time to research, they depended on studies by local administrators, who disliked such tasks and turned to chiefs and elders for their information. Customary law is often seen somewhat like common law in that it evolves according to precedent.[94] There is some truth to this, but customary law is more flexible because it is oral and because it is dependent on the chief and his authority. Traditional land law recognized a series of linked rights: first, rights of those who first cleared the land and could distribute it; second, rights of the cultivator, which could not be removed as long as he used the land; and finally, rights of centralized states, which often overruled traditional rights.[95]

The crucial questions for slaves were the ability of masters to stake out property rights to lands the slaves worked and their ability to control distribution of unused lands. These rights did not always hinder the emancipation of slaves. Thus, the Senegalese administration wanted to increase the amount of land under cultivation. For the chiefs more land under cultivation meant more tax revenue, more gifts, more hands to work the "chief's field." Even in populous areas, the flight of enemies of the chief would occasionally leave land uncultivated. The land thus made available was often assigned to migrating groups of emancipated slaves, whose presence was desired. The French approach to land law was most important in Masina, Futa Jallon and Futa Toro, where high population density and establishment of Muslim law meant that all arable land was claimed. Any slave seeking freedom from a master's control had to leave. But land was a significant variable elsewhere. In the peanut basin, population densities were high even before the development of peanuts, but slave imports meant that there was no free land at the turn of the century. This was why this area became a nursery for Mouride colonization efforts. In areas like Saalum, where uncultivated land was available, intensively worked and manured lands nearest the village were more valuable and were claimed by free families. Among the Songhay, the process was similar. Thus, for Olivier de Sardan, "this liberation was a legal construct: it left to nobles and chiefs their lands and their powers. Those slaves who could returned to their native villages. For the others, nothing changed . . ."[96] Fuglestad argues that the response of the chiefs to the loss of slaves after 1906 was to reinterpret customary law to enable the nobility

to reassert its hold over former slaves, who were slowly reduced to the status of rent-paying tenants, cultivating land belonging to the nobility. This new concept of land tenure paved the way for formation of large estates in the West [of Niger], and their corollary, a landless rural proletariat. But it also resulted in a permanent and pernicious climate of social tension and unrest and in a long series of land disputes.[97]

In the Terres Neuves of Bawol and Saalum, the Mouride *shayukh* cleared the land and claimed property rights. The *shayukh* do not collect rent from their *talibés*, but they receive gifts and labor on their fields. They control vast areas and are still able to use political influence to get new lands. Their authority is articulated in terms of their religious position, but they remain the owners and, for those without land, the best access to it.[98]

Famine and poverty

The period from 1899 to 1914 was one of recurrent famines, some fairly local, some involving the whole region.[99] Famines generally involved an increase in pawning and enslavement, often at derisory prices. Famines also led to movement of slaves. In 1901, at San, there were reports of slaves trying to change masters in the quest for guaranteed subsistence.[100] Famine years often led to servile groups seeking better-watered areas. In Dori during a 1917 famine, 3,000 to 4,000 people, mostly *rimaibe*, headed south to seek food.[101] In the lower Senegal, the 1914 famine induced many to move south into the peanut basin.[102] Eastern Senegal was hit by a series of bad years after 1907 culminating in a disastrous famine in 1913. Clark believes that in eastern Senegal, this drought led to more slave departures than the 1905 decree, in part because the French insisted on collecting taxes.[103] Bakel's population remained static while Kayes' dropped from 7,000 in 1905 to 5,800 in 1912. Clark's informants suggest that during this period, and especially in 1913, people pawned children and sold slaves they could not feed, both to Moors and to traders from the peanut basin. Other slave-owners allowed their slaves to scavenge or to migrate to where they could feed themselves. Clark also argues that the ecological crisis of 1907–13 altered the relationship between masters and those slaves who remained, many stopping payments to masters.

In 1912, Clozel wrote that one out of three slaves had left the sahel, partly as a result of three dry years (1909–11), partly as a result of continued raiding. The report also indicated a desire to limit movement to the Gambia. Ponty's marginal comments indicate continued opposition to efforts to tie people down.[104] Former slaves also had to face the state's hunger for taxes, which cut deeply in areas with a very poorly developed money economy. Large areas had enough rainfall to produce a surplus, but little possibility of converting that surplus into money. In 1914, cultivators in Guinea were paying about a third of their product as taxes.[105] At Banankuru, children were being pawned in 1901 because of famine, in 1904 because of tax problems.[106] During the worst of the famines, the death toll was high. In July 1914, fourteen deaths a day were reported at Sanga, almost seven a day at Bandiagara and Douentza.[107] The young and strong went looking for food or work, but famine decimated the old, the sick and the very young. For some, problems of famine and taxation must have heightened a sense of vulnerability. Security in the harsh world of the Sudan lay in relationships that could afford protection, and that often meant for the former slave nurturing links with his former master. In the absence of convincing data, we can only guess that early twentieth-century famines cut both ways, pressing slaves to leave marginal areas and masters incapable of protecting them, but inducing them to be cautious about breaking links elsewhere.

First World War

The war proved that slavery remained a real issue in many African societies. With staff reduced and attention focused on other problems, administrators responded in different ways. Two incidents demonstrate how different French commandants could be. One involved a conservative administrator, Louis Tauxier, the other a liberal one in Guinea named Liurette. In 1918, Tauxier became commandant at Nioro.[108] When a new commandant came to Nioro, he was generally greeted by Moors who claimed the return of their departed slaves. They were probably surprised to find in Tauxier "a benevolent listener prepared to welcome their claims."[109] Tauxier agreed to return to them any slave who had fled within the previous year. Authorizations were written in Arabic. These were sometimes individual, sometimes collective. Tauxier's clerk said that on some days he wrote fifty. Events turned violent as Moors circulated in villages, demanding their slaves, especially women and children. Arnaud, sent to investigate, described caravans of slaves being led away chained by the neck. The Moors then extended their efforts to the neighboring cercles of Kita and Nara, where they were less successful. When it became known what Tauxier had done, he was quickly withdrawn. The new administrator immediately reasserted his authority over the Moors and began trying to recover the slaves dragged away. It is not clear how successful he was. Tauxier insisted that slaves were not forced to leave with their masters. Once Tauxier was removed, the only question for his superiors was whether he should receive an official reprimand. The file includes few enclosures.[110]

At least one case had the opposite effect. It took place at Kumbia on the border of Portuguese Guinea, a cercle created from the *diwal* of Labé. After being conquered by Labé late in the nineteenth century, Kumbia was colonized by Fulbe nobles, who settled their slaves in the area. It thus had a large slave population. The first years of the war saw flight from slavery and from conscription. Commandant Liurette dealt with the problem by reorganizing the cercle to place slaves under chiefs of servile origin. The result was conflict over land. In addition, many reports claim that slave chiefs could not cope with their responsibilities. Many masters withdrew into either Portuguese Guinea or the Casamance, and Liurette was replaced by a more conservative administrator, Lalande, who tried to reverse the situation, reimposing Fulbe chiefs and using forced labor to establish authority.[111] This made things worse and Inspector Brevié was sent in. As in Bamako, more than a decade earlier, he talked to the slaves and found that they saw Lalande's reforms as a return to slavery. He did not, however, believe that chiefs could be found among the former slaves.[112] On his recommendation, another commandant was sent in, who cooled off the situation, but not before about 26,000 slaves freed themselves.[113] For those who remained, control by masters was still effective. During the inter-war years, courts usually supported the rights of masters over their slaves and the administration often tracked down slaves who fled the *rundé* or reneged on their obligations.[114]

Rejection of liberalism

The biggest problem, however, was that the thinning of the French presence and an increase in demands made on African societies led to a series of revolts, most of them in desert and savanna regions and most of them the result of hostility of the colonized to conscription and taxation.[115] In areas bordering British colonies men fled to avoid conscription. The war increased the isolation of the hierarchy and, therefore, its dependence on African collaborators and its vulnerability. Most important, it increased the power of the chiefs and increased concern with control. The first effort to bolster the chiefs came before the war when Guinea in 1913 stopped local administrators from bringing chiefs before the courts without approval of the Governor. Interestingly, revolts did not take place in Guinea or anywhere where France had effectively coopted and used traditional rulers. With control eroding, many senior administrators felt that the colonial state should strengthen the chiefs. Some were men who long had reservations about Ponty's *politique des races*. Clozel, who became Governor-General when Ponty died suddenly in 1915, had used chiefs effectively in the Ivory Coast. Similarly, Merlin, who became Governor-General in 1919, was the author of a law code which used customary law and supported a pro-chief policy. Clozel gave instructions that administrators were to rely on local traditions in choosing chiefs. In 1917, Van Vollenhoven further reinforced the position of the canton chiefs with a circular that recommended traditional rules for designating chiefs, increased honors, made more difficult administrative sanctions against them and protected their status.[116] Chiefs were paid for providing recruits, and the regime turned a blind eye to their methods.[117]

The increasing reliance on the chiefs was followed after the war by movement away from another of Ponty's ideas, reliance on the market. This rejection of liberalism has sometimes been linked to the renaissance of patriotism and the rise of the right wing in France.[118] The roots of the new policies, however, were much more in events within Africa.[119] First, the re-evaluation of the chiefs was very much a response to the revolts and to the continuing problem of maintaining control. Second, the pre-war period also saw the development of demands by African elites that the colonial administration could not satisfy. They culminated in 1914 in the election of a Senegalese, Blaise Diagne, as deputy from the Four Communes. The response to these was a more repressive policy. In 1920 Merlin reformed the General Council into a Colonial Council on which the votes of elected city-dwellers were counterbalanced by appointed chiefs. He also began a surveillance of African elites similar to earlier surveillance of Muslim leaders.[120]

Conklin also argues that many policy-makers were disappointed with the results of slave emancipation. They accepted Ponty's argument that the former slaves were willing to work, but were disappointed in their production of export crops. Conklin accepts this argument, but it is not correct. Freed slaves produced cloth and gold for local markets and they migrated to Senegalese peanut and Ivoirian cocoa fields. They were the primary source of labor for the dramatic increase in exports during the decade before the war. The problem is that many key figures in French West Africa continued to believe that Africans were lazy, that they would work only until their granaries were filled. They believed that development could only come from coercion. The result was the large-scale use of forced labor and forced cultivation. Forced labor was used to construct railroads, to build roads and to dig irrigation canals.[121] This reliance on coercion even further increased dependence on the chiefs, who were able to use the power the state gave them for their own ends. They received whatever new technology was introduced, were able to acquire lands and could force peasants to work those lands.

The most influential intellectual of the period was Delafosse. He was Director of Political Affairs for both Clozel and Van Vollenhoven and influenced Merlin. Delafosse respected African cultures and supported the use of African law and African chiefs. He also argued that slavery no longer existed:

... from the moment that we ended wars between tribes and expeditions by conquering chiefs, we closed off the only source of slavery and there was no longer any need to proclaim abolition: if some slaves remained in West Africa, they would disappear and the generation that follows ours would not have a single one. There would remain only domestic and agricultural serfs, what we call improperly *captifs de case*. These are people born of slaves and their descendants. According to native custom, they cannot be sold, which distinguishes them from slaves, but they can also not be freed and their descendants remain attached to the family of their masters or lords until the end of time. Such is the theory. In practice, the serfs have simply become a sort of proletariat; the institution has transformed itself into a social class.[122]

Delafosse then argued that it was possible gradually to extend rights to this class. He warned that "certain exterior forms of respect on the part of the serfs toward the nobles" would persist, but he did not think the state should intervene as long as "no native had to submit to any kind of prejudice because of his origin."[123] Whatever Delafosse intended, his analysis provided a justification for benign neglect. The major policy-makers of the period had no desire to reopen old questions.[124] They had also developed new forms of labor coercion that seemed more appropriate to the times. This meant two things to former slaves. First, they had to deal with high taxation and forced labor, both of which are still remembered with great bitterness, particularly in Mali. Second, chiefs, who were often the largest slave-holders, became more powerful. Peasants, whether of slave origin or not, had to work the chief's field one day a week, give him gifts, and defer to him and his values. Commandants, who never liked slave–master hassles, had good reason to ignore complaints from former slaves against chiefs or masters. Ironically, the shortage of labor was due more to underpopulation than to a reluctance to work. The use of coercion and reinforcement of chiefship had the effect of restricting the flow of labor to areas where it was wanted.

Conclusion

The exodus of slaves in the western Sudan was not unique, but the scale of it was not equalled anywhere else in Africa. It was not, however, the first. The Gold Coast in 1874 was the first tropical African colony to abolish slavery, but Dahomey was the first area outside Senegal to experience large-scale emancipation. Dodds, who conquered Dahomey in 1894, abolished the slave trade and freed the slaves of high officials in an effort to cut their power. He is often seen as having abolished slavery. Those who were allied to the French were more successful at maintaining control, but most of those who lived in slave villages left their masters either to return to earlier homes or to set up elsewhere. Many, however, stayed and renegotiated the conditions of their servitude.[125]

The closest parallel to the western Sudan was northern Nigeria, which has been studied by Lovejoy and Hogendorn. After the conquest, Lugard moved quickly to end slave-raiding and long-distance slave-trading. Lovejoy and Hogendorn estimate that roughly 10 percent of the slaves left their masters, perhaps 200,000 people. By contrast, some adjacent areas under French rule experienced a drop in population as high as 50 percent.[126] Fearing a decline in food production and an increase in lawlessness, Lugard moved strongly to stop the departures. Children born after 1901 were technically freed, but others had to pay for their freedom. Fugitive slaves were denied access to land and the right to move freely. All slave matters except enslavement and trading were consigned to the Islamic courts. Eventually, taxation policies forced masters to loosen their control over their former slaves, but the ruling elites of the north continued to control land and labor until late in the century.[127]

Elsewhere, the pattern varied. Almost everywhere, there was some movement. Some states, like the slaving polity of Dar-al-Kuti, crumbled with defeat. As their oppressors fled, slaves just moved out, either to go home or to set up their own communities.[128] In others, slaves preferred to stay where they were. In Somalia, Italian abolition of slavery undercut the plantation system. Slaves, many of them from very distant areas, built their own communities in the fertile Juba and Shebelle valleys.[129] In Buganda, most slaves seem to have stayed and were folded in to the Ganda kinship system.[130] The Germans pursued a rather piecemeal approach to slavery in East Africa, which culminated in the meaningless proclamation in 1905 that children born after that date were legally free. Though only about 10 percent of the slave population received liberty certificates, a majority had probably escaped from slavery by 1914.[131] There was no mass liberation in Portuguese Africa though slavery was legally abolished in 1910.[132] Slavery was not abolished in Sierra Leone until 1928,[133] but the most strongly pro-slavery colony was the Sudan, where little was done about slavery and a clandestine slave trade was tolerated into the 1930s. Sikainga argues that many slaves freed themselves, especially during the period after conquest.[134]

The biggest weakness in the literature on emancipation is an emphasis on colonial policy and a failure to recognize slaves as actors. Morton argues that Cooper underestimates the scale of flight from slavery, but both Cooper and Morton describe a rapid breakdown of the plantation system on the East African coast and both recognize the importance of the slaves. Slaves did not flee to earlier homes, which were often still insecure in the 1890s, but they formed separate communities and sought wage labor as porters, in the cities and in railroad construction. The colonial state was unable to control access to land.[135] Cooper describes for Zanzibar a complex struggle between slaves and masters to control work, in which even the backing of the colonial state could not block the transition to a squatting system under which the former slaves established a considerable measure of autonomy.

Thus, the massive exodus described in this study is unique only in its size. Everywhere, slaves sought either to leave or to establish control of their work lives. "Never," Cooper wrote, "has a slave community regretted its freedom; never, even in the face of the most dire poverty, has it wished to return to the security and oppression of slavery."[136] This surprised colonial observers, who everywhere saw slaves as indolent and passive. Except where the political order disintegrated, as at Dar al-Kuti, there was always a struggle to control both the work lives and family lives of the former slaves. Cooper continues that in many areas, emancipation

has been a time of disillusionment as well as joy. The individual plantation owner may have ceased to be lord and master over his slaves, but the planter class did not lose its power. From the perspective of abolitionists, workers and employers in a free society interacted as individuals in the market place, selling and buying labor. But in case after case, a particular class – under the equally hallowed ideals of private property – kept land from the eager hands of ex-slaves and vigorously applied the instruments of the state and the law to block ex-slaves' access to resources and markets, to restrict their ability to move about, bargain, or refuse wage labor, and to undermine their attempts to become independent producers. At the same time, freed slaves fought hardest against the regimentation of gang labor and the efforts of planters to determine when and how any member of a laborer's family would work.[137]

13 After the War: renegotiating social relations

> ... Everyone was free to go where they wished. Now it was each person for
> himself. Few remained because masters did not give enough help to slaves.
> But those who set themselves up close by continued to come and greet their
> master every morning. Nevertheless, the word slave no longer remained.
>
> Ex-slave informant, Senegal[1]

For the slaves, the most important thing about World War I was that an army
of African slaves went forth once more to serve France, this time on the
battlefields of Europe. While the war shifted colonial policy in a more authoritarian direction, its most immediate result was another movement of liberation. The First World War impacted on slavery because a largely slave army
was conscripted to fight it. Many years later, after another war, a colonial
governor suggested that the Fulbe of Futa Jallon contributed to the emancipation of the slaves by always choosing them when the colonial state demanded men.[2] In this, the Futa Fulbe were not unique. The demand by the
colonial state for soldiers led to a significant erosion of the masters' hegemonic position in many areas. From the first, during the nineteenth century,
those who served in the French army used that service to break the chains of
previous servitude. If they returned to places where they had been slaves, it
was to liberate relatives. Sometimes these relatives were not eager to follow
long-lost brothers or sons, to discover unknown fathers, or to throw off
husbands to join earlier mates; but others followed ex-*tirailleur* kin to new
communities, often in or near French posts. Former *tirailleurs* were often
reluctant to submit to the highly arbitrary nature of French authority. "These
people," an administrator in Buguni complained, "do not wish to recognize
any authority once they have returned to civilian life."[3] Many, however,
benefited from their relationship with the French to better themselves and
find secure employment.

Return of the tirailleurs

On completion of the conquest, the French military began to look to Africa
for soldiers to defend France itself. The French birth rate in the late nineteenth
century was much lower than the German rate. On the eve of World War I,
the ratio of population between the two countries was about 4:7. The French

216

thus turned to the colonies to compensate for the deficiency, and in particular to Africa, whose soldiers had a reputation for being loyal and courageous.[4] Recruitment began in 1912 and was stepped up when the war began. Some slaves were willing, if not eager to go, but in most areas, recruitment was resisted. It led to revolts and large-scale flight, either to the bush or to British colonies. Some whole villages fled, in other cases just the young men.[5] Where slaves were still controlled by masters, the common response was to send them, especially in Fulbe and Soninke areas.[6] Sometimes, enlistment bonuses were paid to masters for manumission. Other slaves were granted liberty when conscripted.[7] Some *tirailleurs* arranged for the master to receive remittances in expectation of manumission. Freed slave communities like Wasulu were also major sources of recruits. The French tried to break the association of slavery and military service, and in particular to get chiefs to send their sons.[8] Some served and were rewarded later with chiefships, but about three fourths of the *tirailleurs* were of slave origin.[9] Only where slaves were few or such distinctions unimportant was there a significant recruitment of free men. About 180,000 *tirailleurs* served in Europe.

The administration knew who the *tirailleurs* were and expected them to make demands after the war not only on the state, but on chiefs and former masters. At the beginning of demobilization in 1919, Governor-General Angoulvant distributed a fourteen-page circular warning local administrators to expect conflict. He pointed out that *tirailleurs* had served France well and suggested that they could be useful collaborators. Commandants were asked to listen to the veterans, be tactful and recognize their rights, but to maintain authority.[10] Authority broke down in many areas. Clark and Manchuelle suggest that the war did more than the 1905 decree to destroy slavery among the western Soninke. Veterans refused to accept the authority of masters. Many had learned to read or picked up other useful skills. Many created separate villages. The commandant at Bakel confiscated land from the ruling Bathily lineage for rebellious veterans. Those who remained with masters usually renegotiated the terms of their dependence, frequently substituting money payments for labor. Many cut all formal obligations, maintaining only symbolic roles like food preparation for major ceremonies. Others did not even do that.[11] Manchuelle suggests that the increase in labor migration after the war resulted from the erosion of the authority of family heads over both their sons and their slaves.[12] We see similar patterns elsewhere. Thus Kane describes problems in Futa Toro with veterans after demobilization: refusal to pay taxes, demands for land, and hostility to chiefs.[13] Roberts reports that when the *tirailleurs* returned, "they used the opportunity to renegotiate once again the condition of their participation in households. They bargained for better food rations, working conditions, and marriage options."[14]

The most intense conflict was in Guinea and was directed not at the state, but at chiefs and former masters.[15] A group in Kissidugu rejected the authority of a canton chief, and when the administration backed the chief, moved away.[16] On the Guinea coast, veterans were reluctant to accept authority: "They have acquired under the colours a rather extensive notion of their rights, which is fine. Unfortunately, they have not developed an awareness of their duties."[17] Change was greatest in upper Guinea. In Kankan, when returned *tirailleurs* asked to leave, the governor asked the commandant to temporize in the hope that they would slip back into an earlier dependence.[18] Nevertheless, the first quarter of 1920 saw a 4 percent drop in population, much of it in slave settlements near Kankan, and later that year, the exodus spread to other parts of the cercle.[19] In Beyla, the administrator reported: "The return of the demobilized *tirailleurs* has made the once servile population understand that nothing ties them any longer to the land they have until now cultivated for others, and they wish today either to leave or to work the land without any rent."[20] The masters insisted that the land was theirs. The administrator could not accept "expropriation without compensation," but he feared a massive departure. A year later, many from Bouzie announced that they too wished to leave. When *métayage* contracts were suggested, only two accepted. The rest left.[21]

In Macenta, former *tirailleurs* did not want to leave, but simply to free themselves from all obligations and to get official recognition of their liberation: "No more in 1921 than in 1912 can we issue liberty papers, but they attach great importance to seeing the domination of those who employed them publicly lifted, in possessing a piece of paper which juridically confirms their new situation and that of their family."[22] A year later, the commandant suggested sharecropping contracts to a delegation of ex-*tirailleurs*, but only two signed. The reason was simple: "In regions where sharecropping contracts have been signed, the soil is not all of the same quality, large areas are not productive and there are only small areas of good land. The freed persons are as a result forced to accept contracts because they cannot live elsewhere, all good land being in the hands of masters."[23] But Macenta was lightly peopled. Fertile well-watered land was available. "They experience, furthermore, a legitimate desire to cut their former ties, to know the joy of working for themselves, of tasting family life free from fear of a brutal separation, of forming new villages and trying a communal life."[24]

Merlin, newly appointed Governor-General, assured the governor that he saw neither a social nor an economic problem in the exodus. He suggested that commandants urge former slaves to remain near former masters, but insisted that they had the right to go where they wished.[25] There is a marginal comment on one report, probably from Merlin: "Guinea has waffled too much on this question of slaves. If a radical measure had been taken in 1905, as in the Sudan, we would not still have to deal with such delicate questions."[26] In spite of this, information sheets on chiefs still asked for a number of years the number of "servants" and wives.[27] The veterans did not remain a radical force, largely because they were freed from such obligations of ordinary Africans as the *indigénat* and forced labor. They also received preference for government jobs, and filled most posts that demanded a limited education: messengers, orderlies, gardeners, concierges, guards and railway workers.[28] Many moved to cities and towns or became petty entrepreneurs. They were among the first, for example, to drive trucks or taxis.[29] This contributed to their well-being and removed potential troublemakers from rural communities.

Once post-war disruptions were over, a quiet class struggle resumed. As we saw in the previous chapter, this struggle took place under conditions not favorable to the former slaves. They had exchanged one form of labor coercion, slavery, for another, forced labor and forced cultivation and the local commandant was likely to support the chief if he was challenged. In spite of this, the struggle continued. Masters were often able to maintain their grip, but most former slaves gradually increased their autonomy. There were two important factors in this. The first was the increasing mobility of both former slaves and former masters. Ex-slave migrants often returned to relations of subordination, but they did not have to. Where home was not a satisfying place, slaves could develop new lives elsewhere. The second was a gradual breakdown of village and household. Freed from fear of raiders, people were able to move out of larger villages. The French tried to limit the breakup of the village, but it continued. Similarly, large households broke into smaller units. Within noble households, the existence of numerous slaves had earlier kept junior members within the family. Most of the reasons for large households no longer existed. More and more young men earned money for their own brideprice and left their father's house as soon as they had family of their own. What this means is that there was a continual erosion of the power of authority figures, village chiefs, masters, elders over the mass of dependants, everyone except the *chef de canton.*

Senegalese peanut basin

In Senegal, these developments were linked to economic growth. Peanut production grew during the inter-war years, most dramatically in Sine-Saloum, where it was already 100,000 tons in 1914. By the 1930s, Sine-Saloum averaged 250,000 tons a year, which was often over half of Senegal's production. The annual flow of *navetanes* averaged at peak 60,000 to 70,000, to which we can add at least another 20,000 to the Gambia.[30] One effect of the *navetanat* is that some decided to stay. Scattered across Saalum are villages of Bambara, Fulbe and Turka.[31] Many Wolof villages have a stranger ward. Baldé shows that many Futa Jallon Fulbe who settled in Senegal were of servile origin.[32] The same was probably true of Bambara and Soninke. There was also movement within the region as groups and individuals sought good land and favorable relations with local chiefs. Of the twenty-eight villages in the arrondissement of Medina Sabakh, six are ex-slave villages under ex-slave chiefs. Five were founded in the inter-war period and the sixth after 1945.[33] By 1920, most slave households in southern Saalum organized their own productive activities and arranged their own marriages.[34]

Unhappy as many chiefs were about loss of their slaves, they profited from settlement of new people on their lands. The area around Thyssé-Kaymor illustrates this. For example, one ex-slave family originated in a group of Tukolor villages about 20 km from Kaymor. They first settled in the Gambia, and then, about 1926, moved to Thyssé-Kaymor, where they formed a separate hamlet near the larger village. By 1975, Al Hajj Musa Ba, the leader of this community was one of the most successful peasants in the village. His family of over sixty worked as a single unit until 1972, when it split into three households. This was unusual. The patriarch prided himself on being the first in the village to build a concrete house and one of the first to adopt agricultural machinery.[35] About the same time, a former slave named Biraan Turé moved with his family to the almost deserted hamlet of Sam, a kilometer or two from Sonkorong. "I was alone with my family," he claimed. There was one other man there, who soon left. Turé cleared the land and gradually increased the scale of his operations. He became one of the more successful peasants, soon grew enough millet to take in *navetanes* and accumulated a large herd of cattle. Turé claimed to be 103 years old when I interviewed him in 1975. The four households in Sam were all his offspring.[36]

Kleene and Venema show how *jaam* who remained with their masters in Sonkorong gradually asserted their autonomy. Sonkorong, a village founded by a Muslim military leader, had large slave holdings. One of the five wards was composed of *jaam*, who moved out of their masters' compounds to live separately. Its name, Santhiabi, means "the place of people of different origin." Others remained for a while with former masters. Even those who physically distanced themselves continued to pay *assaka* and call on *jambur* to preside over marriages and naming ceremonies.[37] In the early 1920s, two members of the ruling Cissé family moved out of Sonkorong with two households of former slaves.[38] Each of the three families claimed rights to land it cleared. The hamlet was called Ndakhar Karim after Karim Cissé, who continued to live there. Gradually, other Cissé slave households moved to Ndakhar Karim. About ten years after it was founded, two *jaam* households left to create Ndakhar Bakhary "to distance themselves from their former master in order to be freer without losing their rights, in particular, their rights to land."[39] They did so on the advice of a marabout and may well in the process have shifted the payment of *assaka* from the slave-owner to the marabout. In 1934, another *jaam* household moved out from Ndakhar Karim to form Ndakhar Aly Coumba and in 1955, on the death of the founder of Ndakhar Bakary, two *jaam* households split from it. This story underlines much about the process of emancipation. Slaves attached to the Cissé family had enough autonomy in 1920 to clear their own land, but they had to move to the edge of the cultivated area to do so. In 1920, the slaves were still linked to the Cissés, but by 1974, there was no longer any economic dependence.[40] *Jaam* controlled land they or their fathers had cleared, but continued to pay taxes through the larger village.

We get a different picture from Irvine's study of a village in southern Kajoor during the late 1960s. *Jaam* were worse off in "Kir Matar" than in southern Saalum. They did not have land of their own and still worked for their ex-masters:

The master–slave relationship . . . is a permanent bond that exists at least in potential even today, when few slaves live in their master's compound and work for him full-time. Even if a slave denies his station and moves away to escape it, Nobles still remember who their slaves were; and the bond remains residually because the Slave or his descendants can come back and reinstate it . . . there are only a handful of slaves living in the master's compound and working exclusively for him. Other slaves have their own compounds, but retain some relationship with their master in which they work for him part-time or on special occasions, such as house-building or harvesting.[41]

Jaam tried to distance themselves from former masters by moving to other parts of the village, but remained dependent on them for land. They also continued to dig and clean latrines.[42]

Working in Ballanghar, a Gambian village not far from Kaymor, just after the war, Ames described a situation more like Kaymor. *Jaam* could get land or permission to clear land a half-hour walk from the village. They sometimes worked the former master's field and paid a tithe from their own harvests. Social relationships confirmed their inferior status:

Jam are still expected to show deference in the presence of the free born. However, some of them have taken advantage of the freedom given them by the British and as one elderly freeborn man put it, they "throw their hats as far as they can." Jam still take off their shoes when greeting their masters and respectfully address them as "grandfathers."
... Not all jam, of course, follow these patterns; some of them avoid such behaviour to the extent that they are permitted to do so by society. These individuals emphasize the fact that not all jam act in such a "degrading fashion," and maintain, on occasion, that they too are really freeborn, since their ancestors did not become jam until they were captured.[43]

Many *jaam* were able through hard work and the fortune of having a large family to accumulate a good bit of wealth.

Fragmentation of *jaam* communities and continued control of political and religious offices by elite families meant that former slaves still lived in a society controlled by former masters. Traditional links are strong in Kir Matar, where shortage of land made it difficult for *jaam* to assert their independence. Even money cannot erase the stigma of servile origins. A man who purchased his freedom in order to marry a *jambuur* woman eventually moved to the city, where it is easier to hide one's origin, but he is still regarded as *jaam* in Kir Matar. So are "children of one foot," the offspring of *jambuur* fathers and *jaam* mothers.[44] Even in Kaymor and Ballanghar, *jaam* pay *assaka* to former masters and, in 1974, three Kaymor *jaam* still lived in their master's compound.[45] In much of Senegal, a former slave making the pilgrimage to Mecca must first buy his freedom under traditional law. One *jaam* informant from Kaymor angered the heir to his master by not approaching him with a proper deferential spirit. The heir said he should have asked the price. Instead he came in, put 18,000 francs CFA on the table (about $70 US) and announced that he was going to Mecca.[46]

The question of *assaka* is crucial. Informants say that *assaka* is 10 percent of the harvest. In the ENEA studies, most budgets for *jaam* families did not mention *assaka*, but four that did list *assaka* at from 0.6 percent to about 3 percent of household expenses. Others lump it into a catchall category called *divers*, which also involves payments to marabouts and usually runs about 7 or 8 percent. Irvine presents only one *jaam* budget with *assaka* a little over 5

percent of family income.[47] It is clear that *assaka* has become a small obligation and, for many, a token one.

Former slaves have moved to Kaymor, where there was still uncultivated
land. Movement was away from Kir Matar, which in 1970 was only 12
percent *jaam*.[48] Irvine's informants claimed that there were many more in
earlier times. She could not verify how many more, but Kir Matar is a Muslim
village in an area that imported large numbers of slaves in the 1880s. People
say that many left for the Ferlo, an area of Mouride expansion, and the city.
Villagers believe that the urban Wolof population is 80 percent *jaam* and
nyenyo[49] – southern Kajoor was an area of recruitment for Mouride *daras*.
Irvine's study suggests that where land was not available, the more ambitious
slaves left and the rest remained poor.

Several court cases illustrate other disabilities that persisted. In one Kajoor
case from 1957, a widow sued because, after her husband's death, his former
master seized his papers and sold his possessions. She sued for the papers and
the right of their son to succeed. The court awarded her the papers, but denied
the succession, which was granted only on appeal.[50] In a second case, a wife
left her husband when she found out that he was of servile origin. He sued, but
the court gave her a divorce and allowed her to keep all of her bridewealth.[51]

We thus had in the peanut basin a very complex process of change as slaves
took charge of their productive and reproductive lives. By 1930, it is unlikely
that many masters could claim the labor of slave children. Social barriers
remained important and *jambuur* maintained control of the mosque, but
economic distinctions broke down. Where *jaam* could get land, they could
become wealthy. There are also activities where slave origins do not inhibit a
person. In Kaymor, *jaam* and *jambuur* work together in cooperative labor
groups. Five of the eleven members of the Sonkorong cooperative council
were *jaam* in 1980, and three of its first four presidents were *jaam*, all of them
successful peasants. Venema identified 126 influential men for an elite study.
Of these, 26 percent were *jaam*. Venema argues that the *jaam* were under-
represented because 42 percent of the households were *jaam*, but his data
suggest a breakdown of status distinctions.[52]

Soninke

The balance between persistence and change is equally striking among the
Soninke. We again see the importance of land. The Soninke inhabited dry
areas. Their best land was in low-lying flood plains that benefited from the
limited rainfall. This meant small communities with limited amounts of good
land, which were firmly under the control of established families. Changes in
land law during the colonial period did not facilitate access of freed slaves to
land.[53] Manchuelle has argued that among the western Soninke, between 5
percent and 20 percent of the slaves left in the original exodus.[54] I am
skeptical of this estimate, but it is clear that pre-war droughts and returning
veterans were equally important. Ibrahima Bathily suggests that pawning of

slaves declined after 1920, and one of Adams' informants said that after World War I, "slaves began to feed their own families."[55] Former slaves, Saint-Père wrote of Guidimaxa in the 1920s, "can go where they wish or marry as they wish; their children belong to them; they can acquire property, they inherit and obtain land."[56] But they were still tied to their masters. In his words, they were no longer *esclaves*, but became *serviteurs*. They could neither marry the free nor become village chiefs. Masters gave former slaves land as sharecroppers, and children of *serviteurs* worked as domestics in the household of the master, "who raises the children with his own children, whose games and work they share."[57]

Gumbu, one of the towns most effected by the exodus, has been studied by Meillassoux. Many of those who remained continued to work the lands of their masters until about 1920. After that date, only slaves of important marabouts worked for them, but others continued to repair their masters' houses, masters maintained social distance and former slaves remained deferential. Meillassoux argues that complete emancipation only came from leaving.[58] All writers depict a process of negotiation. Slaves and masters did not sit down and bargain, but the changed balance of power within society forced each side in this struggle to adapt. One of Michel Samuel's informants explains: "They [the masters] consider it necessary to free people before they revolt, but always imposing a condition: if you wish to rest, you can rest, softening the conditions of the slave's work, and holding out the possibilities that exist when you remain with a noble family."[59]

The harshest view of the Soninke came from a reform-minded chief, Ibrahima Diaman Bathily: "These so-called servants are no more than slaves, still working for their masters, often under constraint and without support or remuneration, except sometimes the tax paid by masters or mistress."[60] Bathily was a schoolteacher and amateur scholar from the royal family of Gajaga, who was named Chef de Canton of Goye Inférieur in 1944. Within the limits of his office, he sought to modernize agriculture and reform Soninke social structure. The question of slavery was a crucial part of his program. His notes show how limited change had been for most former slaves:

. . . servants are still given at marriage as part of the dowry, gifts that could be pawned up to 1920 and later that could be inherited from direct and collateral kin . . . The greatest evil, worse than slavery, is inheritance from dead servants. It is the master or the mistress who inherits from a servant regardless of the age and number of children . . . As soon as a servant (even married or with children) dies, the master seals the granary of the deceased. He takes possession of all of his property without concern for widows and orphans belonging to his fellow man. If the deceased and his wife belong to him, he leaves the survivors a part of the property . . .[61]

The former slaves were Soninke, they had "no other national soil, no hearth other than the place of their birth." Like colonial officers of an earlier generation, Bathily proposed contracts, but recognized that contracts would have little meaning without land: "They should have farm land, enjoy their lands in full property, with the same freedom as those who under the vain title of masters, are perched on their shoulders, sucking their blood like the leeches or vampires that they are."[62] Opposed by many of his people and without support from the French, Bathily was frustrated in his efforts and committed suicide in June 1947.

Manchuelle believes that Bathily's view of slavery was distorted because it was based on an archaic form of slavery which prevailed in the royal village.[63] He argues that after the First World War there was a new form of contract, which incorporated elements of traditional *woroso* "serfdom." I doubt that Bathily understood less than French observers and I do not think the *nansoka* contract was generous. Saint-Père wrote about Guidimaxa in the 1920s that former slaves worked the owner's lands or received land as sharecroppers. Their children still served.[64] A generation later, Boyer described *nansoka* contracts among the Kingi Jawara. The worker was given a plot of land and seed, and was fed during the growing season. Five parts of the crop went to the master, two to the cultivator.[65] In the 1960s, Pollet and Winter described for Jafunu a somewhat better situation in which former slaves worked for their masters every morning until they got married. They then received land and paid for that land with two days of labor a week and a small part of the harvest.[66] All accounts suggest that former masters remained in control.

All this was the product of an intense struggle. Some *woroso* left early. Others established autonomous communities, which limited the claims of former masters. The masters controlled land, controlled access to migratory networks, and could coerce. The departures continued. Soninke slaves from Guidimaxa were still moving back to Wasulu and Sikasso in 1929.[67] But the *woroso* migrants were Soninke; they left family behind and were more likely to use revenue from migratory labor to establish their autonomy than to break away.[68] If the former master could not provide land, the former slave could either move to another landlord or work elsewhere.[69] Pollet and Winter describe Dyahunu in the 1960s:

Liberty, granted by a foreign power against the will of the masters, did not make them nobles. They remained second class citizens, scorned by free men. They could marry only slave women and had acquired neither a right to chiefship nor landed property . . . But the slave no longer belongs to a noble or is in the power of a master even though he maintains ties with him. Although of inferior condition, he is a member of society. His family is regulated by the patrilineal principle. . . he is circumcised by the blacksmith, can put on pants [a rite of passage for the adult male], marries according to a procedure which is not exactly that of the nobles, but increasingly resembles it, owns property, follows the precepts of Islam, participates in councils (while being very reserved). Most important, he is no longer obligated to use his labor power for another . . . He is free in his movements to the point of being able to found villages of culture.[70]

Former master and former slave addressed each other as father and son or elder brother and younger brother. Continued submission gave them not only land, but also access to migratory networks. After 1905, labor migration, to the peanut basin, to the Congo, and later to France, eroded patriarchal authority, but strengthened social hierarchy. In the cities of both Senegal and France, migrants lived and ate in dormitory-like rooms with other men from the same clan or village, at least during the early years of migration. They helped each other get jobs, shared expenses and, when disaster struck, pooled resources to ship home or bury an unfortunate colleague. The price that former slaves paid for participation in this system was reaffirmation of their inferior status. In France, it was cooking and cleaning. Eventually, younger ex-slaves rebelled at the subservience expected of them. Michel Samuel has described the "revolt" of a group of young ex-slaves in France who insisted that cooking be shared. When a noble suggested that nobles pay a larger share of the costs, the leader of the slaves responded "that our refusal is not in any way involved with our not wishing to play our part. The essence of our revolt is purely and simply to be exploited no longer."[71]

Soninke society was marked by a weak state and patriarchal households, which included not only the patriarch's children, but also his brothers' families, slaves and clients. The freeing of slaves diminished the household's patrimony. Work elsewhere brought individual income. Slave, son and brother could now pay their own brideprice from earnings as migrants. Former slaves negotiated their own marriages. Extended family relations remained important, especially in migration, where they provided work, lodging and security, but the household was diminished in both size and strength. In spite of this, migrating slaves generally came home and continued to accept the hegemony of masters. Weigel suggests that families remaining behind were essentially hostages. In contrast, Manchuelle argues that former slaves got enough benefits to remain within the system. Descendants of slaves also have the right to ask for help when in financial difficulty, but the price they pay is that they have to acknowledge their inferiority regularly. The slave must remain humble in the presence of the noble, he cannot sit on the same mat, he serves as an intermediary and a spokesman, and he does not eat rice.[72]

Tokolor

The cercles of Futa Toro had the highest slave percentages in Senegal in the 1904 study, but research on the Tokolor has devoted little attention to transformation of slave–master relations. Moustapha Kane argues that few slaves left the Futa Toro because laborers and conscripts were needed there. Such concerns often linked commandants and chiefs, but this explanation is not adequate. We can, however, infer other variables from Kane's thesis. First, conquest of the Futa had been long and difficult. Faced with hostile elements, the French actively supported their clients. In the 1890s, that support involved the right to seize the slaves and cattle of Abdul Bokar Kane and the Futanke returning from the Sudan. Second, with demand for slaves high in the peanut basin during the 1890s, Futa Toro probably imported few new slaves. Thus, by 1905, the percentage of those recently enslaved was relatively small. Third, though land was scarce, the north bank was opened up for settlement with the decline of raiding by Moors after 1902. In 1908, Inspector Demaret suggested that many slaves were cultivating land in what had become Mauritania.[73] These new lands were opening up just as the exodus was taking place elsewhere. They had always been part of the Futa, but raiding by Moors made them unsafe during much of the nineteenth century. Leservoisier describes on the north bank the kind of sharecropping the French tried to create in many areas.[74] *Rimaibe* gave between a third and half of their crop to the landowner under a contract called *rempeccen*. There is, however, he says, no mention of *rempeccen* in colonial studies of land tenure and the contracts were not submitted to any administrator. Finally, Omar Kane has suggested that a key difference between Tokolor and Soninke was that Tokolor did not have slave villages. This may have meant a greater integration of slaves into Tokolor life.[75]

As among the Soninke, former slaves were often able to improve their economic conditions at the price of accepting lower status. According to Abdoulaye Diop: "After their liberation, not having any land, they remained on the land of their former masters as sharecroppers. Many became artisans, particularly weavers, in order to free themselves economically."[76] Migration was not for Tokolor *rimaibe* the outlet it was for other slaves. Former slaves migrated, but in smaller numbers than their percentage of the population. The only group over-represented among migrants is the *torodbe*. At first, this seems surprising, but the *torodbe* are the most numerous status group. They include the most powerful, but there is little wealth in the Futa, which has been economically stagnant since the 1890s. Most *torodbe* lineages were latecomers to the river. Only the powerful have land. In addition, pride limits the ways in which they work. Former slaves had at the time of Diop's research a higher average income because, as in Futa Jallon, they were willing to work as both sharecroppers and weavers. Diop also suggests that former slaves could not leave without the permission of their masters.[77] Delaunay argues that the rates of migration of nobles and *rimaibe* were identical, but agrees with Diop that the low rate of *rimaibe* emigration was because they had higher incomes. He also argues that *rimaibe* could become completely free only by leaving.[78]

Those without slaves

In decentralized societies where slavery was not important, it seems to have disappeared. These societies rarely exploited the labor of others or did so only late in their history. They also tended to integrate those born in the society. In part, the best data is the absence of data. In Wasulu, almost everyone I met descended from someone who had been a slave. I did not hear anyone referred to as a slave today. In Meillassoux's collection on slavery, many authors writing on hierarchical societies include a paragraph on the colonial period. Those writing on decentralized societies ignore servile relationships in the twentieth century. There is nothing in the ethnographic literature to suggest that slave origins are important in any of the egalitarian societies of southern Mali or the forest zone of Guinea.

Among the Minianka, slavery disappeared as the Minianka reasserted their egalitarian norms.[79] The Jola and the Sereer probably had no traditional form of slavery. Both got involved in selling slaves to Europeans and both kept a certain number for themselves, but exploitation of slave labor never became important. Linares argues that Jola took slaves primarily to be ransomed or sold. Jola slaves did work that was not very different from that of others. The deeper structures of society did not change, and thus, under colonial rule, slave origins ceased to be important.[80] The Sereer state was created by outsiders on top of a strongly egalitarian village society. Sereer Siin was part of a Wolof state system. It participated in the Atlantic slave trade, but slaves and casted artisans were found mostly around the capital of Diakhao. Slave holdings were low, and slave origins rapidly lost their importance during the colonial period.[81] Gastellu argues that "today, every trace of slavery has disappeared and the term is used only in joking relationships."

Bambara and Malinke

In many other areas, slave descent is relatively unimportant. Toulmin found slavery irrelevant for understanding work relations in a Bambara village:

. . . ex-slave households are still known as such and they maintain systems of marriage alliance separate from those of nobles. Ex-slave families tend to intermarry because, while a noble family is eager to take a woman from these households in marriage, it is very hard for the ex-slave household to gain a woman for marriage in exchange. Thus, rather than lose all their women in unreciprocated exchanges, they prefer to marry among themselves. Outside the field of marriage, however, no trace of slavery remains in terms of the relationship between ex-slave and master household; the latter is unable for instance to demand any labor service from the former.[82]

Lewis and Grosz-Ngaté were also concerned with work. Lewis argues that there was a sector of the Bambara peasantry that resisted any involvement in the slave economy of pre-conquest Segu. Slave origins were not important in the village he studied and he is convinced that slavery was never important. Bambara peasants there invested in social networks rather than in accumulation of slaves.[83]

Grosz-Ngaté elaborates. She studied the Sana Bambara not far from Maraka Sinsani. Slaves were more numerous in Maraka and *tonjon* communities than in *horon* (free peasant) villages. In *horon* villages, slaves lived within the family compound, worked alongside the family, and were mostly women bought as wives for members of the family or for male slaves. When the slave trade ended and slaves were free to leave, the substance of slave–master relations was rapidly eroded. In the Maraka town of Sibila, there is a *woloso* quarter. In the *horon* villages of Sana, there is no distinctive group of slave descent.[84] Perhaps the most telling variable is that while some *horon* refused to weave, others found it an excellent dry season supplement to their incomes.[85] The stigma that exists among the Maraka, who see weaving as slave work, does not exist among the *horon*. In *horon* villages studied by Toulmin,

Lewis and Grosz-Ngaté, there was no systematic exploitation of slave labor and, thus, no denigration of agriculture as slave work.

Slavery was more important in Malinke areas of the upper Niger. Leynaud and Cissé estimate that the area was 10 to 15 percent *woloso* in the early 1960s.[86] Though they argue that there was a significantly higher percentage in earlier times, they believe that most slaves stayed where they were after 1905. The upper Niger had neither a major political center nor a major commercial city, and thus was probably an area where slave holdings were relatively small. As with Wolof *jaam*, *woloso* gradually asserted their autonomy by moving to the periphery of settled areas or to what had been rainy-season villages, usually rain-fed areas rather than irrigated lands near the river.[87] They benefited from the weakening of the traditional household and from labor migration. They are often confidants of chiefs, but they also continue to do slave tasks like running messages. Though the young were hostile to what they see as archaic values, many *woloso* remained "timid and unobtrusive."[88]

In some poor areas, slavery disappeared because slaves left. In Wolof areas, there is a difference between the peanut basin and elsewhere. In Jolof, Audiger wrote in 1957, most of the slaves had gone except for the crown slaves at Yang-Yang, the traditional capital. Some were sold during famine years for needed grain. Others profited from economic opportunities to move elsewhere.[89]

Slave trade

The number of prosecutions for slave trading dropped sharply during and after the First World War. For West Africa as a whole, the number of convictions dropped from 192 in 1907 to 4 in 1921 (see Table 13.1). In Sudan, there were ten slave-trade cases between 1918 and 1923, four between 1923 and 1926, and none during the subsequent five years.[90] In Niger, there were twenty-two prosecutions between 1930 and 1935.[91] Nevertheless, a small trade persisted. Kidnapping was a problem until after World War II, mostly in the desert-side area. Chiefs were regularly removed for trading in slaves. Slaves could be moved, mostly by nomads, but only in small groups. In the 1930s the French collaborated with the British in fighting a trade that went through Chad to Sudan and Egypt. It involved mostly children, some kidnapped, others sold or pawned by desperate parents. On one occasion, forty children were freed in Niger.[92]

A major concern was the slave trade to Saudi Arabia. Though Ibn Saud banned slave imports in 1934, the pilgrimage provided an effective cover for the trade and sale of slaves an easy way of paying for it.[93] In 1954, Dominique Traoré wrote a series of articles in the Catholic weekly *Afrique Nouvelle* on the trade. He interviewed a young man born a slave in the Niger Bend region, who was taken to Mecca by his Tuareg master. The party consisted of the slave-owner, his wife and three children, and five slaves, who were all sold in Mecca. The article charged that about 1,000 slaves a year were exported from Africa and that the trade was well organized.[94]

Table 13.1. *Prosecutions for slave trading in French West Africa**

1906	147	1919	21
1907	192	1920	16
1908	107	1921	4
1909	58	1930	5
1910	58	1931	15
1911	27	1932	5
1912	30	1933	6
1913	21	1934	6
1914	45	1935	3
1915	22	1936	8
1916	19	1937	0
1917	19		
1918	12		

* "Rapport sur la Question de l'Exchange en A.O.F." submitted by Gov. Gen. to Minister of Colonies, 30 Nov. 1926, ARS, 2 K 4 (1926).

Islam

The mosque became an important battleground in the class struggle that succeeded emancipation. In the wake of the exodus, there were reports of regression to pre-Islamic religions, usually linked to former masters being forced either to herd or to cultivate and echoing the claim that Islam was declining in Banamba.[95] In the long run, this was not true. The more entrepreneurial either hired people or took in migrants – or, in some cases, became full time traders. Clerics, who used slave labor to underwrite their religious vocation, found that in a market economy they could depend directly on gifts from believers and labor of their *talibés*.[96] Former slaves, who had little instruction and often clung to traditional cults, converted or became stricter Muslims, even in Wasulu where Islam was long associated with the hated Samori.[97] In areas like Futa Jallon, where they were not welcome in established mosques, *rimaibe* built their own.

Islam often was a factor in emancipation. Slaves received freedom by serving in various jihads and sought freedom when they fled to various Muslim reformers. During the colonial period, many of the most dynamic movements were those that stressed the equality of all believers. We have seen the social action of the Mourides. A similar role was played by the Hamallists in the Sudan. Shaykh Hamallah was from a branch of the Tijaniya that differed from the mainstream largely in the organization of beads in the rosary.[98] Born in 1883 or 1884, the son of a Beydan trader and a slave woman, Hamallah early developed a reputation for mysticism and asceticism. He never preached in public or solicited gifts, but he taught and wrote letters to other clerics urging them to reform their behavior. He was more concerned with teaching the illiterate and the recently converted than with training scholars.

Hamallah developed a following among slaves, *harratin* and poorer Fulbe in the Nioro area and early formed villages of his disciples. Many of his

followers refused to pay the *zakkat*. This threatened *beydan* tribes and established *tijani* clerics, who began attacking his followers and put pressure on the
French to remove him. By 1917, his influence had spread to Bamako. Like
Amadu Bamba, Hamallah was not openly hostile to the French. Marty
suggested in 1916 that Hamallah's supporters were more reliable than the
Moors.[99] The French were, however, nervous about popular Muslim teachers
and anxious to maintain the authority of collaborating religious leaders and
chiefs. Hamallah refused to send his children to French schools, never attended Bastille Day ceremonies, and would not visit the commandant unless
summoned. In 1925, when he was exiled to southern Mauritania, the movement grew more radical. In Froelich's terms, "he raised the lower classes
against the aristocrats, the poor against the rich, the young against the
old."[100] The French responded by moving him to Algeria and then to France,
where he died in 1943.

Hamallah urged former slaves to reject claims of their masters. His villages
gathered the disenfranchised. At one point, there was a virtual war with the
Tenwajib, a *beydan* tribe, who attacked Hamallist villages, stole cattle, beat
men, abducted women and children. In 1940, a Hamallist band attacked the
main Tenwajib encampment and massacred more than 400 people. A break-
away movement under Yakuba Sylla, a Soninke disciple, moved in a more
radical direction:

To gain admission, followers had to make a full public confession of their sins,
renounce all finery and fancy clothing, and give their jewels to the community. They
built separate villages where everybody worked in common, earnings being handed
over to the local head of the sect . . . Yakubist villages consisted chiefly of people who
had previously lived in a dependant position: slaves fleeing from their patrons, wives or
concubines fleeing from their husbands, youth fleeing from their parents.[101]

After 1946, the Hammalists were linked to the radical Rassemblement Démocratique Africain.

If Islam had egalitarian elements, it also legitimated slavery and advised
obedience. Thus, according to one of Samuel's informants, "The marabout
made slaves understand that the slave's paradise came only with the master's
consent."[102] Islam was the cornerstone of a hegemonic ideology for local
elites, who maintained a monopoly of religious offices. In many areas, a
person of slave origin could not become an imam. In the Futa Jallon, *Rimaibe*
were not obligated to pray, or even to attend the mosque. If they attended,
they had to sit in the back, and sometimes their right to wear the traditional
grand boubou was challenged. The imam and muezzin were always Fulbe.[103]
A Fula performed naming ceremonies for *rimaibe* children, and up to the
1960s the sacrifice of a ram at the Tabaski festival was also done by a Fula.[104]
Key events were marked by gift exchange, which underlined continued submission by *rimaibe*.

Islam could, however, be a two-edged sword, used to support the pretensions of masters or to undercut them. Derman cites a case in which a Fula
gave the child of one of his slaves to a chief as a gift. The local cadi maintained

that the transaction was contrary to Islamic law. His arguments were not persuasive, but he then went to North Africa to study for several years. Upon his return, he reopened the case, arguing that no one had the right to separate the child from its mother.[105] The response of *rimaibe* was not to retreat from Islam, but to seek a quranic education and, often, to create schools and mosques in the *runde*. Many challenged Fulbe religious ascendancy. Botte tells of a World War II *rimaibe* veteran, who was challenged in 1946 when he took his place with Fulbe. It took two years of argument and examination before he was allowed his place. Only in the last quarter of the twentieth century have *rimaibe* been accepted, albeit reluctantly, as Muslims.[106]

Resurgence of pawning

If the 1920s saw increasing autonomy for former slaves, the depression years saw a resurgence of pawning.[107] The problem was economic. The colonial state responded to a drop in revenues by cutting back on staff and tightening tax collection. In cash-crop areas, people generally found ways to pay their taxes. In poor areas, where migrant labor was the major source of cash, many were forced to pawn children. The colonial state had paid little attention to pawning.[108] Most Africans treat pawning as significantly different from slavery because the pawn remains a member of his or her original lineage and can be redeemed. In the absence of clear title to land or other mortgageable possessions, people were the only security for debts. In two cases discussed here, the pawns were all girls.

In the middle of 1934, a Catholic senator, Gustave Gautherot, wrote the Colonial Minster that fathers at Ouahigouya were forced to sell their daughters to pay their taxes, and that the administrator, Le Houx, was involved. The sales took place even though the White Fathers offered to pay the tax for some families if they promised not to sell their daughters.[109] The Governor claimed that the information was exaggerated, but Le Houx essentially conceded the charges:

This was not exactly the sale of a daughter by her father, but more a kind of pawning practised at the instigation of village chiefs. The child was given by her close relatives to a third party during the absence of her father who had gone to the chief to pay his tax. The amount of the agreed loan, a mere 20 francs, was used to pay the tax, after which the father was freed.[110]

Even without administrative prodding, pawning would have taken place. Hurt by both depression and drought, Ouahigouya produced little for market, relying on the income of migrants. With the drop in prices, demand for Mossi labor was reduced.

The second case was in Guinea. In 1932, as an economy measure, Jallonke Sangalan was divided between four Fulbe cantons. In 1936, an African clerk wrote the district administrator about the requisition of young girls. With the collapse of prices, many Jallonke migrants could not find work and those who found it returned with reduced incomes. In addition, drought affected the region, and locusts devoured what survived.[111] When some Jallonke could not pay their tax, the Commandant pressed Chief Alfa Mamadou Diallo to find a way to collect. When Diallo responded that people could only pay if they pawned their daughters, the Commandant answered "that the Jallonke had to manage as best they could to find the money and that he did not want to know how they got it."[112] Diallo interpreted these instructions as a go-ahead. He called those who could not pay to "furnish a number of girls to the Bara market, where they met with heads of Fulbe families who had money, livestock or cloth. In the presence of their parents, these girls were given to their acquirers and the product of these sales was given to the canton chiefs."[113] Of forty-five girls brought to Bara, twenty-four were pawned. They ranged in ages from seven to sixteen. By time the case was investigated in 1936, two were married and four had fled. Other girls were pawned separately by their fathers, in all seventy-four.[114]

The Sangalan affair raised two questions. First, was this an involuntary exchange of persons? If so, it was a violation of the 1905 decree. Second, could women be pawned without their permission?[115] Some of the girls were taken as wives, while others became concubines. This brought the Catholic church into the picture. The Church sought the creation of marriage that was voluntary, monogamous and divinely sanctioned. "Slavery," Holy Ghost Superior General Le Roy wrote, "persists and is maintained in conditions all the more odious in that only the woman is subjected to it."[116] Church attitudes converged with those of the French Left, which came to power in 1936. The administration thus found itself looking both at pawning and at marriage.[117]

When the administration asked for information, it found a dramatic increase in pawning. In Kutiala, there were at least 300 pawns in 1937. In Bandiagara, pawning of women and girls increased among both Fulbe and Maraka after 1930.[118] Of fourteen Masina informants, eleven said it was common, some vividly describing financial pressures and coercion by guards sent to collect taxes.[119] Sikasso, Satadugu and Tougan all reported an increase: "During recent years of poor crops, some young girls were sold by their parents, who were pressed by necessity, but these sales were often sanctioned by marriage."[120] In Segu in 1935, there were over 1,000 pawns.[121]

The girls were returned to their parents.[122] The Fulbe chiefs were stripped of their positions and imprisoned and Sangalan was reorganized to reduce Fulbe authority over the Jallonke.[123] Administrators in both cantons moved to eliminate pawning. At the same time, there was an effort to minimize political consequences. Letters moved up the chain of command, each trying to prove to his superior that pawning was not a morally objectionable institution. The Resident in Kulikoro argued: "Neither the moral nor the material situation of the pawned persons suffers any diminution. Free they are and free they remain . . . Indeed, the people pawned are better treated and better considered by their creditors than domestics in other locations. It is not rare that a child pawned winds up in the new family by marriage."[124]

With pawning, the labor contracted was that of a third and probably unwilling party, whose freedom was constrained until the loan was repaid. The length of service was indefinite.[125] Moreover, the pawn did not receive a wage, since the value of her labor served as interest on the original loan. It was clearly a violation of the 1905 decree.[126] Brevié's response was not to abolish pawning, but to reform it. He suggested that a daily wage rate be set and that as soon as the labor delivered equalled the amount of the debt and interest, the debt should be considered as discharged.[127] The administration still had to distinguish between pawning, sale and marriage, between bridewealth payments, loans and commodity transactions. For Marius Moutet, Popular Front Minister of Colonies, the practices reported could not be reconciled with "liberty of the individual, and more generally, with the dignity of man."[128] The result was two circulars. The first, in June 1936, provided that no marriage could be contracted by girls younger than fourteen or boys younger than sixteen and that consent of both spouses was essential to the validity of the marriage.[129] The second analyzed pawning and the role of the depression in increasing its use. Brevié discounted the use of wages due the pawn to reduce the debt, because that would consecrate "a custom that cannot be conciliated with our conviction on the respect for liberty and human dignity." He therefore suggested that the courts use the 1905 decree, but he insisted that they do so prudently, using persuasion and education where possible. In other words, he told them not to push hard and to use light penalties if any at all.[130]

The problem was already resolving itself. Incomes were rising and rose even more after the war. Oral sources suggest that pawning declined with the end of the depression and disappeared during the war. It is striking, however, that there was not a major increase in pawning during the disastrous famine years from 1968 to 1983.[131] In fact, those famines had the opposite effect. They were so massive that they completely destroyed the power of nomadic groups that still controlled servile agriculturalists. There has been no resurgence of pawning because household heads no longer have the authority to deliver their children.

After World War II

In 1939, the *tirailleurs* went off to war again. Both the army that defended France unsuccessfully in 1940 and the one that liberated it in 1944 had many African conscripts – over 200,000 men each. There are no estimates of the number of men of slave origin among them. Many former slaves were called up, probably more than random selection would indicate, but it was no longer a slave army. The organization of conscription made it hard for others to avoid service.[132] Chiefs had some influence on who went, but they were under pressure to send their own sons and those of the elites.[133] Nevertheless, recruitment was high in areas with a tradition of military service like Wasulu, or where military service made emancipation possible. Men of slave origin were also important among the cadres.[134] They returned to a different world, one in which Africans became French citizens and had the vote. There were no parallels to the social conflicts that took place after World War I, but the Second World War contributed to further social change. Enlistments were heavy, for example, among the *rimaibe* of Futa Jallon. Those who returned had money. Some of it was spent on consumer goods, but much went into buying land or investing in small business. Those who invested in land often became relatively prosperous farmers, including a large group that went into rice.[135]

The post-war situation led to what was probably the last major slave rebellion in the desert-side area in 1946.[136] It took place largely in the bend of the Niger and in the Kayes-Nioro area. Despite earlier movements of emancipation and French efforts to undercut Tuareg control of *bella* after a revolt in 1916, about 50,000 *bella* remained under the control of their Tuareg masters either in their own camps or under the direct control of their masters within the cercles of Niafunke, Gundam, Timbuktu and Gao.[137] Then, in 1946, at Menaka, among the Imajoren Tuareg, "there was an explosion. The word liberation spread like wild fire. The *bellas* arrived at the post to seek the 'peace paper.'" Many took stock with them. Others left fields unharvested. Overnight, the authority of chiefs and masters disappeared as Tuareg struggled to save their herds and keep a few *bella* in their camps.[138] The commandant tried to arbitrate between the two groups, divide the stock and form the *bella* into nomadic fractions of Black Tuareg.[139] That was not the desire of the *bella*. By 1949, *bella* near Gao were heading south to look for better lands. The commandant was told to control vagabondage and aimless wandering, but also "to remedy the real causes of the departures in better regulating conflict between masters and slaves and in improving the conditions of the *bella* population."[140]

Further west, there were similar problems at Yelimané and Nioro. Between Kayes and Nioro, about 30,000 *harratin* lived in agricultural villages, paid annual dues to and were taxed through their *beydan* masters. Many *harratin* traveled with their masters in their transhumant migrations, but reports state that desert-side *harratin* were increasingly limiting the demands of their masters. In 1944, a border rectification transferred some districts to Mauritania in an effort to establish a more rational border between Sudanese agriculturalists and Mauritanian nomads. The problem was that Moors of the Hodh came to the Sudan every dry season and pastured their herds at the villages of their *harratin*. In Mauritania, masters were protected, but in Sudan, *harratin* were exposed to "propagandists of new ideas." Yelimané was populated largely by former slaves. As increasing numbers of *harratin* took refuge at Nioro and Yelimané, many *beydan* refused to come south for fear of losing remaining *harratin*. Others took hostages. The Commandant in Nioro expected the smooth liberation of agricultural villages, but feared that freeing the *harratin* would lead the *beydan* to quit the desert. He undertook negotiations to avoid that.[141] The French still worried about keeping population in the desert, but both Moor and Tuareg increasingly had difficulty controlling desert-side populations. In general, the years since 1945 have seen a southward movement of *bella* and *harratin* seeking both better-watered land and freedom from their former masters.[142]

And yet old attitudes persisted. A 1950 report by the Governor of the Sudan underlines how little some French administrators had learned. It spoke of preventing separation of children from parents and using Quranic law to control mistreatment and redemption. There was some recognition of human rights, but also fear of detribalization, vagabondage and laziness. Contracts were still seen as a way of dealing with these problems.[143] The slave–master link also persists. Even after the revolt of the *harratin*, some former slaves remained with their masters. An administrator from Nioro wrote in 1952, as numerous earlier administrators had written, that some left and some stayed. Those who left, he wrote, did so "because of mistreatment, a desire for freedom or a spirit of adventure." As for those who stayed:

What exactly are their relations with their master? They owe the same days of work as collaterals and descendants. In addition, a tithe from their harvest . . . Finally, all weavers must weave for the master. In exchange, the masters protect them and give them gifts and sometimes favor them over their own sons, who are workers of inferior quality. A day of work must be provided by each circumcised male, noble of not, to the chief of the slaves, who has taken care of them during the period of circumcision.[144]

Conclusion

Thus, from World War I on, change was steady but uneven. In some areas, it was limited. Suret-Canale argues:

. . . attempts made by the administration to transform traditional slavery and serfdom in Masina, Fouta-Djalon and elsewhere into share-farming on big landed estates do not seem to have met with success, except in so far as they replaced terminology that was judged "embarrassing" by another acceptable to bourgeois views. For the chiefs, "rights" always continued to be exercised over men and the fruits of their labor, rather than over the abstract "landed estate", the very notion of which was often the opposite of local reality.[145]

And yet, that change was real. By 1920, we are dealing overwhelmingly with *woloso* and *rimaibe*, who had rights. The former slaves also had mobility. If there were limits on mobility, they were the problem of earning a living elsewhere and social ties to communities in which they were born and raised. The potential freedom of the slave limited the master's options and forced him to think about tying slaves more effectively into the local community. The small size of the slave family increased its vulnerability, but with time, some slaves built up family ties while the households of masters shrank. Slaves had some advantages in this process. The most important was their willingness to work hard and to do work that free men refused to do. Where land was available, slaves often had higher incomes than the freeborn. The right to own land was contested in some areas, but only briefly.[146]

For the colonial regime the major reward from freeing the slaves was the creation of a labor reserve. In an important article on the Lagos general strike of 1897, A.G. Hopkins argues that the colonial government could not break the strike because there was no ready pool of workers who could be engaged at the wage offered.[147] This was because the largest potential pool of labor was tied down by slavery. For French West Africa, as for Lagos, an increase in production depended on freeing labor from the restraints of traditional society. Ponty recognized this, albeit somewhat cautiously. The First World War ironically contributed to a second great wave of liberation, but also to a shift away from such liberal policies. By the time the war came, the French understood how much the smooth functioning of colonial rule depended on the chiefs. The men who came to power between the wars were as concerned with order as with development.

14   A question of honor

Slavery having disappeared as a structure, it is discourse and behaviour that constitutes our only access to the reality. Today, though slavery has been abolished for more than a half-century on the level of power as much as production, daily language abounds with references to the noble–slave contradiction, perpetuating the valorisation of one and the symmetrical contempt of the other.   J.-P. Olivier de Sardan[1]

Though the FulBe no longer have any rights over the RiimaayBe they used to own, the memory of the old relationship is still very much alive in both groups. Individuals vary considerably in how they feel about the past, but it is fair to say in general that the FulBe regret the coming of the French, the loss of sovereignty, and the "'theft" of their RiimaayBe labor force, while the RiimaayBe are glad of it.   Paul Riesman[2]

Slavery casts a long shadow into the colonial period and when adjustments in relationships must be made they are made within the weakened idiom of the known world, just as the relationships of the slave period had been accommodated within the idiom of pre-existing kinship systems.
                                        Martin Chanock[3]

In 1958, several months after the referendum that gave France's African colonies self-government, Robin Maugham visited Timbuktu under the auspices of the British and Foreign Anti-Slavery Society. He interviewed both slaves and masters and actually bought a slave.[4] In Timbuktu, slaves had the right to freedom and many took it. Some fled to the city, where they could find work in the quarries, could become prostitutes or could farm. But there were still many *bella* living in Tuareg camps outside the city. Slaves were sometimes sent into the city to work if there was not enough for them to do in the camps. They could be sold, but only if they agreed to the sale. One chief paid for his trip to Mecca by selling several slaves there. They were often harshly treated. Those who fled were beaten or attacked and followed into the city. Those safely established in the city were often visited and reminded that the French were leaving. Maugham was convinced that many *bella* remained both because of coercion and because they accepted their role. "Of course a slave can go to the Commandant," one informant told him,

and the Commandant will tell him that by law he is not a slave, and by law his master is not his master. But the slave probably knows that already. In his head he knows that he is a free man. But in his heart he does not believe it. He knows he is a Bela [sic] – and a Bela is a slave. If he buys his freedom from his master, that is different. But otherwise, he believes that he belongs to his master, and so do his children.[5]

The slave Maugham bought was freed before witnesses under Quranic law.[6]

Slavery remained important in the desert and slave origins remained meaningful in desert-side regions and in many areas once subject to centralized polities, but it has disappeared in much of the rest of the region. It is almost totally gone in the cities. To be sure, the researcher is often told about begging relationships, and some wealthy families maintain former slaves as family retainers. An American friend was provided with a servant several years ago, who turned out to be a "slave" of the friend who made the arrangement. As Olivier de Sardan suggests above, slavery has disappeared as a structure, but still lives in a discourse that shapes the lives of those descended from both slaves and masters.

Nationalist politics

One clear evidence of this discourse is the role of the fight against slavery in the emergence of radical nationalist parties. These issues have not been important in Senegal. People of slave origin participate actively in public life, though not extensively at the highest levels. There was no effort to organize or attack the vestiges of earlier social relations because these had only limited importance. Guinea and Mali were different. In Guinea, slavery was an important issue. The Parti Démocratique de Guinée (PDG), the Guinean branch of the Rassemblement Démocratique Africain (RDA), was founded in 1946. Like many radical political groupings, the PDG was concerned both with reforming African society and with ending colonial rule. In Guinea, that meant attacking chiefship and "feudal" relationships.[7]

Botte believes that a decisive step in breaking structures of authority was the grant of French citizenship and the end of forced labor and the *indigénat* in 1946.[8] Intimidation, however, kept the PDG from taking root in the Futa. Militants were attacked and sometimes driven from the region. This brought home to Touré and the PDG that the major barrier facing them was the traditional chiefs. The PDG recruited at first outside the Futa, and from 1953, organized a network of cells within the *rundes* of the Futa, an effort facilitated by the separation of *runde* and *fulasso*. They also increasingly encouraged *rimaibe* to complain against the excesses of the chiefs. In a special election for Deputy in 1954, Futa votes were crucial in a narrow defeat. In 1956, however, Touré was elected Deputy, and a year later, the PDG swept all parts of the country in territorial elections, taking fifty-eight of sixty seats.[9] The PDG in the Futa was largely a party of *rimaibe* and poor Fulbe.

In power, the PDG proceeded immediately to replace the chiefs by elected local committees, on which *rimaibe* and poor peasants were strongly represented. In doing so, they destroyed French control of the electoral process and created the basis for decisive rejection in 1958 of De Gaulle's Fifth Republic constitution. After independence, Touré announced "definitive suppression" of slavery and banned all reference to the previous status of servile people. As a result, Fulbe began to refer sarcastically to former *rimaibe* as "Fulbe of September 28" (date of the independence vote).[10] Today, they are usually referred to as *rundebe*, people who live in the *runde*. The Touré regime followed up on their promises when, in 1962, the state took over all land, and *rimaibe* were given rights to it. They served on governing councils and cooperative boards, sometimes, when their membership was challenged, *runde* and *fulasso* were allowed to remain separate.[11] The process has continued since the death of Touré and so has conflict. Slave origins are not yet irrelevant. In 1987, Fulbe unsuccessfully challenged selection of a man of slave origin as prefect of Labé. Marriage between males of slave descent and noble women is rare unless the male is rich and the woman from a poor family. Moreover, old habits do not die. Rivière wrote in 1974:

> . . . many elderly former serfs do not feel themselves totally separate from their masters and continue the same polite deference toward them as before, give them symbolic gifts instead of tribute, and it is always among them that are recruited the butchers, dancers, and healer-magicians . . .[12]

Some observers would go further and argue that it is not just the habit of deference that lasted. The history of the rural social structure during the Touré years has yet to be written, but the works of Rivière, Botte and Wynkoop are a beginning. While Botte provides a picture of continuing struggle, Wynkoop's thesis shows how old elites adapted to a revolutionary situation. In Koubia, the nobility kept control of the machinery of state and eventually won control of the local party organization. There are three major population groups in Koubia, nobles, former slaves, and indigenous peoples. When the economy collapsed, all three had to find other ways of making a living. The nobles had better access to capital and goods. Many of them thus moved into trade. The few with better education and contacts were able to get better jobs. They were thus able to maintain their control over their lands, and through their control over credit and employment, they were able to provide a fragile security for those former slaves who operated within the system: "While noble households use their customary claims on slaves to extract production and labor, slave households rely on customary relations with nobles for credit, often needed during the hungry season to buy food."[13] Subservience had its rewards. The former slaves had greater access to land and work than indigenous inhabitants.[14] It is not clear from Wynkoop's account what the total obligation of a former slave is, but the basic obligation is a tithe. The form rent takes is negotiable and can be either work, cash, or a share of the crop.

In Mali, there is much less published information available about social conflict. The Sudanese branch of the RDA, the Union Soudanaise, was probably the most serious of the early socialist parties in Africa. It was committed to equality and the major opposition party, Fily Dabo Sissoko's PSP, was strong in areas where slave labor was still being exploited. Once in power, the Union Soudanaise tried to re-shape rural society and create new forms of cooperation.[15] There were campaigns of *sensibilisation et de conscientisation* in Masina which clearly had as one of their purposes the organisation of the *rimaibe*.[16] The Union Soudanaise may have been successful with *rimaibe*, but their broader program failed because they tried to impose on the peasantry models of social organization that the peasants did not want. Social equality was unfortunately linked to the heavy hand of the state.

When the United Nations had another inquiry on slavery in 1963, Guinea did not respond. Mali's response was one of the most detailed and was marked by a fervor which suggested the importance of the question to the new regime. It claimed that the 1905 decree

> was designed to prevent attempts by former masters to regain control of slaves or persons of servile status. But the decree was never applied in practice, because the colonial regime substituted a collective system of slavery for the previous system and allowed the black peoples living near the Sahara to remain slaves *de jure*. The independent Republic of Mali liberated the Bellahs and Haratines.[17]

Persistence

Given the erosion of slavery by a market economy, the attack on it by both colonialists and nationalists, and the resistance of slaves themselves, we must ask why any vestigial relationship persists. My original hypothesis was that slavery would most completely disappear in cash crop areas. Then, I read Ames' thesis. Though former slaves in Ballanghar could get land outside the village, they sometimes worked the former master's field and gave him a "tithe" from their own harvests. They were still expected to show deference, though not all did. A generation later, Mohammed Mbodj and I worked in several Wolof villages on the other side of the border and found a similar situation. Though the *assaka* had become for most a token payment, most *jaam* still paid it. A *jaam* could not go to Mecca without purchasing his freedom. A former slave could not become an imam. *Jaam* generally did the cooking at weddings, funerals and naming ceremonies and were still expected to show deference. At the same time, they could accede to important offices such as head of the cooperative or local party leader, they served on elected councils and many were economically well off. Why then in an area of major economic change did symbols of submission and payment of dues persist? This is Ames' argument:

> First of all, it has been noted that jam receive adequate compensation for performing their traditional tasks in all the ceremonies held by the freeborn. Secondly, they are entitled to beg from their masters anything they need, although they are not always successful. However, the most effective reinforcement of the freeborn–jam relationship today (as probably in the old days also) is religious. Unlike the freeborn, jam are not educated in Koranic schools; all they are expected to know is how to pray. Jam are told that if they work for their masters in the fields, present tithes (hassaka), and behave respectfully, they will be blessed and go to heaven. The threefold ideal of working hard, being respectful to one's elders – in this case one's masters – and praying regularly to receive blessings, is one of the most important devices of social control in the culture.[18]

Ames' analysis is sound, but does not go far enough. We have seen that in and close to the desert, coercion was clearly a factor, but coercion was not important in coastal Senegal after the First World War. I think that there were other variables. The first was economic insecurity. The twentieth century saw some difficult years and some harsh obligations. The tendency for the peasant was to maintain as many insurance policies as possible. The preservation of links between masters and former slaves meant that each could turn to the other in moments of need, albeit in different ways. The master was forced to concede a constant and important reduction in obligations just as household heads had to concede a reduction in hours to *navetanes* and a younger age of economic autonomy to their own sons. The masters had some leverage in that they controlled key institutions of rural life. They were both the canton and village chiefs and they ran the mosque. They tightened their control where they could, for example, in their use of Islam.

The former slave could collect on his insurance policy only by deferential behavior and begging, but in the process, he confirmed his submission. Descendants of masters often talked of what they gave descendants of slaves and claimed that the relationship cost them more than they received. One day, a friend told me that his father had a slave. When I asked what the relationship consisted of, he said that this old man regularly came to his father to ask for money. His father had inherited the man. When I asked if the man had any children, I was told that he had a son, who taught school. Did the son have any contact with my friend's family, I asked? No, I was told, never, not even greetings on special occasions. Similarly, Ames tells us that many former slaves refused to behave as *jaam*.

The second factor was acculturation. From the 1890s on, masters had to find ways to get slaves to accept their inferior status. The exodus of people who remembered another home helped in some ways. Once they had gone, the people who remained were all people who participated in the culture of the dominant group. They had been raised to their roles. Miner suggests that the "practice of separating children from their parents . . . may account for the almost complete acculturation of *bella* to Tuareg ways of life."[19] For the *bella* child, life in the Tuareg camp involved not only learning the language, but learning submission, learning to play the role to which he or she would be consigned. Maugham's picture of the *bella* is of a people sometimes angry, but cowed and fearful. That is one reason why service in the French army was important. For many it broke that attitude of submission. But for others, dependence involved security and the acceptance of their role.

Memories and silences

We cannot simply see people being acculturated to inferior roles. To understand fully why former slaves continue to accept some form of hegemony of their former oppressors, we must explore the deeper recesses of memory. Colonizers, descendants of the masters and the descendants of the slaves all have their memories, which shaped and still shape behavior.

The European record is marked by silences which were deliberate and were complicated by conscious distortion or selection of information. Faidherbe developed a formula that permitted France to ally itself to slavers and to tolerate slavery while seeming to be hostile to it. His formula worked as long as he and his successors could control what the metropole thought was happening in Africa. Darrigrand and Schoelcher destroyed Faidherbe's formula, but his successors constantly tried to regain control over both images of the present and memories of the past. In this, they were aided by the concern of many administrators not to put compromising matter on paper. Administrators often lied, usually were highly selective in the information they collected and passed up the chain of command, and sometimes were downright sloppy. Governors and commandants were often not familiar with instructions given a few years earlier or with events that had only recently taken place. Their views seem to have been determined more by colonial culture and by some kind of collective folk memory than by clear evidence about what went before. They were strongly influenced by their intermediaries, by chiefs who shaped their view of local law and culture, by clerks and guards who sometimes controlled access, and by interpreters who could shape what they said and what they heard. Thus, it was easy for them to accept and pass off the more benign images of African slavery. If nothing else they could focus on the situation of the *woloso* and not on the slave raid, the slave market or the slave caravan, and often, even their images of *woloso* life were idealized.

Thus there was a consistent discourse on slavery parroted by colonial writers even after the exodus made a mockery of its distortions and simplifications. Over and over again, higher authority was reminded that France promised to respect African institutions, often by the people who made those promises in France's name. The issue thus became not the morality of slavery, but the integrity of French promises. Colonial administrators recognized that vast amounts of wealth were tied up in slave property and often felt that violating those property rights was more offensive than ignoring the human rights of the slaves. They also saw the masters as benign figures. Saint-Père in the 1920s wrote that Soninke masters treated their slave children like their own. Was he taken in by blissful pictures of children at play? Did he really believe that masters did not differentiate between their own offspring and those of their slaves? And then, there is the image of the slave. How do we equate the picture of slaves as lazy, improvident and lacking direction with a picture of a million slaves walking home hungry and emaciated, but determined to reassert control of their lives.[20]

Prakash has written that by defining something as slavery, colonial rulers could declare it abolished and not worry about the relations of power and exploitation that remained.[21] Or they could label what remained with a term that made it more acceptable. Hostility to slave-trading and to slavery justified making war against Amadu and Samori or stripping Bokar Biro of his slaves. But once administrators abolished "slavery," they could talk of "natives living with other natives" without paying any attention to conditions of those lives. They did notice how slaves lived. The novels of Oswald Durand and Robert Arnaud are quite vivid. Africans learned that if a master defined a slave as his wife, he was within the law. But the wives of Aguibou and Moussa Molo took issue with this. Pawning could be ignored if it were simply seen as a credit transaction or a casual exchange between neighbors. Thus, a commandant could treat marriage to a pawn as evidence of the benign nature of pawnship without asking what the power relationships were. Most important, were they aware that converting master–slave relationships into sharecropping contracts merely reinforced the control masters had over their former slaves? Saurin certainly knew this. Most local communities continue to this day to use the traditional term for slave.

African memories

Europeans were outsiders, mostly men who came for a short time. The past and the present they packaged were generally not ones they lived. The masters were men with a history, who defined themselves by that history. Descendants of slave-owners, even casted artisans, can give genealogies, often fifteen or more generations back. They can link themselves to events and people long dead. The discourse of the masters is more complex than that of the colonizers. The masters define themselves through their histories, which indicate that there is no stigma of slavery in their male ancestry. Societies of the western Sudan were often structured on dualities. For Bazin, the opposition between *jonya*, the state of being a slave, and *horonya*, the state of being a free man, was central to Bambara culture.[22] For Diop, there was among the Wolof a more complex opposition of class and order.[23] Western writers on Wolof or Mande societies often rank the different statuses, but this does not capture the complexity of differences. Slave and artisan were linked to the free and noble in different ways, but they were important to the noble in that they represented what the noble was not.[24]

Descendants of slaves and masters agree on some things. Both present a harsher view of the past than colonial observers did. Both stress that slaves were owned and could be sold. "Anybody can sell his property," Baabu Khoja Siise, a *jaambur* said. Both stress the master's power. "The *jaam* did everything the master wished. He had no right to anything," Samba Ba, a Kaymor *jaam*, remembered. A Fula in Masina defined slavery thus:

What is slavery? Three elements composed slavery: power, whip and rope. Power: the master gives orders to his slave to do something and he cannot question them. He has to do whatever is asked of him. He cannot question his master. Whip: if he refuses to do so, you take the whip and whip him to remind him that he is chattel. Someone could kill, sell or feed the slave to the crocodiles in the river without caring that he is a human being. Rope: if it pleases the master or if the slave has misbehaved, the master can tie his legs and bring him to the market place to be sold. My son, this is what we called slavery. When you cannot do this to your slave, do not fool yourself. You do not have slaves anymore.[25]

Both have a similar picture of emancipation. They stress the formation by slaves of their own households and working for themselves, in other words, control over their productive and reproductive lives. "They remained where they were, but worked for themselves," a Kaymor *jaam* said.[26] The context, however, is different. For the masters, it is pride in the power they exercised over others. For them, the freed persons were still *jaam, woloso* and *rimaibe.* For the slave, the context is remembrance of a humiliating powerlessness. "The slave was a property," Biraan Ture remembered bitterly, "like the goats, who could be sold whenever desired . . . The *jaam* had to work every day under the orders of the master, like his animals."[27] When asked the slave's obligation, Bakary Gueye said "To work and suffer in silence." When asked what the master owed the *jaam*, he suggested that "you who distinguish between *jaam* and *jaambur* can figure that out for yourself."

Mbus Fadi Siise was nostalgic for the old days: "With the coming of the white man, the slave no longer respected his master . . . Some continue to accept that they are *jaam*, but no one dare call them slaves any longer." Later in the same interview, Siise picked up another theme that runs through the masters' discourse. The *jaam* who pays *assaka* to his master "can ask anything of him at any time . . . they have become kin and everything happens within this framework." Regrets for lost power were stronger in Masina. A Fulbe informant defined what was lost: "The breakdown of slavery leads to the breakdown of the society. Even your child will not respect you any more. Today, you cannot choose a wife for your son. When the law says no one can have a slave, this leads to no one owning his own son."[28] Usman Ndiaye, chief of Kaymor village, presented a more paternalistic view in suggesting that "the master should help his *jaam*; it looks bad if the *jaambur* eats and the *jaam* does not eat or has difficulties." A master in Masina had a similar view of the master's generosity: "Those who agreed to live with their former masters, could benefit from the latter's generosity and work his fields. The former master willingly pays his tax. This situation is more advantageous for the former slaves than for the master."[29]

The *jaam* were terser, but less taken with the generosity of the masters. Asked what masters owed their slaves, Biraan Ture responded, "a hoe at the beginning of the rainy season. He can also make gifts, but not everyone did that." One of Botte's *rimaibe* informants remarked "Now they no longer say 'you are our servants,' but they say 'you are family.' Their mouth says it, but inside they are unhappy that we no longer have labor obligations to them."[30] Pollet and Winter cite a slave informant:

The master was bad. One could not even break wind without being beaten. We never received presents. When a slave was sick there was only Allah to take care of him . . . They [slaves] possessed no property except their meagre personal harvest, which they could sell to the Moors and pay a bride price or buy a goat. It was impossible to save money to buy your freedom . . .
    They only wore a cotton cloth. If one of them put on a better cloth, the nobles would say "You are acting like a noble," tie you up and beat you.[31]

Former slaves in the Futa Jallon have long been denied not only the right to sit in the front in the mosque but, often, the right to wear a white boubou. There was also, however, an element of pride in some of the slave accounts.

Layen Njobu Sow had moved to the edge of the village to get land. "I am the one who cleared this land," he said.[32] "No one contests these lands." And Baabu Caam, chief of a *jaam* village, suggested that in material terms, the situation of former *jaam* "was better than that of their former masters."[33]

These remarks by descendants of slaves were culled from many interviews. It was harder to penetrate the mentality of the slave because it is impolite to confront someone of slave descent with the fact that you know he is of slave descent. This was brought home to me in Kaymor when the village chief's nephew, who had attached himself to our party, blurted out in the middle of an interview, "Who is your master?" The informant's sixty-year-old younger brother took over the interview and answers to questions got shorter and shorter, polite but less informative. It is rare that the descendants of slave-owners are that crude. In one village, I used as my intermediary a Peace Corps volunteer who spoke Wolof well and had excellent rapport with the villagers but, after living there for eighteen months, was oblivious to the fact that one ward of the village was made up of people of slave descent.

Those of slave descent generally did not want to recognize their antecedents even where those antecedents were well known. In my Kaymor interviews, only two informants spoke of slavery in the first person. Both were successful farmers and persons of some status. The first claimed to be 103, had created his own hamlet, and was a prosperous peasant. The second was a man known as the Bur Sonkorong whose status depended on exploiting his servile origins. He organized work parties and celebrations, served as a spokesman for the more powerful, and enjoyed some of the license former slaves have. Still, he indicated slave origins only in referring to a grand-parent who had been pawned. Other informants responded to more indirect lines of questioning, but former slaves were generally the worst informants. They had no genealogy or one that was patently false. They had no history except the history involved in their demeaning status. Pollet and Winter cite an informant who knew he was of Dagara origin, but had forgotten his clan. The Wasulunke also talked about informants who did not remember their clan. In the Futa Jalon, *rimaibe* clearly know and identify with their roots.[34]

Reclaiming an earlier identity is perhaps claiming an honorable past or, as Botte argues, resistance to acculturation, but that acculturation has taken place. The conflict is whether to become Fulbe or whether to become something else. One of Botte's Kissi informants defines his dilemma: "I cannot consider myself Kissi because I was born and grew up in the Futa Jallon. It is only that my ethnic group is Kissi. I am of Kissi origin, but as I do not speak the language, I cannot consider myself a Kissi. I am a Fula because I speak the Fula language."[35] For many *rimaibe*, becoming free meant becoming Fulbe.[36] They often reproach their masters for not giving them the Muslim education that would have facilitated assimilation. It is not enough to become Fulbe by decision of the state. Those who can, often seek to do so either through Islam or, for the richer, by paying for their manumission.[37] And both master and slave think about the uneven flow of women. Fulbe men take *rimaibe* wives, but would consider it shameful to marry their daughters in the *rundes*.[38]

The struggle between slave and master is most vivid in interviews done for me in Masina. I had a full picture of events between 1908 and 1914, but I had no documentation on the inter-war period and, for the most recent period, a disparity between the work of Salmana Cissé and French researchers. I arranged for a friend, Aly Kampo, to do some interviews for me. Of the fourteen people, he interviewed, two were *rimaibe*. The Fulbe informants talked freely and gave a master's perspective. Not only did they regret a lost power, but many still saw the *rimaibe* as slaves with no rights to land they worked or houses they built on Fulbe lands. They described a sharp split among *rimaibe* between those who had nothing to do with former masters and those who carefully maintained ties.

Rimaibe informants were terse, surly and not very informative. One was interviewed in the presence of the village chief. Most of his answers were a single sentence. He claimed not to know the origins of his parents or the name of his "master." Though he had worked on forced labor levies, he spoke of neither deaths nor flights common to most tales of forced labor. He had no idea whether most slaves left their masters or stayed.[39] The second informant was more forthcoming, but still provided little information on slave life. He was a weaver, who worked for a tailor and lived in his compound. Surprisingly, he was a former *tirailleur* who had returned to an earlier relationship. His master's presence may have shaped the interview. Thus he talked about their being "brothers" and about faithfulness. On his parents, he said: "They were treated like children of their master. Even after emancipation, my father lived with his master. They then came together to Konn where I was born . . . [After emancipation] many slaves went back to their native villages. My father did not go back to Jenne. He remained faithful to his master." Roberts did seventy interviews among the Maraka in 1976 and 1977, but only two were with slaves. Both were fairly short interviews, valuable mostly for limited references to the experience of slavery.[40] Bernard Moitt had only one informant of slave origin in Kajoor and this person never admitted it.[41] Few scholars working in this area have opened up the rich fund of slave memories.

Honor and sexuality

Several themes run through memories of slavery. One is the clinging to status. The former slaves are sometimes better off than their former masters, but masters cling to status distinctions. A second is that some former slaves use the master's culture, sometimes consciously, often to their economic advantage. The third is a discourse on honor. Slavery is a self-reinforcing system. It reinforces itself not only through the ways it educates the children, but also through the ways it sets people apart. The slave is a foreigner. More important for those born in the community, the slave is lacking in honor.[42] For Patterson, this is rooted in their being saved from death. Slaves have the right to beg.

In fact, they are expected to beg. Many, of course, like the teacher referred to above, refuse to beg and thus stake out a claim to be honorable. The former slave who becomes a practising Muslim is also staking out a claim to honor. *Rimaibe* reproach the Fulbe for not instructing them.

The lack of honor is also displayed in ritual roles. Thus, chiefs often had a slave who made public proclamations for them, and many marabouts still use such spokesmen because it would be unseemly for a noble person to shout, even into a bull-horn. The Bur Sonkorong profits from his own modern adaptation of these roles just as griots often profit from their monopoly of music and theater. Furthermore, Ames suggests that *jaam* would make accusations that a free man would not make: "It is said that the slaves are fearless and without shame, even able to accuse a person of adultery in public, which a freeborn could never bring himself to do."[43] Role-playing can, of course, take many forms. Peter Weill feels that slaves consciously exploit the noble's code of honor, inviting him to weddings and naming ceremonies and turning to him in moments of need.[44] Others confirm this. When asked if he participated in Fulbe ceremonies, a *rimaibe* from Masina responded "If there is something to be gained, I go."[45] Masters in Masina were also frank: "When a slave becomes rich and powerful, he builds a house outside his master's compound."[46]

The ultimate expression of honor and dishonor lay in the realm of sexuality. Thus, Ames continues: "Freeborn men show a lessened restraint in their behavior toward jam and other lower class women. They may caress them in public, and tell risqué stories in their presence as they never would with women of their own class."[47] For the freeborn woman, one of the horrors of enslavement was to be suddenly removed from a situation where her sexuality was carefully controlled and her virginity valued to one where her body was someone else's property and subject to that other's will. Cheikna Keita's old slave retainer was first taken as a teenage girl. During her first weeks of captivity, she and her friends were raped every night by *sofa*. The first time she was sold, she found herself in a situation where she would be taken into a hut at night by a group of the men in the family and used sexually until the men were tired.[48] Once in a family, however, she was treated with respect.

This approach to slave women crops up in many other analyses. Thus, in 1958, Tuareg nobles still considered *bella* women as theirs to take. Maugham describes a group of young men sending a girl out to collect firewood, then following and raping her.[49] Orsini commented in 1966 that "in the absence of television," a Saharan host provided his guest with a slave woman.[50] Meillassoux writes that in Gumbu, members of the master's family can always have sexual relations with slave women.[51] Perhaps the most vivid example of this was the obscene dances slave women did in many West African societies. Arnaud describes such a dance in a novel based on his pre-World War I service in the Futa Jallon.[52] In it three young slave women, stripped down to several pieces of cloth, did an intense frenetic dance to obscene refrains, simulating sexual intercourse and making lascivious movements. Others have commented on such dances.[53]

The custom of slave women doing obscene dances died out during the colonial period. Samori banned them and they are abhorrent to strict Muslims, but they are crucial in understanding slavery. As in other slave societies, the male slave was often seen as a "Sambo," a happy-go-lucky individual interested primarily in the pleasures of the moment. The female slave was seen as licentious and promiscuous. Even where sexual activity is not an issue, the strength of relations between former masters and slaves is often not similarities, but differences. Riesman refers to Fulbe men enjoying the free atmosphere of *rimaibe* villages and visiting them regularly.[54] Vincent also describes Fulbe in Masina visiting their *rimaibe*. The interaction is highly dependant. Vincent says that the Fulbe of Masina will often help the *rimaibe*, will discuss problems over tea or console him when the latter tells innumerable stories while crying like a child. Vincent argues on the basis of this interaction that *rimaibe* are loyal to their masters because of the latter's kindness and generosity. I read his data as a description of role-playing by *rimaibe*.[55]

The modern counterpart of these slave dances are dances, which are no more licentious than those done any evening in North American discos, but are condemned as immoral by strict Muslims. The dances involve much rhythmic shaking of the body. As a result, they have been banned in many villages in Senegal. In others, they are done only by young people of slave or caste descent. Ernst comments that in the village he studied in Mali, "*jon* worked more land than the *horon* did and under the same terms as *horon*, but they danced and drummed during celebrations and were the messengers sent to announce a birth or death."[56] The importance of the dancing is that some people are given license to do what others find immoral. Those who give them license set them apart and provide a justification for their inferior status.

Just as slaves are often believed to be more sexual, so too they are often believed to have darker powers. The powerful thus fear the ability of the powerless to bewitch them. Thus, Miner wrote:

Within Timbuctoo the Songhoi consider Abaradyu to be particularly infested with genii . . . the blacksmiths of this suburb are thought to have potent supernatural power, but the Songhoi usually think of the Gabibi and Bela as being the strongest in the "black arts . . . Like the marabouts, the Gabibi deny such control of genii even when they are professional makers of charms.[57]

We see a variant of the theme of honor and shame in Riesman's work on the Djelgobe Fulbe of northern Burkina Faso.[58] This is a pastoral area, though one in which local Fulbe were able to accumulate large holdings of slaves in the nineteenth century. The *rimaibe* still make up over 40 percent of the Poular-speaking population, but they no longer have political or economic obligations. They live separately from each other, but any services they give are either reciprocated or remunerated. A few are servants of village and regional chiefs and are proud of the relationships. The Fulbe have more wealth because they own herds. The *rimaibe* do not herd, and thus are not tied down during the dry season, but they do more different kinds of work. Many migrate for the season. Others make bricks, build houses, engage in carpentry, weave cloth, or work in other ways. They are more involved in the money economy and, as a result, have solid houses, more possessions, better clothes and richer foods.[59]

Unlike other areas, *rimaibe* have not tried to become Fulbe. The difference between them is primarily in the strict code of behavior called *pulaaku*, which marks the Fulbe here and elsewhere. They speak softly and display a great deal of self-control and self-restraint. They do not eat in front of others and are very discrete about various bodily functions. *Rimaibe* tend to be loud, boisterous and aggressive, and are seen as coarse and shameless, the antithesis of Fulbe behavior. Riesman does not describe a sexual component, nor does he see Islam as an area where *rimaibe* can try to become honorable. Underlying *pulaaku* are the Fulbe lineages, which give them a sense of tradition. The *rimaibe* social structure is more atomized. They have no past and no lineages. They take pride only in their work, their products and their possessions. As for their attitude to the Fulbe, most of them

... don't like the FulBe much, make fun of them behind their backs, and yet are not ashamed of being descendants of captives. They see that time when their fate was decided as a terrible epoch, when the law of the jungle prevailed, when the strong ate the weak and the ruthless ate those with scruples; what was done then cannot be undone.[60]

The quest for honor is present not only in Islamization, but in the way ex-slave groups recreate their past. The most impressive example of this is Olivier de Sardan's recording of the memories of a group of *horso* from a large Songhay slave village.[61] It is the fullest presentation we have of slave memories, treating war and peace, domination and liberation. Their narrative is in some ways a claim to honor. They describe the subjection of all of the Songhay by the Tuareg. Thus, the nobles too were slaves. And when the French freed the slaves, those who remembered other homes left. The informants did not leave because they were *horso*. They had land. They fought alongside the warriors and received slaves as a reward. In spite of this, masters tried and failed to keep control by force. In a similar way, De Bruijn and Van Dijk describe a reinterpretation of tradition by the *rimaibe* of Hawre. They claim that they were the original inhabitants and were cheated out of their rights.[62]

Conclusion

Honor thus defined not only the boundary between slave and non-slave, but also the identity of the non-slave. It has always been difficult to label those who are not slaves. Some speak of them as the freeborn.[63] Others call them nobles, though they are a large group and not necessarily privileged. They are best defined as having honor, which essentially means being neither caste nor slave.[64] The distinction within the society between those who are honorable and those who are not was crucial to a hegemonic ideology which enabled ruling elites to control both agricultural slaves and the more privileged slave warriors. It was important to what was essentially an economic relationship in which slaves provided most of the work.

As the ability of masters to extract wealth from slaves declined, as some slaves became wealthier than the nobles, the honorable class clung all the more intensely to status distinctions. The mosque became an important battleground. The prohibition against former slaves becoming imams is probably a twentieth-century phenomenon. Earlier, the issue would rarely have arisen. Insistence on the stigma of slavery was essential to maintaining distance. The prohibition against marriage with slaves also became stronger. Certainly marriage with slave women was accepted in traditional societies, and in at least one rare case, trusted male slaves were accepted as sons-in-law.[65] Crucial to all of this, and harder to maintain, is the notion that those of slave descent are less able to control their sexual desires. For the slaves, the initial battle was to get control over both their productive and reproductive life. They tried to do the former either by moving away or by trying to get access to land. They did the latter by asserting the right to negotiate their own marriages, by accumulating and bequeathing their property, by rejecting the claims of the honorable on their wives and children. In creating a family, by becoming Muslim, by seeking education, by dressing properly, by behaving in an honorable manner and by assimilating the culture of their masters, the former slaves became more honorable. Masters thus struggled to maintain the distinctions while slaves fought to reduce them.

The question of honor was an asset to the slave in the economic struggle. The most consistent refrain in the discourse of the freeborn is that they spend more on their former slaves than they receive from them. Generosity was important to the idea of honor. Life is insecure in most areas involved in this study and French policy made it difficult for any peasant to achieve a comfortable standard of living. For the slaves, begging brought in needed resources and deference was the best way to deal with authority. In order to be able to seek help from families of former masters they had to maintain some vestige of the former relationship. This meant giving gifts, acting in a deferential way, cooking for weddings and naming ceremonies, carrying messages, and sometimes doing a little role-playing. It meant inviting the honorable to preside over certain kinds of festive occasions.

Colonial administrators often refer to a flight from freedom. They talk about slaves having been so brutalized that they could not cope with freedom and eagerly returned to their masters. There is no evidence that this was ever so on any significant scale. Most of my data would suggest just the opposite, that most slaves worked hard to establish their autonomy and were by and large successful. And yet, the question of hegemonic ideology is crucial. Some of those who remained with their masters probably believed that this was meant to be and, perhaps, that they were inferior. Hegemonic ideology, in particular religion and child-rearing, were designed to achieve that end. Today, many of the young and most of the educated are impatient with these traditional values. In a sense, Ibrahima Diaman Bathily was the voice of a new Africa. Today, young people, particularly the educated, want to be done with questions of slave or caste status. The young, however, are reluctant to marry without approval of their families. Marriage thus remains the key barrier to the integration of those of slave or artisan descent.

The real heroes of this story are those who sought freedom, people who made the long march to distant homes, sought freedom in the new towns and cities and people who struggled to assert their autonomy. In North America, we honor those who rose above slave origins, people like Frederick Douglass, Harriet Tubman, Booker T. Washington or George Washington Carver, whose accomplishments are all the more remarkable when their modest roots are considered. Their West African counterparts are invisible. Only Ki Zerbo's biography of his father stands out as a celebration of triumph over slavery, and Ki Zerbo's father spent only a few years in slavery. Though much of the elite in the countries I have studied is probably of slave descent, I have never had a person casually talk about slave origins. The traders of nineteenth-century Senegal were often of slave origin.[66] Some even started accumulating while still in slavery. The first educated were usually either slaves or the sons of chiefs. Early Christians were predominantly slaves. Chiefs were often asked to send their sons to school. Many did so, but others sent slaves. We will never know how many. This means that many teachers and clerks were of servile origins. The same thing is true of the army. With time, the permanent cadres of the army were recruited from the sons of former soldiers, usually of slave origins. Many former soldiers became policemen, messengers or guards. Finally, urban people have generally benefited more from education and economic opportunity than their rural cousins. In 1848, both Goree and Saint Louis were cities with heavy slave majorities, and in the century after 1848, the cities were clearly an important destination for former slaves. "Dakar," one of my friends told me, "that is democracy," by which he meant that Dakar was big enough for a person to be anonymous. It is certain that a large part, perhaps a majority of the population of Dakar, Conakry and Bamako was of slave origin until very recently.

There is thus a dramatic story here which will never be told in full. French sources often speak of crime and vagabondage. They do not tell of Christian converts, of the nascent proletariat, or petty traders, who sought to master a new world and free themselves from the chains of the old. Nor did these people tell their children what they had accomplished. They did not do so because they wanted to be honorable. This was a goal that could best be achieved by inventing a genealogy. One is told from time to time that certain politicians or military leaders were of servile origin. Hopefully, this is becoming irrelevant to political life. What is most important, however, is not the success of a few, but the unsung achievement of hard-working *rimaibe*, *woloso*, *bella*, *horso* and *jaam*, who became modernizing peasants and who earn more money than their former masters.

Appendixes

APPENDIX 1   HOW MANY SLAVES?

How many slaves were there in the West African territories? This is a question we can never answer with precision. There are, however, enough data for us to venture a rough estimate. There are two major sources about the numbers of slaves in French West Africa. These are the responses to the slave questionnaires of 1894 in the Sudan and 1904 for all of French West Africa. In addition, there are local studies and censuses. There are major problems in using colonial data. Administrators were often ill informed about the societies they ruled and lacked the personnel to do a really efficient job of data collection. Furthermore, slavery was a touchy question. African slave-owners had good reason not to report fully their slave holdings because they feared French intentions. Similarly, many administrators were nervous about potential unrest and were hostile to any action against slavery. Many administrators in both 1894 and 1904 refused to estimate the slave population; others simply "eyeballed" it. Fortunately, we have more rigorous studies made by social scientists in the second half of the century which suggest that almost all early administrators underestimated the number of slaves.

Nevertheless, these are the data we have. Furthermore, there are some patterns and ways of checking them. In producing global estimates, I have used the following method. I start with the 1904 estimates.[1] First, where I have absolute numbers, but no percentages, I use 1904 or 1905 population data to produce percentages. Second, where I have only percentages, I use the reverse process to estimate the number of slaves. Third, for those cercles where I have no data, I use analogy to similar cercles and analysis of their ethnic mix, political situation and geographic position. Finally, where there are other more reliable data, I use them. The charts attached use the 1904 figure where available. When I reject the original figure, I have placed that original figure in parentheses.

For the Sudan, the 1904 questionnaire suggests about 700,000 slaves, making up about 18 percent of the population.[2] The relatively low figure can be explained by the absence of slaves in many densely populated areas in the southern tier of the colony. The Sahel cercles were reported at about 40 percent slave. Certain cercles, however, were obviously under-reported. The Tuareg and Fulbe were large slave-holders, generally with servile majorities. The southernmost Tuareg were outnumbered by their Bella by eight or nine to one. For Songhay areas (Gao), Olivier de Sardan has estimated the servile population at about from two thirds to three quarters of the total.[3] We must also revise upward estimates of the *rimaibe* populations of Masina. While the French stopped counting slaves among other ethnic groups by 1908, the *rimaibe* were seen as virtually a distinct ethnic group and thus were regularly counted. In 1952, Charpentier did a *mémoire* on the sub-division of Jenne, which suggested that some Fulbe areas were as much as 70 to 80 percent *rimaibe*. A decade later, Jean Gallais (1967) reported 42,592 *rimaibe* out of a Fulbe-speaking population of 85,502.

That works out to 50 percent. Only a few years later, a government demographic survey of the area controlled by the Office du Niger reported the *rimaibe* as 53.6 percent of the 111,575 Fulbe speakers in the area. The *rimaibe* had not fled the delta in massive numbers, but they were more likely to leave than the Fulbe and their mortality rate is even today marginally higher.[4] The figures Inspector Saurin used in 1908, about 30,000 *rimaibe* and 8,000 Fulbe, are probably accurate. I have altered the chart to suggest 60 percent, but this is a modest estimate. This all raises the estimated slave population to 21 percent, but I think that the actual percentage was at least a quarter and perhaps as high as a third, over half in the Sahel, near major political centers and around *juula* and Maraka towns. I am convinced that the figures given for Bafulabe, Medine, Kury, Dunzu and Ouagadougou were lower than the actual numbers. It is also quite probable that administrators in Kayes, Nioro, Niafunke, Segu, Bamako, Satadugu and Sokolo underestimated the actual number of slaves.

GUINEA

For Guinea, the 1904 reports are more complete and the estimates of slave population are higher. Less reasoning by analogy is necessary. The result is a global estimate of almost 35 percent. Some districts, however, are inexplicably low. Rio Nunez was the largest exploiter of slave labor on the coast. I have raised the estimates from 11 percent to 60 percent, near the 65 percent given for the Rio Pongo. It is also clear that the estimates are low for many of the Futa Jallon cercles. Saurin was skeptical of these figures as was Noirot, who reviewed slave data in a letter in 1905. His figures showed the slave population estimates for all of Guinea at slightly under 27 percent of the population, largely because he operated with a higher estimate of total population than the 1904 census. He was, however, skeptical of his own figures. For the Malinke cercles of the upper Niger, he suggested raising the figures by 5 percent. For the Futa Jallon and the coastal cercles, he argues that slaves were at least as numerous as the free.[5] A contemporary, LeClerc, administrator of the Futa, suggested in 1905 that slaves made up at least two thirds of the population of the Futa.[6]

These estimates were confirmed by the work of later scholars. In 1940, Vieillard estimated the free:slave ratio at about two free to one slave in the lower Futa and about even in the central Futa cercles. This was after widespread slave emigration. A few years later, Richard-Molard did a survey which reported *rimaibe* at about 33 percent near Labé and 27 percent in several districts in Koubia in the northeast Futa, but he admitted that his method probably undercounted.[7] A 1954–55 demographic survey suggested that there 202,000 slaves left among 852,000 Fulbe-speakers. This is less than a quarter, but to Suret-Canale, it meant that there was probably a slave majority before conquest.[8] Not only had many *rimaibe* left, but those remaining probably had a higher mortality and a lower birth rate. I have altered the Futa figures to reflect estimates by LeClerc and Viellard. Only LeClerc's estimate explains the data later given by Vieillard and Richard-Molard. I have, however, only estimated Futa percentages at 60 percent and 50 percent, respectively. In Lower Guinea, I have sharply revised Rio Nunez, which may well have had the highest slave percentages on the coast.[9] The Mellacorée figure is probably low, but I have left it. Of the remaining figures, Kurusa is too high, probably because the census reported a very low total figure, but Kankan, the major commercial center in Samori's empire, is clearly too low. The errors here may balance each other. I would estimate a slave population of 685,000 with slaves more than 50 percent of the total population. Slaves probably represented about half the total population of Guinea.

Table A1.1. *Estimated slave population of Haut-Sénégal-Niger*

Cercles	Total population	Slaves	% Slave
Bafulabe[a]	59,805	15,000	25
Bamako	177,149	61,999	35
Bamba	34,012	13,604	40
Bandiagara[b]	197,870	49,467 (20,000)	25
Bobo-Dioulasso[c]	236,000	46,000	20
Buguni	95,592	3,340	4
Jenne[d]	69,635	41,781 (15,981)	60
Dori	88,475	41,500	47
Gao	46,011	34,508 (8,000)	75 (17)
Gumbu	66,947	33,473	50
Kayes	71,421	30,000	42
Kita[e]	56,624	27,500	49
Koury[f]	224,266	33,639	15
Koutiala	223,403	22,300	10
Lobi	188,900	8,000	4
Medine	4,931	650	13
Niafunke	59,597	23,838	40
Nioro	114,228	45,688	40
Ouagadougou	1,477,982	147,790	10
Raz-el-Ma	1,952	1,600	82
Satadugu[g]	34,194	6,839 (1,500)	20 (4)
Segu[h]	140,610	56,244 (25,150)	40 (18)
Sikasso	164,410	50,000	30
Sokolo	34,770	13,300	38
Timbuktu	22,232	13,579	61
TOTAL	3,891,016	821,639	21

[a]This number is low, given the population of Mandinka, Fulbe and Soninke. The adjacent cercles, Kayes and Kita, had much higher estimates.

[b]Other documents suggest much larger slaves holdings for Bandiagara. Comm. Destenave, "Rapport sur la Captivité dans les États d'Aguibou," ANM, 1 E 156, suggests that among the Fulbe, there were two *rimaibe* for each Pullo, among Bambara an equal number and one slave for each two Futanke. He clearly excluded the large slave-holdings of Aguibou, which were being increased in 1898.

[c]This is probably accurate. Slaves were estimated at two thirds of the *juula* population and a third of the Fulbe, but holdings were small among the more numerous Bobo.

[d]Revised upward on the basis of contemporary estimates and later research. Saurin, Report on Jenne, Meray Mission, ARS, 4G 10, calculated that 30,000 of the 38,900 Fulbe-speakers were *rimaibe* and that one of three Bambara- and Bozo-speakers were slaves. See also Charpentier 1952 and Gallais 1967, I: 143–44.

[e]The author of the Kita report put the slave population at between one half and two thirds, but in giving a more concrete estimate, took half and rounded it off. The actual number was probably higher.

[f]This figure is probably low. More than half of the population were Bobo and Samo who had very few slaves, but 40 percent were Maraka and Fulbe, people who raided heavily among their chiefless neighbors. I assume a slave majority among the Maraka and Fulbe, but have not altered the figure because I have no evidence.

Table A1.1. *(cont.)*

[g]There are references in reports from Satadugu to slave flight, but it is not clear whether flight
was to or from Satadugu. Leynaud and Cissé 1978: 11 estimated the population of slave descent
in Malinke areas of the upper river at 10 to 15 percent, but suggest that it was much higher
before conquest. I have, therefore, revised the figure upwards, but by a modest amount.
[h]This is a difficult one. The 1894 report from Segu (ARS, K 14) suggests that there were $4\frac{1}{2}$
slaves for every free person. The heavy concentration of both military and agricultural slaves in
and around Segu may have distorted the perceptions of the importance of slaves, but 18 percent
was clearly low. Some slaves departed or were freed. The five years after the 1894 report also
saw many new slaves both in the suppression of revolts and in the conquest of Sikasso. I
suggest 40 percent, but there could well have been a slave majority.

Table A1.2. *Estimated slave population of Guinea*

Cercles	Total population	Slaves	% Slave
Boussourah	7,380	800	10.8
Dingiray[a]	30,074	12,932 (10,900)	43 (36.2)
Ditinn	135,954	81,572 (15,000)	60 (11)
Dubreka	76,630	38,315	50
Faranah	39,092	3,600	9.2
Friguiabe	68,000	34,000	50
Kade	20,000	13,000	65
Kankan[b]	57,000	10,500 (10,000)	18.4 (17.5)
Kissidugu	39,786	1,989	5
Koin	56,746	28,373	50
Kurusa[c]	34,430	31,700	92.1
Labé	187,315	112,389 (60,000)	60 (32)
Medina Kouta	26,133	13,100	50.1
Mellacorée	75,000	25,000	33.3
Ouassou	13,000	4,300	33.1
Rio Nunez	51,767	31,060 (5,680)	60 (11)
Rio Pongo	115,000	75,000	65.2
Sigiri	45,856	12,600 (12,000)	27.5 (26.2)
Timbis	117,546	70,527 (20,000)	60 (17)
Timbo	84,189	50,513 (30,000)	60 (35.6)
Touba	17,620	10,572 (8,000)	60 (45.4)
Yambering	48,839	24,920	51
TOTAL	1,347,357	686,762 (465,677)	51 (34.6)

[a]An 1898 census reported Dingiray as 43 percent slave. ANG, 2 D 71. It was probably at least
that.
[b]The 1894 report, reported that Kankan, before its attachment to Guinea, was one third slave,
but the area under French control was smaller than in 1904. The first census reported only
19,485 people. Both are probably low, but I cannot prove that. Kankan was an important
commercial center for Samori. The area around the city was intensively worked by slave labor
and saw massive departures in 1911 and again after the return of the *tirailleurs*.
[c]This is clearly much too high, probably because total population is being underreported.

SENEGAL

When I first tried to estimate slave population, I did not attempt Senegal. Senegal had gone through a decade of change. Furthermore, it had been policy in Senegal to turn a blind eye to slavery. No one counted slaves and few wanted to know how many there were. Some of the cercles clearly ignored slavery or treated the large numbers of slaves working for themselves as free men. Given the constant reports of a large flow of slaves to Kajoor and Bawol, the largest slave concentrations should have been in Tivouane and Thiès. Kaolack reported slaves as a third of total population, but Sine-Saloum was only beginning to take off economically in 1904. There had been a massive movement of slaves into lower Senegal and the Peanut Basin. My revisions produce a figure of about 30 percent. I would guess the real figure at 35 to 40 percent of total population.

These estimates would produce a figure of over 1,800,000 for the three colonies as a whole. If my guesses are correct, the actual number was well above 2 million. Deherme has estimated 2 million for the whole of French West Africa without Mauritania. If we add in Mauritania and assume similar under-reporting in Dahomey and the Ivory Coast, the total for French West Africa was probably between 3 and 3.5 million. This would have been over 30 percent of the total population of the federation.

Table A1.3. *Estimated slave population of Senegal*

Cercle	Total population	Slaves	% Slave
Bakel	56,000	38,000	68
Casamance	140,000	14,000	10
Dagana	58,000	29,000	50
Kaedi	36,000	18,600	51.7
Kaolack	154,000	51,282	33.3
Louga[a]	101,000	20,200 (10,000)	20 (9.9)
Matam	68,000	20,000	29.4
Niani-Ouli	28,000	5,000	17.9
Podor	71,000	18,600	26.2
Tivouane[b]	125,000	50,000 (15,000)	40 (12)
Thies[c]	218,000	65,400 (26,000)	30 (12)
TOTAL	1,055,000	330,082 (245,482)	31.3 (23.3)

[a]Jolof, the cercle of Louga, was a major military force in the 1880s. Though some of the area was too dry for peanuts, the better watered area around Louga became an important producer. I assume that the slave population was over 20 percent, even after some early colonial emigration.

[b]Tivouane was Kajoor. Cruise O'Brien (1975: 27) suggests that slave holdings in the old peanut basin were between half and two thirds of the population. The actual figure for Tivouane was probably over half, but I have been cautious here.

[c]Much of the cercle of Thiès also profited from the same import of slaves that populated Kajoor, but a part of the cercle was inhabited by acephalous peoples with few slaves. Only 750 slaves were enumerated among the 50,000 persons in the Serer Provinces. Report on Thiès, ARS, K 18.

APPENDIX 2   SELECTED LIBERTY VILLAGES UP TO THE EXODUS

Cercle	1894	1895	1897	1900	1902	1903	1905	1908
Bafoulabe		519						
Bamako		1074						
Bandiagara						59	96	139
Bissandugu	57	4						
Buguni	32	90	149	61	25	55	86	14
Jenne					48	71	84	59
Gumbu		16	249	331	140	172	175	274
Issa-Ber							236	
Kankan	18		108					
Kayes		1006	824	816	742	869	927	1387
Kita	13		132	207		100	91	104
Kurusa	18	27	17					
Koury							34	55
Koutiala				13			38	
Medine	1484	273	391	54	54	758	49	
Nioro	821	358	488	622	828	481	481	535
Ouahigouya						21	47	95
Raz-el-Ma				28			163	
Satadugu			56	78	464	580	578	771
Segu		187	118	293	299	329	256	
Sigiri	857	915	825					
Sikasso						470	80	
Sokolo		50	86	192	215	328	265	431

APPENDIX 3   SAMPLE BREAKDOWN OF MEN, WOMEN AND CHILDREN

Cercles	% Men	% Women	% Children
Buguni	35.5	37.8	26.8
Gumbu	24.4	47.8	27.9
Kayes	33.3	48.4	18.4
Nioro	25.5	49.4	25

APPENDIX 4   A SAMPLE OF ENTRIES AND DEPARTURES,
LIBERTY VILLAGES

Cercle and Year	Population at end of year	Entries	Departures
Kayes 1897	824	151	262
Kayes 1900	816	237	175
Kayes 1907	1,335	351	37
Kayes 1908	1,387	483	331
Koury 1905	33	201	208
Koury 1906	59	241	208
Koury 1907	27	155	188
Nioro 1895	358	144	114
Nioro 1896	393	184	102
Nioro 1907	1,102	584	498
Nioro 1909	485	101	151
Segu 1900	293	181	270
Segu 1905	256	67	222

APPENDIX 5 SLAVE PRICES, PRE-1904

1827	Sambatikilia	average price	30 bricks salt[1]
1878	Bundu	young man or woman	2 pieces guinea or 30 bricks salt
	Kajoor	average	125 to 150 fr[2]
1879	Saint Louis	adult	250 to 300 fr
		child	150 to 200 fr[3]
		man for a cow, four for a horse	
1885	Kuntu	tax valuation	250 fr
1890	Kayes	general	260 to 275 fr[4]
1892	Nioro	tax valuation	150 & 175 fr[5]
1894	Kita	8-year-old male	80 fr
		12-year-old male	120 fr
		15-year-old male	150 fr
		girl, 18–20	300 fr[6]
1894	Kerouane	average price	190 fr
	Beyla	healthy girl	250 fr
		young girl	6,000 to 7,000 kola
			a cow & 50 fr
			32 kg salt
			13 to 16 pagnes[7]
	Bissandugu	nubile woman	200 to 300 fr
		healthy male	150 fr
1894	Buguni	woman	200 fr
		man	80 fr
		boy	120 to 150 fr
		girl	150 to 175 fr[8]
	Kissi	ordinary slave	200 fr
		young girl	250 to 300 fr
	Kurusa	woman	50 to 250 fr
		man	85 to 200 fr
		little girl	125 to 150 fr
		boy	125 to 175 fr
		children	45 to 50 fr[9]
	Medine	healthy woman	250 to 300 fr
	Nioro	adult woman	200 fr
		man, 20 to 40	180 fr
		children	100 to 150 fr
1899	Gambia	average price	£10 to £25 (200 to 500 fr)[10]
1901	Banankuru	pawned children	10 to 60 fr[11]

Note: Prices are often given in guinea, esp. for 1894 reports – translated into 10 francs per guinea[12]

Notes

1 SLAVERY IN THE WESTERN SUDAN

1 On the export trade in slaves and its impact on Africa, see Lovejoy 1983, esp. chs. 1 and 2; Manning 1983 and 1990; Klein 1992a. On the trans-Saharan trade, see Austen 1990 and 1992; Malowist 1966; Kaké 1979; Levtzion 1973: 174–78.
2 Lovejoy 1983, chs. 3–5; Manning 1990; Curtin 1969; Rawley 1981; Inikori 1992.
3 Searing 1993; Klein 1983b. For another view, see Inikori 1992. See also Fisher and Fisher 1970: ch. 3.
4 Ca da Mosto 1937; Fernandes 1951. Walter Rodney (1966) claimed that slavery did not exist on the upper Guinea coast, but his argument was questioned by Elbl (1983 and 1985). On medieval slavery, see Malowist 1966; Levtzion 1973: 117–19; Hunwick 1985; Tymowski 1970a and 1970b; Kodjo-Niamkey 1976 and 1988.
5 Curtin 1975: 155; Meillassoux 1971: 55.
6 Moses Finley (1968) preferred the more neutral term "slave society" because he was offended by the way the concept of a mode of production was used by Communist historians. I am using the term to describe societies where the major source of productive labor was slaves. I reject the concept of a unilineal theory of social evolution; I speak of modes in the plural and am not concerned here with Marxist theoretical debates. See Jewsiewicki and Letourneau 1985; Terray 1969; Coquery-Vidrovitch 1969.
7 Meillassoux 1971: 55. See also A.G. Hopkins 1973: ch. 2.
8 Meillassoux 1971: 31–34 and 71–74.
9 Tamari 1991. An excellent discussion of caste is Diop 1981. See also Camara 1976; McNaughton 1988.
10 Ly 1966 and 1967; Patterson 1982: ch. 3; Bazin 1975; Riesman 1974, ch. 7. For comparison, see Glassman 1995: 79–80.
11 Oyo became a slaving power in the mid-seventeenth century; Law 1977. Asante dominated the hinterland of the Gold Coast after defeating Denkyera in 1702; Rodney 1969; Fynn 1971; Wilks 1975. The Bambara state of Segu was founded in 1712; Roberts 1987b; Bazin 1972 and 1975. Muslims in the Futa Jallon begin a struggle for control of that strategic area in the 1720s; Rodney 1968a; Barry 1988a.
12 Law 1976 and 1980; Fisher 1972–73; Webb 1993.
13 Rodney 1969; Inikori 1977; Curtin 1975.
14 Meillassoux 1986 (1991); Lovejoy 1983: chs. 3–6.
15 On the Maraka, see Roberts 1988; Buna, see Boutillier 1969, 1971, 1975 and 1993; on Bonduku, see Handloff 1982 and Terray 1974, 1987b, 1995; on Kong, see Bernus 1960 and Green 1984 and 1986.
16 These estimates are based on inquiries made by the colonial administration in 1894 and 1904. See ARS, K 18–22. The 1904 survey is the most important source of data on slavery at the dawn of colonial rule.

17 Boutillier 1969 and 1975.
18 Roberts 1980c, 1981 and 1987b.
19 Diallo 1994; Echenberg 1971b.
20 See Héritier 1975 and Linares 1987 on incorporation of small-scale societies in slaving. On the Jola, see also Mark 1985: 22–31; Baum 1986: ch. 4.
21 Cercles were the smallest districts under a French commandant's authority. They were divided into cantons, each under an African chief.
22 Lovejoy 1978 and 1979b refers to these villages among the Hausa as plantations. Other scholars working on the Sudan shy away from this term because of differences in the way labour was organized.
23 The low-density model is close to that presented in Miers and Kopytoff 1977. See Klein 1978, Lovejoy 1979b, Kopytoff 1979, Cooper 1979. The high-density model is close to that of Meillassoux 1986 (1991). On reproduction, see Meillassoux 1983.
24 The southern tier had relatively high populations, but some peoples seem to have been decimated by slave raiders. On the Tanda, see Curtin 1975: 177–78.
25 Roberts 1980c; Bazin 1975 and 1982; Bazin and Terray 1982. See Curtin 1975: 156–68 for a controversial model on enslavement.
26 Klein and Robertson 1983. On slave demography, see Manning 1983 and 1990: chs. 3–6.
27 Binger 1892, I: 103; Mage 1968 (1868): 437–38; Klein 1968: ch. 4; Robinson 1985b: 154, 194.
28 Falola and Lovejoy 1994; Klein and Roberts 1978; "Problème présent du travail servile en Côte d'Ivoire (1931)," ARS, 2 K 5 (26); "Coutumes du Sénégal (1907)," ARS, 1 G 330; "Essai sur les coutumes Peulhes," Fonds Vieillard, IFAN, Dakar. See also reports on slavery, Bamako, ARS, K 19, Kong and Bonduku, ARS, K 21.
29 E. Barat, "Coutumes Juridiques (1897–1900)," ARS, 1 G 229; Report on Slavery, Kaolack, ARS, K 18; Gallais 1967, I: 294.
30 Bazin 1975: 143; Reports on slavery, Tivouane, ARS, K 18; Bamako, Diebugu, Yatenga, ARS, K 19; Kong, ARS, K21.
31 Monteil 1924: 190; Reports on Slavery, Nioro, ARS, K 14; Gumbu, Kita, Segu, ARS, K 19.
32 On Segu tonjon, see Roberts 1987b: ch. 2; Bazin 1975.
33 This is an inaccurate use of captif. I will use captive only for those still in transit and not yet incorporated in any society. See Meillassoux 1986: 117–18 (1991: 116–17).
34 Bazin 1975: 141; Roberts 1987b: 122; Meillassoux 1975b; Olivier de Sardan 1975 and 1983; Derman 1973: 27–32. Many of these were already slaves; slave villages were more vulnerable to raids.
35 Meillassoux 1986 (1991): 117–18. See Joseph Ki Zerbo 1983 for a description of seasoning in a nomad camp.
36 The Wolof use the term jaam for both those acquired and those born in the house, but they distinguish between them.
37 Derman 1973: 27–30; Sanankoua 1990: 110; Meillassoux 1986 (1991): 35–39.
38 Meillassoux 1986 (1991): 122–25; Olivier de Sardan 1984.
39 Moore 1738: 33; see also Durand 1802 and Mollien 1820.
40 Interviews, Mbodj-Klein collection: Biraan Kumba Siise, Biraan Ture, Al Haj Abdu Siise. Kampo collection: Alpha Mamadou Sendeque, Bada Bocoum.
41 Report on slavery, ARS, K 19, Bamako. Meillassoux 1986 (1991): 124 agrees that all slaves could be sold, though there were pressures against the master doing so. See also Bazin 1975: 159; Olivier de Sardan 1976: 56; Terray 1982: 126.
42 Report on slavery, ARS, K 18, Dagana.
43 Cooper 1977: 159 describes a similar work regime on the East African coast.

44 Meillassoux 1986 (1991): 118; Derman 1973: 36–37. See also Reports on Slavery, Beyla and Kissi, ARS, K 14; Bakel and Matam, ARS, K 18; Bandiagara and Nioro, ARS, K 19. See also Roberts 1978: ch. 6.
45 Meillassoux 1986 (1991): 118–19. See also Ames 1953: 15–18; Report on Slavery, Tivouane, ARS, K 18.
46 The low figure is from Yoro Dyao, a Senegalese chief, who had good reason to understate slave obligations; Rousseau 1929. The high figure is Meillassoux 1975b: 236 on the Soninke.
47 The *muud* was a measure of volume, which was not the same in all areas. Curtin 1975, II: 57–61 gives it as 1.75 litres. Most commandants gave it as 3 kg. A slave owed 150 muud at Gumbu, 100 at Nioro, 90 at Bandiagara. The alternative was paying cowries, 10,000 for a man, 8,000 for a woman among Fulbe near Jenne. Where slaves wove, they also owed a certain amount of cloth.
48 Monteil 1924: 192.
49 Meillassoux 1975b: 249.
50 Pollet and Winter 1971: 239.
51 Bazin 1975; Izard 1975; Olivier de Sardan 1975; Klein 1977a.
52 Hunwick 1985.
53 Meillassoux 1975b: 249–50; Ames 1953: 10–11; Roberts 1978: ch. 7, 1996: ch. 2 and 1984.
54 Derman 1973: 37–39; Baldé 1975: 197; Report on Slavery, Nioro, ARS, K 14.
55 Thus, Wilbur 1943: 243 explains that his thesis on Chinese slavery "was originally conceived of as one way to learn more about the condition of the lower classes in Han times, but it now appears to reveal much more about the ruling group, and to contribute only indirectly to a knowledge of the common people."
56 Patterson 1982: ch. 1; Meillassoux 1986 (1991): 23–35.
57 Bazin 1975; Izard 1975; Olivier de Sardan 1975; Klein 1977a.
58 Klein 1968: 11–17. In the Kajoor of Lat Dior, the second most powerful figure was the Farba, Demba Warr Sall. Sall was the most important chief in Kajoor after the conquest; Diouf 1990: ch. 19.
59 Diouf 1990: 92–96; Boulègue 1977; Colvin 1972.
60 Roberts 1987b: ch. 2; Bazin 1975 and 1982; Monteil 1924.
61 Searing 1993: ch. 4; Brooks 1970. On slave merchants in Niger, see Baier 1980: 63.
62 Meillassoux 1986 (1991): 12–15; Miers and Kopytoff 1977; Klein 1978; Cooper 1980; Lovejoy 1979 and 1983: ch. 1; Kopytoff 1979b.
63 Patterson 1982: 19. Curtin 1975: 34–36 also refers to the slave as an "artificial kinsman."
64 Meillassoux 1975b: 224 and 1986 (1991): 34–36; Riesman 1974: 88.
65 Interviews, Mbodj-Klein collection, Senegal 1975: Biraan Kumba Siise, Biraan Ture, Al Haj Musa Ba, Mbus Fadi Siise, Habib Niang.
66 Bazin 1975: 142; Monteil 1924: 193; Binger 1892: I, 20.
67 Tauxier 1921: 265; Report on slavery, Kissi, ARS, K 14; Raz el Ma and Kita, ARS, K 19.
68 Reports on Slavery, Kurusa, ARS, K 14; Yatenga and Medine, ARS, K 19.
69 Sanankoua 1990: 110.
70 Patterson 1982: 187.
71 Klein 1983; Meillassoux 1983; Olivier de Sardan 1983. Most sources say that a master had to provide a wife for a slave. I have yet to see any statement of obligation to a female slave.
72 Riesman 1974: 83.
73 Ames 1953: 14.

74 Monteil 1924: 219; Rousseau 1929: 294; Reports on Slavery from Nioro, Kita, Dori, Sikasso, Bamako and Jenne, ARS, K 19.
75 Reports on Slavery, Kaedi, Louga, Dagana, ARS, K 18.
76 Klein 1983 a and b.
77 Meillasoux 1991: 138.
78 Nieboer 1910; Goody 1980.
79 On China, see Wilbur 1943 and Watson 1980b. On other Asian systems, see Watson 1980a; Reid 1983; Patnaik and Dingwaney 1985.
80 Goody 1980: 23. See also Baks *et al.* 1966; Domar 1970; Cooper 1977: 155–56.
81 Gray and Birmingham 1970: 18. Goody 1971: 32 argued that it was not just women and slaves, but the means of destruction, guns and horses, that were the basis of power.
82 The model of an open society in Watson 1980b: 9–13 is based on Miers and Kopytoff 1977.
83 Cooper 1977: 5–6, 1980 and 1981. His analysis is based on Meillassoux 1975a.
84 On demographic impact, see Manning 1990: chs. 3 and 4. See also Inikori 1982; Klein 1992a and 1994; Rodney 1966; Fage 1975 and 1980.
85 Reports on slavery, Timbuktu, Jenne, Kita, Bourem in ARS, K 19.
86 According to Meillassoux 1975: 238–42 and 1986 (1991): 119–21, the *komo xoore* could not move from Gumbu, marry a freeborn person or be elected to office. See also Olivier de Sardan 1982.
87 Monteil 1924: 193; Report on slavery, Beyla, ARS, K14; Sokolo, ARS, K 19.
88 Roberts 1987b: 126–28.
89 Roberts 1987b: 120.
90 Meillassoux 1971: 193. In a later calculation, Meillassoux 1986 (1991): 298 estimated that a male slave could produce his replacement cost in about four years.
91 Report on Slavery, Podor, R. du Laurens, 22 Feb. 1904, ARS, K 18.
92 Genovese 1972: 295–324.
93 Finley 1968.
94 Meillassoux 1986 (1991): 99–116.
95 Patterson 1982: 185–86.
96 Patterson 1982: 101. These comments are based on Hegel's reflections on the dialectical link between Lord and Slave in Hegel 1910: 228–40. See also Davis 1975: 559–64.
97 Cooper 1977: ch. 1; Davis 1966: ch. 2 and 1975: 559–64; Genovese 1972; Lovejoy 1981; Cooper 1981; Roberts 1981.
98 Terray 1975.
99 B. Barry 1978 and 1988a and b: 216–20. See also I. Barry 1971.
100 Smith 1954: 39.
101 Finley 1968.
102 See Patterson 1982: 51–52 on rituals of enslavement.
103 Roberts 1981: 179.
104 Cooper 1981: 277; Lovejoy 1981: 208–15.
105 Cooper 1981: 286.
106 See for comparison Miers and Roberts 1988; Grace 1975; Cooper 1980; Lovejoy and Hogendorn 1993.
107 Cohen 1971.
108 Kanya-Forstner 1969.
109 Klein 1993a; on India see Temperley 1972; on the Gold Coast, McSheffrey 1983 and Dumett and Johnson 1988. See also Miers and Roberts 1988.

2 ABOLITION AND RETREAT. SENEGAL 1848–1876

1 Daget 1971 and 1990: ch. 7; Drescher 1968: ch. 6.
2 Necheles 1971: ch. 10; Drescher 1980.
3 Daget 1980 and 1990: ch. 9; Brasseur 1988; Jennings 1988. In Drescher's terms, there was "little formal defense of slavery in principle, but also very little by way of attacks on it"; Drescher 1968: 156.
4 Daget 1975 and 1981: 201.
5 Daget 1971: 55–57.
6 Daget, 1981: 202–3; Jennings 1985 and 1988.
7 Curtin, 1981: 88. During peak years of the eighteenth century, 2,000 to 2,500 were exported from Senegambia.
8 In Algeria, the situation that most resembled Senegal, abolition also exacerbated problems. See Emerit 1949.
9 Manchuelle 1987: ch. 1; McLane 1986.
10 Webb 1985; Stewart 1973: 54–65; Curtin 1975, I: 215–18. The extraction of gum was particularly unpleasant because the tree was very thorny. Unlike salt production, it was done only by slaves. On Mauritanian salt, see McDougall 1980 and 1990: 254–55.
11 Searing 1993: 167–75; Robinson 1975a: 29–31; Webb 1993: ch. 6.
12 Webb 1985: 202.
13 Thompson 1989: chs. 1 and 2.
14 Schnapper 1961; Brooks 1970; Curtin 1975: 105–8.
15 Brooks 1976b; Curtin 1975, I: 119–21; Marcson 1976; Ka 1981. The European population of the colony was not much over 1 percent of the population. Saint Louis had only 235 Europeans in 1845, of whom 97 were women. Curtin 1975, I: 139.
16 Barry and Harding 1992; Ka 1981.
17 Brooks 1970.
18 Searing 1993: ch. 3; Bathily 1986: 554.
19 Guèye 1965: 247.
20 Thompson 1989: 55 claims that in 1843, about half of the *laptots* were free.
21 Marcson 1976: 27–28 calculated the profit on purchase of a slave at 13 to 20 percent. The slave generally received two meals. Government rations in 1836, which included 250 grams of meat, normally cost about .25 francs per day per slave. See also Deherme 1994; Kane 1984.
22 See appeals for indemnification. ARS, N 9 and 10.
23 Kane 1984: 64.
24 Appeals against the Indemnity Commission, ARS, N 10.
25 Deherme 1994: 170. Some women invested heavily in *pileuses*. For example, Charlotte Alotte owned twenty slaves, ten of them *pileuses*. Appeals against Commission de l'Indemnité, ARS, N 9 and N 10.
26 Marcson 1976: 20–28; M. Kane 1984.
27 Guèye 1969: 252.
28 Searing 1993: 182. The failure to reproduce cannot be explained by conditions of slavery. Free blacks had a slightly higher mortality rate. The excess of deaths over births is probably explained by the urban disease environment.
29 Zuccarelli 1962: 421. The last such proposal was made months before the Revolution of 1848. See report of 4 October 1847, ANSOM Sénégal XIV 15a.
30 Barry 1972: 213–36; Hardy 1921.
31 Marcson 1976: 142; Delaunay 1984: 44–46.
32 Zuccarelli 1962. See Renault 1976 on recruitment for sugar islands.

33 Gov. Baudin to Citoyen Min. 25 April 1848. ANSOM, Sénégal XIV 15.
34 Gov. to Min. 23 Aug. 1848, ANSOM Sénégal XIV 15a.
35 Guèye 1965: 641–45; Pasquier 1967; Gov. to Min., 23 Aug. 1848, ANSOM Sénégal XIV 15a.
36 Gov. to Min. 8 Sept. 1848. ANSOM XIV 15a.
37 Guèye 1965: 645.
38 Min., Arago to Gov. Baudin. 7 May 1848. ANSOM Senegal XIVa.
39 Mbodj 1993; Ka 1981. For an opposed view, see Pasquier 1967.
40 Gov. to Min. 27 Sept. 1851. ANSOM Senegal XIV 12.
41 Deposition of Mariam Kamata, ANSOM, Sénégal XIV 15a. The dossier contains several cases of slaves quickly sold to avoid the emancipation. Prosecutor Vincent Larcher wanted to act, but was restrained by Governor Baudin who could not imagine depriving masters of slaves without some form of indemnification. See covering letter of 3 Feb. 1849.
42 These fears were repeated in all correspondence from Governor to Minister in 1848 and early 1849. ANSOM Sénégal XIV 15a.
43 Barry 1972: 239–80.
44 Kane 1986 and 1974; Robinson 1975b: ch. 1 and 1985b: ch. 2.
45 Bathily 1985 and 1989; Barry 1988a: 136–41; Curtin 1975, I: 68–75 and 179–82; Delaunay 1984: 39–43.
46 Diouf 1990; Colvin 1972 and 1974.
47 Klein 1977a; Searing 1993.
48 Baudin to misc. rulers, 15 Feb. 1848, ARS 3 B 64, cited in Diouf 1990, 152.
49 Min. to Commissaire de la République, 7 May 1848, ARS, K8; Renault 1971, 8.
50 Poulet 1994; on links of Devès family to African rulers, see Manchuelle 1984 and Robinson 1975a: 121–22.
51 Report of 18 April 1849, ANSOM, Sénégal XIV 15a.
52 Gov. to Min. 3 Feb. 1849. ANSOM Sénégal XIV 15a.
53 Gov. Baudin to Min. 22 Aug. 1848, ANSOM Sénégal XIV 15 a.
54 Gov. to Min., 12 Feb. 1848, ANSOM Sénégal XIV 15a.
55 Min. to Gov. 25 Oct. 1848, ANSOM Sénégal XIV 15a.
56 Gov. to Dir. des Colonies, 26 Dec. 1848 and 12 Feb. 1849. ANSOM Sénégal XIV 15a.
57 ANSOM Sénégal XIV 15a.
58 Procureur de la République to Direction des Colonies, 23 March 1849. ANSOM Sénégal XIV 15a. Larcher was under attack because of seven prosecutions, all involving slaves brought illegally into or sold out of Saint Louis. Larcher was anxious to prove that his actions did not jeopardize the security of the colony.
59 Procureur de la République to Direction des Colonies, 15 Feb. and 23 Mar. 1849. ANSOM Sénégal. XIV 15a.
60 Gov. Baudin to Direction des Colonies, 2 March 1849. ANSOM Sénégal XIV 15a. Baudin wanted to indemnify in cases where he could not return the slaves, but he probably knew that Paris would never accept such a financial commitment.
61 Saint-Martin 1989: 233–49; Barrows 1974a and 1978. There is no good biography of Faidherbe, but see Delavignette 1946 and Hardy 1947.
62 Brooks 1970 and 1976a.
63 Robinson 1985b: 204–11.
64 Echenberg 1991: 7–11, 19–20. Most soldiers were ransomed, that is to say, purchased for military service, after which they owed a fourteen-year commitment. See Thompson 1989: chs. 3 and 4 on recruitment and training of *laptots*.
65 Renault 1972, 83–86.

66 Renault 1972: 86–87; Minutes of Conseil d'administration meeting of 10 April 1855; Gov. to Min., 25 April 1855. ANSOM Sénégal XIV 15b.

67 Min. to Gov. 21 June 1855. ANSOM Sénégal XIV 15 b.

68 Decree of 18 October 1855, ARS K 11.

69 Decree of 14 Nov. 1857, ARS K 11.

70 Moitt 1993.

71 Minutes of Conseil d'Administration, 5 Dec. 1857. ANSOM Sénégal XIV 15b.

72 In 1862, the *conseils de tutelle* were suppressed and administration of the system was assigned to the chief of the judicial service.

73 Mbodj 1993.

74 Deherme 1994.

75 Confidential circular of 15 Novembre 1862, ANSOM Sénégal XIV 15 d. Also in ARS, 2 D 292. Both Faidherbe and Jauréguiberry put anti-slavery clauses in treaties, but more often a protection for the local state than a prohibition of its slaving activities. For example, a treaty with Toro signed 25 March 1863, ARS K 12, provided that "No free man from Toro can from this time forth be reduced into slavery." On Jauréguiberry, see Saint-Martin 1989: 475–93. See also Deherme 1994.

76 Roche 1976: 72; R.P. Kieffer, Report on Carabane, CSE 159 B III. See also Leary 1970: 80.

77 For the Gambian Mandinka the Soninke were pourers of libations, that is to say pagan Mandinka. They are not the same as the Soninke of the Upper Senegal Valley, who are generally known in the Gambia as Serewulli or Sarakolle. See Quinn 1972: ch. 3; Klein 1968: chs. 4 and 5.

78 Comm. Sédhiou to Comm. Gor. 20 Jan. 1866, ARS, Fonds du Sénégal, 2 D 293. On slaves "born in the house" running away, see Comm. Sédhiou to Comm. Gor., 2 April 1866. On the flight of slaves being moved from Saalum to the Futa Jallon, see Comm. Sédhiou to Comm. Gor. 24 June 1866. See also letter of 15 April 1969. All in ARS, 2 D 293. See also Roche 1976: 117–14; David 1980: 15–20.

79 Robinson 1975a: 28–69; Saint-Martin 1989: 339–69.

80 Diouf 1990, 171–80; Saint-Martin 1989: 409–44.

81 Diouf 1990: 247–43; Barry 1988a: 299–302; Colvin 1974; Klein 1968: 79–93. See also Political Reports, ARS, 2 B 35.

82 Gov. to Min. 14 Feb. 1871. ARS 2 B 35; Diouf 1990: 235–43.

83 Johnson 1971: ch. 2; Idowu 1966.

84 Johnson 1971: 30–36; Pasquier 1960.

85 Min. to Gov., 28 Dec. 1854, ARS, K 11.

86 Gov. to Min., 15 Dec. 1857. ANSOM, Sénégal XIV 15b. One witness bought a fifteen-year-old girl for fifteen pieces of guinea and a six-year-old boy for three pieces. The Pipy case seems to have shaken Carrère out of his usual complaisance. He freed only a little over 1,000 slaves in twelve years. Gov. to Min, 23 Nov. 1867. ARS K 11.

87 Barrows 1974a: 292–96. It is ironic that Faidherbe was earlier transferred from Guadeloupe for being a Negrophile. He later dedicated his book *Le Sénégal* to Victor Schoelcher. His mistress, a Khassonke woman, bore him a son, who later served in the French army.

88 Clark 1990: 186–88; Bathily 1986: 534–62.

89 Clark 1990: 138–41; Bathily 1986: 561–62.

90 Instructions to posts at Saldé, Matam and Bakel, cited in Renault 1972: 94–95.

91 Renault 1972: 95–96; Robinson 1975a.

92 ARS 13 G 148, cited by Robinson 1975a: 113.

93 État des captifs réfugiés à Podor, ARS 13 G 124/ 11 to 14.
94 M. Kane 1984: 18–23 suggests that the vast majority of the slaves at Saint Louis came from the upper river area.
95 Samb 1985.
96 See Instructions to Commandant, Saldé, 9 May 1867, in Renault 1972: 95–96. Slaves from Kajoor were to be freed only if enslaved after the annexation of Kajoor. If already slaves, they were to be expelled on the master's claim.
97 Min. to Gov. 11 June 1868, ANSOM, XIV 15b.
98 Gov. to Min. n.d. 1865. ARS, K 11. Pinet-Laprade was then commandant at Gorée.
99 Gov. to Comm. Gorée, 4 Feb. 1874, ANSOM, Sénégal XIV 15c.
100 Comm. Gorée to Gov. 16 Feb 1874, ANSOM, Sénégal XIV 15c.
101 Gov. to Comm. Gorée, 24 March 1874, ANSOM, Sénégal XIV 15c.
102 Comm. Gorée to Gov., 8 May 1974, ANSOM, Sénégal XIV 15c.
103 Diouf 1990: 248–54; on Amadu Shaixu, see Robinson 1975a and Klein 1972; on Sidia, see Saint-Martin 1974.
104 Diouf 1990, 256; Comm. Thiès to Gov. 6 March 1869, ARS 13 G 264.
105 Most of what follows is based on research by Mohammed Mbodj, which he has not yet published. See also Gray 1940: 117.
106 Weil 1984: 81–86.
107 Annual Report 1868, PRO, Banjul.
108 Cohen 1971: ch. 1.

3   SLAVERY, SLAVE-TRADING AND SOCIAL REVOLUTION

1 Botte 1994: 109.
2 Echenberg 1971b: 6.
3 For an overview of this period, see Barry 1988a, Part 4; Person 1974; Barry and Suret-Canale 1974.
4 Curtin 1975, I: p. xxii.
5 Curtin 1975, I: 4–6; McDougall 1986. On commodity trade, see Hopkins 1973: ch. 4; Austen 1987; Flint and McDougall 1987.
6 Curtin 1975, I: 156–57.
7 Barry 1972 and 1988a; Bazin 1975 and 1982; Bazin and Terray 1982; Roberts 1987b; Bathily 1986; Klein 1972 and 1992a.
8 Bazin and Terray 1982: 24.
9 Meillassoux 1971: 69 and 1986 (1991): 143–75; Manning 1990: ch. 2.
10 Lopes 1988; Niane 1989; Mané 1978; Hawkins 1980: ch. 2.
11 Rodney 1968a and b and 1970.
12 Fuglestad 1983; De Latour 1982; Klein 1968.
13 On Kong, see Bernus 1960 and Green 1984 and 1986; on Buna, see Boutillier 1969, 1971, 1975, 1993; on Bobo-Dioulasso, see Quimby 1972. On Bonduku, see Terray 1974 and 1995 and Handloff 1982.
14 Wilks 1975: 64–71.
15 Brown 1969: 101–2; Gallais 1967: I, 92–93.
16 Law 1991: 340–44. On Oyo, see Law 1977: 225–28.
17 Inikori 1982; Manning 1990: ch. 4.
18 Roberts 1980b: 171; Green 1984: ch. 2. On the central Sudan, see Lovejoy 1980.
19 Klein 1992a; H. Klein 1983; Geggus 1990. This position has been attacked by Inikori 1992.
20 Slave warriors often kept boy captives to carry their gear and supplies on cam-

paigns. These boys could eventually be incorporated in the army. See Raffenel 1856: 435–59.

21 Curtin 1975: 176; Becker 1986 and 1988; Manning 1990: ch. 3. Geggus 1990 shows that the further the source in the interior, the higher the ratio of men to women.

22 On hides, see Curtin 1975: 218–21; Boulègue 1986, II: 489–91. On food security, see Becker and Martin 1975; Becker 1986 and 1988; Bathily 1989: 278–82 and 339–48; Barry 1988a: 161–68; Boulègue 1986, II: 482–88; Curtin 1975, I: 109–11 and 168–73.

23 Roberts 1987b, ch. 2; Bazin 1975; Meillassoux 1975a and 1986 (1991); Boutillier 1975; Izard 1975; Klein 1978.

24 Lovejoy and Richardson 1995a and b. See also Terray 1982.

25 Klein 1971.

26 White 1971; Fisher 1971; Echenberg 1971a; Robinson 1985b: 329–34; Roberts 1987b: ch. 3.

27 Rodney 1966. See also Fage 1980.

28 Fernandès 1951: 69; Ámada 1964.

29 Linares 1987; Mark 1985: 22–31; Baum 1986: ch. 4. Though the Jola were raided for slaves over the whole period of the Atlantic trade, their population increased sufficiently for them to absorb most of the Baynuk and push forward the frontier of settlement. This is probably because they assimilated most of their slaves.

30 Jonckers 1987: 122–31. On the Bwa, see Capron 1973: 70–91. Hubbell 1996 describes a similar process for Dafina.

31 Sanneh and Curtin disagree on whether the Jaxanke were primarily traders or clerics. Curtin 1971; Sanneh 1976b: 55. Both activities were linked to each other and, as Sanneh argues, to the exploitation of slave labour.

32 The Jaxanke almost always built their villages far from political centers. Sanneh 1979.

33 Trimingham 1962; but also see response of Willis 1971.

34 On Pir in southern Kajoor, see Robinson 1975a and b.

35 Levtzion 1986a and b and 1987. See also Sanneh 1979.

36 Ba and Daget 1955: ch. 2; Klein 1968: ch. 4; Hawkins 1980; Last 1967; Hiskett 1984.

37 Irwin could find no written documents on the jihad in Liptako. Irwin 1981: 203–5.

38 Robinson 1975b: 26–27.

39 White 1971; Beachey 1962.

40 Miers 1975: 261–70.

41 Bah 1985: 234–40; Robinson 1985b: 250–51 and 331–33; Saint-Martin 1970.

42 White 1971; Crowder 1971; Fisher and Rowlands 1972.

43 Fisher and Rowlands 1972: 220; Smaldone 1977: ch. 6; Ba and Daget 1955: 36–40.

44 Olivier de Sardan 1982; Kimba 1981: 64–66.

45 Law 1980. Few armies were more than a third cavalry. Echenberg 1971b: 100.

46 On those without a social base see Holden 1965; Echenberg 1971b; Cordell 1985. On horses and guns, see Webb 1993.

47 Bah 1985. If they could not breach a wall, European armies would have faltered at major fortresses, as happened with Samori at Sikasso.

48 The traditional elite squandered much of their revenue on drink. The frugal Muslims bought weapons. Klein 1968 and 1977b.

49 Stewart 1973: 13–18; Norris 1969.

50 Barry 1972 and 1988a: 88–95; Curtin 1971; Norris 1969; Ritchie 1968. Kane 1986: 456–59 argues that the Hassani and Denianke were "pillagers who rejected those obligations which flowed from their commitment to Islam. It was because they were traitors to Islam that they were considered as enemies."

51 Some also carried arms. Stewart 1973: 54–65; McDougall 1985: 103.

52 Barry 1988a: 143–44; Curtin 1971a and 1971b; Gomez 1992; Bathily 1989: 308–12.
53 Kane 1986: 360.
54 Kane 1974 and 1986; Robinson 1975a and 1985b: 59–71; Barry 1988a: 154–60.
55 Robinson 1975a: 16.
56 Roger 1829: 151 and 209–10.
57 Kane 1986: 359–61; Robinson 1975a: 22.
58 Robinson 1975a: 13–18; Roger 1829; Park 1816: 261–63; Colvin 1972: 167–79 and 599–601; Durand 1802: 240–42; Diouf 1990.
59 Robinson 1985b: 65. See also Robinson 1975a: 19–27.
60 Robinson 1975a: 113.
61 Barry 1988a: 144–54; Rodney 1968a; Botte 1991.
62 Rodney 1968a: 277; Levtzion 1975: 207; Barry 1988a: 145. The seventeenth-century hide trade provided exchange for many pastoral groups; Curtin 1975: 220–21.
63 Rivière 1984.
64 Goerg 1986: ch. 2.
65 The Alfaya descend from Karomoko Alfa, the original leader. The Soriya descend from Ibrahima Sory, the most successful military leader: Diallo 1972; Rodney 1968a: 278–80.
66 Diallo 1972.
67 Barry 1988a: 208–45.
68 Ismael Barry 1971; Botte 1988.
69 Barry 1988a, 208–20. On the Wali of Gumba, see Verdat 1949; Suret-Canale 1966; Sanneh 1986.
70 Gallais 1967: I, 87; Sanankoua 1990: ch. 1.
71 Gallais 1967: I, 77–93.
72 Brown 1969: iii.
73 Gallais 1967: I, 92–93.
74 Brown 1969: 102.
75 Brown 1969: 101.
76 Brown 1969: 102. This image of the Ardos remains vivid in the oral traditions. See interviews, Kampo Collection: Bada Bocoum. Belko Tambura, Amirou Tahikiri, Mamadou Guisseh.
77 Brown 1969: 103–10; Sanankoua 1990: 33–42.
78 Ba and Daget 1955: 23–28. On Amadu's ambivalent links to Sokoto, see Stewart 1986.
79 Ba and Daget 1955: ch. 2; Gallais 1967: I, 93–96; Sanankoua 1990: 42–48. Ahmed remained hostile to Jenne. Caillié 1830, I: 461 wrote "that the great trade of that town interfered with his religious duties and drew aside the true believers from their devotions." Thus, he built his capital, Hamdullahi off the major trade routes. On Ahmed's anti-merchant orientation, see Azarya 1980.
80 Ba and Daget 1955: 32–35 report that at Nukuma, 1,000 of Amadu's supporters, of whom only 40 had horses, faced 200,000 of the allied army. This is undoubtedly an exaggeration, but many in the delta undoubtedly waited for the outcome of the battle before supporting Amadu.
81 Ba and Daget 1955: ch. 4; Monteil 1932: 106–14; Gallais 1967: I, 93–96; Sanankoua 1990: ch. 3.
82 Gallais 1967: I, 93–96; Marty 1921: II, 137–38; Johnson 1976.
83 Brown 1969: 209; Sanankoua 1990: 93–100.
84 Johnson 1976.
85 Johnson 1976; Gallais 1967: I, 148 ff.
86 Sanankoua 1990: 111; Brown 1969: 116 and 126; Ba and Daget 1955: 40. Some of

the new *ulema* may been of slave origin. The *ulema* was quite small at the time of the jihad, but expanded dramatically soon afterwards. Freed slaves had the option of advancing socially by seeking a Muslim education. It is unlikely that such information would ever get recorded by the oral tradition. All the tradition tells us is that slaves served and were freed.

87 Robinson 1985b: 365–70. On Umar, see also Roberts 1987b: ch. 3; Oloruntemehin 1972; Saint-Martin 1970; Willis 1978.
88 Cruise O'Brien 1988.
89 Robinson 1985b: 117; Willis 1978.
90 The *fergo* continued to the last years of the Umarian regime. See Robinson 1975a: 54 and 1985b: 219–31. Hanson estimates that over 50,000 emigrated, probably a fifth of the population of the Futa.
91 Mage 1968: 163; Robinson 1985b: 256–57.
92 Robinson 1985b: 186–90; Roberts 1987a: 77–79; Hanson 1996: 31.
93 Roberts 1987a: 84–88, 95–99.
94 Masina traditions reproach both the attack on fellow Muslims and the brutality of the victors. See Sanankoua 1990: ch. 7.
95 Thiero 1985; on the way in which resistance shaped Umarian Segu, see Roberts 1980c and 1987a: 95–100.
96 Hanson 1996: 9.
97 Hanson 1996:46. A slave was also appointed in Koniakary.
98 Hanson 1996: ch. 1.
99 On Tijani, see Robinson 1985b: 311–16; Caron 1891: chs. 4 and 13.
100 Robinson 1985b: 108.
101 Robinson 1985b: 119–20.
102 Robinson 1985b: 152–53.
103 Soleillet 1887: 441 says that in the Sudan men taller than a gun were often put to death. See also Klein 1983; Meillassoux 1983.
104 Robinson 1985b: 154.
105 Mage 1868: 153; Robinson 1985b: 187.
106 Robinson 1985b: 275.
107 Robinson 1985b: 183–84.
108 Robinson 1985b: 329–34 estimates that 1,500 to 1,800 small arms per year passed through Bakel and Medine.
109 Robinson 1985b: 216.
110 Bah 1985: 139–42; Robinson 1985b: 216.
111 Samori's empire was often referred to as Wasulu. This is incorrect. Wasulu was only incorporated in the 1880s and was the area that suffered most from his conquest.
112 Person 1968: I, 201 and 214–19. On another *juula* state-builder absorbed by Samori, see O'Sullivan 1976.
113 Person 1968: I, 294–316.
114 Person 1968: II, 973–82.
115 Person 1968: II, 837–39; Peroz 1891: 323–39.
116 Person 1968: II, 929–32.
117 Person 1968: II, 906–12.
118 Person 1968: II, 912–19 and 942.
119 Person 1968: II, 747–800
120 Rondeau 1980: 264.
121 Rondeau 1980: 285.
122 Holmes 1977; Rondeau 1980: ch. 3; Person 1968: II: 745–49; Collieaux 1924.

123 Roberts 1987b: 107–12; McDougall 1990; Klein 1992b.
124 Roberts 1987b: 101–4. The French *ligne de ravitaillement*, which lay to the south, was an alternative route, but much less important for slave traders. Baillaud 1902: ch. 3.
125 Binger 1892, I: 130. See also Person 1975, III: 1762–63.
126 McDougall 1980 and 1985.
127 Baillaud 1902.
128 Baillaud 1902: 35–37.
129 Baillaud 1902: 112.
130 Lovejoy 1978 and 1979a; Hogendorn 1977.
131 Klein 1987. See Appendix 2. All except Gao reported about 40 percent, and Gao was clearly under-reported. Olivier de Sardan 1984: 191 suggests that the actual slave percentage in Songhay areas was between two thirds and three quarters.
132 Lenz 1887: 287–99.
133 Shroetter 1992. This revises upward the estimate of Miège 1961, who suggested 3,500 to 4,000 a year.
134 Abitbol 1979: 204 also talks of 3,000 to 4,000 a year.
135 *Chroniques*, #73, Jan. 1897, AWF.
136 Report on Situation in Soudan, ANSOM, Soudan IV 1.
137 Cordell 1983; McDougall 1988.
138 Report on slavery, Sokolo, 1904, ARS, K 19.
139 Binger 1892: I, 320–21.
140 Binger 1892: I, 30–31. See also Amselle 1977; Roberts 1980b.
141 Binger 1892: I, 385.
142 Keita 1959.
143 Commercial report, Médine, ANM, 1 Q 70. The largest was 176. By comparison, Salaga regularly received caravans of between 500 and 2,000 slaves, mostly from Hausaland.
144 Roberts 1980 speaks of caravans with thirty or forty traders. Gallieni 1885: 455 speaks of caravans leaving the upper Senegal with twenty to sixty traders.
145 Binger 1892 I, 498.
146 Mage 1868: 192.
147 Binger 1892: I, 26.
148 In 1894, when the trade was under attack, one broker had only five girls between six and ten years old and a thirty-year-old male. A second had five girls aged ten to thirteen, three adult women and a boy. Comm. Kayes to Gov. 12 June and 27 Sept. 1894, ANM, 1 E 173. Other brokers had moved away or diversified. Korientza also had three brokers. Lt. St. Martin to Resident Masina, 11 May 1902, ANM, 1 E 23. See also correspondence from Médine to Kayes, ARS, 15 G 116.
149 Johnson 1986: 343–45.
150 Echenberg 1971b: 121–28.
151 On Liptako, Irwin 1981: 108–32; Irwin 1973: ch. 3; On Masina, Stewart 1986.

4 SENEGAL AFTER BRIÈRE

1 Diouf 1990: 268.
2 Saint-Martin 1966: 60.
3 Kanya-Forstner 1969: 55-60.
4 Fozard 1975: 155–65 and Kanya-Forstner 1969: 60–72.
5 Ndiaye 1968: 467.

6 Min. to Gov. 11 June 1868. ANSOM, Sénégal XIV 15 b.
7 Note, Jan. 1868, ANSOM, Sénégal XIV 15b; Gov. to Min. 23 Nov. 1867, ARS, K 11. Bazot objected to administering the redemption process, but in the absence of documents, I do not know why. Governor Pinet-Laprade got him transferred.
8 See his personnel file, ANSOM, EE 596(1).
9 Darrigrand to Gov., 28 May 1875, ANSOM, Sénégal XIV 16.
10 Procureur to Chef du Service Judiciaire, ANSOM, Sénégal XIV 16.
11 There was no significant flight to Gorée. Comm. Boilève claimed that no slaves had been turned over to their masters between 1867 and 1875, but some runaways were shipped to Joal and Portudal. "Question des captifs au Sénégal," ANSOM, Sénégal XIV 15d. Goree was probably too far from the mainland for most runaways.
12 Acting Gov. to Min., 8 Aug. 1878; Gov. to Min., 8 Dec. 1878, ANSOM, Sénégal XIV 15c.
13 Gov. to Min, 27 Aug. 1878 and 1 Feb. 1879, ARS, K 11. See also Harrison 1988: 11–15; Cruise O'Brien 1967; Robinson 1988: 415–23.
14 "Note pour le Ministre," ANSOM, Sénégal XIV 15d.
15 Min. to Gov., 17 Jan. 1879, ANSOM, Sénégal XIV 15d; Renault 1972, 14.
16 Gov. to Min., 25 Jan. 1879, ANSOM, Sénégal XIV 15d; Gov. to Comm. Dakar, # 36, 1979, ARS, K 11.
17 Min. to Gov. 17 Feb. 1879 ANSOM, Sénégal XIV 15d.
18 Prosecutor to Gov., 28 May 1875, ANSOM, Sénégal XIV 16; Compte-Rendu des Assises, 12 Nov. 1878, ANSOM, Sénégal XIV 15c.
19 Ndiaye 1968; Manchuelle 1984. Idowu 1969b and 1971. Ndiaye suggests that Darrigrand was a part of an anti-Brière cabal, but he began before Brière arrived, consistently opposed interference with the judiciary and insisted on enforcing the law.
20 Manchuelle 1984. The request by the General Council in 1881 for strict enforcement of the 1848 law was surprising because *habitants* often traded in slaves. Idowu 1968: 253. This resolution may have reflected hostility to Brière.
21 *La France*, 3 Oct. 1879. *La Lanterne*, 10 and 14 Oct. 1880. This story was why Jauréguiberry put pressure on Brière. Min. to Gov. Sen. 4 Oct. 1879, ANSOM, Sénégal XIV 15d. Ironically, Jauréguiberry was a Protestant and was close to the Protestant Mission when he was Governor. Fozard 1975: 155–65.
22 Schmidt 1994.
23 *JORF*, 2 March 1880.
24 ANSOM, Sénégal XIV 15 d; Renault 1972: 33.
25 See Brière of 23 Feb. 1880 and 8 June 1880, ANSOM, Sénégal XIVd.
26 Gov. Brière to Min., 8 June 1880 and 23 Oct. 1880, ANSOM, Sénégal XIV 15d. See also correspondence, ARS, 13 G 311; Ndiaye 1968.
27 Comm. Dagana to Gov. Sen., 1 August 1882, ARS, 13 G 311.
28 Comm. Dagana to Gov. 12 Oct. 1880, cited in Deherme 1994.
29 Post Diary, 17 May 1881, ARS, 13 G 111.
30 *Moniteur du Sénégal*, 9 Feb. 1881; Renault 1972: 33–34; Schoelcher 1882, I: 232–35.
31 Manchuelle 1984: 478; Ndiaye 1968. Brière continued to argue that freeing slaves would attract vagabonds to French posts and alienate those willing to cooperate with the French *marche civilisatrice* toward the Niger. Brière de l'Isle to Min. 23 March 1881, ANSOM, Sénégal XIV 15 e.
32 Schoelcher 1882: I, 270.
33 Schoelcher 1881 in ANSOM, Sénégal XIV 15e.
34 Circular of 27 Oct. 1881, ARS, 2 D 5.
35 Monthly political reports, ANSOM, Sénégal I 66. Canard was recalled in June

after a short term. *Moniteur du Sénégal*, 15 June 1882. He had always been unsympathetic to runaways. In 1871, while Commandant at Gorée, he overruled the Prosecutor in one case and delivered a runaway to her master, who killed her; Deherme 1994.

36 Min. to Gov. Sen., 31 Jan. 1882, ANSOM, Sénégal XIV 15 d.

37 Min. to Gov., 12 June 1882, ARS, 13 G 25.

38 Schoelcher 1882 II: 188 ff. Vallon was hostile to the policy he was supposed to enforce. Gov. to Min., 27 July 1882 and 1 Nov. 1882, ANSOM, Sénégal I 67.

39 Report of 18 March 1882, cited in Deherme 1994. Reports on slave-trade cases which Canard sent to Paris in 1881 and 1882 suggest that the French often turned a blind eye to slave transactions.

40 Circular to Commandants du Cercle, 8 Jan. 1884, ARS, K 12. Cited in Renault 1972: 37.

41 Diouf 1990: 268. See also Lat Dior's letters in ARS, 13 G 260.

42 Diouf 1990: 255–86; Moitt 1985: ch. 4. On Lat Dior see also Diop 1966, Colvin 1972 and 1974. In 1865, the Commandant at Thiès told chiefs at Saniokhor and Jander to welcome "strangers who wished to clear land and cultivate"; 6 June 1865, ARS, 2 D 259.

43 Diouf 1990 stresses the slave issue. See also Ganier 1965.

44 In 1887 Saer Maty Ba in Rip and Soninke marabout Mamadu Lamine in the upper Senegal were defeated; Klein 1968; Hrbek 1976 and 1979. In 1890, Alburi Njay and Abdul Bokar Kan were defeated and fled east to join Amadu; Robinson 1975a.

45 Moitt 1985: ch.5 and 1989.

46 Brooks 1976a; Bowman 1987.

47 Report on slavery, Dagana, 1904, by R. Manetche, ARS, K 18.

48 Circular to Commandants du Cercle et Chefs du Poste, 8 Jan. 1884, ARS, K 12.

49 Robinson 1985b: 219–31; Hanson 1990 and 1996: 43–47.

50 Hanson 1996: 72–87; Ganier 1968.

51 Gov. Sen. to Min., 18 Dec. 1889, ARS, K 12. See also various reports ARS, 2 B 75 and 13 G 181 and 182 and Renault 1972: 38–43.

52 Comm. Dagana to Gov., 31 May 1883; telegram 28 Sept. 1883; Report for Jan. 1884, ARS, 13 G 311.

53 Comm. Dagana to Gov. 19 July 1886, ARS, 13 G 113.

54 Comm. Sup. to Gov. Sen., 4 Jan. 1889, ARS, 15 G 32.

55 Chef, Service Judiciaire to Gov., 16 Dec. 1885; Procès-Verbal, 18 Dec. 1885, ARS, K 12.

56 See for example Comm. Dagana to Gov., 11 May 1881, ARS, 13 G 111. In Kajoor, Awa Kebe, a slave of Lat Dior's freed at Saint Louis, tried to return home. Lat Dior tore up her papers, but her brother arranged through Lat Dior's creditors to redeem her. Gov. Sen. to Min. 20 March 1882, ANSOM, Sénégal XIV 15 d.

57 Comm. Dagana to Gov. Sen. 1 Nov. 1882, ARS, 13 G 311. Some slaves feared to return, but petitioned the administration for help in recovering children. Thus, see petition of 1 March 1883 of a former slave who fled Fulbe near Dagana and was afraid his child would be sold. ARS, K 12.

58 Comm. Dagana, 15 July 1881, ARS, 13 G 111.

59 Comm. Dagana to Dir. Aff. Pol., 31 May 1883, ARS, 13 G 112. Though told to confiscate slaves, the Commandant thought that only one of the Fulbe in question intended to emigrate. Who, he asked, should he believe, masters or slaves? On instructions to free, see Dir. de l'Intérieur to Comm. Dagana, 25 June 1885, ARS, 13 G 112.

60 Bulletin, Dagana, ARS, 13 G 112.

61 Deherme 1994.
62 Comm. Dagana to Dir. Aff. Pol., 15 July 1881, ARS, 13 G 111.
63 Min. to Gov. Sen., 12 June 1882, ARS, 13 G 25.
64 Instructions to Comm. Podor, cited in Deherme 1994.
65 Comm. Dagana to Dir. Aff. Pol., ARS, 13 G 112.
66 Comm. Dagana to Gov. 19 July 1886, ARS, 13 G 113.
67 Gov. to Min., 5 Feb. 1889 and 18 Dec. 1889, ARS, K 12. Idowu 1968 suggests that Clément-Thomas and his successor, Henri Lamothe, also wanted to free themselves from the General Council.
68 Robinson 1987. See also Robinson 1975b; Charles 1971 and 1977.
69 Idowu 1968; M. Kane 1987. Disannexation was attacked in the General Council both for protecting slavery and for limiting the authority of the Council. See Minutes, 19 Dec. 1892, ARS.
70 Jeng 1978: 95 ff. See also Swindell 1980.
71 Pa Alhaggie Sampa Saidy, 16 April 1977, cited in Jeng 1978: 95.
72 Quinn 1972: chs. 5–7; Klein 1968: ch. 4, 1972 and 1977b; Gray 1940; Barry 1988a: 267–72.
73 Klein 1968: ch. 5; Quinn 1972: 158–63.
74 Klein 1968, 101–2.
75 D'Arcy to Blackall, 15 Nov. 1866, PRO, London. Cited in Jeng 1978: 168.
76 Admin. Gambia to Gov.-in-Chief, 26 July 1869, PRO, Banjul.
77 Comm. Kaolack to Comm. Gorée, 4 April 1862, ARS, 13 G 319.
78 Said about Biram Cissé by his grandson, Baabu Xoja Cisse, Ndimba Touba, January and February 1975, Klein-Mbodj collection.
79 Hay to Holland, 2 March 1887, PRO, London, CO 87/130.
80 Barry 1988a: 326–31; Leary 1970: 122–57; Roche 1976: 132–45; Quinn 1972: 170–74.
81 Roche 1976: 214–17; Barry 1988a: 326–29.
82 Barry 1988a: 326–27.
83 Jeng 1978: 166–67.
84 Jeng 1978: Table 7.
85 Colonial Office to Admin. Gambia, 3 May 1893, PRO, London, CO 87/143. See also Travelling Commissioner's Reports, PRO, London, CO 187/149.
86 Curtin 1975: 230–31; Bathily 1985, II: 569–72; Mage 1868: 38–40.
87 *Annual Report on The Gambia*, 1848. Tillibunka means people of the east. See also Bérenger-Féraud 1879: 195–96 and 308–9.
88 Roche 1976: 117–24.
89 David 1980: 15–19.
90 Swindell 1980; David 1980: ch. 1; Adams 1977: 40.
91 Klein 1989a; Goerg 1986: 77–78. On Tuba, see Sanneh 1976b and Suret-Canale 1970.
92 David 1980: 20–27; Klein 1968: 177–78.
93 Bowman 1987: 96–98.
94 Manchuelle 1987: 113–26.
95 Manchuelle 1989 a and b. See also Thompson 1989 and 1992.
96 Frey 1888: 239.
97 Notes sur l'organisation des *laptots* au Sénégal, ANSOM CC 3 1183. There is no date, but Manchuelle estimates it as about 1880.
98 Manchuelle 1987: 169. Manchuelle here uses Walter Elkan's distinction between "migrants" and "proletarians"; Elkan 1960.
99 Gov. to Min., 18 Feb. 1882, ARS, K 12; 27 Mar. 1882, ANSOM, Sénégal XIV 15e.

See also Renault 1972: 37.
100 Vallière's Conseil d'Administration recommended that he stop freeing slaves. Diouf 1990: 242.
101 Deherme 1994; Moitt 1993.
102 Robinson 1975a: 113–14.
103 Father Kieffer, Bulletin de la Communauté, 31 October 1880, CSE, 160 B I. On a child-buying expedition to Siin, see Duboin to Schwindenhammer, 10 Feb. 1878, CSE, 160 A II. Meillorat 1884 told Catholic readers that redeemed children would be instructed in the Catholic faith, given good work habits and taught a skill. See also Annales Religeuses de St. Joseph de Ngasobil, ARS.
104 Echenberg 1986 and 1991. See also Barrows 1974a, 1974b and 1978.
105 See for example Comm. Dagana to Gov. Senegal, 29 April 1881, ARS, 13 G 111.
106 Renault 1972: 21–23.
107 ARS, 13 G 185.
108 Dr. Collomb to Comm. des Cercles, 4 March 1885, ARS, 13 G 185.
109 Comm. Dagana to Gov. Sen., 29 April 1881, ARS, 13 G 111. See also Jauréguiberry to Gov. Vallon, 4 Oct. 1882, ARS, 2 B 54.
110 Gov. to Min. 23 May 1882, ANSOM, Senegal XIV 15 d.
111 Suret-Canale 1971, 60–62; Manchuelle 1986. See Conklin 1989 on Republican agendas in colonial policy.

5   CONQUEST OF THE SUDAN: DESBORDES TO ARCHINARD

1 Galliéni 1885: 435.
2 Capt. André Ballieu, Report on Slavery, Bafulabe, 15 May 1894, ARS, K 14.
3 Kanya-Forstner 1969; Hargreaves 1974 and 1985.
4 De Benoist 1987; Harding 1972.
5 Frey 1888: 472–94; Kanya-Forstner 1969: 137–41.
6 Report of 1 Nov. 1884 to Gov. Sénégal, ARS, 15 G 83.
7 Cohen 1974.
8 Malowist 1966; Hopkins 1967; Tymowski 1970a.
9 Kanya-Forstner 1969: ch. 1.
10 Gallieni 1885; Michel 1989; Kanya-Forstner 1969: 72–83.
11 Kanya-Forstner 1969; Méniaud 1931; Ward 1976.
12 Fozard 1975; Kanya-Forstner 1969: 64–68. From 1883 to 1885, commandants had explicit instructions to avoid military conquest. Hargreaves 1974: 60–61. The decision to build the railroad was linked to the Trans-Sahara project. With the massacre of the Flatters expedition in 1881, that utopian idea died, but rail enthusiasts still won support of the Chamber for a rail line between the Senegal and Niger rivers.
13 Ndiaye 1968; Kanya-Forstner 1969: 67–68.
14 Méniaud 1931, I: 146 and 154.
15 Roberts 1987b: 101–2. On relations between Beledugu and the Futanke, see Ward 1976. See also Oloruntemehin 1968 and 1972.
16 Gallieni seems to have assumed that Amadu would know little about his efforts in Beledugu and that Beledugu chiefs would ask no questions about his destination. When he told one chief that the French wanted neither territory nor captives, the chief responded: "All that you say is very wise, but what proves that you are not lying? Al Hajji also came thirty years to this country, speaking to us of deliverance, or the abolition of tithes, promising us great wealth, but he deceived us and once master of the country, treated us as slaves." Quoted by Ward 1976: 97 from Gallieni

to Gov. Sen., 12 June 1880, ANSOM, Mission 16 Gallieni 1880.

17 Meillassoux 1968: 3–7; Ward 1976: 106–14; Méniaud 1931: 162–81; Oloruntemehin 1972: ch. 8; Perinbam 1996.

18 Person 1968, II: 663–95; Cissoko 1988: 299–306; Saint-Martin 1967: ch. 12; Méniaud 1931, I: 142–232.

19 Gov. Sudan to Comm. Kita, no. 1, ARS, 15 G 142.

20 Comm. Bafulabe to Comm. Sup., n.d., 1887. ANM, 1 E 186. Gallieni said that if she was married to her master, she was free.

21 Comm. Bafulabe to Comm. Supérieur, 19 June 1883, ANM, 1 E 186. Captives taken in the 1885–86 campaign were "freed" and assigned to household heads, but were to be available whenever the Commandant wanted to take inventory. Capt. Mamadou Racine to Comm. Sup. p.i., 21 Aug. 1887, ANM, 1 E 179. It is unlikely that many took inventory, and with frequent changes of command, most never got to know their commands.

22 Comm. Bafulabe to Comm. Sup., 19 June 1883, ANM, 1 E 186. See similar complaints from Niagassola in 1886, ANM, 1 E 58.

23 Person 1968, II: 663.

24 On Capt. P.L. Monteil's critique, see Kanya-Forstner 1969: 136.

25 Roberts 1987b: 142–46.

26 Borgnis-Desbordes' speech of 5 February 1983 in *Moniteur du Sénégal*, 20 March 1883.

27 Instructions for Comm. Sup., 1883–1884, ARS, 1 D 76.

28 Cissoko 1988: 299–322. See also Cissoko 1969.

29 Cissoko 1969: 896–98 and 908–12.

30 Gallieni 1885: 317.

31 Michel 1989: 119.

32 Monteil 1896–98.

33 Echenberg 1991: 13; Méniaud 1931, I: 84–85; Frey 1888: 390–93.

34 Echenberg 1991: 11–19.

35 Report, Niagassola, Oct. 1890, ANM, 1 E 58.

36 Echenberg 1971b: 127–28; Méniaud 1931: 84–85; Frey 1888: 390–93.

37 Monteil 1896–98: 138.

38 Carpeaux 1913: 11.

39 Frey 1888: 77–85; Méniaud 1931: I, 66–68.

40 Letter, 19 Jan. 1891, probably to Comm. Sup., ARS, 15 G 132.

41 Frey 1888: 391–92. Frey also describes about 200 "freed" and virtually naked women shivering in a French camp on a 10 °C night; 1888: 128.

42 Once in Senegal, a whole village was placed with two chiefs as hostages because they could not pay a fine. Someone in the governor's office realized what was likely to happen, and quickly sent out a new administrator. When the new administrator tried to round up the hostages, 140 had disappeared. See Klein 1968: 205–207.

43 Archinard to Etienne, 8 Jan. 1891, ARS, 15 G 21.

44 Capt. Philippe, Comm. El Oualedji to Comm. Northern Region, 1984, ANM, 1 E 178; Major Elsener, Comm. Northern Region to Gov. Sudan, 14 Sept. 1894; Capt. Gerard, Gundam to Comm. Northern Region, 1 Sept. 1894, ANM, 1 E 178.

45 *Diaire*, Segu, 18 and 19 July 1896, AWF.

46 Asst. Comm. Bafulabe to Musa Sisoko, Chief of Bambugu, ANM, 1 E 186.

47 I am grateful to Comm. Louis Baron for discussing his research on the colonial army.

48 This section profits from conversations with Comm. Louis Baron on his research on the officers of the French colonial army.

49 Mgr. Hacquard to Dir. de l'Oeuvre de la Sainte Enfance, Nov. 1894. Corres. Officielle 1892–1911, AWF. The narrator in Carpeaux 1913 has a large entourage, which includes a coquettish young female slave.
50 *Diaire*, Segu, April 1896, AWF.
51 See ANM, 1 E 191 for a series of slave reclamations.
52 *Diaire*, Segu, April 1896, AWF.
53 *Diaire*, Segu, 24 and 25 July 1896, AWF.
54 Report of Apostolic Vicar to the Propaganda, 12 Sept. 1892, CSE, 163 B II. At the officer's mess, the conversation was frequently about sex, presumably when the missionaries were not present. Monteil quotes Trentinian as suggesting that it was the older officers, those least able to do it, who talked about it the most and in the greatest detail. Monteil 1896–98: 42.
55 Monteil 1896–98: 240–41. He apparently had children by two of these women.
56 Person 1968, II: 1123.
57 Lt. Adjoint to Comm. Sup., 18 Dec. 1891, ARS, 15 G 132; *Diaire*, Segu, Jan. 1896.
58 Méniaud 1931: 193–273.
59 Frey 1888: 264–417; Bathily 1970 and 1985: ch. 5; Hrbek 1976 and 1979.
60 Gallieni 1891.
61 Frey 1888: 408–9; Bouche 1968: 80; Clark 1994c.
62 Bouche 1968: 85.
63 Order 185, 18 Dec. 1888, ANM, 15 G 154.
64 Order 217, 5 Jan. 1889, ARS, 15 G 155.
65 Order 15, 11 July 1891, ARS, 15 G 156.
66 Order 420, 2 April 1890, ANM, 1 D 102.
67 Order 117, 2 May 1893, ARS, 15 G 155. The order explicitly denied the master the right to refuse.
68 "Note sur les Villages de Liberté," 16 Nov. 1895, ANM, 1 E 180. See also Bouche 1968: 83.
69 Thus, in Kayes, 449 slaves were liberated between 1 January 1893 and 1 June 1894. The children were distributed, thirty-one to Europeans, twenty-nine to the Catholic mission, sixty to "natives from the lower river," and twenty-eight to diverse native subjects. ANM, 1 E 134.
70 Bouche 1968: 85-87.
71 Comm. Bafulabe to Comm. des Cercles, 2 Aug. 1887, ANM, 1 E 68.
72 ANM, 1 E 143. See Appendix 3. Many were reluctant to go to the new villages because of fear of raids by the Moors. Comm. Nioro to Lt. Gov. Soudan, 4 April 1896, ANM, 1 E 60.
73 Trentinian's Circular 8, 10 March 1897, ANM, 1 E 149 complained about inadequate statistics in reports, for example entry and departure data that did not add up.
74 Bouche 1968: 98; Deherme 1908: 478.
75 Bouche 1968: 98-100. One officer asked what to do with caravans under ten. They probably paid in cowries or trade goods.
76 Archinard, Order 376, 17 May 1889, ARS, 1 D 97; Order 157, Instruction to Commandants, ARS, 15 G 159. See also Bouche 1968: Ch. 5. Archinard also insisted that the freed slave, regardless of age or sex, be assigned to an established household head, who fed the freed slave and made sure he or she worked.
77 Order 195 of 29 Dec. 1891, ARS 15 G 156. Humbert wanted to encourage flight from Samori, but did not have enough grain. On grain problems, see Roberts 1980a.
78 Report of 1 July 1898, ANM, 1 E 123.

79 Comm. Bafoulabe to Del. Gen., 29 April 1900, ANM, 1 E 186.
80 Comm. Nioro, 2 July 1894, ANM, 1 E 164. Lists of freed slaves from Senegal often gave only a personal name. See also Clark 1994c.
81 Clark 1994c.
82 Bouche 1968: 107–8, 113–14. Her data are different from mine.
83 Order # 113 of 21 Nov. 1888, ANM, 1 D 93.
84 Political Report, 1 May 1887, ANM, 1 E 18.
85 Frequent repetition of these orders suggests that they were not effective. Order 120 of 3 May 1893, ARS, 15 G 155; Archinard correspondence with Kita in ANM, 1 Q 17 and other orders, ANM, 1 D 93.
86 Fall 1993: chs. 1 and 2.
87 Hanson 1996: ch.4.
88 Michel 1989: 68–127; Person 1968: II, 776–82. See also Gallieni 1891 and Méniaud 1931: I, 275–307.
89 Kanya-Forstner 1969: 147–50; Peroz 1891: ch. 5.
90 Person 1968, II: 747.
91 Kanya-Forstner 1969: 148–50.
92 Kanya-Forstner 1969: ch. 7. Méniaud 1931 is very hagiographic.
93 Ward 1976: ch. 3. See also Thiero 1985.
94 Report on meeting with Bambara chiefs, 11 April 1890, ARS, 15 G 172.
95 Instructions to Resident, 16 April 1890, ARS, 15 G 172; Monographie Ségou, ANM, 1 D 127; Ward 1976: 194–96; Kanya-Forstner 1969: 196–98; Méniaud 1931: I, 391–524; Roberts 1987b: 154–60. Archinard was so suspicious of Mari Diara that he ordered the Resident to favor Bojan.
96 There is no clear evidence of a plot in the Bamako archives.
97 Situation Politique des Royaumes de Ségou et de Sansanding, Sept. 1892, ANM, 1 E 71. See also Notice Historique sur le Royaume du Ségou, 1896, ANM, 1 D 55.
98 Chroniques, Segu, July–Sept. 1896, AWF.
99 On confiscation of slaves belonging to Umar's sons, see Ordre 575, ARS, 15 G 156. On use as laborers, see Segu Political Report May 1897, ANM, 1 E 71.
100 Notice Historique sur le Royaume du Ségou, 1896, ANM 1 D 55. This is one of the few documents actually to itemize a slave distribution, but unfortunately some crucial pages are crumbling.
101 Archinard to Etienne, 6 Nov 1890, ARS, 15 G 21.
102 Nioro Political Reports, May and June 1893, ANM, 1 E 60; Comm. Kita to Gov. Sudan, 18 Sept. 1894; Comm. Kita to Comm. Sup., 16 Oct. and 12 Nov. 1894, ANM, 1 E 203; letters of 18 June 1896 and 16 July 1897 from Comm. Bafoulabe, ANM 1 E 186. In addition, three slaves were told to take two of Bojan's sons to the School for the Sons of Chiefs in Kayes. Presumably, they were trusted slaves, but once safely away from the Massassi, they left the boys and disappeared. Lt. Gov. Sudan to Gov. Gen. 15 Sept. 1899.
103 Roberts 1991.
104 Comm. Sup. to Sous-Secrétaire d'Etat, 8 Jan. 1891, ARS, 15 G 21.
105 Kanya-Forstner 1969: 195–96.
106 "After the flight of Amadu, the warrior slaves of Kohmodi, of Muntaga, of Bassiru and Amadu came to me to ask for a new master." Archinard to Sous-Séc. d'État, 8 Jan. 1891, ARS, 15 G 21. Warriors were given to Mademba, women to Nto and to important persons in Jenne and Sinsani. See Capt. de Lartigue, "Notice Historique sur la Région du Sahel," ANSOM, Fonds Trentinian. Also ANM, 1 D 51.
107 Hanson 1996: 153–55; M. Kane 1987: ch. 3; Gov. Lamothe to Sous-Séc. d'Etat, 6 June 1893, ANSOM, Fonds Lamothe; De Lartigue, "Notice Historique sur la

région du Sahel," ANSOM, Papiers Trentinian. On Futanke who remained in Karta, see Jean Bertin, "Les Toucouleurs Boundounkes (1954)," ANM, 1 D 51.

108 Kanya-Forstner 1969: 181–89.
109 Oloruntemehin 1972: 305. Tijani was a strong ruler. When Caron proposed a protectorate, Tijani responded: "How can France protect me since it is I who protect traders. This country is mine. God put it in my charge." Caron 1891: 173. Tijani is poorly studied. See Oloruntemehin 1972: 162–66.
110 This generalization is based on a crumbling document whose date has disappeared, but it is clearly from the moment of conquest and lists who was subject to whom in each area. ANM, 1 D 47. See also Lt. Bunas to Gov. French Sudan, 31 May 1894, ANM, 1 E 55.
111 "Rapport sur la captivité parmi les Etats d'Aguibou," ANM 1 E 156. Destenave's estimate for the Futanke is deceptive because he treats crown slaves as Futanke.
112 H. D'Arboussier, Annual Report, Djenné, 1901, ANM, 1 E 29.
113 Henri D'Arboussier, Annual Report, Djenné, ANM, 1 E 29. See Destenave (Note 111) on absence of mixture.
114 Kanya-Forstner 1969: 200–1.
115 Instructions for Comm. Jenné, 20 May 1893, ANM 1 E 236.
116 Kanya-Forstner 1969: 201–2; Baillaud 1902; Roberts 1987b: ch. 4.
117 There are few studies of Senegalese traders in the Sudan, but see Diouf 1990, a study of Hamet Gora Diop, a trader at Medine linked to Devès and Chaumet. Diop maintained agents in Sudanese cities and accumulated property in Saint Louis. He sold arms, but there is no evidence in his books that he dealt with slaves.
118 See political report, 4 April 1892, ANM, 1 E 16 and all commercial reports from Kita and Bafulabe.
119 Comm. Buguni, 25 Feb. 1894, ANM, 1 E 27.
120 Rapport sur la captivité dans les états d'Aguibou, 1895, ANM 1 E 156.
121 Order 420, 2 April 1890, ARS, 1 D 102.
122 *Chroniques*, Segu, January 1896, AWF; De Benoist 1987: 103–4.
123 "Mission de Kita (Soudan Français)," *Annales*, IX (1894), 41–57. Earlier reports claimed an active slave trade in Kita. Father Barthet wrote the Propaganda that every day slave caravans passed in front of the mission. Barthet to Propaganda, 10 August 1892, CSE, 163 B II.
124 Order 13, 1892, ARS, 15 G 156.
125 Order 104 of 4 Oct. 1890, ARS 15 G 156.

6   SENEGAL IN THE 1890S

1 Hunwick 1992. The original source is al-Ghazali.
2 Quoted by Hargreaves 1985: 5.
3 Idowu 1966 and 1971; Johnson 1971: 55–62.
4 On public letter-writers, see Klein 1968: 214–16.
5 Restraints on arbitrariness are rarely addressed in the literature on colonial rule. See, however, Idowu 1968 on a case in which the head of the judiciary, Ursleur, attacked the execution without trial of three Senegalese accused of assassinating an administrator. Ursleur was speedily transferred to New Caledonia.
6 Comm. Sup. to Gov. Sén., 13 July 1887, ARS, unclassified.
7 Undersecretary of State to Gov. Sénégal, n.d., ARS, K 12.
8 Johnson 1971: 159. Interestingly, Isaac was first elected to the Chamber from Guadeloupe in 1885 when Prosper Darrigrand refused to run. Manchuelle 1984 and 1992.

9 Isaac to Etienne, 18 June 1887 and Etienne to Gov. 4 July 1887, ANSOM, Senegal XIV 15 d.
10 Comm. Montségur to Comm. Sup. des Troupes, ANSOM Sénégal XIV 15d.
11 Etienne to Isaac, 15 October 1887, ANSOM, Senegal XIV 15 d.
12 Comm. des Cercles to Comm. Bafulabe, 2 Nov. 1887 and 15 April 1890, ANM, B 66.
13 Gov. to Min., 17 September 1894, ANSOM, Fonds Lamothe.
14 On the Devès family, see Manchuelle 1984.
15 Idowu 1966.
16 Minutes of Conseil General, 20 and 22 December 1897, ARS. In contrast, two years earlier, the Saint Louis Chamber of Commerce criticized those responsible for attacks on slavery in the interior. "All agricultural labour in the Sudan as in Senegal, is provided by slaves." See extract of Chamber of Commerce proceedings, 2 March 1895, ANSOM, XIV 17.
17 Renault 1971, II: chs. 8–10.
18 Hargreaves 1985: 4–9.
19 Miers, 1975: 240-49; Renault 1971, II: 291–312.
20 Miers 1967: 168.
21 But see Temperley 1972 and Klein 1993b.
22 The Propaganda was determined that such monies were not to be used for ordinary expenses of the mission. See Mgr. Barthet, Quinquennial report, 22 Aug. 1897. CSE, 163 B IV. On the use of the Propaganda funds, see Bouche 1968: ch. 16.
23 Mgr. Barthet, Quinquennial report CSE 163 B IV. Amadu gave Gallieni a twelve-year-old male slave and Gallieni gave the boy to the mission. R.P. Guérin to R.P. Barillec, 23 May 1881. CSE, 63 B IV.
24 Just before the Brussels conference Le Roy wrote a pamphlet arguing that only effective colonial rule would end slavery. See Le Roy 1889. Apparently, Pope Leo XIII was unhappy with this pamphlet, though correspondence in the Holy Ghost archives does not indicate why. When the Mother House of the Holy Ghost Fathers heard about the Pope's discontent, Le Roy had already left to become Bishop in Gabon, but they apologized profusely in his name. R.P. Emonet to Cardinal Préfet de la Propagande, 4 Feb. 1890, CSE, 62B I. It did not keep him from being elected Superior-General. See his speech to the Congress of the International Society for Social Economy, Annales, XI (1896), 83–86.
25 See Mgr. Barthet to Catholic deputy Le Myre de Villers, 12 Sept. 1890, CSE, 163 B 1. See also reports in CSE, 63 B IV.
26 Min. to Gov. Sen., 24 Feb. 1892; Gov. Sen. to Min., 6 July 1892, ANSOM, Senegal XIV 17. There was not yet a Colonial Ministry, but Etienne kept a tighter grip on colonial issues than most ministers. Correspondence went to him rather than to the Minister. He pressed the administration to observe the Brussels treaty and take the slave-trade issue seriously. See Deherme 1994 (1906).
27 On Muslim slave law, see Hunwick 1992: 6–10; Samb 1985.
28 Convention of 12 December 1892, ARS, K 12; Gov. Sen. to Min. 6 Feb. 1893, ANSOM, Fonds Lamothe; Moitt 1989: 37.
29 Gov. Gen. to Min. 5 Dec. 1895, ANSOM, AOF XIV 1/514.
30 Renault 1971: 45.
31 Gov. Gen. to Min., 5 Dec. 1895. ANSOM, AOF XIV 1/514.
32 Manchuelle 1987: 294–95 argues that this was a move toward sharecropping. I see only a change in terminology. Sharecropping as a solution to the slavery problem came fifteen years later.
33 See ARS, K 13. One caravan of twenty-seven had twenty-four women. Sixteen were

under sixteen years of age. Another stopped in Sine-Saloum contained five women, ten girls and two boys and no adult males. Admin. Sine-Saloum to Dir. Aff. Pol. 23 July 1893, ARS K 13. See also Guèye 1965: 201–8.

34 Comm. Dakar-Thiès to Gov., 12 June 1893, ARS, K 13.
35 J.J. Crespin to Gov. Sen., 3 Nov. 1893 and 17 April 1894, ARS, K 13.
36 Political report, 3rd quarter, 1901. ARS, 2 D 247.
37 Comm. Sine-Saloum to Gov. Sén. 1893, ARS, K 13.
38 Comm. Nioro to Comm. Sup., 5 Nov. 1895, ARS, 13 G 322; Admin. Sine-Saloum to Gov. Gen., Oct. 1895, ARS, 13 G 325.
39 Gov. Sén. to Bur Saalum Guédel Mbodj, 23 Jan. 1894, ARS K 13.
40 Deherme 1994.
41 Dir. Aff. Pol. to Comm. Pout, 7 April 1894, ARS, K 13.
42 Telegram, 22 Nov. 1893 cited in Deherme 1994.
43 Gov. to Comm. Podor, 25 March 1893, ARS, K 13.
44 Instructions from Dir. of Native Affairs, 18 Aug. 1899, cited in Comm. Allys response to slavery questionnaire, ARS, K 18.
45 Dir. of Polit. Affairs to Admin. Sine-Saloum, 26 July 1889, ARS, 13 G 321; Dir. of Polit. Affairs to Admin. Sine-Saloum, 19 Jan. 1892, ARS, unclassified.
46 Claims register, Sept. 1899. ARS, 13 G 202.
47 Dir. Native Affairs to Comm. Tivouane, 18 March 1901, cited in Report on Slavery, Tivouane, ARS, K 18.
48 Proclaimed 25 April 1895 and applied first in areas below McCarthy Island. PRO, CO 87/148. See minutes of Legislative Council, 27 December 1894, CO 89/8 and confidential report, 23 March 1893, PRO, CO 87/143.
49 PRO, CO 87/143/7.
50 See Report of J.H. Ozanne, Travelling Commissioner, North Bank Province, 1 July 1896, enclosure 1 to PRO, CO 87/152/43.
51 Travelling commissioner C. Sitwell to Colonial Office, 10 Sept. 1899, PRO, CO 87/159.
52 Travelling Commissioner's Report, North Bank Province, 30 June 1898, PRO, CO 87/156.
53 Thus the 1896 Annual Report claimed that "without any violent measures, the whole fabric of slavery is gradually and rapidly crumbling to pieces."
54 R.B. Llewellyn to Colonial Secretary, 2 May 1898, PRO, CO 87/155.
55 J.H. Ozanne to Gov. Gambia, 30 June 1898, PRO, C.O. 87/156/68.
56 Comm. Nioro to Comm. Sup., Nov. 1895, ARS, unclassified.
57 The Travelling Commissioner's Report, Upper River Province, 2 July 1903, PRO, CO 87/169, reports a village chief complaining "that slaves belonging to his district were running away, and to this he added that his people suffered a great deal from slaves who had run away returning and enticing others to follow them." Report of 14 Jan 1903, PRO, CO 87/168/2.
58 Polit. Rep. May 1903, Niani-Ouli, ARS, 2 D 136. The administrator was convinced that slaves fled in the spring because they were lazy and wanted to avoid work. It is more likely that they left when granaries were low and the planting season near. See also Journal de Poste, ARS, 2 D 47.
59 Journal de Poste, Niani-Ouli, 29 May 1901, ARS, 2 D 247. The situation was different on the Ivory Coast–Gold Coast border. There, Ghana abolished slavery early, and slaves were more likely to be freed on the British side of the border. Terray 1987a: 272–73, 284–86; Handloff 1982.
60 Quinn 1972, chs. 7 and 8; Quinn 1971; Roche 1976. On slaves sent by Musa Molo to the Bur Saalum, see Annual Report, North Bank Province, 1894, PRO, Banjul.

Reports on Fodé Silla, Fodé Kaba and Musa Molo are in PRO, C.O. 87/144 and 145. In 1898, Molo made return of runaways a condition of an agreement with the British. He claimed that the French returned runaways. See Memo of 19 January 1898 on meeting, enclosure to 2 Feb. 1898, PRO, London, CO 87/155.

61 Journal de poste, 13 Nov. 1899, ARS, 13 G 202; Moitt 1989: 31–36.
62 Report on Slavery, 26 Jan. 1904, ARS, K 18.
63 Comm. Kaedi to Dir. Native Affairs, 30 Dec. 1899. ARS, 2 D 136.
64 Comm. Kaedi to Dir. Native Affairs, 9 Jan. 1900 or 1901, ARS, 2 D 136.
65 Dir. Native Affairs to Comm. Kaedi, 31 Oct. 1899, ARS, 2 D 136.
66 See for example ARS 13 G 195 from Bakel, 2 G 3/63 from Matam, 2 G 3/61 from Dagana.
67 Comm. Kaedi to Dir. Native Affairs, 28 May 1901, ARS, 2 D 136.
68 Comm. Kaedi to Dir. Native Affairs, ARS, 2 D 136; Comm. Kaedi to Dir. Native Aff., 13 May 1901, ARS 2 D 136.
69 For examples of such views, see responses to inquiry of 1903 on slavery in ARS K18. For further discussion see below, Chapter 8.
70 Political report, Bakel, 8 July 1897, ARS, 13 G 200.
71 Letter from Admin. Sine-Saloum, ARS, K 13. Noirot argued that change would only come with changes in technology and in the economy: "I have a profound certainty that the introduction of the plow, the development of roads and the use of carts will do more to undermine slavery than all the decrees issued up to this point."
72 Political Report, 15 Sept. 1886, ARS, 2 B 75. See also Diouf 1990: ch. 19.
73 Chef. Judicial Service to Min., 19 July 1887, ANSOM, Sénégal XIV 15 d. This is the Chief's version of Governor Genouille's words.
74 Gov. Sén. to Min., 14 Nov. 1886, ANSOM, Sénégal XIV 15 d.
75 Report of 20 Feb. 1897, ARS, 13 G 200.
76 Travelling Commissioner, North Bank Province to Admin. Gambia, 72, 28 June 1894 and 84, 31 July 1894, PRO, CO 87/146. I interviewed in this village in 1962. At one point, a man started arguing with my informant. He was a descendant of the chief of the slaves in the 1894 rising. He told me about the revolt, but the argument quickly subsided into what seemed good-natured banter.
77 Manchuelle 1987: 232–34. Bathily 1985, II: 705 quotes an 1888 letter from slave-owners in Gidimaxa: "Understand governor, that our situation is lost. We are cultivators and we cannot cultivate without slaves. They have fled to you." Cissoko 1988: 307–11 describes damage to Khasso done by these flights.
78 See monthly reports, ARS, 13 G 188. Many went into the liberty village and others sought new masters. Comm. Bakel, to Comm. Sup., 15 April 1889, ARS, 13 G 189.
79 Comm. Matam to Comm. Bakel, 20 Aug. 1895, ARS, 13 G 236; Rapport politique et militaire, Bakel, Oct. 1895, ARS, 13 G 198.
80 Rapport politique et militaire, Bakel, Nov. 1895, ARS, 13 G 198; Manchuelle 1987: 293–96. Chaudié was told to enforce the Brussels convention.
81 Comm. Bakel to Dir. Aff. Pol., 28 Oct. 1895, ARS, 13 G 197.
82 Comm. Bakel to Dir. Aff. Pol., 23 March 1896, ARS, 13 G 197.
83 Corres. from Comm. Bakel to Aff. Pol., ARS 13 G 197.
84 Comm. Bakel to Dir. Aff. Pol., 94, 3 June 1896, ARS, 13 G 197.
85 Comm. Bakel to Gov. Sén., 5 May 1896, ARS, 13 G 197.
86 Monthly report, July 1896, ARS, 13 G 199.
87 Dir. Aff. Ind. to Gov. Gen., ARS, 2 G 1/7.
88 Monthly Report, July 1896, ARS, 13 G 199.
89 There is no copy of these instructions, but De Roll Montpellier refers to them in his letter to Merlin, 7 Sept. 1896, ARS, 13 G 199. I often found references to instruc-

tions which I could not find in the archives. I am convinced that when the law or colonial policy was to be violated, instructions were often oral. Governors toured and administrators regularly passed through the capital.

90 Comm. Bakel to Gov. Sén., 17 July 1896, ARS, 13 G 197.
91 Monthly report, Bakel, Sept. 1896, ARS, 13 G 199. See also Manchuelle, 1987, I: 293–94. Selibaby lost 872 from its tax rolls, about 40 percent of its recorded population.
92 Copie du registre des réclamations, Bakel, Nov. 1897, ARS, 13 G 200. Cited by Manchuelle 1987: 295. Manchuelle cites other colonial data to suggest that this attitude was widespread. Pollet and Winter cite a similar text from Banamba, in which an old Maraka slave told the administrator, "We would ask nothing more than to remain in this country if we could work in peace and be free from the worst vexations and ill treatment that the Maraka constantly inflict on us." Pollet and Winter 1971: 254.
93 Bathily 1985: 705 suggests many flights to the Gambia until after 1900. Medine reports many arrivals and departures during this period. ANM, 1 E 60. See also Registre de réclamations, ARS, 13 G 202.
94 Monthly Report, Bakel, 5 July 1898, ARS, 13 G 201.
95 ARS 10 D 1.
96 Huchard's newspaper, *L'Afrique Occidentale*, frequently opposed the administration. See Johnson 1971: 136.
97 Fatou Camara to Dir. Native Affairs, 25 July 1899 and subsequent correspondence, ARS, 2 D 315.
98 For a Gambian case where the daughter was assimilated to another culture, see J.H. Ozanne to Gov. Gambia, 30 June 1898, PRO, London, CO 87/156/68.
99 Manchuelle 1987: 287–92.
100 On the campaign of 1890–91, when Tokolor allies of the French seized slaves of Abdul Bokar Kan, see M. Kane 1987: ch. 2.
101 Hanson 1996: 153–55; Saint-Martin 1970: 161; Kanya-Forstner 1969: 195–96; M. Kane 1987: ch. 3.
102 Report of Dodds campaign, ANSOM Sénégal 69, cited in M. Kane 1987: ch. 3.
103 Political Report, 9 June 1891, ARS, 2 D 11/1. Cited and Translated in M. Kane 1987: ch. 3.
104 See reports on slavery in Futa Toro cercles, ARS, K 18.
105 On the Kru, see Samarin 1989:33; on the Moroccans and Chinese, Manchuelle 1987: 211; on the Piedmontese, Méniaud 1931, I: 66.
106 Manchuelle 1987: ch. 5. The Soninke were particularly numerous among the emigrants. There were slaves among them but, as in the river area, they were not predominant among Soninke migrants. Admin. Gambia to Sec. State for Colonies, 21 May 1903, PRO, CO 87/168/70. See also correspondence in ANSOM, Senegal XIV 21.
107 On forced labour, see Fall 1993.
108 Lamothe explained to Etienne in 1892 that he had, as instructed, avoided "using certain terms which could be poorly understood or badly interpreted, especially by metropolitan opinion." The word in question was disannexation. Gov. to Sous Séc. d'Etat, 17 Dec. 1892, ANSOM, Fonds Lamothe.
109 Klein 1968: 160–61.

7   THE END OF CONQUEST

1 Monteil 1896–98: 191.
2 Report on slavery, Kurusa, 1894, ARS, K 14.

3 Kanya-Forstner 1969: 202–14.
4 Cited by Kanya-Forstner 1969: 215. On Grodet, see Ghomsi 1968.
5 Méniaud 1931: 477–78; Kanya-Forstner 1969: 215–17; Bonnier 1926.
6 In 1880, a juula told one of Gallieni's officers that the major source of slaves was the area between the branches of the upper Niger. This included Wasulu. Gallieni 1885: 320–21 and 597–99; Bayol 1888: 61–62.
7 Amselle 1990: chs. 5 and 6; Samake 1984.
8 In many Wasulu communities, there are remnants of what were very substantial walls. In others, one can follow the trace of walls that once included large villages. In Bulukura, a small village of about 300 people, the wall was about 3 m high, with places for marksmen. The diameter of the enclosure was about 150 m. In the market town of Ntentu, there was both an inner and outer wall. I could not completely trace the outer wall, but one informant, Musa Samake, claimed that it was a kilometer long. Fonds Klein-Bagayogo.
9 Amselle 1990: 166–67.
10 Samake 1984: 58–68; Amselle 1990: 138–39; Report on Wasulu, 5 May 1896, ANM, 1 E 27. See also Jonkoro Doumbia, Klein-Bagayogo collection.
11 Holmes 1977: 169.
12 Bah 1985: 173–79.
13 Person 1968, II: 1049–141.
14 Binger 1892, I: 65.
15 Binger 1892, I: 52–55. Binger was the first European to write about this area. The first three chapters of his book contain vivid descriptions of the destruction caused by repression of the revolt.
16 Collective interview, Dokoro Samake and Musa Samake, Ntentu, February 1989, Bagayogo-Klein collection.
17 Lt. Margaine, Report on Buguni, n.d., ANM, 1 E 27; see also Samake 1984: 68–73; Méniaud 1931: 483–92.
18 The French stopped one caravan with 500 slaves. The Commandant at Buguni executed forty *sofa* guarding the caravan. Comm. Panier des Touches to Gov. Sudan, 23 Jan. 1894, ANM, 1 E 191. 445 of these slaves had been taken at Ntentu, 49 men, 380 women and 16 children. Report for Jan. 1894, ANM, 2 D 76. See also Ntentu interview, Bagayogo-Klein collection.
19 Undated report, early 1894, ANM, 1 E 27.
20 Journal de Poste, Buguni, 1893–94. ANM, 1 E 97.
21 According to the first census, Report of 12 March 1894, ANM 1 E 27, most people were grouped in four villages with over 1,000 each. There were 1,463 at Buguni. There were 375 in Ouolosébougou, further north, and nine villages had 6 to 27 each. Only a fifth of them were children. A tenth were slaves. By the end of 1895, many had returned to other villages and Buguni was down to about 200. Report of Capt. Porion on trade routes, 1 Oct. 1895, ANM, 1 E 97.
22 Lt. Margaine, report, undated, 1894, ANM, 1 E 27.
23 Holmes 1977: chs. 7 and 8; Ward 1976: ch. 5.
24 Comm. Buguni to Gov. Sudan, 3 April 1894, ANM, 2 D 76. One pretender even heard court cases. See entries of 2 and 3 Aug. 1898, Journal de Poste, Buguni, ANM, 1 E 27.
25 On a *tirailleur* who had thirty slaves and sold seventeen, Comm. Buguni to Gov. Sudan, 28 March 1899 and 22 June 1899, ANM, 1 E 191.
26 Kanya-Forstner 1969: 217–23; Méniaud 1931, I: 473–518. Bonnier did not scout the area around the camp and had few guards posted.
27 Kanya-Forstner 1969: 224–36.

28 Later, as a general, Mangin was the major exponent of using an African army in France. See Echenberg 1991: 28–32.

29 Gov. Grodet to Min. Colonies, 10 Jan 1895, ANSOM, Soudan I 7. The slaves were freed under the 1848 law which prohibited French citizens holding slaves. Quiquandon was a protege of Gallieni.

30 Gov. Sudan to Comm. Northeast, 25 Jan. 1894, ANM, 1 D 2; Ghomsi 1968: 79–91. Results of the inquiry are in ARS, K 14.

31 Gov. Sudan to Comm. Eastern Region, 24 Sept. 1894, ARS, 15 G 168.

32 See Ordre 268, 30 Dec. 1894 for Bamako and 292 of 16 May 1895 for Nioro, Kita, Bafulabe and Bakel. Ordre 293 of 17 May 1895 extended the ban to the whole colony and provided that caravans coming into or leaving the colony were to have all porters listed on passes so that they could not be sold. No child appearing to be less than sixteen could be used as a porter. ANSOM, Soudan XIV 1.

33 Gov. Sudan to Min., # 788, 17 Sept. 1894, ANSOM, Soudan I 7. Grodet asked the Commandant in Timbuktu about distribution of Tuareg prisoners and particularly of Tuareg women being given to *tirailleurs*; Guillaumet 1894.

34 Comm. Segu to Gov. Sudan, 15 Oct. 1895, ANM, 1 E 71.

35 Comm. Northeast to Gov. Sudan, 4 Aug. and 12 Nov. 1894, ANM, 1 E 177.

36 Gov. Grodet to Min., 18 July 1894, ANSOM, Soudan XIV 1.

37 Comm. Northeast to Gov. Sudan, 14 Jan. 1895, ANM, 1 E 176 on closing of markets at Segu; Comm. Medine to Gov. Sudan, 27 Sept. 1894, ANM, 1 E 174 on clandestine slave market at Medine. See also Comm. Kayes to Gov. Sudan, 27 Sept. 1894, ANM, 1 E 173 and Report of Interpreter Mohammed ben Said, n.d., ANM, 1 E 174.

38 Comm. Northeast to Gov. Sudan, 24 April 1894, ANM, 1 E 176.

39 Ordre 301 of 29 June 1895, ARS, K 19. Humbert banned the export of slaves to Senegal, but there is no evidence that his order was enforced. See Ordre 165, ARS, K 19.

40 Gov. Grodet to Comm. Northeast, 27 Sept. 1894, ANM, 1 E 176.

41 Gov. Grodet to Comm. Northeast, 25 Jan. 1895, ANM 1 E 176. Paying the tax indicated that they did not belong to anyone else.

42 Chroniques # 69, Jan 1896, White Fathers, AWF.

43 Kanya-Forstner 1969: ch. 9.

44 Min. of Colonies C. Chautemps to Gov. Gen. Chaudié, 11 Oct. 1895, ANM, 1 E 232. These instructions were in the Bamako archives, which means that they were communicated to Trentinian.

45 Circular 8, 22 July 1895, ARS, 15 G 157.

46 Circular 92, 17 March 1897, ANM 1 E 183.

47 *Diaire*, Segu, 6 Feb. 1897, AWF.

48 *Diaire*, Segu, 12 March 1897, AWF. Trentinian was clearly anxious to get along with the missionaries. The wife of a man in the liberty village was about to be sold. The missionaries pleaded her case and the next day the local commandant blocked the sale.

49 Comm. Nioro to Comm. Gumbu, n.d. 1897, ANM, 1 E 235.

50 Instructions to Commandants, ANM, 1 E 230.

51 De Benoist 1987: 52–56.

52 Gallieni to Etienne, 17 Sept. 1887, copy in CSE, 159 B VI. See also Archinard to R.P. Montel, 7 Sept. 1888, CSE, 159 B VI. Grodet cut the subsidy, but he could not do without the missions. See De Benoist 1987; Harding 1972.

53 Missionaries frequently commented on the warmth of their reception by a Protestant Commandant. See R.P. Cros, "Mission de Kita (Soudan Français)," *Annales*,

IX (1894), 41–57; Gouraud 1939: 57.
54 Hacquard to Dir. de l'Oeuvre de la Ste. Enfance, 27 Oct. 1899, AWF.
55 Within months of the opening of the mission at Kupela in Burkina Faso, there were 120 children at the school. A. Hacquard to Cardinal Préfet de la Propagande, 8 Nov. 1900, Corres. Offic. 1892–1911, AWF.
56 The Holy Ghost Fathers, though also opposed to slavery, seem to have been more tolerant of the ways of the military. "All that we can expect today," Father Cros wrote in 1892, "is in effect, that the merchants do not mistreat their slaves, that they are not exposed for sale in public markets and that they carry passes which must be counter-signed at every post." Cros 1894.
57 *Chroniques*, 68, Segu, AWF.
58 Mission diaries itemize comings and goings during the first years. Sick children could be purchased for as little as 25 francs. Occasionally, orphans were found wandering around the market.
59 Bouche 1968: ch. 12; A. Hacquard to Mgr. de la Passardière, 6 Aug. 1900, Corres. Officielle 1892–1911. See also *Chroniques*, Segu, 67, July 1895, AWF.
60 Cros 1894.
61 Hacquard to Mgr. dela Passardière, 6 Aug. 1900, Corres. Officielle 1892–1911, AWF. Other slaves, Hacquard wrote, "had the honour of being closer to his [the commandant's] person."
62 De Benoist 1987: 99–100; Bouche 1968: 177–210.
63 *Chroniques*, 69, Segu, July–Sept. 1896, AWF.
64 *Chroniques* 69, Segu, July–Sept. 1896. One woman, married to a corporal, found her brother in slavery. When she asked about a ransom, the master threatened to sell the boy and he fled to the mission at Kita. *Diaire*, Segu, 29 Dec. 1899, AWF.
65 Thus, a Somono master agreed to turn a ten-year-old boy over to his mother for 22,000 cowries. *Diaire*, 10 Sept. 1895, Segu, AWF.
66 *Chroniques*, 73, Segu, 10 Sept. 1897, AWF.
67 *Diaires*, Banankuru, 17 and 20 May 1900, AWF.
68 A. Hacquard to Propagation de la Foi, 25 Oct. 1900, Corres. Offic., 1892–1911, AWF.
69 A. Hacquard to Cardinal Préfet, Congrégation de la Propagande, 8 Nov. 1900, Corres. Offic. 1892–1911, AWF. They paid about 60 francs each for slaves, probably paid in food, and 30 for pawns.
70 H. Bazin, Rapport sur les Oeuvres Anti-Esclavagiste, AWF, i/074/015.
71 *Chroniques*, 73, Segu, 4 Aug. 1897, AWF.
72 *Chroniques*, 73, Segu, 4 Aug. 1897, AWF; A. Hacquard to Mgr. de la Passardière, 6 Aug. 1900, Corres. Offic. 1892–1911, AWF.
73 A. Hacquard to R.P. Livinhac, 31 May 1895, AWF, 1/071. See also A. Hacquard to Dir. de l'Oeuvre de la Ste. Enfance, 27 Oct. 1899, Corr. Offic. 1892–1911, AWF.
74 H. Bazin to R.P. Livinhac, 21 Dec. 1901, AWF, I 074/024.
75 *Diaire*, Segu, 21 Feb. 1899, AWF.
76 A. Hacquard to Cardinal Préfet de la Propagande, 27 Oct. 1899, Corr. Offic. 1892–1911, AWF.
77 De Benoist 1987: 92–97; Circular to all Commandants B 1 050, 7 Sept. 1895, Corres. Offic. 1892–1911, AWF.
78 Holmes 1977; Warms 1987: ch. 4; Tymowski 1981.
79 Bah 1985: 173–79 and 181–210. Construction of walls involved a massive use of slave labour, often several thousand at a time; Tymowski 1981.
80 Imbert, n.d. The version I saw was a bound and mimeographed volume available at the Institut des Sciences Humaines in Bamako.

81 Imbert n.d.: 279.
82 Imbert n.d.: 278.
83 Imbert n.d.: 294.
84 Imbert n.d.: 294.
85 *Diaire*, Ségou, 31 May 1898, AWF. In the same diary, there is a reference (3 May 1898) to another campaign, after which officers and non-coms played cards for slaves.
86 *Chroniques*, Segu, 82, April 1899, AWF, 181–85.
87 Journal de Poste, Buguni, Feb. 1895, ANM, 1 E 27.
88 See all interviews, Bagayogo-Klein collection. See also Journal de Poste, ANM, 1 E 27 for 1894 and 1895.
89 Clerk Ségeur to Comm. Buguni, 10 June 1899, ANM, 1 E 27.
90 ANM, 1 E 125.
91 Comments on Buguni Political Report, 20 Jan. 1898, ANM, 1 E 27.
92 Quarterly reports, Sikasso and Koury, 2nd Terr. Militaire, ARS, 2G 1/11 and 2 G 1/19.
93 Kambou-Ferrand 1993: 384. On the problem of outsider chiefs, see Klein 1968: ch. 10.
94 Chef de Bataillon Simonin, Annual report 1900, ARS, 2 G 1/18. According to Case, the defeat of Samori deprived Wasipe in northern Ghana of its major source of slaves, but the trade continued into the twentieth century. It simply moved from market to home. Case 1979: 374–81. See on Mossi, Dim Delobsom 1932: 89–92; Tauxier 1912: 50.
95 Lt. Colonel Millard, Comm. 2nd Terr. Militaire to Gov. Gen., 24 Aug. 1901, ARS, 2 G 1/19.
96 Chef de Bataillon Simonin, Annual report 1900, ARS, 2 G 1/18.
97 "Premier Coup d'Oeil sur Tombouctou," *Diaires*, 1895 Timbuktu; see description of Timbuktu in *Chroniques*, 70, April 1896, AWF. See also Lenz 1887; Dubois 1897.
98 Father Mahiet in *Chroniques*, 73, Timbuktu, Jan. 1897, AWF.
99 Father Mahiet to Mgr. Livinhac, 15 July 1897, *Diaire*, Timbuktu, AWF.
100 A French officer claimed that in 1894 the trade with the Arab lands was less important than that with the Tuareg and the various oases. Rapport sur le situation au Soudan, 10 Feb. 1894, ANSOM, Soudan IV 1. Another document from the same period mentions traders from Arawan, Ghadames, Tuat and Tadjakant, all in the desert. Situation Politique, 1 October 1893, ANSOM, Soudan IV 1. Cordell 1983 and McDougall 1992 argue persuasively that the Sahara absorbed large numbers of slaves.
101 Frère Henri to Mgr., 24 April 1896, AWF, 071/466/467.
102 Father Mahiet to Mgr. Livinhac, 15 July 1897, *Diaire*, Timbuktu, AWF.
103 *Chroniques*, 80, Timbuktu, Oct. 1898, AWF. They were soon back up to fifteen children. Few descriptions of slavery are as pathetic as those of disease-ridden market children and frightened victims of raids.
104 H. Bazin to Mgr. Livinhac, 25 July 1902, AWF, I 074/034. Some missionaries got along well. One, Father Dupuis, became a local linguist, and after leaving the church in 1904, took a wife and raised a family. He took the name Yacouba and remained in the Sudan until his death in 1945. See De Benoist 1987: 77.
105 A Wasulunke liberty village at Bafulabe asked permission to return in December 1898. When this was not forthcoming, many left without passes in the spring of 1900. See reports, ANM, 1 E 16
106 Comm. Bafulabe to Lt. Gov. Sudan, May 1899, ANM, 1 E 16.

107 Quarterly reports for 1899 and 1900, Bamako, ANM, 1 E 18.
108 *Diaires*, 1899, AWF.
109 Circular 87, 27 Jan. 1899, ARS, 15 G 162.
110 Circular 87, 27 Jan. 1899, ARS, 15 G 162.
111 Ordre 6, Comm. West Region, 11 Feb. 1899, ARS 15 G 162.
112 The question of the dependants and their strategies has been most effectively explored in Wright 1993.
113 Thus, a political agent in Buguni helped merchants avoid the trade tax. When arrested, he had four wives, six female slaves aged between fifteen and eighteen and six male slaves. Slaves were sold on his account in Bamako and local people worked his fields. He provided a slave woman for one of the commandants and expected presents from those who wished to see him. Comm. Buguni to Lt. Gov. Sudan, 21 March 1897, ARS, 15 G 171. In Kita, a policeman was collecting millet, sheep, slaves and precious metals. The interpreter tried to get rid of the major witness by sending her back to her village. Monthly Report, June 1898, Kita, ARS, 15 G 135.

8   THE IMPOSITION OF METROPOLITAN PRIORITIES ON SLAVERY

1 Gov.-Gen. E. Roume, Circular 82 of 20 Feb. 1906, transmitting new decree on slavery to Lt. Governors of all colonies, ARS, K 24.
2 Johnson 1978 labels Ponty a Republican paternalist. I do not share this view. Within the context of the colonial administration, he was a liberal in that he believed in the market and preferred less restraint on the individual, but he was also an astute bureaucratic politician, who was willing to take risks, but not too many. For a negative evaluation of Ponty, see Arnaud 1922.
3 *JORF*, Débats. Many colonial ministers knew little about the colonies when they took over the portfolio. See Kanya-Forstner 1969.
4 Min. Colonies Albert Decrais to All Governors, 6 Jan. 1900, CSE, 62 B V; also ANM, A 20.
5 Del. Gen. Ponty to all administrators, HSN, 7 March 1900, ANM, A 20.
6 Del. Gen. Ponty Circular of 18 Oct. 1900, ARS, K 18, 37. See also his letter to Gov. Gen., 15 Sept. 1900. ARS, K 15.
7 Ponty, Circular of 1 Feb. 1901. ANM, A 20.
8 Comm. Bonnassies to Del. Gen., ANM, 1 E 19.
9 Del. Gen. Ponty to all Admin., 11 Oct. 1903, ARS K 15.
10 Monthly Report, HSN, Aug. 1902. ARS, 2 G 2/6; reports on slavery, Eastern Bawol, Dagana, ARS, K 18.
11 Gov. Gen. to Min. 27 May 1903, ANSOM, Sénégal XIV 28 bis. See also response to questionnaire on slavery, ARS, K 19; reports on Mossi, Aug. and Sept. 1902, ARS 2 G 2/10. On Korientza market, see Capt. Dagues to Comm. 1st Terr. Militaire, 14 May 1902, ANM, 1 E 23; see Comm. 2nd Terr. Militaire to Gov. Gen., 24 April 1901, ARS, 2 G 1/19 on trade in Koutiala and Mossi cercles; and ARS, 2 G 2/10.
12 Comm. 1st Terr. Militaire to Gov. Gen. Monthly Report, July 1902, ARS, 2 G 2/10.
13 See for example, in Tenkodogo, punishment of two chiefs who seized women and girls, a kidnapping case, and a band of slave raiders who had seized seventeen people. Monthly report, May 1902, ARS, 2 G 2/10. Many of the 1904 reports on slavery indicate prosecutions for *faits de traite* or seizure of persons. ARS, K 18 and K 19.
14 Monthly reports, Sokolo, ANM, 1 E 75. See also Report, Sokolo, 1904, ARS, K19.

15 Comm. 1st Terr. Militaire to Gov. Gen., 6 Mars 1902, ARS, 2 G 2/8.
16 Annual report San, 28 February 1901, ANM, 1 E 67. One administrator called the Bobo cantons "a nursery for slaves." Political Report, San, 1 Aug 1904, ANM, 1 E 67. See also Father Templier to Mgr. Bazin, *Chroniques*, 96, Ougadougou, Oct. 1902, AWF.
17 Reports of Native Justice, HSN, ARS, M 117. There were more political cases. Thus in Kita, during the fourth quarter of 1903, forty-four men were charged with trying to avoid or defraud census-takers, seventeen for refusal to pay taxes, nine for refusal to provide porters.
18 Fall 1993: 98–103; Pheffer 1975.
19 Comm. Kita to Del. Gen., 18 Sept. 1900, ANM, 1 E 47. The Commandant claimed that porterage for grain alone would demand the whole population of the cercle for two and a half months. With construction entering Kita, ten work camps had to be prepared with 600 to 700 work-days each. In the spring of 1901, Kita was hit by smallpox. Political report, 30 April 1901, ANM, 1 E 47.
20 Annual report, Kita, 1900, ANM, 1 E 47; Political Report, Kayes, ANM, 1 E 44.
21 Political Report, HSN, 27 April 1900.
22 Monthly report, Nioro. ARS, 2 G 1/14.
23 Political Reports, HSN, 12 April 1900, ARS, 2 G 1/12.
24 Political reports, Bafulabe, ANM, 1 E 16.
25 Political report, Bafulabe, June 1905, ANM, 1 E 16.
26 Ordre 7 of Comm. Western Region, 14 Feb. 1899. ARS, 15 G 162.
27 Political report, Kayes, 1 April 1900. ANM, 1 E 44.
28 See political reports, Bafoulabe, 1899, ARS.
29 Political reports, Bafulabe, 1901, ANM, 1 E 17; Annual Report, Bafulabe, 1901, ANM, 1 E 16; Political Report, HSN, April 1902 ARS, 2 G 2/6.
30 Political Report, Medine, 1901, ANM, 1 E 60; Polit. Report, HSN, 1901, ARS, 2 G 1/14. On Bamako, see polit. report, Jan. 1904, ARS, 2 G 4/13. In the margin of a Medine report, Ponty wrote: "It is the job of the Commandant de Cercle to find them work. There is no shortage at Kayes." Polit. Report, August 1901, ANM, 1 E 60.
31 Political Report, Kita, April 1904. ARS, 2 G 4/13. See also reports in ANM, 1 E 47.
32 Report on slavery, Kita, ARS, K 19.
33 Political Report, Bafulabe, April 1901, ARS, 2 G 1/14; Political Report, Bafulabe, 30 April 1901, ANM, 1 E 16.
34 Del. Perm. to Gov.-Gen., 12 June 1904, ARS, 2 G 4/13.
35 Report, 22 May 1901, ANM, 1 E 19; Roberts 1987b: 190–91.
36 Reports on Slavery, ARS, K 19.
37 Report on Slavery, Léo, ARS, K 19.
38 Political Reports, Nioro, March 1901, ARS, 2 G 1/14 and December 1904, ARS, 2 G 4/13.
39 Monthly reports, Segu, April and May 1902, ARS, 2 G 2/16.
40 Monthly reports, May to Sept., 1903, Bandiagara, ANM, 1 E 23.
41 Monthly report Segu, July 1904, ARS, 2 G 4/13.
42 Annual report, Buguni, 1903, 29 Feb. 1904, ANM, 1 E 27.
43 Annual Report, Bamako, 1905, 2 Feb. 1906, ANM, 1 E 19.
44 Journal de poste, Niani-Ouli. ANS, 2 D 247.
45 Political Report, Niani-Ouli, May 1903, ARS, 2 D 136.
46 Gov. Gen. AOF to Gov. Gambia, 11 June 1903, encl. to Conf. of 3 July 1903, PRO, CO 87/168. See also Roume 1994. The Brussels treaty provided for extradition in cases of attacks on personal liberty.

47 Gov. Gambia to Colonial Office, 5 October 1903. PRO, CO 87/170. See also other correspondence in CO 87/168 and 169.
48 Joucla 1905.
49 Kanya-Forstner and Lovejoy 1994: 2–3. See also Conklin 1989: ch. 2.
50 Joucla 1905. See also Report on Slavery, Saint Louis, ARS, K 18.
51 Min. G. Doumergue to Gov. Gen. 31 Oct. 1903, ARS, K 27. Also in ANSOM, Sénégal XIV 28. Bernard Moitt's research on the adoption system is still unfortunately not published.
52 Lt. Gov. C. Guy to Gov. Gen., 22 Nov. 1903. ARS, K 27, #28.
53 Gov. Sen. to Gov. Gen., 4 May 1904, ARS, K 23.
54 Arrêté of 24 November 1903, ARS, K 27. Also in *JOAOF*.
55 Instructions to Verrier Mission, 4 Oct. 1904. ARS 4 G 4. I have not seen any report from this mission.
56 Min. Col. to Gov. Gen., 13 April 1905, ARS, K 24.
57 Gov. Gen. to Min. Col. 27 Oct. 1905, ARS K 24 contains responses of Lt. Governors to the inquiry. See also Cordell 1990.
58 Gov. Gen. to Sec. Gen., 33, 3 Dec. 1903, ARS, K 27.
59 The system dated to 1887, but originally applied only to Senegal. Asiwaju 1979; Renault 1972.
60 Decree of 10 Nov. 1903, 50, ARS M 79. See also Renault 1971: 53–54.
61 Merlin circular of 10 Dec. 1903, ANSOM, Sénégal XIV 28. Also in ARS, K 16, 43. Part of it is reprinted in Renault 1972: 100. See also Roume 1994; Lt. Gov. C. Guy to Gov. Gen., 27 Jan 1904, ARS, K 23.
62 Boutillier 1968; Renault, 1972.
63 Merlin (see note 61).
64 See Merlin's harsh assessment of the quality of the reports in the summary he prepared for Roume. Report, Feb. 1905 to Gov.-Gen., ARS, K 16. See also Boutillier 1968.
65 Some of the cases cited in Moitt 1993: 70–82 illustrate the variability of administrative behavior.
66 Report of Slavery, Tivouane, 29 Jan. 1904, ARS, K 18.
67 Report on slavery, Thiès, 4 Feb. 1904, ARS, K 18.
68 Gov. Gen. to all Lt. Governors, July 1905, ARS, K 24.
69 See esp. Gov. Gen. to Proc.-Gen. 26 May 1904, ARS, K 24.
70 ARS, K 27, # 37.
71 Proc. Gen. to Gov. Gen. 3 Dec. 1903, ARS, K 16.
72 Anonymous 1905.
73 Gov. Gen. E. Roume to Procureur Général, # 114, 2 June 1905. Mbaye Guèye 1965 explains the 1905 law as a response to the murder of the son of a former colonial minister, Chautemps, in April 1904. Chautemps was killed by a Wolof noble accused of seizing slaves. Nothing in the archives shows a connection between this incident and the 1905 law, but it may have pushed Roume to act more rapidly.
74 Roume's report is in ANM, 1 E 81 and ARS K 16. Poulet's is in ARS, K 17. Both have been published in Kanya-Forstner and Lovejoy 1994.
75 This speech was printed in the *JOAOF* and *Bulletin du Comité de l'Afrique Française*, Jan. 1906, p. 15.
76 Lt. Gov. Camille Guy, Circular of 5 March 1906, ARS, K 24.
77 Lt. Gov. Ivory Coast to Gov. Gen., 16 March 1906 and his circular of 10 March 1906, ARS, K 24.
78 Circular of 17 March 1906, ANG, 2 A 3.
79 Fuglestad 1983: 54–78; Salifou 1988: 166–88.

80 Bernus *et al.* 1993.
81 Lord Salisbury proudly announced after signing the Anglo-French convention of 1890: "We have given the Gallic cockerel an enormous amount of sand. Let him scratch as he pleases." Porch 1986: 127.
82 Bernus 1981: 95–104; Kambou-Ferrand 1993: 351–56; Porch 1986.
83 Bonte 1993; Chassey 1978: 15–47.
84 See Baier 1980: 47–49 for an analysis on how this autonomy made it possible for many slaves to move from servicing transhumant cycles of the Tuareg to become independent entrepreneurs. Obligations varied, but were usually between 80 and 100 kg a year; Bernus and Bernus 1975: 33. *Bella* near Timbuktu owed their masters 150 kg of millet per male and 75 kg. See Report on Timbuktu in 1894, ARS, K 14; Reports on Sumpi, Ras-el-Ma and Douzou, ARS, K 19.
85 Olivier de Sardan 1984: ch. 9. See "Directives Générales pour les Officiers Commandant les Circonscriptions Administratives du Territoire Militaire," enclosure with Meray report, ARS, 4 G 11. Though contemptuous of the *bellas*, it advocated weakening traditional links. The liberations sometimes involved rather larger communities, in one case 1,400 persons. See Political Report, Oct. 1901, First Military Territory, ARS, 2 G 1/15; Gov. Gen. Roume to Min., 5 May 1907, ♯ 819, ANSOM, AOF I 14. See also political reports from Gao, 1899–1906, ANM, 1 E 36.
86 Political Report, Dori, June 1902, ARS, 2 G 2/8 and 6 Feb. 1901, ARS 2 G 1/15; Kambou-Ferrand 1993: 356–61.
87 Cited by Bernus 1981: 108.
88 Report of Justice Indigène, Military Territory, 4th quarter 1910 and decision of 10 June 1911, ARS, M 122.
89 Inspector Maurice Meray, Report on Timbuktu, 8 Dec. 1909, ARS, 4 G 11. Political reports for 1907 and 1908 show a continuing struggle for autonomy among Tuareg and Fulbe slaves. For Timbuktu, ANM, 1 E 79; for Dori, ANM, 1 E 32; For Gao, ANM 1 E 36. See also political reports in ARS 2 G. On Tuareg struggle to keep control of Songhay villages, see *Chroniques*, ♯ 132, Nov. 1907, AWF.
90 This is higher than the estimates of 1904, but many observers think that most of the desert-edge population was servile. Olivier de Sardan 1984: 189–94. Robert Arnaud estimated the ratio of free to slave as one to ten in southern Niger. Cited in De Latour 1987: 147.
91 On resistance to Arma, see reports from Gao, esp. Political Report, 1 May 1899, ANM, 1 E 36.
92 Political Report, Gao, 1 May 1899, ANM, 1 E 36; Political Reports, Gao, 1st Military Territory, Feb.–May 1901, ARS, 2 G 1/15. On Songhay, see Olivier de Sardan: 1984: ch. 9. On flight from Timbuktu, ANM, 1 E 79.
93 Fuglestad 1983: 55–62; Kimba 1981: 87–93; Porch 1986: ch. 12. See also Vigné d'Octon 1900. Voulet and Chanoine were both killed, as was Lt. Col. Klobb, commander of the unit sent to stop their rampage.
94 Rothiot 1988: 85; De Latour 1987.
95 Rothiot 1988: Part 2; on his rival, Bayero, see Kimba 1981: 101–6.
96 Bernus 1981: 109–10.
97 Mission Robert Arnaud, ARS, 11 G 4, cited in Kimba 1981: 203. Kimba questions this, arguing that slaves fought alongside their masters. There is not necessarily a contradiction.
98 Cited in Kimba 1981: 205–6.
99 Roume 1994 (1905): 103 did not believe that Africans could understand the abstract idea of liberty.

9 WITH SMOKE AND MIRRORS: SLAVERY AND THE CONQUEST OF GUINEA

1 Admin. Paul Guebhard on Futa slavery, 15 July 1903, ARS, 7 G 84.
2 Goerg 1986: 108–10 and 337–40; Suret-Canale 1971: 42–45.
3 Reports of Inspector Saurin on Faranah and Ditinn, ANSOM, Contrôle 908.
4 Suret-Canale 1966 and 1971 writes of the harshness of French colonial methods and Cohen 1971 describes the eclectic nature of the early colonial service, but neither fully captures what a rag-tag group much of the first generation was.
5 Slaves were probably about half of the population of Guinea and at least a quarter of the Sudan. See Appendix 1.
6 Goerg 1986: 213–14.
7 Cousturier to Gov.-Gen., 5 Oct. 1892, ARS, 7 G 77; McGowan 1975: ch. 8; Barry 1988a: 379.
8 R. de Beeckman to Lt. Gov., 3 June 1885, ARS, K 12. See also case of Hyppolite d'Erneville, Gov. to Min., 24 April 1883, ANSOM Senegal XIV 15e.
9 Mgr. Lorber to Cardinal Ledochowski, 9 March 1897 and 23 March 1898, CSE, 193 B VII.
10 Comm. Benty to Gov. 15 and 22 Nov. 1881, ARS, 7 G 21.
11 The colonial inspectors were a carefully selected group responsible directly to the colonial minister. They could be sent anywhere in the empire to examine administration and the execution of policy. Though there were only twenty-six inspectors in 1905, Guinea was such a problem that it was visited at least three times between 1904 and 1911. Cohen 1971: 59–60. The inspectors were generally skilled men who made a meticulous examination of the records of the office studied. Copies of their reports are not widely available in African archives, but they were seen by all concerned. The administrator reviewed got the chance to respond, and the Lt. Governor and Governor-General also made comments. The Inspector then got the last word, all of this on large multi-column forms.
12 Saurin, "Captivité en Guinée," ANSOM, Contrôle 909. Only four years earlier, another inspector, Rheinhart, visited the Futa and interrogated Hubert, the Commandant, on slavery. Rheinhart, however, accepted what Hubert told him. He wrote that strong measures had been taken to stop the trade, that the administration tried to ameliorate the condition of slaves, that slaves would not work without coercion, and that there was a danger of slave-owners fleeing to Sierra Leone or Portuguese Guinea. Report, 9 Jan. 1904, ANSOM, Guinée XIV 3.
13 Arcin 1911: 593–94; Goerg 1986.
14 Rodney 1968b and 1970.
15 Barry 1988a, 123–27; Rodney 1970; Mouser 1971 and 1983; Rivière 1968; Goerg 1986: ch. 1. On women in the Eurafrican communities, see Mouser 1983 and Brooks 1983.
16 Barry 1988a: 190–96; Lloyd 1949; Mouser 1971.
17 Goerg 1986: 23–58; Barry 1988a: 190–208; Suret-Canale 1970: 40–53; Rivière 1968.
18 The *feitorias* in the Portuguese dominated Rio Grande and Geba were similar to French operations. Most entrepreneurs in both came from Senegal. Hawkins 1980: 2–3 and 125–51.
19 Palm oil was used mostly to make soap, but French consumers would not buy the yellow soap made from palm oil. Marseilles soap-makers found that they could make an attractive soap from a mixture of peanut oil and olive oil. See Klein 1968: 36–38; Schnapper 1961: 118–28. On the peanut, see Brooks 1976a and Guiraud 1937. On Guinea, see also Famechon 1900: 98–99 and 138.
20 Comm. Boké to Gov. Sén., 4 Oct. 1868, ARS, 7 G 7. See Goerg 1986: 77–78; Klein

1989a: 203–7; McGowan 1975: ch. 6. From that time forth, many commandants commented on the industry and productivity of the Tubakayes. See, for example, Monograph, Rio Nunez, 1912, ANG.

21 Curtin 1971b sees the Jaxanke primarily as traders. Sanneh 1976b and 1979: ch. 6 stresses their clerical vocation and argues that slave labour provided economic support for their clerical activities. There is probably an element of truth in both analyses. See also Suret-Canale 1970.

22 Goerg 1986: 76–79 and 105–8.

23 Arcin 1911: 664–66; Goerg 1986: 337–40.

24 Fall 1993: 78.

25 Goerg 1980 and 1986: 108–10 and 337–47; Suret-Canale 1960a. See also Annual Report for Agriculture, ARS, 2 G 5/12.

26 Bouet-Willaumez 1848; Schnapper 1961; Brunschwig 1963: 58–63.

27 McGowan 1975 and 1990.

28 Goerg 1980: 471; McGowan 1975: ch. 6.

29 McGowan 1975: ch. 6.

30 Goerg 1986, 124–25. On Conakry, a hitherto unimportant site, see Goerg 1986, 249–74.

31 Barry 1988a: 221–45; McGowan 1975: ch. 6; Demougeot 1944.

32 Barry 1988a, 221–45; Hawkins 1980: chs. 2–4; Lopes 1988: 204–50; McGowan 1975: ch. 4.

33 Hawkins 1980: ch. 4.

34 Barry 1988a: 331–38; Quinn 1971; Quinn 1977: 174–77; Roche 1976; Sanneh 1976b: 329–32; Lt. Legou, Report on Hamdullahi, 1891, ARS, 7 G 77.

35 Hawkins 1980: ch. 2; Mané 1978; Lopes 1988: 204–50.

36 Barry 1988a: 238–45. Much data in Hawkins and Lopes supports Barry's analysis, but a lot is not clear about the servile groups and their actions. Oral traditions describe events in ethnic terms because of their concern to legitimate.

37 This paragraph is based on unpublished research of Andrée Wynkoop in the Labé archives. I am grateful for her assistance.

38 I. Barry 1992: 103–37.

39 McGowan 1975: ch. 7; Kanya-Forstner 1969: 151–53.

40 Hargreaves 1963: 265–67.

41 Hargreaves 1963: 267–71; I. Barry 1992: 105. It was not clear who was protecting whom. Bayol knew that the Almamy did not want a French presence and had no choice on where he went and how he left.

42 On Fulbe diplomacy, see I. Barry 1992: 95–148.

43 McGowan 1975: ch. 7; Barry 1988a: 347–72.

44 Barry 1988a: 372–84; McGowan 1975, ch. 8.

45 I. Barry 1992: 147; McGowan 1975: ch. 8; Verdat 1949; Suret-Canale 1964.

46 McGowan 1981; Barry 1976. See also miscellaneous reports, ARS, 7 G 78. Alfa Yaya was, like Bokar Biro, an autocratic figure who threatened the checks and balances of the Futa political system. His father, Alfa Ibrahima, chose another son, Aguibou, as his successor. Yaya was the son of Ibrahima and a Kaabu princess and had spent much of his early life among the Malinke. Only in 1892 did he have secure control of Labé.

47 I. Barry 1992: 191–99.

48 Letter of 2 August 1893, ARS, K 13; Klein 1968: ch. 8; Debien 1964.

49 Noirot to Lt. Gov. Guinée, "Lettre sur l'Extinction de la Captivité," 25 July 1904, ANSOM, XIV 3.

50 I. Barry 1992: 206–12.

51 Ordinance 3 of Futa Jallon, ANSOM, Guinée XIV 3; Report on meeting, 13 July 1897, ARS, K28; Arcin 1911: 592–93. The chiefs also agreed to new taxes and to a court system.
52 Arcin 1911: 593.
53 Noirot, "Lettre sur l'Extinction de la Captivité," 25 July 1904, ANSOM XIV 3.
54 Inspector Saurin, "La Captivité en Guinée en 1908," Guyho Mission, Report 163, 20 Feb. 1908, ANSOM, Contrôle 909.
55 Much that happened between 1897 and 1904 was offensive to the chiefs, but they benefited from taxation policy and probably increased their control over their slaves. I. Barry 1992: 180–329.
56 Rapport politique et économique, Jan. 1899, 185, ARS, 7 G 80.
57 Testimony before inquiry, 1905, ANG, 2 D 115.
58 Deposition of administrator Thoreau-Levaré, ANG, 2 G 115.
59 Europeans resented the fact that masons spent more time working for Hubert's concubines than for them. Deposition of L. Coutu, ANG 2 D 115.
60 Deposition of Paul Guebhard, ANG 2 D 115.
61 Report of Henri Cosnier, 28 Nov. 1907, ARS, 7 G 61.
62 Deposition of teacher Fourcade, ANG, 2 D 115.
63 Letter of 13 May 1905, ANG, 2 D 115.
64 Report to Gov. Gen., 25 Jan. 1909, ANG, 2 D 115.
65 ANSOM, Guinée XIV 3 contains documents from the investigation.
66 Lt. Gov. Guinée to Gov. Gen., Oct. 1907 and Gov. Gen. to Min., 15 Oct. 1907, ANSOM, Guinée XIV 3.
67 Political Report, Dec. 1902, ANM, 1 E 68. See also ARS, 2 G 3/1 for political reports from 1903.
68 Political report, Labé, July 1905, ARS, 7 G 60.
69 Annex to Political Report, May 1905, ARS, 7 G 61; Report of 28 Jan. 1904, ANSOM, Guinée XIV 3 and ARS, K 20.
70 See the report of Paul Guebhard in Timbo to Admin. Futa, 30 June 1902, ANG, 2 D 197.
71 Report, Kurusa, June 1895, ANM, 1 E 157. See also ANG, 2 D 200; ARS, 7 G 80; Arcin 1911: 586.
72 Telegram, 7 Dept. 1900, ANSOM, Guinée XIV 3.
73 Lt. Gov. to Comm. Kadé, 12 Oct. 1900, ANSOM, Guinée XIV 3.
74 Telegram to Comm. Faranah, 13 Aug. 1900. ANSOM, Guinée XIV 3. Maclaud told a new administrator at Timbi not to mention slaves or discuss slave problems. Comm. Futa to Comm. Timbi, 6 Aug. 1900, 20, ARS 7 G 82. On freeing of local slaves, see Comm. Faranah to Lt. Gov. Guinée, 13 Sept. 1902, ANG, 2 D 88.
75 Comm. Futa to Lt. Gov. Guinée, 25 Jan 1902, ANG, 2 D 100; Comm. Timbo to Comm. Futa, 30 June 1902, ANG, 2 D 197.
76 Monthly report, Boké, 2 Feb. 1903, ANG, 2 D 32; Comm. Boké to Lt. Gov. Guinée, 3 Nov. 1902, ANG, 2 D 32.
77 On Sankaran, see report from Kurusa, 3 Aug. 1900, ANG, 2 D 191. Slave markets were held openly there. See Report of 15 Jan. 1902, ANG, 2 D 191. On Faranah, see the 1908 monograph, ANG, 1 D 11. In 1898, 43 percent of Dingiray was slave. Only two villages were under 20 percent slave. ANG, 2 D 71. Six years later, the estimated slave population was down by over 4,000. Report on Dingiray, ARS, K20.
78 Comm. Kurusa to Lt. Gov. Guinée, 14 Aug. 1901, ANG, 2 D 184. On Toma and Guerzé, see H. Pobéguin to Lt. Gov. Guinée, 26 April 1903, ANSOM, Guinée XIV 3. Saurin, Rapport sur la Captivité, 1908, mentions many slaves being returned to masters.

79 Comm. Dingiray to Lt. Gov. Guinée, 15 June 1899, ANG, 2 D 71.
80 Bulletin Politique, Dingiray, March 1900, ANG, 2 D 71.
81 Comm. Dingiray to Lt. Gov. Guinée, ANG, 2 D 73.
82 Lt. Gov. Guinée to Comm. Dingiray, 16 Oct. 1900, ANSOM Guinée XIV 3.
83 Comm. Dingiray to Lt. Gov. Guinée, 2 Oct. 1902, ANG, 2 D 73.
84 Polit. Report, Dingiray, July 1903, ANG, 2 D 73.
85 Fall 1993: ch. 3; Mangolte 1968. See Inspector General Guyho, 31 March 1908 on
    Saurin's reports, ARS, 4 G 6.
86 Saurin, Report on Labé, ANSOM, Contrôle 908; Comm. Faranah to Lt. Gov., 28
    Feb. 1903 ANG 2 D 88; see also reports from Ditinn and Timbo, ARS, 4 G 6.
87 Comm. Futa to Lt. Gov. Guinée, 10 Aug. 1901, ANG, 2 D 100.
88 Comm. Faranah to Lt. Gov. Guinée, 20 Nov. 1901, ANG, 2 D 88.
89 Comm. Faranah to Lt. Gov. Guinée, 28 Feb. 1903, ANG, 2 D 88.
90 Comm. Faranah to Lt. Gov. ANG, 1 D 11; Comm. Timbo to Lt. Gov. 23 Feb 1908
    and 29 Feb. 1908, ANG, 2 D 263; Lt. Gov. to Gov. Gen., 30 July 1909, ANS, 7 G
    63 and 30 April 1910, ANG 2 B 53.
91 I. Barry 1992: 266–70.
92 Lt. Gov. Cousturier to Gov. Gen., 272, 13 Dec. 1895. ANSOM, AOF XIV 1. See
    also Cousturier to Min., 8 Nov. 1898, ANSOM, Guinée XIV 3. Saurin made clear
    a decade later that these claims were untrue.
93 Saurin, Report on Faranah. On flight to Faranah, see Political reports of 8 Nov.
    1898, 6 Dec. 1898 and 20 Aug. 1900, ANG, 2 D 88.
94 Lt.Gov. Guinée to Comm. Benty, 15 of 1901, ANSOM, Guinée XIV 3.
95 Saurin, "Captivité," ANSOM, Contrôle 909.
96 Lt. Gov. Tautain to Min., 24 Sept, 1902, ANSOM, Guinée XIV 3.
97 Circular 81 of 17 Sept. 1902, ANSOM, Guinée XIV 3.
98 Journal de poste, 21 Oct. 1902, ANG, 1 D 47.
99 Comm. Boffa to Lt. Gov., 13 Oct. 1902, ANG, 2 D 13. On other coastal cercles, Lt.
    Gov. to Comm. Boké, 6 Dec. 1902, ANSOM, Guinée XIV 3. On Labé, Comm.
    Labé to Lt. Gov., 29 Nov. 1902, ANG, 2 D 198.
100 Lt. Gov. Guinée to Comm. Boké, 6 Dec. 1902, ANSOM, Guinée XIV 3.
101 Circular of 18 April 1903, ANSOM, Guinée XIV 3. Both Noirot and Henri
    Pobéguin, Commandant of Upper Guinea, objected to this policy. Pobéguin saw
    it as retraction of what had just been done. H. Pobéguin to Lt. Gov. Guinée, 26
    April 1903, ANSOM, Guinée XIV 3.
102 Famechon to Lt. Gov. Guinée, 5 April and 8 May 1903 and Roume's response to
    Lt. Gov. Guinée, 6 June 1903, ANSOM, Guinée XIV 3. See also Pobéguin, 26
    April 1903 and Noirot to Lt. Gov. Guinée, 31 March 1903, ANSOM, Guinée XIV
    3.
103 Arrêté of 9 Dec. 1903, ARS, M 125 and ANSOM, Guinée XIV 3.
104 Saurin, "Captivité en Guinée," ANSOM, Contrôle 908.
105 ARS, M 125.
106 Saurin, Report on Labé, ANSOM, Contrôle 908.
107 Lt. Gov. Guinée to Gov. Gen., 24 Sept. 1903, ARS, K 28.
108 Political Report, Sigiri, October 1903, ARS, K 27.
109 I. Barry 1992: 310.
110 Saurin, Report on Timbo, 7 Jan. 1908, ANSOM, Contrôle 908.
111 Comm. Futa to Comm. Ditinn, 31 March 1901, enclosure to Saurin, "Captivité,"
    ANSOM, Contrôle 909.
112 Lt. Gov. Guinée to Gov. Gen., 2 July 1904, ANSOM, Guinée XIV 3; Gov. Gen.
    p.i. to British Consul, 3 Aug. 1904; Comm. Mellacorée to French Consul, Free-

town, 6 April 1904, ARS K27. The French feared the Futa elite moving to Portuguese Guinea or Sierra Leone. The British were disturbed about Sierra Leoneans being sold in Guinea.

113 Acting Gov. Gen. to Lt. Gov., 27 Sept. 1905, ANG, 11 B 38.

114 A year later, an administrator in Boké was chastised when he presided over the division of an inheritance of sixty-three slaves. Lt. Gov. Guinée to Admin. Boké, 13 April 1907, ANSOM, Guinée XIV 3.

115 Gov. Gen. to Lt. Gov. Guinée, 16 Nov. 1905, ANG, 11 B 38.

116 Report by Administrator Lescure on Captivity, 22 Dec. 1905, ANSOM, Guinée XIV 3.

117 Lt. Gov. Frézouls to Gov. Gen., 26 Dec. 1905, ANSOM, Guinée XIV 3.

118 Lt. Gov. Frézouls to Comm. Futa Jallon, 23 July 1905 and 4 Sept. 1905, ANSOM, Guinée XIV 3 and ANG 2 D 115.

119 Comm. Leclerc to Lt. Gov. Guinée, 1 Dec. 1905, ANSOM, Guinée XIV 3.

120 Lt. Gov. Frézouls to Comm. Leclerc, 15 Jan. 1906, ANSOM, Guinée XIV 3. For similar instructions stressing non-recognition, Frézouls to Comm. Liurette, Haute Guinée, 24 Oct. 1905, and Lt. Gov. Richard to Comm. Boffa, 14 June 1906, ANSOM, Guinée XIV 3.

121 Lt. Gov. Frézouls to Comm. Leclerc, 16 Jan. 1906, ANSOM, Guinée XIV 3.

122 Circular of 17 March 1906, ANG, 2 A 3.

123 Inspector General Guyho, 31 March 1908, ARS, 4 G 6 and ANSOM, Contrôle 909.

124 Mgr. Segala, Apostolic Prefect to Cardinal Ledochowski, CSE, 193 B VII.

125 Mgr. Francisco Segala to Cardinal Gotti, 3 Dec. 1903, CSE, 193 B VII.

10 THE BANAMBA EXODUS

1 Keita 1959.

2 Annual Report, Bamako, ANM, 1 E 19.

3 Comm. Bonassies to Res. Logeais, 23 July 1902, ANM, 1 E 19.

4 Klein and Roberts 1980. Banamba was the most important of seven Maraka towns. Tuba was important as a center of learning and of the slave trade. See also Roberts 1987b and McDougall 1990.

5 Baillaud 1902: 294; Mage 1868: 64–66; Soleillet 1887: ch. 20.

6 Cited in Saurin report on Banamba, Meray Mission, 23 Feb. 1910, ARS, 4 G 10.

7 Discussed only in Saurin, "Banamba," ARS 4 G 10.

8 Political Report, Bamako, April 1905, ANM 1 E 19; Comm. Vidal to Lt. Gov. HSN, 25 June 1905, ANM, 1 N 27.

9 Political Report, Bamako, May 1905, ANM, 1 E 19; Annual Political report, ANM 1 E 12; Saurin, "Banamba," ARS 4 G 10.

10 Roume, telegram to Fawtier, 23 May 1905, ANM, 1 N 27; Roume telegram to Fawtier, 26 May 1905 and Fawtier telegram to Roume, 14 June 1905; ARS, 15 G 170.

11 Roume's telegrams to Fawtier, 21 and 26 1905; Fawtier telegram, 29 May 1905, ARS, 15 G 170.

12 Fawtier telegram, 29 May 1905, 15 G 170; Comm. Vidal to Lt. Gov. Fawtier, 25 June 1907, ANM 1 N 27.

13 Annual report, Sudan, 1905, ANM 1 E 12; Fawtier Report, 26 June 1905, ARS, 170. *Tirailleurs* surrounded a meeting at Tuba, then forced the Maraka to evacuate the village, but found only four guns. Residents probably hid their guns elsewhere. Report of Capt. Angeli, 1 June 1905, ANM, 1 N 27.

14 Fawtier, Report of 26 June 1905, ARS, 15 G 170.

15 Comm. Vidal to Lt. Gov., 25 June 1905, ANM, 1 N 27.

16 Report on slavery, Bamako, ARS, K 19.

17 Comm. Vidal to Lt. Gov., 25 June 1905, ANM, 1 N 27.

18 Political Report, Bamako, 1 April 1906, 1 E 19. Ponty indicated in a marginal comment that he intended to let them go. Polit. Report, Bamako, Feb. 1906, ANM, 1 E 19. See also reports in ARS, 2 G 6/6, esp. Lt. Gov. HSN to Gov. Gen., 28 May 1906.

19 Lt. Gov. Sudan to Res. Banamba, 1 R 17.

20 Political Report, HSN, May 1906, ARS, 2 G 6/6.

21 Saurin thought the actual number more than twice that. Many slaves were wary of the French and did not seek passes. See Report on Banamba, ARS, 4 G 10. French censuses indicate a drop of about 12,000 in tax rolls over a two-year period, but since slaves were under-reported, as Brevié argued earlier, the number may have been much higher.

22 Political Report, Bamako, May 1906, ANM 1 E 19.

23 General Report, Bamako, 1906, ANM, 1 E 19.

24 *Diaires*, Patiana, 15 May 1906, AWF. At the time, departures in Patiana were rare, but within a year, the number increased.

25 Political Report, Bafulabe, June 1906, ANM, 1 E 17.

26 Pol. Reports, Segu, March to July 1907, ANM, 1 E 72.

27 Polit. Rep., Bafulabe, May 1907, ANM, 1 E 17

28 See Political Reports, 1908, ANM, 1 E 76.

29 Political Report, Feb. 1908, ANM 1 E 38; Admin. Gumbu to Lt. Gov. HSN, 21 April 1908, ANM, 1 E 197.

30 Echenberg 1971b; Héritier 1975; Hubbell 1996.

31 Personal communication, Andrew Hubbell. See Hubbell 1996.

32 See political reports, ARS, series 2 G. Also in ANSOM, Sénégal I 97 ter. On Dori, see reports from 1908 and 1909, ANM, 1 E 32. On Nioro, ANM, 1 E 212.

33 Bilma had only 19 over two years, but at Bamba there were 311 at the liberty village in 1910. See Report, Bamba, 31 Dec. 1910, ANM 1 E 122 and Bilma, 31 Dec. 1909, ANM, 1 E 124. Suppression of a budget line for Bamba's liberty village caused a raised eyebrow in Inspector's Report on Bamba, 30 Jan. 1910, ARS, 4 G 11.

34 Memel-Foté 1988: 402–18 and 633–38. See Clozel circular of 10 March 1906. Weiskel 1980: 147 says that Clozel issued an emancipation decree in 1905, that was not meant to be enforced. He does not mention Clozel's 1907 speech, nor do Terray or Chauveau. In northern and central Ivory Coast, many recently purchased victims of Samori's last wars went home or took refuge with the French between 1898 and 1903. Others were freed in suppressing Baule resistance. See Weiskel 1980: chs. 4 and 5; Chauveau 1987; Terray 1987a.

35 On Dingiray, Political Report, Aug. 1908, ANG, 2 D 76; political reports in 2 D 73 and 75. On Kankan, Political Report, Guinea, 11 Aug. 1911, ARS, 2 G 11/11 and Gov. Gen. Ponty to Lt. Gov. Guinea, 44 of July 1911, ARS, K 28.

36 Political reports, ANG, 2 D 91, 2 D 185 and 2 D 190.

37 On Rio Pongo, political reports, ANG, 2 D 239; on Rio Nunez, ANG, 2 D 37; on Mellacorée, Comm. Mellacorée to Lt. Gov. Guinea, 3 Jan. 1908, ARS, 2 G 7/12 and ANG, 2 D 95.

38 Political reports, Timbo, March and July 1909, ANG, 2 D 76; Timbo and Mamou, ANG 2 D 263; quarterly political reports for 1909 and 1910, ARS, 2 G 9/13 and 2 G 10/19.

39 Political Report, 10 July 1907, ANG, 2 D 203.
40 Journal de poste, ANG, 1 D 50; Pol. Rep., May 1908, ANG, 2 D 263.
41 Sanneh 1979: 136–38 and 235; Sanneh 1976b; Suret-Canale 1970; Comm. Kadé to Lt. Gov. Guinea, 14 April 1911, ANG, 2 B 59 and Pol. Rep., Kadé, Sept. 1911, ARS, 2 G 11/11.
42 Political Report, Faranah, 31 August 1910, ANG, 2 D 93.
43 Olivier de Sardan 1984: ch. 9. Movement from Dori involved resettlement of *bella* and departure of *rimaibe*. See political reports in ANM, 1 E 32.
44 Rothiot 1988: 249–52. Kimba 1981 thinks that the biggest movement of liberation came after 1920.
45 Olivier de Sardan 1976, 140.
46 Comm. Gorgol to Commissaire du Gov. Gen., Rapports politiques 1906–1938, Archives Nationales, Mauritanie, cited in Kane 1987: Conclusion. At Dagana, the 1903 law code led to many slaves being liberated in 1904. Monthly report, July 1904, ARS, 2 4/51.
47 Guyho Mission,1908, ANSOM, Contrôle 909; correspondence, Dagana, ARS, 13 G 326; "Notice sur le Cercle de Matam," ARS, 2 D 10/7.
48 Political Reports, Timbo, Aug. and Sept. 1910, ANG, 2 D 264.
49 Political Report, Kita, ANM, 1 E 48. See also *Chroniques*, Kita, Feb. 1908, AWF.
50 Annual report, 1910 and 1911, Issa-Ber; Polit. Rep., Issa-Ber, July 1911, ANM, 1 E 43. See Saurin Report on Comm. Rocaché at Issa-Ber, who mishandled these cases, ARS, 4 G 11.
51 Political Reports, Sokolo, 1911, ANM, 1 E 76; Gumbu, Pol. Rep., March and May 1908, ANM, 1 E 38.
52 Saurin, Report on Gumbu, Feb. 1910, ARS, 4 G 10.
53 See Boxes 10.2, 10.3. See also *Diaires*, Patyana, 12 April 1907, AWF.
54 Reports on Sokolo and Issa-Ber, ARS 4 G 11.
55 For a murder in Kita that almost went unpunished because the interpreter was paid off, see *Diaires*, Kita, 6 Nov. 1911, AWF.
56 Political Report, Bafulabe, Aug. 1910, ANM, 1 E 17.
57 Study by Procureur Général, 17 Nov. 1903, ARS, K 27. See also ANM, 1 E 182.
58 *Diaires*, Kita, AWF. Shortly afterwards, thirty slaves belonging to Samba's "Alcali" were freed.
59 Correspondence, 1911, ANM, 1 E 185. There is no indication of the outcome, but such cases were numerous.
60 Political Report, Sikasso, June 1909, ANM, 1 E 73.
61 See Pol. Rep., Tivouane, June 1906, ARS, K 27 on claims to children held in Kajoor; on cases before the *Chambre d'Homologation*, see ARS, M 147. See also Inspector Demaret's 1908 reports on Senegal river cercle, ANSOM, Contrôle 909.
62 Saurin, Report on Banamba, ARS, 4 G 10. Also Dokoro Samake, Ntentu; Kani Tumani Bagayogo, Kossiala; Mamadu Jakité, Kalana, Klein-Bagayogo interviews in Wasulu.
63 Habib Niang, Jigimar. Klein-Mbodj interviews.
64 Res. Yelimané to Comm. Nioro, 5 March 1908, ANM, 1 E 212.
65 Tour of Feb.–Mar. 1912, Bakel, ARS, 2 D 4/32. Roberts 1988: 195 describes a similar strategy at Sokolo.
66 ANM, 1 E 125. Reports are not available for all cercles.
67 ANM, 1 E 34.
68 ANM, 1 E 150.
69 On Bandiagara, ANM, 1 E 123; on Issa-Ber, ANM, 1 E 133; on Kita, ANM 1 E 136; on Nioro, ANM 1 E 143. For many cercles, there are few reports available, only

two for San, one for Bobo-Diulasso.
70 J. Bertin, "Les Toucouleurs Boundounkés (1954)," ANM, 1 D 51.
71 Political Reports, June and July 1907, ANM, 1 E 72.
72 Political Report, July 1912, ANM, 1 E 48.
73 Roberts 1988: 298.
74 Lt. Gov. HSN to Comm. Segu, 25 May 1907, ANM, 1 E 77. See also Lt. Gov. Peuvergne to Comm. Segu, 10 Feb. 1908, ANM, 1 E 77.
75 Ponty to Comm. Gumbu, 14 March 1908, ANM, 1 E 197. On Nioro, Lt. Gov., HSN to Comm. Nioro, 27 May 1908, ANM, 1 E 212.
76 Circular of 12 Nov. 1906, ANM, 1 E 182.
77 ANSOM, Soudan I 11 for final versions.
78 Gov. Gen. Ponty to Min., 13 Jan. 1913, ARS, 17 G 39.
79 Circular of Lt. Gov., HSN to Nioro, Segu, Kayes, Kita, Bamako, Satadugu, and Issa-Ber, 10 Feb. 1908. See Bouche 1968: 160.
80 Bouche 1968: 259–66. Ponty was unhappy when the liberty village at Sikasso emptied. He wanted it shifted to the tax roles. See his instructions of 3 May 1907, ANM, 1 E 73.
81 Bouche 1968: 254–57.
82 Min. to Gov. Gen., 27 Feb. 1908, ARS, K 26.
83 Gov. Gen. Ponty to Lt. Gov. Guinée, 24 April 1908, ANG, 11 B 48; Gov. Gen. Ponty to Lt. Gov. HSN, 24 April 1908 with decree of 28 May 1908, ANM, 1 E 184. See also Lt. Gov. HSN to Comm. Nioro, 29 June 1908, ANM, 1 E 212. The decree could have been interpreted to ban economic aspects of domestic slavery, but there is no evidence it was ever used to do so. It also could have been used against labor agitation because it barred threats, violence and deception to induce a worker to break a contract.
84 *JOAOF*, 14 Dec. 1908.
85 Lt. Gov., HSN to Gov. Gen., Quarterly Report, 28 May 1909, ARS, 2 G 9/12.
86 Political Report, Bafulabe, Sept. 1908, ANM, 1 E 17 and Ponty's response, Lt. Gov. HSN to Comm. Bafulabe, 10 June 1907, ANM, 1 E 186.
87 Comm. Brocard to Lt. Gov., Senegal, 8 Oct. 1907, ARS, unclassified.
88 Response to Saurin Report on Issa-Ber, ARS, 4 G 10.
89 Etats Trimestriels des Jugements, HSN, ARS, M 119.
90 Rougier 1930 estimated the total loss at 10,000, but that is incompatible with census data, which tended to underreport. Some departures continued even after 1908. A 1910 political report suggested 20,000, which is more likely. See Rapport Politique d'ensemble du Soudan, 1910, ANM 1 E 12. See also Roberts 1988: 288.
91 Roberts 1988: 299–300. Roberts reports some hiring of labor before 1906. On Bambara work groups, see Lewis 1979 and Grosz-Ngaté 1986. Marty 1920, I: 40 suggests importance of Quranic students.
92 Annual Report Bamako, 5 Jan. 1907, ANM, 1 E 19; quarterly report, 14 Oct. 1906, ARS, 2 G 6/6.
93 Political report, May 1909, ANM, 1 E 19.
94 Saurin, Report on Banamba, 23 Feb. 1910, ARS 4 G 10. See McDougall 1990 on Banamba salt trade.
95 Rougier 1930; Rougier, Report on Islam in Banamba, ANM, 1 D 33. See also Marty 1920, vol. IV: 63–84, 176–79.
96 See Annual Report Bamako, 1910, ANM, 1 E 19; Report on Banamba, 23 Feb. 1910, ARS, 4 G 10.
97 Saurin on Segu, 6 Jan. 1910, ARS, 4 G 10.
98 Political Report, Comm. Issa-Ber, ANM, 1 E 43.

99   Lt. Gov. HSN to Gov. Gen., Quarterly Report, 4 June 1910, ARS, 2 G 10/17.
100 Second Quarter Report, ARS, 2 G 6/3.
101 Annual Report, Kita, 1909, ANM, 1 E 48.
102 Consul-General, Dakar, to Gov. Gen., 24 Dec. 1910 and Gov. Gen. W. Ponty to
     Consul General, 26 of 22 Feb. 1911, ARS, K 26. On Dahomey, where the French
     encouraged a mass exodus, see Manning 1982: 188–93.
103 Report on slavery, Bamako, ARS, K 19.
104 Political reports, Kita, ANM, 1 E 48.
105 Meray Report on Secretary General, 2 Nov. 1909, ARS, 4 G 11.
106 On Kutiala, ANM, 1 E 50; on Kury, see Lt. Gov. HSN to Comm. Kury, 19 April
     1907, ANM 1 E 204.
107 Roberts 1988: 292.
108 Manning 1982: 192 estimates the departures from the Fon kingdom of Dahomey
     after Dodds freed slaves there at one quarter to one third of the slave population.
     Of course, both of us are talking about the first wave.
109 Father Templier to Mgr. Livinhac, 8 Mar. 1906, AWF, I/074/118. In 1902, the
     missions had 700 orphans. R.P. Hippolyte Bazin to Dir., Oeuvre de Sainte
     Enfance, 25 Oct. 1902 and his report on schools and orphanages, Corres. Off.
     1892–1911, AWF.
110 Mgr. H. Bazin to Mission Ouagadougou, 19 Jan 1903, *Diaires*, White Fathers,
     Ouagadougou, AWF. De Benoist 1987: 111–20.
111 This account is based on the diaries from Kupela, AWF. Father De Benoist 1976:
     176–80 is sceptical of the tale of Goguely's rather kinky behavior, but I see no
     reason to doubt it. According to the diary, he earlier had about twenty girls
     rounded up to be his "wives." He claimed to be a Catholic and several years later,
     when he returned to the area as a civilian administrator, was regarded by the
     missionaries as a friend. De Benoist argues that the missionaries were insensitive
     in their approach to traditional society, but the persecution took place with the
     authorization and participation of the commandant.
112 *Diaire*, Banankuru, July 1904. AWF. The Commandant was Carrier, who later
     commandeered mission girls for his pleasure at Kupela. Carrier thought that the
     mission was inciting slaves to leave their masters. See *Diaire*, Kita, March and
     April 1905 on harassment of Christians there.
113 *Diaire*, Kita, AWF. All diaries contain cases of intercession both with the adminis-
     tration and with the master.
114 *Chroniques*, Banankuru, 143, Nov. 1907, AWF.
115 *Chroniques*, Kita, Jan. 1909, 157, AWF.
116 *Chroniques*, Timbuktu, 124, Feb. 1906, AWF.
117 De Benoist 1987: 231–34; *Diaires*, Ouagadugu, June and July 1908, AWF. On
     1901 famine, see *Chroniques*, Banankuru, 89, Jan 1901, AWF; Gov. Gen. to Min.,
     535 of 27 May 1903, ANSOM, Sénégal IV 28.
118 *Diaire*, Ouagadougou, June and July, 1908, AWF.
119 *Diaire*, Patyana, 25 April 1907, AWF. This letter may have been inspired by the
     Alla-ma-son case (see box 3). On similar tensions at Kita, see *Chroniques*, Kita,
     161, May 1909, AWF.
120 Annual Report, Kita, *Chroniques*, 161, 1908–1909, AWF. See a case from Din-
     guira, in which two men with clubs invaded the mission to take away a daughter
     who refused to marry her father's choice. *Diaires*, Dec. 193, AWF.
121 De Benoist 1987: 163–64; on family policy, see Alexandre LeRoy, "Le Relèvement
     de la Famille en Afrique," CSE, 63 B V. On orphanages, see De Benoist 1987:
     211–12.
122 Suret-Canale 1971: 61.

11   FRENCH FEARS AND THE LIMITS TO AN EMANCIPATION POLICY

1 Kampo collection.
2 Cooper 1987. See also Cooper 1980, esp. ch. 2.
3 Pouncy 1981; Tamuno 1972: 324–25; Phillips 1989: ch. 2; Craven and Hay 1994.
4 Speech of 14 Dec. 1908, *JOAOF*, 19 Dec. 1908.
5 On sharecropping in France, see Weber 1976: 117 and 126–27.
6 This issue is also discussed in Klein 1983.
7 Caron 1891: 206 argued that Masina was more valuable than Timbuktu because of its agricultural production.
8 Political Report, May 1895, ANM, 1 E 24. In their treaty with the Amirou, the French promised not to intervene in slave matters. See slavery questionnaire, Bandiagara, ANM, 1 E 23, and Marty, 1920, II: 181–88. The French reported on *rimaibe* even after they stopped collecting data on slaves because they were seen as a separate ethnic group.
9 Saurin referred to 30,000 slaves and 8,000 Fulbe. Report on Djenné, 14 Jan. 1910, ARS 4 G 10. There were also non-Fulbe in the inner Delta. Comm. Destenave estimated in 1894 two *rimaibe* for each Fula, equal numbers of slave and free among the Bambara, while the Futanke were two-thirds free. "Rapport sur la Captivité dans les Etats d'Aguibou," ANM, 1 E 156.
10 Annual Report, Djenné 1909, ANM, 1 E 30. Another source gave it as 180 for men and 90 for women. Comm. Djenné to Lt. Gov. HSN, 24 Dec. 1908, ANM, 1 E 30.
11 Annual Report, Djenné, 1909, ANM, 1 E 39. Johnson and Gallais refer to both *jamgal* and *jégom*. Gallais 1967, I: 129–31; Johnson 1976. As becomes clear below, the *jégom* or sixth, replaced the *jamgal*. The original error was in Marty 1920, II: 276–78. Contemporary informants speak only of *jamgal*.
12 Gallais describes a rice cultivating family with six active members aged fifteen or above, which produced 4.6 tons in 1958. They produced well above their needs, and with fish supplementing their diet and supplementary income from off-season labor, were relatively comfortable. If they had had to pay *jamgal*, there would have been little surplus. Gallais 1967, I: 203–11.
13 Report on tour, 1 March 1912, Djenné, ANM, 1 E 30.
14 Saurin, Report on Djenné, ARS, 4 G 10.
15 Cissé 1978: 89–90.
16 Political reports, Djenné, June and July 1903, ANM, 1 E 29.
17 Political report, Djenné, Dec. 1905, ANM, 1 E 29.
18 Annual Report, Djenné, 1907, ANM, 1 E 29.
19 In 1894, a year after the conquest, increased demand for labor contributed to slave flight. Report on Slavery, Djenné, ARS, K 14.
20 Political Report, Djenné, July 1908, ANM, 1 E 29.
21 Political Report, Djenné July 1907, ANM, 1 E 29.
22 Political Report, Djenné, Oct. 1908, ANM, 1 E 29.
23 Tour report, 24 Dec. 1908, ANM, 1 E 192. See also Acting Gov. Gen. Liotard to Min., 1791, 22 Aug. 1908, ANSOM, Soudan I 11; Monthly reports and Annual Report, Djenné, ANM, 1 E 29. Comm. Djenné to Lt. Gov. HSN, 24 Dec. 1908, ANM, 1 E 192. See also Marty, 1920: II, 276–78.
24 "La location à la forme métayère, le sol appartenant aux Peuls." Annual Report, Djenné, ANM, 1 E 29; Annual Report, Djenné, ANM, 1 E 30. Clozel justified the agreement in comments on Saurin's Jenne report. ARS, 4 G 10.
25 Cissé 1978: 26–49; Comm. Febvre. Political Report, Feb. 1910, ANM, 1 E 30
26 Decree of 24 July 1906, cited in Cissé 1978: 66–70.

27 The Tenenkou meeting is not well remembered in Masina. Of more than a dozen people whom Kampo interviewed, only Amadu Cissé of Sevaré knew about it.
28 Tour report, 1909–10, Djenné, ANM, 1 E 30.
29 Political Report, Djenné, April 1909, ANM, 1 E 30.
30 Saurin report, quoted by G. Febvre, Political Report, Djenné. Feb. 1910, ANM, 1 E 30.
31 Annual Report, Djenné, ANM, 1 E 30. By 1910, Fulbe were also collecting *jaka* or *zakkat*, a tithe on the harvest for the state. Monthly report, Feb. 1910, ANM, 1 E 130.
32 Political Report, Djenné, Feb. 1910, ANM, 1 E 30.
33 Various reports, Djenné, ANM, 1 E 30.
34 Political report, Djenné, Dec. 1912, ANM, 1 E 30.
35 A.A. Lalarde, Tour Report, April–May 1912, Djenné, ANM, 1 E 30; Tour Report, 30 Nov. 1910 and "Rapport sur la Politique Générale," Mopti, ANM, 1 E 55.
36 Political Report, Djenné, Sept. 1913. ANM, 1 E 30. See also reports from Mopti.
37 Lalarde tour report (see Note 35 above).
38 Annual Report, Jenné, ANM, 1 E 130, suggested providing land for the *rimaibe*.
39 Cissé 1978: 29. Cissé's picture of the relationship between Fulbe and *rimaibe* is supported by conversations with other Malian scholars. Gallais 1967 and Vincent 1963 give a more benign picture. Vincent had difficulty getting Fulbe budget data, but he felt that *rimaibe* were better off than Songhay and Bambara in the same area and had a closer relationship with former masters than the *bella*.
40 Cissé 1978: 139–50.
41 Cissé 1978: 151–61. Gallais argues that *rimaibe* obligations had been reduced to token payments. Gallais 1967: I, 131, 160–61. See also Comm. Mopti to Lt. Gov. Sudan, 18 Feb. 1935, ANM, 2 E 135.
42 Cissé 1978: 92–94. The assaka was traditionally one tenth of the harvest, one thirtieth of the cattle and one fortieth of the sheep and goats. Vincent 1963: 106 speaks of the *rimaibe* obligation as *murgu*. For a more accurate use of the term, see Lovejoy 1993.
43 Cissé 1978: 99–102.
44 Interview, Bada Bocoum, Kampo interviews.
45 Cissé 1978: 161.
46 Cissé 1978: 191.
47 Comm. Mopti to Lt. Gov. Sudan, 18 Feb. 1935, ANM, 2 E 135.
48 Comm. Kury to Lt. Gov. HSN, 19 April 1907, ANM, 1 E 204.
49 Circular of Lt. Gov. Clozel to Cercles of Issa-Ber, Bandiagara, Sokolo, Gumbu and Nioro, 29 July 1908, ANM, 1 E 212.
50 Comm. Gumbu to Lt. Gov. HSN, 21 April 1908 and 15 July 1908, ANM, 1 E 197.
51 Comm. Hombori to Comm. Masina, ANM, 2 E 3.
52 Annual Report, Bandiagara, 1910, ANM, 1 E 23; Tour report, Douentza, 31 May 1912, ANM, 1 E 24. De Bruijn and Van Dik describe a similar situation in Hayre, where Fulbe lost all control over slaves and many left.
53 Lt. Gov. HSN to Comm. Gumbu, 28 Sept. 1908, ANM, 1 E 197.
54 Reports on slavery, Rio Nunez and Rio Pongo, ARS, K 20.
55 Correspondence, Boké, 1906, ANG, 2 D 33. See for 1907, reports from Boké, ANG, 2 D 34. On this case, see Klein 1989a.
56 Poulet Circular, ANG, 2 A 4.
57 Rapport Politique, 8 March 1909, ANG, 2 D 37.
58 See monthly political reports, ANG, 2 D 34 and 2 D 36. For a more limited exodus from Rio Pongo, see ANG, 2 D 238.

59 Journal de Poste, Boké, ANG, 2 D 36; Political Report, 8 March 1909, Boké, ANG, 2 D 37.
60 Political Report, 8 March 1909, ANG, 2 D 37.
61 Comm. Boké to Lt. Gov., Guinea, 13 April 1909, ANG, 2 D 37.
62 Political Report, Boké, May 1909, ANG, 2 D 37.
63 Political Report, June 1909, ANG, 2 D 37.
64 Comm. Mellacorée to Lt. Gov. Guinée, 29 Sept. 1907 and 3 Jan. 1908, ANG, 2 D 94; see also ANS, 2 G 7/12.
65 Political Report, April 1908, Mellacorée, ANG, 2 D 95.
66 Political and Commercial Reports, Rio Pongo, ANG, 2 D 239.
67 Political report, Rio Pongo, July 1909, ANG, 2 D 239; Lt. Gov. Guinea to Comm. Mellacorée, 28 June 1912, ANG, 2 B 65. The Governor could not accept a work obligation of six hours per day, six days a week. Monographie, Mellacorée 1908, ANG, 1 D 14.
68 Monograph, Forecariah, ANG, 1 D 14, claimed that slavery was almost complete- ly gone by 1912 in the Mellacorée.
69 Political and Commercial Report, 1909, Rio Pongo, ANG, 2 D 239.
70 Political reports, Rio Pongo, April 1910, ANG, 2 D 242 and Sept. 1912, ANG, 2 D 19. See also Marty 1921: 119.
71 Circular 16, Lt. Gov. Richard, 17 March 1906, ANSOM, Guinée XIV 3; I. Barry 1992: 286–315.
72 Poulet Circular 48 of 22 April 1908, ANG, 2 A 4. There do not seem to be any responses in the archives to his request.
73 Lt. Gov., Guinée to Comm. Pita, 3 June 1908, ANG, 2 B 36.
74 Lt. Gov. Guinea to Comm. Kissidugu, 18 Feb. 1909, ANG, 2 B 47. See also Lt. Gov. Guinea to Comm. Boké, 25 Jan. 1909, ibid.
75 Letters to Faranah, Kindia, Timbo, Ditinn, Dingiray, ANG, 2 B 37. See also Liotard's instruction to Boké, 6 May 1909, ARS, 2 B 4 and to Kurusa, 12 May 1910, ANG, 2 B 36.
76 Harrison 1988: 49–51; Lombard, 1967: 106–23; Marty 1915. On French attitudes, see also Robinson 1988.
77 Harrison, Ingawa, and Martin, 1987: 501–4.
78 I. Barry 1992: 301–2 speaks of small acts such as refusal to serve on tribunals or seizure of liberty papers.
79 Ponty, "Situation Politique dans le Fouta-Djallon," to Lt. Gov. Guinea, 662, 25 September 1909, ARS, 7 G 86.
80 See Ponty response, 31 March 1914 to Rheinhart report, ARS, 4 G 17.
81 Gov. Gen. Ponty to Lt. Gov. Guy, 1 Nov. 1910, ARS 7 G 63.
82 This section is based on Harrison 1988: ch.5; I. Barry 1992: 495–505; Verdat 1949; Sanneh 1986; and Suret-Canale, 1964 and 1970. See also Charles Pherivong, "La Situation Politique," 23 Feb. 1911, Pherivong Mission, ANSOM, Contrôle 912.
83 Sanneh 1986 gives more credence to the plot than Harrison 1988 or Suret-Canale 1964. Verdat 1949 accepted official explanations.
84 Baldé 1974: 55 suggests that 11,000 slaves left for Casamance or Guinea-Bissau. See also I. Barry 1992: 438–65.
85 Suret-Canale 1971: 76; see also Harrison 1988: ch. 5.
86 See letters from the Labé commandant, ANG, 2 D 200.
87 I. Barry 1992: 495–525.
88 Circular of 4 March 1911, ARS, 7 G 63.
89 Circular, 31 Aug. 1911, ANG, 2 A 12.
90 Circular of 18 Sept. 1911, ANG, 2 A 12.

91 Circular of 26 Sept. 1911, ARS, 7 G 63. Also in ANG, 2 A 12.
92 I. Barry 1992: 567.
93 Lt. Gov. Guy to Gov. Gen., "La Société Foula et l'action française," 15 April 1911, ARS, 7 G 87.
94 Lt. Gov. Guinea to Gov. Gen., 17 July 1911, ANG, 2 B 59.
95 Political Report, Kadé, April 1911, ARS, 7 G 63.
96 Report, Tuba, ARS, 2 G 11/11. Suret-Canale 1970 suggests that the population of Tuba dropped from over 7,000 to about 3,000.
97 Circular of 2 Jan. 1912, ANG, 2 A 12.
98 Quarterly report, 4th quarter, 1910 on large movements from Mali, Koin, Tuba, Dingiray. ARS, 2 G 10/19. See Rapport d'ensemble, 1911, ARS, 1 G 11/1; on Dingiray, ANG, 2 D 76; on Telimélé, third quarter report, 1912, ANG, 2 B 62; on Kankan, ARS, 2 G 11/11.
99 Political Report, 4th quarter, 1909, ANG, 2 D 263. See also first quarter 1910, reports from Suarella, Ditinn and Mamou; Political report, 2nd quarter, 1907 and Rapport sur les anciens captifs libérés, 5 July 1908, Timbo, ANG, 2 D 263.
100 Saurin report, 19 Dec. 1907, ANSOM, Contrôle 908. See also Monthly reports, Faranah, ANG, 2 D 93. On flight to Portuguese Guinea, Lt. Gov. to Comm. Mali, 7 Aug. 1909, ANG, 2 B 51.
101 Political Report, Timbo, Feb. 1911, ANG, 2 D 264. See also Political report, Labé, Feb. 1912, ANG, 2 D 200.
102 Monthly reports, Kurusa, ANG, 2 D 185; Pherivong mission, Report, 10 April 1911, ANSOM, Contrôle 912.
103 Lt. Gov. to all Administrators, 31 October 1911, ARS, 7 G 63.
104 Political Report, 2nd quarter, 1912, ANG, 2 B 65. Neither the reorganization of the Futa in 1912 nor the contracts slowed up the departures. Timbo, reduced to a subdivision of Mamou, dropped from 40,000 in 1912 to 25,000 in 1917 because of slave flight and fear of recruitment. 4th quarter Report, ARS, 2 G 17/9.
105 I. Barry, 1992: 296.
106 Lt. Gov. Guy to Gov. Gen., 30 Oct. 1911, ANG, 2 B 60; Quarterly Report, Guinea, 4th Quarter, 1911, ARS, 2 G 11/11; Political Report, Timbo, 29 April 1912, ANG, 2 D 264; Political Report, Labé, Nov. 1911, ANG 2 D 200; 2nd quarter report, Guinea, ARS, 2 G 13/14; polit. report, Timbo, 29 April 1912, ANG, 2 D 264.
107 Report, 2nd quarter, 1913, ARS, 2 G 13/14.
108 Lt. Gov. Guy to Comm. Tugué, 22 Dec. 1911, ANG, 2 B 60. See also Lt. Gov. to Comm. Dingiray, ARS, 2 B 60 and ANG, 2 B 61; reports of 3rd and 4th quarters, ARS, 2 G 11/11.
109 Lt. Gov. to Comm. Forecariah, 17 Aug. 1912 and Lt. Gov. to Comm. Dingiray, 12 July 1912, ANG, 2 B 65;
110 Richard-Molard 1953a and 1953c.
111 Ponty, "Situation Politique dans le Fouta Djallon," ARS, 7 G 86.
112 Condé 1972: 16–19. See on land law, Vieillard 1939.
113 On Kadé, 1 Sept. 1911, Lt. Gov. Guinea to Comm. Kadé; on Kankan, Lt. Gov. Guinée to Comm. Kankan, 21 Oct. 1911, ANG, 2 B 59.
114 Gov. Gen. Ponty to Lt. Gov. Peuvergne, 5 March 1913, ARS, 7 G 64.
115 Rheinhart report, 7 April 1914, ARS, 4 G 17.
116 Rheinhart Report on Timbo, 16 March 1914, ARS, 4 G 17.
117 An area of 600,000 to 700,000 people, the Futa had nine cercles and three lesser posts in 1911. It was administered by 9 administrators, 9 assistants, 18 clerks and 175 guards. Lt. Gov. Guy to Gov. Gen., "La Société Foula et l'action française," 15 April 1911, ARS, 7 G 87. See I. Barry 1992: 28.

118 This concern was evident in a discussion in 1924 of making former *rimaibe* court assessors. The idea was rejected because the chiefs were too committed to tradition and contemptuous of slaves. Justice Report, 1925, ARS, 3 M 8.

119 Durand 1935. Throughout there is a notion of blood. Many of Tene's supporters are of mixed Malinke-Fulbe descent and supposedly possess Malinke solidity and Fulbe intelligence. Commandant at Pita in 1928 and 1929, Durand was later governor of Senegal. On introduction of plowing in part of the Futa, see Derman 1973: 135.

120 Durand 1935: 21–22. Durand spoke of a *captif* several times, but preferred *serviteur, servante* or serf. Derman 1973 translates all these terms as serf.

121 Durand 1935: 72.

122 Durand 1935: 38.

123 ARS 2 K 6 (26).

124 Vieillard was a young scholar-administrator, who died in World War II. His notes are available at the Institut Fondamental d'Afrique Noire in Dakar and are an invaluable source on the inter-war Futa. See also Vieillard 1939 and 1940.

125 Derman 1973: 34–36. Vieillard and Derman suggest a heavier labor obligation than the 1931 report. Obligations were always variable, depending on personalities of the actors and the relative balance of power between *rimaibe* and Fulbe. See also Baldé 1975.

126 Wynkoop 1991: 63.

127 Derman 1973: 132–33. See also Dupire 1994: 428–32.

128 Derman 1973: 56.

129 Derman 1973: 51–54 and 154–62; Baldé 1975: 213. On the case of a *tirailleur*, who used savings to buy land, see Derman 1973: 135–36.

130 Fonds Vieillard, chemise 92. In the Futa a slave child was often given as a servant to the bride and sometimes to the groom. Vieillard cites a 1933 inheritance case in which each heir received a slave.

131 Derman 1973: 65 and 79–110.

132 H. Baldé 1957.

133 Derman 1973: 116–19; Dupire 1994.

134 Derman 1973: 200. This was particularly true of those who made money. H. Baldé 1957.

135 Wynkoop 1991: 58–64; Baldé 1974. See also David 1980: 141–54.

136 Derman 1973: 157.

137 Baldé 1974: 263.

138 Baldé 1974: 266–78.

139 Hacimou Baldé 1957 suggests 300,000.

140 Baldé 1975.

141 Botte 1994. Writing about Adamawa in Cameroon, Ver Ecke 1994 describes a similar process in which *rimaibe* try to become Fulbe while the Fulbe stubbornly exclude them.

142 Ponty response to Rheinhart report, 31 March 1914, ARS, 4 G 17.

143 Lt. Gov. Lebretoigne du Mazel, Situation Politique, 1913, ARS, 7 G 64. His 3rd quarter report, Guinea, 1913, ARS, 2 G 13/14, suggests that material conditions should have been improved before dealing with complex social questions. Similarly, Deherme remarked that "Sentimental abolitionism fails to recognize that slavery was progress and that there is a kind of abolition that is properly a regression." Deherme 1994 (1906): conclusion.

144 Marty 1921, I: 449–50.

12   LOOKING FOR THE TRACKS. HOW THEY DID IT

1 Bloch 1953: 54–55.
2 Cruise O'Brien 1975: 28.
3 Kopytoff 1988: 485–87. I have since revised my estimates upward. See Appendix 1.
4 Meillassoux 1975b: 246. See also Baldé 1975: 212; Roberts 1988; Fuglestad 1983; Olivier de Sardan 1984: 195.
5 Memel-Foté 1988: 402–8 describes emancipation in the Ivory Coast in these terms.
6 Saurin report on Tivouane, 15 Nov., 1907, ANSOM, Contrôle 909. The numbers went from five in 1903 to sixty-eight in 1905 and back down to fourteen in 1907.
7 See Mbodj-Klein interviews from southern Saalum; Moitt 1985: 234–43; Irvine 1973: 437–47.
8   Interview, A.H. Baba Niang, Sonkorong, Mbodj-Klein collection.
9 Interview, Alpha Siré, Keur Jibi, Mbodj-Klein collection.
10 Habib Niang, Jigimar, Mbodj-Klein collection.
11 Moitt 1985: 234–43.
12 David 1980, 453–61. David suggests that between 5 percent and 10 percent of all Senegalese came to Senegal as *navetanes* or descend from *navetanes*. In addition, many people moved from elsewhere in Senegal into the peanut basin.
13 Pheffer 1975.
14 Poulet 1994 (1905).
15 Roberts 1987a, 1992 and 1996.
16 Rapport d'Ensemble, 1911, ANS, 2G 11/6. See Moitt 1985: 244–45.
17 Moitt 1985: 250–51.
18 Moitt 1985 and 1989.
19 Report on slavery, Podor, 22 Feb. 1904, ARS, K18.
20 See Klein 1968: 177–78 on French efforts to reduce demands on migrants.
21 Pélissier 1966: 496–500; David 1980.
22 Pélissier 1966: ch. 9; David 1980: 20–34.
23 Pélissier 1966: 344–47.
24 Klein 1968: 223–29.
25 Paul Marty, "Le Groupement de Bou Kunta," ARS, 13 G 67; Marty 1917. His real name was Cheikh Abou Mohammed ben Abou Naama. See also Marty 1917; Robinson 1987.
26 Marty 1917.
27 Gov. Gen. to Min. 4 March 1915, ARS, 19 G 1.
28 On charisma, see Worsley 1957; Cruise O'Brien 1988.
29 Robinson 1987. See also Cruise O'Brien 1971 and 1975; Copans 1973 and 1980; Copans *et.al.* 1972; Sy 1969; Pelissier 1966: 301–62; Coulon 1981; Dumont 1975; Marty 1917: I, 217–332; Ba 1982.
30 Cruise O'Brien 1971: 141–43. These words are now used by all Mouride *talibés* in making their submission.
31 The French were unhappy about fighting, but generally ignored Fulbe complaints. Cruise O'Brien 1971: 196–99; Cruise O'Brien 1975: 64–72; Klein 1968: 223–29.
32 Cruise O'Brien 1975: 64–65.
33 Copans 1980: 88.
34 The southern Saalum is predominantly Tijaniya. Though there was land between villages, few sites were large enough for a whole village. Padaff was settled on a site deserted after a conflict between village and canton chiefs. Elsewhere, I talked to Mourides of both servile and free origins, but the large ex-slave following of Mouride *shaykhs* often came up in casual conversation.
35 Keur Bakary in eastern Saalum was not a Mouride village, but it was over half

jaam, and two thirds of them were Mouride. Of the *jambuur,* about 60 percent were tijani. Goupakh Keur Gamou was the slave settlement of a Tijani family in the canton of Medina Sabakh, but it was majority Mouride.

36 ENEA report, Keur Bakary, 1974–75. Sy 1969: 56–57, 143–44 stresses Amadu Bamba's egalitarian message.
37 Copans 1980: 117. For a more complete version, see Copans 1973.
38 Couty 1972: 116.
39 Rocheteau 1972: 242.
40 Roch 1972, 140–42; Couty 1972: 191; Rocheteau 1972, 237–39.
41 Copans 1980: 106.
42 See maps and discussion by Gérard Brasseur in 1977: 76–78 and Mission Portères, 1952, ARS.
43 Cruise O'Brien 1971: 59.
44 Klein 1968: 223–29. By 1912, there were about 7,000 Mourides along the new line of rail. Comm. Sine-Saloum to Gov. Sen., 7 Jan 1912, ARS unclassified.
45 Cruise O'Brien 1971: 83–84 and 1975: 41. Pélissier 1966: 122 argues that the Tijaniya is more egalitarian because it recruited primarily from *jaambur,* but Cruise O'Brien argues that through submission Mouride *talibés* got land and thus independence.
46 Marty 1917, I: 217–332.
47 Sira Bagayogo, aged ninety-one, Ntentu, Bagayogo-Klein collection. Her father was a *sofa.* His wives refused to accompany him, but after Samory was finished, he headed home, where he found four brothers, who helped him get started.
48 Annual report, Buguni. 1910, ANM, 1 E 28.
49 See Roberts 1988: 288 on Bamako. I also spoke to informants who talked of people flocking in to Bamako during this period.
50 Sira Bagayogo, Ntentu, Klein-Bagayogo interviews.
51 Dokoro Samake, Ntentu, Klein Bagayogo collection.
52 Tiemoko Doumbia, Bulukura, Bagayogo-Klein collection. Dokoro Samake spoke of men learning about ways to earn money while working as porters.
53 In Kossiala, the village chief apologized for not knowing the history of the village. He explained that as a young man, he had been a hunter. He would provide game meat for villages in exchange for food and lodging, often spending over a year away from home. Today, the only big game left is wild boars, which Muslim Wasulunke do not eat.
54 Adams 1977: 73.
55 PRO, Banjul, 2/823. David 1980: 33–34 and 467.
56 David 1980: 34–42 and 113–24. See Ponty's assessment, Gov. Gen. to Min., 1318, 22 June 1908: Gov. Gen. to Min., 1098, 28 May 1911, ANSOM, Soudan I 11.
57 David 1980: 171–205; Pélissier 1966: 427–66.
58 The British paid more attention. See Swindell 1980.
59 Goerg 1986: 337–47; Suret-Canale 1970: 43–45; 1960a; 1969.
60 Political Report, Sigiri, Aug. 1905, ARS, 7 G 61. This commandant complained that his predecessor "liberated *en masse* without worrying about economic consequences."
61 Suret-Canale 1971: 49–51; 1970: 105–6, 119 and 303.
62 The first cases of laborers seeking work can be explained by drought. Political Report, Oct. 1902, ARS, 2 G 2/6. See also Fall 1993: 25–124.
63 David 1980: 34; Fall 1993: ch. 3.
64 1st quarter report, Guinea, 1909, ARS, 2 G 6/9.
65 Lt. Gov. Guinea to Gov. Gen., 30 July 1909, ARS, 7 G 63; and 30 April 1910, ANG,

2 B 53. See ANG, 2 A 7 for circulars regulating porterage and trying to restrict demands on local peoples.

66 Political Report, Mamou, April 1910, ANG, 7 G 63; see also Lt. Gov. Guinea to Gov. Gen., 30 April 1910, ANG, 2 B 53.

67 See political reports, ANG, 2 D 93. See also quarterly reports ARS, 2 G 8/16.

68 Comm. Dingiray to Lt. Gov., 26 April 1914, ANG, 2 D 75.

69 Rouch 1956; Fuglestad 1983: 69 and 87; Olivier de Sardan 1984: 176–77.

70 Political Report, Segu, June 1910, ANM, 1 E 72; Bandiagara, April 1912, ANM, 1 E 55.

71 Echenberg 1991: 11–19 and 25–32. Military service remained important in Wasulu. Many of my informants were veterans of World War II.

72 Comm. J. Villeneuve to Lt. Gov. HSN, 1 Dec. 1911, ANM, 1 D 35.

73 Political Report, Nov. 1911, Labé, ANG, 2 D 200.

74 Political Report, Jan. 190, Dingiray, ANG, 2 D 76.

75 Political reports, Kurusa, July to Nov. 1908, ANG, 2 D 190.

76 Baabu Caam, Keur Serigne Thioye, Mbodj-Klein Collection.

77 Biraan Touré, Samb. Mbodj-Klein collection.

78 See among others Baabu Khoja, Alpha Siré, Musa Ba, Samarama Dem. Mbodj-Klein collection. Others like Ibrahima Siise stressed the founding of new villages or hamlets.

79 Mbus Fadi Siise, Thyssé-Kaymor. Mbodj-Klein collection. Sokone developed rapidly as a peanut producer during the early twentieth century and attracted many migrants. It is about 85 km from Kaymor.

80 De la Roncière, Charles. Historique du Fouladou (1869–1902). ARS 1 G 295.

81 2nd Quarter Report, 1911, Guinea, ARS, 2 G 11/11

82 Letter from Bacary, 11 March 1908, ANG, 1 D 95.

83 Almamy Daouda to Comm. Mellacorée, 27 March 1908, ANG, 2 D 95.

84 Swindell 1980: 100–1; Weil 1984: 109–10.

85 Layen Njobe Sow, Ndakhar Karim, Mbodj-Klein collection.

86 Political Report, Gumbu, May 1908, ANM, 1 E 38.

87 2nd quarter report, 1913, Guinea, ARS, 2 G 13/14.

88 Habib Niang, Jigimar, Mbodj-Klein collection.

89 Interview, Al Hajj Musa Ba, Keur Musa Ba, Mbodj-Klein collection.

90 In the Quran, *Assaka* (*zakkat*) is to be given to the poor. Some informants said that *jambuur* gave to the poor and *jaam* to the masters. Some added that the masters then gave to the poor. There is no evidence that this was done. On transformation of *zakkat*, see Van Hoven 1996.

91 See also on Futa Toro, Schmitz 1986: 357.

92 Clozel's 1909 circular included a questionnaire. See Delafosse 1912: 18–25.

93 Delafosse 1912, III: 1–123. See Harrison 1988: ch. 8; Van Hoven 1990; Delafosse 1976 and Robert Cornevin's introduction to the 1972 edition of Delafosse 1912. Delafosse's first involvement with Africa was in 1891 with the Institut des Frères armés du Sahara, a group organized by Lavigerie to stop the Saharan slave trade by force. They were too few to have any effect and were soon withdrawn. Though he wrote little about slavery, Delafosse later served as France's representative to the League of Nations' Anti-Slavery Committee. Clozel was probably the most scholarly colonial governor of his generation.

94 Chanock 1985 stresses the creation and use of custom by colonial rulers. There is little comparable on French Africa, but see Snyder 1981a and 1981b.

95 Cissé 1978: ch. 1 argues that the Dina overrode all other rights in Masina. This was probably true of most Muslim states.

96 Olivier de Sardan 1976: 16–17.
97 Fuglestad 1983: 68–69; Olivier de Sardan 1976: 10 and 16.
98 Cruise O'Brien 1971: ch. 9.
99 Chastanet 1983: 5–36.
100 Annual Report, 1900, San, 28 Feb. 1901, ANM, 1 E 67.
101 Vincent 1963: 126.
102 Delaunay 1984: 69.
103 Clark 1994b: 61–64.
104 1st quarter report, 1912, HSN, ARS, 2 G 12/12. In the version that went to Paris, Ponty edited out everything that suggested that things were not fine in the Sahel. See report of 15 Oct. 1912 to Minister, same dossier.
105 Rheinhart report, 1 May 1914, ARS, 4 G 17. On the misery caused by taxation in well-watered Kurusa, see Comm. Kurusa to Lt. Gov. Guinea, 29 Dec. 1913, ANG, 2 D 185. Women wore old cloths, men wore little and children went completely nude.
106 *Chroniques*, Banankuru, 89, Jan. 1901; 100, Nov. 1903; 103, Jan. 1904, AWF.
107 Political Report, Bandiagara, July 1914, ANM, 1 E 24.
108 Tauxier was an experienced administrator who already had thirteen years in the field. He wrote eleven books and numerous articles on African history and ethnography, for example, Tauxier 1912, 1921, 1942. See Cornevin 1975.
109 Lt. Gov. to Gov. Gen., 2 July 1918, ANM, 1 E 108. My documentation on this incident consists largely of a single report which presents a very negative picture of Tauxier.
110 Telegram to Nara, 4 Feb. 1918, ANM, 1 E 103.
111 Third quarter report, Kumbia, 1917, ARS, 2 G 17/9; 2nd quarter report, 1918, ARS, 2 G 18/4; Quarterly report, ARS, 2 G 19/5. Most of this information comes from Liurette's unhappy superiors. He was an experienced administrator, but I have read none of his reports and do not know the logic of his actions or how far he went in undercutting the authority of chiefs and masters.
112 2nd quarter report, 1918, ARS, 2 G 18/4. Brevié was attached to the Governor's office, not the Inspector General.
113 The population drop was about 16,000 from 1912 to 1919. 3rd quarter report, ARS, 2 G 19/6. See also David 1980: 146–47.
114 Wynkoop 1991: 55–59.
115 Michel 1982: 100–16; Crowder 1975: 561–66; Fuglestad 1973; Kambou-Ferrand 1993.
116 Circular of 15 August 1917. See Van Vollenhoven 1920: 189–211; Hargreaves 1969: 210–14; Ismael Barry 1992: 591.
117 Johnson and Summers 1978.
118 Manchuelle 1987: ch. 6; Van Hoven 1990.
119 Conklin 1989. Manchuelle 1987: ch. 6 sees a struggle within the administration between two factions, one liberal and humanitarian, the other protectionist and authoritarian. The problem is that some men are hard to classify. Among the liberals, Clozel and Delafosse supported the use of traditional chiefs and customary law and Van Vollenhoven stressed that in any situation one person commanded. My argument here is more influenced by Conklin.
120 Johnson 1971: 205–13.
121 The best history of forced labour is Fall 1993. On the controversial Office du Niger, see Magasa 1978; Filopovich 1985; Van Beusekom 1990. On compulsory cultivation of cotton, see Roberts 1996: chs. 6 to 8.
122 Quoted in Michel 1975.

123 Delafosse's daughter has written a loving biography of him. See Delafosse 1976. He spent his last years as French representative on the League of Nations' Temporary Commission on Slavery.
124 But see Marty 1921, 444–52.
125 Manning 1982: 16, 188–93. Manning's analysis is brief, but captures many complexities of the situation. See also Newbury 1960 and Manning 1975. On the Gold Coast, see McSheffrey 1983 and Dumett and Johnson 1988.
126 Lovejoy and Hogendorn 1993: 60–63.
127 Lovejoy and Hogendorn 1993: ch. 6; on southern Nigeria, see Igbafe 1975; Tamuno 1972; Ohadike 1986.
128 Cordell 1988.
129 Cassanelli 1988.
130 Twaddle 1988.
131 Deutsch 1995.
132 Heywood 1988; Isaacman and Rosenthal 1988.
133 Grace 1975.
134 Sikainga 1996: ch. 2 is especially good on slave strategies. See also Daley 1986: 231–39, 439–46; Warburg 1978 and 1981. Fewer than 5,000 slaves were freed through official channels between 1911 and 1922. Sikainga 1996: 51. On manumission of female slaves, see Sikainga 1995. For valuable studies, see Miers and Roberts 1988.
135 Cooper 1980: ch. 5; Morton 1990. Morton unfairly accuses Cooper of painting coastal slavery as benign. See also Romero 1986.
136 Cooper 1980: 1.
137 Cooper 1980: 1.

13 AFTER THE WAR: RENEGOTIATING SOCIAL RELATIONS

1 Layen Njobu Sow, Ndakhar Karim, Mbodj-Klein Collection
2 Gov. Guinea to Gov. Gen., 13 July 1950, ARS, 2 K 15 (174).
3 General report, Buguni, 1913, ANM, 1 E 28.
4 Michel 1982: Part I; Echenberg 1991: 25–32.
5 Michel 1982: 50–57, 100–16; Johnson and Summers 1978: 27; Mbodj 1978. When Mohammed Mbodj and I interviewed in southern Saalum in 1975, we did not find a single person who had served. Informants old enough to be called up all spent the war years in the Gambia or in hiding.
6 Kersaint-Gilly 1924; on eastern Senegal, see Clark 1990: 267 and 1994b: 65; on Guinea, Johnson and Summers 1978: 28; on Niger, see Fuglestad 1983: 93.
7 Clark 1990: 230.
8 This was particularly true in Blaise Diagne's recruitment campaign of 1918. See Michel 1982: chapter 11 and 12.
9 Kersaint-Gilly 1924: 474; Clark 1994b: 65 and interviews done with Mohammed Mbodj and by Aly Kampo.
10 Circular of 25 May 1919, ANG, 7 G 63. On demobilization, see Michel 1982: 414–16.
11 Clark 1990: 230–33 and 1994b: 66–67; Manchuelle 1989a: 101.
12 Manchuelle 1989a: 102; David 1980: 122.
13 Kane 1987: ch. 10.
14 Roberts 1988: 296.
15 For Johnson and Summers 1978 it was anti-colonial protest, but actions were primarily directed against masters.

16 Political report, Guinea 1919, ARS, 2 G 19/6.
17 Report from Dubreka, ARS, 7 G 67.
18 3rd quarter report, Kankan, 1919, ARS, 2 G 19/5.
19 1st and 4th quarter reports, Kankan, 1920, ARS, 2 G 20/8.
20 4th quarter report, 1919, Beyla, ARS 2 G 19/6. In the first quarter of 1921, 1,399
     freed themselves, but remained in the cercle; 532 left. Another 780 left the second
     quarter.
21 Johnson and Summers 1978: 34.
22 4th quarter report, Macenta, 1921, ARS, 2 G 21/11.
23 Political report, Macenta, ARS, 2 G 22/12.
24 Quarterly report, Macenta, 1922, ARS, 2 G 22/12. On Sigiri, see 4th quarter report,
     ARS, 2 G 19/6.
25 Gov. Gen. Merlin to Lt. Gov., Guinea, 16 Aug. 1920, ARS, 2 G 20/8.
26 Attached to Macenta report, 4th quarter 1921, ARS, 2 G 21/11.
27 See ANG, 2 B 17.
28 Michel 1982: 409–14.
29 Echenberg 1991: 133–39; Rivière 1974: 393–94; Baldé 1957.
30 Jeng 1978: 331–35; David 1980: 45–69.
31 David 1980: 453–56, estimates that between 5 percent and 10 percent of the
     population of Senegal is made up of *navetanes* or their descendants.
32 Baldé interviewed in Gapakh Keur Gamou, a village founded by two *rimaibe* from
     the Futa, which was 71 percent slave origin. Most had cut all ties to the Futa. Baldé
     1974: 266–75.
33 Venema 1978: ch. 12.
34 Al Hajj Biraan Turé, Sam, Klein-Mbodj collection.
35 Al Hajj Musa Ba, Keur Musa Ba, Mbodj-Klein colection.
36 Al Hajj Biraan Touré, Sam, Mbodj-Klein collection. At one point, Touré had
     fifteen sons and *navétanes* working under his direction.
37 Al Hajj Biraan Turé, Sam; Samarama Dem, Ndemen; Al Hajj Musa Ba, Keur
     Musa Ba; Ibrahima Siise, Nganda, Mbodj-Klein collection.
38 Venema 1978: ch. 10; Kleene 1974.
39 Kleene 1974.
40 Venema 1978: ch. 10 sees the 1930s as the crucial years.
41 Irvine 1973: 74.
42 Irvine 1973: 185–92.
43 Ames 1953: 16–18. The ENEA village inquiries suggest that many younger *jaam*
     ignore slave–master relations as much as possible. In Padaff, young men often pay
     assaka only when their fathers insist.
44 Irvine 1973: 100–10.
45 Venema 1978: ch. 10.
46 Al Hajj Abdu Siise, Sonkorong, Mbodj-Klein collection.
47 Irvine 1973: 396. Also A.H. Musa Ba, Keur Musa Ba and Samba Ba, Colomba,
     Mbodj-Klein collection.
48 Diop's research in the Wolof heartland also shows a low percentage of slaves. Less
     than 5 percent of his informants claimed slave origins, though 21 percent claimed
     to have slaves. Diop 1981: 208.
49 Irvine 1973: 437–47; Diop 1981: 35–36
50 Silla 1965: 141–49.
51 Silla 1965: 151.
52 Venema 1978: chs. 11 and 12. When I was there, the political *responsable* of Medina
     Sabakh was of slave origin. The President of the cooperative at Keur Bakary was a

jaam.
53 Pollet and Winter 1971: ch. 7; Weigel 1982: 61–77; Samuel 1976: 104.
54 Manchuelle 1987: 297; Manchuelle 1997.
55 Adams 1985: 72.
56 Saint-Père 1925: 182.
57 Saint-Père 1925: 183.
58 Meillassoux 1975b: 246–47.
59 Samuel 1976: 106.
60 Bathily 1969: 86. These are his notes, edited by his nephew, Abdoulaye Bathily.
61 Bathily 1969: 86–87.
62 Bathily 1969: 87.
63 Manchuelle 1987: ch. 5
64 Saint-Pére 1925: 182–83.
65 Boyer 1953: 98 describes a contract in which the master provides only land and receives 10 percent of the harvest.
66 Pollet and Winter 1971: 324–24. See also Weigel 1982.
67 Report of July 1929, Kayes, ANM, 1 E 19, cited in Manchuelle, forthcoming: ch. 6.
68 Saint-Père 1925: 183.
69 Weigel 1982: 66 and 73–77. 22 percent of Weigel's former slave informants got land from someone other than their former master.
70 Pollet and Winter 1971: 255. Like most writers on slavery, Pollet and Winter write as if slaves were men – though most were women. Female slaves had not only the right to marry or sleep with free men, but were often obliged to do so.
71 Samuel 1976: 111–19. One older slave was willing to cook because he was told to do so by the chief of the slaves in his home village.
72 Pollet and Winter 1971: 255–59.
73 Report on Matam, 26 Feb. 1908, ANSOM, Contrôle 909.
74 Leservoisier 1994: 75–81.
75 Personal communication.
76 Diop 1965: 25–26.
77 Diop 1965: 70–72; Cros 1971.
78 Delaunay 1984: 134–36.
79 Jonckers 1987.
80 Linares 1987: 127–31.
81 Gastellu 1981: 35.
82 Toulmin 1992: 33.
83 Lewis 1979.
84 Grosz-Ngaté 1986: 55–58. See also Ernst 1976: 131–33.
85 Grosz-Ngaté 1986: 178. Weaving increased dramatically among *horon* during the drought years of the 1970s and 1980s.
86 Leynaud and Cissé 1978: 118.
87 Leynaud and Cissé 1978: 78–80.
88 Leynaud and Cissé 1978: 118.
89 Audiger 1961: 165.
90 Lt. Gov. Sudan to Gov. Gen., 4 Dec. 1931, ANM, 2 E 134.
91 "Faits de traite, 1933–36," ARS, 2 K 10. See also UNG, 6B/16796/10875.
92 Gov. Gen. to Min., 31 Dec. 1933, ARS, 2 K 10.
93 On the Arabian slave trade, see Miers 1989; Derrick 1975: ch. 6.
94 *Afrique Nouvelle*, 365–67, August 1954. See also *L'Essor*, the newspaper of the RDA, 3 Nov. 1954 and Derrick 1975: ch. 6.
95 Rougier 1930; Marty, 1920: II, 180; Report on Kong, 5 April 1913, ARS, 19 G 2; on

Banamba, Political Report, May 1909, ANM, 1 E 19; 2nd quarter report, HSN, 1909, ARS, 2 G 9/12; Political Report, Suarella, 1st quarter 1909, ARS, 2 G 9/13.

96 Marty 1921: 119 suggests that many Jaxanke of Tuba had to farm, but on p. 134–35 and 146 suggests that at Boké, many turned to teaching and succeeded in forging new links with former slaves.

97 Wasulu has a reputation for resistance to Islam. I was told to bring wine as gifts. This was a mistake. It is now quite Muslim, but Islamization is recent, probably linked to migration.

98 Traore 1983; Brenner 1984: 45–59; Alexandre 1970a; Moreau 1964; Froelich 1962.

99 Alexandre 1970a: 502.

100 Froelich 1962: 242. Traore 1983: 218–19 claims that Hamallah was not concerned with liberation of slaves, and that he had several "serviteurs" himself.

101 Alexandre 1970a: 507. Sylla was deported to the Ivory Coast in 1930 and developed a following there, in Sudan and Niger. See Traore 1983: 138–47 and 205–13.

102 Samuel 1976: 106.

103 Fonds Vieillard; Derman 1973: 211–23. Dupire 1994: 268 remarks that some Fulbe treat the offspring of a slave concubine as inferior. This is contrary to Muslim law.

104 Vieillard 1939 and 1940; Derman 1973: 219.

105 Derman 1973: 29.

106 Botte 1994: 131. On the *foulanisation* of *rimaibe*, see also Dupire 1994.

107 Coquery-Vidrovitch 1976 and 1977. For more detail, see Klein and Roberts 1987.

108 Ortoli 1939: 320; Paulme 1940: 106. On pawning as a response to famine, see Robert Arnaud, "Rapport sur l'esclavage en Haute Volta," submitted to Gov. Gen., 26 Nov. 1931, ARS, 2 K 5 (26). Arnaud was the only respondent to this inquiry who mentioned pawning.

109 Mgr. Thevenoud to Gov. Gen., 21 Dec. 1933, ARS, 2 K 8 (26); Senator Gautherot to Min., 12 June 1934, ARS 2 K 8 (26). Though Gautherot and Thevenoud threatened to go to the anti-slavery society, they never did so. Catholic missions preferred to operate behind the scenes.

110 Comm. Le Houx to Lt. Gov. Sudan, 2 June 1934, ARS, 2 K 8 (26); Lt. Gov. Du Fousset to Gov. Gen., 20 July 1934, ARS, 2 K 8 (26).

111 Inspector Cheruy, Report, 30 December 1936, ANSOM, Aff. Pol. 541–4.

112 Gov. Gen. to Min. Col., 17 Nov. 1936, ANSOM, Aff. pol. 541–4.

113 Gov. Gen. to Min. Col., 17 Nov. 1936, ANSOM, Aff. pol. 541–4.

114 Lt. Gov. Guinea to Gov. Gen., 27 Feb. 1937, ARS, 2 K 7.

115 Ortoli 1939.

116 Note of 12 March 1933, CSE, 62 B 1.

117 Circular to all Lt. Govs., 25 June 1936, ANSOM, Aff. pol. 541–4. On mission policy in Senegal, see CSE, 62 B and 649 A.

118 Report of 16 Jan. 1933, ANM, 1 D 210.

119 See Kampo interviews in Masina.

120 Report from Tougan, 23 Jan. 1934; Sikasso, 19 Jan. 1934; Satadugu, 15 Jan. 1934, ANM, 1 D 210.

121 Extrait du procès-verbal de passation de service concernant le cercle de Ségou, 30 April 1935, ANM, 1 D 211.

122 Comm. Ouahigouya to Lt. Gov. Sudan, 2 June 1934, ARS, 2 K 8 (26); on Sangalan, Lt. Gov., Guinea to Gov. Gen., ARS 2 K 13 (26).

123 Gov. Gen. to Lt. Gov., Guinea, 1 June 1937, ANSOM, Aff. pol. 541–4.

124 Res. Kulikoro to Comm. Bamako, 17 July 1935, ANM, 1 D 200. See also Lt. Gov. Sudan to Gov. Gen., 20 July 1934; Gov. Gen. to Min., 6 Oct. 1934, ARS 2 K 8 (26).

125 Inspecteur des Affaires Indigènes, "Contrat de mise en gage," 14 June 1934, ANM, 1 D 211.
126 Note from Procureur-Général 4 Sept. 1934, ARS, 2 K 8.
127 Gov. Gen. to Lt. Gov. Sudan, n.d. 1934, ANM, 1 D 211.
128 Min. Col. to Gov. Gen., 30 Dec. 1936, ANSOM, Aff. pol. 541–4.
129 Circular, Gov. Gen. to all Lieutenant Governors, 26 June 1936, ANSOM, Aff. pol. 541–1.
130 Circular 296, 10 May 1937, ARS, K 13 (26).
131 De Latour 1980: 126–27 cites a type of voluntary slavery.
132 Personal communication, Myron Echenberg.
133 Lawler 1992: 13 says that all social classes were called up. Slave status is not an issue in Lawler's book, perhaps because she interviewed largely in two areas where slavery was not important, Man and Korhogo.
134 Rivière 1975: 173.
135 Rivière 1974.
136 Gov. Sudan to Gov. Gen., 9 Feb. 1950, ANS, 2 K 15 (174).
137 Gov. Sudan to Gov. Gen., #16, January 1950, ARS, 2K 15 (174).
138 Gov. Sudan to Gov. Gen., 7 July 1950, ARS 2 K 15 (174). *Bella* were about 43 percent of a population of 25,000. The nobles were less than 5 percent.
139 Capt. Forgeot, Report on Bellah, n.d., ARS, 2 K 15 (174).
140 Dir. Pol. Aff. to Gov. Sudan, 9 Sept. 1949, ARS, 2 K 15 (174).
141 Comm. Nioro to Gov. Sudan, 6 April 1948; Gov. Sudan to Gov. Gen., ARS, 2 K 15 (174).
142 On the continuing southward movement of *harratin* seeking "to escape the close attentions of their former masters," see Toulmin 1992: 22.
143 Gov. Sudan to Gov. Gen., 16, January 1950, ARS, 2 K 15 (174).
144 J. Luciani, Monograph of Kaarta-Soninke, 1952, ANM, 1 D 51.
145 Suret-Canale 1971: 420–22.
146 Olivier de Sardan 1984: 394–95. See also Cissé 1978: 150.
147 Hopkins 1966.

14   A QUESTION OF HONOR

 1 Olivier de Sardan 1984: 29.
 2 Riesman 1992: 15.
 3 Chanock 1985: 15.
 4 Maugham 1961: chs. 10 and 11.
 5 Maugham 1961: 164.
 6 Maugham 1961: 201–3.
 7 Rivière 1975: 174–77; H. Baldé 1957; Botte 1994.
 8 Botte 1994: 112.
 9 Suret-Canale, 1966; Rivière 1974; Baldé 1957.
10 M. Baldé 1974; H. Baldé 1957; Rivière 1975: 176.
11 Botte 1994: 121–24.
12 Rivière 1974: 396.
13 Wynkoop 1991: 124.
14 Wynkoop 1991: 71–72.
15 Ernst 1976.
16 Cissé 1978: Introduction.
17 Awad 1966: 99. Senegal's response, like most responses, simply detailed its laws dealing with both the ownership and trade in slaves.

18 Ames 1953: 18.
19 Miner 1953: 40.
20 Marty 1921, I: 449–50.
21 Prakash 1990.
22 Bazin 1975. See also Olivier de Sardan 1984.
23 Diop 1981.
24 A noble could take a slave wife or concubine. Many rulers descended from slave concubines. A noble could not marry a member of the artisan castes. In spite of this the artisans were economically better off than slaves because of the way they were linked to the powerful.
25 Alpha Mamadu Sendeque, Kampo collection.
26 Musa Ba. Abdu Siise, a *jaambur*, put it in almost the same words. Mbodj-Klein collection.
27 Biraan Ture, Mbodj-Klein collection.
28 Alpha Mamadu Sendeque, Kampo collection.
29 Boreima Boré, Kampo collection.
30 Botte 1994: 117.
31 Pollet and Winter 1971: 249.
32 Klein-Mbodj collection.
33 Klein-Mbodj collection.
34 Suret-Canale 1969b; Botte 1994: 112–14.
35 Botte 1994: 118. Most of Botte's *rimaibe* informants knew where their ancestors came from, their clans and their totemic taboos. See also Dupire 1994.
36 De Bruijn and Van Dijk 1993: 99; Ver Ecke 1994: 42.
37 Dupire 1994: 273. For comparison, see Glassman 1991 on the struggle of slaves and former slaves to become Swahili.
38 Botte 1994: 122–24.
39 Belko Tambura, Sare Seyni, Kampo collection
40 Roberts 1980d.
41 Moitt 1985.
42 My reflections about honor are very much influenced by Ly 1966. This thesis has unfortunately never been published, but its argument is summed up in Ly 1967. See also Bazin 1975; Olivier de Sardan 1984: 27–39; Pollet and Winter 1971: 237–61.
43 Ames 1953: 17. Pollet and Winter 1971: 432 make the same point.
44 Personal communication.
45 Belko Tambura, Kampo collection.
46 Alpha Mamadu Sendeque, Kampo collection.
47 Ames 1953: 17. Some of the license given to slave women was also given to casted women, particularly to griottes. There was a taboo against sexual relations with griottes, which was coupled to a belief that they were specially adept at the sexual arts.
48 Keita: 1959.
49 Maugham 1961: 167–68.
50 Orsini 1966.
51 Meillassoux 1975b: 228–30. See also Pollet and Winter 1971: 26 and 250; Olivier de Sardan 1976: 19 and 1984: 35–39; Klein 1983a: 87–88.
52 Arnaud 1910.
53 See also Pollet and Winter 1971: 246. A former slave woman described the dances to Maria Grosz-Ngaté. Personal communication.
54 Riesman 1977 (1974): 121.
55 Vincent 1963: 130.

56 Ernst 1976: 131–33.
57 Miner 1953: 97–98. The Gabibi were serfs of the Arma, the descendants of the Moroccans, who conquered the area in 1591. See Baldé 1957 on such beliefs in Futa Jallon.
58 Riesman 1977 (1974) and 1992.
59 Riesman 1992: 61.
60 Riesman 1992: 15. In this book, Riesman tries to understand why similar approaches to child-rearing produce radically different personality structures. On *pulaaku*, see also Ver Ecke 1994 and Breedveld and De Bruijn 1996.
61 Olivier de Sardan 1976. Olivier has used interviews with slaves more effectively than any other scholar working in the area. See Olivier de Sardan 1984. The most interesting methodological work is Diawara 1985 and 1989, but his discussion of slave traditions focuses on the royal slaves. See also Botte 1994; Pollet and Winter 1971 and some of the articles in Meillassoux 1975a.
62 De Bruijn and Van Dijk 1993: 103.
63 See also Olivier de Sardan 1984: ch. 2.
64 Bazin 1975; Olivier de Sardan 1982 and 1984: 27–39.
65 Baier 1980: 177.
66 Robinson 1987.

APPENDIX 1   HOW MANY SLAVES?

1 Except where specified, the source is ARS, K 18 to 22.
2 Deherme's 1906 report gave an estimate of 600,000 for Haut-Sénégal-Niger. Kanya-Forstner and Lovejoy 1994: 166.
3 Olivier de Sardan 1984: 191. Robert Arnaud, an astute early colonial administrator, gave an even higher estimate of ten to one. De Latour 1987: 147.
4 Hill, Randall and Sullivan 1982.
5 ANS 22 G 19.
6 Admin. Futa Jallon to Lt. Gov. Guinea, 1 Dec. 1905, ANSOM Guinée XIV 3.
7 Richard-Molard 1953c, 85–93. He simply counted the slave population of the *rundes*, but a significant number of *rimaibe* lived in the *fulassos*: concubines, wives, retainers.
8 Suret-Canale 1969b.
9 Some missionaries estimated the slave population on the coast at 80 percent. Msgr. Lorder to Cardinal Ledochowski, Propaganda, CSE, 193B VII.

APPENDIX 5   SLAVE PRICE, PRE-1904

1 Caillié 1830, I: 316.
2 Soleillet 1887.
3 V. Schoelcher interpellation in Senate, 1 March 1880, JO de 2 mars 1880. Citing Villeger in *Eglise Libre*, 26 Sept. 1879.
4 Comm. Kayes to Comm. Sup., 20 March 1890, ANM 1 E 191.
5 ANM 1 Q 74
6 P. Cros, "Mission de Kita (Soudan Francais)," *Annales*, (1894), 41–57.
7 ARS K14
8 Report on slavery, ARS, K 14.
9 ARS, K 14.
10 Travelling Commissioner Cecil Sitwell to Col. Off., 10 Sept. 1899. PRO, CO 87/59
11 White Fathers, *Chroniques*, Jan. 1901.
12 White Fathers, *Chroniques*, Jan. 1901.

Bibliography

I ORAL SOURCES

1 MBODJ-KLEIN COLLECTION (SENEGAL)

Alpha Siré, Keur Jibi, 18 January 1975
Biraan Kumba Siise, Thyssé-Kaymor, 19 January 1975
Biraan Ture, Samb, 19 January and 12 February 1975
Baabu Xoja Siise, Ndimba Tuba, 21 January 1975
Al Hajj Musa Ba, Keur Musa Ba, 23 January 1975
Samba Ba, Colomba, 24 January 1975
Al Hajj Baba Niang, Sonkorang, 27 January 1975
Al Hajj Abdu Siise, Sonkorang, 29 January 1975
Mbus Fadi Siise, Thyssé-Kaymor, 6 February 1975
Keba Ramata Siise, Bur Sonkorang, 7 February 1975
Usman Njay, Bumi Kaymor, 10 February 1975
Layen Njobu Sow, Ndakhar Karim, 12 February 1975
Habib Niang, Jigimar, 13 February 1975
Samarama Dem, Ndemen, 18 February 1975
Ibrahima Siise, Nganda, 20 February 1975
Baabu Caam, Keur Serigne Thioye, 23 February 1975

2 KAMPO COLLECTION (MASINA), AUGUST 1984

Alpha Mamdou Sendeque, Konna
Bada Bocoum, Mopti
Belko Tambura, Sare Seyni
Amirou Tahikiri, Tahikiri
Amadou Cissé, Sevaré
Boreima Boré, Koniba Boré
Mamadou Guisseh

3 BAGAYOGO-KLEIN COLLECTION (WASULU)

Tiemoko Doumbia, Bulukura, 10–12 February 1989
Jonkoro Doumbia, Bulukura, 10 February–5 March 1989
Dokoro Samake, Ntentu, 14–15 February 1989
Musa Samake, Ntentu, 14–15 February
Siré Bagayogo, Ntentu, 16 February 1989
Kani Tumani Bagayogo, Kossiala, 27 February–1 March 1989
Mamadou Jakite, Kalana, 3 March 1989

II   ARCHIVES AND LIBRARIES CONSULTED

Archives Nationales, Dakar, Senegal
Library of Institut Fondamental d'Afrique Noire, Dakar
Archives Nationales, Bamako, Mali
Institut des Sciences Humaines, Bamako, Mali
Archives Nationales, Conakry, Guinea
Bibliothèque Nationale, Conakry, Guinea
Archives Nationales, Section Outre-Mer, Aix-en-Provence, France
Archives de la Congrégation du Saint Esprit, Chevilly-Larue, France
Archives of the White Fathers, Rome
United Nations Archives, Geneva
Public Record Office, Banjul
Public Record Office, London
Rhodes House, Oxford University
Centre des hautes études administratives sur l'Afrique et l'Asie

III   UNPUBLISHED SOURCES

Ames, David. 1953. Plural Marriage among the Wolof in the Gambia, Unpublished
  PhD thesis, Northwestern University
Atchebro, D. D. 1990. La Société des Nations et la Lutte contre l'Esclavage 1922–1938,
  Mémoire, Institut Universitaire des Hautes Etudes Internationales
Baldé, Hacimou. 1957. Le Foutah et l'esclavage, Mémoire, ENFOM
Baldé, Mamadou Saliou. 1974. Changements sociaux et migration au Fuuta-Jalon.
  Les Peul du Fuuta dans le milieu rural sénégalais, Doctorat du 3e cycle, Univer-
  sité de Paris-V
Barrows, Leland C. 1974b. General Faidherbe, the Maurel et Prom Company and
  French Expansion in Senegal, Unpublished Ph.D. thesis, UCLA
Barry, Ibrahima. L'occupation toucouleur du Macina, Mémoire, Ecole Normale
  Supérieur, Bamako
Barry, Ismael. 1971. Contribution à l'étude de l'histoire de la Guinée: les Hubbu de
  Fitaba et les almami du Futa, Mémoire de Maîtrise, Institut Pédagogique de
  Kankan
  1992. Le Fuuta Jaloo face à la colonisation, Unpublished doctoral thesis, Université
  de Paris-VII
Bathily, Abdoulaye. 1985. Guerriers, tributaires et marchands. Le Gajaaga (ou
  Galam), le Pays de l'Or. Le développement et la regression d'une formation
  économique et social sénégalaise c. 8e–19e siècle, Unpublished thesis, Université
  de Dakar
Baum, Robert M. 1986. A Religious and Social History of the Diola-Esulalu in
  Pre-Colonial Senegambia, Unpublished Ph.D. thesis, Yale University
Bazin, Jean. 1972. Commerce et predation: l'état bambara de Ségou et ses commu-
  nautés marka, Conference on Manding Studies, London (SOAS)
Boulègue, Jean. 1986. La traite, l'état, l'islam. Les royaumes wolofs du dix-cinquième
  au dix-huitième siècle, Unpublished thèse d'état, Université de Paris-I
Brown, William A. 1969. The Caliphate of Hamdullahi, c. 1818–64, Unpublished
  Ph.D. thesis, University of Wisconsin
Case, Glenna. 1979. Wasipe under the Ngbanya, Unpublished Ph.D. thesis, North-
  western University
Charpentier, G. 1952. Avec les Peuls de la subdivision de Djenné, Mémoire 1975,
  CHEAM

Cissé, Salmana. 1978. L'esclavage "domestique" dans la partie Gourma du Moyen Niger: Structure sociale et comportement de classe, Thèse du 3e cycle, Université de Paris-VII

Cissoko, Sekene Mody. 1969. Contribution a l'histoire politique des royaumes du Khasso dans le Haut-Sénégal. Des origines a la conquête française (XVIIe–1890), 2 vol., Unpublished thèse d'état, Universite de Paris-I

Clark, Andrew. 1990. Economy and Society in the Upper Senegal Valley, 1850–1920, Unpublished Ph.D. thesis, Michigan State University

  1994c. Freedom Villages and the Demise of Slavery in the Upper Senegal Valley (West Africa), 1887–1910, Unpublished paper, African Studies Association, Toronto

Colvin, Lucie. 1972. Kayor and its Diplomatic Relations with Saint-Louis-du-Sénégal, 1763–1861, Unpublished Ph.D. thesis, Columbia University

Conklin, Alice. 1989. A Mission to Civilize: Ideology and Imperialism in French West Africa, 1895–1930, Unpublished Ph.D. thesis, Princeton University

Copans, Jean. 1973. Stratification sociale et organisation du travail agricole dans les villages Wolof Mourides du Sénégal, Doctorat du 3e Cycle, Ecole Pratique des Hautes Etudes

Copans, Jean, P. Couty, J. Roch, G. Rocheteau. 1972. Maintenance sociale et changements économiques au Sénégal. Doctrine économique et pratique du travail chez les Mourides, Paris, ORSTOM

Cordell, Dennis. 1983. Black Africa and the Sahara: The Demographic Implications of the Muslim Slave Trade in the Late Nineteenth Century, Paper presented to American Historical Association, San Francisco, 1983

  1990. The Sexuality of Eunuchs: Emasculation, Masculinity, and Gender in Africa and Elsewhere, Paper presented to Conference Toward a History of Gendered Man in Africa, University of Minnesota, April 1990

Couty, P. 1972a. Emploi du temps et organisation du travail agricole dans un village wolof mouride: Darou Rahmane II, Paris, ORSTOM

  1972b. Travaux collectifs en milieu wolof mouride: Darou Rahmane II, Paris, ORSTOM

Cros, C. R. 1971. Les migrations et la colonisation rurale au Sénégal. Quelques changements sociaux en milieu rural, Doctorat du 3e cycle, Université de Toulouse

Daget, Serge. 1986. Les Aléas de l'abolition de la traite au Sénégal, Colloque international pour le tricentenaire du Code Noir, Dakar, Senegal

Deutsch, Jan-Georg. 1995. What Happened to All the Slaves? Colonial Policy, Emancipation, and the Transformation of Slave Societies in German and British East Africa (Tanganyika), c. 1890–1930, Paper presented to African Studies Association, Orlando, Florida, November 1995

Diallo, D. 1971. L'Organisation politico-sociale du Diwal du Labé dans la Confédération Musulman du Fouta Djallon, Mémoire, Institut Polytechnique Gamal Abdul Nasser, Kankan

Diawara, Mamadou. 1985. La Dimension sociale et politique des traditions orales du Royaume de Jaara (Mali) du XVe au milieu du XIXe Siècle, Doctorat du 3e cycle, EHESS

Echenberg, Myron. 1971b. African Reaction to French Conquest: Upper Volta in the Late Nineteenth Century, Unpublished Ph.D. thesis, University of Wisconsin

Elbl, Ivana. 1983. Slavery and the Slavery Trade in Coastal West Africa and the Opening of the Atlantic Trade, Unpublished paper, Canadian Association of African Studies

1985. West Africa and the Portuguese Trade, Unpublished Ph.D. thesis, University of Toronto

Filipovich, Jean. 1985. The Office du Niger under Colonial Rule: Its Origins, Evolution and Character (1920–1960), Unpublished Ph.D. thesis, McGill University

Fondacci, P. 1946. Maures et serviteurs au pays nomades d'Afrique (Mauritanie, Soudan). Monograph # 811, CHEAM

Fozard, Lyte Mitchell. 1975. Charles-Louis de Saulces de Freycinet: the Railway and the Expansion of the French Empire in North and West Africa 1877–1923, Unpublished Ph.D. thesis, Boston University

Garner, Reuben. 1970. Watchdogs of Empire. The French Colonial Inspection Service in Action, 1815–1913, Unpublished Ph.D. thesis, University of Rochester

Ghomsi, Emmanuel. 1968. Le Gouverneur Albert Grodet au Soudan Française (Novembre 1893 à Juin 1895), Mémoire de maitrise, Université de Dakar

Green, Kathryn. 1984. The Foundation of Kong: A Study in Dyula and Sonongui Ethnic Identity, Unpublished Ph.D. thesis, Indiana University

Grosz-Ngaté, Maria. 1986. Bambara Men and Women and the Reproduction of Social Life in Sana Province, Mali, Unpublished Ph.D. thesis, Michigan State University

Guemas, M. 1957. Bellahs et Harratines, Mémoire, Ecole Coloniale

Guèye, Mbaye. 1969. L'Esclavage au Sénégal du XVIIe au XIXe siècle, Thèse du 3e cycle, Université de Nantes

Handloff, Robert. 1982. The Dyula of Gyaman: A Study of Politics and Trade in the Nineteenth Century, Unpublished Ph.D. thesis, Northwestern University

Harmon, Stephen. 1988. The Expansion of Islam Among the Bambara under French Rule: 1890–1940, Unpublished Ph.D. thesis, University of California, Los Angeles

Hawkins, Joye Bowman. 1980. Conflict, Interaction, and Change in Guinea-Bissau: Fulbe Expansion and its Impact, 1850–1900, Unpublished Ph.D. thesis, UCLA

Holmes, LeVell. 1977. Tieba Traore, Fama of Kenedougou: Two Decades of Political Development, Unpublished Ph.D. thesis, University of California, Berkeley

Hornac, Jean. 1947. Le Rachat des hormas au Trarza, Doc. 2180, CHEAM

1953. Le problème des serviteurs en Mauritanie Monograph 2,202, CHEAM

Hubbell, Andrew. 1996. Patronage and Predation: A Social History of Colonial Chieftaincies in a Chiefless Region – Souroudougou (Burkina Faso), 1850–1946, Unpublished Ph.D. Thesis, Stanford University

Idowu, H. O. 1966. The Conseil Général in Senegal, 1879–1920, Unpublished Ph.D. thesis, University of Ibadan

Imbert, G. (n.d.). Une Epopée française au Soudan de 1894 à 1899 avec les spahis de Laperrine, ed. P. Deloncle, Typescript

Irvine, Judith. 1973. Caste and Communication in a Wolof village, Unpublished Ph.D. thesis, University of Pennsylvania

Irwin, Paul. 1973. An Emirate of the Niger Bend: A Political History of Liptako in the Nineteenth Century, Unpublished Ph.D. thesis, University of Wisconsin

Jeng, A. A. O. 1978. An Economic History of the Gambian Groundnut Industry 1830–1924: The Evolution of an Export Economy, Unpublished Ph.D. thesis, University of Birmingham

Ka, I. 1981. L'évolution sociale à Saint-Louis du Sénégal du XIXe siècle au début du XXe siècle, Thèse du 3e cycle, Université de Dakar

Kane, M. 1984. L'esclavage à St. Louis et à Gorée à travers les archives notariées: 1817–1848, Mémoire de maîtrise, Université de Dakar

Kane, M. M. 1987. A History of the Fuuta Tooro, 1890s-1920s: Senegal under Colonial Rule, Unpublished Ph.D. thesis, Michigan State University

Kane, Omar. 1986. Le Fuuta Tooro des Satigi aux Almaami (1512–1807), Doctorat

d'Etat, Université de Dakar
Keita, Cheikna. 1959. Les survivances de l'esclavage et du servage en Afrique noire, Mémoire, Ecole Nationale de la France d'Outre-Mer
Kleene, Paul. 1974. Unités experimentales du Sine Saloum: régime foncier et possibilités de restructuration agraire a N'Dakhar Karim. Institut de Recherches Agronomiques Tropicales et des Cultures Vivrières (unpublished)
Leary, Frances. 1970. Islam, Politics and Colonialism. A Political History of Islam in the Casamance Region of Senegal (1850–1914), Unpublished Ph.D. thesis, Northwestern University
Le Boulleux, L. 1963. L'esclavage dans l'ouest saharien, Mémoire 3824, CHEAM
Lewis, John V. 1979. Descendants and Crops: Two Poles of Production in a Malian Peasant Village, Unpublished Ph.D. thesis, Yale University
Lopes, Carlos. 1988. Les Kaabunke: Structures Politiques et Mutation, Doctorat ès lettres, Université de Paris-I
Ly, Babacar. 1966. L'honneur et les valeurs morales dans les sociétés oulof et toucouleur du Sénégal, Etude de Sociologie, Unpublished thèse du 3e cycle, Paris
Manchuelle, François. 1987. Background to Black African Emigration to France: The Labour Migrations of the Soninke, 1848–1987, Unpublished Ph.D. thesis, University of California, Santa Barbara
Marcson, Michael D. 1976. European–African Interaction in the precolonial period: Saint Louis, Senegal, 1758–1854, Unpublished Ph.D. thesis, Princeton University
Mbodj, Mohammed. 1978. Un Exemple d'économie coloniale, le Sine-Saloum (Sénégal) de 1887 à 1940: Cultures arichidières et mutations sociales, Unpublished thèse du 3e cycle, Université de Paris-VII
McDougall, E. Ann. 1980. The Ijil Salt Industry, Unpublished Ph.D. thesis, University of Birmingham
McGowan, Winston. 1975. Futa Jallon and the Foundation of French Colonial Rule, 1794–1895, Unpublished Ph.D. thesis, School of Oriental and African Studies, London
McLane, Margaret. 1992. Economic Expansionism and the Shape of Empire: French Enterprise in West Africa, 1850–1914, Unpublished Ph.D. thesis, University of Wisconsin
Memel-Foté, Haris. 1988. L'esclavage dans les sociétés lignagères d'Afrique noire: Exemple de la Côte d'Ivoire précoloniale, 1700–1920, Thèse d'état, Université de Paris and Ecole des Hautes Etudes en Science Sociales
Miers, Suzanne. 1986. Britain, the League of Nations and the Suppression of Slavery, Ninth International Economic History Congress, Berne
    1988. Britain and the suppression of Slavery in Ethiopia, Eighth International Conference on Ethiopian Studies, Addis Ababa
Moitt, Bernard. 1985. Peanut Production and Social Change in the Dakar Hinterland: Kajoor and Bawol, 1840–1940, Unpublished Ph.D. thesis, University of Toronto
Monteil, Charles. 1896–98. Journal d'un jeune administrateur colonial stagiaire 1896–1897–1898, Manuscript
Mouser, Bruce. 1971. Trade and Politics in the Nunez and Pongo Rivers, 1790–1865, Unpublished Ph.D. Thesis, Indiana University
O'Sullivan, John. 1976. Developments in the Social Stratification of Northwest Ivory Coast during the Eighteenth and Nineteenth Centuries: From a Malinke Frontier Society to the Liberation of Slaves by the French – 1907, Unpublished Ph.D. thesis, UCLA
Olivier de Sardan, Jean-Pierre. 1981. Contradictions sociales et impact colonial, Doctorat ès-lettres, Université de Paris-VII

Orsini, P. 1966. Survivance des "Non-Libres" au Sahara et particulièrement à Tindouf. CHEAM 4074

Pheffer, Paul. 1975. Railroads and Aspects of Social Change in Senegal 1878–1933, Unpublished Ph.D. thesis, University of Pennsylvania

Pouncy, Hilliard. 1981. Colonial Racial Attitudes and Colonial Labor Laws in British West Africa, 1815–1946, Unpublished Ph.D. thesis, Massachusetts Institute of Technology

Quimby, Lucy. 1972. Islam among the Dyula of Kongbougou from 1880 to 1970, Unpublished Ph.D. thesis, University of Wisconsin

Reyss, Nathalie. 1983. Saint-Louis du Sénégal à l'époque précoloniale. L'Emergence d'une société métisse, 1650–1854, Thèse du 3e cycle, Université de Paris-I

Rivière, Claude. 1975. Dynamique de la stratification sociale en Guinée, Thèse du doctorat d'état, Université de Paris-V

Roberts, Richard. 1978. The Maraka and the Economy of the Middle Niger Valley, 1712–1905, Unpublished Ph.D. thesis, University of Toronto

Roberts, Richard. 1980d. Maraka Historical Texts. Transcripts of Oral Data Collected in the Segu Region of the Republic of Mali, 1976–1977. Typescript

Robinson, David. 1987b. Brokerage and Hegemony in Senegal, Conference on New Perspectives on Colonial Africa, University of Illinois, March 1987

Roch, J. 1972. Emploi du temps et organisation du travail agricole dans un village wolof mouride: Kaossara. ORSTOM

Rondeau, Chantal. 1980. La Société Senufo du Sud Mali (1870–1950) de la tradition à la dépendance, Unpublished thèse du 3e cycle, Université de Paris-VII

Rothiot, Jean-Paul. 1984. Zarmakoy Aouta: les débuts de la domination coloniale dans le cercle de Dosso 1898–1913, Unpublished thesis, Université de Paris-VII

Samake, Maximin. 1984. Pouvoir traditionnel et conscience paysanne: Les Kafow de la région de Bougouni – Mali, Unpublished thèse du 3e cycle, Ecole des Hautes Etudes en Sciences Sociales

Samb, Babacar. 1985. La Legislation islamique relative à l'esclavage: la fosse entre la loi et son application effective, Colloque International pour le Tricentenaire du Code Noir, Dakar

Silla, O. 1965. Les castes dans la société ouolof. Aspects traditionnels, persistances actuelles, Mémoire, Ecole Pratique des Hautes Etudes

Sugy, Catherine. 1975. Economic Growth and Secular Trends in the Precolonial Sudanic Belt, Unpublished Ph.D. thesis, Columbia University

Thiero, Seydou. 1985. Les Ngolosiw et la décadence du Fanga du Segou 1818–1893, Mémoire Fin d'étude, Ecole Normale Supérieure, Bamako

Thompson, J. Malcolm. (n.d.). Mechanics, Firemen, and Laptots: West Africans in the French Colonial Marine, 1864–1887, Working Papers, Social History Workshop, University of Minnesota

    1989. In Dubious Service: The Recruitment and Stabilization of West African Maritime Labor by the French Colonial Military, 1659–1900, Unpublished Ph.D. thesis, University of Minnesota

Van Beusekom, Monica. 1990. Colonial Rural Development: French Policy and African Response at the Office du Niger, Soudan Français (Mali), 1920–1960, Unpublished Ph.D. thesis, Johns Hopkins University

Ward, Jennifer. 1976. The Bambara–French Relationship, 1880–1915, Unpublished Ph.D. thesis, University of California, Los Angeles

Warms, Richard. 1987. Continuity and Change in Patterns of Trade in Southern Mali, Unpublished Ph.D. thesis, Syracuse University

Wynkoop, Andrée. 1991. The Political Economy of Migration: A Case Study of the

Impact of Out-Migration in Rural Guinea, Unpublished Ph.D. thesis, Boston University

IV PUBLISHED WORKS

Atlas National du Sénégal. 1971. Paris
Abitbol, Michel. 1979. *Tombouctou et les Arma*. Paris
Adams, Adrian. 1977. *Le long voyage des gens de fleuve*. Paris
Adams, Adrian. 1985. *La Terre et les gens du fleuve*. Paris.
Alexandre, Pierre. 1970a. A West African Islamic Movement: Hamallism in French West Africa. In Ali Mazrui and Robert Rotberg, eds., *Protest and Power in Black Africa*. New York, 497–512
    1970b. Chiefs, Commandants and Clerks: Their Relationship from Conquest to Decolonisation in French West Africa. In M. Crowder and O. Ikime, eds., *West African Chiefs*. New York, 1–13
Álmada, Alvares de. 1964. Tratado Breve dos Rios de Guiné. In Antonio Brasio, ed., *Monumenta Missionaria Africana – Africa Ocidental (1570–1600)*. Vol. III. Lisbon
Amselle, Jean-Loup. 1977. *Les négociants de la savane. Histoire et organisation sociale des Kooroko (Mali)*. Paris
    1985. Lignage, esclavage, contrat, salariat: l'évolution de l'organisation du commerce à longue distance chez les Kooroko (Mali). In C. Coquery-Vidrovitch and P. Lovejoy, eds., *The Workers of African Trade*. Beverly Hills, 123–36
    1990. *Logiques métisses: Anthropologie de l'identité en Afrique et ailleurs*. Paris
Amselle, Jean-Loup and Elikia M'Bokolo, eds. 1985. *Au coeur de l'ethnie: ethnies, tribalisme et état en Afrique*. Paris
Anonymous. 1905. L'odieux traffic. *Action Coloniale*: 439–47
    1907. *Instructions à l'usage des administrateurs du Haut-Sénégal-Niger*. Paris
    1939. *Coutumiers Juridiques de l'Afrique Occidentale Française*. Paris
Arcin, André. 1911. *Histoire de la Guinée française*. Paris
Arnaud, Robert. 1910. *Le Commandant et les Foulbe*. Paris
    1922. *Le Chef de Porte-Plume*. Paris
    1932. Les formes anciennes de l'esclavage dans la boucle méridionale du Niger. *Etudes de sociologie et d'ethnologie juridique* 2: 23–64
Asiwaju, A. I. 1979. Control through Coercion: A Study of the Indigenat Regime in the French West African Administration, 1887–1946. *BIFAN* 41: 35–71
Audiger, Jeanne. 1961. Les Ouolofs du Bas-Ferlo. *Cahiers Outre-Mer*. 54: 157–81
Austen, R. 1987. *African Economic History*. London.
Austen, Ralph. 1990. Marginalization, Stagnation and Growth: The Trans-Saharan Caravan Trade in the Era of European Expansion, 1500–1900. In J. D. Tracey, ed., *The Rise of Merchant Empires: Long-Distance Trade in the Early Modern World 1350–1750*. Cambridge, 311–50
    1992. The Mediterranean Islamic Slave Trade Out of Africa: A Tentative Census. In E. Savage, ed., *The Human Commodity: Perspectives on the Trans-Saharan Slave Trade*. London, 214–48
Awad, Mohammed. 1966. *Report on Slavery*. New York, United Nations
Azarya, Victor. 1978. *Aristocrats Facing Change: The Fulbe in Guinea, Nigeria and Cameroon*. Chicago
    1980. Traders and the Center in Massina, Kong and Samori's State. *IJAHS* 13: 420–56
Ba, Amadou Hampaté and Marcel Cardaire. 1957. *Tierno Bokar. Le Sage de Bandiagara*. Paris

Ba, Amadou Hampaté and Jacques Daget. 1955. *L'empire peul de Macina*. Dakar

Ba, Oumar, ed. 1976. *La Pénétration française au Cayor*. Dakar

ed. 1982. *Ahmadou Bamba face aux autorités coloniales (1889–1927)*. Dakar

Bah, Thierno Mouctar. 1981. Les forts français et le controle de l'espace dans le Haut-Sénégal, 1855–98. In *Le sol, la parole, et écrit. 2000 ans d'histoire africaine*. Paris

1985. *Architecture militaire traditionelle et poliorcétique dans le Soudan Occidental*. Yaounde

Baier, Stephen. 1980. *An Economic History of Central Niger*. Oxford

Baillaud, Emile. 1902. *Sur les routes du Soudan*. Toulouse

Baks, C., J.C. Breman and A.T.J. Nooij. 1966. Slavery as a System of Production in Tribal Society. *Bijdragen tot de Taal-, Land-, en Volkenkunde van Nederlandsche-Indiê* 122: 90–109

Baldé, Mamadou Saliou. 1975. L'esclavage et la guerre sainte au Fouta Jallon. In C. Meillassoux, ed., *L'esclavage en Afrique précoloniale*. Paris, 183–220

1986. Crises et mutations sociales au Futa-Jalon. In M. Adamu and A.H.M. Kirk-Greene, eds., *Pastoralists of the West African Savanna*. Manchester, 267–82

Barrows, Leland C. 1974a. The Merchants and General Faidherbe: Aspects of French Expansion in Senegal in the 1850s. *RFHOM* 61

1976. Faidherbe and Senegal: A Critical Discussion. *ASR* 19: 95–118

1978. Louis Léon Cesar Faidherbe (1818–1889). In P. Duignan and L.H. Gann, eds., *African Proconsuls*. New York, 51–79

1980. Some Paradoxes of Pacification: Senegal and France in the 1850s and 1860s. In R. Dumett and B.K. Swartz, eds., *West African Cultural Dynamics*. The Hague, 515–44

Barry, Boubacar. 1972. *Le Royaume de Waalo*. Paris

1976. *Bokar Biro: Le dernier grand almamy du Fouta Djallon*. Daka

1978. Crise politique et importance des révoltes populaires au Futa Dyalon du XIXe siècle. *Afrika Zamani* (8–9)

1988a. *La Sénégambie du XVe au XIXe siècle. Traite négrière, Islam et conquête coloniale*. Paris

1988b. Traite négrière et esclavage interne au Sénégal au XVIIIe siècle. In S. Daget, ed., *De la traite à l'esclavage*. Paris, 213–22

Barry Boubacar and Leonhard Harding, eds. 1992. *Commerce et commerçants en Afrique de l'ouest: Le Sénégal*. Paris

Barry, Boubacar and Jean Suret-Canale. 1974. The Western Atlantic Coast to 1800. In J.F.A. Ajayi and M. Crowder, eds., *History of West Africa*. 2nd edn., Vol. I. London

Barth, Heinrich. 1957–58. *Travels and Discoveries in North and Central Africa*. 3 Vols. London

Bathily, Abdoulaye. 1970. Mamadou Lamine Dramé et la résistance anti-impérialiste dans le Haut-Sénégal, 1885–1887. *Notes africaines* 125: 20–32

1972. La conquête française du Haute Fleuve (Sénégal) 1818–1887. *BIFAN* 34: 67–112

1986. La Traite atlantique des esclaves et ses effets économiques et sociaux en Afrique: Le cas du Galam, royaume de l'hinterland sénégambien au dix-huitième siècle. *JAH* 27: 269–93

1989. *Les Portes de l'Or. Le royaume de Galam (Sénégal) de l'ère musulmane au temps de négriers (VIIIe–XVIIIe siècle)*. Paris

Bathily, Ibrahima D. 1969. Notices socio-historiques sur l'ancien royaume Soninké du Gadiaga. *BIFAN* 31: 31–105

Bayol, Jean. 1888. *Voyage en Sénégambie, Haut Niger, Bambouck, Fouta Djallon et Bélédougou, 1880–1885*. Paris

Bazin, Jean. 1975. Guerre et servitude à Ségou. In C. Meillassoux, ed., *L'esclavage en Afrique précoloniale*. Paris, 135–82

1982. Etat guerrier et guerres d'état. In E. Terray and J. Bazin, eds., *Guerres de lignages et guerres d'états en Afrique*. Paris, 319–74

Bazin, Jean and Emmanuel Terray, eds. 1982. *Guerres de lignages et guerres d'états en Afrique*. Paris

Beachey, R. W. 1962. The Arms Trade in East Africa during the Late Nineteenth Century. *JAH* 3: 451–67

Becker, Charles. 1986. Conditions écologiques, crises de subsistence et histoire de la population à l'époque de la traite des esclaves en Sénégambie au 17e et 18e siècles. *CJAS* 20: 357–76

1988. Les effets démographiques de la traite des esclaves en Sénégambie: esquisse d'une histoire des peuplements du XVIIe à la fin du XIXe siècle. In S. Daget, ed., *De la traite à l'esclavage*. Vol. II. Paris, 71–110

Becker, Charles and Victor Martin 1975. Kayor et Baol, royaumes sénégalais et traite des esclaves au XVIII siècle. *RFHOM* 62: 270–300

Benoist, Joseph-Roger de. 1987. *Eglise et pouvoir colonial au Soudan français*. Paris

Bérenger-Féraud, J.-L. 1879. *Les peuplades de la Sénégambie: Histoire, ethnographie, moeurs et coutumes, légendes*. Paris

Bernus, Edmond. 1960. Kong et sa région. *Etudes Eburnéennes* 8: 239–324

1981. *Touaregs nigériens. Unité culturelle et diversité régionale d'un peuple pasteur*. Paris

Bernus, Edmond and Bernus, Suzanne. 1975. L'évolution de la condition servile chez les Touaregs sahéliens. In C. Meillassoux, ed., *L'ésclavage en Afrique précoloniale*. Paris

Bernus, Edmond., P. Boilley *et al.*, eds. 1993. *Nomades et commandants: Administration et sociétés nomades dans l'ancienne A.O.F*. Paris

Binger, Louis-Gustave. 1891. *Esclavage, Islamisme et Christianisme*. Paris

1892. *Du Niger au Golfe de Guinée par le pays du Kong et de Mossi, 1887–1889*. Paris

Bloch, Marc. 1953. *The Historian's Craft*. New York

Boilat, P. D. 1853. *Esquisses sénégalaises*. Paris

Bolt, Christine and Seymour Drescher, eds. 1980 *Anti-Slavery, Religion and Reform: Essays in Memory of Roger Anstey*. Folkestone, Dawson

Bonnier, G. 1926. *L'occupation du Timbuctou*. Paris

Bonte, Pierre. 1993. L'émir et les colonels, pouvoir colonial et pouvoir émiral en Adrar mauritanien. In E. Bernus *et al, Nomades et commandants. Administration et sociétés nomades dans l'ancienne A.O.F*. Paris

Botte, Roger. 1988. Révolte, pouvoir, religion: les Hubbu du Futa Jalon (Guinée). *JAH* 29: 391–413

1991. Les Rapports nord–sud, la traite négrière et le Fuuta Jaloo à la fin du XVIIIe Siècle. *Annales ESC*: 1411–35

1994. Stigmates sociaux et discrimination religeuses: l'ancienne class servile au Fuuta Jaloo. *CEA* 34: 109–36

Bouche, Denise. 1949–50. Les villages de liberté en A.O.F. *BIFAN* 11: 491–540, 12: 135–214

1968. *Les villages de liberté en Afrique noire française 1887–1910*. Paris

Bouet-Willaumez, Edouard. 1848. *Commerce et traite des noirs aux côtes occidentales d'Afrique*. Paris

Boulègue, Jean. 1977. Lat-Sukaabe Fal ou l'opiniâtreté d'un roi contre les échanges inégaux au Sénégal. *Les Africains*. Paris, 167–96

Bousquest, G. N. 1952. Des droits de l'esclave. Fragment extrait de l'Ih'ya' de Ghazali. *Annales de l'Institut des Etudes orientales* 10: 420–22

Boutillier, Jean-Louis. 1968. Les Captifs en AOF. *BIFAN* 30: 513–35

1969. La Ville de Bouna de l'époque précoloniale à aujourd'hui. *Cahiers ORSTOM* 6: 3–20

1971. La cité marchande de Bouna dans l'ensemble économique Ouest-africain précolonial. In C. Meillassoux, ed., *The Development of Indigenous Trade and Markets in West Africa*. London, 240–52

1975. Les trois esclaves de Bouna. In Claude Meillassoux, ed., *L'esclavage en Afrique précoloniale*. Paris, 253–80

1993. *Bouna. Royaume de la Savane ivoirienne. Princes, marchands et paysans*. Paris

Boutillier, Jean-Louis *et. al.* 1962. *La Moyenne Vallée du Sénégal*. Paris

Bowman, Joye. 1986. Abdul Njai: Ally and Enemy of the Portuguese in Guinea-Bissau, 1895–1910. *JAH* 27: 463–80

1987. "Legitimate Commerce" and Peanut Production in Portuguese Guinea, 1840s–1880s. *JAH* 28: 87–106

Boyer, G. 1953. *Un peuple de l'Ouest africain*. Dakar

Brasseur, Gerard. 1977. Repartition de la population en 1971. *Atlas National du Sénégal*. Dakar

Brasseur, Paule. 1985. Les campagnes abolitionnistes en France (1815–1848): L'Afrique sans l'Afrique. In Serge Daget, ed., *De la traite à l'esclavage*. Vol. II. Nantes, 333–42

1988. L'esclavage, les campagnes abolitionistes et la naissance de l'oeuvre de Libermann. *Libermann 1802–1852. Une pensée et une mystique missionaires*. Paris

Breedveld, Anneke and Mirjam De Bruijn. 1996. L'image des fulbe. Analyse critique de la construction du concept de *pulaaku*. *CEA* 36

Brenner, Louis. 1984. *West African Sufi. The Religious Heritage and Spiritual Search of Cerno Bokar Salif Taal*. London

Brooks, George. 1970. *Yankee Traders, Coasters, and African Middlemen*. Boston

1976a. Peanuts and Colonialism: Consequences of the Commercialization of Peanuts in West Africa, 1830–1870. *JAH* 16: 29–54

1976b. The Signares of Saint-Louis and Goree: Women Entrepreneurs in Eighteenth Century Senegal. In E. Bay and N. Hafkin, eds., *Women in Africa*. Stanford, 19–44

1983. A Nhara of the Guinea-Bissau region: Mae Aurelia Correia. In C. Robertson and M. Klein, eds., *Women and Slavery in Africa*. Madison, 295–319

Brunschwig, Henri. 1960. *Mythes et réalités de l'impérialisme colonial français 1871–1914*. Paris

Brunschwig, Henri. 1963. *L'Avènement de l'Afrique Noire*. Paris

Ca da Mosto, Alvise. 1937. *The Voyages of Cadamosto*. London

Caillié, René. 1830. *Journal d'un voyage à Toumbouctou et à Jenné dans l'Afrique centrale*. Paris

Camara, Sory. 1976. *Gens de la parole. Essai sur la condition du rôle des griots dans la société Malinké*. Paris

Conrad, David and Barbara Frank, eds. 1995. *Status and Identity in West Africa: Nyamakalaw of Mande*. Bloomington

Capron, J. 1973. *Communautés villageoises Bwa. Mali–Haute Volta*. Paris

Caron, E. 1891. *De Saint-Louis au port de Tombouctou. Voyage d'une cannonière française*. Paris

Carpeaux, Louis. 1913. *Mon roman au Niger*. Paris

Carrère, Frédéric and Paul Holle. 1855. *De la Sénégambie française.* Paris

Cassanelli, Lee. 1988. The Ending of Slavery in Italian Somalia: Liberty and the Control of Labor, 1890–1935. In S. Miers and R. Roberts, eds., *The End of Slavery in Africa,* Madison, 308–31

Chanock, Martin. 1985. *Law, Custom and Social Order. The Colonial Experience in Malawi and Zambia.* Cambridge

Charles, Eunice. 1971. Ouali N'Dao: The Exile of Alboury N'Diaye. *African Historical Studies* 4: 373–82

1977. *Precolonial Senegal: The Jolof Kingdom.* Boston

Chassey, Francis de. 1978. *Mauritanie 1900–1975. De l'ordre colonial à l'ordre néo-colonial entre Maghreb et Afrique Noire.* Paris

1979. *L'évolution des structures sociales en Mauritanie de la colonisation à nos jours. Introduction à la Mauritanie.* Paris

Chastanet, Monique. 1983. Les crises de subsistances dans les villages soninké du cercle du Bakel. Problèmes méthodologiques et perspectives de recherches, *CEA* 23: 5–36

Chauveau, Jean-Pierre. 1987. La colonisation "appropriée." Essai sur les transformations économiques et sociales en pays baule (Côte d'Ivoire) de 1891 au début des années 1920. In M. Piault, ed., *La Colonisation: Rupture ou Parenthèse.* Paris, 57–122

Cissé, Salmana. 1986. Le delta intérieur du Niger: organisation spatiale. In M. Adamu and A.H.M. Kirk-Greene, eds., *Pastoralists of the West African Savanna.* Manchester, 283–97

Cissoko, Sékéné Mody. 1975. *Tombouctou et l'Empire Songhay.* Dakar

1986. *Contribution à l'histoire du Khasso dans le Haut-Sénégal des origines à 1854.* Paris

1988. *Le Khasso face à L'Empire Toucouleur et à la France dans le Haut-Sénégal 1854–1890.* Paris

Clark, Andrew. 1994a. Internal Migrations and Population Movements in the Upper Senegal Valley (West Africa). *CJAS* 28: 399–420

1994b. Slavery and its Demise in the Upper Senegal Valley, 1890–1920. *S&A* 15: 51–71

Cohen, William B. 1971. *Rulers of Empire: The French Colonial Service in Africa.* Stanford

1974. The Imperial Mirage: The Western Sudan in French Thought and Action. *JHSN* 7: 417–45

Collieaux, M. 1924. Contribution à l'étude de l'histoire de l'ancien royaume de Kenedougou. *BCEHSAOF* 14: 365–432

Colvin, Lucie. 1974. Islam and the State of Kajor: A case of Successful Resistance to Jihad. *JAH* 15: 587–606

Condé, A. 1972. *Guinée: Albanie d'Afrique ou néo-colonie américaine?* Paris

Cooper, Frederick. 1977. *Plantation Slavery on the East Coast of Africa.* New Haven

1979. The Problem of Slavery in African Studies. *JAH* 20: 103–26

1980. *From Slaves to Squatters. Plantation Labour and Agriculture in Zanzibar and Coastal Kenya, 1890–1925.* New Haven

1981. Islam and Cultural Hegemony: The Ideology of Slaveowners on the East African Coast. In P. Lovejoy, ed., *Ideology of Slavery in Africa.* Beverley Hills, 271–307

1987. Contracts, crime and agrarian conflict: from slave to wage labor on the East African coast. In D. Hay and F. Snyder, eds., *Labor, Law and Crime.* London

Copans, Jean. 1980. *Les marabouts de l'arachide, la confrérie mouride et les paysans du*

Sénégal. Paris

Coquery-Vidrovitch, Catherine. 1969. Recherches sur un mode de production africaine. *La Pensée* 144: 61–78. Tr. in M. Klein and G.W. Johnson, eds., 1973. *Perspectives on the African Past.* Boston

1976. L'Afrique coloniale française et la crise de 1930: crise structurelle et genèse du sous-développement. *RFHOM* 63: 386–424

1977. Mutation de l'impérialisme français dans les années 30. *AEH* 4: 103–52

Cordell, Dennis. 1985a. *Dar al-Kuti and the Last Years of the Trans-Saharan Slave Trade.* Madison

1985b. The Labor of Violence: Dar al-Kuti in the Nineteenth Century. In C. Coquery-Vidrovitch and P. Lovejoy, eds., *The Workers of African Trade.* Beverley Hills, 169–92

1986. Warlords and Enslavement: A Sample of Slave-Raiders from Eastern Ubangi-Shari 1870–1920. In Paul Lovejoy, ed., *Africans in Bondage.* Madison, 335–65

1988. The Delicate Balance of Force and Flight: The End of Slavery in Eastern Ubangi-Shari. In S. Miers and R. Roberts, eds., *The End of Slavery in Africa,* Madison, 150–71

Cordell, Dennis, Joel Gregory and Victor Piché. 1996. *Hoe and Wage. A Social History of a Circular Migration System in West Africa.* Boulder

Cornevin, Robert. 1968. L'un des plus grands proconsuls français: William Merlaud-Ponty. *France-Eurafrique* 197: 33–37

1975. Louis Tauxier (1871–1942). *Hommes et Destins,* Vol. I, Paris, 582–83

1976. Introduction. Maurice Delafosse, *Haut-Sénégal-Niger.* Paris

Coulon, Christian. 1981. *Le Marabout et le Prince. Islam et pouvoir au Sénégal.* Paris

Courtet, M. 1903. *Etude sur le Sénégal.* Paris

Craton, Michael, ed. 1979. *Roots and Branches.* New York

Craven, Paul and Douglas Hay. 1994. The Criminalization of "Free" Labour: Master and Servant in Comparative Perspective. *S&A* 15: 71–101

Cros, R. P. 1894. Mission de Kita (Soudan français). *Annales* 9: 41–57

Crowder, Michael, ed., 1971. Introduction. *West African Resistance: The Military Response to Colonial Occupation.* London

1975. The French Suppression of the 1916–17 Revolt in Dahomeyan Borgu. *Journal of the Historical Society of Nigeria.* 8: 179–97.

Crowder, Michael and Obaro Ikime, eds. 1970. *West African Chiefs.* New York

Cruise O'Brien, Donal. 1967. Towards an "Islamic Policy" in French West Africa. *JAH* 8: 303–16

1971. *The Mourides of Senegal.* Oxford

1975. *Saints and Politicians. Essays in the organisation of a Senegalese peasant society.* Cambridge

1988. Introduction. *Charisma and Brotherhood in African Islam.* Oxford

Curtin, Philip. 1969. *The African Slave Trade. A Census.* Madison

1971a. Jihad in West Africa: Early Phases and Interactions in Mauritania and Senegal. *JAH* 12: 11–24

1971b. Pre-colonial trading networks and traders: The Diakhanké. In Claude Meillassoux, ed., *The Development of Indigenous Trade and Markets in West Africa.* London, 228–39

1975. *Economic Change in Precolonial Africa. Senegambia in the Era of the Slave Trade.* Madison

1981. The Abolition of the Slave Trade from Senegambia. *The Abolition of the Atlantic Slave Trade.* Madison

Daget, Serge. 1971. L'abolition de la traite des noirs en France de 1814 à 1831. *CEA* 11:

14–58

1975. Le trafic négrier illégal de 1814 à 1860: historiographie et sources. *Annales de l'Université d'Abidjan* 3: 25–53

1980. A Model of the French Abolitionist Movement and its Variations. In Christine Bolt and Seymour Drescher, eds., *Antislavery, Religion and Reform*. Folkestone, 64–79

1981. France, Suppression of the Illegal Trade, and England, 1817–1850. In James Walvin and David Eltis, eds., *The Abolition of the Atlantic Slave Trade*. Madison, 193–217

ed. 1985. *De la traite à l'esclavage*. Colloque International sur la traite des Noirs. Nantes. 2 Vols. Paris

1990. *La Traite des noirs*. Paris

Daget, Serge and F. Renault, 1985. *Les traites négrières en Afrique*. Paris

Daly, Martin. 1986. *Empire on the Nile. The Anglo-Egyptian Sudan, 1898–1934*. Cambridge

David, Pierre. 1980. *Les Navetanes*. Dakar

Davis, David Brion. 1966. *The Problem of Slavery in Western Culture*. Ithaca

1975. *The Problem of Slavery in the Age of Revolution 1770–1823*. Ithaca

Debien, Gabriel. 1964. Papiers Ernest Noirot. *BIFAN* 26: 676–78

De Bruijn, Mirjam and Han van Dijk. 1993. State Formation and the Decline of Pastoralism: the Fulani in Central Mali. In John Markakis, ed., *Conflict and the Decline of Pastoralism in the Horn of Africa*. London

1994. Drought and Coping Strategies in Fulbe Society in Haayre (Central Mali): A Historical Perspective, *CEA* 34: 85–108

Deherme, Georges. 1994 (1906). L'esclavage en Afrique occidentale française: étude historique, critique et positive. In P. Lovejoy and S. Kanya-Forstner, eds., *Slavery and its Abolition in French West Africa*. Madison, 111–206

1908. *L'Afrique occidentale française: action politique, action économique, action sociale*. Paris

Delafosse, Louise. 1976. *Maurice Delafosse: le Berrichon Conquis par l'Afrique*. Abbeville

Delafosse, Maurice. 1912. *Haut-Sénégal-Niger*. Paris

De Latour, Eliane. 1980. Shadows Nourished by the Sun: Rural Social Differentiation among the Mawri of Niger. In M. Klein, ed., *Peasants in Africa*. Beverley Hills, 105–41

1982. La paix destructrice. In J. Bazin and E. Terray, eds., *Guerres de lignages et guerres d'états en Afrique*. Paris

1987. Le Futur Antérieur. In M. Piault, ed. *La Colonisation: Rupture ou Parenthèse?* Paris, 123–76

Delaunay, Daniel. 1984. *De la captivité à l'exil: Histoire et démographie de migrations paysannes dans la Moyenne Vallée du fleuve Sénégal*. Paris

Delavignette, Robert. 1946. Faidherbe. *Les Constructeurs de la France d'Outre-Mer*. Paris, 232–63

Demougeot, A. 1944. *Note sur l'organisation politique et administrative du Labé avant et depuis l'occupation française*. Dakar, IFAN

Demougeot, A. 1949. L'Esclavage et l'émancipation des Noirs au Sénégal. *Tropiques* 312 (July): 10–17

Derman, William. 1973. *Serfs, Peasants, and Socialists: A Former Serf Village in the Republic of Guinea*. Berkeley

Derrick, Jonathan. 1975. *Africa's Slaves Today*. London

Devisse, Jean. 1988. L'exportation d'êtres humains hors d'Afrique: son influence sur l'évolution historique du continent. *De La traite à l'esclavage.* Vol. I. Paris, SFHOM, 113–20

Diallo, Ousmane. 1961. Evolution sociale chez les Peuls du Fouta-Djalon. *Recherche africaine* 4: 73–94

Diallo, Thierno. 1972. *Les Institutions politiques du Fouta Dyalon au XIXe siècle.* Dakar, IFAN

Diallo, Youssouf. 1994. Barani: une chefferie satellite des grands états du XIXe siècle. *CEA* 34: 359–84

Diawara, Mamadou. 1989. *La graine de la parole: Dimension sociale et politique des traditions orales du royaume de Jaara (Mali) du XVème au milieu du XIXème siècle.* Stuttgart

Diawara, Mamadou. 1989. Women, Servitude and History: the Oral Historical Traditions of Women of Servile Condition in the Kingdom of Jaara (Mali) from the Fifteenth to the Mid-Nineteenth Century. *Discourse and its Disguises: The Interpretation of African Oral Texts.* Birmingham, Centre of West African Studies

Dim Delobsom, A. A. 1932. *L'empire du Mogho Naba, coutumes des Mossi de la Haute Volta.* Paris

Diop, Abdoulaye Bara. 1965. *Société toucouleur et migration.* Dakar

   1966. Lat Dior et le problème musulman. *BIFAN* 28: 493–539

   1981. *La société Wolof. Tradition et changement. Les systemes d'inégalite et de domination.* Paris

Diouf, Mamadou. 1990. *Le Kajoor au XIXe siècle.* Paris

   1992. Traitants ou négociants? Les commerçants Saint Louisiens (2e moitié du XIXe s.–début XXe s.) Hamet Gora Diop (1846–1910) – Etude de Cas. In B. Barry and L. Harding, eds., *Commerce et commerçants en Afrique de l'Ouest: Le Sénégal.* Paris, 107–53

Domar, Evsey. 1970. The Causes of Slavery or Serfdom: A Hypothesis. *Journal of Economic History* 30: 18–32

Drescher, Seymour. 1968. *Dilemmas of Democracy: Toqueville and Modernization.* Pittsburgh

   1980. Two Variants of Anti-Slavery: Religious Organization and Social Mobilization in Britain and France, 1780–1870. In Christine Bolt and Seymour Drescher, eds., *Anti-slavery, Religion and Reform.* Folkestone

Dubois, Felix. 1897. *Tombouctou la mystérieuse.* Paris

Dumett, Raymond and Marion Johnson. 1988. Britain and the Suppression of Slavery in the Gold Coast Colony, Ashanti and the Northern Territories. In S. Miers and R. Roberts, eds., *The End of Slavery in Africa.* Madison

Dumont, Fernand. 1975. *La pensée religieuse de Amadou Bamba, Fondateur du mouridisme.* Dakar

Duperray, A.-M. 1984. *Les Gourounsi de Haute-Volta.* Wiesbaden

Dupeyron, G. 1959. Bintagoungou, Village de Faguibine: budgets et niveaux de vie. *Cahiers d'Outre-Mer* 12: 26–55

Dupire, Marguerite. 1970. *Organisation sociale des Peul. Etude d'ethnographie comparée.* Paris

   1994. Identité ethnique et processus d'incorporation tribale et étatique. *CEA* 34: 265–80

Durand, J.-B.-L. 1802. *Voyage au Sénégal 1785–1786.* Paris

Durand, Oswald. 1935. *Terre Noire.* Paris

Echenberg, Myron. 1971a. Late Nineteenth Century Military Technology in Upper Volta. *JAH* 12: 241–54

   1975. Paying the Blood Tax: Military Conscription in French West Africa, 1914–

1929. *CJAS* 9: 171–92

1980. Les migrations militaires en Afrique occidentale française 1900–1945. *CJAS* 14: 429–50

1986. Slaves into Soldiers: Social Origins of the Tirailleurs Sénégalais. In Paul Lovejoy, ed., *Africans in Bondage: Studies in Slavery and the Slave Trade*. Madison, 311–33

1991. *Colonial Conscripts. The Tirailleurs Sénégalais in French West Africa, 1857–1960*. Portsmouth, N.H.

Elkan, Walter. 1960. *Migrants and Proletarians: Urban Labour in the Economic Development of Uganda*. London

Emerit, M. 1949. *La Révolution de 1848 en Algérie*. Paris

Ernst, Klaus. 1976. *Tradition and Progress in the African Village. The Non-Capitalist Transformation of Rural Communities in Mali*. London

Fage, John. 1975. The Effect of the Export Slave Trade on African Populations. In R.P. Ross and Richard Rathbone, eds., *The Population Factor in African Studies*. London

1980. Slaves and Society in Western Africa, c. 1445–c.1700. *JAH* 21,289–310

Faidherbe, Léon. 1889. *Le Sénégal*. Paris

Fall, Babacar. 1993. *Le travail forcé en Afrique occidentale française (1900–1945)*. Paris

Falola, Toyin and Paul Lovejoy, eds., 1994. *Pawnship in Africa. Debt Bondage in Historical Perspective*. Boulder

Famechon, M. 1900. *Notice sur la Guinée française*. Paris

Fernandes, Valentim. 1951. *Description de la côte occidentale d'Afrique: Sénégal au Cap de Monte*. Bissau, Centro de Estudos da Guinea Portuguesa

Finley, Moses. 1968. Slavery. *International Encyclopedia of the Social Sciences*. New York, 307–13

Fisher, Humphrey. 1971. Firearms in the Central Sudan. *JAH* 12: 215–40

1972–73. He Swalloweth the Ground with Fierceness and Rage: the Horse in the Central Sudan. *JAH* 13–14: 13:369–88, 14: 355–79

Fisher, Allan and Fisher, Humphrey. 1970. *Slavery and Muslim Society in Africa*. London

Fisher, Humphrey and Virginia Rowlands. 1972. Firearms in the Central Sudan. *JAH* 12: 215–40

Flint, John and E. Ann McDougall. 1987. Economic Change in West Africa in the Nineteenth Century. In J.F.A. Ajayi and Michael Crowder, ed., *History of West Africa*. Vol. II. London

Franke, Richard and Barbara Chassin. 1980. *Seeds of Famine. Ecological Destruction and the Development Dilemma in the West African Sahel*. Montclair, N.J

Frey, Henri. 1888. *Campagne dans le Haut Niger (1885–1886)*. Paris

1890. *Côte Occidentale d'Afrique*. Paris

Froelich, J. C. 1962. *Les musulmans d'Afrique noire*. Paris

Fuglestad, Finn. 1973. Les revoltes des Touareg du Niger (1916–1917). *CEA* 13: 82–120

1983. *A History of Niger 1850–1960*. Cambridge

Fynn, John K. 1971. *Asante and its Neighbours*, 1700–1807. London

Gallais, Jean. 1967. *Le Delta intérieur du Niger. Etude de geographie regionale*. Dakar

Gallieni, Joseph. 1885. *Voyage au Soudan français (Haut-Sénégal et pays de Ségou), 1879–1881*. Paris

1891. *Deux campagnes au Soudan français, 1886–1888*. Paris

Ganier, G. 1965. Lat Dyor et le chemin de fer de l'arachide, 1876–1886. *BIFAN* 27: 223–81

1968. Maures et Toucouleurs sur les deux rives du Sénégal. *BIFAN* 30: 182–226

1973. Jean Bayol et Victor Ballot dans les Rivières du Sud. *RFHOM* 60: 549–88

Gastellu, Jean-Marc. 1981. *L'égalitarisme économique des Serer du Sénégal.* Paris

Gatelet, L. 1901. *Histoire de la conquête du Soudan française 1878–1899.* Paris

Geggus, David. 1990. Sex Ratio, Age and Ethnicity in the Atlantic Slave Trade: Data from French Shipping and Plantation Records. *JAH* 30: 23–44

Genovese, Eugene. 1972. *Roll, Jordan, Roll: The World the Slaves Made.* New York, Random House

Glassman, Jonathan. 1991. The Bondsman's New Clothes: The Contradictory Consciousness of Resistance on the Swahili Coast. *JAH* 32: 277–312

1995. *Feasts and Riot: Revelry, Rebellion, and Popular Consciousness on the Swahili Coast, 1856–1888.* Portsmouth, N.H.

Goerg, Odile. 1980. La destruction d'un réseau d'échange précolonial: l'exemple de la Guinée. *JAH* 21: 467–84

1986. *Commerce et colonisation en Guinée.* Paris

1988. Deux modalités d'adaptation à l'abolition de la traite atlantique: le Rio Nunez et le Rio Pongo (actuelle Guinée). In Serge Daget, ed., *De la traite à l'esclavage.* Vol. II. Paris, 557–74

Gomez, Michael. 1992. *Pragmatism in the Age of Jihad: The Precolonial State of Bundu.* Cambridge

Goody, Jack. 1971. *Technology, Tradition and the State in Africa.* Cambridge

1980. Slavery in Time and Space. In James Watson, ed., *Asian and African Systems of Slavery.* Berkeley, 16–42

Gouraud, Henri. 1939. *Souvenir d'un Africain: au Soudan.* Paris

Grace, John. 1975. *Domestic Slavery in West Africa.* New York

Gray, John M. 1940. *A History of the Gambia.* Cambridge

Gray, Richard and David Birmingham, eds., 1970. *Pre-Colonial African Trade: Essays on Trade in Central and Eastern Africa Before 1900.* London

Green, Kathryn. 1986. Dyula and Sonongui Roles in the Islamization of the Region of Kong. *Asian and African Studies* 20: 103–23

Guèye, Mbaye. 1965. L'affaire Chautemps (avril 1904) et la suppression de l'esclavage de case au Sénégal. *BIFAN* 27: 543–59

1966. La fin de l'esclavage à St. Louis et à Gorée en 1848. *BIFAN* 28: 637–67

Guillaumet, Eduard. 1894. *Tableaux Soudanais.* Paris

Guiraud, Xavier. 1937. *L'arachide sénégalaise.* Paris

Hanson, John. 1990. Generational Conflict in the Umarian Movement after the Jihad: Perspectives from the Futanke Grain Trade at Medine. *JAH* 31: 199–216

1994. Islam, Migration and the Political Economy of Meaning: Fergo Nioro from the Senegal River Valley, 1862–1890. *JAH* 35: 37–60

1996. *Migration, Jihad, and Muslim Authority in West Africa: the Futanke Colonies in Karta.* Bloomington, Indiana

Harding, Leonhard. 1972. *Franzosische Religonspolitik in WestAfrika: "Soudan Français" 1895–1920.* Berlin

Hardy, Georges. 1921. *La mise en valeur du Sénégal de 1817 à 1854.* Paris

1947. *Louis Faidherbe.* Paris

Hargreaves, John D. 1963. *Prelude to the Partition of West Africa.* London

1969. *France and West Africa.* London

1974. *West Africa Partitioned: The Loaded Pause, 1885–89.* London

1985. *West Africa Partitioned: The Elephants and the Grass.* London

Harrison, Christopher. 1988. *France and Islam in West Africa, 1860–1960.* Cambridge

Harrison, C., T.B. Ingawa and S. M. Martin. 1987. The Establishment of Colonial Rule in West Africa, c. 1900–1914. In J.F.A. Ajayi and M. Crowder, eds., *History of West Africa*. Vol. II. London, 485–545

Hegel, G.W.F. 1910. Lordship and Bondage. In *Phenomenology of the Mind*. Tr. J.R. Baillie. London

Héritier, Françoise. 1975. Des cauris et des hommes: production d'esclaves et accumulation de cauris chez les Samo (Haute-Volta). In C. Meillassoux, ed., *L'esclavage en Afrique précoloniale*. Paris, 477–507

Heywood, Linda. 1988. Slavery and Forced Labor in the Changing Political Economy of Central Angola, 1850–1949. In S. Miers and R. Roberts, eds., *The End of Slavery in Africa*, Madison, 415–36

Hill, Allan, Sara Randall and Oriel Sullivan. 1982. *The Mortality and Fertility of Farmers and Pastoralists in Central Mali, 1950–1981*. London: Centre for Population Studies, London School of Hygiene and Tropical Medicine

Hiskett, Mervyn. 1984. *The Development of Islam in West Africa*. London

Hogendorn, Jan S. 1977. The Economics of Slave Use on Two "Plantations" in the Zaria Emirate of the Sokoto Caliphate. *IJAHS* 10: 369–83

Holden, Jeff. 1965. The Zabarima of North-West Ghana. *Transactions of the Historical Society of Ghana* 8: 60–86

Hopkins, Anthony G. 1966. The Lagos Strike of 1897: an Exploration in Nigerian Labour History. *Past and Present* 35: 133–55

   1967. Underdevelopment in the Empires of the Western Sudan. *Past and Present* 37: 149–56

   1973. *Economic History of West Africa*. London

Hrbek, Ivan. 1976. A Fighting Marabout. The Beginning of Mamadu Lamin's Struggle in Senegal. *Praha-Archiv* 44

   1979. The Early Period in Mamadou Lamin's Activities. *Studies in West African Islamic History*. London, 211–32

Hunwick, John. 1985. Notes on Slavery in the Songhay Empire. In J.R. Willis, ed., *Slaves and Slavery in Muslim Africa*. Vol. II, London, 16–32

   1992. Black Africans in the Mediterranean World: Introduction to a Neglected Aspect of the African Diaspora. In Elizabeth Savage, ed., *The Human Commodity*. London, 5–38

Idowu, H. O. 1968. The Establishment of Protectorate Administration in Senegal, 1890–1914. *JHSN* : 247–65

   1969a. The Establishment of Elective Institutions in Senegal, 1869–1880. *JAH* 9: 261–77

   1969b. Assimilation in 19th Century Senegal. *CEA* 9: 194–218

   1971. Café au lait: Senegal's Mulatto Community in the Nineteenth Century. *JHSN* 6: 271–88

Igbafe, Philip. 1975. Slavery and Emancipation in Benin, 1897–1945. *JAH* 16: 409–30

Inikori, Joseph. 1977. The Import of Firearms in West Africa, 1750–1807: A Quantitative Analysis. *JAH* 18: 339–68

   1982. *Forced Migration: The Impact of the Export Slave Trade on African Societies*. London

   1992a. Export Versus Domestic Demand: The Determinants of Sex Ratios in the Transatlantic Slave Trade. *Research in Economic History* 14: 117–66

   1992b. Africa in World History: The Export Slave Trade from Africa and the Emergence of the Atlantic Economic Order. *UNESCO General History of Africa*. Vol. V. B.A. Ogot, ed. Berkeley and Los Angeles

Irwin, Paul. 1981. *Liptako Speaks: History from Oral Tradition in Africa*. Princeton

Isaacman, Allen and Anton Rosenthal. 1988. Slaves, Soldiers and Police: Power and

Dependency among the Chikunda of Mozambique, ca. 1825–1920. In S. Miers and R. Roberts, eds., *The End of Slavery in Africa*, Madison, 220–53

Izard, Michel. 1975. Les captifs royaux dans l'ancien Yatenga. In Claude Meillassoux, ed., *L'esclavage en Afrique précoloniale*. Paris, 281–96

Jennings, Lawrence. 1976. French Policy Towards Trading with African and Brazilian Slave Merchants, 1840–1853. *JAH* 17: 515–28

1985. Slave Trade Repression and the Abolition of French Slavery. In Serge Daget, ed., *De la traite à l'esclavage*, Vol. II, Nantes, 359–72

1988. *French Reaction to British Slave Emancipation*. Baton Rouge

Jewsiewicki, Bogumil and Jocelyn Letourneau, eds. 1985. *Mode of Production: The Challenge of Africa*. Quebec

Johnson, G. Wesley. 1971. *The Emergence of the Black Politics in Senegal: The Struggle for Power in the Four Communes, 1900–1920*. Stanford

1978. William Ponty and Republican Paternalism in French West Africa (1866–1915). In Peter Duignan and Lewis Gann, eds. *African Proconsuls*. New York and London

Johnson, Marion. 1976. The Economic Foundations of an Islamic Theocracy. *JAH* 17: 481–96

1986. The Slaves of Salaga. *JAH* 27: 341–62

Johnson, R. W. and A. Summers. 1978. World War I Conscription and Social Change in Guinea. *JAH* 19: 25–38

Jonckers, Danielle. 1987. *La Société Minyanka du Mali*. Paris

Joucla, E. 1905. L'esclavage au Sénégal et au Soudan, état de la question en 1905. *Bulletin de la Société des anciens élèves de l'école colonial* 19: 1–13

Kaké, Ibrahma Baba. 1979. The Slave Trade and Population Drain from Black Africa to North Africa and the Middle East. In UNESCO, *The African Slave Trade*, 164–74

Kambou-Ferrand, J.-M. 1993. *Peuples voltaïques et conquête coloniale 1885–1914 Burkina Faso*. Paris

Kane, Omar. 1974. Les Maures et le Fouta Toro au XVIIIe siècle. *CEA* 14: 237–52

Kanya-Forstner, A. S. 1969. *The Conquest of the Western Sudan. A Study in French Military Imperialism*. Cambridge

Kanya-Forstner, A. S. and Paul Lovejoy, eds. 1994. *Slavery and its Abolition in French West Africa: the Official Reports of G. Poulet, E. Roume, and G. Deherme*. Madison

Kersaint-Gilly, Felix de. 1924. Essai sur l'évolution de l'esclavage en Afrique occidentale française: son dernier stade au Soudan français. *BCEHSAOF* 7

Ki Zerbo, Joseph. 1983. *Alfred Diban, premier chrétien de Haute-Volta*. Paris

Kimba, Idrissa. 1981. *Guerres et sociétés. Les populations du Niger occidental au 19e siècle et leurs réactions face à la colonisation*. Niamey

Klein, Herbert. 1983. African Women in the Atlantic Slave Trade. In Claire Robertson and Martin Klein, eds., *Women and Slavery in Africa*. Madison, 29–38

Klein, Martin. 1968. *Islam and Imperialism: Sine Saloum 1847–1914*. Stanford

1971. Slavery, the Slave Trade and Legitimate Commerce in Late Nineteenth Century Africa. *Etudes d'histoire Africaine* 2: 5–28

1972. Social and Economic Factors in the Muslim Revolution in Senegambia. *JAH* 13: 419–42

1977a. Servitude among the Wolof and Sereer of Senegambia. In Suzanne Miers and Igor Kopytoff, eds., *Slavery in Africa*. Madison

1977b. Ma Ba ou la résistance forcée à la conquête française en Sénégambie. *Les Africains*. Paris, 171–203

1978. The Study of Slavery in Africa. *JAH* 19: 599–609

1983a. From Slave to Sharecropper: An Effort at Controlled Social Change in the French Soudan. *Itinerario* 8: 102–15

1983b. Women and Slavery in the Western Sudan. In M. A. Klein and C. Robertson, eds., *Women and Slavery in Africa*. Madison, 67–88

1987. The Demography of Slavery in Late Nineteenth Century. In Joel Gregory and Dennis Cordell, eds., *African Population and Capitalism*. Boulder, 50–61

1989a. Slave Resistance and Slave Emancipation in Coastal Guinée. In S. Miers and R. Roberts, eds., *The End of Slavery in Africa*. Madison, 203–19

1989b. Studying the History of Those who would rather Forget. *History in Africa* 16: 209–17

1992a. The Impact of the Atlantic Slave Trade on the Societies of the Western Sudan. In Joseph Inikori and Stanley Engerman, eds., *The Atlantic Slave Trade: Effects on Economies, Societies, and Peoples in Africa, the Americas and Europe.* Durham, 25–48

1992b. The Slave Trade in the Western Sudan during the Nineteenth Century. In Elizabeth Savage, ed., *The Human Commodity. Perspectives on the Trans-Saharan Slave Trade*. London, 39–60

ed. 1993a. *Breaking the Chains: Slavery, Bondage and Emancipation in Africa and Asia*. Madison

1993b. Slavery and Emancipation in French West Africa. In Martin Klein, ed., *Breaking the Chains: Slavery, Bondage, and Emancipation in Modern Africa and Asia*. Madison, 171–96

1994. Simulating the Atlantic Slave Trade, *CJAS* 28: 296–99

Klein, Martin and Paul Lovejoy, 1979. Slavery in West Africa, in J.S. Hogendorn and H.A. Gemery, eds., *The Uncommon Market: Essays in the Economic History of the Atlantic Slave Trade*. New York, 181–212

Klein, Martin and Richard Roberts, 1980. The Banamba Slave Exodus of 1905 and the Decline of Slavery in the Western Sudan, *JAH* 21: 375–94

1987. The Resurgence of Pawning in French West Africa, *AEH* 16: 23–37. Reprinted in Paul Lovejoy and Toyin Falola, eds., *Pawnship in Africa*, Boulder, 303–20

Klein, Martin and Claire Robertson, eds. 1983. *Women and Slavery in Africa*. Madison

Kodjo-Niamkey, Georges. 1976. Contribution à l'étude des tribus dites serviles du Songhai, *BIFAN* 38: 790–812

1988. Razzias et développement des états du Soudan occidental, in Serge Daget, ed., *De la traite à l'esclavage*. Vol. II. Paris, 19–36

Konaré, Alpha Omar. 1983. *Sikasso Tata*, Bamako

Kopytoff, Igor. 1979. Commentary. In Michael Craton, ed., *Roots and Branches*, New York, 62–76

1988. The Cultural Context of African Abolition. In S. Miers and R. Roberts, eds., *The End of Slavery in Africa*, Madison, 485–503

Labouret, Henri. 1955. Le servage étape entre l'esclavage et la liberté en Afrique occidentale, *Afrikanistiche Studien*, Berlin

Last, Murray. 1967. *The Sokoto Caliphate*. New York

Law, Robin, 1976. Horses, Firearms and Political Power in Pre-Colonial West Africa. *Past and Present* 72: 112–32

1977. *The Oyo Empire c.1600–c.1836*. Oxford

1980. *The Horse in West African History*. London

1991. *The Slave Coast of West Africa 1550–1750*. Oxford

ed. 1995. *From Slave Trade to "Legitimate" Commerce: The Commercial Transition in Nineteenth-Century West Africa*. Cambridge

Lawler, Nancy. 1992. *Soldiers of Misfortune: Ivoirian Tirailleurs of World War II*.

Le Roy, Alexandre. 1889. L'esclavage africain. *Annales apostoliques* 4: 124–42

Legassick, Martin. 1966. Firearms, Horses and Samorian Army Organization. *JAH* 7: 95–116

Lenz, Oskar. 1887. *Voyage au Maroc, au Sahara et au Soudan*. Paris

Leservoisier, Olivier. 1994. L'évolution foncière de la rive droite du fleuve Sénégal sous la colonisation (Mauritanie). *CEA* 34: 55–84

Levtzion, Nehemia. 1971. Notes sur les origines de l'Islam militant au Fouta Djalon. *Notes africaines* 132: 94–96

    1973. *Ancient Ghana and Mali*. London

    1985. Slavery and Islamization in Africa. In J. R. Willis, ed., *Slaves and Slavery in Muslim Africa*. Vol. I. London, 182–98

    1986a. Rural and Urban Islam in West Africa: an Introductory Essay. *Asian and African Studies* 20: 7–26

    1986b. Merchants v. Scholars and Clerics: Differential and Complementary Roles. *Asian and African Studies* 20: 27–43

    1987. The Eighteenth Century Background to the Islamic Revolutions in West Africa. In John Voll and Nehemia Levtzion, eds., *Eighteenth Century Renewal and Reform in Islam*. Syracuse

Leynaud, Emile and Youssef Cissé. 1978. *Paysans Malinke du Haut Niger*. Bamako

Linares, Olga. 1987. Deferring to the Trade in Slaves: The Jola of Casamance, Senegal in Historical Perspective. *HIA* 16: 113–39

Lloyd, Christopher. 1949. *The Navy and the Slave Trade*. London

Lombard, Jacques. 1967. *Autorités traditionelles et pouvoirs européens en Afrique noire*. Paris

Lovejoy, Paul. 1978. Plantations in the Economy of the Sokoto Caliphate. *JAH* 19: 341–68

    1979a. The Characteristics of Plantations in the Nineteenth Century Sokoto Caliphate (Islamic West Africa). *American Historical Review* 84: 1267–92

    1979b. Indigenous African Slavery. In Michael Craton, ed., *Roots and Branches: Current Directions in Slave Studies*. New York, 19–61

    1980. *Caravans of Kola: The Hausa Kola Trade, 1700–1900*. Zaria

    ed. 1981. *The Ideology of Slavery in Africa*. Beverly Hills

    1983. *Transformations in Slavery: A History of Slavery in Africa*. Cambridge

    ed. 1986a. *Africans in Bondage*. Madison

    1986b. Fugitive Slaves: Resistance to Slavery in the Sokoto Caliphate. In Gary Okihiro, ed., *In Resistance: Studies in African, Caribbean, and Afro-American History*. Amherst

    1986c. Problems of Slave Control in the Sokoto Caliphate. *Africans in Bondage. Studies in Slavery and the Slave Trade*. Madison

    1988. Concubinage and the Status of Women Slaves in Early Colonial Northern Nigeria. *JAH* 29: 245–66

    1990. Concubinage in the Sokoto Caliphate (1804–1903). *S&A* 11: 159–89

    1993. Murgu: The "Wages" of Slavery in the Sokoto Caliphate. *S&A* 14: 168–85

Lovejoy, Paul and Jan Hogendorn. 1993. *Slow Death for Slavery: The Course of Abolition in Northern Nigeria, 1897–1936*. Cambridge

Lovejoy, Paul and David Richardson. 1995a. Competing Markets for Male and Female Slaves: Prices in the Interior of West Africa. *IJAHS* 28: 261–94

    1995b. The Initial "Crisis of Adaptation": The Impact of British Abolition on the Atlantic Slave Trade in West Africa, 1808–1820, in R. Law, ed., *From Slave Trade to "Legitimate" Commerce*. Cambridge, 32–56

Ly, Babacar. 1967. L'Honneur dans les sociétés oulof et toucouleur du Sénégal (Contribution à l'étude des valeurs morales africaines). *Presence Africaine* (67): 32–67

Ly-Tall, Madina. 1991. *Un Islam militant en Afrique de l'ouest au XIX siècle: La Tijaniyya de Saiku Umar Futiyu contre les pouvoirs traditionels et la puissance coloniale.* Paris

Magasa, Amadu. 1978. *Papa-commandant a jeté un grand filet devant nous. Les exploités des rives du Niger 1902–1962.* Paris

Mage, Eugene. 1968 (1868). *Voyage dans le Soudan occidental (Sénégambie-Niger), 1863–1866.* Paris

Malowist, Marian. 1966a. Le commerce d'or et d'esclaves au Soudan occidental. *Africana Bulletin* 4: 49–72

1966b. The Social and Economic Stability of West Africa in the Middle Ages. *Past and Present* 33: 3–16

Manchuelle, François. 1984. Métis et colons: la famille Devès et l'émergence politique des Africains au Sénégal, 1881–1897. *CEA* 24: 477–504

1986. Origines républicaines et philanthropiques et la politique d'expansion coloniale de Jules Ferry (1838–1865). Proceedings of the French Colonial Historical Society

1989a. Slavery, Emancipation and Labour Migration in West Africa: The Case of the Soninke. *JAH* 30: 89–106

1989b. The Patriarchal Ideal of Soninke Labor Migrants in West Africa: From Slave Owners to Employers of Free Labor Migrants. *CJAS* 23: 106–25

1992. Le rôle des Antillais dans l'apparition du nationalisme culturel en Afrique Noire Francophone. *CEA* 32: 375–408

1997. *Willing Migrants.* Athens, Ohio

Mané, M. 1978. Contribution à l'histoire du Kaabu, des origines au XIXe siècle. *BIFAN* 40: 87–159

Mangolte, J. 1968. Le chemin de fer de Konakry au Niger, 1890–1914. *RFHOM* 55: 37–105

Mann, Kristin and Richard Roberts, eds. 1991. *Law in Colonial Africa.* Portsmouth, N.H.

Manning, Patrick. 1975. Un document sur la fin de l'esclavage au Dahomey. *Notes africaines*, 147: 88–92

1982. *Slavery, Colonialism and Economic Growth in Dahomey, 1640–1960.* Cambridge

1983. Contours of Slavery and Social Change in Africa. *American Historical Review* 88: 835–57

1990. *Slavery and African Life. Occidental, Oriental and African Slave Trades.* Cambridge

Mark, Peter. 1985. *A Cultural, Economic, and Religious History of the Basse Casamance since 1500.* Wiesbaden

Marty, Paul. 1915. *La Politique indigène du Gouverneur-Général Ponty en Afrique occidentale française.* Paris

1917. *Etudes sur l'Islam au Sénégal.* Paris

1920. *Etudes sur l'Islam et les tribus du Soudan.* Paris

1921. *L'Islam en Guinée. Fouta-dialon.* Paris

Maugham, Robin. 1961. *The Slaves of Timbuktu.* New York

Mbodj, Mohammed. 1993. The Abolition of Slavery in Senegal, 1820–1890: Crisis or the Rise of a New Entrepreneurial Class? In M. A. Klein, ed., *Breaking the Chains: Slavery, Bondage and Emancipation in Modern Africa and Asia.* Madison, 197–211

McDougall, E. Ann. 1985. The view from Audagust: Warriors, Clerics and Merchants in Southern Saharan Society, 8th through 15th Centuries. *JAH* 26: 1–32

1986. The Economics of Islam: The Rise of the Kunta Clan. In Nehemia Levtzion and Humphrey J. Fisher, eds., *Rural and Urban Islam in West Africa*. Boulder

1988. A Topsy-Turvy World: Slaves and Freed Slaves in Mauritanian Adrar. In S. Miers and R. Roberts, eds., *The Ending of Slavery in Africa*. Madison, 362–88

1989. Setting the Story Straight: Louis Hunkanrin and "Un forfait colonial". *History in Africa* 16: 285–310

1990. Banamba and the Salt Trade of the Western Sudan. In David Henige, ed., *West African Economic and Social History: Studies in Memory of Marion Johnson*. Madison, 151–70

1992. Salt, Saharans, and the Trans-Saharan Slave Trade: Nineteenth Century Developments. In Elizabeth Savage, ed., *The Human Commodity*. London, 61–88

1995. In Search of a Desert-Edge Perspective: the Sahara–Sahel and the Atlantic Trade c. 1815–1890. In R. Law, ed., *From Slave Trade to "Legitimate" Commerce*. Cambridge, 215–39

McGowan, Winston. 1981. Fula Resistance to French Expansion into Futa Jallon. *JAH* 22: 245–62

1990. The Establishment of Long-Distance Trade between Sierra Leone and its Hinterland, 1787–1821. *JAH* 31: 25–42

McLane, Margaret. 1986. Commercial Rivalries and French Policy on the Senegal River, 1831–1858. *AEH* 15: 39–68

McNaughton, Patrick. 1988. *The Mande Blacksmiths: Knowledge, Power and Art in West Africa*. Bloomington

McSheffrey, Gerald. 1983. Slavery, Indentured Servitude, Legitimate Trade and the Impact of Abolition in the Gold Coast, 1874–1901. *JAH* 24: 349–68

Meillassoux, Claude. 1968. *Urbanisation of an African Community: Voluntary Associations in Bambako*. Seattle

1970. Le commerce pré-coloniale et le développment de l'esclavage à Gubu du Sahel Mali. In C. Meillassoux, ed., *The Development of Indigenous Trade and Markets in West Africa*. London, 182–95

ed. 1971. *The Development of Indigenous Trade and Markets in West Africa*. London

ed. 1975a. *L'Esclavage en Afrique précoloniale*. Paris

1975b. Etat et conditions des esclaves à Gumbu (Mali) au XIXe siècle. In C. Meillassoux, ed., *L'Esclavage en Afrique précoloniale*. Paris

1978. Rôle de l'esclavage dans l'histoire de l'Afrique occidentale. *Anthropologies et Sociétés* 2: 117–48

1983. Female Slavery. In M.A. Klein and C. Robertson, eds., *Women and Slavery in Africa*. Madison

1986 (1991). *Anthropologie de l'esclavage: le ventre de fer et d'argent*. Paris. Tr. into English by Alide Desnois as *Anthropology of Slavery*. 1991. Chicago

Meillorat, E. 1884. La meilleure solution d'un grand problème. *Echo des Missions d'Afrique* (July): 93–98

Méniaud, J. 1931. *Les pionniers du Soudan avant, avec, et après Archinard*. Paris

Michel, Marc. 1975. Une programme réformiste en 1919: Maurice Delafosse et la politique indigène en Afrique Occidentale Française. *CEA* 15: 313–27

Michel, Marc. 1982. *L'Appel à l'Afrique: contributions et réactions à l'effort de guerre en A.O.F. (1914–1919)*. Paris

1989. *Gallieni*. Paris

Miège, Jean-Louis. 1961. *Le Maroc et l'Europe (1830–1894)*. Paris

Miers, Suzanne. 1967. The Brussels Conference of 1889–1890: The Place of the Slave

Trade in the Policies of Great Britain and Germany. In Prosser Gifford and W.R. Louis, eds., *Britain and Germany in Africa*. New Haven

1975. *Britain and the Ending of the Slave Trade*. New York

1989. Diplomacy Versus Humanitarianism: Britain and Consular Manumission in Hijaz 1921–1936. *Slavery and Abolition*. 10: 102–28

Miers, Suzanne and Igor Kopytoff, eds. 1977. *Slavery in Africa*. Madison

Miers, Suzanne and Richard Roberts, eds. 1988. *The End of Slavery in Africa*. Madison

Mille, Pierre. 1912. La Fin du régime de l'esclavage. *L'Action Nationale* 4: 500–8

Miner, Horace. 1953. *The Primitive City of Timbuktu*. Princeton

Moitt, Bernard. 1989. Slavery and Emancipation in Senegal's Peanut Basin: The Nineteenth and Twentieth Centuries. *IJAHS* 22: 27–50

1993. Slavery, Flight and Redemption in Senegal 1819–1905. *S&A* 14: 70–86

Mollien, Gaspard. 1820. *Voyage dans l'intérieur de l'Afrique*. Paris

Monteil, Charles. 1924. *Les Bambara du Segou et du Kaarta*. Paris

1932. *Une Cité soudanaise. Djenne*. London

Moore, Francis. 1738. *Travels into the Inland Parts of Africa*. London

Moreau, R. L. 1964. Les Marabouts de Dori. *Achives de Sociologie Religeuse* 17: 113–34

Morton, Frederic. 1990. *Children of Ham. Freed Slaves and Fugitive Slaves on the Kenya Coast, 1873 to 1907*. Boulder

Mouser, Bruce. 1983. Women-slavers of Guinea-Conakry. In C. Robertson and M.A, Klein, eds., *Women and Slavery in Africa*. Madison, 320–39

Ndiaye, Francine. 1968. La Colonie du Sénégal au temps de Brière de l'Isle (1876–1881). *BIFAN* 30: 463–512

Necheles, Ruth. 1971. *The Abbé Gregoire: The Odyssey of an Egalitarian*. Westport, Connecticut

Newbury, Colin. 1960. An Early Inquiry into Slavery and Captivity in Dahomey, *Zaire* 14: 53–67

Niane, Djibril Tamsir. 1989. *Histoire des Mandingues de l'Ouest*. Paris

Nieboer, H. I. 1910. *Slavery as an Industrial system*. The Hague

Norris, H. T. 1969. Znaga Islam during the Seventeenth and Eighteenth Centuries. *Bulletin SOAS* 32

Northrup, David. 1988. The Ending of Slavery in the Eastern Belgian Congo. In S. Miers and R. Roberts, eds., *The End of Slavery in Tropical Africa*, Madison, 462–82

O'Sullivan, John. 1980. Slavery in the Malinke Kingdom of Kabadougou. *IJAHS* 13: 633–50

Ohadike, Don. 1986. *Anioma*. Athens, Ohio

Olivier de Sardan, Jean-Pierre. 1969. *Les voleurs d'homme*. Niamey

1973. Esclavage d'échange et captivité familiale chez les Songhay-Zarma. *Journal de la Societé des Africanistes* 43: 151–67

1975. Captifs ruraux et esclaves imperiaux du Songhay. In C. Meillassoux, ed., *Esclavage en Afrique précoloniale*. Paris

1976. *Quand nos peres étaient captifs*. Paris

1982. *Concepts et conceptions songhay-zarma (histoire, culture, société)*. Paris

1983. The Songhay-Zarma Female Slave: Relations of Production and Ideological Status. In C. Robertson and M. A. Klein, eds., *Women and Slavery in Africa*. Madison, 130–43

1984. *Les Sociétés Songhay-Zarma (Niger-Mali). Chefs, guerriers, esclaves, paysans*. Paris

Oloruntemehin, B. O. 1968. Resistance Movements in the Tukolor Empire. *CEA* 29

1972. *The Segu Tokolor Empire*. New York
Ortoli, H. 1939. Le Gage des personnes au Soudan français. *BIFAN* 1: 313–24
Ould Cheikh, A. W. 1991. Herders, Traders and Clerics: The Impact of Trade and Warfare on the Evolution of Moorish Society. In John Galaty and Pierre Bonte, eds., *Herders, Warriors, and Traders: Pastoralism in Africa*. Boulder
    1993. L'évolution de l'esclavage dans la société maure. In Edmond Bernus *et al.*, eds., *Nomades et commandants*. Paris
Park, Mungo. 1816. *Travels into the Interior Districts of Africa*. London
Pasquier, Roger. 1960. Villes du Sénégal au XIXe siècle. *RFHOM* 47: 387–426
    1967. A Propos de l'émancipation des esclaves au Sénégal en 1848. *RFHOM* 54: 188–208
    1983. Les traitants des comptoirs du Sénégal au milieu du XIXe siècle. *Entreprises et entrepreneurs en Afrique, XIXe et XXe siècles*. Paris
Patenostre, D. 1930. La captivité chez les peuples du Fouta-Djallon. *Outre-Mer* 2: 241–54, 353–72
Patnaik, Utsa and Majari Dingwaney, eds. 1985. *Chains of Servitude: Bondage and Servitude in India*. New Delhi
Patterson, Orlando. 1982. *Slavery and Social Death*. Cambridge
Paulme, Denise. 1940. *Organisation sociale des Dogon*. Paris
Pélissier, Paul. 1966. *Les Paysans du Sénégal*. Saint Yrieix
Perinbam, B. Marie. 1980. The Julas in Western Sudanese History: Long-Distance Traders and Developers of Resources. In Raymond Dumett and B.L. Swartz, eds., *West African Cultural Dynamics*. The Hague, 455–76
    1986. Islam in the Banamba region of Eastern Beledugu, c. 1800–c. 1900. *IJAHS* 19: 637–57
    1996. *Family Identity and the State in the Bamako Kafu, c. 1800–c.1900*. Boulder
Péroz, E. 1891. *Au Soudan français: souvenirs de guerre et de mission*. Paris
    1905. *Par vocation*. Paris
Person, Yves. 1968–75. *Samori. Une revolution dyula*. Dakar
    1974. Esclavage et captivité dans la société Malinke. La traite clandestine et la Côte de Rivières. *Bulletin de liaison des Professeurs d'Histoire et de Géographie d'Afrique et Madagascar* 1: 33–71
Phillips, Anne. 1989. *The Enigma of Colonialism. British Policy in West Africa*. London
Piétri, C. 1885. *Les Français au Niger*. Paris
Pollet, E. and G. Winter 1971. *La Société Soninke (Dyahunu, Mali)*. Brussells
Porch, Douglas. 1986. *The Conquest of the Sahara*. Oxford
Poulet, Georges. 1994 (1905). Enquête sur la captivité en A.O.F. In P. Lovejoy and S. Kanya-Forstner, eds., *Slavery and its Abolition in French West Africa*. Madison, 19–92
Poussibet, F. 1979. Réflexions sur l'esclavage au Sahara et au Sahel malien. *Notes africaines* 162: 36–42
Prakash, Gyan. 1990. *Bonded Histories: Genealogies of Labor Servitude in Colonial India*. Cambridge
Quinn, Charlotte. 1971. A nineteenth century Fulbe state. *JAH* 12: 427–40
    1972. *Mandingo Kingdoms of the Senegambia. Traditionalism, Islam and European Expansion*. Evanston
Raffenel, A. 1846. *Voyage dans l'Afrique occidentale*. Paris
    1856. *Nouveau voyage dans le Pays des Nègres*. Paris
Rawley, J. 1981. *The Transatlantic Slave Trade: A History*. New York
Renault, François. 1971. *Lavigerie, l'esclavage africaine et l'Europe*. 2 Vols. Paris
    1972. *L'abolition de l'esclavage au Senegal: l'attitude de l'administration française,*

1848–1905. Paris

1976. *Libération d'esclaves et nouvelle servitude: les rachats de captifs africains pour le compte des colonies françaises après l'abolition de l'esclavage.* Abidjan and Dakar

1988. Problèmes de recherche sur la traite transsaharienne et orientale en Afrique. In S. Daget, ed., *De la traite à l'esclavage.* Vol. I. Paris, 37–54

Richard-Molard, Jacques. 1948–49. Démographie et structure des sociétés negro-peuls, parmi les hommes libres et les serfs du Fouta Djallon (région de Labé, G.F.). *Revue de géographie humaine et d'ethnologie* 4: 45–51

1953a. Essai sur la vie paysanne au Fouta-Djalon. *Présence Africaine* 15: 155–251

1953b. Les traits d'ensemble du Fouta-Djalon. *Présence Africaine* 15: 143–54

1953c. Notes demographiques sur la région de Labe. *Présence africaine* 15: 83–94

1953d. Les densités de population au Fouta-Djalon. *Présence africaine* 15: 95–106

Riesman, Paul. 1974. *Société et liberté chez les Peul Djelgôbé de Haute Volta.* Paris. English edition published as *Freedom in Fulani Social Life* (1977), Chicago

1992. *First Find your Child a Good Mother. The Construction of Self in Two African Communities.* New Brunswick, N.J.

Ritchie, C. A. I. 1968. Deux textes sur le Sénégal 1673–1677. *BIFAN* 30: 289–353

Rivière, Claude. 1968. Le long des côtes de Guinée avant la phase coloniale. *BIFAN* 30: 727–50

1971. Les bénéficiaires du commerce dans la Guinée précoloniale et coloniale. *BIFAN* 33: 257–84

1974. Dynamique de la stratification sociale chez les Peuls de Guinée. *Anthropos* 69: 361–400

1984. Sociologie des guerres au Fouta-Djalon précolonial. *Cultures et développement* 16: 553–81

Roberts, Richard. 1980a. The emergence of the Grain Market in Bamako, 1883–1908. *CJAS* 14: 37–54

1980b. Long Distance Trade and Production: Sinsani in the Nineteenth Century. *JAH* 21: 169–88

1980c. Production and Reproduction of Warrior States: Segu Bambara and Segu Tokolor. *IJAHS* 13: 389–419

1980–81. Linkages and Multiplier Effects in the Ecologically Specialized Trade of Precolonial West Africa. *CEA* 20, 135–48

1981. Ideology, Slavery and Social Formation: The Evolution of Slavery in the Middle Niger Valley. In Paul Lovejoy, ed., *Ideology of Slavery in Africa.* Beverly Hills, 171–200

1984. Women's Work and Women's Property: Household Social Relations in the Maraka Textile Industry of the Nineteenth Century. *Comparative Studies in Society and History* 26: 229–50

1987a. French Colonialism, Imported Technology, and the Handicraft Textile Industry in the Western Sudan, 1898–1918. *Journal of Economic History* 47: 461–72

1987b. *Warriors, Merchants and Slaves. The State and Economy in the Middle Niger Valley, 1700–1914.* Stanford

1988. The Ending of Slavery in the French Soudan, 1905–1914. In S. Miers and R. Roberts, eds., *The Ending of Slavery in Africa.* Madison, 282–307

1991. The Case of Faama Mademba Sy and the Ambiguities of Legal Jurisidiction in Early Colonial French Soudan. In K. Mann and R. Roberts, eds., *Law in Colonial Africa.* Portsmouth, 185–201

1992. Guinée Cloth. Linked Transformation within France's Empire in the Nineteenth Century. *CEA* 32: 597–627

1996. *Two Worlds of Cotton: Colonialism and the Regional Economy in the French Soudan, 1800–1946*. Stanford
Robinson, David. 1975a. *Chiefs and Clerics. Abdul Bokar Kan and Fouta Toro 1853–1891*. Oxford
1975b. The Islamic Revolution of the Futa Toro. *IJAHS* 8: 185–221
1985a. French Islamic Policy and Practice in Late Nineteenth Century Senegal. *JAH* 29: 415–36
1985b. *The Holy War of Umar Tal. The Western Sudan in the mid-Nineteenth Century*. Oxford
1987. The Umarian Emigration of the late 19th century. *IJAHS* 20: 245–70
1988. French "Islamic" Policy and Practice in late 19th Century Senegal. *JAH* 29: 415–36
1991. Beyond Resistance and Collaboration: Amadu Bamba and the Murides of Senegal. *Journal of Religion in Africa* 21: 149–71
1992. Ethnography and Customary Law in Senegal, *CEA* 32
Roche, Christian. 1976. *Conquête et résistance des peuples de Casamance (1850–1920)*. Dakar
Rocheteau, Guy. 1972. Système mouride et rapports sociaux traditionels. Le travail collectif agricole dans un communauté pionnière du Ferlo occidental. In J. Copans *et al.* eds. *Maintenance Sociale et changements économiques au Sénégal. Doctrine économique et pratique du travail chez les Mourides*. Paris, ORSTOM
1975a. Société Wolof et Mobilité. *Cahiers ORSTOM* 12: 3–18
1975b. Pionniers Mourides au Sénégal: colonisation des terres neuves et transformations d'une économie paysanne. *Cahiers ORSTOM* 12: 19–53
Rodney, Walter. 1966. African Slavery and Other Forms of Social Oppression on the Upper Guinea Coast in the Context of the Atlantic Slave Trade. *JAH* 7: 431–43
1968a. Jihad and Social Revolution in Futa Djallon in the Eighteenth Century. *JHSN* 4: 269–84
1968b. A Reconsideration of the Mane Invasions of Sierra Leone. *JAH* 8: 219–46
1969. Gold and Slaves on the Gold Coast. *Transactions of the Historical Society of Ghana* 10: 13–28
1970. *A History of the Upper Guinea Coast, 1545–1800*. Oxford
Roger, J. F. 1829. *Kelédor, histoire africaine*. Paris
Romero, Patrica. 1986. "Where Have all the Slaves Gone?" Emancipation and Post-Emancipation in Lamu, Kenya. *JAH* 27: 497–512
Rothiot, J.-P. 1988. *L'Ascension d'un chef africain au début de la colonisation*. Paris
Rouch, Jean. 1956. *Migrations au Ghana (Gold Coast)*. Paris
Rougier, F. 1930. L'Islam à Banamba. *BCEHSAOF* 13: 217–63
Roume, Ernest. 1994 (1905). Rapport au Ministre des Colonies. In P. Lovejoy and S. Kanya-Forstner, eds., *Slavery and its Abolition in French West Africa*. Madison, 93–110
Rousseau, R. 1929. Le Senegal d'autrefois. Etude sur le Oualo. Cahiers de Yoro Dyao. *BCEHSAOF* (1–2): 133–211
Roux, E. 1911. *Manuel à l'usage des Administrateurs et du personnel des Affaires Indigènes*. Paris
Saad, Elias. 1983. *Social History of Timbuktu*. Cambridge
Saint-Martin, Yves. 1966. *Une source d'histoire coloniale du Sénégal: les rapports de situation politique*. Dakar
1967. *L'empire toucouleur et la France: un demi-siècle de relations diplomatiques (1864–1893)*, Dakar
1970. *L'Empire Toucouleur, 1848–1897*. Paris

1974. Léon Sidia Diop. Une assimilation manquée. *Mélanges Deschamps*. Paris, 285–97

1989. *Le Sénégal sous le second Empire*. Paris

Saint-Père, J.-H. 1925. *Les Sarakhollé du Guidimakha*. Paris

Salifou, André. 1988. *Histoire du Niger*. Paris

Samake, Maximin. 1988. Kafo et pouvoir lignager chez les banmana. L'hégémonie gonkorobi dans le Cendugu. *CEA* 28: 331–54

Samarin, William. 1989. *The Black Man's Burden: African Colonial Labor on the Congo and Ubanghi Rivers, 1890–1900*. Boulder

Samuel, Michel. 1976. Les Contradictions internes à la paysannerie continuent à Agir au sein de la migration en France. In Pierre-Philippe Rey, ed., *Capitalisme négrier. La marche des paysans vers le prolétariat*. Paris, 69–138

Sanankoua, Bintou. 1990. *Un empire peul au XIXe siècle: La Diina du Maasina*. Paris

Sanneh, Lamine. 1976a. The Origins of Clericalism in West African Islam. *JAH* 17: 49–72

1976b. Slavery, Islam and Jakhanke People of West Africa. *Africa* 46: 80–97

1979. *The Jakhanke: The History of an Islamic Clerical People of the Senegambia*. London

1986. Tcherno Aliou, the Wali of Goumba: Islam, Colonialism and the Rural Factor in Futa Jallon, 1867–1912. *Asian and African Studies* 20: 73–102

Schmidt, Nelly. 1994. *Victor Schoelcher et l'abolition de l'esclavage*. Paris

Schmitz, Jean. 1985. Autour d'al-Hajj Umar Taal. Guerre sainte et Tijaniyya en Afrique de l'Ouest. *CEA* 25: 555–65

1986. L'Etat géomètre: les *leydi* des Peul du Fuuta Tooro (Sénégal) et du Maasina (Mali). *CEA* 26: 349–94

Schnapper, Bernard. 1961. *La politique et le commerce français dans le golfe de Guinée de 1838 à 1871*. Paris

Schoelcher, Victor. 1880. *L'Esclavage au Sénégal*. Paris

1882. *Polémique Coloniale*. Paris

Searing, James. 1988. Aristocrats, Slaves, and Peasants: Power and Dependency in the Wolof States, 1700–1850. *IJAHS* 21: 475–503

1993. *West African Slavery and Atlantic Commerce: The Senegal River Valley, 1700–1860*. Cambridge

Shroeter, Daniel. 1992. Slave Markets and Slavery in Moroccan Urban Society. In Elizabeth Savage, ed., *The Human Commodity: Perspectives on the Trans-Saharan Slave Trade*. London, 185–213

Sikainga, Ahmad. 1995. Shari'a Courts and the Manumission of Female Slaves in the Sudan, *IJAHS* 28: 1–24

1996. *Slaves into Workers: Emancipation and Labor in Colonial Sudan*. Austin

Smaldone, Joseph. 1977. *Warfare in the Sokoto Caliphate: Historical and Sociological Perspectives*. New York

Smith, Mary F., ed. 1954. *Baba of Karo. A Woman of the Muslim Hausa*. London

Snyder, Francis. 1981a. *Capitalism and Legal Change: An African Transformation*. New York

1981b. Colonialism and Legal Form: The Creation of Customary Law in Senegal. In D. Hay and F. Snyder, eds., *Labor, Law and Crime*. London

Soleillet, P. 1887. *Voyage à Ségou*. Paris

Starrett, Priscilla. 1981. Tuareg Slavery and Slave Trade. *S&A* 2: 83–113

Stewart, Charles. 1973. *Islam and Social Order in Mauritania*. Oxford

Stewart, Charles. 1986. Frontier Disputes and Problems of Legitimation: Sokoto–Masina Relations, 1817–1837. *JAH* 17: 497–514

Sundiata, I. K. 1980. *Black Scandal. America and the Liberian Labor Crisis, 1929–1936.*
Philadelphia

Suret-Canale, Jean. 1960a. L'économie de la traite en Afrique noire sous domination
française (1900–1914). *Recherches africaines* 2: 3–39

1960b. La Guinée dans le système colonial. *Présence Africaine* 29: 9–44

1964. A propos du Ouali de Goumba. *Recherches Africaines*, 160–64

1966. La fin de la chefferie en Guinée. *JAH* 7: 459–93

1969a. La Guinée dans le système colonial. *Présence africaine* 29: 9–44

1969b. Les origines ethniques des anciens captifs au Fouta-Djallon. *Notes africaines*
123: 91

1970. Touba in Guinea – Holy Place of Islam. In Christopher Allen and R.W.
Johnson, eds., *African Perspectives*. Cambridge, 53–81

1971. *French Colonialism in Tropical Africa 1900–1945*. New York

Swindell, Kenneth. 1978. Family Farms and Migrant Labour: The Strange Farmers of
of the Gambia. *CJAS* 12: 3–17

1980. SeraWoolies, Tillibunkas and Strange Farmers: the Development of Migrant
Groundnut Farming along the Gambia River, 1848–95. *JAH* : 93–104

Sy, C. T. 1969. *La confrérie Sénégalaise des Mourides*. Paris

Tamari, Tal. 1991. The Development of Caste Systems in West Africa. *JAH* 32: 221–50

Tamuno, T. N. 1972. *The Evolution of the Nigerian State. The Southern Phase 1898–
1914.* London

Tardits, Claude. 1987. *Princes et serviteurs du royaume*. Paris

Tauxier, Louis. 1912. *Le Noir du Soudan, pays mossi et gourounsi*. Paris

1921. *Le Noir de Bondoukou*. Paris

1942. *Histoire des Bambara*. Paris

Temperley, Howard. 1972. *British Antislavery, 1833–1870*. London

Terray, Emmanuel. 1969. *Le marxisme devant les "sociétés primitives": deux études.*
Paris

1974. Long Distance Exchange and the Formation of the State. *Economy and
Society* 3: 315–45

1975. La captivité dans le royaume abron du Gyaman. In C. Meillassoux, ed.,
L'Esclavage en Afrique précoloniale. Paris, 389–454

1977. Class and Class Conciousness in the Abron Kingdom of Gyaman. In M.
Bloch, ed., *Marxist Analyses and Social Anthropology*. London, 85–135

1982. Réflexions sur la formation du prix des esclaves à l'intérieur de l'Afrique de
l'ouest précolonial. *Journal de la Société des Africanistes* 52: 119–44

1987a. Le royaume abron de Gyaman de 1875 à 1910: de l'indépendance à
l'établissement du pouvoir blanc. In Marc Piault, ed., *La Colonisation: rupture ou
parenthèse*. Paris, 229–99

1987b. Le Royaume abron de Gyaman. In C. Tardits, ed., *Princes et serviteurs du
royaume*. Paris

1995. *Une histoire du royaume abron du Gyaman. Des origines à la conquête coloniale,*
Paris

Thesee, Françoise. 1988. Au Sénégal, en 1789. Traite des nègres et société africaine
dans les royaumes de Sallum, de Sin, et de Cayor. In S. Daget, ed., *De la traite à
l'esclavage*. Vol. I. Paris, 223–46

Thompson, J. Malcolm. 1992. When the Fires are Lit: The French Navy's Recruitment
and Training of Senegalese Mechanics and Stokers, 1864–1887. *CJAS* 26: 274–
303

Toulmin, Camilla. 1992. *Cattle, Women and Wells. Managing Household Survival in the
Sahel*. Oxford

Traore, A. 1983. *Cheikh Hamahoullah: Homme de foi et résistant.* Paris
Trimingham, J. Spencer. 1962. *History of Islam in West Africa.* Oxford
Twaddle, Michael. 1988. The Ending of Slavery in Buganda. In S. Miers and R.
   Roberts, eds., *The End of Slavery in Africa.* Madison, 119–49
Tymowski, Michel. 1970a. L'économie et la société dans le bassin du moyen Niger. Fin
   XVI–XVIIIe siècles. *Africana Bulletin* 12: 9–63
   1970b. Les domaines des princes du Songhay. *Annales: Economies, Sociétés, Civilisa-
   tions* 6: 1637–58
   1981. Le Développement de Sikasso, capitale du Kenedugu, en tant que siège du
   pouvoir politique et centre urbain. *RFHOM* 68: 436–45
UNESCO. (1979). *La traite négrière du XVe au XIXe siècle.* Paris
Van Hoven, ed. 1990. Representing Social Hierarchy. Administrators-Ethnographers
   in the French Sudan: Delafosse, Monteil. *CEA* 30: 179–98
   ed. 1996. Local Tradition or Islamic Precept. The Notion of *zakat* in Wuli (Eastern
   Senegal), *CEA* 36: 703–22
Van Vollenhoven, Joost. 1920. Un âme de Chef. Paris
Venema, L. Bernhard. 1978. *The Wolof of Saloum: Social Structure and Rural Develop-
   ment in Senegal.* Wageningen
Verdat, Marguerite. 1949. Le Ouali de Goumba. *Etudes Guinéennes.* 3: 3–81
Ver Ecke, Catherine. 1994. The Slave Experience in Adamawa: Past and Present
   Perspectives from Yola (Nigeria). *CEA* 34: 23–54
Vieillard, Gilbert. 1939. *Notes sur les coutumes des Peuls au Fouta Djallon.* Paris
   1940. Notes sur les Peuls du Fouta-Djalon. *BIFAN* 2: 87–210
Vigné d'Octon, Paul. 1900. *La Gloire du Sabre.* Paris
Vincent, Yvan. 1963. Pasteurs, paysans et pecheurs du Guimballa (Partie Centrale de
   l'Erg du Bara). *Nomades et paysans d'Afrique occidentale.* Nancy, 36–157
Warburg, Gabriel. 1978. Slavery and Labour in the Anglo-Egyptian Sudan. *Asian and
   African Studies* 12: 221–45
   1981. Ideological and Practical Considerations Regarding Slavery in the Mahdist
   State and the Anglo-Egyptian Sudan: 1881–1918. In P. Lovejoy, ed., *The Ideology
   of Slavery in Africa.* Beverley Hills, 245–70
Watson, James L., ed. 1980a. *African and Asian Systems of Slavery.* Berkeley and Los
   Angeles
   1980b. Slavery as an Institution, Open and Closed Systems. In J. L. Watson, ed.,
   Asian and African Systems of Slavery. Berkeley and Los Angeles, 1–15
   1980c. Transactions in People: The Chinese Market in Slaves, Servants, and Heirs.
   In J.L. Watson, ed., *Asian and African Systems of Slavery.* Berkeley and Los
   Angeles, 223–50
Webb, James L. 1985. The Trade in Gum Arabic: Prelude to French Conquest in
   Senegal. *JAH* 26: 149–68
   1993. The Horse and Slave Trade between the Western Sahara and Senegambia.
   JAH 34: 221–46
   1995. *Desert Frontier: Ecological and Economic Change along the Western Sahel
   1600–1850.* Madison
Weber, Eugen. 1976. *Peasants into Frenchmen. The Modernization of Rural France,
   1870–1914.* Stanford
Weigel, J.-Y. 1982. *Migration et production domestique des Soninke du Sénégal.* Paris
Weil, Peter. 1984. Slavery, Groundnuts, and European Capitalism in the Wuli King-
   dom of Senegambia, 1820–1930. *Research in Economic Anthropology* 6: 77–119
Weiskel, Timothy. 1979. Labor in the Emergent Periphery: From Slavery to Migrant
   Labor among the Baule Peoples, 1880–1925. In Walter Goldfrank, ed., *The*

World-System of Capitalism: Past and Present. Beverly Hills, 207–33

1980. *French Colonial Rule and the Baule Peoples. Resistance and Collaboration 1889–1911.* Oxford

White, Gavin. 1971. Firearms in Africa: An Introduction. *JAH* 12: 173–84

Wilbur, C. Martin. 1943. *Slavery in China during the Former Han Dynasty: 206 B.C.–A.D. 25.* Chicago

Wilks, Ivor. 1975. *Asante in the Nineteenth Century.* Cambridge

Willis, John Ralph. 1971. The Western Sudan from the Moroccan Invasion (1591) to the Death of al-Mukhtar al-Kunti (1811). In J. F. A. Ajayi and M. Crowder, eds., *History of West Africa.* New York, 441–83

1978. The Torodbe Clerisy: A Social View. *JAH* 19: 195–212

1985a, ed. *Slaves and Slavery in Muslim Africa.* London

1985b. Jihad and the Ideology of Enslavement. In J.R. Willis, ed., *Slaves and Slavery in Muslim Africa.* Vol. I. London, 1–15

Willis, J. R. 1989. *In the Path of Allah: The Passion of Al-Hajj Umar.* London

Worsley, Peter. 1957. *The Trumpet Shall Sound: A Study of "Cargo" Cults in Melanesia.* London

Wright, Marcia. 1993. *Strategies of Slaves and Women: Life Stories from East/Central Africa.* New York

Zuccarelli, François. 1962. Le régime des engagés à temps au Sénégal (1817–1848). *CEA* 7: 420–61

Index

OTHER BOOKS IN THE SERIES